Labyrinths of Democracy:
Adaptations, Linkages,
Representation, and Policies
in Urban Politics

The Urban Governors Series

Labyrinths of Democracy:

Adaptations, Linkages, Representation, and Policies in Urban Politics

Heinz Eulau
Stanford University
and
Kenneth Prewitt
University of Chicago

The Bobbs-Merrill Company, Inc. Indianapolis   New York

Heinz Eulau, Stanford University
Kenneth Prewitt, University of Chicago

Coeditors, The Urban Governors Series

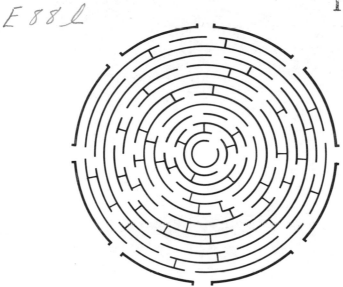

The Labyrinth, or Maze, was first designed as a prison.
The ancient Egyptians built a labyrinth similar to the
one shown here.

The labyrinth was a building with many confusing paths and pas-
sageways.

According to legend, Daedalus built it for King Minos of Crete.
Minos wanted it as a prison for the monster called the Minotaur.
He sacrificed seven Greek youths and seven maidens to the Mino-
taur every year.

Theseus, the son of a Greek king, went into the labyrinth, killed the
Minotaur, and found his way out of the twisting passages. Ariadne,
Minos' daughter, had given him a ball of thread to unwind as he
went in. He followed the thread and escaped.

Buildings with confusing and seemingly endless networks of passages are found in many amusement parks. A modern labyrinth of
this nature is sometimes called a maze, and is used for testing skill
in escape. Many toys and games are based on the pattern of the
labyrinth. Psychologists use mazes in experiments to test the reactions of animals.

v

Preface

The quality of urban life is, in part at least, in the hands of a few who govern the many. How cities are governed and the policies stemming from governance are questions of great immediacy and importance. This comparative study of 82 city councils in the San Francisco Bay region is, however, something less than a study of urban governance, and it should not be so considered. What contribution it may make to the understanding of urban problems would only be an accompaniment to the major theme. That theme is the problem of how the distance between governors and governed, between the representatives of the people and the represented, can be minimized so that the values of democracy can be maximized. In this perspective, the 82 councils and cities are best thought of as real-world laboratories where one can observe the workings out of some, by no means all, of the governing processes relevant to democracy. Other aspects of governance in the 82 cities are treated by our collaborators in companion volumes of *The Urban Governors* series, published by The Bobbs-Merrill Company.

But the research reported here is also something less than a full-fledged inquiry into the problems of democracy. It had its origins in a long-standing passion for parliamentary processes, on the one hand, and a research seminar on legislative behavior, on the other. What parliaments and seminars have in common is the tendency to talk (French: *parler*), though the nature of the talk in one differs significantly from its nature in the other. Yet, both share the assumption that talk makes men rational and, therefore, free. Talk in the seminar (Latin: *seminarium*, pertaining to seed) germinated the idea of research on small legislative groups now come to fruition. But why small legislative groups? For the simple reason that city councils, and many of them, were easily accessible to observation and interview. In the absence of funding, this seemed a reasonable choice to make in a research seminar that was to do something more than talk.

The original aim was to replicate, in a new setting, previous research on legislative behavior in American states. But because they are relatively small groups, city councils also promised some novel lines of inquiry, notably into legislative interaction, which would have been difficult to execute in larger legislative bodies. Finally, though we were rather vague at the time about this aspect, the council seemed suitable to rigorous comparative treatment as an institution in its own right. This, we thought, would be helpful in overcoming the false dichotomy made between the behavioral and institutional approaches in the study of political things.

These, then, were our initial enthusiasms—replication, small-group analysis, and genuine comparative analysis—mostly methodological concerns. What came later is reported elsewhere in this volume and in its companion volumes. This book differs from the others in *The Urban Governors* series in that it consistently treats the council as the unit of analysis rather than the individuals who compose it. There is much in the total research not used in this volume, again for a very simple reason. Not all the data collected at the individual level are amenable to group-level transformation; besides, we had enough empirical data to satisfy our theoretical interests, and introducing even more data would have made the labyrinth of governance through which we try to take the reader still more labyrinthine than it now is.

A great many persons and organizations helped in the research that spanned a decade. Our greatest debt, perhaps, is to the 435 anonymous city councilmen—89 percent of those whom we approached—who were willing to sit still, some up to five hours, and answer our questions. We hope that nowhere in this volume have we betrayed our promise of strictest confidence. All names appearing in quotations from interview protocols are fictitious substitutes for real names.

Initiation of the project was the result of an invitation to Eulau by the Department of Political Science, University of California, to spend the academic year 1961–62 in Berkeley as visiting legislative research professor. This professorship was established by the University in connection with the California Legislative Internship Program, supported by the Ford Foundation. The program also provided a summer grant for analyzing the pretest interviews and revising the interview schedule. Dwight Waldo, then Director of the Bureau of Public Administration, and Eugene C. Lee, as Acting Director, were most helpful in providing office space and giving initial logistic support. Victor Jones, an old friend, gave much-needed advice on Bay Area governmental problems. Sidney G. Tarrow, now at Cornell University, was the project's first research assistant and worked indefatigably in getting the project started and on the road to its first pretest.

Meanwhile, correspondence with an invisible college of colleagues throughout the country who had done some work on local legislative politics yielded working papers or questionnaires that were most useful in preparing our own drafts. We wish to express our thanks to Charles R. Adrian, Robert J. Huckshorn, J. Leiper Freeman, Herbert Jacob, Kenneth Janda, Charles S. Liebman, Dwaine Marvick, and Henry J. Schmandt, who have probably forgotten that, ten years ago, they came to our aid. Our indebtedness to John C. Wahlke, William Buchanan, and Leroy C. Ferguson, pioneers in the behavioral study of legislatures, is recorded throughout this volume and the other publications of the City Council Research Project.

The project would not have been possible without the active encouragement of Henry W. Riecken, then Director of the Social Science Division of the National Science Foundation, who suggested that we seek Foundation funding even before political science had been included in its programs. The substantial initial grant was renewed twice, and we are most grateful to Howard Hines, who succeeded Riecken as Director of NSF's Social Science Division, for his patience and confidence.

With funding assured, it was possible to assemble a research team and, from 1964 on, the City Council Research Project, housed in the Institute of Political Studies, a facility of the Department of Political Science, Stanford University, became a major research and research training organization. Prewitt and Betty H. Zisk (now at Boston University) were the first members of the team. They were joined, in due time, by Gordon Black (now at Rochester University), Thomas E. Cronin (now at the Brookings Institution), Robert Eyestone (now at the University of Minnesota), Katherine Hinckley (now at Rice University), Helmut Kramer (of the Institute for Advanced Study, Vienna, Austria), Charles Levine (now at the University of Illinois, Chicago), Ronald O. Loveridge (now at the University of California, Riverside), and Peter Lupsha (now at Yale University). While we are willing to take some credit for the education they received as members of the CCRP, we acknowledge the uncounted hours they devoted to interviewing and coding the interviews as well as to assembling the census, budget, and election data that we are using. It was just plain fun (and occasionally agony) to work with all of them. Moreover, though they were graduate students then, their role in CCRP needs proper appreciation. CCRP was centrally directed, but each collaborator contributed to the design of the research and was free to utilize the commonly collected data as he saw fit. Each of the dissertations that came out of CCRP and each monograph in *The Urban Governors* series therefore reflects the writer's own theoretical and substantive interests, and each writer is alone responsible for what he has written.

Although some of the final interviews were conducted by members of the CCRP team, the bulk were undertaken by a group of professional interviewers, including Jean J. Andrews, Sheryl Brown, Marion N. Fay, Helen M. Smelser, Sofia K. Thornburg, Mary E. Warren, and Betty E. Urquhart. Peter Lupsha served as field coordinator; Jean Stanislaw, Sally Ferejohn, Andy Ellis, and Lauren Eulau as research aides; and Virginia Anderson and Lois Renner as project secretaries. We are most grateful to all these men and women for their conscientious work on a project whose future they perhaps perceived only dimly but influenced clearly.

What is now well known as SPSS (*Statistical Package for the Social Sciences*), but was only an idea in the heads of its talented authors when our research began, was an indispensable mediary between us and the computer. Two of the creators of SPSS overlapped this research at both Stanford University and the University of Chicago; both of them, C. Hadley Hull and Norman Nie, must accept some responsibility for the mountain of print-out we accumulated. Many ideas that we pursued would have eluded us had the nearly 500 initial variables not been so easily analyzed, given the flexibility and elegance of SPSS and the constant advice of Hull and Nie. Sue Hull and Linda Fields also performed admirably and without complaint as computer advisors.

At Stanford's Institute of Political Studies we enjoyed the company of many colleagues who took a lively interest in our work, notably Gabriel A. Almond, Richard A. Brody, Richard Fagen, and Sidney Verba. Arlee Ellis, administrative assistant of the Department of Political Science, made life easy for both of us in so many ways that we cannot begin to list them. Her friendliness and warmth make the Institute more than just another office building.

During the later stages of data processing and analysis Prewitt enjoyed the benefits which accompany the position of Senior Study Director at the National Opinion Research Center, University of Chicago. He is grateful to the excellent staff at NORC, and especially to Norman Bradburn, then Director.

There are other people who, in one way or another, had a hand in what we were doing. Harmon Zeigler of the University of Oregon and M. Kent Jennings of the University of Michigan, themselves involved in a study of small decision-making groups—school boards—were significant others at the periphery of our work, and occasional exchanges of work in progress as well as conversations helped to clear up any number of problems of mutual interest. Robert L. Peabody, an old friend, excited our interest in bargaining behavior and made available to us the questionnaire on "bargaining, hierarchy and legislative outcomes" he was using in his work on the U.S. House of Representatives. If we inadvertently stole some of his ideas, we are sure that he will be gratified by reading this confession. Numerous conversations with J. David Greenstone, University of Chicago, suggested lines of inquiry.

A training grant from the National Institute of Mental Health made it possible to conduct, in the summers of 1969 and 1970, two seminars on problems of micro-macro analysis which used the CCRP data for training purposes. We wish to thank Kenneth Lutterman of NIMH for making this possible.

Last, but not least, there is Barbara Sullivan, who typed the manuscript not only once but twice, tables and all. No secretary in memory has been as fast, accurate, conscientious, and good-humored about it all as she.

Heinz Eulau and Kenneth Prewitt

CONTENTS

Contents

TABLES

FIGURES

Part I

Theory, Method, Context

INTRODUCTION

Theorizing about political things demands being self-conscious about one's assumptions, biases, values, perceptions, and inferences concerning politics. Perhaps more than is the case in any other arena of human affairs, the study of politics is subject to normative and cognitive biases that distort and disguise reality. If theorizing is to be anchored in empirical reality and to explain that reality, therefore, it is best pursued in the course of research and in the context defined by the research problem. Theorizing takes place throughout the research process, from its inception to its conclusion, and its conclusion hopefully is the beginning of new theorizing, for only in this way can we neutralize the biases and correct the distortions that arise in the study of political things. Theorizing, then, not only means formulating assumptions and propositions about one's problems but also reformulating them in the process of study and in the context of the data at hand. For this reason, theorizing, methodizing, and describing contexts are intimately related.

This is not to say that "grounding" theory in the empirical data is the only or best strategy of theorizing.[1] For grounding theory in data can be circular and indeterminate. But if letting theory flow from the data is unsatisfactory, so is its opposite—using data only

---

[1] On "grounded theory," see Barney G. Glaser and Anselm L. Strauss, *The Discovery of Grounded Theory: Strategies for Qualitative Research* (Chicago: Aldine Publishing Company, 1967).

to test some previously postulated or theory-derived hypotheses. No theory is so sound and consistent that the task of research is simply to prove or disprove its propositions. In its present stage, political theory is unevenly developed; some aspects of politics can be approached with confidence when prior theorizing is germane, whereas other aspects lack even minimal theoretical guidance. The wise strategy is, therefore, to let inquiry follow the deductive route where prior theoretical knowledge can guide it and to let it follow the inductive route where prior knowledge is dubious or missing. This is the strategy adopted in this research. Theorizing, methodizing, analyzing, and generalizing go hand in hand. At some times we let theory order the data; at other times we let the data stimulate theory.[2]

What we grope for, in the explicitly theoretical chapter that follows but even more so throughout this study, is theoretical knowledge about conditions, processes, and results of governance. The quest for theoretical knowledge should not be confused with a quest for theory. The history of political inquiry is studded with theories that fail to explain the problems of governance. It cannot be otherwise, for all theories, even if couched in universal language, are bounded by time and place and, more likely than not, are partial theories at best. If theoretical knowledge gained from empirical inquiry is to be useful and valid, it will also be temporary and partial. Insofar as such temporary and partial theorizing is generalizable or generalized, it is always subject to modification or falsification. Our theoretical stance, therefore, even if at times sounding unduly didactic or doctrinaire, is always tentative. This is precisely the reason why we prefer to say that what we are about is "theorizing" rather than "theory construction."

Theories of governance are partial in a number of senses. They are partial because they proceed from normative assumptions about particular types of regimes—as when one speaks of theories of democracy, dictatorship, or totalitarianism. Second, theories of governance are partial because they are about parts of the govern-

---

[2] Our indebtedness in this formulation to Robert K. Merton should be obvious; see his "The Bearing of Sociological Theory on Empirical Research" and "The Bearing of Empirical Research on Sociological Theory," in *Social Theory and Social Structure* (rev. ed.; Glencoe, Ill.: The Free Press, 1957), pp. 85–117.

ing process—as when one theorizes about the separation of powers, cabinet responsibility, judicial activism, federalism, or bureaucratic rationality. Finally, theories of governance are partial because they do not take account of all possible variables and propositions linking these variables, and indeed explicitly rule out all but a few variables—as when attention is given to bargaining and exchange, coalition behavior, political participation, conflict and competition, group politics, or allocation and distribution. And last, but not least, theories of governance are partial because they are necessarily contextual.

Yet, from time immemorial, men in search of understanding governance have sought to discover principles so pervasive and universal that they would reduce the complexity of political life to a simple formula. Aristotle found the principle in the good life, Machiavelli in power, Locke in a social contract, Bentham in pleasure, Marx in the class struggle, and so on.[3] What, one wonders, makes for the resilience of the quest for a formula? The question cannot be answered simply and unequivocally, nor is it our obligation here to answer it. But we do suggest that the search for formulas has less to do with the phenomena of politics than with the ancestral quest for order, certainty, and first causes. Paradoxically, then, precisely because politics is so disorderly, there has been a continuing search for a single principle that would explain and bring order into the great diversity of political things. Not the diversity of political phenomena, however, but what Freud once called the "omnipotence of thought," it seems to us, is the harbinger of this traditional search.[4] Because we *feel* and *believe* that human relations, and political relations in particular, must be governed by some universal principle, we *see* and *experience* them as if they were, in fact, disclosed by the principle. And if, upon inquiry, we cannot find what the principle tells us we should find, we tend to blame our definitions, theories, and methods—because common sense tells us that the thing expressed in word or thought

---

[3] William T. Bluhm, *Theories of the Political System* (Englewood Cliffs, N.J.: Prentice-Hall, 1965), is especially useful as it pursues this theme through history and makes it contemporary.
[4] See the chapter on "Animism, Magic and the Omnipotence of Thought" in Sigmund Freud, *Totem and Taboo* (New York: Dodd, Mead & Co., 1918).

must be there. But common sense, the history of science has shown time and again, is a poor compass on a voyage into the land of the unknown.

The search for formulas persists despite the changing temper of the times, and it persists today in political science. The models of our own day are more sophisticated, more empirically grounded, less metaphysical, and less normative than in the past, but they continue a long tradition of political inquiry. As a result, the gap between theory and empirical fact is often widened rather than closed, and empirical fact can remain as theoretically rootless as any untested hypothesis can be empirically footloose.

Our task in this volume is more modest than searching for comprehensive theoretical closure in the tradition of the ancients or their modern successors. As we shall point out in Chapter 1, our search is for theoretical knowledge of governance through legislative and representational processes under highly restricted contextual conditions. Though we do not follow the routes charted by contemporary theorists like Almond, Deutsch, or Easton, we are clearly indebted to them, if in each case only partially. Our indebtedness to Dahl, Key, Lasswell, and Truman is visible throughout, but we depend on these eclectics in the eclectic manner that they themselves promoted.

As our study is concerned with governance, one might expect that we would and could draw with benefit on studies of political power. But power is elusive, and it is elusive precisely because it is so pervasive, so pernicious—and so invisible. Once we begin to inquire into the phenomenon of power, the reality to which it presumably refers recedes ever more into the background. The search for power seems to involve infinite regression. There always seems to be power behind power. There appears to be no end of the line. As March concluded after many years of inquiry into the "power of power," the concept "gives us surprisingly little purchase in reasonable models of complex systems of social choice."[5]

We assume therefore that governments do govern, and that they do so more or less responsively. It is the relative influence of gov-

---

[5] James G. March, "The Power of Power," in David Easton, ed., *Varieties of Political Theory* (Englewood Cliffs, N.J.: Prentice-Hall, 1966), pp. 39–70, at 70.

ernors *and* governed that deserves empirical inquiry. This is not a matter of definition or a priori assumptions. In any case, however, the assumption that governors do govern is more viable than the assumption that they are mere pawns in the hands of power structures or interest groups or even electorates—for the very simple reason that relevant hypotheses can be falsified under specifiable conditions, while hypotheses about power cannot.

Pluralists, so-called, are probably right in concentrating on actual decisions as their bases of inference about the workings of power, but decision, however conceptualized—with or without a focus on power—does not seem to provide a satisfactory frame of reference in the comparative analysis of governance. The difficulties involved are both theoretical and empirical.[6] Attention to decisions is most useful in the study of single cases of low generalizability. But viable generalizations about governance to be derived from the study of decisions require the availability of many cases.[7] In principle, this is possible; in practice, it is not.

From a theoretical standpoint, models of decision-making seem to be attractive because they include well-defined sets of political actors—governmental and nongovernmental—who make calculated choices among well-defined alternatives. Such models would seem to reduce the complexities of governance to theoretically and operationally manageable form. But if applied to political reality, these models become extraordinarily cumbersome, as their creators are anxious not to exclude any factors conceivably relevant to decision-making.[8] When all factors must be considered, decision means a long series of antecedent, concurrent, and subsequent activities; the empirical study doing justice to the model comes to re-

---

[6] But to say, as some pluralists do, that those who make the most important decisions are the powerful is only tautological: is it power that enables them to make the decisions, or is it their decisions that give them power?

[7] Although it is often said that case studies are rich sources of hypotheses for future systematic research, few follow-up studies are made. James A. Robinson, in *Congress and Foreign Policy-Making* (Homewood, Ill.: Dorsey Press, 1962), demonstrated the difficulties involved in using a great many cases prepared by different authors for the purpose of systematic theorizing.

[8] See the essay by Herbert McClosky, "Concerning Strategies for a Science of International Politics," in Richard C. Snyder, H. W. Bruck, and Burton Sapin, eds., *Foreign Policy Decision-Making* (New York: The Free Press, 1962), pp. 186–205.

semble the rich narrative of the historian.[9] Moreover, decisional
models attribute more rationality to decision-makers than they are
likely to muster and master in a complex world. In the political
process as we know it, it is often by no means clear what the goals
of public decisions are. Indeed, it is one of the tasks of politics to
evolve and settle on alternative goals. This will involve a good deal
of conflict over "substantive rationalities" that decisional models
cannot handle.[10] Finally, decisional studies tend to deal with
atypical and often crisis situations rather than with the routine
processes of governance that are the rule rather than the exception.
As Shklar has put it, "in short, the decision-makers are not decisive
and the crisis view of government as perpetual choice and change
is artificial."[11]

Governors may not be powerful or decisive, but perhaps they
behave like thermostats that control the temperature of a room.
Whatever governors are responsive to—God's will, power wielders,
electorates, interest groups, or the public interest—they might be
thought of as regulatory devices which, in receiving negative or
positive feedback, make governance a system of communications.
But cybernetic or communication models of governance are at
best analogues, and while analogues are suggestive, they rarely ex
plain anything. As all social relations involve communication, a
model equally applicable to learning things, selling things, reporting things, or deciding things will tell us little about the particular
thing we want to explain. The political process involves communication and, in some respects, feeds on feedback, but there is
more to governance than inputs, conversion, and outputs.

In their more pyramidic form as "systems" models, theories of
the polity are both so abstract and intricate that their utility in
empirical work is low. It is not only difficult to derive concrete and
testable hypotheses from these constructions, but, if taken in earn-
est, they would require a research design stultifying to both the

---

[9] And this is the reason, of course, why decisional studies, like historical studies,
end up being case studies of the spectacular.
[10] See John C. Wahlke, Heinz Eulau, William Buchanan, and Leroy C. Ferguson, *The Legislative System: Explorations in Legislative Behavior* (New York:
John Wiley and Sons, 1962), pp. 378–379.
[11] Judith N. Shklar, "Decisionism," in Carl J. Friedrich, ed., *Rational Decision*
(New York: Atherton Press, 1964), pp. 3–17, at 16.

political imagination and political reality. This is not to say that systems models do not give suggestive leads into the labyrinth of governance. But it is precisely in their ambition to describe the labyrinth in its full intricacy that systems models fail to analyze the substances that may be hidden there.

Our own approach is different. We view governance as a set of problem-solving (but also problem-creating) activities that intervene between man and his environment. Governance, it seems to us, is not a set of routines to be administered but a set of problems to be solved. Because we have a healthy respect for the great diversity of political life, we are trying to avoid both itemistic description of detail and glittering generalities. We self-consciously try to steer between brute empiricism and abstract scholasticism. This self-consciousness is all the more important in theorizing when empirical investigation does not take off just from behavioral assumptions but also from normative axioms. Much of the theorizing and analyzing in the chapters to follow proceeds from assumptions and valuations associated with democratic theories. While these assumptions and valuations are not themselves empirically demonstrable, and while empirical inquiry cannot show them to be false, they pervade all stages of the research process, even if they are not always explicitly articulated. If the reader is interested in discovering where we come out, he may wish to turn at this point to the Epilogue, which is not so much a "conclusion" as a glimpse into the future.

Chapter 1

Theorizing About Governance

That small groups of men manage the affairs of large collectivities is evidence of political ingenuity and inventiveness. How this happens has fascinated the political imagination from the ancients to the moderns; that it continues to happen despite the spread of democratic ideology challenges contemporary political thinking. Even in democracies, Gaetano Mosca noted in 1883, "the need for an organized minority persists, and that in spite of appearances to the contrary, and for all the legal principles on which government rests, this minority still retains actual and effective control of the state."[1] The elite theorists had discovered a principle of universal applicability.[2] Despite egalitarian slogans and democratic forms of government, the distance between rulers and ruled remains.

---

[1] This is Mosca's own description of his *Teorica dei Governi*, published in 1883, as reported in *The Ruling Class*, first published in 1896 (New York: McGraw-Hill, 1939), p. 331.

[2] This, indeed, was the burden of the argument made by Mosca when he wrote that "in all societies—from societies that are very meagerly developed and have barely attained the dawnings of civilization, down to the most advanced and powerful societies—two classes of people appear—a class that rules and a class that is ruled. The first class, always the less numerous, performs all political functions, monopolizes power and enjoys the advantages that power brings, whereas the second, the more numerous class, is directed and controlled by the first. . . ." *Ibid.*, p. 50.

Not content just to assert this principle, the elite theorists went further and declared democracy itself to be impossible. In their opinion, popular sovereignty is unobtainable, whether under socialism or capitalism, for the reality everywhere is the presence of a ruling minority.[3] In Michels's words, "leadership is a necessary phenomenon in every form of social life," and "every system of leadership is incompatible with the most essential postulates of democracy."[4] Universal rule of the many by the few is due to human differences and to social complexity. Elite rule is inevitable because some people are superior to others;[5] and the differentiation in society between the few who manage things and the many

---

[3] In part, this formulation was intended to refute the economic determinism of Marx. Marxian "science" held that the differentiation between rulers and ruled was a consequence of economic arrangements. Terminate these arrangements, private ownership of the modes of production, and you eliminate the division of society into two classes, rulers and ruled. Against this was pitted the positivism of the elitist school. Eliminating the economic base of the current ruling class does not eliminate rulers, it only shifts the source of their power. Private property may come and go, but the division of society into the rulers and ruled persists. The historical evidence gives the edge to the elitists on this count; few serious scholars today believe that societies can be governed (coordinated) without a division of political labor, that is, without rulers and ruled. This is not to say that serious scholars have given up the notion that the exploitation of one class by another can be eliminated by terminating private ownership of the modes of production. Socialist theoreticians and practitioners thrive despite the theoretical difficulty of imagining a social order without some form of government. An important revision and application of Marx can be found in Ralf Dahrendorf, *Class and Class Conflict in Industrial Society* (Stanford, Calif.: Stanford University Press, 1959). Dahrendorf writes: "in post-capitalist as in capitalist industrial enterprises there are some whose task it is to control the actions of others and issue commands, and others who have to allow themselves to be controlled and have to obey. Today as a hundred years ago there are governments, parliaments, and courts the members of which are entitled to make decisions that affect the lives of many citizens, and there are citizens who can protest or shift their vote but who have to abide by the law. Insofar as either of these relations can be described as one of authority, I would claim that relations of domination and subordination have persisted through-out the changes of the past century" (p. 71).
[4] Robert Michels, *Political Parties* (New York: Collier Books, 1962), p. 364.
[5] This is the burden of Machiavelli's *virtu,* Pareto's distinction between the lions and the foxes—those superior at force or cunning—Michels's "force of will," Lasswell's "intense deference needs" of the powerful, and the formulations of many others. For a critique, see James H. Meisel, *The Myth of the Ruling Class* (Ann Arbor: University of Michigan Press, 1958).

who are managed is necessary because social coordination requires a division of political labor.[6]

The elite theorists were correct to note that direct—or, as it is now fashionable to call it, participatory—democracy has been so rare in the annals of mankind and its maintenance has proven so fragile that, for all practical purposes, it can be considered a special case outside the range of what we think of as the problem of governance. But in challenging the hopeful assumptions about popular rule characteristic of the nineteenth century, elite theorists actually stimulated a deepening concern with democracy—what it means and how it works. Though persuasive in arguing that leadership by the few prevails in all political societies, elite theorists have been less successful in establishing the logical impossibility of democracy. It is not at all self-evident that a division of political labor implies the negation of democracy. Lasswell and Kaplan, for instance, reject "the common supposition that to put the concept of elite to the fore in political science is to deny from the outset the possibility of democratic institutions"; and they continue: "whether a social structure is democratic depends not on whether or not there is an elite, but on the relations of the elite to the mass —how it is recruited and how it exercises its power."[7] Lipset, directly commenting on Michels, accepts "the technical impossibility of terminating the structural division between rulers and ruled within a complex society" and accepts that "elites always have special group interests which are somewhat at variance with those of the people they represent." But this does "not mean that democracy is impossible; rather [it suggests] the need for a more realistic understanding of the democratic potential in a complex society."[8]

At issue is not the existence of the few who govern and the many

---

[6] This, of course, is especially the contribution of Max Weber. See especially Talcott Parsons, ed., *Max Weber: The Theory of Social and Economic Organization* (New York: Oxford University Press, 1947). Also Reinhard Bendix, *Work and Authority in Industry* (New York: John Wiley and Sons, 1956); and, for a deviant case, Seymour M. Lipset, Martin Trow, and James Coleman, *Union Democracy* (Glencoe, Ill.: The Free Press, 1956).

[7] Harold D. Lasswell and Abraham Kaplan, *Power and Society* (New Haven: Yale University Press, 1950), p. 202.

[8] Seymour M. Lipset, "Introduction," in Michels, *Political Parties*, p. 34.

who are governed, but the relationship between them under different conditions of governance. Indeed, because the relationship is variable, it is of scientific interest. For if governors and governed are inextricably linked in a mutual relationship which establishes the polity, the problem of governance can be reformulated more generally as the problem of the relationship between the few and the many.

On Governance: Committing the Whole

The community organizes itself through governance—that is, by a part of the community giving direction to the collective affairs of the whole. A social and human collectivity is purposive and relies on governance to achieve its purposes. Governance means that the whole is given direction as it seeks to adapt itself to and cope with the challenges arising from collective existence in multiple environments. These environments set limits to what can and cannot be done to achieve whatever goals are stipulated. In short, governance is concerned with the relationships among a polity's several parts as well as with the relationship between the parts and the whole that is the polity.

Like other terms of common discourse in social affairs, "governing" is an ambiguous word. Yet, we want to use it in a special sense. Let us exclude, therefore, what we do not mean. We do not equate it with "ruling"—the exercise of authority over others. Governing may involve ruling, but it is not identical with it. For instance, the city council has authority over city employees and, in this sense, rules over the city administration and its services. But it is not the ruler, for instance, over the citizens, though it may regulate their conduct or, through its decisions, have an effect on their ways of living. For, by the same token, the citizens, through elections and other means, could be said to rule over the council. Ruling, it seems to us, is too limited a term for what takes place as the council responds to citizens, supervises the administration, issues ordinances, provides services, and raises taxes.

Much the same can be said of identifying governing with exercising power. While it is naive to assume that those who govern are always the powerful because of the officiality of their position, it does not follow that the powerful, if identifiable, do the governing. One need not assume one or the other in focusing on governing behavior, and we treat the issue of power as essentially moot. The council may or may not be powerful in this perspective; it may be the effective holder of power or it may be merely the agent of others who are powerful in the community. Our interest, therefore, is not in the origins, location, or exercise of power but in the process of governing.

It is easier to say what something is not than what it is. Govern, the root term, derives from the Latin *gubernare,* which in turn stems from the Greek *kybernan.* The Greek term was probably first used in connection with seafaring, in which the Greeks excelled, and it was used by them to denote the activity involved in bringing the ship to port. That is, *kybernan* or govern meant steering the ship in a straight course or maintaining a smooth course. If a straight and smooth voyage was forthcoming, both the ship as a whole and its crew as individuals would reach port safely. The now somewhat outdated metaphor of "ship of state" reflects this ancient meaning of govern. Recently the term "governor" has been picked up by students of homeostatic systems, especially in the fields of communication and systems analysis, who are concerned with the equilibrium-maintaining functions of complex engineering and communication systems. However, we believe that the classical conception of *gubernare* or *kybernan* is more appropriate to the kind of governing behavior in which we are interested.[9] For though these terms also imply such acts as directing, regulating, or controlling, they do not imply the existence of a closed system such as is commonly associated with modern cybernetic models. And as

---

[9] In a letter to *Science* 150 (12 November 1965): 827–828, Panos D. Bardis writes: "It was Plato who first employed the word 'cybernetics,' meaning 'the steersman's art.' In fact, the Athenian philosopher used the word quite frequently. In his *Gorgias* (511c-d), for instance, Socrates says to Callicles, 'I will speak to you about a greater art, that of cybernetics, which saves, not only souls, but also bodies and possessions, from the greatest dangers.' In the *Statesman* (299b-c), the Stranger suggests to the younger Socrates that a law be passed to prevent people from 'persuading other younger men to essay cybernetics and medicine not according to the laws.' And in the *Cleitophon* (408b), we find 'the cybernetics of men, as you, Socrates, often call politics.' "

we shall assume that council governing behavior is essentially open and anything but automatic, the ancient usage is more appropriate. For it makes discretion rather than automation the quintessence of governing behavior.[10]

In governance the whole is committed by its parts, be the parts the few or the many. Who the governors are is always a matter of determining who commits the whole in purposive action. Governance, therefore, is mostly by committee, and the expression "committee of the whole" known in legislative practice is a convenient shorthand for saying that every member participates in committing the whole. A referendum is of the same character. Although theoretically the electorate as a committee of the whole participates in committing the community, in fact not all citizens participate and only a majority of the actual voters commit the population. A committee, then, is always a part of the whole and therefore smaller than the whole. That very small committees normally govern— that is, commit—very large wholes is the fascinating problem of governance.

It is not an accident that committee and commit have the same etymological root. Both derive from the Latin *committere*, which has a variety of politically significant meanings. One meaning is to lead together, tie together, bring together, join together, fit into one another, combine, or unite.[11] A second meaning is to accomplish, realize, achieve, let something happen, begin, or initiate.[12] A third meaning is to hand over or surrender, leave, give up, yield up, or resign, and entrust, deposit, or confide to.[13] All these verbs convey a sense of human relatedness and political relevance. To commit means bringing parts together and fitting them into each other to make a unified whole; it means taking the initiative

---

[10] As so often, Harold D. Lasswell was ahead of his contemporaries in recognizing this. See his "Current Studies of the Decision Process: Automation versus Creativity," *The Western Political Quarterly* 8 (September 1955): 381–399, where he concludes: "Even in an automatizing world some top-level choices must be made. In that sense at least discretion is here to stay."

[11] The German words are *zusammenfuehren, zusammenfuegen, verbinden, vereinigen.*

[12] The German equivalents are *etwas zustandebringen, etwas stattfinden lassen, anfangen, beginnen.*

[13] The German terms are *uebergeben, ueberlassen, anvertrauen.*

and acting creatively; and it means turning something over but also binding or obligating the other. Governing involves all these things and, of course, more.

Committee, too, is part of this etymological family that derives from *committere*. A commission is the task or authority given to act for, or in behalf and in place of, another; commissary means one to whom some charge or office is committed by another (usually a superior); commitment means both the state of being committed and the act of committing. A committee, the dictionary tells us, is "a body of persons appointed or elected to take action upon some matter or business, as by a court or legislature."

The synonymous richness of "commit" reveals the poverty involved in restricting the meaning of governance to rule, power, domination, or authority. The phenomena referred to by these terms are by no means absent in governance, but they are at best special aspects of governing as committing the whole. Quite apart from the fact that they involve gradations of more or less governing, they do not exhaust the multiplicity of behavior patterns characteristic of governance and implicit in the term commit.

Our focus in exploring governance is on the relationship between a unit assigned governing responsibilities (the council) and the community. This relationship varies not only from regime to regime, from democracy to dictatorship, but also within any kind of regime. In democracies it is especially diverse and complex because the governed are assumed to participate, and in some measure do participate, in committing the polity. Nevertheless, we take it for granted that the council, the governing few, plays a role in committing the community more continuously and decisively than do other actors, whether they are what we call the "active stratum," the electorate, organized interests, spontaneously formed issue groups, or individual citizens. However, in focusing on the council, we do not intend to theorize about the legislature alone. The choice of the council as the research target is a matter of convenience; it provides an entry into problems of governance far broader than council behavior. This choice, however, limits what we can do, both in theorizing and data analysis.

The council stands in a double relationship of commitment to the community it governs. On the one hand, it is charged, com-

missioned, or committed to govern and to do all the things that
governing involves. On the other hand, it commits the community
through the actions it initiates and the policies it pursues. Out of
this reciprocal relationship arise some of the more interesting
issues of governance.

On Governance: Mediating the Environment

Governing is more than making decisions, mobilizing and allocating resources, articulating interests and satisfying claims, exchanging trust and services, striving for and manipulating influence, competing for office, setting directions, choosing among
alternative courses of action, adopting policies, persuading the
doubtful, rewarding friends and punishing enemies, regulating
behavior, solving conflicts, maintaining order, planning for the
future, and so on and so forth. Governing involves all these things,
but just as the whole is more than the sum of its parts, so governing
is more than the sum of the multitude of behavioral patterns that
it implies.

Governing is, above all, mediating or intervening between man
and his environment. All of the behaviors that governing implies,
and in whatever forms of conduct they find expression, are means
by which man seeks to manage his environment. "Man and his environment" is, of course, only a figure of speech. There are many
persons and many environments. Any person is a complex biological, psychological, and sociological phenomenon. The simplest
person-to-person relationship is even more complex, for each
person in the relationship constitutes a context for the other
person.

As the number of persons involved in human relationships increases and spreads over ever larger space, complexity increases
enormously and with it the separation of person and environment.
When hundreds, thousands, and millions of people come to constitute a community, the physical and natural environment in all
its complexity and diversity not only sets conditions of survival
but challenges the human response.

The coming together in a community creates a social environment which in some respects is even more intricate than the physical environment. Not surprisingly, man probably knows more about nature than about himself, and he has in many respects been more successful in coping with the problems stemming from the physical environment than with those stemming from his own nature. Nevertheless, man has faced the challenges of his multiple environments, including the social environment, by inventing social institutions and, especially, institutions of governance.

Governing means intervening between man and man as well as between man and his environment. For it is through governing that a unit is related to its environment and comes to terms with it by adjusting to it or controlling it. This, we suggest, is the meaning of governing in its broadest sense. The variations of "unit-governance-environment" are legion, differing from locality to locality, region to region, and nation to nation, just as they do from person to person, group to group, organization to organization. Analysis, then, centers on the problems created for governing at the unit-in-environment interface. The focus on governing conceived as problem-solving (but also problem-creating) and therefore mediating the relationship between units and their multiple environments makes governance not a routine to be administered but a set of issues to be solved.

Focus on Problems: Internal and External

Certain problems of governance are internal, arising out of political and organizational relationships; others are external, stemming from the position of government between the community and its social and physical environments. These problems of governance can be subsumed under four concepts—adaptation, linkage, representation, and policy. The problems involved occur in small as well as in large cities, in democratic as in dictatorial regimes, in developed and less developed nations. Problems of adaptation stem from the need to cope with internal processes and external environments as limiting conditions of governance; problems of linkage arise out of the distance between the governors and the governed; problems of representation derive from the governing group's variable responsiveness to demands made by the governed; and problems of policy are rooted in uncertainties of choice in the face of environmental challenges and in the face of opportunities not clearly understood.

No community exists without governance, for by definition a community is a set of persons bound to each other through joint efforts in conducting collective affairs. Even the most anarchic group one might imagine governs itself by common norms and understandings, implicit or explicit. Governance is a collective or systemic phenomenon immanent in any social situation in which people interact for the purpose of solving their collective problems and achieving collective goals. Indeed, it is through governance that the collective is brought into existence. In this perspective, drafting and adopting a constitution is an act of governance whereby problems of adaptation, linkage, representation, and policy are anticipated.

Where to begin theorizing about governance is an arbitrary decision. If one deals, as we do, with ongoing governing units, it is plausible to begin with how the unit solves the problem of adaptation through organizational structures and processes.

Organization and Collective Adaptation

That the council governs the community is taken as axiomatic; in actions and nonactions the council commits the community. But it may do so more or less effectively and successfully. Its effectiveness or ineffectiveness depends in part on how it organizes itself for action, which, in turn, affects linkages and policies.

A governing group, set off as it is from the general population, develops ways of conduct that facilitate or impede its adaptation. In their ascent to office the group's members have undergone a series of experiences not shared by the general population. This gives them a sense of common fate that is reinforced by their increasing interaction and sharing of experiences as they face the issues of governance. On the one hand, therefore, there is a tendency for the group to become more cohesive, integrated, and self-sufficient—a tendency that may be conducive to task performance. On the other hand, cohesion can turn into exclusiveness, integration into rigidity, and self-sufficiency into isolation. The problem of adaptation consists, therefore, in maintaining a balance between the group's need for internal solidarity and its ability to respond to external demands.

The governing group organizes itself in a variety of ways: it develops an internal status order; it cultivates a preferred governing style and pursues appropriate practices; it experiences its own social climate; it develops characteristic interaction patterns; it orients itself to action by differentiating between and assigning relevant roles; it evolves a decision structure. All these internal processes and structures, partly formal but mostly informal, are adaptive mechanisms that affect governance.

By adaptation is meant, then, the behavioral fit between the unit and its environments. Behavior will vary with the degree of complexity characteristic of both the internal environment (milieu) and the external environment (context). In other words, the structures and processes evolving internal to the council are responses to its internal complexity, to the complexity of the external situation, and to the particular mix of internal and external complexity. For our purposes, the council's own size is an indicator of internal complexity, while the population size of the city it governs is an indicator of external complexity. In response to these two dimensions of complexity the council's adaptive behavior produces organizational structures, processes, and behavioral patterns.

Adaptive behavior involves adjustment to but also active control of the environment. Adaptation may have both short-term and long-term consequences. If current practices and organizational patterns work, they will be institutionalized; but in groups subject to continuous renewal of their members a good deal of adaptation will only fit with the immediate situation.

Constitutive Processes as Linkages

Elections and their prior companion processes—recruitment and campaigning—serve to establish linkages between the council and the community which in some measure offset tendencies for the governing group to be unduly isolated from the public. This is a matter of degree because even in democratic settings publics may be indifferent to who governs and because governing groups may deliberately want to isolate themselves.

Oligarchic tendencies are less likely in democratic than in bureaucratic organizations, but they can occur. Their appearance in democratic regimes does not prove either hypocrisy, as populist ideologues would have it, or the impossibility of democracy, as elitist ideologues believe. Even though the division of a community into governors and governed is a fact of political life, the participation of an electorate in the decision as to who shall govern is not a formal and empty gesture, and it is not without consequences for other aspects of governance. Not the least important consequence of elections is that they make possible the eviction of incumbents. However, if elections are to bring about changes in the governing group, they will have to meet certain conditions.

One important condition is that there be effective competition for electoral support. This means, minimally, that there be more than one candidate for any one open post in the government, for it is only in having a genuine choice between alternatives and perhaps in the opportunity to remove leadership that the community can be said to be self-governing. This is not a trivial matter. Under conditions of competitive elections the probationary nature of political tenure is assured. It is this probationary nature of elective office which forcefully reminds governors of the distinction between the relatively stable and permanent structure of government and their own relatively short and temporary tenure —that they do not somehow "own" their offices in perpetuity.

Competitive elections also imply that, at any given time, the composition of the governing group varies with shifting social groupings and interest coalitions. Although the governing group resembles more the active stratum from which it is recruited than the electorate at large, it is subject to shifts in the preferences and strengths of electoral groupings beyond the active stratum. The threat of electoral defeat should make governors responsive to actual or imagined voter preferences. The effectiveness of electoral sanctions is predicated, of course, on the assumption that governors wish to stay in office—an assumption that cannot always be taken for granted; but where and when it holds, political decisions are likely to be responsive because electoral sanctions facilitate responsible discharge of the public trust.

Elections are only the last in a series of events that enter the constitutive process. Linkages among the governing group, the active stratum, and the mass electorate are also encouraged if the recruitment process is relatively open so that any would-be challenger has at least the chance of running for office and if the candidates—both incumbents and challengers—present themselves to the electorate in a vigorous election campaign. By thus establishing linkages between the governors and the governed, recruitment processes, campaigning, and elections counteract oligarchic tendencies in democracies, though they may not completely eliminate them. These themes are continued in Part III. Suffice it to say here that if recruitment is open, if campaigning is vigorous and elections are competitive, there is more of a probability that through the circulation of governors both procedural and substantive goals of democracy will be realized.

Petitioning Processes as Linkages

Constitutive processes are not the only means by which the governors are informed about the governed and subjected to the consent of the governed. Democratic governance rests also on the public's direct influence on the programs adopted in behalf of the community. Referenda are direct instruments of governance, but they are sporadic and cumbersome to use. Equally direct and more continuous are linkages occurring during the interelection period through petitioning and related activities and structures.

Petitioning is used here to refer not only to the specific claims and demands made by lobby groups or individual citizens in regard to particular issues; it also refers to the emergence of broad clusters of interests and spokesmen for these interests which constitute something we call a "dual system of representation." The dual system is particularly important in a democracy because abundant organizational life and organizational activity can counter the feeling of powerlessness of the isolated individual. When groups become politically activated, they provide a means whereby citizens can press their preferences on the leadership. In turn, when the governing groups feel isolated, as is easily the case in mass societies, they can consult with and mobilize groups in their own support.

Group activity, therefore, augments the significance of the vote by connecting political leadership with interest groupings in the society. And organizations have resources in addition to electoral strength: they can arouse their members in support of or in opposition to proposed programs, they control information possibly useful to governors, and they have contacts that may aid or hamper the governing process. Organized interests are listened to and thus facilitate democracy despite the distance separating the average citizen from the political leadership. Groups occupy "space" between governors and governed, helping to join the decisions of the former to the preferences of the latter. Groups not only communicate to the governors, but keep their members informed about the programs and performance of governing bodies in matters salient to their members. Theorizing along these lines is continued in Part IV.

Constitutive and petitioning linkages appear in varying degrees. "Linkage" is little more than a metaphor, but it directs attention to the persistent problem in democratic politics of connecting the few who manage the community's affairs with the many whose affairs are managed. All governance implies linkages, as even the despot seeks information of the whereabouts and wealth of his subjects, if only to draft them into his army or to collect taxes. But linkages take different forms depending on the nature of the regime. Democratic procedures seek to maximize communication between governors and governed both upward and downward.

Representation as Political Activity

Linkages between the governors and the governed, whether through constitutive or petitioning processes, are not to be mistaken for political representation. Whether representation *emerges* from the relationship between governors and governed depends on certain conditions that facilitate or hinder it. Representation of course has many meanings. As we shall use the term, representation takes place if and when councils act in political ways *responsive* to the preferences expressed by the public, or groups and sectors within the public, and select programs and adopt policies in general accordance with those preferences. A nonresponsive council pays less heed to publicly expressed preferences and takes action according to other criteria.

The invention of representation was one of the great innovative acts of political engineering. It does not matter that the origins of representation are shrouded in mystery and that its development from antiquity through the Middle Ages to modernity has often been discontinuous and taken many forms. As an act of governmental engineering repeatedly renewed as political societies adapt themselves to the changing conditions and consequences of political life, or as they seek to control these conditions and consequences through political intervention, representation solves a significant problem—namely, how a human community of any size larger than a group with continuous face-to-face interaction of all members can maintain itself as a community and can organize for collective action.[14]

Representation as a tool of governance presumes that the problems stemming from community size are not soluble unless there is a division of labor between those who, by governing, make public decisions for the community and those who, by commissioning others to make these decisions, permit themselves to be governed. Representation, therefore, whatever its form, is based on the fact that in any large community not all can directly participate in governance. What is problematic is the relationship between governors and governed; and whatever form representation has taken, it is the most critical issue of all governance. Tyrants,

---

[14] While it is always hazardous to seek an explanation of societal phenomena in terms of a single factor, it is probably true that the destruction of the Greek city state and of the Greeks' failure to find a viable federal solution through representation contributed to the Roman conquest. Not that the Greeks in fact lacked representative institutions. But they did not comprehend them, and their lack of comprehension contributed to the failure of the Greek polity. See Heinz Eulau, "Changing Views of Representation," in Ithiel de Sola Pool, ed., *Contemporary Political Science* (New York: McGraw-Hill, 1967), pp. 61–64.

dictators, oligarchs, benign kings, popes, cabals, juntas, colleges of cardinals, and parliamentary cabinets have been concerned about their relationships with the governed. In regimes aspiring to be democratic, the character of the representational relationship between the governing few and the governed multitude is of foremost importance. For, in a democracy, the degree to which the governors are responsive to the preferences of the governed is the *sine qua non* of whether democracy in fact exists.

This is not to say that we wish to define democracy in terms of its representational system alone. The properties of democracy are numerous, and no single property is a defining characteristic. But representation—the participation of the governed in the process of governance through their representatives—is a necessary condition of mass democracy.

It would take us too far afield to theorize about the relationship between governors and governed beyond the research arena in which we conduct our inquiry. But we do begin with an assumption only grudgingly conceded in most theorizing about democracy —namely, that even in a democracy there are a few who govern and a great many who are governed. One need not be an elite theorist to concede this. Representative democracy means that citizens have an *opportunity* to participate in governance; it does not mean that they in fact do or necessarily will participate. But even if, as is not the case, all citizens were to cast ballots in elections and seek to influence governance through petitioning, their participation would still be incommensurate with the participation of those elected to office. It is in the nature of representative democracy that there are representatives and represented, and it is due to the greater involvement of the former and the lesser participation of the latter that problems of governance arise. By providing for representation, representative democracy acknowledges the inevitability of there being a difference between representatives and represented. Moreover, because they are set off from the represented by virtue of being chosen, the tendency is for representatives to constitute a body of the elect or select that is separate and different from the general body of citizens. There is, then, a constant question of whether the representatives are representing.

These and other notions about representation, especially the relationship between responsiveness and electoral accountability, are more fully treated in Part V. The point to be made here is that though the same institutions which make for linkages between governors and governed are also likely to make for responsiveness in representation, theorizing should distinguish between the creation of linkages and the emergence of representation. Otherwise there will be the mistaken presumption, made by many observers, that just because the institutional trappings of representative democracy are present, the activity of representation is also surely taking place. Although linkage institutions may well facilitate the responsiveness of the governors to the governed, they should not be confused with responsiveness as the defining criterion of representation.

Public Policy and Collective Adaptation

The test of a governing body's responsiveness is, ultimately, in the kind of policies it pursues—that is, in the ways in which it commits the community. What makes the test difficult to carry out is that even unresponsive governors may succeed in formulating and following policies that do what policies are supposed to do, namely, either adjust the community to environmental challenges or control these challenges. The test is difficult for two reasons. First, responsiveness on the governors' part is likely to be judged on the part of the governed according to a short-run perspective. Yet policies are long-run affairs—we shall think of them as standing decisions—which, because they are cumulative and incremental, may benefit or harm the community despite short-term fluctuations in policy-making, whether responsive or not. As standing decisions, policies develop over time and come to constitute a policy environment that is in many respects autonomous.

Second, insofar as policy is a long-term rather than a short-term response, it can be said to be "caused" by environmental conditions; but as policy is itself a sequence of behavioral patterns through time, it has a reactive effect on the external environment.

As policies cumulate through time they come to constitute an environment of their own that persists because, insofar as policy proves rewarding, the behavioral patterns involved in responding to environmental challenges have proved rewarding and therefore are continued. But it is just for this reason that the values or goals that policy-makers pursue in responding to the social and natural environments are not independent of the interdetermined relationship between environment and policy. If this is so, it goes a long way toward explaining what has been called "incremental decision-making," though this formulation places the explanatory accent elsewhere.[15] Empirically, it means that current policies do not deviate widely from the goals implicit in policy as a response to the environment. Psychologically, it means that policy has a momentum of its own, unless environmental challenges are so overwhelming that innovative behavioral responses are called out.

The effect of governing structures and processes on policy can best be examined in a situation in which policy and environment appear to be in disequilibrium. The most general working hypothesis would be that the volitional element in policy decision-making, including the kind of responsiveness on the part of governors which representative democracy implies, will be optimized when policy development is out of step with the needs and challenges of the social and physical environment.

At issue, it seems to us, is the rate of change in the relationship between environmental conditions and policy response. Equilibrium assumptions about the relationship tend to neglect entropy—the probability of complete disorder in the relationship. Development assumptions tend to be preoccupied with entropy. Undoubtedly an environment may be "used up" by inappropriate policies. For instance, a governing group attempting to increase taxes and appropriations ad infinitum will encounter increasing resistance from its economic environment as the point of exhaustion is approximated. But societies also have regenerative capabilities that

---

[15] The model of decision-making implicit here is similar to Lindblom's "successive limited comparisons." See Charles E. Lindblom, *The Intelligence of Democracy* (New York: The Free Press, 1965), pp. 148–151; and Ira Sharkansky, *The Politics of Taxing and Spending* (Indianapolis: The Bobbs-Merrill Company, 1969), pp. 113–125.

make entropy or complete disorganization unlikely. There is always the possibility that the degenerative and regenerative tendencies in the relationship between environment and policy are compensatory. This may give an impression of stability in the relationship between policy and environment, while, in fact, development takes place. The probability of entropy is therefore very low. That some change always takes place may be taken for granted; but the rate of change may vary from very high to very low.

What we cannot, and must not, ignore is that while the relationship between the policy environment and the social-physical environment—what we shall call the "eco-policy system"—powerfully constrains governing structures and processes, it also has, paradoxically, a liberating consequence for governance. This is especially significant in democratic polities where the governing few are expected to be responsive to the governed many. Precisely because the policy environment reduces the options open in policy-making, it frees the governing unit from having to consider all rationally possible alternatives. Not all challenges and pressures from the physical or social environment need be perceived as problems requiring a solution. What is perceived and dealt with depends on the state of the policy environment. The ongoing policy environment legitimizes demand; and claims made on the governing group that go beyond the legitimate definition of demand will not be responded to. In limiting the options open to the policy-making group, the policy environment actually increases the amount of discretion available to governors in their representational activities. The policy environment fixes, so to speak, the range of activity within which responsiveness is *not* a criterion of democratic representation.

Democratic Governance Revisited

We have come full circle. The theme that pervades our theorizing—admittedly partial theorizing—about governance is the interdetermination of adaptive political behavior and purposive political behavior. Adaptive behavior is largely a response to a manifold of environmental conditions, social and physical, that constrain governance; purposive behavior is largely oriented by norms and values that liberate governance. In the language of a timeworn dualism, theorizing about governance seems to be impossible without pitting free will against determinism. But the issue need not be formulated in this manner, for the very simple reason that so formulated it is insoluble as long as men disagree on what is possible and what necessary.

In accepting as axiomatic that in most polities a few govern the many, we do not mean to imply that the rule of elites is necessary or that it is desirable. But, it seems to us, the axiom directs attention to some of the more interesting questions one can ask about governance, such as the governing group's adaptation as a unit to its internal and external environments, its linkage structures and processes that reduce the distance between governors and governed, its representational style and responsiveness that might be rooted in electoral accountability, and its policies that commit the many through the action of the few.

We have explicitly said very little about political conflict, though it is a theme that is latent throughout. Conflict occurs within the governing group as it seeks to adapt itself to its tasks; it occurs both within the politically active stratum and the electorate; it is built into the struggle of interest groups for access and consideration; and it pervades the choice of alternative policies. But as we wanted to theorize about governance as a systemic phenomenon and not about conflict, our focus of attention has been more on the mechanisms that resolve conflict than on those that institutionalize it.

Although some of the statements that have gone into our theorizing have referred to the individual city councilman or citizen, the units of our theorizing are conceptualized as collectivities, that is, as real groups rather than statistical artifacts. We have in part done so because real-world language speaks in terms of collectivities. Some of the methodological and technical problems involved are treated in the next chapter.

However, we chose the group level of theorizing and analyzing for another reason as well. If the controversy in political theory between elitists and democrats as well as in research between those who discover monolithic and those who discover pluralistic power structures has taught us anything, it is that governance depends less on the attributes, roles, norms, or values of the governors and the governed as individuals and more on systemic variations from one regime to the other, from one territory to the other, or from one organization to the other. These systemic variations and their interdependencies, it seems to us, have more explanatory power in the comparative study of governance than do variations at the individual level of analysis, though the latter may be more useful for predictive purposes in a particular case. What is called institutional bias is something that is systemic and cannot be understood at the level of the individual. For instance, the exclusion of certain issues from the agenda of governance that stems from a prevailing value system and the tendency of incremental budgeting that is deeply rooted in organizational inertia are such biases. The very context of governance in which our research has been carried out is permeated by the middle-class culture of American society. These biases vary from one arena to the next and are therefore best treated as systemic properties of governance.

In short, then, theorizing at the group level of analysis permits the empirical linking of certain phenomena that would be impossible at the level of individuals. Democracy itself is, of course, a systemic phenomenon, and its variations, which are manifold, can best be understood as systemic phenomena.

Chapter 2

Devising Methods and Procedures

Just as theory changes and unfolds in the process of research, so does method. And just as theory brings order to theorems, hypotheses, and inferences, so does method bring order to the collection and analysis of data. Because research is a process through time, it has a natural history. In turn, because it has a natural history, there are likely to be shifts in the theoretical and methodological orientation between the time when the research is reported and the time when it was designed, normally several years earlier. This is so because research is itself a learning experience. The natural history of a research enterprise, especially one that uses social survey data, therefore has a pervasive impact on the development of theory as well as on the development of methods and procedures. This is the case with the research reported here, for what we set out to do and what we ended up doing are not the same thing.

Natural History of the Research

The research was originally planned as a series of related studies about decision-making and other behavioral patterns in small legislative groups. The earliest design was modeled on *The Legislative System,* which explored legislative behavior in four American states.[1] It differed only in its deliberate choice of small legislative groups. At that time, such groups had not been widely investigated.[2] It was proposed, therefore, to undertake a comparative study of city councils in the context of the local community.

Three methodological difficulties encountered in the study of large legislatures were avoided. First, the large size of state assemblies of the houses of Congress makes systematic analysis of the legislature's interpersonal structures by way of survey research difficult, if not impossible.[3] Yet these structures are important properties of the legislative body. The small size of councils permits the application of survey techniques in the study of interpersonal relations and group properties.

Second, a state or national legislature is usually remote from its environment; this precludes detailed analysis of contextual variables relevant to legislative behavior. The proximity of the city council to its environment promises research payoffs not attainable with available research technology in the study of larger legislative bodies.

Third, at the time of initiation, most legislative studies had been in the nature of case studies. The choice of large institutions as

---

[1] See John C. Wahlke, Heinz Eulau, William Buchanan, and Leroy C. Ferguson, *The Legislative System: Explorations in Legislative Behavior* (New York: John Wiley and Sons, 1962).

[2] Ralph K. Huitt had published his influential "The Congressional Committee: A Case Study," *American Political Science Review* 48 (June 1954), and Samuel Patterson had dealt with the small-group aspects of the legislature in "Patterns of Interpersonal Relations in a State Legislative Group: The Wisconsin Assembly," *Public Opinion Quarterly* 23 (Spring 1959). But none of the important congressional committee studies by Richard F. Fenno, Charles O. Jones, James A. Robinson, Robert L. Peabody, or John F. Manley had appeared, though some were contemporary with the initiation of the research. Two studies also noteworthy in this connection and contemporary with the inception of the research are Alan Fiellin, "The Functions of Informal Groups in Legislative Institutions: A Case Study," *Journal of Politics* 24 (February 1962); and Wayne L. Francis, "Influence and Interaction in a State Legislative Body," *American Political Science Review* 56 (December 1962). These and other relevant studies are reviewed in Heinz Eulau and Katherine Hinckley, "Legislative Institutions and Processes," in James A. Robinson, ed., *Political Science Annual* (Indianapolis: The Bobbs-Merrill Company, 1966), Vol. 1, pp. 85–189.

[3] See, for instance, Chapter 10, "The Bonds of Friendship," drafted by William Buchanan, in Wahlke et al., *The Legislative System*, pp. 216–235.

research sites had, with the exception of *The Legislative System,* prevented the comparative analysis of legislatures. As a result, the generalizations current about legislative behavior were necessarily tenuous. City councils were numerically rich, fertile, and readily accessible legislative arenas. Their choice as research sites facilitates the application of survey analysis in comparative legislative study.

From a substantive point of view, the research as planned was also expected to contribute to what had been called "the lost world of municipal government." Reviewing the literature, Lawrence J. R. Herson had found most texts on local government antiquated, resting on theoretical and empirical foundations long destroyed. The study of city government, he pointed out, "lacking, for example, its first comparative study of the American city council—has yet to amass much of this necessary knowledge."[4]

The flowering of research on local government and politics in the intervening years is now a matter of record. At the time, the literature offered little guidance. Much of the contemporary writing was bogged down in the inconclusive controversy over community power structure.[5] Although some of the questions in the survey instrument were stimulated by this controversy, it did not loom large as a research interest. Only a few other studies then available were directly relevant to the research on city councils.[6] Useful as

---

[4] Lawrence J. R. Herson, "The Lost World of Municipal Government," *American Political Science Review* 51 (June 1957): 330–345, at 340.

[5] The literature now is legion. But see Nelson W. Polsby, *Community Power and Political Theory* (New Haven: Yale University Press, 1963); Terry N. Clark, ed., *Community Structure and Decision-Making: Comparative Analyses* (San Francisco: Chandler Publishing Company, 1968); and Willis D. Hawley and Frederick M. Wirt, eds., *The Search for Community Power* (Englewood Cliffs, N.J.: Prentice-Hall, 1968).

[6] Freeman had reported a case study of factional conflict in a city council, seeking to account for the sources and consequences of the conflict. Huckshorn and Young had interviewed city administrators about voting patterns of city councils in the Los Angeles area. Schmandt had examined the characteristics and political attitudes of city councilmen in Milwaukee suburbs. A team of researchers under the leadership of Kammerer had studied council-manager tenure and turnover in relation to community stability in ten Florida cities. Mills and Davis had published seven cases of decision-making processes. And there was the contextual study of a small town in upstate New York by Vidich and Bensman which paid special attention to the relationship between formal and

these studies were, they left an enormous gap in the knowledge of governing behavior at the local level.

But the primary objective of the research was not to contribute to the study of local government and politics. Rather, it was to be a contribution to the study of legislative institutions, for the underlying assumption was that legislative decision-making is a generic process which can be studied in various concrete settings. The council project was designed both to replicate and to explore. In its component studies the project would draw on theoretical notions and hypotheses developed in earlier work on the legislative process. But a great deal of the research remained exploratory, guided only by the most general questions about the legislative process in community decision-making. For this reason it was advisable to leave the research design somewhat open. As it turned out, this was a happy decision. For the analysis reported here would otherwise have been impossible. In any case, we expected that certain circumstantial variables, notably the small size of the council and its local setting, would raise fresh questions concerning familiar propositions about the legislative process.

The research was planned to be both disciplinary and interdisciplinary. Traditionally, the study of governmental institutions had been the province of political science, and political scientists had long studied the workings and social consequences of legislatures. But as attention turned to the individual legislator, the study of legislative bodies became increasingly interdisciplinary. Political researchers drew on formulations about social structures developed by sociologists and about social behavior developed by

---

informal decision-making processes. See J. Leiper Freeman, "A Case Study of the Legislative Process in Municipal Government," in John C. Wahlke and Heinz Eulau,, eds., *Legislative Behavior* (Glencoe, Ill.: The Free Press, 1959), pp. 228–237; Robert J. Huckshorn and Charles E. Young, "Study of Voting Splits in City Councils in Los Angeles County," *Western Political Quarterly* 13 (June 1960): 479–497; Henry J. Schmandt, "The City and the Ring," *The American Behavioral Scientist* 4 (November 1960): 17–19; Gladys M. Kammerer, Charles D. Farris, John M. DeGrove, and Alfred B. Clubok, *City Managers in Politics: An Analysis of Manager Tenure and Termination* (Gainesville: University of Florida Press, 1962); Warner E. Mills, Jr., and Harry R. Davis, *Small City Government: Seven Cases in Decision-Making* (New York: Random House, 1962); and Arthur J. Vidich and Joseph Bensman, *Small Town in Mass Society* (Princeton: Princeton University Press, 1958).

social psychologists. The shift of emphasis from institution to individual would have important consequences for the research. A wider range of variables became important—from demographic and ecological factors external to the legislative group to the interrelations and personal attributes, attitudes, and roles of the participants in the legislative arena. The assumption was that an institution is never more and never less than the patterned and regularized behavior of the individual human actors who compose it. However, as the final research proposal put it, "our foci of attention remain real groups as interactional and institutional units, or aggregates of actors classified in sets that are theoretically meaningful."

In retrospect, it is only candid to admit that we were not fully aware of the implications of this injunction. Our research design called for interviews with several hundred councilmen; we intended to study these councilmen as "aggregates of actors classified in sets that are theoretically meaningful." But we were vague about how the councils were to "remain real groups as interactional and institutional units." In short, at the design stage we did not really face the methodological problem of moving from the level of individual behavior to the level of collective behavior.

Inferences about the behavior of a collective made from information about individual behavior are possibly misleading in that they risk the "individualistic" or "compositional" fallacies.[7] Data about individuals as such are not sufficient to permit testing of propositions about the behavior of collective actors. For instance, knowing that 60 percent of the individual councilmen in the San Francisco Bay Area favor regional transportation does not tell us how many councils hold this view. The 60 percent may be distributed throughout the region in such a way that every council has a majority favoring regional transportation, or in a way that only councils concentrated in a few counties take a favorable stand.

A collective unit of action consists of parts, and the whole must be empirically reconstructed from the parts—an operation different from inference, which is purely conceptual. If construction

---

[7] See Morris R. Cohen and Ernest Nagel, *An Introduction to Logic and Scientific Method* (New York: Harcourt, Brace, 1934), p. 377.

does not occur, it is possible only to test propositions about the behavior of individuals *in* larger units, but not about the behavior *of* these units.[8] Yet most propositions of politics are not propositions about individual actors but about collective actors—on the sound assumption that collective units are, in fact, *real* decision-makers.

The theme can be developed in a different way. Insofar as political research is behavioral in being based on the individual person as the unit of analysis, it deals with the behavior of individuals in collectivities and not with the behavior of collectivities. The study involves similarities or differences in the behavior of the individual members of nations, bureaucracies, or legislatures. This is legitimate inquiry and easy enough. More difficult is the identification of the factors that make for these similarities or differences. Explanation is often sought in extraneous social-structural or speculative cultural conditions that are introduced *post hoc* and are not part of the data set itself. What is involved is an arbitrary shift in the level of analysis: concepts that refer to collective phenomena are used to explain individual behavior. Or, as the case may be, individual behavior is used to explain collective phenomena by way of inference. At issue, however, is the need to test propositions about the behavior of collectivities *in their own right.*[9] These propositions can only be tested at these units' own level and cannot be tested at the level of subunits or individual members.

The recognition that our theoretical interests required that we treat the council as a unit on its own level of analysis came slowly. The recognition was brought about by a shift in theoretical orien-

---

[8] For instance, in their study of four state legislatures, Wahlke et al., *The Legislative System,* treat the attitudes, perceptions, orientations, and norms *of* individual legislators and compare the distributions of individual responses *in* the legislatures rather than the structures of behavior patterns *of* the four legislatures as collectivities. However, it should also be pointed out that in chapters 16 and 17 these authors seek to reconstruct the legislature's "role structure" out of the individual data.

[9] There are other problems as well not of immediate interest in our research, such as the problem of how different level units are related or of how a unit on one level has an impact on or causes the behavior of a unit on another level. For related problems, see John H. Kessel, George F. Cole, and Robert G. Seddig, *Micropolitics: Individual and Group Level Concepts* (New York: Holt, Rinehart and Winston, 1970), pp. 1–15, "Introduction."

tation that occurred once we had an opportunity to look at the data, especially those pertaining to the relational, emergent, and contextual properties of the councils. Awareness of these properties was made possible by the research design—the availability of many small units in different contexts that could be more easily looked at in terms of both their components (the individual members) and as wholes. Because the councils had properties that could be related to each other analytically only at the council's own level—such as council size and the population size of the city, or council decision structure and budgeting behavior—theorizing had to be accommodated. Once theorizing moved from propositions about the behavior of individual legislators to propositions about legislative structures and processes, it was clear that the entire analysis had to be conducted at the council level. This required making data about individuals commensurate with group-level data.

Meanwhile what had begun as a small, unfunded enterprise grew into a large, well-funded one. From a graduate seminar it turned into a research and research-training project with a large student and professional staff. As additional Ph.D. candidates came into the project, each with his own ideas of what data would be required to meet his substantive interests, the research design underwent many changes. The original interview questionnaire, pretested in 1962 in six cities around Berkeley, was revised in 1962–1963 and again tested in six cities, this time in the Palo Alto area.[10] The third and final pretest was conducted in 1965 in a number of cities outside the San Francisco Bay counties. New research interests that could not be accommodated in the interview instrument spilled over into a self-administered questionnaire that respondents were asked to fill out at the end of the interview and return by mail. The new interests also stimulated a larger collection of various types of aggregate data than had been originally planned. In addition to demographic and ecological data available from the U.S. Census, budget data were collected in all cities for a period of eight years,[11] and aggregate electoral statistics for a

---

[10] Betty H. Zisk and Kenneth Prewitt joined the project at that time.
[11] This was done by Robert Eyestone, who joined the project in 1965.

period of ten years.[12] While the Ph.D. dissertations and later monographs, published in *The Urban Governors* series, are mostly based on data about individual councilmen, the analyses reported in this book use the council as the unit of analysis.

The Level of Analysis Problem

Our theoretical interests came to focus on the council as a decision-making group with systemic properties, such as its policies, that are not reducible to individual behavior and on properties emerging from individual behavior that are transformed in the process of emergence, like representation as a collective response. We therefore had to confront the level of analysis problem as the most critical methodological issue of the research. While some data were aggregate statistics not reducible to the level of the individual, especially those that described the environmental, electoral, and developmental context of the council, other data were individual data, especially those concerning interpersonal relations among councilmen or their perceptions, attitudes, and behavior.[13]

To cope with the level of analysis problem we distinguish between an object unit and a subject unit. By *object unit* is meant the unit whose behavior is to be analyzed, in our case the city council. By *subject unit* is meant the unit whose behavior is observed in order to construct the behavior of an object unit. The distinction between object and subject units is purely conceptual. In empirical reality an object unit can be the subject unit, as when the individual person is both the object whose behavior is to be analyzed and the subject of observation.[14]

---

[12] The electoral data were collected by Gordon Black in cooperation with Willis D. Hawley of the Institute of Governmental Studies, University of California, Berkeley.

[13] For a more comprehensive statement of the level of analysis problem, see Heinz Eulau, *Micro-Macro Political Analysis* (Chicago: Aldine Publishing Company, 1969), pp. 1–19, "Introduction: On Units and Levels of Analysis."

[14] See Ernest R. Hilgard and Daniel Lerner, "The Person: Subject and Object of Science and Policy," in Daniel Lerner and Harold D. Lasswell, eds., *The Policy Sciences* (Stanford, Calif.: Stanford University Press, 1951), pp. 16–43.

The conception of the individual person as object and subject of analysis is simpler than the conception of a group as object and subject. This is so because a group as a group is more difficult to observe than an individual person. But conceptually a group, like an individual, can be both object and subject of analysis. Moreover, the conceptual distinction serves to clarify what is meant by *level of analysis*. If we say that a unit is both object and subject, we are in effect saying that the behavior of the unit is both observed and analyzed at its own level.

By itself this formulation is a shorthand expression of little practical use. But it is of formal logical use. It implies the logical possibility of observing the unit at *another level* while analyzing it *at its own level*. In other words, if the object unit is a group, the notion of level of analysis suggests that it may be observed at its own or at another level. The conception of level of analysis does not tell us automatically at which level the group is to be observed, whether at a lower level in terms of subunit properties, at its own level, or at a higher level of, say, the level of intergroup relations.

The methodological question then is what subject units are to be chosen as foci of observation in order to characterize the behavior of the object unit. The choice cannot be a matter of convenience. Moving from one level, the level of the object unit, to another level where a subject unit is observed may be necessary if the object unit cannot be fully observed at its own level. But such movement to another level should not be arbitrary, as it so often is.[15] Rather, if the level of analysis is determined by the choice of a subject unit, that choice must be made in terms of the *theoretical standpoint of the observer*.[16]

---

[15] David Singer has rightly complained that choice of level is often "ostensibly a mere matter of methodological or conceptual convenience." Speaking of his own discipline of international relations, he writes: "We have, in our texts and elsewhere, roamed up and down the ladder of organizational complexity with remarkable abandon, focusing upon the total system, international organizations, regions, coalitions, extranational associations, nations, domestic pressure groups, social classes, elites, and individuals as the needs of the moment required." See J. David Singer, "The Level of Analysis Problem in International Relations," *World Politics* 14 (October 1961): 77–78.

[16] The importance of the "standpoint of the observer" has been a perpetual theme in the writings of Harold D. Lasswell. See especially his "General Framework: Person, Personality, Group, Culture," in *The Analysis of Political Behavior* (New York: Oxford University Press, 1948), pp. 195–234.

There are limits on the observer's movement from one level of analysis to another. In the language of the philosophy of science, the issues are reduction and construction. Reductionism, an issue much debated in the past, holds it to be desirable, and even necessary to analyze larger units in terms of the smallest elements into which they can be decomposed, on the assumption that events occurring at a simpler level are also more fundamental.[17] In response to radical reductionism some analysts insist on observing units as wholes.[18] The issues raised by this debate concern us less as philosophical matters than as procedures of analysis. Reduction is sound practice if the object is in fact reducible and if there are theoretical reasons for doing so.[19] But once the object unit has been reduced and its properties observed at the lower level of analysis, it often makes good sense to reconstruct it as a whole. Reconstruction is especially important if the unit contains some nonreducible characteristics (integral properties of a group) and if it is a significant actor in politics, as is the case with the city councils.

In the present research, relevant observations occur at different levels, some higher and some lower than the council's own level. We observe the council at its own level in terms of such integral properties as its size, constitution, or policies. We can reduce the council to lower-level subject units, such as committees, factions, cliques, or individuals, ascertain their properties, and reconstruct the council by appropriate procedures; for instance, from studying individual perceptions and attitudes we can construct the council's "policy map"; or from studying interpersonal relations we can

---

[17] See Ernest Nagel, *The Structure of Science* (New York: Harcourt, Brace & World, 1961), pp. 345–358, 541–544.
[18] For a persuasive statement, see Helen M. Lynd, *On Shame and the Search for Identity* (New York; Science Editions, 1958), pp. 74–132. For other aspects of the "part-whole" problem, see Daniel Lerner, ed., *Parts and Wholes* (New York: The Free Press, 1963).
[19] Donald E. Stokes has suggested that analytic reduction of the institutional phenomena of politics to the level of the individual has at least these advantages: (a) it allows us to generalize the phenomenon under review; (b) it increases our power to predict or explain variations of gross phenomena; and (c) it permits observations at a lower level of analysis, which may be more generous in a sampling sense. See Donald E. Stokes, "Analytic Reduction in the Study of Institutions," a paper delivered at the 1966 Annual Meeting of the American Political Science Association, New York, pp. 5–6.

construct cliques and the council's decision structure. Finally, we can select as higher-level subject units certain attributes of the council's social or physical environment which are then treated by assignment as contextual properties; for instance, whether the council has an active interest group environment, whether it has a competitive electoral context, or whether it is located in a city with a developed policy environment.

Reduction, construction, and assignment allow for comparison and correlation that would otherwise be impossible. Because individuals cannot be compared with groups, either the properties of individuals must be constructed into group properties, if the object unit is the council, or council properties must be reduced to individual properties, if the object unit is the councilman. Similarly, one cannot correlate the properties of the council as an object unit with the properties of the city environment, for instance, whether it is more or less urban. But an environmental characteristic can be assigned to the council as a contextual property, so that one can speak of urban and rural councils. One can then correlate the contextual property with some other council property, even those constructed from individual data.

Group Properties and Their Construction

Level of analysis is a general methodological problem in all the sciences; it was aggravated in our research because of the relatively late decision to conduct the analysis at the council level—that is, to treat the councils rather than the councilmen as the objects of analysis. Had we better anticipated where we were going and had we had a clear idea about group-level comparison, the entire data collection process would have proceeded differently. As it was, by the time we had reformulated our theoretical notions and concluded that the problems of interest required analysis of groups, we had a mass of individual data, on the one hand, and a mass of aggregate data, on the other. In other words, we had subject unit data that had to be brought to the level of the unit about whose behavior we were theorizing—the city council.

The problem of data transformation forced us to clarify the

properties of the council as our object unit.[20] The data base of the properties to be compared or correlated had to be unambiguous. This conceptual clarity was necessary because it affects the operations performed on data gathered on different levels of organizational complexity. It affects *what* data are transformed, *how* the data are transformed, and the *way* in which transformed data are interpreted.

There has been attention to this, but the nomenclature has differed. In general, properties at the object unit's own level are called global, integral, or syntality variables; those stemming from subunits or members are variously called population, aggregative, or analytical variables; and those derived from the environment are called structural or contextual variables.[21] To clarify our own usage, the following chart may be helpful.

Nomenclature of Unit Properties

Property is constructed from information about:	Nomenclature of	
	Sociologists	Eulau–Prewitt
Unit itself	Integral Global Syntality	Integral
Members (subunits)	Population Aggregative Analytical	Distributive
		Relational Structural
Environment (superunits)	Contextual Structural	Contextual

[20] For a fuller discussion of the data transformation problem, see Heinz Eulau, "The Legislative System and After: On Closing the Micro-Macro Gap," in Oliver Walter, ed., *Political Scientists at Work* (Belmont, Calif.: Wadsworth Publishing Company, 1971), pp. 171–192.

[21] The two most useful references are Paul F. Lazarsfeld and Herbert Menzel, "On the Relation Between Individual and Collective Properties," in Amitai Etzioni, ed., *Complex Organizations* (New York: Holt, Rinehart and Winston, 1965), pp. 422–440; and Hanan C. Selvin and Warren O. Hagstrom, "The Empirical Classification of Formal Groups," in Theodore M. Newcomb and Everett K. Wilson, eds., *College Peer Groups* (Chicago: Aldine Publishing Company, 1966), pp. 162–189.

Integral Properties

Integral properties belong only to the group as a whole—for example, the group's length of existence (its age as distinguished from the median age of its members); its wealth (the money in its treasury as against the individual wealth of its members); its language, size, or boundaries. Other integral properties are the group's constitution or laws, including its membership criteria or decision rules, often found in documents that are themselves, in a literal sense, properties of the group. Similarly, properties denoted by such terms as authority or officiality, defining the group's external relations, are integral. Finally, there are properties related to the group's action or performance as a whole, notably its decisions and policies such as are found in legislative statutes, court opinions, or fiscal expenditures. These outputs are properties of the group, not of its individual members. As integral properties, decisions, policies, and other outputs arise or emerge from member interactions, but they are different from the attributes of individual members such as their policy views or vote stands.

Distributive Properties

A group is composed of members with their own integral properties such as age, race, income, or education. These attributes exist independently of group membership, but they can be transformed into group properties because they are distributed within the group. A group's distributive properties are always properties upon which some mathematical or statistical operations have been performed. Ratios, measures of central tendency and dispersion, or proportions are common. Thus, by using the median as cutting point, we speak of young or old groups and of highly or poorly educated groups.

Individual attitudes, perceptions, beliefs, orientations, identifications, expectations, values, or other psychological characteristics can also be treated at the group level as distributive properties. Although these individual characteristics may not be unrelated to membership in the group, it is possible to characterize the group in terms of the distribution of such attributes. For instance, a group is said to be consensual in a matter of policy if a specified proportion of the members share the same view. Consensus, in this sense, is a distributive property of the group. In short, a group's distributive properties are the result of reducing the group to its members and then constructing group properties out of member characteristics through some kind of mathematical computation.

Relational Properties

By definition a group is a set of members who interact with each other and stand in specifiable relationships to each other. This quality distinguishes an action group from an aggregate of persons. While an aggregate, say, individuals in a voting precinct or census tract, has distributive properties, it has no relational properties. Relational properties emerge from interactions between and relationships among members of a social unit and can be ascertained only through observation of or information about such relationships. They are not derived from either member characteristics or integral group characteristics. Group characteristics such as cohesion or tension and group practices like compromise, bargaining, or other forms of exchange are relational properties. So also are a group's informal organizational norms or rules of the game, though these are difficult to observe, as is evident in the vagueness of concepts like social climate or political culture.

Relational properties are distinguished from integral properties in that they are minimally reducible to dyadic relationships; they are distinguished from distributive properties in that they are arithmetic products not of individual member characteristics but of intermember relationships. However, they are not the same as particular patterns of interaction in the group. Such patterns represent structural properties. Relational properties are undifferentiated qualities characterizing the group as a whole. Measures such as Rice's "index of cohesion" or the Proctor-Loomis "index of expansiveness" are sociometric devices used to summarize a group's relational properties.

Structural Properties

If the interactions among group members are so patterned that the positions of the members vis-à-vis each other can be ascertained, we speak of structural properties. Although group structure tells us a great deal about how members relate to each other, it is necessary to distinguish between relational and structural properties; but the distinction is not always easy to make. One difference is that relational properties can be reduced to dyads; structural properties cannot be similarly reduced. It can be said of a group that it is generally harmonious, even though every member is not always cooperative and friendly with every other member. But it cannot be said of a group that its authority structure is pyramidical without making an assumption about the standing of every member as the occupant of a position within that structure. Structural properties change less readily as a result of personnel turnover than do relational properties.

Structural properties take many forms. A status structure may resemble a pyramid, a diamond, or a flat box. A communication structure may look like a line, a fork, or a wheel. In other words, structures are aspects of behavior patterns or relationships which can be divorced from time yet which are also subject to change through time. A structure can be likened to a snapshot of the group's behavioral processes. It catches the positions and statuses occupied by group members, determining the flow of transactions and interactions in the group and being determined by them.

If the patterns of interaction are lasting and formally recognized, they become independent of the group's members and their behavior. An organizational chart symbolizes the group's structure as a property that has become institutionalized. There may also be informal structures that are more or less flexible and subject to change as particular members move into and out of positions or statuses and redefine their mutual relationships.

The tendency to reify concepts sometimes leads to confusion in the use of the notion of structure. Institutionalized groups, such as the family, the factory, or the government, are sometimes referred to as structures. But structures are not things in the way stones are things: they are properties of things, as a stone may be round, square, or flat. Denoting a thing by its properties may confuse the thing with its properties. Structure does not refer to a thing like a group but only to some property of the group. By structural properties, then, we refer to specifiable organizational patterns among group members.

Contextual Properties

Contextual properties are assigned from the characteristics of a group's environment. The context may be a higher-level unit—as when a committee is located in a legislature—or it may be what is conventionally thought of as environment—an urban environment or a middle-class environment. Contextual properties result from a group's inclusion or location within a higher level of social organization. The data transformation procedure involved is simple and straightforward; it does not require particular new ways of constructing relevant indicators.

The property assigned to the council may itself be distributive, structural, or integral. For instance, the city council may be located in a city with a home rule charter—an integral property; with a power elite—a structural property; or with a heterogeneous population—a distributive property. Contextual properties must not be confused with the group's properties that are generated at its own level or are constructed from lower-level subject units. Being located in a rich suburb does not mean that the council is rich or that it is composed only or necessarily of rich persons.

Problems of Analysis

"Government" has not been a very fashionable concept of political analysis in recent years. As investigators strove for analytic rigor, individuals and their behavior promised more successful research payoffs. Governing groups remained objects of analysis, but they seemed too complex to be readily manipulable as subject units in research. The disuse into which the term "comparative government" fell is symptomatic. Large collectivities like legislatures or bureaucracies, not to mention nation-states, are difficult to comprehend as a whole; and though their actions as wholes could be identified in decisions or policies, the comparison of collective actors was not high on the agenda of political research.

Yet, the fact remains that governance—the activity of governments—is largely a collective phenomenon that involves not only the behavior of individual actors and their interactions and transactions but also the behavior of the governing unit as a whole. The

neglect of government behavior has recently been remedied by
studies of institutional outputs, especially budgets, as indicators of
collective governing performance. These studies are important because they permit inferences to be made about the policy behavior
of governments or governmental institutions. But they do not inform directly on many other facets of governance as a collective
phenomenon.

Councils are governing units small enough to facilitate the kind
of data transformation needed to study them at their own level
and numerous enough to permit comparative analysis. Nevertheless, the number is still sufficiently small to create analytic problems. It is best, therefore, to harness a variety of modes of analysis
to come to grips with these problems.

Causal Analysis

Most group properties are immanent or emergent phenomena;
any satisfactory explanation of why they take the form they do in
particular groups requires analytic reduction. That is, to *account*
for many council properties is possible only at the level of the
members whose interactions and collective performance make an
aggregate into an action group. This is not the research task we set
for ourselves. The purpose of analytic reduction and construction
in this study is to bring all measures to the same level of analysis,
that of the city council, so that the interrelationships among council properties can be analyzed.

One consequence of this strategy is to make it almost impossible
to disentangle independent and dependent variables. As Thibaut
and Kelley succinctly put it in speaking of social interaction, "each
subject's behavior is at the same time a response to a past behavior
of the other and a stimulus to a future behavior of the other; each
behavior is in part dependent variable and in part independent
variable; in no clear sense is it properly either one of them."[22] To
apply this perspective to the present research suggests, first, that
councils are purposive collective actors, and, second, that a

[22] John W. Thibaut and Harold H. Kelley, *The Social Psychology of Groups*
(New York: John Wiley and Sons, 1959), p. 2.

council responds to environmental stimuli as a collectivity. By this logic, council properties are collective adaptations.

They are not caused by individual-level processes, which are subsumed at the group level in the measures that serve as variables for analysis. Neither are the properties caused by the environment. An association between city size, used to index environmental complexity, and task differentiation in the council is an association between a contextual and a structural property of the council. The one does not cause the other. The association can only be interpreted to mean that council structures are collective adaptations to the complex environment. Of course, the association alerts us to the need to introduce city size as a control when looking at relationships among council properties, but to control by city size is deliberately to reject it as a causal explanation for the patterns and relationships in the data. Otherwise we would be writing a book about the importance of size in politics, which is not our intent.

This is not to say that we altogether avoid causal analysis. In a few instances we use a causal model for heuristic reasons more than for explanatory ones. Although causal inference in nonexperimental research is very fashionable, it tends to make for more certainty about natural-state phenomena than the data collected in field research warrant. It is preferable to assume that even the application of a causal design to the kind of data generated by survey research always involves "as if" propositions rather than "true" statements.

Much current research on political behavior and political processes using comparison as its mode of inference assumes that the phenomena of political life are continuous—that, in the language of the Romans, *natura non facit saltum*. Whatever the validity of this assumption in regard to natural phenomena, it is open to doubt in regard to social phenomena. There has been some perplexity over recent findings that the relationship between political structures or processes and policy outputs is discontinuous. But this perplexity derives from the assumption of continuity rather than from the findings. Models that basically ignore the time dimension are partly responsible. The system model, for instance, posits the continuity of input, conversion, output, and feedback processes, and it treats discontinuities as noise or malfunctions that need only be removed to assure the flow of communications or transactions. But the system model is basically an engineering model and not an explanatory model of why things are what they are. If one assumes the possibility of discontinuity through time, that is, if variables are not related in a theoretically meaningful and empirically demonstrable manner, it does not follow that they are socially insignificant.

Contextual Analysis

Because a social phenomenon cannot be explained in a causal sense does not mean that it is any less real than a phenomenon that is causally explained. Many of the properties we deal with are emergents, that is, properties that in principle cannot be reduced to causes. There may be between them and their presumed causes what Northrop has called "epistemic correlations" or what Margenau has called "rules of correspondence,"[23] but these correlations are not available for causal inference. George Herbert Mead has argued that insofar as a phenomenon is an effect, there is in the effect an emergent that in turn conditions the context or environment. If this is so, there are two logical implications. First, the effect cannot be deduced from a so-called cause, and second, the context cannot be known before its emergence.[24] One need not totally agree with Mead's rejection of the mechanistic assumptions of cause and effect to appreciate his insight into the possibility of contextual as an alternative to causal analysis.

Contextual analysis is not substituting a multi-factor for a single-factor design. Lasswell and Kaplan specifically warn against confusing interdetermination and multiple causation. "But more is involved than multiple causes," they point out; "there are multiple effects as well, and more important, there are patterns of interaction in which it is impossible to distinguish between cause and

---

[23] F. S. C. Northrop, *The Logic of the Sciences and the Humanities* (New York: The Macmillan Company, 1947), Chapter VII, pp. 119–132: "Epistemic Correlations and Operational Definitions"; and F. S. C. Northrop and Henry Margenau, *The Nature of Concepts, Their Inter-Relations and Role in Social Structure* (New York: Foundation for Integrated Education, 1950).

[24] George H. Mead, *Mind, Self and Society* (Chicago: University of Chicago Press, 1934), pp. 198, 329–334.

effect."[25] Contextual analysis involves, again in Lasswell's terms, the principle of situational reference: "Empirical significance requires that the propositions of social science, rather than affirming unqualifiedly universal invariances, state relations between variables assuming different magnitudes in different social contexts."[26] Comparative contextual analysis is a complement to causal analysis; it is used not just because there are data problems that causal analysis cannot handle, but because it is a theoretically rewarding approach in its own right.

Structural Analysis

Contextual analysis is essentially structural rather than functional. Indeed, because of the ambiguity surrounding the concept of function in contemporary social science, we avoid it in this book. Despite persuasive arguments in favor of proceeding from the study of functions—whatever the meaning of the term—to the study of structures,[27] it seems to us that the alternative strategy is equally plausible. If functions (whether activities and their consequences, or purposes) are easily identifiable and structures are not, an economical research strategy calls for beginning with functions. If, on the other hand, structures are more easily identifiable than the functions they perform, structural analysis recommends itself as a first step.[28]

---

[25] Harold D. Lasswell and Abraham Kaplan, *Power and Society* (New Haven: Yale University Press, 1950), p. xvii.
[26] *Ibid.*, p. xxi. Also see Heinz Eulau, "The Maddening Methods of Harold D. Lasswell: Some Philosophical Underpinnings," *Journal of Politics* 30 (February 1968): 3–24. Also in *Micro-Macro Political Analysis*, Chapter 5, pp. 119–137.
[27] For a discussion of the issues involved, see Don Martindale, ed., *Functionalism in the Social Sciences* (Philadelphia: American Academy of Political and Social Science, February 1965).
[28] It is probably not accidental that political science began its investigations with a concern for the structuring of political activity. Many of the units of structural interest to the political scientist were "givens" because they were based on law and hence easily visible. The study of legislatures, executives, courts, and bureaucracies was followed by the study of more or less formal associations such as parties, interest groups, and mass media whose structures were somewhat more difficult to identify. These inquiries were followed, in turn, by the study of formations most difficult to specify, such as elites, social classes, or informal groups. We are not saying that this sequence has been strictly linear; we are

In fact, most contemporary studies of small political or politically relevant groups, whether formal, semiformal, or informal,
are of both a structural and functional kind. Some research is explicitly concerned with examining the consequences of a group's
existence, practices, and policies for the functioning of the whole
political system or some of its subsystems.[29] In such research, the
group is largely treated as an internally undifferentiated unit. Another type of research approaches small political groups as structurally autonomous units—autonomous in the biological sense, as
when an organism responds or reacts independently *of* the whole,
and not in the legal sense of being independent *from* the whole. In
these studies, it is primarily the functional problems of the group
itself and the consequences of members' behavior for the solution
of these problems that are of interest.[30]

Structural analysis focuses on the relations among the properties
that give the group its structure. Of course, structural analysis is
not an end in itself. It may be used to study the tasks which the
council performs for the community (one use of function), its own
internal organizational problems such as integration (another use
of function), or the consequences of membership for the individuals who compose it or for the community (another use of function). Despite these utilities, structure as an analytic construct
has been given short shrift in political science, partly and probably because of the theoretical emptiness of the older formal, in-

---

merely saying that, in general, the bulk of structural analysis has followed this
sequence. Moreover, a functional orientation was by no means altogether absent
in the older structural analyses. Functional analysis as such became prominent
in political science only when it became apparent that the conventional structural categories were inadequate in coping with such phenomena as charismatic
leadership, mass movements, stateless societies, and so on.

[29] See, for instance, Herbert McClosky and Harold E. Dahlgren, "Primary Group
Influence on Party Loyalty," *American Political Science Review* 53 (September
1959): 757–776.

[30] See, for instance, Richard F. Fenno, Jr., "The House Appropriations Committee as a Political System: The Problem of Integration," *American Political Science Review* 56 (June 1962): 310–324; Charles O. Jones, "The Role of the Congressional Subcommittee," *Midwest Journal of Political Science* 6 (November
1962): 327–344; and John F. Manley, "The House Committee on Ways and
Means: Conflict Management in a Congressional Committee," *American Political Science Review* 59 (December 1965): 927–939.

stitutional approach. But structural analysis is a critical concern of political science, just as it is of continuing concern in biology, geology, chemistry, linguistics, and almost every other science.[31] For all political activity, whether that of an individual or a group, or even of an amorphous mob on the streets, is limited or constrained by the structure that obtains in the unit.

To avoid formalism, it is of the utmost importance to distinguish between group and structure, terms quite often used interchangeably. Otherwise structures are treated as if they were collective actors. But structures cannot act; only individuals or groups, if they follow certain decision rules, can act. While a group has structures, by virtue of the fact that its properties are related to one another in more or less characteristic ways, a structure is not a group. Structure is an analytic concept that refers to the patterns of relationship among the group's properties, whereas group refers to a concrete set of interacting persons, whatever the structure of their interactions may be.

The distinction between group and structure is less important in research mainly concerned with the effects of a group's practices and policies on other aspects of the polity, for such research treats the group as a global and internally undifferentiated unit. But in the kind of comparative group-level analysis attempted here, the distinction between group and structure is crucial. For while groups serve as the units whose behavior is analyzed, structures serve as variables that facilitate explanation.

Configurative Analysis

Comparative analysis, to warrant its name, must involve more than simple juxtaposition of objects that may be similar or dissimilar. The description of similarities and differences has its own rewards and is certainly an important aspect of comparison. But, as a method, comparison is expected to yield empirical generalizations or inductive inferences that transcend the unique descrip-

---

[31] David E. Apter is one of the few contemporary political scientists seriously concerned with the "structural approach," though his formulation differs from our own. See David E. Apter, *The Politics of Modernization* (Chicago: University of Chicago Press, 1965), pp. 16–20, "The Structural Approach."

tive statement. In comparative perspective, what first appears unique is, in fact, an instance or case in a universe of instances that partake of some degree of uniformity and regularity. Only upon the discovery of uniformities and regularities can it be said that a case is so deviant that it can be called unique. Comparative analysis is, therefore, a rudimentary form of statistics. But comparison as statistics has been difficult in what is conventionally called comparative politics for two reasons: first, the behavior systems (units) to be comparatively treated, such as nation-states, subnational organizations, or institutions like legislatures and bureaucracies, are physically so large that their properties cannot be readily managed; and second, the number of these systems usually available for comparison is too small for statistical manipulation.

While statistical treatment of a relatively large number of small units, as in this research on 82 city councils, overcomes some of these difficulties, sole reliance on statistics is insufficient to fulfill the promises of comparative analysis. Even if more cases were available, multivariate analysis would quickly exhaust them. For this reason, comparative analysis is well advised to fall back on less rigorous procedures to survey the broad canvass of relationhips among group properties. Put differently, it is not enough to rely for inference on bivariate or even multivariate analyses that are statistically sound. To exploit fully the theoretical possibilities of the data, whether treated causally or contextually, it is desirable to inspect the total configuration of relevant numerical distributions and statistically measured associations among group properties. If this can be done contextually, analysis and interpretation are correspondingly enriched.

Configurative analysis has the virtue, therefore, of placing deviations from normal distributions or expected associations in perspective. In the configurative perspective it is the balance between concordance and discordance in the data that serves as the criterion for assessing the bulk of the evidence rather than particular bits of evidence. Although configurative analysis begins by inspecting items of evidence, it is the *gestalt* of items that influences interpretation. The method involved is perhaps more subjective than one might wish it to be, and its test is more a matter of subjective probability than statistical probability. But subjective probability is not arbitrary, because it is subject to modification as a "degree of rational belief."[32] For the results of analysis are subject to change as new evidence becomes available and makes revision necessary. Configurative analysis, in accepting subjective probability as its test, is sensitive to the fact that what we observe and measure are only partial indicators of the natural, ecological, social, cultural, economic, or political phenomena that constitute reality.

Data Transformation and Problems

Not all the data collected by the City Council Research Project are used in this study, and not all individual-level data were made amenable to group-level analysis. Data transformation could be direct, through computation and through what we shall call imputation, or indirect through classification. In general, direct transformation means that there is a conceptual parallelism between individual and group properties and that the group property derived from individual-level data has the same theoretical meaning as the individual-level datum from which it is derived. Classification involves a second step—either the ordering of transformed data or the creation of new properties through cross-tabulation of transformed data. Each type of procedure involves a variety of techniques that are fully described in relevant footnotes when a measure is introduced or in Appendix B. Some general observations about these procedures are in order.

Computation

Computation was used to develop council-level measures whenever the individual interview data could be meaningfully transformed through mathematical manipulation.

---

[32] The notion of "subjective probability" stems from John Maynard Keynes, *A Treatise on Probability* (London: Macmillan, 1921). For a succinct discussion, see Bruno De Finetti, "Probability: Interpretations," *International Encyclopedia of the Social Sciences* (New York: Macmillan and Free Press, 1968), Vol. 12, pp. 496–505.

Computation may involve the application of measures of central tendency such as the mean, median, proportion, and so on. Or it may involve sociometric measures, graphs, and other scoring devices. For instance, it is possible to construct such distributive properties as the council's median tenure, its average opinion on an issue, or the proportion of members holding an identical role orientation. It is possible to construct the degree of agreement that may characterize the group or the pervasiveness of relational properties, such as the degree of mutual affect or respect that obtains in the council. It is possible to measure and graph some aspects of its structure, such as social differentiation, stratification, pattern of interaction, internal political division, or role structure.

Computation can be used whether the bits of information collected from members are respondent or informant data. For instance, the articulation of norms by respondents can be computed and the resultant statistic may be used as an informant indicator of this relational property. Similarly, if all or most councilmen inform us about the council's social environment, this information can be computed to yield an indirect measure of a contextual property. Or information given by one member about his colleagues' voting behavior can be taken into account in constructing the council's decision-making structure. The success of computation would also seem to depend on the visibility of the phenomenon being computed. The more visible the phenomenon, the more reliable are the results of computation. For instance, whether the council is split into factions is a highly visible phenomenon, and we should expect that the group's members will give trustworthy responses.

Computation of a group's properties may seem hazardous in the case of small groups of five, seven, or nine members. For it is obvious that the fewer the number of observations possible, the more likely is it that the measurements will be subject to random or idiosyncratic errors in member responses. The only criterion available to judge the reliability of computed group properties is the results that are obtained in analysis. In fact, computed group properties are meaningfully related to assigned or imputed group properties.

Whatever the weakness of a measure computed from small numbers, it is probably still more accurate than a single observation. Direct observation of a council's behavior by a single observer increases the probability of bias in observation; the more independent observations that are available, the more bias is reduced. No outside observer can see as much as group members themselves see.

Just as the assignment of contextual properties does not involve the ecological fallacy, so the construction of unit properties through computation does not involve the compositional fallacy. Group properties are not inferred from member properties but constructed out of them.

Imputation

Imputation[33] is the name we give a procedure of transformation that uses individual respondent or informant data interchangeably and that is more qualitative than quantitative, though it may involve reliance on a loose count of the relevant information. It was made possible by the largely open-ended interview schedule we used (Appendix C), for the interview generated rich, elaborate descriptive material on many topics. City councilmen are not different from other politicians in at least one respect: they like to talk. Stories, anecdotes, and discursive responses to specific questions provided much of the information used in the imputational coding. The quotations scattered throughout the text and in Appendix B for illustrative purposes give ample evidence of the richness of the data.[34] For the purpose of imputation, particular

---

[33] The etymology of "imputation" gives a clue to the meaning we give it. *Imputare*, the Latin verb, can be translated to mean "to bring into reckoning," while "reckon" is related to the German verb *rechnen*, which may mean, as does reckon, "to count, compute, calculate." Imputing a property from information about individuals to a group involves at least some "loose" calculation in addition to "ascribing" or "attributing" the property.

[34] In most of our imputational coding, the absence of the trait was the residual code category. That is, if insufficient information was forthcoming to impute a given property, such as tension, the council was coded as not having the property.

questions, sets of related questions, or major parts of the interview were read simultaneously for *all* members as if they constituted a single document of the group as a whole. The coding was done jointly by the authors. Imputation, as will appear, is a literally "more or less" precise way of data transformation.

A missing respondent's characteristics may be ascertained from information given about him by other respondents. For instance, we might wish to determine the extent to which a given governing style relevant to group performance is valued in the group as a whole. The property in question is basically distributive. As in the case of computation, a criterion is set—say, three out of five members should possess the relevant style and it should be salient. Let us assume that one member in a five-person council has not been interviewed and no other external information is available; that two members report a benevolent style in their council work; and that two others report a pragmatic style. In this case, if at least two of those interviewed (regardless of what they say about themselves) report that the noninterviewed member pursues a benevolent governing style, the group as a whole is characterized by that style. Had the procedure been strict computation, the group could not have been meaningfully classified.

Similarly, imputational transformation of individual into grouped data can deal with more complex properties. For instance, let us take the council's "representational response style." If councilmen seldom mention any groups or groupings in the public, or if they fail to describe an actual case of council responsiveness to public pressures, or if they simply assert that they know what is best for the community and act upon it, the council as a whole is said to have a self-defined image of representation. If most respondents make references to occasionally active neighborhood organizations or to other transitory groups wanting, say, a stoplight at a given corner, or to temporary campaign organizations, and if they indicate that they have responded to pressures from such groups and have attempted to placate them, then the council as a whole is characterized as responsive to issue-groups. Finally, if the councilmen define a fairly well-organized public, attentive to what the council is doing, and if the respondents indicate (usually by citing an illustrative case) that they are responsive to these attentive publics, then the council as a whole is imputed the property of being responsive to attentive publics.

In this procedure, then, individual remarks and accounts are used as information about the response style of the group. It may be that an individual respondent himself is not responsive in one way or another, yet he may describe the group as acting that way. The individual data are used solely as informant data, and the transformation procedure, though dealing with a basically distributive property of the group, is quantitative in a very restricted sense.

Similarly, it is possible to ascertain some relational properties by imputational transformation. For instance, such interpersonal strategies as bargaining, compromising, coalition building, and so on are relational properties that can be ascertained by using respondent information and transforming it into group properties. A council may be characterized as bargaining or coalition building when only one respondent gives a detailed account, which, however, must be corroborated by at least one supportive statement (though, usually, there is more than one such corroboration) and which is not contradicted by other members.

Similar procedures can be used to impute contextual properties which, if more direct data were available, would probably represent aggregated characteristics of the context. For instance, one may impute the extent to which the public has a favorable image of the council or the extent to which it is supportive of the council.

On the least precise end of transformation through imputation, there are properties that can only be apprehended by an observer looking at a thing as a whole. Even if the thing is in principle reducible, reconstruction of the whole from its individual parts is impossible because the whole is more than the sum of its parts. For instance, a tree has a trunk, branches, and leaves. We can describe the tree in terms of its component parts, but we cannot easily reconstruct it as a whole once we have disassembled it. We may wish to characterize the tree as massive, as is a giant redwood, or we may wish to characterize it as delicate, as is a young birch.

This is not the place to speculate about the reality of such qualitative, irreducible properties of a thing. From the operational standpoint pursued here, it matters little if the property inheres in the thing or is the product of the observer's insight or is the resultant of some transaction between the observer and the thing. But as one observes almost any group, either directly as a participant or through a two-way mirror or more indirectly by studying reports from individual participants, one is invariably impressed by the fact that the group as a whole appears to be characterized by qualities that can only be apprehended as wholes. For instance, what one may call the group's social climate, admittedly a vague concept, is a property that eludes reduction and can only be constructed from behavioral patterns in the group as a whole.

The procedure involved in transforming information gathered from individual participants into a property of the group as a whole involves seeing a *gestalt* of many aspects of the group's behavior. In other words, there must be pervasive evidence that the property in question is actually present. Cues for characterizing the group's atmosphere as tense, for instance, are taken from references throughout all interviews to an internal power struggle or to the competition for status, and from the frequent negative or derogatory references made by members about each other.

Imputation, in contrast to computation, may appear to be a very subjective way of transforming data collected from and about individuals, or information about the group and its context, into group properties. It does, however, involve some calculation, ranging from loose counting that combines respondent and informant data to a holistic view of the group. While there is inevitably much coder judgment in the procedure, this judgment is not arbitrary. It is tutored by a respect for either the quantity of information or for the quality of information. Not to use such information in the study of collective behavior and to rely solely on exact data—that is, on data that can be unequivocally counted—would deprive the analyst of valuable and, we believe, usable knowledge. While the reliability of this kind of information may be less than that of data based on computation, it is at least as reliable as the information that can be gathered through participant observation or the data collected from a single informant. Social science is hardly in a position to ignore such information. The guiding criterion in imputational transformation is that the group property constructed by this procedure is directly founded on information from the members of the group about themselves, about other members, or about the group as a whole.

Classification

Data transformation through classification makes for the creation of new variables at the group level of analysis when appropriate concepts have been formulated. As Lazarsfeld and Barton put it, "before we can investigate the presence or absence of some attribute in a person or a social situation, or before we can rank objects or measure them in terms of some variable, we must form the concept of that variable."[35]

In some cases, clarification of concepts leads to simple assignment of the council to one or another category that may or may not be mutually exclusive; for instance, as discussed in Chapter 5, once the conceptual distinction is made between compromising and bargaining, councils are directly assigned to one or another class as a result of imputational coding. However, because the number of cases falling into a joint compromising-and-bargaining class would be so small as to be analytically useless, we opt for assigning these cases to the bargaining category on the assumption that bargaining may be accompanied by compromising but that compromising need not engender bargaining. By analytically treating bargaining and compromising as mutually exclusive events which they are not in empirical reality, we sacrifice information of possible interest; but we do so because we are more concerned in such cases with the presence or absence of one or the other property than with their possible joint occurrence.

A great many classifications are based on the results of computations that initially permit rank-ordering of the councils on a given property. Wherever rank-ordering proves feasible, the resultant continuum is divided into quartile, tercile, or dichoto-

[35] Paul F. Lazarsfeld and Allan H. Barton, "Qualitative Measurement in the Social Sciences: Classification, Typologies and Indices," in Lerner and Lasswell, *The Policy Sciences*, p. 155. For some of the problems involved in classification, see Giovanni Sartori, "Concept Misinformation in Comparative Politics," *American Political Science Review* 64 (December 1970): 1033–1053.

mized distributions that serve as analytic categories. Although we also use interval scale measures directly in computing correlation coefficients where appropriate, we prefer the strategy of collapsing the data into classes for a number of reasons.

In the first place, the particular values initially obtained from computation are of no import and little use in the kind of broad comparative study of councils as wholes on their own level of analysis that is undertaken here. Second, these values are often so close or even the same, with a great many ties, that rank-order correlations would often yield specious quantitative results. Third, as many other classifications are at best nominal scales without an inherent order, dichotomized or trichotomized classification of rank-ordered data facilitates their correlation with nominal typologies, once theoretical assumptions are introduced so that we can think of the latter as at least quasi-ordinal. Finally, it is our experience that classed data more readily lend themselves to theoretical and interpretive—that is, analytically richer—exploitation than do unclassed data, no matter how sophisticated the statistical analysis that can be performed on them.

Other classifications are directly provided by the research instrument. This is the case, for instance, with the decision structure typology described in Chapter 9. We are dealing here with natural types in the real world. This is not to say that there are no ambiguous cases where judgment has to be applied in classifying one or another council. But this ambiguity does not stem from lack of analytic clarity; rather it stems from inadequate data collection.

Finally, classification can be based on cross-tabulation of non-correlated properties, such as the electoral context typology introduced in Chapter 12 or the policy development typology explicated in Chapter 24. These typologies are inherently multivariate because they are based on two dimensions explicitly brought into the classification. As a result of such fusing of variables, the ordering power of any one category in the classification may differ from one dependent variable to another. Nevertheless, the theoretical power of the typology is probably greater than that of any of the single variables that are cross-tabulated to constitute the classification.[36]

---

[36] For a discussion of the statistical aspects of the analysis, see Appendix B2.1.

Chapter 3

Constructing Contexts

There is no social unit—whether an individual, a small group, a large association, or a territorial organization—that is not a "unit-in-environment." Only for analytic reasons is the single constellation "unit-in-environment" decomposed into a unit and its multiple environments. For only if the unit is set off from its multiple contexts is it possible to examine empirically the mutual interdependence of unit and environment or the interdependencies of the unit's own properties in different contexts.

The immediate environment of the city council is the city for which it makes decisions. The city is a multidimensional environment. It is a physical environment, a social environment, an economic environment, and a political environment, and this is not an exhaustive list. What, in Chapter 12, we shall describe as the "electoral context" or, in Chapter 23, as the "policy environment" are components of the total environment that is the city. As a totality, each city is itself located in an even more comprehensive environment—the metropolitan region.

Council-in-city-in-region eludes analysis because it would minimally require two metropolitan research arenas. But this research was conducted, for reasons pointed out in the Preface, in the single region composed of eight counties adjoining San Francisco Bay.[1] Whatever the relevance of the metropolitan context to

---

[1] Not included is the city-county of San Francisco because its Board of Supervisors is a much more professionalized legislative body than the other city councils in the region.

council activities and processes, it does not enter the analyses presented in the following chapters.[2] Moreover, though cities are more or less connected with one another, intergovernmental relations and council involvement in these relations are not part of the analysis. Rather, it is the city environment in its various dimensions that serves as the context for analyzing the structures, processes, behavior patterns, relationships, and policies of city councils.

Some of the contexts in which councils are constituted, exist, and act, such as the electoral context or the policy environment, are fully described in later chapters. The task here is to spell out, first, what is meant by environment generically, though our concern is less with defining the concept than with the uses to which it may be put once its meaning is clarified; and second, what is meant by the city's "physical and social environment." In particular, the urban environment in its physical and social aspects must be conceptualized in ways that are conducive to treating it as a theoretical variable in its own right.

Environment: What a Unit Is Not

Environment has been called "the aggregate of all the external conditions and influences affecting the life and development of an organism, etc., human behavior, society, etc."[3] Simple and neutral as this definition appears to be, it can give rise to extraordinary complications. In the first place, whenever two concepts are counterposed, as are organism and environment, there is the possibility that the counterposition will become a dualism obstructing scientific inquiry. Prominent examples of dualisms are the counterposi-

---

[2] Our collaborator, Thomas E. Cronin, has made the metropolitan context and councilmen's behavior and orientations toward this context the focus of another companion volume to this study. See Thomas E. Cronin, *The Metropolitan Crucible: Intergovernmental Relations* (Indianapolis: The Bobbs-Merrill Company, forthcoming).

[3] We do not blush to cite this definition from Webster's *New Collegiate Dictionary*. It is also quoted in the lead-off paragraph of the article on "environment" by Marston Bates, *International Encyclopedia of the Social Sciences* (New York: Macmillan and Free Press, 1968), Vol. 5, p. 91.

tions of soul and body, of force and matter, and of the individual and society. The dualism of organism and environment does not escape the predicaments that have characterized these other dualisms.[4] They pervade the controversies of determinists and possibilists in geography and the controversies of environmentalists and hereditists in biology and psychology.

Second, there is the possibility of teleology—of ascribing to the environment purposive qualities that are thought to be immanent in it. The environment is said to influence, control, or direct the behavior of the organism. This attribution of purpose to the environment through the use of action words may be metaphorical license, but especially in causal analysis is this usage likely to occasion deceptive interpretations of the relationship between organism and environment. The tendency to anthropomorphize the environment is less dangerous when the environment referred to is the social or human rather than the natural or physical environment, because people do in fact act with purposes in mind; but even in this connection the tendency to treat the human environment as if it were an actor creates analytic difficulties.[5]

Finally, the dualism of organism and environment creates problems of boundary setting. Working at high levels of conceptual abstraction, some theorists stress the analytic need for setting off the system whose functioning they seek to explain from an environment that is not part of the system. They therefore come to be preoccupied with the boundaries that presumably separate system from environment. However, after having specified the boundaries, they must seek to overcome them by postulating, often in complicated ways, the interactions or exchanges between system and environment.[6] In the course of definitional elaboration, both con-

---

[4] We have elsewhere discussed some of the intellectual problems that a dualism can create. See Heinz Eulau, "The Maddening Methods of Harold D. Lasswell: Some Philosophical Underpinnings," *Journal of Politics* 30 (February 1968): 8.

[5] See Harold and Margaret Sprout, "Environmental Factors in the Study of International Politics," *Conflict Resolution* 1 (December 1957): 309–328, who tend to write off the teleological implications of the vocabulary of action in discourse about environment. But their article remains the only serious conceptual treatment of environment in political science.

[6] See, for instance, David Easton, *A Framework for Political Analysis* (Englewood Cliffs, N.J.: Prentice-Hall, 1965), Chapter V, pp. 59–75: "The Environment of a Political System."

cepts—system and environment—tend to be reified and become useless as analytic tools in empirical inquiry.

We mention these difficulties not because we are interested in conceptual exegesis or criticism but because they sensitize us to the great care we must take in using the concept of environment. As we prefer to work with concepts that are close to the concrete "things" with which we are concerned, we hope to avoid some of the familiar difficulties that the terms organism and environment engender. Ordinary language use will again guide us.

It seems to us that in ordinary language environment is used in two ways. First, we speak of the environment as something that the "environed thing" (or unit, as we shall call it) is not. For instance, the city council is not the city, but the city is the council's environment. As cities differ in regard to many things, for instance, size and density of population, the council's environment is said to differ from city to city, depending on population size and density. Presumably, council behavior in one environment differs from council behavior in another environment. Implicit in this usage, then, is the assumption that a unit's behavior varies with varying environments. Nothing is said, of course, about how it varies or why it varies as it does. In other words, no hypotheses are entertained about the nature of the relationship between unit and environment. Saying that the environment is simply what the unit is not may help in clarifying the terms, but in the absence of hypotheses about the nature of the relationship between unit and environment the distinction is purely descriptive and theoretically empty.

In a second usage, we say that what is significant *in* the environment of a thing or unit is another thing or unit. In other words, it is not a case of the environment being what the unit is not, but rather the unit in connection with something else constitutes the environment. For instance, we may say that as they are a group, councilmen are the most significant factors in each other's environment. In shorthand language, the council is a factor in each member's environment. Councilmen A and B do not exhaust all the things in their own respective environments; rather, their interaction constitutes a special environment. In this usage, then, the environment is an emergent phenomenon that would not be there if there were no relationship between two things.

This explication can be extended to physical or natural factors as well. It is not "nature" (for instance, oceans or mountains) that constitutes the environment of the unit man, but rather it is man's relationship to nature that constitutes the environment. A mountain range or an ocean crossed by man are different from a mountain range or ocean not crossed. The mountain range or ocean are factors *in* man's environment only insofar as man places himself in a relationship with these factors.[7]

This second usage avoids some of the difficulties that the counterposition of unit and environment can occasion. In the first place, the danger of dualistic treatment is minimized. The unit is not set off from its environment but is part of it. The environment would not be "there," for the unit to be *in* it, if the unit did not stand in an identifiable relationship with something else. We speak of "unit-in-environment" rather than of "unit and environment." Just how unit-in-environment works is a matter of empirical determination. The relationship between unit and significant other factors in the environment may be one of mutual role expectations—as between councilmen; or it may be cognitive and evaluative—as when the council perceives a problem and does something about it; or it may be causal—as when the council responds to a competitive electoral situation by increased campaign activity; or it may be instrumental—as when the council allocates or reallocates available resources; or it may be cultural—as when the council shares community norms concerning what kind of place the city ought to be.

Second, the conception of unit-in-environment is nonteleological. The environment does not "force" the unit to behave in certain ways; it does not "influence" the unit's action, and so on. The environment presents conditions or circumstances within which the unit behaves, but as the unit is in the environment, the en-

---

[7] George Herbert Mead, speaking of organic evolution, gives this illustration: "If an animal has eyes, it has an environment that has color; if it has ears, it lives in a world of sounds; if it has taste, its environment is sapid; if nostrils, its world is odorous." See George Herbert Mead, *Movements of Thought in the Nineteenth Century* (Chicago: University of Chicago Press, 1936), p. 140.

vironment may change as the unit's behavior changes. It is not the environment that determines the behavior of the unit, but rather it is the unit-in-environment that behaves in characteristic ways. An urban council behaves in different ways from a rural council, or a council exposed to an active group life in the city acts in ways different from a council not so exposed.

Finally, if we think of unit-in-environment rather than of unit and environment, neither the unit nor the environment appear to be sharply bounded. The unit's boundaries are porous and flexible. The unit is more or less permeable. For instance, for some purposes the city manager becomes "part of" the council in a very immediate sense. This permeability of the unit is a critical property of its structure. The physical environment is similarly penetrable. The unit not only adapts itself to the environment of which it is a part by establishing linkages, performing services, internalizing environmental norms, perceiving conditions, or responding to challenges, but it also penetrates and regulates the environment. The distinction between unit and environment becomes one of observational standpoints. What is unit and what environment is a matter of looking at the same phenomena from different perspectives.

Environment, then, is an analytic term that we use to designate things which, in various ways, "hang together" in a complex arrangement of parts. This hanging together may involve social interaction, as between city councilmen; it may involve symbolic interaction, as between candidates in electoral competition who are never in direct contact with each other; or it may involve cognitive interaction, as when the council deals with conditions in the city.

Whatever the form of the relationship between one thing or unit and another, certain things are abstracted out of the whole, because one cannot treat everything at once, and then reconstituted as environment. The environment is never caught in its wholeness. It is decomposed by the participant or by the observer, and certain parts that stand in meaningful relationship to each other are said to be in each other's environment. Whatever environment one refers to abstractly—natural, material, social, cultural, economic, political, and so on—only some aspects serve as surrogates of the whole. For instance, we may speak of the urban environment, but we mean to say that some things are meaningfully related to each other—for instance dense population, commercial establishments, broad tax base, and so on. It is the particular set of relationships among particular things that makes for the emergence of an environment in which each unit is related to other units or things.

The distinction is sometimes made between "operational environment" and "psychological environment."[8] The operational environment is said to exist apart from the unit's cognitions, though it limits or constrains the unit's behavior regardless of whether it is perceived. The psychological environment, on the other hand, is said to be the environment that is the unit's focus of attention. From the perspective of unit-in-environment pursued here, the distinction is conceptually not necessary. For whether perceived or not, the environment is a property of the environed unit. A big-city council as contrasted with a small-city council is a unit whose environment is a big city. We mean to say that a council that has as its environment a big city shares with other things in the city the quality of being "big cityish." Being big cityish is a contextual property of the council. Whether this quality or property of the unit, stemming from its environmental context, is perceived is of no conceptual importance, though relevant perceptions may have significant consequences for the unit's behavior.

A Conception of Urbanism

If, as contextual treatment assumes, council conduct in all its manifestations—as adaptations, linkages, or policies—is in part a response to challenges from the urban environment, it is necessary to select indicators of this environment that trigger or contain relevant behavioral patterns and processes. There is good reason to believe that population size, density, growth, and diversity are revealing indicators of urbanism. One need not accept Herbert Spencer's organismic analogy to appreciate his observation that "along with increase of size in societies goes increase of structure.

---

[8] Sprout, "Environmental Factors in International Politics," p. 318.

. . . The social aggregate, homogeneous when minute, habitually gains in heterogeneity along with each increment of growth; and to reach great size must acquire great complexity."[9] Durkheim, in turn, recognized that as population density increases, social interaction also increases, and with it social complexity: "The division of labor develops, therefore, as there are more individuals sufficiently in contact to be able to act and react upon one another. If we agree to call this relation and the active commerce resulting from it dynamic or moral density, we can say that the progress of the division of labor is in direct ratio to the moral or dynamic density of society."[10]

Population size, density, and heterogeneity have consequences not only for social organization and structure but also for the psychic aspects of collective and individual behavior. Following Simmel's discussion of the social-psychological concomitants of urbanism,[11] Robert E. Park described the city as "a state of mind, a body of customs and traditions, of the organized attitudes and sentiments that inhere in these customs and are transmitted with this tradition."[12] Louis Wirth, finally, linked both social-structural and social-psychological variables to ecological factors. For sociological purposes, he wrote, "a city may be defined as a relatively large, dense, and permanent settlement of socially heterogeneous individuals."[13] However, unlike other theorists who worked with ideal-typical constructs of society,[14] Wirth did not expect to find

---

[9] Herbert Spencer, *Principles of Sociology* (New York: D. Appleton and Company, 1892), Vol. I, p. 459.

[10] Émile Durkheim, *The Division of Labor in Society*, translated by George Simpson (New York: The Free Press, 1960), p. 257.

[11] Reprinted in Kurt Wolff, ed., *The Sociology of Georg Simmel* (New York: The Free Press, 1950), pp. 409–424.

[12] Robert E. Park, "The City: Suggestions for the Investigation of Human Behavior in the Urban Environment," in Robert E. Park, Ernest W. Burgess, and Roderick D. McKenzie, *The City* (Chicago: University of Chicago Press, 1925), p. 1.

[13] Louis Wirth, "Urbanism as a Way of Life," in Paul K. Hatt and Albert J. Reiss, Jr., eds., *Cities and Society: The Revised Reader in Urban Sociology* (New York: The Free Press, 1957), p. 50.

[14] See Ferdinand Toennies, *Fundamental Concepts of Sociology*, translated and supplemented by Charles P. Loomis (Chicago: University of Chicago Press, 1940), for *Gemeinschaft* and *Gesellschaft;* Henry S. Maine, *Ancient Law* (London, 1861; New York: Beacon Press, 1963), for status and contract; Durkheim,

abrupt and discontinuous variations as a community's size increased. He suggested as a general hypothesis that "the larger, the more densely populated, and the more heterogeneous a community, the more accentuated the characteristics associated with urbanism will be."[15]

Contemporary empirical studies find that population size and related variables are by far the dominant component properties of the urban environment. Hadden and Borgatta, in an extensive factor-analytical study, show that when population size is related to other variables indicative of the city's specialized activities and processes, "it is an inescapable conclusion that sheer size has a tremendous effect on many structural aspects of cities."[16]

When speaking of the city's physical and social environment, therefore, one means, among other things, the conditions associated with population size, density, and heterogeneity.[17] With increasing size and density, the city as a physical structure becomes more complex and intricate. Size and density have economic consequences on the ways in which people earn their livings. The division of labor and specialization in the wake of population growth make for highly interdependent forms of economic coordination and accelerated exploitation of natural resources; but they also generate new economic and social capabilities to meet the needs of large populations.

At the level of interpersonal relations, increasing size and density, aided by increasing diversity, make for a host of problems stemming from intergroup differences of cultural, social, and ethnic kinds. They tend to reduce the effect of informal social

---

The Division of Labor in Society, for *solidarité mécanique* and *organique;* and Howard Becker, *Through Values to Social Interpretation* (Durham, N.C.: Duke University Press, 1950), for sacred and secular societies.

[15] Wirth, "Urbanism as a Way of Life," in *Cities and Society,* p. 51.

[16] Jeffrey K. Hadden and Edgar F. Borgatta, *American Cities: Their Social Characteristics* (Chicago: Rand McNally, 1965), p. 40.

[17] In the following synopsis, we draw particularly on the following: Leo F. Schnore, *The Urban Scene: Human Ecology and Demography* (New York: The Free Press, 1965); Philip M. Hauser and Leo F. Schnore, *The Study of Urbanization* (New York: John Wiley and Sons, 1965); and Leonard Reissman, *The Urban Process: Cities in Industrial Societies* (New York: The Free Press, 1964).

controls in favor of laws and regulations enforced by bureaucratic organizations and instrumentalities. Although the image of the modern city as an undifferentiated mass of people characterized by anonymity, impersonality, standardization, and disorganization is exaggerated, population growth does have effects on the nature of social relationships and on individual adaptation to the changing human environment.

Moreover, although in the modern city social organization may be increasingly based on contract rather than on status, new forms of social stratification, based on economic differentiation or differences in influence and prestige, emerge as the population increases in size and density. Social stratification in turn develops along areal lines. Williams and his associates found that "whole sections of cities are identified with particular industrial and commercial activities and entire neighborhoods are given over to one racial, ethnic, or otherwise socially differentiated group."[18] The same process of differentiation based on social stratification appears to make for differences between cities in the metropolitan region. As new cities evolve, differences in the social-class character between smaller, more homogeneous (whether upper or lower class) and larger, more heterogeneous cities become evident. Cities, it appears, are not only maintaining but often developing distinct and characteristic "public life styles."[19]

Synoptic as this conception of the urban environment is, it suffices to justify the use of population size as the major surrogate indicator of the urban context, its challenges and pressures. This is not to say that the context is wholly captured by population variables. But it is clear, statistically speaking, that a significant amount of variance in council behavior is produced by population size.

---

[18] Oliver P. Williams, Harold Herman, Charles S. Liebman, and Thomas R. Dye, *Suburban Differences and Metropolitan Policies: A Philadelphia Story* (Philadelphia: University of Pennsylvania Press, 1965), pp. 17–18.
[19] See Oliver P. Williams, "Life-Style Values and Political Decentralization in Metropolitan Areas," in Terry N. Clark, ed., *Community Structure and Decision-Making: Comparative Analyses* (San Francisco: Chandler Publishing Company, 1968), pp. 427–440.

Demographic Peculiarities of Bay Region Cities

While population size is a generally valid surrogate indicator of city characteristics associated with urbanization, especially physical complexity and social heterogeneity, it is appropriate to take note of some demographic and ecological peculiarities of San Francisco Bay Area cities. As the correlation coefficients in Table 3–1 show, the relationships between population size and density, on the one hand, and further indicators of urbanism, on the other, even though positive or negative in the direction one would expect on the basis of the size-density model, are consistently weak, with only a few exceptions.

Table 3–1

Correlation Coefficients (r) for Relationships
Among City Size, Density, and Selected Demographic
Variables in 82 Cities of the San Francisco Bay Region

	Population	
	Size	Density
Size	—	.36
% Nonwhite	.53	.33
% Unemployed	.17	−.03
% Manufacturing employment	.13	.05
% Moving to county, 1955–1960	.09	.01
Median value of rental unit	.01	.15
% with income under $3,000	.01	−.09
% Foreign-born	−.01	−.05
Median school years	−.02	.11
% Four years high school	−.09	.07
% in white collar jobs	−.10	.10
Median family income	−.14	−.12
% with income over $10,000	−.14	−.09
Median market value of home	−.16	−.18
% Owner-occupied house	−.22	−.17

To interpret these results, one must appreciate the historical growth pattern of the San Francisco Bay region. Unlike most other metropolitan areas, the region's urban development did not follow the normal concentric pattern, with industrial and commercial activities gravitating toward the central city, and subsequently, as the core city is no longer able to hold its growing population, with suburbs sprawling out from the center and filling the empty spaces between it and older outlying cities which come to be the metropolitan fringe. As James E. Vance, Jr., has persuasively shown, the San Francisco Bay region is not a conurbation—a group of cities originally formed to exploit a common natural resource and since grown together.[20] Rather, the region is composed of cities originally formed for different reasons and since grown farther apart. As a result, many of these cities are largely self-sufficient employing or residential areas. Moreover, from the beginning, the Bay region consisted of multiple urban centers, with San Francisco specializing in commerce, banking, and food distribution and the East Bay cities containing most of the region's industries and warehousing. More recently, the San Jose–Palo Alto area has become a center of light manufacturing and the aerospace industry. The dispersion of economic centers has continued to increase, with food distribution now being decentralized in at least four subregional centers, large shopping areas springing up throughout the region, and commercial and industrial activity developing in both its northern and southern parts.[21]

Given this historical growth pattern, it is not surprising that the correlation coefficients between the population variables and other indicators of urbanization are low. Only the relationship between population size and the proportion of nonwhites is substantial, conforming with the common observation that the black population is concentrated in the large cities and finds it difficult

---

[20] James E. Vance, Jr., *Geography and Urban Evolution in the San Francisco Bay Area* (Berkeley: Institute of Governmental Studies, 1964).
[21] Our collaborator Robert Eyestone has imaginatively used the notion of the San Francisco Bay region as consisting of "urban realms" in a companion volume to show varieties of policy development in different subareas of the region. See Robert Eyestone, *The Threads of Public Policy: A Study in Policy Leadership* (Indianapolis: The Bobbs-Merrill Company, 1971).

to move into the suburban or fringe cities (although Negroes are found in several nonincorporated ghetto areas).

Even the relationship between population size and density is lower in the Bay region cities than elsewhere.[22] This can be partly explained by the positive relationship between growth in population and growth in land area. Although cities grow in population, they also expand their land areas, thus reducing density.

Size as Context and Variable

Although city size can be accepted as a valid surrogate variable for the structural and even social-psychological aspects of urban life, how it is used in analysis imposes different constraints on interpretation. Primarily, we view city size as a context which gives meaning to the phenomena or relations among phenomena within it. How size as a contextual property of councils is interpreted depends, therefore, a good deal on the phenomena to be contextually analyzed and interpreted. For instance, in Chapter 11 it is found that certain measures of political competition are more highly interrelated in small cities than in large cities. Size is here construed to mean that the context is characterized by more or less political intimacy in the population. And on the assumption that political intimacy aggravates the potential for conflict, the finding that different measures of political competition are more highly related in the small (read "intimate") city becomes plausible.

City size can also be directly related to a dependent variable whose variance is to be explained. But this usage has limited theoretical advantages. At best, it alerts the analyst to the possibility that if variables related to size, but also to each other, are not controlled by size—that is, treated contextually—there is the risk of spurious inference. Indeed, city size as such is not a particularly interesting interpretative variable. What makes it interesting is the particular interpretation that it can be given if it serves as a control variable descriptive of the urban context.

---

[22] For instance, Schnore, *The Urban Scene,* p. 318, reports a zero-order correlation coefficient of .55 for city size and density in 213 urbanized areas of the country.

This is most evident in our handling of size operationally. Because size is a continuous variable, any classification of cities in terms of size is necessarily arbitrary. Ideologists, whether speaking in praise of the small community or denouncing it, are hard put to attach a precise numerical value to what they mean by "small" or "large." If, for instance, the criterion is face-to-face interaction and the "naturalness" of social relationships, it is still difficult to say whether the "small community" is one of 2,500 people, 10,000, or, as in the Athenian *polis,* 30,000.[23] It is for this reason that we make the most arbitrary but least whimsical choice of all by dichotomizing the cities exactly at the median, with the result that 41 cities with a population of less than 17,000 are characterized as small, while 41 cities with a population of more than 17,000 are characterized as large.[24]

The main handicap of this procedure is that the category "large cities" has a wider range than the category "small cities." A city with a population of 17,000 may, in some respects, seem "closer" in character to a city of 3,000 than to a city of 100,000.

Council size is also an important variable because it is a surrogate for what one may call its "milieu" or internal environment. Of the 82 councils, 67 have five members and 15 have seven or nine members (one council has 13). Defining the five-member councils as small and all those with seven or more members as large may be to ignore, perhaps even to violate, some aspects of empirical reality. It may well be that seven-member councils are more "like" five-member councils than they are "like" nine-member councils. But if one were to deal with council size in a more refined fashion than the dichotomy here adopted, the small numbers involved would make for even more data instability than is now the case. In opting for the dichotomy of small and large councils as defined, therefore, we are wholly aware of its arbitrariness. Its validity depends on its discriminative power in analysis.

If both city and council size are introduced into analysis, the analytic problem is confounded. Of the 67 small councils, 39 are

---

[23] Robert A. Dahl, "The City in the Future of Democracy," *American Political Science Review* 61 (December 1967): 957.
[24] In some cases we are also working, mainly for descriptive purposes, with a trichotomy—cutting city size at 10,000 and below for "small" cities, at 50,000 and above for "large" cities, with cities of 10,000 to 50,000 being called "medium."

situated in small cities, 28 in large cities. Of the large councils, only two are in small cities and the rest in large ones. As a result of these distributions, we can control for city size really only in the case of the small councils. Therefore, we shall compare small councils in small cities with those in large cities, and we shall compare both with large councils, ignoring the fact that two of the latter are located in small cities.[25]

The Political Environment

Although the physical and social environments of Bay Area cities are highly diverse, they share many political and governmental features that reflect the ethos of nonpartisanship in local affairs. Most of the cities have a council-manager or council-administrator form of government, and most of them have the same general form of election.[26] In the great majority of cities, the councilmen, including the mayor, are elected at large; in a few, the mayor is elected separately; in some, candidates are named from particular districts, though all voters cast ballots for all candidates regardless of district; and some have runoff elections in the absence of absolute majorities. These differences are not numerically significant enough to be treated as variables.

The most important political feature shared by all the cities is that, legally and formally, they have nonpartisan elections—that is, the party affiliations of the candidates are not listed on the ballot.[27] The parties are not precluded from supporting or opposing candidates if they wish to do so, but in most cities they are not manifestly active in council elections. Of the 435 councilmen who were interviewed, only 17 reported having had the support of a

---

[25] While these two councils could have been dropped from the analysis, we opted against doing so after seeing that the two cities, though small by our arbitrary definition, sufficiently resembled large cities in other respects that assigning them to the large category for purposes of jointly examining city and council size did not distort the analysis.

[26] The role of the city manager and his relations with the council are explored in another companion volume to this study by Ronald O. Loveridge, *City Managers in Legislative Politics* (Indianapolis: The Bobbs-Merrill Company, 1971).

[27] See Eugene C. Lee, *The Politics of Nonpartisanship: A Study of California City Elections* (Berkeley: University of California Press, 1960).

party organization in the previous election. Eighty-seven percent
of the respondents felt that local government would be "worse off"
if councilmen were elected on a party ticket, and 84 percent felt
that "better people" are elected in nonpartisan than in partisan
elections. Eighty-two percent reported never having been con-
tacted by a party organization or party group on issues pending
before the council, and 68 percent denied finding it sometimes
useful to consult with anybody in either of the two major parties.[28]

These one-sided distributions testify to the pervasiveness of the
nonpartisan ethos in the municipal political environment, but
they do not preclude that a form of latent partisanship may also be
present. Careful inspection of the interviews, council by council,
revealed that there is no kind of party activity at the municipal
level, either in elections or otherwise, in 50 cities. Where party
activity in one form or another appears seems to depend largely, as

Table 3–2
Relationship Between Party Activity
at the Local Level and City Size

| | City Size | | |
	Small N = 40	Large N = 41	Total N = 81
No party is active	90%	34%	62%
Republicans are active	0	2	1
Democrats are active	5	29	17
Both parties are active	5	35	20
	100%	100%	100%

Table 3–2 shows, on city size. Parties are generally more active
in larger cities, and their activity may spill over into municipal
affairs. Nevertheless, because of the lopsided number of cities evi-

---

[28] The questions on which these data are based can be found in Appendix C,
Questions 72–77. The data are more fully analyzed in Gordon Black, *The Arena
of Electoral Competition* (Indianapolis: The Bobbs-Merrill Company, forthcoming).

dently without latent or manifest partisanship,[29] the problem was set aside, and the nature of the political environment, at least in its party aspect, will not be explored in this volume. Instead, we shall be working with a measure of "electoral context" that theoretically permits more relevant treatment of the problems posed in this study.

---

[29] "Latent partisanship" was explored in a preliminary study based on pretest data; see Heinz Eulau, Betty H. Zisk, and Kenneth Prewitt, "Latent Partisanship in Nonpartisan Elections: Effects of Political Milieu and Mobilization," in M. Kent Jennings and Harmon Zeigler, eds., *The Electoral Process* (Englewood Cliffs, N.J.: Prentice-Hall, 1966), pp. 208–237.

Part II

Social Organization as Collective Adaptation

INTRODUCTION

The city council is five, seven, or nine persons formally commissioned through electoral selection. This implies that, *ab initio,* it is merely an aggregate of individuals who happen to hold office in the same city. But five strangers meeting more or less often do not govern. The council governs, and the council is not an aggregate but a group of interacting men or women who collectively carry out common tasks. The council, then, is constituted in two respects—through formal and informal recruitment and election processes (which will be treated in Part III), but also organizationally by evolving internal structures that transform an aggregate into a decision-making group.

The council's social organization is a means of coordinating, integrating, regulating, and directing the work of its members. Social organization is collective adaptation to the need for becoming a decision-making group that can govern as well as adaptation to the challenges presented by the common task of governing.

The emphasis is on collective adaptation because how a group gets its work done is not simply a matter of each member's relationship with every other member, though interindividual relations are at the root of the council's jelling as a group. Rather, there are conditions in the interpersonal situation that are independent of person-to-person relations and over which individuals have basically no control, such as the number of paired relationships in the group due to its size or the multiple networks of interaction due to the size of the population in the external environment. Were it otherwise, social organization could be satisfactorily accounted for as the outcome of personality. Personality factors do play a part in how a group organizes itself, but it is impossible to account for organization in terms of personality precisely because such analysis does not deal with the impact of social complexity on the emergence of group properties and their interdependencies.[1]

The most significant factor in the individual councilman's political life space is other councilmen and, similarly, the most significant factor in the council's political environment is the body of citizens it represents and governs. Out of the triple bonding of the relationships involved—councilman with councilman, councilman with council, and council with citizenry—arises the problem of collective adaptation. To be effective as a member of the council, the individual councilman learns to work with his colleagues. In the process of these interpersonal adjustments councilmen develop forms of behavior more or less conducive to coping as a collectivity with the problems of governance. The forms of behavior prevailing in the council are constrained by the bonds that constitute the internal and external context. Collective adaptation is the council's *modus operandi* determined by and taking place within its dual environment.

Of the factors affecting collective adaptation none is therefore more crucial than the sheer number of interacting persons. What two persons do or can do in relating to each other is very different from what three persons do or can do. As a group increases in size, individual affective and cognitive processes are transformed into group properties, interaction patterns become more complicated, mutual adjustment becomes more difficult, and social orga-

---

[1] This is perhaps one of the reasons why Sigmund Freud's venture into group analysis is neither convincing nor acceptable. The basic point of *Group Psychology and the Analysis of the Ego* (1921) is that groups are formed as a result of members' common identification with a leader. But this emphasis on the leader as the *deus ex machina* is at most a very partial explanation of collective adaptation. Undoubtedly, some emotional attachments among group members are probably necessary conditions of group life, but they need not be centered in a leader and they need not be exclusively affective. Groups faced with the responsibility for performing, especially, may be held together by cooperative modes other than leadership.

nization replaces spontaneous behavior. This is so because with an absolute increase in size the number of interpersonal relationships increases exponentially. A five-member council is characterized by ten relationships; a seven-member council by 21; and a nine-member council by 36 relationships.

The council's size is not alone in affecting collective adaptation. Councilmen are not the participants in a small-group laboratory experiment that purposefully isolates the group from its external environment. Rather, councilmen interact in response to and in the context of citizens and community associations. The size of the citizenry is as critical a factor in collective adaptation as is the council's own size. As population increases, the number of relationships between the council and individual citizens or civic groups also increases. The task of governance in a complex environment is objectively different from that in a relatively simple environment, and external complexity influences the council's organization just as does internal complexity.

This is not to say that council and city size have independent and always different consequences for social organization. They may in fact reinforce each other or they may be at odds with each other. They may have different consequences for different modes of organization. These are empirical problems for whose solution there are, at present, no firm theoretical guidelines, and we do not propose to test only a priori propositions about the effects of social complexity. For, and this requires emphasis, our interest is not in the consequences of internal or external complexity as such for the council's social organization. Both council size and city size are, in this connection, surrogate variables for a host of sociological or social-psychological dimensions in the council's life space whose interpretative uses are more attractive for the purpose of grounding theory in data than for the purpose of testing hypotheses about the effects of size as such.

We shall explore in the following chapters the independent and joint consequences of council and city size on the emergence of council properties and structures, largely to obtain a feel for the implications of size as a surrogate of complexity. Our primary focus, however, is the emergence of social organization as a solution to collective adaptation *within* more or less complex contexts rather than the effects of context on social organization and collective adaptation. Our task is to observe, if not explain, how the council *becomes* a viable decision-making unit through a social organization that is adapted to conditions of varying complexity in its internal and external environment. Our approach is action- and actor-oriented in the sense that political behavior is conceived as a transaction between actor and context of action.

The overwhelming reality facing any legislative group is that, sooner or later, it must make decisions which, for all practical purposes, involve a choice between only two alternatives. It can only say "yea" or "nay" to a proposition before it. This very simple circumstance has a far-reaching impact. While the council is characterized by a variety of other properties and processes, its most distinctive social process is voting. As voting is a repetitive process, the council's most pervasive structural feature is its decision structure—the relatively stable pattern that emerges from the voting situation when councilmen take stands either with or against each other. Indeed, it is the agreed-on decision rules in terms of which voting is conducted that make the council a collective unit of action. We shall explicate, in Chapter 9, three different analytic dimensions of the decision structure.

Although the decision structure is an almost defining property of a legislative body, it is not the only structure that matters in collective action. Like other persons joining together in groups, councilmen expect to derive from membership on the council certain advantages or benefits which they could not obtain by acting alone and whose achievement is in fact predicated on collective choice-making. By being joined together, the needs, goals, or purposes of individual councilmen also become the needs, goals, or purposes of the council. Of course, not all individual purposes will become the group's purposes, and not all the group's purposes will be an individual member's purposes. The goals of individual councilmen and those of the council may be at odds. Nevertheless, whatever an individual member's motivation for joining, or however precise or ambiguous the council's goals, the development of collective expectations as to what the council should do in the performance of its mandate and in legislating for the community is a significant social process.

In the course of interacting with one another to achieve their individual goals, councils form expectations as to the legitimacy of these goals and as to the conduct appropriate to their attainment. As individual goals are legitimized and, as a consequence, accepted as worthy of support, council goals emerge and the members orient themselves to collective action in terms of these goals. Out of this subtle interplay of goal expectations and orientations to action develops a role structure that is more or less differentiated. Whatever its content or form, the role structure is a critical property of the council's social organization. In its absence the council would find it difficult to coordinate its activities in ways conducive to the achievement of its collective goals. Chapter 8 is devoted to an explication and analysis of the council's role structure.

Even if voting on the part of each council member can be assumed to be rational, it does not follow that collective decision-making is similarly rational. It is by no means uncommon that, in setting goals and choosing means, criteria other than rationality intrude on council decision-making, especially if the values to be maximized are controversial and the goals remain vague. The role and decision structures may be rooted not in rational considerations but in political or social circumstances that reduce the possibility of rational behavior. Personal relations and interactions in the council stemming from private motives may interfere with or constrain the definition of council goals. The council's interactive structure is therefore an important property of its social organization.

The council, like any group, has a communication network that facilitates or impedes the transmission of explicit information and inadvertent cues among the members. Lines of communication are variously structured as councilmen interact with each other more or less frequently and more or less formally. The messages exchanged in a particular setting may be more or less politically relevant. As will be shown in Chapter 7, differences in communication between political, public-formal, and private-informal settings give the council's social organization its characteristic structure of interaction.

Just how the council organizes itself for legislative action also depends a good deal on the personal relations among its members. These relations may be warm, friendly, and collegial; they may be tense and antagonistic; or they may be disinterested and impersonal. Out of the feelings accompanying interpersonal relations emerges a social climate or group atmosphere that is a characteristic property of any social organization. It will be seen in Chapter 6 that the council's social climate is an especially critical property because it seems to intervene between some aspects of social organization that are mainly responses to the council's internal complexity and others that are responses to external complexity.

Legislatures develop patterns of governing behavior that distinguish them from administrative or judicial groups. This is not to say that bargaining, compromising, coalition formation, or exchanges of trust and confidence are exclusive features of legislative organization. These practices can also be found in governing groups whose tasks and organizational structures are not formally legislative. And legislatures may in some respects resemble administrative groups. But the legislature is a more genuinely political group than either a court or an administrative bureau. Insofar as practices like bargaining or coalition formation are prominent features of council conduct, the social organization is politicized. This is also true of the council's governing style—the premises underlying governance. The governing style may be political if the legislative process is experienced as a political game to be won or lost; it may be pragmatic if legislative action is seen as primarily based on factual and practical considerations; or it may be paternalistic and benevolent if the council presumes to act on the basis of its own conception of what is best for the community and in the public interest. Governing styles and practices will be reviewed and analyzed in Chapter 5.

A variety of particularized social relations permeate the council. Familiar social relations like friendship, respect, or expertise may be more or less widely shared in a legislative group as a whole. Other relational properties, which we shall introduce in Chapter 4, are cosponsorship in the promotion of proposals, the anticipation of potential opposition to legislation, and opinion leadership in decision-making. Of concern here is the incidence of such social relations in the council as a whole and the interdependencies among them.

Although the council is formally a body of equals, differential evaluations made by members when they seek out others as friends, experts, cosponsors, and so on give rise to social stratification or a status order. This is as likely in elected bodies as in any other type of association. Whatever their genesis, social evaluations separating the member who gets most of what there is to get from the member who gets least vary from council to council. The status order therefore may be highly egalitarian or it may be as stratified as it is in formally hierarchical groups. Stratification, whatever its shape, is a persistent and pervasive property of the council's social organization. Chapter 4 includes a description of the council's status order.

So little is known about small legislative groups that a description of social organization is valuable to analysis. In addition to description, however, the interrelationships among the properties are analyzed. This is accomplished in a cumulative fashion, each chapter incorporating properties described in previous chapters, so that the emergence of the council's social organization can be observed as it unfolds. The resulting picture is complicated; there are many properties and typical structures of these properties, and there are interdependencies among the properties that are themselves structured in typical ways. But complication is inevitable because it is multiple structures and multiple relationships among them which give to any group its social organization.

We can think of social organization only if the independent parts stand in orderly and predictable relationships to one another. This presents two difficulties. First, there is no way of knowing whether all the component properties have been discovered; if not (which is likely), at least some of the structural links making for social organization remain undetected. In the absence of a comprehensive theory of small legislative groups as social organizations, caution is called for, if only to avoid the self-deception that one has in fact discovered the council's social organization.

Second, though order and predictability must be assumed if we are to speak meaningfully of social organization, it does not follow that there is a single causal model that represents the true organization. As the data are cross-sectional and synchronic, it is better to assume reciprocal causation or interdetermination among council properties rather than asymmetries. For practical purposes, properties will at times be treated as independent, intervening, dependent, or contextual variables, depending on the theoretical issue under review. This is especially the case in Chapter 10 where we examine the interdependencies of style, social climate, interaction, role differentiation, and decision structure.

Descriptive and analytic difficulties notwithstanding, social anatomy of the type attempted in the following chapters is desirable in political science. It shows structural differentiation as the process probably most conducive to collective adaptation. How the council is internally organized makes a difference in its external relations. One can, of course, study a political unit's foreign relations and policies without probing into its internal structure. Especially if many governing groups of like character are available for analysis, significant inferences can be drawn about how they adapt to external conditions and pressures. But such analysis ignores an important link in the chain of governance. For how a governing group adapts to or controls the external environment is not independent of how it deals with problems of internal organization.

Chapter 4

Social Relations and Stratification

The council is a group of five, seven, or nine persons brought together for the purpose of coping with public issues and making decisions—not as individuals but as a collectivity. Even if there has been a complete turnover in membership and all incumbents are new recruits, as an *institutionalized* group the council does not begin its work anew after each election. Rather, the individuals meeting as a council are predisposed to act and conduct themselves in rather predictable ways. Before joining together they already know a good deal about council tasks and practices. Formal rules and informal norms of conduct are transmitted by means of written records or through word of mouth. Expectations of what councilmen should do as a group are known to new members as a result of anticipatory socialization. A minimal bond exists between councilmen even if actual interaction has not yet occurred, and many councilmen know each other prior to election.

However, these minimal understandings do not make the council jell. Only as it proceeds with its tasks will the council's initial bondedness gradually undergo changes that make for collective adaptation. Different kinds of social relations occurring in the group under different conditions of social complexity come to play an increasingly important part in its social organization. They also give rise to a status order or system of stratification as a result of social differentiation among council members.

Types of Social Relations

Social relations refer to the nature of the bonds that give the council its essential wholeness.[1] While bonds of friendship or mutual deference may be more or less pervasive and give the council characteristic qualities of some consequence, of more import are the social relations that stem from its mandate to govern the city. Although the tasks of governance at the local level are relatively limited, they are sufficiently diverse and difficult to make for a division of labor and the acceptance of expertise or specialization.

Councilmen also relate to each other as political animals. They seek each other out for political support, appreciate each other's opposition, and follow each other in matters of political opinion. They recognize and value colleagues who, for whatever reasons, make their views felt and by force of argument give leadership. Proposals for legislation or action have a better chance of success if cosponsored by at least two members.[2] At the same time, councilmen take note when colleagues oppose their goals. Out of these social relations emerge group properties that are eminently political. To measure the council's various social relations, individual responses to a number of sociometric questions were summed at the group level by way of an "expansiveness index."[3]

Friendship

It is often suspected that friendship is an important consideration in political practice, yet surprisingly little is really known about it.[4] This is partially due to the politician's reluctance to

---

[1] See Robert K. Merton, *Social Theory and Social Structure* (rev. ed.; Glencoe, Ill.: The Free Press, 1957), p. 317.

[2] Cosponsorship as used here is not identical with coalition formation as used in Chapter 5. Cosponsorship is a condition of coalition formation, but cosponsorship does not necessarily lead to coalition formation as a governing practice.

[3] For a description of the expansiveness index, see Appendix B4.1.

[4] But see Samuel Patterson, "Patterns of Interpersonal Relations in a State Legislative Group: The Wisconsin Assembly," *Public Opinion Quarterly* 23 (Spring 1959): 101–109; Alan Fiellin, "The Functions of Informal Groups in Legislative Institutions," *Journal of Politics* 24 (February 1962): 72–91; William

admit that so particularistic a criterion as friendship will influence his public conduct. Indeed, some councilmen would deny the relevance of friendship altogether: "I'll vote with somebody if I agree with him, and vote against him if I disagree. Personal relations don't carry much weight"; or "The councilmen who are good friends are often the ones who vote differently; if friendship played a part, they wouldn't."[5] But the place of friendship in politics is difficult to treat meaningfully also because politicians can claim that "all are my friends." If such responses mean anything, they mean that friendship is a cheap commodity; and if it is cheap, it is unlikely to be politically consequential.[6]

But not all councilmen are so evasive. Some are candid, and their candor is enlightening. They recognize the informal pressures on political belief or conduct generated by friendship: "If there are three members of the council whose wives play bridge together and they golf together, it's almost axiomatic that they'll think along the same lines. If they get along socially, they'll get along politically." While friendship is thus recognized as a very pervasive bond that penetrates political behavior to the point where it is indistinguishable from other aspects of interpersonal relations, other respondents admit its salience only in situations that, paradoxically, are indifferent to them: "Occasionally there's an issue of no strong feeling either way. One consideration is who is supporting it and who is opposing it. I think you support a friend." Friendship may also be relied on as a decisional criterion in a situation in which a choice is difficult rather than a matter of indifference: "If you are on the fence, and some fellow is sincere, and I'm not sure, I would go along with my friend."

Whatever the particular content of the responses about friend-

Buchanan, "The Bonds of Friendship," in John C. Wahlke, Heinz Eulau, William Buchanan, and Leroy C. Ferguson, *The Legislative System: Explorations in Legislative Behavior* (New York: John Wiley and Sons, 1962), pp. 216–235.
[5] The quotations come from answers to this question: "From your experience, would you say that personal friendships among the councilmen play an important part in the way they vote, some part, or no part at all?" The measure of friendship was constructed from nominations to a follow-up question: "Whom among all the councilmen do you personally like best?"
[6] For this reason, responses of this nature were treated as nonresponses in constructing the measure of friendship.

ship, they suggest that friendship in politics may be a *political* variable. And as our analysis proceeds, it will be seen that friendship as a group property is related to the directly political properties of the council more than to others.[7]

Respect

In a governmental group like the city council, the respect or mutual deference generated among its members is an important component of its social organization. Respect means that a member's words or deeds are given attention and consideration, even though they may be a source of disagreement or conflict, and that there is an appreciation of the individual member as a person of significance because he possesses some virtue which accrues to the benefit of the council. Respect is rooted in a variety of attributions, some of them institutional, some broadly cultural, and some highly personal. Some attribution may be circular, as when a member is said to be respected because of his formal position as mayor, for he may have been chosen mayor because he is respected. Seniority of tenure on the council may be a source of respect. More often, it is the contribution which the individual is seen to make to the council as a group that is appreciated. His dedication to the council's work, long hours put in on council business, being helpful to others and cooperative, and similar qualities are considered worthy of respect.[8] In addition to these institution-related sources, there are external criteria, largely of a status-relevant sort, that serve as bases of deference. Success in one's business or profession, educational achievement, or prestige in the community are recognized as deserving respect within the council.

---

[7] Although friendship is a property in interpersonal relations that would not seem to be amenable to analysis at the level of the group as a whole, it is possible to conceive of the council as being more or less saturated by ties of friendship among its members. Our concern is not with "who likes whom?" but with the pervasiveness of friendship choices in the council.

[8] The respect measure was constructed from nominations in response to this question: "Who, among the present councilmen, would you say is the *most respected?* I mean the kind of man a new member would look up to when he's just learning about the council and how it works? What makes for his being so respected?"

Expertise

No matter how small a governing group, the demands made on it are likely to make for a division of labor among its members. Although city councilmen are amateurs called upon to make decisions on a variety of public issues brought before them or considered on their own initiative, they bring to the common task a rich and diverse background of interest, experience, or knowledge that, in the aggregate, benefits the council.

Councilmen specialize in a wide range of subject matter, a range as wide as the activities carried on in a particular city. There are specialists in planning and zoning; in public safety problems, including fire and police; in fiscal matters, from taxing to budgeting and accounting; in amenities such as recreation facilities and cultural undertakings. Specialization in these subjects may be grounded in private occupational or professional training and experience, in personal interest and ability, or in experiences due to prior participation in the city's auxiliary government such as planning commissions, police boards, library committees, and so on.[9]

Expertise is not the the same thing as specialization, and in some councils the notion of expertise was rejected. One reason might be that members "all shift commissions and know a little about each one but not too much about any one of them." Another reason would be that though "some have more experience and activity than others, none of them have a depth of background that makes them an expert." Expertise was not considered necessary in a council "confronted mostly with amendments and modifications of existing ordinances." The amateurish condition of the council would be given as a reason: "No one becomes an expert at something they only spend a few hours a week at." Other councils felt that expertise should come from the manager, the city attorney, and the administrative staff: "In a city manager type of government it is important to have an able, expert manager and council-

[9] The expertise measure was constructed from nominations in response to this question: "I would like to ask you about other councilmen in this connection (i.e., the councilman's self-identification as an expert). Is there another councilman, or several, who is especially expert on some aspects of council work?"

men with sound judgment. We bring in experts on important issues."

Opinion Leadership

Though the council is composed of persons whose votes count equally, this does not mean that their voices are heard equally. Some members are more likely to have their opinions and judgments prevail than others. They may be more articulate, persuasive, forceful, or convincing in presenting their arguments. Their success in occupations or professions relevant to council business or their experience in municipal affairs may give them an advantage in having their opinions accepted. Their prestige in the community, and council awareness of the need for community support, may be a factor. In conflict settings their leadership in factions may mark them as opinion leaders. Whatever the source of their influence, opinion leaders are easily recognized by their colleagues.[10]

However, in some councils opinion leadership is denied because the council self-consciously claims to be equalitarian: "We all come out even; we all listen to one another and share"; or "We operate pretty democratically; each person has a chance to speak, and we all try to come to an intelligent decision." Factionalism may interfere with opinion leadership: "As a rule I used to be most listened to; but now, with the split, the coalition gets together and decides most matters before we even come to the council session."

Cosponsorship

Promoting projects geared to the solution of community problems is something individual councilmen may espouse, but it is something they can seldom do on their own. They will seek out others able and willing to cosponsor a proposal, for a jointly spon-

---

[10] The opinion leadership measure was constructed from nominations to this question: "Who among the present council members would you say are the most likely to have their opinions accepted by the other councilmen?"

sored project is more likely to obtain attention, credence, and support. Of course, cosponsorship may be seen in strictly political terms, as a matter of mobilizing support:[11] "I like to have on my side those people who see the merits of the issue. However, on polar questions, it is advantageous to have someone from the other side as cosponsor." For other councilmen, cosponsorship may be more a matter of instrumental than political association. The respondent would point to some attribute of a colleague that he himself does not possess: "He fills in the holes that I don't think of. He thinks of problems in a different way." Other councilmen would be singled out as cosponsors because of their knowledge or experience: "He is a brilliant man, a professor of political science. I always check with him on key problems."

In some councils, however, there is no expectation at all that an individual member will solicit support for legislation or a course of action. As a result, cosponsorship does not appear as a relational property of the council. Asked whom they would like to have join them as cosponsors, respondents in some councils would reply: "We work as a majority to raise anything. It requires a majority to move. We play no power politics. We are all individuals and we all act that way. No. There is no one with whom I would like to cosponsor a measure. And it doesn't work that way."

Cosponsorship refers to something different from a coalition. While considerations of political advantage are not absent in cosponsorship, it is a more temporary pattern of alignment than is coalition formation. The choice of cosponsors is largely determined by the nature of the problems or proposals, while the formation of a coalition is undertaken with an eye on the relatively permanent advantage that may accrue from being in a steady partnership. Whereas cosponsorship is a possible base for the emergence of a stable coalition, cosponsorship arrangements are not usually of a permanent character.

---

[11] The cosponsor measure was constructed from nominations to a question which was a follow-up to a previous question about city problems: "On a key problem as we just talked about, is there any council member you would especially like to have join you as a cosponsor of a proposal you might have?"

Opposition Potential

In small face-to-face governing groups like councils, opposition from colleagues is part of the social organization. But it is by no means clear whether such opposition is harmful or helpful. It may be detrimental if unchecked or carried too far; but insofar as another's potential opposition is taken into account in an actor's own conduct as a form of anticipated reaction, it may serve as a cathartic agent that prevents mistakes in judgment or action.

Opposition is affected by many considerations.[12] It can be feared from colleagues who are perceived as friends or allies: "He's a very effective arguer and a real good friend; if he opposed something, I'd wonder if I were right." Opposition can come from ideological antagonists: "We don't see eye-to-eye in approaches to our community. His main concern is for the business community and I have a broader concern for all." Other respondents expressed concern about opposition which disrupts the council: "He has a way of fouling a whole issue up. Once he gets hold of it, he loses all perspective of the way it was planned."

Finally, but to a lesser extent, opposition is rooted in the council's power constellation: "He has a lot of political pull—maybe not himself, but the group he represents"; or "He controls two votes besides his own." Opposition is especially troublesome if it cannot be anticipated: "You never know how he is going to jump; he switches from one half hour to the next"; or "He is the one who is unpredictable; he sways back and forth. You never know what he will do."

The Matrix of Social Relations

The distribution of the social ties that bind council members and transform an aggregate of individuals into a group gives each council a characteristic social matrix. In a political group, its

---

[12] The question on which the opposition potential measure was based reads as follows: "If there is disagreement on the council in regard to some key problem, which members' opposition would you be most concerned about?"

explicitly political relations are likely to be more highly inter-related with one another than with its instrumental or honorific relations. And if politics has this power of harnessing kindred social relations, one should expect that the resulting matrix will be more symmetrical than chance would have it. Because the shape of the matrix is difficult to predict, our procedure is heuristic. Table 4–1 is roughly ordered in terms of the strongest coefficients obtained for the relationships between each kind of social relations and all the others.

The intuitively political relations—opinion leadership, opposition potential, and cosponsorship—are most strongly related to one another, while they are generally not strongly related to expertise and respect. In other words, if a council is more politicized on one kind of social relations, it is also more politicized on a proximate kind. Opinion leadership, opposition potential, and cosponsorship clearly constitute a political subset in the council's social matrix.

Most intriguing in Table 4–1, however, is the set of correlations between friendship and the more explicitly political properties. The coefficients between friendship and the three political properties, while not as high as among these properties themselves, are at least substantial. The correlations seem to confirm what textual analysis had already hinted—that friendship as a relational property has a political dimension, that it is perceived and practiced

Table 4–1
Correlation Coefficients for Relationships
Among Council Social Relations

	Cosponsorship	Opposition potential	Friendship	Expertise	Respect
Opinion leadership	.73	.68	.64	.37	.46
Cosponsorship	—	.65	.54	.50	.05
Opposition potential		—	.54	.42	.58
Friendship			—	.46	.20
Expertise				—	.25

in a political frame of reference. By way of contrast, respect is arbitrarily related to the political properties, including friendship, though it is strongly related to opposition potential. The latter is not altogether surprising. As some of the comments in the interview protocols had indicated, opposition is more likely to be a matter of concern when it comes from colleagues who are highly regarded than from those who are held in low esteem. The weak correlations between cosponsorship, friendship, and expertise, on the one hand, and respect, on the other, are corollary results: respect as an honorific variable does not seem to enter as much into the interpersonal calculus. Expertise, finally, seems to occupy a middling position. While its relationship with respect is quite weak, it is moderately or substantially related to the more political properties.

The matrix of social relations reveals some inner logic or plausible order. It does not tell us anything, except possibly by inference to individual-level assumptions, about the etiology of relationships in the council's social organization. But it suggests that the council's informal social ties are not haphazard or whimsical but, rather, subject to some implicit laws of emergence.

Complexity and Social Relations

If there are laws of emergence implicit in an organization and especially in an informal social organization, they are best conceived as responses to complexity. In general, both the character and richness of social relations in the council as well as their interdependencies are likely to be affected by the size of the group and/or the size of the population with which it interacts in the process of governing. Where the net of social relations inside and/or outside the council is complex, the bonds of friendship, respect, expertise, cosponsorship, opinion leadership, and opposition potential that constitute the council's social matrix should be pervasive and interrelated.

What we find, however, as Table 4–2 shows, is that the size of the council but not the size of the city affects the type of social organization that emerges. If we compare small councils in large

Table 4–2
Relationships Among Council Relational Properties,
Council Size, and City Size

Proportion high on relational property	Large council N = 15	Large city small council N = 28	Small city small council N = 39
Friendship (g = .13)	53%	50%	44%
Respect (g = .16)	67	46	49
Expertise (g = .22)	60	46	41
Opinion leadership (g = .29)	80	36	44
Cosponsorship (g = .35)	73	43	39
Opposition potential (g = .32)	60	57	39

and small cities, in only one case—opposition potential—does the difference in the proportion of councils high on the expansiveness index exceed 8 percent.

Although large councils are in all cases more highly permeated by a given property than are small councils, opinion leadership and cosponsorship stand out. These properties, more than the others, appear to be especially important in how councils respond to internal complexity. Large councils are evidently dependent on the availability of persons who, for qualities that make them opinion leaders, can give orientation to the council as a whole or, perhaps, to factions on the council. Similarly, the need to mobilize internal support through cosponsorship is greater in the more complex interactional setting of the large council.

More problematical in this connection is the role of friendship. It is only very weakly related to the council's internal complexity. That it is not more pervasive in the small councils is understandable. In the small group, friendship, especially if it involves politi-

cal ties, can be a source of trouble unless all members share in it—
an unlikely outcome even in a triad if friendship is to mean
anything. But one might have expected friendship to be more pervasive in the large councils. The result here does not mean, however, that friendship is unimportant. It merely indicates that its
genesis has not much to do with internal and, for that matter, external complexity. As we shall note later on, its emergence as a
relational property may be connected with the conflict situation
that prevails in the council.

Both respect and expertise are moderately related to internal
complexity. Perhaps mutual deference reduces political tension in
the larger councils, for, as noted in Table 4–1, respect is quite
strongly related to opposition potential (.58).

It does not follow, of course, that because all six kinds of social
relations are more or less positive responses to the council's internal complexity, they will also be invariably more interdependent
in the more complex than in the less complex settings. Yet, the
presumption is strong that they are. And, as Table 4–3 shows, the
large councils (most in large cities) appear to be characterized, on
balance, by greater interdependence of the relational properties
than the small councils in large cities, and the latter more so than
the small councils in small cities. Close scrutiny of Table 4–3 shows
that of the 15 correlations possible in each of the three council-
city size matrices, the rank-order of the coefficients is as follows:

Rank of coefficients:	Large councils	Small councils in large cities	Small councils in small cities
First	9	4	2
Second	3	9	3
Third	3	2	10

While it is difficult, if not impossible, to say just why a given
relationship is more or less strong in one or another council-city
setting, the evidence is quite convincing that the more complex
the total (internal and external) environment, the more will social
relations be highly interdependent. Social complexity, it appears,
makes for a tighter net of social relations than does social sim-

Table 4–3
Correlation Coefficients Among Council Social Relations,
by Council Size and City Size*

	Cosponsorship	Opposition potential	Friendship	Expertise	Respect
Large Councils					
Opinion leadership	.82(1)	1.00(1)	1.00(1)	1.00(1)	.71(1)
Cosponsorship	—	.27(3)	.68(2)	.78(1)	—.26(3)
Opposition potential		—	.60(2)	.75(1)	.56(2)
Friendship			—	.89(1)	—.20(3)
Expertise				—	.56(1)
Small Councils					
Large Cities					
Opinion leadership	.72(2)	.67(2)	.78(2)	.40(2)	.11(3)
Cosponsorship	—	.33(2)	.74(1)	.13(3)	—.17(2)
Opposition potential		—	.74(1)	.44(2)	.67(1)
Friendship			—	.41(2)	.41(1)
Expertise				—	.52(2)
Small Councils					
Small Cities					
Opinion leadership	.66(3)	.66(3)	.51(3)	.00(3)	.52(2)
Cosponsorship	—	.86(1)	.31(3)	.57(2)	.15(1)
Opposition potential		—	.31(3)	.19(3)	.54(3)
Friendship			—	.22(3)	.15(2)
Expertise				—	—.17(3)

* Numbers in parentheses indicate rank of coefficient for each correlation among
council city size clusters.

plicity. Put differently, the council responds to the demands of
complexity by greater integration of its social organization.

Stratification

Social relations saturate the council's interpersonal life space
and also give rise to a status order or system of stratification among
members. Although councils, like all legislatures, are composed

of men and women who are formally equal by virtue of each having one and only one vote, informally there emerge structures of social differentiation (stratification) that restrict the equal influence of councilmen on decisional and other outcomes.

The evidence in support of this proposition is overwhelming. In both the Congress and state legislatures, hierarchical rather than equalitarian forms of organization are typical. Interactions among members are selective, and they are of different degrees of intensity. Some members are sought out because they possess attributes that are personally attractive or politically useful to others. As these attributes cumulate more in some members than in others, distinctions come to be made in the membership so that social differentiation ensues and an informal status order develops. Selective interaction and social stratification are endemic features of legislative bodies.

The relationships that councilmen maintain toward each other can be thought of as political resources. This is true not only of those interactions that are directly political, like cosponsorship, opinion leadership, or opposition potential, but also of those that are honorific or instrumental, like respect or expertise. The values implicit in interpersonal relations are in short supply. Because some members of the council are sought out more than others, and because the values involved in social selection are scarce, there develop status differences among the members which make stratification a typical feature of legislative life.

Status is not a one-dimensional phenomenon and there is no single status order. A council member who, in the judgment of his peers, is a desirable cosponsor may not be valued highly as a friend or expert. Yet, the councilman who is frequently selected on all or most of the dimensions already identified—opinion leadership, cosponsorship, and so on—occupies a generally higher status than his colleague who receives few nominations. Therefore, in searching for a single measure of council stratification, we opted for an additive index.

As each councilman's composite status can be measured by the number of actual choices he received compared to the number he might have received on all six dimensions if all other members had chosen him, it is possible to rank the members of the council on a social distance scale from high to low status. Operationally, the arithmetic difference between the person of highest status and the person of lowest status can serve as an index of council stratification. The resultant council score is best thought of as a measure of the span of the council's social hierarchy.[13]

Stratification and Complexity

Because councils are more or less stratified, the part played by differentiation in social organization is of some interest. One would expect that social complexity and stratification are positively related because complexity in human relations simply provides more opportunity for social differentiation than does sim-

---

[13] The pattern of stratification may, of course, differ from one council to the next. Status refers to the relative rank of council members. In some councils, the social distance between the member most highly valued and the person least valued may be very great; in other councils, the difference in ranking may be very small. As a result, the council as a whole may be more or less stratified. But the model underlying the stratification index assumed continuity rather than discrete classes. We note, therefore, as shown in Table 4A, that although there is no real discontinuity in the distribution of the councils on the index, the overall distribution of scores is somewhat skewed toward the higher, more stratified end of the continuum. The highest score for the full array (.709) is farther from the mean (.389) than the lowest score (.125). When the distribution is dichotomized, however, the skewing is only moderately toward the lower end in the less stratified councils and toward the higher end in the more stratified councils. In other words, even dichotomized categories can be considered "true"

Table 4A
Deviations of Extreme Stratification Scores from Means

Stratification category	Score Values			Differences	
	Low limit	Mean	High limit	Low to mean	High to mean
Total array (N = 82)	.125	.389	.709	.264	.320
Lower half (N = 41)	.125	.276	.375	.151	.099
Upper half (N = 41)	.389	.503	.709	.144	.206

representations of the underlying model. Although some of the variance is disguised by treating continuous data categorically, the resultant simplification is conducive to cross-tabulation and correlation with discontinuous properties. For a description of the stratification index, see Appendix B4.2.

Table 4–4

Relationship Between Council Status Order
and Council and City Size

Stratification	Large council N = 15	Large city small council N = 28	Small city small council N = 39
High	67%	54%	41%
Low	33	46	59
Gamma = .32	100%	100%	100%

plicity. The research question turns to the conditions under which more or less stratification occurs. Is it more related to internal or external complexity in the council's social environment?

Table 4–4 shows that the relationship between stratification and complexity is moderate and positive, in the expected direction. A highly stratified status order appears most often in the large councils and least often in the small councils of small cities. Moreover, as Table 4–5 further indicates, internal and external complexity make about equal contributions to the variance in the relationship. When council size is controlled by city size, the value of the coefficient is .27; when city size is controlled by council size, its value is a very similar .25. Both internal and external complexity have an impact, if only a moderate one, on the emergence of a

Table 4–5

Correlation Coefficients for
Relationships Between Stratification
and Council and City Size

Correlation of stratification with:	Gamma
Council size (zero-order)	.40
Council size controlled by city size (large cities only)	.27
City and council size combined	.32
City size (zero-order)	.24
City size controlled by council size (small councils only)	.25

more highly stratified status order. Evidently, faced with the complexities stemming from size of council and city, especially the larger councils in the larger cities but also the smaller councils in large cities organize themselves informally by concentrating their attention on a "star" whose high status, being legitimized by common choice, is conducive to collective adaptation.

Stratification and Social Relations

Social differentiation is an attribute of human collectivities, from the smallest to the largest. Yet, stratification will vary with the incidence of social relations, conceived as resources, in different councils. In some councils, the members may be very reluctant to specify others as cosponsors or friends, and so on, while in other councils they may be very free in doing so. It is not unreasonable to assume that where social relations are very pervasive and abundant, there will be more opportunity for social differentiation. But where social relations are scarce, the status order is likely to be more equalitarian or less stratified.

Because stratification emerges from the kind of social relations that permeate the council in varying degree, the contribution each makes to the status order can inform us about the political relevance of stratification—what is more and what is less valued in the process of social differentiation under varying conditions of internal and external complexity.

Table 4–6 is informative in a number of respects. As shown in Part A, the predominantly politicized kinds of social relations— cosponsorship, opposition potential, and friendship, but not opinion leadership—evidently contribute more to molding the council's status order than do the less politicized properties of expertise and respect. Stratification seems to be more grounded in political than honorific or instrumental social differentiation.

However, if one inspects the different relationships in their contextual settings, Part B of Table 4–6 reveals considerable variability. Cosponsorship and stratification are more closely related in the simpler internal and external environments, while opposition potential is more interdependent with stratification in the

Table 4–6
Correlation Coefficients for Relationships
Between Social Stratification and Social Relations,
in Large and Small Cities and Councils

Relationship between stratification and social relation	Co-sponsorship	Opposition potential	Friendship	Expertise	Opinion leadership	Respect
Part A						
All councils by council size	.52	.52	.51	.40	.30	.34
All councils by city size	.52	.52	.49	.37	.33	.29
All councils	.54	.54	.50	.38	.33	.29
Part B						
Small councils in small cities	.71	.19	.41	.09	.41	.04
Small cities	.76	.30	.40	.22	.49	.15
Small councils	.52	.52	.52	.42	.30	.37
Small councils in large cities	.17	.80	.64	.74	.20	.74
Large cities	.24	.70	.58	.51	.15	.42
Large councils	.45	.56	.38	.00	.00	—.45

more complex internal and external environment. The relationship between friendship and stratification is substantial in the simpler and quite strong in the more complex environments. Opinion leadership and stratification are more closely related in the simpler than the complex settings.

The strongest interdependence with stratification—in the cases of opposition potential, friendship, expertise, and respect—occurs in the small councils of large cities, that is, in the context where internal simplicity and external complexity meet. But instead of reducing the strength of the relationships, the ambiguity of the situation evidently has the effect of increasing it. In other words, if a council with a relatively simple internal but complex external context is highly permeated by certain kinds of social relations, it tends to evolve a highly stratified status order. Stratification is a response to both the internal and external environment. But this varies with the degree to which a council is saturated by particular kinds of social relations.

Chapter 5

Governing Practices and Styles

Any work group, and especially a governing unit, evolves distinctive practices which facilitate, and sometimes impede, the performance of its collective tasks. These are the behavioral ways in which groups go about their work. Not meant are the standard rules and procedures which, by ordinance or charter, specify how the council should go about its business, such as time and place of meetings or study sessions, preparation and distribution of the agenda, duties of the presiding officer, time limits on debate, preparation of minutes, or establishment of committees.[1] Rather, we mean the informal ways in which the council approaches its governing tasks. Implicit in these ways, moreover, are some underlying common orientations that, for lack of a more apt term, will be called the council's "governing style."

By "governing practices" we mean, more specifically, such behavioral phenomena as bargaining, compromising, exchanging information, coalition building, and other forms of conduct. The term "practices" rather than "tactics" is used because the endeavor is not to assess the rationality or optimality of the governing process, but to discover what practices are employed to expedite the council's business and whether these vary under different conditions of internal or external complexity.

By governing style is meant the set of underlying premises as

---

[1] See George S. Blair and Houston I. Flournoy, *Legislative Bodies in California* (Belmont, Calif.: Dickinson Publishing Company, 1967), pp. 78–89.

to how the business of governing is or should be transacted. These premises may be latent or manifest beliefs, ideal or actual norms, intrinsic or extrinsic values. Perhaps the notion of operational code comes close to what is meant here by governing style.[2] In classical parlance, for instance, one governing style was expressed by the formula: "the government is best that governs least." A governing style may be only vaguely recognized by councilmen themselves because they live by it or because customary ways of doing things are so well established that alternatives are simply not contemplated. Governing style, then, refers to the council's general approach to its governmental activities. It is likely to influence its governing practices.

The effects of constraints stemming from complexity are especially severe in small, face-to-face groups in which the individual is exposed to social pressures for conformity that, his probable protestations notwithstanding, inhibit unconventional behavior. Not only is the individual councilman under pressure to accept prevailing governing styles that may well antedate his own incumbency, but he is also likely to abide by prevailing practices if only to get along. Both governing styles and practices are group properties that may be more or less conducive to collective adaptation in the face of variable conditions of complexity.

Governing Practices

Five governing practices were identified as characteristic council properties. They must be described and explicated before analysis can proceed.[3]

Exchange: General and Limited

Involved in this practice is the frank transmission of attitudes, views, or opinions of a private nature that cannot be transmitted

---

[2] See Alexander L. George, *The "Operational Code": A Neglected Approach to the Study of Political Leaders and Decision-Making* (Santa Monica, Calif.: Rand Corporation, 1967).

[3] For a description of how governing practices were coded and illustrations, see Appendix B5.1.

in public. Exchange therefore tends to establish mutual trust and confidence in the group as a whole or, where the group is split, among the members of a faction.[4] Exchange may be practiced among all or most members or only among some members. It was possible to distinguish between "general exchange" and "limited exchange" and to classify the councils accordingly.

What is exchanged is not factual information but information about feelings, doubts, or convictions. If it were a matter of factual information, it could be exchanged in public session. Rather, the practice is designed to find out where another member stands on an issue or to clarify one's own stand before a public commitment is made. It contributes to the unity of the group as a whole or to that of a faction. The cost of such private exchange is low because, if exchange is not reciprocated, it is likely to cease.[5]

Bargaining

Bargaining is a practice in which every one party to the bargain will gain something.[6] It involves trading off things more valued by one legislator but less by another for other things more valued by the latter but less by the former. Although councilmen were often reluctant to admit that bargaining went on in their council, they would give evidence of implicit logrolling in "going along" with a proposal in expectation of receiving reciprocal support at a later time. In general, there seems to be more approval of tacit trading

---

[4] For a theoretical discussion of "social exchange" as used here, see Peter M. Blau, *Exchange and Power in Social Life* (New York: John Wiley and Sons, 1964), pp. 88–114. See also George C. Homans, *Social Behavior: Its Elementary Forms* (New York: Harcourt, Brace & World, 1961), pp. 30–50.

[5] See Alvin W. Gouldner, "The Norm of Reciprocity," *American Sociological Review* 25 (April 1960): 161–178.

[6] In coding council practices, the components of two sets were treated as mutually exclusive: general and limited exchange as one pair, compromising and bargaining as another. While general and limited exchange are mutually exclusive in logic, this need not be true of bargaining and compromise. Although councils emphasizing compromise as a practice invariably disavow bargaining, bargaining councils may yet practice compromise. But as it could be assumed that bargaining councils would also practice compromise, we opted for a mutually exclusive classification. Coding a council as both bargaining and compromising would not have yielded additionally significant information.

than of explicit bargaining where the terms of the deal call for a tangible *quid pro quo*.

Sometimes councils use the word "compromise," but it is clear from the context that the practice referred to is bargaining: "Bargaining at council session does take place—but not behind the scenes. An example? If a councilman wants a stop sign in a certain place, but the police chief says it should be on a different corner, let's say a block away, the council might split—some with you and some with the police chief. But if another proposal is coming up with a similar problem, you can usually make a compromise and get some to go along with you in exchange for your going along with his request. You have to give a little."

Compromise

As interpreted here, compromise means exchanging a part of a valued thing in order to safeguard another part. It means settling a disagreement over two alternatives by recourse to a third: A wants x and B wants y. The settlement is z. Neither side gets all it wants, but it also does not lose all that might be lost if there were a stalemate. Compromise means avoiding a stalemate by searching for a mutually satisfactory middle ground or common solution which a majority or all can support.

Although the words "bargaining" and "compromise" were often used interchangeably by respondents, in coding the councils into one or the other category, as sharp a distinction as possible was made between them. The task of distinguishing was somewhat eased by the fact that compromise was almost universally approved as a practice while bargaining was either disapproved or denied.

A compromise may be negotiated by the parties themselves or it may be negotiated by an uncommitted member. He will vote with one side or another only if it is willing to make concessions to the other side. In this case the compromise will lead to a majority vote or unanimity.[7] One of two conditions seems necessary for a success-

---

[7] This is of course not the only possible outcome. One side may offer side payments to the uncommitted voter in exchange for his support without making any concessions to the other side. But this strategy may not work if the minority is intense.

ful compromise: both sides must be flexible in their approach to decision-making, or both sides must assume that each side has asked for more than it really wants. Both these conditions, behavioral flexibility and reciprocal expectations, are among the "rules of the game" that facilitate the legislative process.[8]

Coalition Formation

Coalition is a characteristic of any group or subgroup that is basically united, but as a governing practice it may be more or less consciously and persistently pursued. A distinction must therefore be made between coalitions that result inadvertently from exchange, bargaining, or compromise and coalition formation as a deliberately pursued practice to build a winning majority. Coalition is here defined therefore as a purposive or goal-oriented alliance between two or more members of a group for some indeterminate period of time.[9] The crucial element in this definition is that the activity involved in coalition formation be purposive and goal-oriented.

A council was coded as a coalition-forming group only when there was strong and direct evidence that members made deliberate efforts to attract sufficient votes to win for a legislative purpose. Minority factions in stable conflictual situations will attempt coalition building in order to attract a member of the majority to their side, or a majority faction will engage in coalitional activity in order to maintain the loyalty of a marginal member. But it does not follow that coalition formation is the only feasible means of winning in these cases.

In general, the evidence of coalition formation in the interviews was unambiguous and strong. A variety of procedures seem to be involved—getting others involved in a proposal, persuading them

---

[8] As Aaron Wildavsky shows in *The Politics of the Budgetary Process* (Boston: Little, Brown, 1964), reciprocal expectations of this sort are often entertained in budget-making.

[9] This definition is a composite of definitions in William Riker, *The Theory of Political Coalitions* (New Haven: Yale University Press, 1962), p. 12, and William Gamson, "A Theory of Coalition-Formation," *American Sociological Review* 26 (June 1961): 373–382.

through reasoned argument or presentation of facts, taking care of their needs, making promises, and so on.

Ministration

The practice called for lack of a better term "ministration" is difficult to define and illustrate. It refers to the formal process of government, the invocation of the council's authority, reliance on law or statute as guidelines in policy-making. The council is seen as having a clear-cut mission or mandate defined for it by legal prescription or electoral approval, and it goes about its work in a formal and businesslike manner. Ministration is a practice that may replace other, more political practices when politics is of low salience, but it may also be associated with other practices.

The Cluster of Practices

Council governing practices are likely to be interdependent, depending on the degree to which they are politicized. To explore this interdependence, Table 5–1 cross-tabulates exchange with the remaining governing practices; it provides some interesting insights. In the first place, ministration is predominantly practiced in councils in which no private exchanges, whether of the limited

Table 5–1
Relationships Between Exchange
and Other Governing Practices

| | *Exchange** | | |
Other practices	Limited N = 24	General N = 39	None N = 19
Ministration	17%	36%	79%
Bargaining	63	21	5
Coalition formation	38	26	11
Compromising	21	33	11
None	0	8	5

* Percentages total more than 100 because councils may have more than one practice.

or general kind, occur. Moreover, a few other practices are common in these nonexchange councils. Ministration is a formal practice not generally interdependent with other, more political practices.

Second, bargaining is strongly related to limited exchange as is—if to a lesser extent—coalition formation, while compromising is more characteristic of councils practicing general exchange. One suspects that there is a generic configuration of practices consisting of limited exchange, bargaining, and coalition formation. Although the number of cases becomes very small, Table 5–2 is suggestive. While in the general exchange councils it makes no difference whether bargaining or compromising intervene in shaping the formation of coalitions, in limited exchange councils the tendency toward coalitional politics noted in Table 5–1 (38 percent) is measurably strengthened when bargaining is also practiced (53 percent). It is feasible to think of limited exchange, bargaining, and coalition formation as "hard" political practices in contrast to ministration, general exchange, and compromise. And these hard practices should be congenial to the council whose governing style is predominantly political.

Practices and Complexity

Governing practices should be adaptive responses to complexity. One would expect that the hard practices—limited exchange, bargaining, and coalition formation—would be especially pro-

Table 5–2
Relationships Among Compromise, Bargaining,
and Coalition Formation, Controlled by Exchange

Coalition formation	Limited Exchange		General Exchange	
	Bargaining $N = 15$	Compromise $N = 5$	Bargaining $N = 8$	Compromise $N = 13$
Present	53%	20%	37%	38%
Absent	47	80	63	62
	100%	100%	100%	100%

Table 5–3
Relationships Among Council Governing Practices,
Council Size, and City Size*

Governing practices	Large council N = 15	Large city small council N = 28	Small city small council N = 39
Limited exchange (N = 24)	67%	29%	15%
Bargaining (N = 24)	67	21	21
Coalition formation (N = 21)	53	21	18
Compromising (N = 20)	27	25	23
Ministration (N = 33)	13	46	46
General exchange (N = 39)	33	43	56

* Percentages total more than 100 because councils may have more than one practice.

nounced in the larger councils (all but two of which are located in larger cities). Table 5–3 presents the data.

The data confirm our expectations and reveal some other results as well. In the first place, the three politicized practices emerge most strongly in the large councils. Moreover, in the case of four practices—bargaining, coalition formation, compromise, and ministration—city size has no effect at all in the small councils. Identical or near-identical proportions of small councils with these properties appear in both large and small cities. Compromise, moreover, is practiced, if at all, irrespective of either council or city size.

But both general and limited exchange are practices on which internal and external complexity seem to have a cumulative effect, though in opposite directions. While limited exchange takes place in two-thirds of the large councils and declines in the small councils with declining city size, general exchange is most widely practiced in the small councils in small cities, less in the small councils of large cities, and least in the large councils. Trust and confidence are widely shared in the small councils in both small and large cities, but are somewhat more frequent in the former than in the latter. In the large councils, however, trust and confidence are restricted—everyone may trust someone, but no one trusts everybody; and the less complex environment of the small city has the effect of restricting limited exchange and stimulating general exchange among councilmen.

The relative contribution of council and city size to governing practices can be more clearly seen in Table 5–4, which presents the coefficients of association between each practice and the two size variables and also controls the latter by each other. When council size is controlled by city size, the reduction in the values of the coefficients is minor. But when city size is controlled by council size, the reductions are in most cases considerable. Only general exchange is exempt. Council practices, it appears, are predominantly adaptations to internal rather than to external complexity.

Table 5–4

Correlation Coefficients for Relationships
Among Governing Practices, Council Size, and City Size

Governing practices	Council size (zero-order)	Council size by city size*	City and council size	City size (zero-order)	City size by council size†
Limited exchange	.77	.67	.61	.55	.37
Bargaining	.77	.76	.49	.34	.03
Coalition formation	.65	.61	.44	.31	.11
Compromise	.07	.04	.06	.00	.05
Ministration	—.70	—.70	—.32	—.15	.00
General exchange	—.35	—.20	—.30	—.33	—.32

* In large cities only.
† In small councils only.

It is possible now to bring together two major findings. It was found, in Chapter 4, that the council adapts itself to internal rather than to external complexity by developing social relations of a political character such as cosponsorship, opinion leadership, friendship, and opposition potential. The larger the council, the more these relational properties are in evidence. It has been found in this chapter that certain eminently political practices—limited exchange of trust, bargaining, and coalition formation—are also more responses to internal than to external complexity. The larger the council, the more these practices predominate. In other words, in organizing themselves as a governing group, councilmen respond more to complexity stemming from the council's size than to complexity stemming from the size of the human environment.

One may ask, then, why it is that council size rather than city size has these consequences in both social relations and practices of a political sort. It may be taken for granted, of course, that as both sets of properties are related to council size, they are themselves interrelated. And, as the first column in Table 5–5 for all cities shows, this is largely the case, though the strengths of the relationships vary a good deal. Cosponsorship, opinion leadership, friendship, and opposition potential, as well as stratification, are more or less strongly and positively related to the more politicized practices and negatively related, in most cases, to the less politicized practices. The most consistent exception is compromise, a practice that comes close to being political, but the relationships are mostly very weak or near-zero.

However, if one inspects all the relationships between relational properties and governing practices separately for small and large cities, the results are impressive. In the cases of cosponsorship, opinion leadership, and friendship especially, the coefficients for the relationships between these properties and the governing practices increase in the large cities and differ even more importantly from the coefficients obtained in the small cities. This is true in 17 out of the 18 possible relationships. These transformations are less frequent in the cases of opposition potential and stratification, precisely those properties that contain within themselves the possibility of conflict.

Table 5–5
Correlation Coefficients for Relationships
Between Council Relational Properties of Political Import
and Governing Practices, by City Size

Relationship between	All cities	Large cities	Small cities
Cosponsorship and:			
Limited exchange	.62	.73	.37
Bargaining	.43	.46	.35
Coalition formation	.40	.50	.21
Ministration	−.13	.07	−.29
Compromise	−.04	−.29	.23
General exchange	−.30	−.59	.09
Opinion Leadership and:			
Limited exchange	.60	.87	−.08
Bargaining	.07	.52	−.60
Coalition formation	.25	.55	−.22
Ministration	−.17	−.46	.13
Compromise	.19	.29	.10
General exchange	−.34	−.53	−.13
Friendship and:			
Limited exchange	.51	.60	.31
Bargaining	.51	.63	.29
Coalition formation	.37	.67	−.16
Ministration	−.36	−.52	−.18
Compromise	−.33	−.53	−.50
General exchange	−.15	−.59	.37
Opposition Potential and:			
Limited exchange	.27	.48	−.33
Bargaining	.15	.11	.08
Coalition formation	.22	.16	.21
Ministration	−.31	−.29	−.29
Compromise	.03	.03	.23
General exchange	−.20	−.56	.29
Stratification and:			
Limited exchange	.12	.09	−.03
Bargaining	.34	.33	.29
Coalition formation	.19	.38	−.16
Ministration	−.25	−.29	−.18
Compromise	.13	−.16	.41
General exchange	−.05	−.39	.37

Governing Styles

Governing practices, we saw, are more or less politicized, and their appearance as well as interdependence vary a good deal from council to council. It is quite clear, however, that implicit in these practices are certain basic orientational assumptions of a normative sort that, for lack of a better term, we call governing styles. At least three distinct styles are characteristic of Bay Area city councils. Giving these styles names is hazardous, for naming invariably has evaluative connotations that may be misleading. The meanings given the labels that were chosen will therefore remain close to the raw material from which the analytic style categories are derived.[10]

The Benevolent Style. This style perhaps comes closest to the "city father" image so idealized in the textbooks on local government. In some respects, the benevolent style is residual; it is residual in the sense that it is probably so pervasive in the culture of nonpartisan politics that, when it is articulated, it is expressed sparingly if not banally. The council works for the good of the city and its citizens; its work is a public service and serving on the council is not a matter of self-interest; the council is open to suggestions from its members, the city staff, and local citizens, but though responsive, it leaves the initiative to others.

The Pragmatic Style. A council has a pragmatic governing style when the emphasis is placed on knowledge, facts, expertise, or the substantive merits of a proposal in proceeding with council business. The pragmatic style stresses planning, meeting problems before they arise, following external standards, and coming to efficient, economically sound, and technically competent decisions.

The Political Style. This style differs markedly from the benevolent and pragmatic styles. Here the council is chiefly seen as an arena in which a political game is played, where advantages may be derived from going along or obstructing, where differences in status and power are seen as important, where there is more em-

---

[10] For a description of how governing styles were coded and illustrations, see Appendix B5.2.

phasis on policy payoffs that may benefit the individual council-man or his particular clientele.

Style and Practices

Governing practices, Table 5–6 shows, are consistently anchored in appropriate governing styles. A political style implies that the council engages in limited exchange, bargaining, and, to a somewhat lesser extent, coalition formation. The pragmatic style varies positively only with ministration, the kind of practice that is matter-of-fact and largely routine. The benevolent style encourages general exchange and, to a lesser extent, ministration and compromise. But compromise, the weak coefficients obtained for all three styles indicate, has little discriminatory power. Overall, councils tend toward a high level of consistency in governing style and governing practices.

Complexity and Governing Style

A council's governing style should be influenced by the complexity of its human environment. In the small town the technical problems of governance are relatively simple and fewer demands are made on the council; a benevolent governing style is likely to be congenial. In the larger city the problems of governing are

Table 5–6

Correlation Coefficients for Relationships
Between Governing Practices and Governing Styles

Governing practices	Political style N = 19	Pragmatic style N = 15	Benevolent style N = 48
Bargaining	.87	—.08	—.77
Limited exchange	.82	—.08	—.71
Coalition formation	.47	—.71	—.04
Ministration	—.90	.59	.28
Compromising	—.12	—.15	.18
General exchange	—.65	—.02	.49

complicated by the spillover effects of community conflicts and disagreements, and the political governing style is more likely to occur.

Table 5–7 does not altogether falsify these propositions, but it shows that the small councils in the larger cities do not differ as much in governing style from the small councils in the smaller cities as one might expect on the assumption that environmental complexity has a significant effect. But the table also suggests that the style typology, though basically a nominal scale, includes an implicit order from most to least politization. Because our major interest is in council *political* behavior, we shall in subsequent analysis emphasize the political style and not pay much attention to the other two styles, characterizing them as nonpolitical. When the relationship between city size and governing style is controlled by council size (for small councils, where alone the test is possible), the coefficient drops to a weak .20 (see Table 5–8). But when the relationship between council size and governing style is controlled by city size (for large cities), the coefficient, though reduced, remains substantial (.42).

Explaining why city size contributes less to the variability in governing styles than does council size is difficult. Like the council's relational properties (Table 4–3), governing styles appear to be adaptations to internal complexity more than to external complexity, although the latter has some effect as well.

It is perplexing to note that it is especially the political style that is taken more in response to council size than to city size.

Table 5–7

Relationships Among Council Governing Styles,
Council Size, and City Size

Governing style	Large council N = 15	Large city small council N = 28	Small city small council N = 39
Political (N = 19)	53%	21%	13%
Pragmatic (N = 15)	7	21	21
Benevolent (N = 48)	40	57	67
Gamma = .36	100%	100%	100%

Table 5–8
Correlation Coefficients for
Relationships Among Governing Styles,
Council Size, and City Size

Correlation of governing styles with: *	Gamma
Council size (zero-order)	.51
Council size controlled by city size (large cities only)	.42
City and council size combined	.36
City size (zero-order)	.35
City size controlled by council size (small councils only)	.20

* The order of the governing styles is: Political > Pragmatic > Benevolent.

One possible explanation is that the political style may be so strongly related to the council's relational properties, themselves more strongly related to council than to city size, that the possible effect of external complexity is partially suppressed. But as Table 5–9 shows, this explanation is not acceptable. While some of the relational properties are strongly or at least substantially related to the political governing style, even after city or council size are held constant, others are not.

More revealing is the fact that the relationships between relational properties and political style, whatever their strength, are all positive in the large cities and all negative in the small cities. If the external environment is complex, it appears, social relations in the council are evidently given political operational meaning; while if the external environment is relatively simple, the same social relations do not take on a political tone. Moreover, when the relationships between social relations and political style are examined by council size, the degree of complexity is much less significant. Insofar as a political style serves as a kind of operational code that shapes social relations, it does so more effectively in the complex environment of the large city than in the simpler setting of the small city. The council's internal context, of course, also has

Table 5–9
Correlation Coefficients for Relationships
Between Council Social Relations and Political Governing Style,
Controlled by City Size and Council Size

Relationship between political style and:	All cities	Large cities	Small cities	Cities partial	Large councils	Small councils	Councils partial
Opinion leadership	.62	.87	-.15	.60	.47	.52	.52
Friendship	.51	.72	-.09	.49	.76	.40	.44
Cosponsorship	.16	.18	-.03	.11	-.57	.13	.08
Expertise	.16	.25	-.09	.14	.11	.05	.06
Opposition potential	.10	.25	-.52	.01	.60	-.24	-.16
Respect	-.22	.25	-.25	-.25	-.20	-.48	-.46
Stratification	.43	.45	.35	.42	.81	.20	.25

a role to play, though it appears to be more arbitrary. If the internal setting is complex, as in the large councils, the political style obstructs cosponsorship ($-.57$) but encourages friendship relations (.76) as well as oppositional behavior (.60).

As city size clearly has an impact on the degree of interdependence between social relations and political style, it may be revealing to control this association by the council's relational properties.

Table 5–10

Correlation Coefficients for Relationships
Between City Size and Political Style, Council Size
and Political Style, Controlled by Social Relations

		Correlation Between:	
Control variables:		City size and political style	Council size and political style
Opinion leadership	High	.85	.60
	Low	−.20	.66
	Difference	1.05	−.06
Friendship	High	.80	.82
	Low	.08	.52
	Difference	.72	.30
Cosponsorship	High	.64	.57
	Low	.50	.87
	Difference	.14	−.30
Expertise	High	.68	.71
	Low	.45	.68
	Difference	.23	.03
Opposition potential	High	.87	.86
	Low	.32	.61
	Difference	.55	.25
Respect	High	.58	.81
	Low	.58	.67
	Difference	.00	.14
Stratification	High	.59	.81
	Low	.50	.22
	Difference	.09	.59

Again, for comparative purposes, Table 5–10 also includes the correlation coefficients for the relationship between council size and style. Two aspects of the table are noteworthy. First, as the measures of difference between the conditional coefficients for each relational property show, where the council is highly permeated by opinion leadership, friendship, cosponsorship, expertise, and opposition potential, *external* complexity is strongly related to the appearance of the political governing style. But, second, the interdependence of *internal* complexity and a political governing style is, with the exception of stratification, not similarly affected by the extent to which the council is permeated by any one of the forms of social relations. Although social relations and governing styles are responses to internal complexity, if certain social relations are pervasive in the council, external complexity and the political governing style are, in fact, interdependent—as had been originally assumed. It seems that just as city size has an impact on the degree of interdependence between social relations and political governing style, so social relations have an effect on the degree of relationship between external complexity and political governing style. There is a great deal of interdetermination among external complexity, high permeation by social relations, and the political governing style, even though, as the partials reported in Table 5–11

Table 5–11

Partial Correlation Coefficients for Relationships
Between City Size and Political Style, Council Size
and Political Style, Controlled by Social Relations

| | *Partial Correlations Between:* | |
Control variables:	City size and political style	Council size and political style
Opinion leadership	.54	.61
Friendship	.54	.72
Cosponsorship	.57	.71
Expertise	.56	.70
Opposition potential	.57	.79
Respect	.58	.78
Stratification	.55	.69

show, council size remains more strongly related to political style than does city size when the relational properties are held constant.

Conclusion

What is one to make of these remarkable results as well as of the earlier findings on the relationships between council social relations and governing practices in large cities? The answer is simple, but it involves a paradox that is a fact of political life. It would seem that in primarily responding to internal complexity in its social relations, governing style, and governing practices, the council is in fact responding, if only indirectly, to the complexity of its human environment. The larger the city and all that size involves —complexity, heterogeneity, social pluralism, and so on—the more likely it is that the council will turn inward and develop a configuration of social relations, governing styles, and practices that is conducive to its internal adaptation, its ability to jell as a group and get along, in the face of what may well be experienced as a complex and puzzling environment. In the small city, on the other hand, there is less pressure for the integration of social relations and governing practices. As in the large cities, the small-city council adapts itself to its internal complexity by evolving appropriate social relations and practices; but its more familiar and less complex human environment does not stimulate it to integrate its social relations and governing practices either in the same degree or at all.

Chapter 6

Social Climate

City councils in session differ in the solemnity of their proceedings, in the degree of camaraderie expressed in words or gestures, and in the level of tension that is evident. In some councils, the members address each other only by surnames, while in others first names are freely used. Some councils rigidly follow Robert's Rules, while in others discussion and voting are informal and relaxed. In some councils, members are carefully listened to, while in others members interrupt each other incessantly. In some councils, the language of discourse is polite and deferential, while in others it is harsh and abrupt. In some councils a member's lack of information leads to patient explanation of facts and circumstances, while in others the uninformed member is ridiculed.

Direct observation of these behavioral patterns is extremely difficult, and to pursue it in a large number of legislative groups, even though they may be small in size, is costly. Because this is so, interviewing has an advantage over observation. Reading two hundred or more pages of open-ended material from interviews in a council provides insight into what we call the council's social climate. Sprinkled throughout the protocols are expressions of warm regard for colleagues, remarks that are unkind or unfavorable, emphasis on the spirit of cooperation, reports of antagonism and conflict, and similar indicators of group atmosphere. And these comments and remarks do not occur randomly, but cluster by council. If they occur in one respondent's protocol, they are echoed in his colleagues'.

It is possible, then, to characterize the council in terms of how members feel about one another and relate to one another emotionally. At the level of the group, we often speak of cohesion or solidarity. Cohesion and solidarity are psychological outcomes of social organization; they can be of great importance to the individual and can affect how he behaves as a group member. But they are also important as group properties. It is for the latter reason that we introduce "social climate" into our analysis.

Any group will have a social climate, and though such a phenomenon can be noticed by the sensitive observer, it is difficult to conceptualize and measure.[1]

Discovering Social Climate

The 82 councils were categorized as having a collegial or an antagonistic social climate.[2] *Collegiality* refers to a spirit of cooperation, teamwork, mutual deference, solidarity, and appreciation that pervades the group as a whole: "We pretty much agree on things as it stands. We are all buddies, first name friends, and when one of us has something on his mind, we just go to each other and discuss it to see how the other feels. If I discover that several feel the matter is important, I will bring the matter up in a meeting."

Antagonism is characterized by the presence of a competitive and perhaps even conflictual struggle for status, power, prestige, or influence among council members: "Edwards was powerful on the council, and now he doesn't like me much. I guess it is because now I'm more powerful than he is and he kind of resents it." Antagonism and tension can also stem from personality clashes, as is evidenced in the following comment: "Psychological natures

---

[1] The conception of a group's "social climate" was first developed by the social psychologist Kurt Lewin in connection with his famous studies of "authoritarian" and "democratic" group structures. See Kurt Lewin, *Resolving Social Conflicts* (New York: Harper and Brothers, 1948), p. 82: "The social climate in which a child lives is for the child as important as the air he breathes. The group to which a child belongs is the ground on which he stands."

[2] For a description of the coding procedures used in classifying councils in terms of social climate, see Appendix B6.1.

and personalities have something to do with it here. There is a lack of leadership. No one respects the others. The dislike between Johnson and me increases with every meeting."

Some councils fall into neither of the two categories. Their social climate is *impersonal* rather than collegial or antagonistic. Here the work is transacted in a businesslike and matter-of-fact manner with a minimum of interpersonal affect. The relationships among councilmen are relatively free of emotional content, being neither warm and indulgent as in the collegial councils nor competitive and deprivational as in the antagonistic councils.

Complexity and Social Climate

Although in organizing their social relations and evolving governing styles or practices, councils are responding more to internal than to external complexity, insofar as these collective properties are themselves interrelated, their interdependence is accentuated in the larger cities. Precisely because the external environment is difficult to cope with, the council will adjust its social ties and governing procedures in ways that are helpful in coming to grips with internal complexity.

If this is to be more than a plausible interpretation, proof is needed for why it is that, as isolated variables, social relations and governing procedures are responses to internal complexity, while, as interdependent variables, they are responses to external complexity. We hypothesize that external complexity gives rise to the council's social climate, which mediates between external complexity and the internal social relations and governing practices.

A first step in what will require an intricate analysis is to show that social climate is more closely related to external than to internal complexity. As Table 6–1 shows, the variations in social climate are mainly rooted in differences of city size rather than of council size. Social climate is predominantly collegial in the small councils in the small cities, while the small councils in the large cities barely differ from the large councils. When, as Table 6–2 shows, council size is controlled by city size, the relationship with social climate is greatly reduced and very weak ($-.11$); but when

Table 6–1
Relationships Among Social Climate,
Council Size, and City Size

Social climate	Large council N = 15	Large city small council N = 28	Small city small council N = 39
Collegial (N = 40)	33%	39%	62%
Impersonal (N = 20)	34	32	15
Antagonistic (N = 22)	33	29	23
Gamma = −.28	100%	100%	100%

city size is controlled by council size, it remains moderate (−.30). Social climate is the first property investigated so far that is more closely related to city size than to council size, suggesting that it may indeed be an important factor that mediates between external complexity and internal relations and processes.

Social Climate and Social Relations

The tendency of social relations to be more responsive to the council's internal complexity than to environmental complexity is due to the intervention of the social climate. This important

Table 6–2
Correlation Coefficients for
Relationships Among Social Climate,
Council Size, and City Size

Correlation of social climate with:	Gamma
Council size (zero-order)	−.27
Council size controlled by city size (large cities only)	−.11
City and council size combined	−.28
City size (zero-order)	−.35
City size controlled by council size (small councils only)	−.30

Table 6–3
Correlation Coefficients for Relationships
Between Social Climate and Social Relations
for Small and Large Cities

Relationships between climate and: *	All cities	Large cities	Small cities
Opposition potential	—.36	—.28	—.40
Opinion leadership	—.32	—.37	—.32
Friendship	—.30	—.45	—.22
Cosponsorship	.00	.19	—.14
Expertise	.25	.29	.28
Respect	.32	.28	.33

* Scale order for climate: Collegial > Impersonal > Antagonistic.

social-psychological dimension of interpersonal relations neutralizes the direct impact of external complexity on social relations. We must examine the relationships between social climate and social relations under varying conditions of urban complexity.

Even though the relationships are overall of only moderate strength, the results obtained in Table 6–3 are revealing. In the first place, looking at the coefficients for all cities, only the zero relationship between social climate and cosponsorship is not what one might expect. In general, the more collegial or less antagonistic the council's social climate, the less emphasis there is on the politicized kinds of social relations—opposition potential, opinion leadership, and friendship—and the more social relations are characterized by expertise and respect.

Second, although with the exception of cosponsorship the signs of the coefficients remain the same in the small and large cities, their values differ in significant ways. In the case of opposition potential, the relationship with social climate declines in the larger cities;[3] in the case of friendship, it increases considerably. The

[3] The reason why the relationship between social climate and opposition potential is strengthened in the smaller cities and reduced in the larger cities lies in the initial relationship between opposition potential and city size. Of all six kinds of social relations, opposition potential is the only one that was more a response to external than to internal complexity (see Table 4–3).

increases do not present interpretative difficulties. They suggest that in the more complex environment of the larger city the social climate does indeed intervene more strongly than in the less complex context of the smaller city, thus neutralizing the effect of external complexity on the council's social relations.

The results obtained in Tables 6–1 to 6–3 can be summarized as follows: while social relations, with one exception (opposition potential), are largely adaptations to internal rather than to external complexity, this is so because external pressures making for politization of social ties are neutralized by a collegial social climate that itself is directly related to external complexity. When the council's environment is simple, its social climate tends to be collegial; and when the climate is collegial, the council's social relations are less politicized. When the external environment is complex, however, the social climate is more likely to be antagonistic; and when the climate is antagonistic, social relations of a political nature are used to cope with the problem of collective adaptation.

One final observation: of the 82 councils, 22, or slightly more than a quarter, are characterized by an antagonistic social climate. This does not mean that they are unable to operate as social groups. Although opposition potential is high, the antagonistic councils rely more on opinion leadership and political friendships than do the collegial councils, thereby offsetting the difficulties that may inhere in their antagonistic atmosphere. But it is also true that they rely less on expertise and do not share in respect.[4]

Social Climate and Governing Style

Councils with a collegial climate characterized by mutual deference and cooperation are more likely to have a benevolent govern-

---

[4] Stratification is not related to social climate. The zero-order coefficient for the relationship is −.04, and the partial coefficient with city size held constant is −.02. This outcome is not surprising in view of the quite diverse interdependencies observed between social relations and social climate in Table 6–3— some negative and some positive. Stratification as such is evidently not a source of political tension.

ing style; councils with an antagonistic climate characterized by competition for status and influence are more likely to approach the task of governing with a political style. Of course, the relationship is probably interdeterminate rather than unidirectional. Table 6–4 shows that the properties are related as expected.

Governing style, we noted, is more an adaptation to internal complexity than to external complexity (Table 5–8). This proved something of a puzzle; we expected governing styles to be responses to problems stemming from the external environment. Introducing social climate into the analysis helps to solve the puzzle. As governing style is related to social climate (Table 6–4) and the latter is related more to external than to internal complexity (Tables 6–1 and 6–2), social climate intervenes between governing style and external complexity by neutralizing the direct impact of the latter. Indeed, it is in the larger cities that the interdependence of governing style and social climate is pronounced ($-.69$), while in the small cities it is weak (.23).

It may be that social climate also affects how internal complexity is related to governing style. We earlier reported that the relationship between governing style and council size, with city size controlled, is .42 (Table 5–8). When the relationship is controlled by social climate, it drops to .30. While the relationship between governing style and climate, controlled by city size, is $-.34$, it drops to $-.21$ when controlled by council size (Table 6–5). Further, the relationship between governing style and social climate is even more reduced in the small councils, while in the large

Table 6–4
Relationships Between Social Climate and Governing Styles

Governing style	Collegial climate N = 40	Impersonal climate N = 20	Antagonistic climate N = 22
Political	5%	20%	59%
Pragmatic	32	10	0
Benevolent	63	70	41
Gamma = −.38	100%	100%	100%

councils it is substantially increased. As in the case of the external environment, social climate neutralizes the effect of—in this case, internal—complexity.

Table 6–5 leaves little ambiguity about the intervening power of social climate between internal and external complexity, on the one hand, and governing style, on the other. Social climate is most effective in neutralizing the effect of complexity in the large councils; it is also effective in the small councils of large cities; but it is not effective in the small councils in small cities.

Although governing style is more a response to internal than to external complexity, social climate intervenes between governing style and *both* internal and external complexity. Even if internal complexity is confounded, as in the small councils of large cities, social climate has the power to shape governing style. Though less so than in the large councils, even in the small councils of large cities does a collegial atmosphere engender a benevolent, and an antagonistic climate a political, governing style. Once social climate, reflecting external complexity, is introduced into the equation, governing style is no longer as exclusively adaptive to internal complexity as initially seemed to be the case. Rather, it appears to be an adaptive response to social climate, especially in the most complex situation of all—the large councils.

Table 6–5
Correlation Coefficients for Relationships
Between Governing Style and Social Climate,
in Large and Small Cities and Councils

Relationship between governing style and social climate in:	Gamma
Small councils in small cities (N = 39)	.18
Small cities (N = 41)	.23
Small councils (N = 67)	—.16
All councils controlled by council size (N = 82)	—.21
All cities controlled by city size (N = 82)	—.34
All councils (N = 82)	—.38
Small councils in large cities (N = 28)	—.46
Large cities (N = 41)	—.69
Large councils (N = 15)	—.92

Social Climate and Governing Practices

Governing practices, it will be recalled, also were responses more to internal than to external complexity (Table 5–3) but were more highly related to social relations in the larger cities (Table 5–4). It remains to explore, therefore, whether social climate intervenes to reduce the direct effect of complexity on governing practices.

A first step, of course, is to establish whether and how social climate and governing practices are related. From all that we know about both property sets, we would expect the more politicized practices—limited exchange, bargaining, and coalition formation—to be associated with an antagonistic climate, and the politically more relaxed practices—general exchange, compromising, and ministration—to be congenial in the collegial climate. Table 6–6 not only confirms these expectations, but also shows great resemblance to Table 5–6. The practices found there to be positively related to the benevolent style are the same here related to the collegial climate, and those related in Table 5–6 to the political governing style are the same that are here related to the antagonistic climate. In the impersonal climate the relationships are more ambiguous. It seems to make for a good deal of bargaining, as does the antagonistic climate, but it appears to be especially unreceptive to compromising.

Table 6–6
Relationships Between Social Climate and Governing Practices

Governing practices	Collegial climate N = 40	Impersonal climate N = 22	Antagonistic climate N = 20
Ministration	.69	−.08	−.83
General exchange	.37	.19	−.63
Compromising	.41	−.57	−.06
Coalition formation	−.62	.14	.58
Bargaining	−.73	.40	.53
Limited exchange	−.78	.02	.79

Table 6–7
Correlation Coefficients for Relationships Between Governing Practices
and Social Climate, in Large and Small Cities and Councils

Relationship with social climate in:	Governing Practices					
	Limited exchange	Bargaining	Coalition formation	Compromise	General exchange	Ministration
Small councils in small cities (N = 39)	−.87	.56	−.53	.33	.49	.61
Small cities (N = 41)	−.74	−.58	−.56	.40	.27	.60
Small councils (N = 67)	−.87	−.54	−.67	.00	.39	.64
All councils controlled by city size (N = 82)	−.84	−.58	−.64	.08	.39	.65
All councils (N = 82)	−.74	−.67	−.59	.27	.39	.69
All cities controlled by council size (N = 82)	−.71	−.66	−.57	.30	.36	.69
Small councils in large cities (N = 28)	−.85	−.53	−.84	.32	.38	.72
Large cities (N = 41)	−.70	−.72	−.58	.20	.42	.77
Large councils (N = 15)	−.29	−1.00	−.26	1.00	.29	1.00

The zero-order relationships between social climate and governing practices suggest that social climate may in fact have an independent effect and thus neutralize the direct impact of complexity on governing practices. Table 6–7 largely confirms this expectation. Especially if one compares the zero-order coefficients with the partials obtained for either council size controlled by city size or city size controlled by council size, the variations are minor except in the case of compromising, which is not related to social climate in the small councils.

To appreciate the impact of social climate on governing practices, it must be recalled that the latter were generally more responsive to internal than to external complexity (Table 5–4). As Table 6–7 shows, council size remains a determinative influence on the relationship between social climate and governing practices, but there are also strong relationships between social climate and governing practices in the more complex larger cities. By neutralizing the direct impact of external complexity on governing practices, social climate facilitates relevant governing procedures that are conducive to the council's collective adaptation to the pressures stemming from the environment.

Chapter 7

Interaction
and Political
Communication

What politicians can and will tell each other depends in part on the social situation in which they find themselves. They may say things to each other or about each other in public that they would not say in private. And they will tell each other things in private that they cannot say publicly. Politicians probably do not differ in this respect from persons in business, church, or university, but public scrutiny of their words and deeds imposes on them a greater need for circumspection than is the case in the private sphere. The result is often paradoxical: in seeking to avoid public scrutiny through private communication they arouse public suspicion that they are holding back what the public is entitled to know.

Be this as it may, communication among council members is not limited to the formal encounters of public (or, for that matter, closed) sessions. They can interact and communicate with each other outside the official meetings, and they do so more or less frequently and more or less intensively. Experimental small-group research is not interested in these "external" interactions for the simple reason that the subjects brought into the laboratory generally do not know each other outside, so that the internal, face-to-face communications are not affected by external relationships.[1]

---

[1] The literature on experimental and other small-group research stressing interaction and communication is enormous. Instead of citing relevant studies by

In the case of real-world groups like city councils the opposite must be given strong credence—namely, that there is a reciprocal connection between what goes on in formal and informal encounters.

The location of the encounter is a clue to, though not evidence of, just what exchanges are likely to occur. What council members say to each other in different situations varies with the type of encounter and the definition given it. Where members exchange information is, therefore, a condition of the council's collective adaptation and social organization. Because of the political sensitivities that may be involved, different social situations will be seized on for different types of communication. For instance, the public nature of formal council sessions may not be conducive to exchanges of information that involve bargaining, coalition formation, or the presentation of tentative proposals not ready for public scrutiny. But the intimate social occasion may also not be conducive to political communication. Indeed, social relationships may be endangered by the exchange of political information, and politicians close to each other socially may avoid political talk in order to lessen the possibility of interpersonal tension or conflict.

Types of Interaction

Three types of interaction situation—labeled private, public, and political only because no more appropriate labels come to mind—serve the purposes of analysis. The meaning given each label is best illustrated by some of the anecdotal material from the interviews.[2]

---

sociologists and social psychologists, we refer the reader to Barry E. Collins and Bertram H. Raven, "Group Structure: Attraction, Coalitions, Communication, and Power," in Gardner Lindzey and Elliott Aronson, eds., *The Handbook of Social Psychology* (2nd ed.; Reading, Mass.: Addison-Wesley Publishing Company, 1969), Vol. 4, pp. 102–204, which includes an excellent bibliography. Political scientists do not generally study political behavior in experimental laboratory settings. The outstanding exception is James David Barber, *Power in Committees: An Experiment in the Governmental Process* (Chicago: Rand McNally, 1966).

[2] For construction and explanation of the interaction measure, see Appendix B7.1.

Private Interaction

While home visiting would seem to be an unambiguous criterion of private interaction, some respondents took exception. As they put it, "I grew up with him," or "I've known him since a kid," or "I have grown up with most of these people and we see each other often in the summer." In addition to long-term acquaintance, a few respondents reported going bowling, fishing, or hunting with one or another colleague.

Those who admitted to visiting in each other's homes were evidently anxious to minimize the political importance of these contacts, either by pointing out that they were neighbors or that they did so in passing. "We're in each other's home mainly on way to council meetings," or "Because we live next door to each other we drop into each other's home; it's not that I'm any friendlier with him." Others explicitly disassociated their social and political contacts: "The ones I see the most often are not the ones I am voting with at present;" or, "I see a lot of Sanford socially; he is a fabulous character, but I disagree with him violently."

The impression these comments give is that the respondents seek to underplay the possible effect of social intimacy on their relationships. Frequent and intimate interaction is either not considered politically salient or its possible impact on the business of the council is disavowed. The assumption that degree of intimacy of social interaction has a cumulative effect on political communication is therefore not warranted.

Public Interaction

Respondents who reported seeing colleagues only at council meetings or in connection with council work were often emphatic that socializing and council work do not mix: "I don't see them any more than this on purpose; I like to have an open mind when I go down, and if I fraternize too much, my opinion gets warped." Or another respondent: "I feel my strength is in not doing that sort of thing—socializing; I feel you shouldn't get too friendly or involved on a job like this." While this type of respondent seemed fairly impersonal in his comments about colleagues, another type revealed some hostility in reporting that they see their colleagues only formally: "I don't trust him, so I wouldn't drink with him; I might say something I didn't want to."

Other respondents reporting only public contacts indicated that they did not have the time for other opportunities or that they worked out of town. "If you are busy," said one, "this business of visiting around in the home, you don't have the time for that, and if they're busy they don't either." Others referred to the Brown Act as prohibiting informal relationships: "There's a law against that [informal discussion]. The Brown Act. It's not right to do that. I work no deals with nobody."

Limiting interaction to the public setting, it seems, is rationalized in terms of diverse motivations or objective circumstances. Insofar as public interaction has political content, the communication is open and direct. In general, however, many respondents in this category probably do not see council business in political terms at all.

Political Interaction

In general, respondents reporting casual contacts seemed politically more aware and sensitive, even though they were cautious in admitting that these contacts had political content. As one councilman said, "The middle column is the closest to the actual situation. We may lunch over a matter with the city council or the city manager. We mix up the groups all the time—part city council, part others." Or another: "There are a lot of functions where we are all gathered and where a lot of discussion does go on."

Some of the respondents who confirmed occasional and casual contacts with their colleagues beyond public council sessions emphasized that this kind of relationship would occur more often were it not for their working in another town: "Smith and Jones are the only two with businesses around here." Or: "Leonard has an office in another city, but we are on the phone four or five times a week." Another respondent said that filling the box on the questionnaire "is rather hard. I'll check it but it's not quite appropriate. All except Pellegrini see each other informally to discuss council meetings. . . . I'll often see them casually on the road and stop and talk. But there's not a great deal of social relationship on a non-council basis."

Some councilmen disavowed too close social relationships, such as home visiting might involve, precisely because they might be politically disadvantageous. As one respondent put it, "I deliberately avoid seeing them socially. I may find or cause added friction where none was before. The wives might quarrel. The same goes for my colleagues." And another commented: "This is such a small town that we see each other every day; once you start getting into people's homes, then it gets all sticky and personal."

Complexity and Interaction

The settings in which council business is transacted should vary with the complexity of the social environment. In the larger city the greater exposure of the council to group pressures and public scrutiny should incline the council to favor informal situations for the conduct of some of its business that will shield it from the public limelight. At the same time, the complexity of the large-city context should reduce opportunities for private and intimate interactions that are more likely to be typical of the simpler small-city setting.

As Table 7–1 shows, different interaction patterns do occur in small and large cities, with council size having little effect. Indeed, if the measures of complexity are controlled by each other, what relationship there may be between internal complexity and

Table 7–1
Relationships Among Interaction, Council Size, and City Size

Interaction	Large council N = 15	Large city small council N = 28	Small city small council N = 39
Political	40%	46%	28%
Public	40	32	28
Private	20	22	44
Gamma = .29	100%	100%	100%

Table 7–2
Correlation Coefficients for
Relationships Among Interaction,
Council Size, and City Size

Correlation of interaction with:	Gamma
Council size (zero-order)	.18
Council size controlled by city size (large cities only)	—.07
Council and city size combined	.29
City size (zero-order)	.46
City size controlled by council size (small councils only)	.38

the interaction situation almost vanishes (−.07), while the effect of external complexity remains close to substantial in the case of the small councils (.38; see Table 7–2). It seems that an external environment that is diverse and complex will call out interaction patterns congenial to politically sensitive transactions more than will a relatively simple context.

Interaction and Social Climate

Forms of interaction are not only responses to complexity. Whether interaction will be political, public, or private should also depend on the council's social climate, which mediates between external conditions and internal relationships. Private, essentially nonpolitical interaction presupposes a congenial social atmosphere, while informal, politicized interaction is probably more characteristic of an antagonistic social milieu. Councils with an antagonistic climate are likely to be composed of cliques or factions whose interactions may be facilitated by informality in interpersonal relations. It may be, of course, that insofar as political interactions cut across lines of cleavage in the antagonistic setting, they may be conducive to the reduction of tensions. Table 7–3 shows that the expected relationships are present and mod-

Table 7–3

Relationship Between Interaction and Social Climate

Interaction	Collegial climate N = 40	Impersonal climate N = 20	Antagonistic climate N = 22
Political	30%	45%	41%
Public	20	40	45
Private	50	15	14
Gamma = −.35	100%	100%	100%

erate. Especially pronounced is the difference between collegial and antagonistic councils in regard to private, nonpolitical interaction. But there are no differences between councils having either an impersonal or an antagonistic climate.

Moreover, social climate does not have the same mediating power between external complexity and interaction that was noted earlier in connection with other council properties. As Table 7–4 reports, when the relationship between interaction and social climate is controlled by city size as well as when the relationship between interaction and city size is controlled by social climate, the partial correlations do not fluctuate sharply, and they fluctuate in the same order. Social climate and external complexity reinforce each other in influencing the nature of interaction patterns,

Table 7–4

Comparison of Correlation Coefficients for Relationships Among Interaction, Social Climate, and City Size

Relationship between interaction and social climate:		Relationship between interaction and city size:	
Zero-order	−.35	Zero-order	.46
Partial by city size	−.31	Partial by social climate	.41
In large cities	−.23	In noncollegial social climate	.32
In small cities	−.40	In collegial social climate	.49

Table 7–5
Cumulative Impact of Social Climate
and External Complexity on Interaction

Interaction	Large city noncollegial* N = 26	Large city collegial N = 15	Small city noncollegial N = 16	Small city collegial N = 25
Political	50%	40%	31%	24%
Public	38	33	50	12
Private	12	27	19	64
Gamma = .43	100%	100%	100%	100%

* Combines antagonistic and impersonal social climates.

though external complexity appears to have somewhat more of a direct effect than does social climate. If the two properties reinforce each other, there should be a cumulative impact. Table 7–5 presents the cross-tabulation.

While the pattern is uneven, it is sufficiently regular to suggest that forms of interaction are responses to environmental complexity and the council's internal social atmosphere. The contrasts are especially sharp in the cases of the large-city, noncollegial councils and the small-city, collegial councils. If the external environment is complex and the internal context not collegial, the council resorts to informal political interaction to cope with the problem of collective adaptation; if the external environment is simple and the internal context is collegial, interactions are likely to have low political salience.

Interaction and Social Relations

Interaction is an important aspect of the council's social organization, though it is not interaction alone that makes for it. The distinct form of interaction with reference to social relations shapes social organization. The path of possible causation is not at issue; in fact, interaction and social relations are in all likelihood interdeterminate properties of the council.

It is well to recall the meanings of the social-relational variables.

Four of these—opinion leadership, opposition potential, cosponsorship, and friendship—were noted to be political forms of social
relations, themselves positively and substantially interrelated but
less related to the instrumental property of expertise and the
honorific property of respect (Table 4–1). One should expect,
therefore, that political interaction will be significantly related to
social relations of the political kind.

Table 7–6 presents the cross-tabulation of interaction and the
six relational properties. In general, the distributions are as expected. In particular, as in earlier analyses, friendship emerges
as a political variable. As also suggested earlier, friendship as a
group property is likely to be especially prominent in conflictual
councils. In this setting, also, interaction and the content of communication are probably politicized. Similarly, cosponsorship and
opinion leadership are related to political interaction.

The relationship between interaction and opposition potential
is, at first glance, curious. High opposition potential appears as a
relational property of councils whose interaction pattern is public
rather than, as one might have expected, political. Perhaps it is
when interaction is public that opposition cannot easily be anticipated, in contrast to the political interaction situation in which the
behavior of opponents becomes known as a result of informal
communication.

Although the results obtained in Table 7–6 make theoretical

Table 7–6
Relationships Between Interaction
and Council Social Relations

| Proportion of councils high on: | Interaction | | |
	Political N = 30	Public N = 26	Private N = 26
Friendship	67%	35%	39%
Cosponsorship	60	39	39
Opinion leadership	60	39	42
Opposition potential	47	62	39
Expertise	50	27	62
Respect	40	54	62

sense, the analysis has ignored the external context in which the relationships between interaction and particular kinds of social relations are enmeshed. But context cannot be ignored, because interaction is related to external complexity. As this is the case, one might suspect that the relationships observed in Table 7–6 are characteristic of councils in the large cities whose environment is complex, and that it accentuates the interdetermination of interaction and social relations.

Introducing relevant controls (Table 7–7) gives remarkable results. There is an accentuation of the relationships between informal, political interaction patterns and the *political* kinds of social relations in the complex settings of the large cities. The obverse holds between private interaction patterns and *nonpolitical* social relations in the simple settings of the small cities. Indeed, three of the relationships—between interaction and friendship, interaction and cosponsorship, and interaction and opinion leadership—almost vanish in the small cities. Moreover, in the simpler context of the small city, political interaction reduces opposition potential, while in the complex larger cities, political interaction intensifies it. Finally, expertise appears as positively related to political interaction in the more complex context as well.

The results confirm the importance of external complexity for interpersonal relations in the council. Although social relations, with the exception of opposition potential, are largely adaptations

Table 7–7
Correlation Coefficients for Relationships
Between Interaction and Social Relations, by City Size

Coefficients between interaction and:	Zero-order	Partial	In large cities	In small cities
Friendship	.38	.37	.70	.02
Cosponsorship	.30	.28	.70	−.18
Opinion leadership	.25	.25	.46	.05
Opposition potential	.09	.02	.40	−.33
Expertise	−.12	−.11	.48	−.67
Respect	−.29	−.30	−.05	−.54

to the council's internal complexity (Table 4–2), it now appears that through the intervention of particular interaction patterns, themselves related to city size, external complexity contributes to shaping the council's social organization. In the complex environment, interaction patterns and social relations are interdetermined as political dimensions of council social organization; in the less complex environment, interaction patterns and social relations are interdetermined as nonpolitical dimensions. Complexity, it appears, makes for political behavior, while environmental simplicity leads to more emphasis on instrumental or honorific relations.

Interaction and Stratification

Even before physically interacting, people will appraise and evaluate each other and make judgments about the possible value to themselves of an anticipated interaction. This is especially likely in political life, for the leading participants are public persons. Councilmen are endowed with qualities that give them status, and status is a powerful constraint on interaction. Whether persons are attracted to each other or whether they avoid each other, and how people approach one another as they enter into interaction, is strongly influenced by their mutual evaluations. These valuative judgments may be realistic or mistaken, but whether one or the other they in turn suggest strategies of approach or avoidance that shape the interaction. Not every encounter leads to or involves interaction, but interaction is inaugurated and shaped by social differentiation.

If these notions are plausible in the dyadic encounter, they are probably even more appropriate in group situations that have passed the formative stage and have become regularized. Although the members of such groups are often formally equal, social differentiation stemming from the unequal distribution of status-relevant attributes shapes interaction and communication. The members of the council, having made evaluative judgments of each other, relate to and interact with each other in terms of the status order implicit in mutual appraisal.

But the implications of stratification for social interaction are problematic. On the one hand, an established stratification system can be divisive simply because interpersonal distinctions are invidious. As a result, the interaction subsequent to social differentiation may be conflictual or even destructive. On the other hand, social differentiation can be integrative because it is predicated on and tends to generate common values which cut across the status distinctions. As a result, social differentiation can have a binding and integrative effect on social organization. As noted in Chapter 6, stratification as such is evidently not a source of political tension in the councils.

Especially in legislative bodies in which decisions are made through voting, status barriers are not tolerable if they interfere with the possibility of successful vote outcomes. Political patterns of interaction are therefore more likely to be found in councils whose stratification is high. Table 7–8 presents the data, for all cities and by city size. Even cursory inspection of the table shows that the hypothesis is confirmed only in the large cities and that it is falsified in the small cities.

But these results do not mean that stratification is of minor import in shaping interaction. This can best be seen if one compares, as in Table 7–9, the coefficients for interaction and stratification, with city size controlled, and the coefficients for interaction

Table 7–8

Relationship Between Interaction and Stratification, for All, Small, and Large Cities

	Stratification					
	All Cities		Small Cities		Large Cities	
	High	Low	High	Low	High	Low
Interaction	N = 41	N = 41	N = 18	N = 23	N = 23	N = 18
Political	44%	29%	28%	26%	57%	33%
Public	29	34	16	35	39	34
Private	27	38	56	39	4	33
	100%	100%	100%	100%	100%	100%
Gamma =	.24		−.17		.52	

Table 7–9

Comparison of Correlation Coefficients for Relationships
Among Interaction, Stratification, and City Size

Relationship between interaction and stratification:		Relationship between interaction and city size:	
Zero-order	.24	Zero-order	.46
Partial by city size	.18	Partial by stratification	.40
In small cities	−.17	In low stratified councils	.11
In large cities	.52	In high stratified councils	.66

and city size, with stratification controlled. The comparison shows not only that external complexity has an unmistakable impact on the kind of interaction that occurs, but that the impact is felt primarily in highly stratified councils. Vice versa, the impact of external complexity is reduced in councils which are low in stratification. While external complexity clearly contributes more to the variance in interaction patterns, stratification significantly intervenes in the complex environment. This is all the more significant because, as was seen earlier in Table 4–5, stratification itself is only weakly related to city size.

Interaction and Governing Styles and Practices

It is possible to deepen our understanding of the meaning of different kinds of interaction by examining the governing styles and practices that are implicated in the interactional patterns. From what we already know about these properties, it can be expected that political interaction will be congenial to a political governing style and to those practices that are especially political —limited exchange, bargaining, and coalition formation. The styles and practices with less political content should be more prevalent in councils having public or private interactional patterns. Table 7–10 presents the data.

Table 7–10
Relationships Between Interaction
and Governing Styles and Practices

	Interaction		
Proportion of councils high on:	Political N = 30	Public N = 26	Private N = 26
Limited exchange	43	31	12
Bargaining	40	31	15
Political style	33	23	12
Coalition formation	30	31	15
Pragmatic style	17	12	27
Compromising	17	19	39
Ministration	40	31	50
General exchange	43	42	58
Benevolent style	50	65	61

There are no surprises in Table 7–10, but the results are all the more remarkable because the interaction variable, on the one hand, and the style and practice variables, on the other, constitute altogether different council properties. The measure of interaction was derived and aggregated from sociometric questions asked of councilmen about their associations, while the style and practice properties were coded directly and judgmentally at the group level from open-ended interview materials. Although the strengths of the relationships vary a good deal from one property to the next, the patterns of distribution are all in the expected direction. Substantively, the data suggest that informal interaction in fact involves a maximum of political behavior and communication.

One should expect, therefore, that the relationships between interaction and styles or practices will be especially salient in the more complex environment of the large cities, where collective adaptation is more likely to assume a political format. Table 7–11 presents the relevant correlation coefficients. It is not only readily apparent that there are considerable increases in the size of the coefficients for the expected relationships in the large cities, but also that the relationships either vanish or are sharply reduced in

Table 7–11

Correlation Coefficients for Relationships
Between Interaction and Governing Styles and Practices
in Large and Small Cities

Relationship between interaction and:	Zero-order	Partial	In large cities	In small cities
Limited exchange	.50	.43	.64	.06
Bargaining	.39	.36	.64	−.02
Political style	.41	.33	.49	.02
Coalition formation	.25	.22	.42	−.02
Pragmatic style	−.21	−.21	−.19	−.23
Compromising	−.38	−.40	−.25	−.55
Ministration	−.13	−.12	−.46	.21
General exchange	−.18	−.11	−.37	.14
Benevolent style	−.17	−.10	−.34	.16

the small cities. Of all the variables, only compromising is fairly strongly related and a pragmatic style very weakly related to private interaction in the less complex setting. Altogether, seven of the nine relationships are accentuated in the expected direction in the more complex environment of the larger cities. In the complex environment, councils are evidently induced to pursue forms of interaction that contribute to collective adaptation by facilitating a political style or politicized practices.

Chapter 8

Task-Role Structure:
Content and Form

The council is a group with a job to do. Its formal
tasks are set by statute or charter that stipulate the work of city
government. Minimally, the council is concerned with police and
fire protection; construction and maintenance of streets and
sewers; zoning and building regulations; and so on. Maximally, its
concerns include the provision of playgrounds, parks, libraries,
and other public amenities; the management of municipally owned
utilities like waterworks, light and power plants, or airports.
Council business covers a wide range of activities, from a matter as
simple, though possibly acrimonious, as a dog leash ordinance to a
matter as complex as a new master plan; or from a minor variance
adjustment to a major urban renewal project.[1]

However, its formal tasks do not define the council as a legislative group; there are latent purposes and goals that give direction
to the performance of formal tasks and determine whether a task
is in fact performed. These purposes or goals are not the same for
each council. They will vary with the complexity of the urban
environment; the economic and human resources available to
carry out given tasks; the citizenry's conception of what constitute

---

[1] For legal and administrative aspects of local government in California, see
Winston W. Crouch et al., *California Government and Politics* (3rd ed.; Engle-
wood Cliffs, N.J.: Prentice-Hall, 1964), Chapter 12: "Cities–Government at the
Grass Roots"; or Bernard L. Hyink et al., *Politics and Government in California*
(5th ed.; New York: Thomas Y. Crowell Company, 1967), Chapter 12: "Local
Government in California."

adequate or desirable municipal services and programs; and the council's own premises as to the goals for which municipal tasks are to be performed.

Insofar as there exists a collective definition of council goals, it is rooted in each councilman's orientation to his job as a purposive actor and his perceptions of what he is expected to do as a member of the council. In other words, what at the level of the individual councilman can be thought of as his "purposive role"[2] cumulates for the council as a group into a collective orientation to the tasks confronting it. As the notion of a legislative group's orientation to its tasks is novel, it requires some explication. This can best be done by anticipating the drift of the argument and analysis to follow.

Councils, it appears, have at least three major options in pursuing their formal tasks. First, they can perform only such tasks as are minimally necessary to *maintain* the city as it is. The goal of this kind of city government is essentially one of housekeeping or protecting the city against the intrusion of forces from an environment that is perceived as hostile. Second, tasks can be performed in response to demands made on the city government by individual citizens and groups, or as a way of mediating conflicts concerning municipal functions among individuals and groups. In responding to pressures and in acting as a broker in conflict situations, the council's orientation is one of *adjusting* city tasks to the changing preferences of people and interests. Finally, the council can approach its tasks not just routinely or opportunistically, but creatively by meeting current city needs or anticipating future needs. Here, the orientation to the council's work is essentially *programmatic*. It seeks to give city government policy direction and/or to plan for the future.

These orientations to action at the group level are constructed from the purposive role definitions of individual councilmen. This is not to say that an individual member's orientation to the council's work is independent of the role structure at the group level. A

---

[2] The concept of "purposive role orientation" was developed by John C. Wahlke, Heinz Eulau, William Buchanan, and Leroy C. Ferguson, *The Legislative System: Explorations in Legislative Behavior* (New York: John Wiley and Sons, 1962), Chapter 11: "The Legislator as Decision Maker: Purposive Roles."

compositional effect may be present that makes individual council-men hold purposive orientations that are immanent in the group situation.[3] As a role orientation is likely to be held in response to the expectations of significant others, and as each member's col-leagues are significant others in the matter of council tasks, there is reason to believe that purposive role-taking is not altogether idiosyncratic. This is especially likely in face-to-face, institutional groups like city councils in which interpersonal pressure to con-form to the group's definition of proper conduct and collective purpose is probably great. Some councils may limit individual options and possibly even punish deviance from prevailing norms; but other councils may be permissive in allowing their members some leeway in defining their roles, perhaps even expecting them to hold different orientations. The conditions under which variations in role differentiation occur may be related to differ-ences in the council's external environment or to differences in other internal structural aspects of the council. Because the unit of analysis here is the council and not the individual councilman, these conditions are of greater interest than the question of com-positional effects, which can remain moot.

More relevant is the question of whether individual role orienta-tions can be used to describe the purposive role structure of the council as a whole. For, at the level of the individual actor, the repertory of role orientations he can hold may be very extensive. This depends on the number and variety of relationships in which he is involved and on the ensuing complexity of the network of such relationships. Each network constitutes a role sector. Multi-ple role-taking within a single sector and across sectors may be harmonious or conflictual, varying with the content of role orien-tations and the degree to which they are held simultaneously or seriatim.[4]

---

[3] For the notion of compositional or structural effects, see Peter Blau, "Struc-tural Effects," *American Sociological Review* 25 (April 1960): 178–193; and James A. Davis, "A Technique for Analyzing the Effects of Group Composition," *American Sociological Review* 26 (April 1961): 215–225.

[4] See Wahlke et al., *The Legislative System*, pp. 3–28. The literature on role theory and role analysis is very large and diverse. For a convenient compendium, see Bruce J. Biddle and Edwin J. Thomas, eds., *Role Theory: Concepts and Research* (New York: John Wiley and Sons, 1966).

The richness of role analysis possible at the level of the individual yields to simplification at the level of the group. This is so because the council's task role structure is conceived as the equivalent of only one role sector at the individual level of analysis. Although it is usual for councilmen to hold several orientations relevant to the performance of council tasks, the notion of a group's role structure directs attention to the *primary* role that the individual takes in orienting himself to purposive action. In other words, the assumption that each councilman will take several intrasector roles is sacrificed to the conception of role differentiation as a structural feature of the council as a unit of action.[5] From the systemic point of view of the council as a purposive role structure, the emphasis shifts to role differentiation *in the group* and away from role diversity *within the person*. What matters from the perspective of group-level analysis is not each member's set of multiple roles in a given network of relationships or role sector; what matters is the role in the set which is more pervasive than any other—what has been called the primary role in the set of purposive orientations.

Operationally, therefore, and without denying or overlooking the possibility and probability of multiple role-taking at the individual level, the effort was made to identify each councilman's primary purposive orientation and to ignore secondary ones.[6] While this procedure involves giving up information of great interest at the individual level, it is theoretically called for to elucidate the council's purposive role structure as it emerges from *inter*individual differentiation among primary orientations. Determining which among several orientations can be considered primary requires, of course, subtle judgment in coding assignments. But if a councilman does articulate two purposive roles, as for instance taking both a policy planning and an interest adjusting

---

[5] See S. F. Nadel, *The Theory of Social Structure* (Glencoe, Ill.: The Free Press, 1957), pp. 63ff., 97ff.

[6] The main question from which role orientations were derived reads: "Now I would like to ask you some questions about the job of city councilman. First of all, how would you describe the job of being a councilman—*what* are the most important things you *should* do as a councilman?" Supplementary information came from this question: "Are there any important differences between what *you* think the job of councilman involves and the way the voters see it?"

role, we determined which of the two was the more salient to his conduct.[7] In cases of doubt, usually due to inadequate interviewing or transcription of responses, corroborative evidence could be found in other parts of the interview.

Maintaining the City as It Is

Since the days of the Progressive movement and its quest to take city government out of politics, a prevailing notion in local governance has been to limit its tasks to caretaking or housekeeping —the idea that government is a routine to be administered rather than a matter of problems to be solved. This passive view of governmental purpose may be yielding to a more active one of safekeeping the city against the inroads of urbanization, but in both views, *maintenance* is the purpose to be served. The council's task is, above all, to see to it that the "good of the community" is served. In this passive view, the good of the community is either self-evident or, as more candid respondents admitted, amounts to saying that what is good for business is good for the community. The conception is one of stewardship. The steward, Webster informs us, is "an officer or employee in a large family, or on a large estate, to manage the domestic concerns, supervise servants, collect rents or income, keep accounts, etc." As if echoing the dictionary definition, a respondent described the job of councilman thus: "He's like the member of the household who gives guidance to the family. He's part of the family and gives leadership in family activity. He provides for safety, recreation, pleasure and education of the children. . . ."

In this benign view, all that is needed and expected is familiarity with the city's problems and reliance on information that can best be obtained from the professional staff. Decisions are to be

---

[7] To illustrate what is meant by a primary as against a secondary role, an example from the world of sports may be helpful. It occasionally happens that a basketball team is directed by a "player-coach," i.e., a coach who also plays on the floor. If one were asked which of these two roles is primary in the individual's own perspective and the social perspective of the other players or spectators, one would probably conclude that it is the role of coach rather than that of player.

made on the basis of "facts" and "study," by looking at things as they are, and they are as they should be. There is no need to innovate because the world of local government is the best of all possible worlds. The council should see to it, a respondent emphasized, "that the employees are good, properly taken care of, paid on commensurate basis, and that the new developments provide for school sites, park sites, that they are kept modern and that the streets meet with the approval of the police and fire departments. See that traffic patterns are right. Those are the general problems that come before the council. There's no distinction between what we should do and what we do."

Yet, there are discordant notes as well. In a more active conception of maintenance, the task of the council is to guard the city against the pressures that come from the metropolitan environment. Maintenance requires conservation: "We here are trying to keep our community intact as it is. We try to preserve the city as it is." The theme appears over and over again: "Maintain the town in its best condition, to preserve the town as it is in its environment and its natural beauty, and to uphold the ordinances as enacted."

Adapting the City to Community Wishes

In the maintenance conception of council tasks there is little room for popular intervention in the governing process. By way of contrast, if the council has an adjustive orientation to its tasks, it is important for it to know the opinions, feelings, and problems of people; the councilman, a respondent pointed out, "should reflect as strongly as possible the opinions and feelings of his constituents in problems that they confront us with. . . . You need to be constantly in touch with people to try to find out what they want."

In a more sophisticated interpretation, the council does not simply listen to but discriminates among the people, and especially the groups, that it serves. By being sensitive to the diversity of local interests and the possibility of conflict, the council approaches its tasks dispassionately, adapting city policies to the variety and pluralism of the community social system. Governing involves brokerage among diverse interests and conflicting viewpoints: "Determine what problems face the community. Determine various views for solution of these problems. Be able to converse with and listen to various segments of the community. Be able to make a decision in view of conflicting viewpoints expressed without losing your own reasonableness."

Programming the City's Future

In a third conception of the council's tasks, the council is seen as a board of directors whose primary task is to determine policy. Administrative matters are to be left to the professionals: "This city council is like a board of directors of a major company. The job of councilman is primarily to determine the policy that will best promote controlled growth and development—commercial and economic—of the city as a residential community." In this view, involvement in administrative detail and ongoing problems is to be avoided because it spells the possibility of "politics": "You shouldn't serve as a politician but as a corporate director. The council is a legislative policy-making body and has no administrative or executive function."

Policy-making may be short-range or long-range. In the long-range conception of the council's tasks, providing for the future is critical: "The councilman's duty is to try to have the scope and foresight as to what should be done, and can be done, in your city. He should ask, 'What is the effect today, next week, and most of all, fifty years from now?'" Rather than taking its cues from public opinion or sentiment, the council should look elsewhere for innovative ideas "to bring things up to the present day and age . . . , to keep in mind what the ultimate community will look like. We have a good master plan. This city will be a model community."

Distributions

The role structure's content, rather than its form, orients council actions. Table 8–1 classifies each council by content of pur-

Table 8–1
Distribution of Councils by Leading Purposive
Role Orientation

Leading purposive role orientation	Councils N = 82
Programming	11%
Adapting	17
Maintaining	23
Programming and adapting (tied)	16
Programming and maintaining (tied)	11
Adapting and maintaining (tied)	22
	100%

posive role orientations and presents the distribution of the 82 councils in terms of their leading role orientations.[8] Half the councils are characterized by a single leading orientation to their tasks, while the other half are characterized by competing orientations. Nearly a fourth of the councils have only a maintaining role orientation. Moreover, the maintaining orientation is associated with the adapting orientation twice as often as with the programming orientation (22 percent versus 11 percent). These combined appearances must not be misinterpreted. For all 82 councils, the association between the maintaining and adapting orientation is $-.65$, between the maintaining and programming orientation, $-.73$, and between the adapting and programming orientation, $-.40$.[9] Although the strength of the coefficients varies, the negative signs in all three combinations suggest that the role orientations are in fact more disassociated than not.

Purposive Role Orientations and Complexity

Council role orientations are more likely to be responses to external than to internal complexity. The council's own size

---

[8] For a description of how the councils were classified in terms of their leading task orientations, see Appendix B8.1.
[9] The coefficients are gammas; a negative sign means that if one orientation is present, the other is more or less absent.

should matter less in the taking of roles which, by definition and
construction, are oriented toward the urban environment. One
would expect, therefore, that in the larger cities the council will
hold orientations that are programmatic or adaptive rather than
maintaining. In the small city governing is still relatively simple.
Councils should see their tasks as being directed toward providing
minimum services and protecting the city as much as possible
against encroachments from the metropolitan environment. As
they do their work relatively free from individual and group
pressures, because there probably is a good deal of citizen agreement on maintaining the city as it is, they also need not concern
themselves too much with the future by planning for orderly
expansion. By way of contrast, councils in the larger cities are
probably more exposed to divergent citizen views concerning the
tasks of government. In some of these cities there will be pressures
to resist further growth and development, while in others government is expected to make the necessary adjustments to an inevitably more urbanized future. But councils in the large cities are
also likely to take the initiative by programming and planning.
We shall pursue these themes in Part VI. Suffice it to point out
here that the programming orientation so crucial to task performance in a rapidly changing metropolitan region is directly related
to the urban condition. In the more heterogeneous and complex
environment of the larger cities, councils orient themselves to
action in terms of plans and programs for the future.

Table 8–2 largely supports these expectations. City size rather
than council size accounts for more of the variation in task
orientations. However, many councils, especially large councils in
the larger cities, also subscribe to the maintaining orientation. In
other words, there is more mix in the larger cities: while councils
see it as their task to program for the future and respond to the
needs created by the external environment, they also feel called
upon to preserve what is worth preserving. As Table 8–3 shows,
holding more than one orientation is much more characteristic of
councils in large cities than of councils in small cities.

The results of Table 8–3 may be spurious, however, because 13
of the large councils are located in large cities so that the multiplicity of orientations there may simply be due to council size
and internal complexity. There is simply more opportunity for

Table 8–2

Relationships Among Purposive Role Orientations,
Council Size, and City Size*

Purposive role orientation	Large council N = 15	Large city small council N = 28	Small city small council N = 39
Programming	60%	54%	18%
Adapting	67	68	41
Maintaining	67	43	62

* Percentages total more than 100 because each council may have more than one orientation.

multiple orientations in the larger councils. But, as Table 8–4 shows, this is not true for all three orientations. When the relationships between council size and orientations are controlled by city size, they are greatly reduced or vanish altogether in the case of programming and adapting but increase only in the case of maintaining. Yet, as Table 8–3 showed, programming and adapting occur together in the large cities more often than the other two possible combinations. Internal complexity, in other words, con-

Table 8–3

Distribution of Purposive Role Orientations by City Size

Purposive role orientations	Large cities N = 41	Small cities N = 41
Programming	7%	10%
Adapting	12	12
Maintaining	7	54
Programming and adapting	32	0
Programming and maintaining	17	4
Adapting and maintaining	25	20
	100%	100%

Table 8–4
Correlation Coefficients for Relationships
Among Purposive Role Orientations, Council Size, and City Size

Correlation of role orientations with:	Program-ming	Adapt-ing	Maintain-ing
Council size	.51	.29	.27
Council size controlled by city size (large cities only)	.13	—.03	.45
Council and city size combined	.54	.41	—.07
City size	.76	.65	—.58
City size controlled by council size (small councils only)	.68	.50	—.36

tributes independently only to the emergence of the maintaining as a second orientation in the larger cities. This is confirmed when city size is controlled by council size. Here the negative relationship between city size and the maintaining orientation is more drastically reduced than when the positive relationships between city size and the other two orientations are controlled by council size.

Role Differentiation and Complexity

The conception of a role structure, or configuration of roles, implies that individual orientations toward the council's tasks are not random occurrences. Rather, it implies that the structure has emerged as a result of processes internal to the council or in response to the exigencies of the tasks confronting it. These exigencies are largely environmental rather than interpersonal, though the emergence of a particular structure may not be unrelated to personal or interpersonal predispositions. But analysis of the role structure as a group property need not concern itself with its

Table 8–5
Relationships Among Purposive Role Structure,
Council Size, and City Size

Differentiation in role structure	Large council N = 15	Large city small council N = 28	Small city small council N = 39
High	67%	61%	44%
Low	33	39	56
	100%	100%	100%

genesis at the level of the individual. A group of like-minded individuals may allocate all available roles among its members, or it may allocate only one role.

The role structure may involve more or less differentiation among roles. One role, two roles, or three roles may be taken. Role differentiation as the most characteristic feature of the role structure refers to the degree of specialization in role-taking. If all three roles appear, differentiation is relatively high. If only one or two roles are taken, differentiation is relatively low. Low differentiation may imply that one role is dominant because many members take it. But correlation of an independent dominance measure and the measure of differentiation ($-.83$) suggested that the two measures are collinear. We therefore opted in favor of the differentiation measure to describe the role structure.[10]

Table 8–5 shows that small councils in large cities have an almost even chance with large councils of being highly differentiated. Put differently, role differentiation is predominantly a response to the exigencies of external complexity and only indirectly affected by council size. Moreover, as Table 8–6 shows, when city size is controlled by council size, the strength of the correlation is only slightly reduced. Role differentiation is not an artifact of internal complexity but is conditioned by the council's urban environment. When the city is large, the role structure is more characterized by differentiation than when it is small.

---

[10] For a description of the role differentiation measure, see Appendix B8.2.

Table 8–6
Correlation Coefficients for Relationships
Among Role Differentiation, Council Size, and City Size

Relationship between role differentiation and:	Gamma
Council size (zero-order)	.32
Council size controlled by city size (large cities only)	.13
Council and city size combined	.33
City size (zero-order)	.38
City size controlled by council size (small councils only)	.33

Role Form, Content, and Complexity

Although role differentiation, like the orientations from which it derives, is a response to external complexity, a council's role structure is the product of some distinctive process of role allocation that has gone on inside the group. One may ask, therefore, how the role structure's form is related to its content. Although conventionally we speak of "form and content," in that order, as if form shaped content or content could be poured into any form—like wine into any bottle—it is more plausible to assume that content shapes form. The problem of relating content to form, or form to content, is complicated because both form and content are analytic and not concrete properties of the emergent role structure. Both, it must be emphasized, are abstractions of individual behavioral patterns. The problem is further complicated by the fact that though structure generally refers to the product or outcome of these behavioral patterns, it also contains a processual component that makes structure something dynamic in its own right. A structure "is," but it also "becomes." It is only because structure is usually observed at one moment in time that it gives the appearance of being rather than becoming.

It is impossible to deal with the operational problem of relating content and form without making some assumptions about causation, even if we cannot observe the flow of cause and effect. From the causal perspective, the role structure's content—the council's task orientations—is a given (itself rooted, as we suggested, in environmental conditions as these impinge on predispositions). The first stage in the emergence of the role structure is probably synchronous with the group's individual members differentiating among alternative orientations to action. Differentiation refers to both process and product. Because individuals differentiate among purposes and, in doing so, are engaged in a process of choice, differentiation emerges as a group product. This is not to say that the individual's act of differentiating among role orientations "causes" differentiation in the role structure. Rather, it is to say that inter-individual differentiation as a process intervenes between and links the structure's form and content.

The task, then, is to discover the "discriminative power" of the role structure's content over its form; in operational language, we ask what contribution any one of the three orientations makes to role differentiation. The constraints imposed by content on the role structure are shown in Table 8–7. It is clear that the programming and maintaining orientations have no impact on role differentiation. Councils with either of these orientations are just as likely to have high as low differentiated role structures. High role differentiation is largely due to the contribution made by the adaptive orientation. Why should this be the case?

Table 8–7
Relationship Between Form and Content
of Purposive Role Structure

Role differentiation	Purposive Role Orientation*		
	Programming N = 31	Adapting N = 45	Maintaining N = 44
High	48%	62%	48%
Low	52	38	52
	100%	100%	100%

* "N" refers to the number of orientations present, not to the number of councils. A council may have more than one leading orientation because of ties.

If our logic is sound, the answer may lie in the content of the role orientations. Although both programming and adapting are orientational responses to external complexity (Table 8-4), they differ in the degree of constraint that complexity may impose on their choice. A programmatic orientation is probably more voluntaristic than an adjusting one, in the sense that though occasioned by external complexity, the council in the large city favorably inclined to programming or planning may actually not do so. In other words, programming is a rational response to the external environment. By way of contrast, once an adapting orientation has been accepted as a premise for action, the council will find it difficult to escape the demands incessantly made on it. As the council in the large city has little leeway in responding to human needs, whether in the nature of direct services or the reconciliation of conflicting interests, the adapting orientation will be taken, if not alone, at least in combination with the other two. And this is in fact what occurs. A glance back at Table 8-3 will show that in the 41 large cities, 32 percent of the councils combined the adapting with the programming orientation and that 25 percent combined it with the maintaining orientation. One should expect, therefore, that it is the adapting orientation which contributes most to the emergence of a highly differentiated role structure. As Table 8-8 shows, it is in the large rather than in the small cities where the adapting orientation has a significant impact on role differentiation. By way of contrast, neither the programming nor the maintaining role makes a positive contribution to role differentiation. Indeed, as Table 8-8 also shows, programming is highly

Table 8-8
Correlation Coefficients for Relationships
Between Form and Content of Purposive Role Structure,
by City Size

Correlation between role differentiation and:	Zero-order	Partial	Large cities	Small cities
Programming orientation	—.17	—.37	—.69	.15
Adapting orientation	.63	.29	.49	.11
Maintaining orientation	—.26	—.22	—.14	—.29

negatively related to role differentiation in the large cities. One may conclude, therefore, that a highly differentiated role structure not only is an appropriate response to external complexity but also contains within itself a factor—the adjusting orientation—which is particularly well suited to the council's collective response to urban complexity.

Role Structure and Interpersonal Relations

Even if there existed a viable theory concerned with possible linkages between a group's role structure and its other structural properties, it would still be difficult to formulate particular hypotheses about relationships between interpersonal processes, on the one hand, and the task role structure, on the other. Indeed, we are hard put to formulate any reasonable hypothesis and therefore proceed empirically to see what the data suggest for inference.

Table 8–9 presents the zero-order and partial coefficients, with city size as control, for all possible associations between differentiation in the role structure and the various interpersonal relationships characteristic of the councils. The table leaves little to the theoretical imagination. The correlation coefficients, whether positive or negative, are overwhelmingly weak. None of the zero-order or partial coefficients reaches a value higher than .29. And even the directly city size–related coefficients do not reveal a pattern that could usefully serve the purpose of grounding theory in the data. The only inference that can possibly be made is that the task structure constitutes an autonomous property of the council that follows its own laws of emergence and crystallization. In selecting appropriate roles and allocating these roles in the council, the social process involved is relatively independent of other social relationships that exist in the council, its system of stratification, its governing styles and practices, its social climate, or political interaction patterns. In confronting its governing tasks, the council apparently does not permit political or personal considerations to affect the selection of the roles that are conducive to the performance of its substantive business.

Table 8–9

Correlation Coefficients for Relationships
Between Purposive Role Differentiation and Social Relations,
Stratification, Governing Styles and Practices,
Social Climate, and Interaction, by City Size

Correlation between role differentiation and:	Zero-order	Partial	Large cities	Small cities
Cosponsorship	−.23	−.28	−.27	−.29
Opposition potential	−.14	−.21	−.33	−.09
Expertise	−.14	−.19	−.20	−.18
Opinion leadership	−.09	−.10	−.14	−.07
Respect	.05	.03	−.07	.15
Friendship	.11	.08	−.07	.22
Stratification	.19	.15	−.13	.40
Political style	.25	.15	.26	−.09
Pragmatic style	.16	.21	.08	.29
Benevolent style	−.27	−.23	−.27	−.19
General exchange	.20	.29	.19	.37
Limited exchange	−.10	−.24	−.37	.02
Compromising	.04	.04	−.10	.16
Bargaining	−.10	−.19	−.11	−.28
Coalition formation	.09	.03	.43	−.48
Ministration	−.07	−.04	.11	−.18
Social climate	−.03	.03	−.13	.21
Interaction	−.06	−.15	−.29	−.03

This interpretation attributes perhaps more rationality to the process of role differentiation than might be warranted. Yet, the fact that the role structure is geared to the conditions of external complexity, on the one hand, but is only minimally related to other internal properties or processes, on the other hand, does on reflection make theoretical sense. If it were otherwise—if the task structure were highly related to the council's internal properties and behavioral patterns—one might suspect that roles are taken not because they are purposive responses to city conditions but because they are more helpful in maintaining the council's internal social and political processes. This is evidently not the case. Rather, both the content and form of the role structure are related to characteristics of the urban environment in a way that suggests purposive behavior. In the large, heterogeneous, and complex cities, adjusting to the multiple preferences and often conflicting wishes of the citizenry as well as programming the city's future through policy planning give the council its task orientation. In the larger cities, moreover, with their greater complexity of governance, there is more role differentiation than in the smaller cities with their simpler governmental problems, resulting in a form of the task structure that is accommodated to diversity.

As a tool of governance, therefore, the task structure should be well suited to meeting environmental conditions and solving the governmental problems occasioned by these conditions. How the task structure is related to the council's political environment— the electoral context, the representational process, the interest group environment, and policy development—is yet to be explored after these variables have been introduced in later chapters.

Chapter 9

Decisional Structures:
Sources and Dimensions

Legislative bodies, large or small, have characteristic decision-making structures. A decisional structure is the prevailing relationship among the legislature's members when the votes are counted. Where, as in England, a strong two-party system guarantees disciplined legislative behavior, the parliamentary structure is bifurcated. Where, as in France or Italy, parliamentary coalitions must be formed among several parties to bring about a majority, the decisional structure is fragmented. In the one-party legislatures of Communist states, the decisional structure is monistic. By way of contrast, in the congressional regimes of the United States, the decisional structure is relatively fluid, often exhibiting different patterns that give it a certain kaleidoscopic quality.

A single voting decision is like a single frame in the moving film of decisions that the legislature makes. There are many such stills over time. But out of these stills emerges, over time, a decisional structure; a pattern of voting alignments evolves that is relatively stable and repetitive. The relationship between any two or more members who, by virtue of their individual stands on many issues, are aligned with each other may be deliberate or circumstantial. If member A and member B, over a long series of decisions, always vote in a similar way, they are associated with each other irrespective of whether they deliberately vote together or come to their decisions independently. These considerations, even if not always articulated, underlie studies of legislative and judicial voting blocs.[1] A variety of techniques using roll-call votes —indices of cohesion and likeness, unidimensional scaling, or sociometric methods—identify a legislative body's partisan alignments, ideological groupings, leadership patterns, and power structure.[2] Such investigations assume that alignment patterns are sufficiently stable and regular that inferences about latent behavioral aspects of the decision-making process can be made from manifest vote outcomes. In the case of the city council, for instance, the assumption can be made that if A and B regularly vote together, they have similar orientations to action. Once a bloc has been identified, the further assumption may be made that in future votes on the same or similar issues the bloc will reappear, thus making for order and regularity in the council's behavior. If then, in the course of time, the votes of some councilmen are consistently cast with the votes of others or in opposition to specified others, we speak of the decisional structure. By decisional structure is meant the recurrent voting alignment that emerges in legislative decision-making.

Voting patterns are the most direct and objective evidence of a council's decisional structure. If each council's votes on all issues were recorded, conventional roll-call analysis could be used. In the case of nonpartisan city councils, bloc analysis based on roll calls is impossible because in most councils votes are either not recorded or, if recorded, names are not reported in council min-

---

[1] See Stuart A. Rice, "The Identification of Blocs in Small Legislative Bodies," *American Political Science Review* 21 (August 1927): 619–627; or John G. Grumm, "The Systematic Analysis of Blocs in the Study of Legislative Behavior," *Western Political Quarterly* 18 (June 1965): 350–362; Duncan MacRae, Jr., *Dimensions of Congressional Voting* (Berkeley: University of California Press, 1958); David B. Truman, *The Congressional Party: A Case Study* (New York: John Wiley and Sons, 1959); Lee F. Anderson et al., *Legislative Roll-Call Analysis* (Evanston, Ill.: Northwestern University Press, 1966).

[2] For some examples of the increasingly sophisticated use of legislative roll-call analysis, see Duncan MacRae, Jr., *Issues and Parties in Legislative Voting* (New York: Harper & Row, 1970) and *Parliament, Parties, and Society in France, 1946–1958* (New York: St. Martin's Press, 1967); Leroy N. Rieselbach, *The Roots of Isolationism* (Indianapolis: The Bobbs-Merrill Company, 1966); Wayne L. Francis, *Legislative Issues in the Fifty States* (Chicago: Rand McNally, 1967); Cleo H. Cherryholmes and Michael J. Shapiro, *Representatives and Roll-Calls: A Computer Simulation of Voting in the Eighty-eighth Congress* (Indianapolis: The Bobbs-Merrill Company, 1969).

utes. As an alternative to roll-call data, each councilman was asked sociometric questions about his own and others' voting behavior. With whom does the respondent vote on controversial issues, and with whom do the others vote?[3]

While the councils' nonpartisanship makes conventional bloc analysis difficult, it has some analytical advantages. In intent, non-partisanship emphasizes the independence of members, who are elected at large and who are assumed to be uncommitted to a political party or to other specific groupings of voters.[4] The presumption is that in contrast to legislatures elected by party ballot

---

[3] The question: "When the council is in disagreement on an issue, would you say there is more or less the same line-up of votes here in (city)? I mean, do some members seem to vote together on controversial issues? If YES: With whom do *you* usually vote on controversial matters? Now, what about the others? Are they united or split? If SPLIT: Who would you say votes most often together when the others are split?"

Implicit in the question was, of course, the assumption that councilmen line up with each other more or less regularly *regardless* of the content of specific issues. If one were to ask this question of legislators or judges on other levels of government, it would be absurd and ridiculous. But at the local level and in the case of small groups, it is neither absurd nor ridiculous.

In the first place, the issues with which a city council deals are considerably less diverse than those facing state or federal legislative bodies or courts. The probability that the same members will line up with one another over many issues is therefore much greater than in legislatures dealing with more complex and diverse matters. Second, in small groups in which interpersonal relations are face-to-face and often intimate, stable factionalism in spite of varying issues is quite likely to result from group pressures to conform to the norms, attitudes, and behavior of those whose affect, respect, or help one values. Third, where different issues do make for shifting coalitions or blocs in the council, one would have reason to expect that councilmen would articulate irregular voting patterns if they occurred. And this, in fact, was the case in 29 out of the 82 councils. Finally, as the analysis will show, the decisional structures identified by the sociometric question do in fact yield empirical relationships with other properties that are clearly not due to chance. If the method only yielded nonsense, one could hardly secure the results that were obtained.

[4] That partisan considerations seem to intrude into council elections was tentatively explored in Heinz Eulau, Kenneth Prewitt, and Betty H. Zisk, "Latent Partisanship in Nonpartisan Elections: Effects of Political Milieu and Mobilization," in M. Kent Jennings and Harmon Zeigler, eds., *The Electoral Process* (Englewood Cliffs, N.J.: Prentice-Hall, 1966), pp. 208–237. See also Eugene C. Lee, *The Politics of Nonpartisanship: A Study of California City Elections* (Berkeley: University of California Press, 1960). See also Oliver P. Williams and Charles R. Adrian, "The Insulation of Local Politics under the Nonpartisan Ballot," *American Political Science Review* 53 (December 1959): 1052–1063.

or proportional methods in other jurisdictions the council is not structured by selection processes. While this assumption may be questionable, the analysis will proceed for the time being as if it were valid.[5]

Three decisional structures were identified.[6] In some councils, no lineups ever occur, and all respondents agree that this is the case. These councils have a *unipolar* decisional structure: all members vote together, although there may be an occasional deviant on a given vote. In a second type of council, there are no reoccurring lineups. These councils have a *nonpolar* decisional structure: there is no set voting pattern, although there may be minority cliques which at times vote together. The voting pattern of the nonpolar council is best viewed not as one which is irregular but as one in which no alignments persist from issue to issue or from meeting to meeting. Finally, in the third type of council, there are factional lineups: members of one faction name themselves as voting together and identify those voting against them, and members of the other faction do likewise. These councils have a *bipolar* decisional structure: the council is divided by a permanent split into two factions, although there may be swing voters who from time to time shift, without, however, disturbing the basic pattern.

Explication of Decisional Structure Typology

Councils provide descriptive material about the sources of or reasons for the occurrence or nonoccurrence of various kinds of

---

[5] Because we are more interested in conceptual than in statistical relationships for the purpose of theoretical explication of the decisional structure's dimensions, we are not dealing here with extraneous variables. As will be seen, though, the decisional structures are variously related, depending on the dimension involved, to city size and council size.

[6] The procedure was first explained in Heinz Eulau and Peter Lupsha, "Decisional Structures and Coalition Formation in Small Legislative Bodies," in Elke Frank, ed., *Lawmakers in a Changing World* (Englewood Cliffs, N.J.: Prentice-Hall, 1966), pp. 150–186. It should be mentioned that what we now term "nonpolar" was called "multipolar" in this article. Theoretical reconsideration of what was there called multipolar suggested that nonpolar was the empirically more appropriate designation. For more detailed explanation of some coding decisions, see Appendix B9.1.

voting patterns.[7] These accounts, summarized in Table 9–1, deepen our understanding of the three types of decisional structure.[8]

Bipolar Structure

The bipolar structure is rooted either in differences stemming from disagreements over basic policy issues or in differences stemming from the different backgrounds or experiences of the membership. Policy differences often have a strong ideological component, involving the role of government, planning, development, taxation, private enterprise, and so on: "It's the progressive against the nonprogressive. We (progressives) are for civil rights, planning, recreation and the view of the city. Our minds reach the same conclusions. We have seen the same facts. We do disagree over labor and the budget among the progressives, though."

Age differences, differences in length of residence, differences in ethnic origin or occupation, and differences in political experience are also sources of continuing voting splits: "Maybe their backgrounds and outlooks are related—e.g., Bonham and Eldridge have lived all their lives here—from well-known families and farming people. Sabbatini and myself both have kicked around the country quite a bit before settling down here—both now in business here."

Personal differences, rooted in mutual dislikes, suspicions, distrust, and personality clashes, are somewhat less frequent sources of conflict, but they too distinguish bipolar from nonpolar structures. Voting splits due to partisanship account for decisional

---

[7] Individual councilmen were asked: "How do you account for the fact that the council divides as it does?" The procedure for coding a council as a whole was imputational: a council was classified into a response category when one respondent's *detailed* account was *corroborated* by at least one supportive statement (usually there was more than one such corroboration). With regard to "personal differences," several unfavorable remarks by one councilman about another were accepted as sufficient evidence for classifying the council, though in most cases more than one respondent made such remarks. Idiosyncratic behavior was treated similarly.

[8] These codings were of course made independently of prior knowledge of the council's decisional structure.

Table 9–1

Council Accounts of Voting Patterns in Three Types
of Decisional Structure

	Decisional Structure		
	Conflictual bipolar	←– – –→ nonpolar	Harmonious unipolar
Sources of voting patterns	N = 20	N = 29	N = 33
Split is due to basic ideological or policy differences	65%	14%	0%
Split is due to differences in background or experience	60	17	0
Split is due to personal differences and difficulties	45	17	0
Split is due to partisan division	20	7	0
Split is due to differences of opinion on particular issues	25	48	0
Split is due to individual members thinking independently and differently	0	31	0
Split does not generally occur; if it occurs, is due to idiosyncratic behavior	10	10	48
Split simply does not occur	0	0	52

NOTE: Cell entries may total more than 100% because a council could be coded in more than one category. A council was coded in one or more of the categories if there was a detailed statement about the sources of voting patterns made by one respondent that was corroborated by another or several others.

structuring in only six councils, four of them bipolar and two of them nonpolar: "The groups have different political philosophies entirely. The majority of 7 are conservative Republicans. The rest are left-wing Democrats."

Nonpolar Structure

There is a clear shift in the pattern of Table 9–1 at the point where voting splits are accounted for in terms of differences of opinion on particular, nonoverlapping issues. In almost half the nonpolar structures (48 percent), but in only a fourth of the bipolar, this explanation is offered. It is clear that these occasional and nonrepetitive situations make for less pervasive conflict on the council than do basic policy differences, differences in background, or personal difficulties: "Some of the councilmen go along with the staff and let staff thinking influence their common sense. It happens on lots of items. For example, Mechan and I voted against participation in the county library system, but the rest went along with the staff recommendation to get the 'free money.' There isn't any one person really because the lineup is not consistent from item to item. We may have six 4–3 votes in a night, but not the same lineup each time."

Similarly, councils stressing group members' "independent thinking" as the source of voting splits tend to be nonpolar. These accounts occurred in almost a third of the nonpolar but in none of the bipolar councils: "No one pressures any of us into a decision, and no one expects we'll all vote the same way, unless we come to our individual conclusions by ourselves and they happen to be the same."

Unipolar Structure

There are no voting splits in unipolar councils, though, as the following quotation illustrates, this may result from informal pressures for conformity as well as from harmony of viewpoint: "There is really no split. I guess this is because we have such similar points of view as to what the people of the town want in the way of government. It is also because we are small and if this in itself does not lead to unanimity on most decisions, then we try to achieve a unanimous vote by persuading dissenters, because we don't want to appear wishy-washy. We want complete agreement on the issues."

Unipolarity in the decisional structure need not mean that the council has not disagreed before the voting takes place. Some comments suggest that it is often the social pressure inherent in the functioning of small face-to-face groups that makes a dissenting member abandon his opposition and accede to the wishes of the others.[9] Although dissenting votes may be cast, these do not disturb the council's basic decisional structure: "There is a four to one split because of Robinson. He doesn't figure into much of what we do."

Dimensions of the Decisional Structure

In speculating about the theoretical dimensions which might be inherent in the typology of decisional structures, it became clear that more than one order could reasonably be assigned to the classification. In fact, three orderings suggested themselves—a conflict to harmony ordering, a fragmentation to integration ordering, and a permissiveness to constraint ordering.

First Ordering: Conflict and Harmony

Any decisional structure will reflect the degree of harmony or conflict that obtains among its members. The unipolar council is the most harmonious. It is a council in which voting splits rarely, if ever, occur. This is not to say that there are no disagreements; it is to say that prior to voting the group resolves any disagreements it may have. At the other extreme of the harmony-conflict continuum is the bipolar council, the group which on important and controversial issues more often than not divides into two stable, permanent factions. Whatever its source, conflict pervades the group and becomes crystallized in the bipolar pattern. The majority faction usually prevails, though it may at times lose as one or another member shifts to the minority. The sources of conflict are numerous and will vary from council to council; there may be lasting ideological differences, splits arising out of personal antagonisms, or commitments to different and hostile constituencies.

---

[9] This is not the sole reason for unanimity, of course, either in unipolar or in nonpolar and bipolar councils. It should be pointed out that unanimity may be the outcome in 90% or more of voting even in nonpolar and bipolar councils. But see Heinz Eulau, "Logics of Rationality in Unanimous Decision-Making," in Carl J. Friedrich, ed., *Rational Decision* (New York: Atherton Press, 1964), pp. 26–54.

If the polarity typology contains a harmony-conflict dimension, nonpolar structures should be located between the two extreme poles. There are issues or personal difficulties that divide the council, but disagreements are neither so enduring nor so intense that councilmen cannot shift from issue to issue and form changing coalitions. As lines of cleavage are temporary, recurrent alignments, as in the unipolar or bipolar situations, do not develop. While nonpolar structures contain conflictual elements, they also contain elements of harmony.

Any variable itself containing the harmony-conflict dimension should therefore be ordered along a linear scale that locates the decision structures from conflict (bipolarity) to harmony (unipolarity). A variable of this sort is opposition potential. Where conflict is pronounced, there should be widespread anticipation of opposition; where there is little conflict, the council's opposition potential should be low. As Table 9–2 shows, although the relationship is weak, opposition potential is ordered by the conflict dimension of the decisional structure.[10]

Friendship, it was noted above, is political rather than personal. Once this is recognized, it is not puzzling to find that friendship is meaningfully related to the conflict dimension of the decisional structure.[11] In councils with sharp factional polarization, members are inclined to value the binding quality of friendship in the otherwise hostile group context. As Table 9–3 shows, in politically harmonious councils expressions of friendship are less likely, probably because interpersonal relations are not strained and friendship is not needed to maintain the group's harmony. The tendency of conflict situations to call forth strong friendship relations is due, of course, to the fact that friendship probably follows factional lines of cleavage. In an analysis based on *individual*

---

[10] The low coefficient reported in Table 9–2 is due to the fact that for the purpose of analysis here the data on social relations were dichotomized. When opposition potential is classified by quartiles, the coefficient is .30. See Heinz Eulau, "The Informal Organization of Decisional Structures in Small Legislative Bodies," *Midwest Journal of Political Science* 13 (August 1969): 350.

[11] We note that in a preliminary analysis of the data, before we had had an opportunity to explore fully the meaning of friendship in the council setting, the relationship between decisional structure and friendship was found to be a puzzle. See Eulau, "The Informal Organization of Decisional Structures," pp. 355–356.

Table 9–2
Conflict Ordering of Decisional Structure
and Opposition Potential

Opposition potential	Conflict bipolar N = 20	←–––→ nonpolar N = 29	Harmony unipolar N = 33
High	55%	52%	42%
Low	45	48	58
Gamma = .17	100%	100%	100%

Table 9–3
Conflict Ordering of Decisional Structure
and Friendship

Friendship	Conflict bipolar N = 20	←–––→ nonpolar N = 29	Harmony unipolar N = 33
High	60%	55%	33%
Low	40	45	67
Gamma = .37	100%	100%	100%

Table 9–4
Intra- and Interfactional Friendship Nominations
in Bipolar Councils

Nominations by	*Nominations Given to*		
	Own faction	Other faction	
Members of majority (N = 108)	81%	19%	= 100%
Members of minority (N = 52)	71%	29%	= 100%

SOURCE: Peter A. Lupsha, *Swingers, Isolates and Coalitions: Interpersonal Relations in Small Political Decision-Making Groups* (unpublished manuscript, 1970), p. 190, Table 8–10.

respondents, it was found that in the bipolar councils members of both majority and minority factions named those belonging to their own subgroups as personally best liked (Table 9–4).

Second Ordering: Fragmentation and Integration

The decisional structure typology also contains a dimension that orders the structures from the most to the least integrated. Non-integrated councils we call fragmented, but this term must not be confused with conflict. Individuals in a group may be only loosely connected and have only minimal common interests. However, such a group need not be a conflictual group. In fact, mutual avoidance may avert conflict. In a group where conflict is highly institutionalized, the structure may be well integrated; in Simmel's terms, the conflict may bind group members together.[12]

Nonpolar councils, it has been noted, are less conflictual than bipolar councils, although they are more conflictual than unipolar ones. If our theoretical reasoning is valid, this is because nonpolar councils are poorly integrated—they consist of multiple factions, cliques, and/or isolates. The pattern of interpersonal relationships is fragmented but not necessarily conflictual. By way of contrast, bipolar structures, though conflictual, are more integrated as two stable factions confront each other. Unipolar structures, of course, are the most integrated. It seems reasonable, therefore, to order the polarity types from high to low fragmentation—nonpolar, bipolar, unipolar—in that order.

If nonpolar councils are the least integrated, one may ask how a majority necessary for decision-making comes about. One way, perhaps a necessary way, in which majorities in loosely knit groups can be formed is through joint sponsorship of proposals. Individuals, cliques, or factions seek each other out as the group moves from issue to issue; the resulting alliances, even though temporary, make it possible to conduct council business. Nonpolar councils should have more cosponsorship than bipolar councils have.

---

[12] See Georg Simmel, *Conflict* (Glencoe, Ill.: The Free Press, 1955), and Lewis Coser, *The Functions of Social Conflict* (Glencoe, Ill.: The Free Press, 1956). See also Robert C. North et al., "The Integrative Functions of Conflict," *Journal of Conflict Resolution* 4 (September 1960): 355–374.

Table 9–5
Fragmentation Ordering of Decisional Structure
and Cosponsorship

Cosponsorship	Fragmentation nonpolar N = 29	←– – –→ bipolar N = 20	Integration unipolar N = 33
High	59%	50%	33%
Low	41	50	67
Gamma = .36	100%	100%	100%

In the bipolar councils cosponsorship is less necessary to create a new alliance but is often necessary to maintain a standing coalition, for unless the bipolar split is very stable, there are always marginal members whose support either faction seeks to retain. In the unipolar structures, of course, cosponsorship is likely to be minimal, though even here the desire to maintain a united front may call for some cosponsorship. As Table 9–5 shows, the expected relationships do in fact occur. The more fragmented the decisional structure (nonpolarity), the more cosponsorship seems to occur; the more integrated the structure (unipolarity), the less is cosponsorship a council property.

In addition to cosponsorship, it seems that opinion leadership serves as an integrating mechanism. Opinion leadership was first analyzed in connection with the study of mass communication.[13]

Table 9–6
Fragmentation Ordering of Decisional Structure
and Opinion Leadership

Opinion leadership	Fragmentation nonpolar N = 29	←– – –→ bipolar N = 29	Integration unipolar N = 33
High	59%	55%	33%
Low	41	45	67
Gamma = .36	100%	100%	100%

[13] See Paul F. Lazarsfeld, Bernard Berelson, and Hazel Gaudet, *The People's Choice* (New York: Columbia University Press, 1948); also Elihu Katz and Paul F. Lazarsfeld, *Personal Influence* (Glencoe, Ill.: The Free Press, 1955).

The mass has a highly fragmented and inchoate structure of inter-personal relations. It is through the emergence of opinion leader-ship that otherwise disjointed opinions and attitudes are collected into organized positions on political issues. Table 9–6 shows that strong opinion leadership emerges most often in small fragmented (nonpolar) legislative groups.

Third Ordering: *Permissiveness and Constraint*

The three decisional structures also differ in the degree to which conformity to expected voting behavior is rewarded and deviation punished. In the nonpolar pattern of voting, a live-and-let-live atmosphere makes for a great deal of permissiveness in political conduct and few constraints are imposed on the individual by the group as a whole, by factions, or by other individuals. Voting is likely to be constrained in bipolar structures where more or less disciplined factions confront each other, where a premium is put on loyalty to the faction, and where there are sanctions asso-ciated with deviation from the factional alliance. If the decisional structures are ordered from those where conduct is least con-strained to those where it is most constrained, unipolar councils will be located in the middle. Although members of a group with a unipolar structure are generally expected to conform to the group's consensus, occasional deviation is permitted because it does not seriously affect the group's basic harmony and inte-gration.

City councils, being essentially volunteer groups, do not have at their disposal the variety of sanctions available to more profes-sionalized and partisan legislatures. One sanction available, how-ever, is the awarding or withholding of respect. In small, face-to-face groups high value is placed on retaining the respect of one's peers.

The conditions under which respect should be less pervasive are encountered in the factional, bipolar council. For one thing, re-spect is withheld from members of the opposing faction. Moreover, deviation from a factional alliance is likely to be punished by the withdrawal of, or at least the nonattribution of, respect. It was found, for instance, on the individual level of analysis that swing-ers in bipolar councils were less respected than those who stuck to

Table 9-7
Permissiveness Ordering of Decisional Structure
and Respect

Respect	Permissiveness nonpolar N = 29	←－－－→ unipolar N = 33	Constraint bipolar N = 20
High	62%	52%	35%
Low	38	48	65
Gamma = .33	100%	100%	100%

their factions.[14] The more permissive context of the nonpolar council should be related to greater attribution of respect, for there is no deviant behavior to be punished. As Table 9–7 shows, if the decisional structures are ordered along the permissiveness-constraint dimension, respect pervades the nonpolar, permissive councils more than it does the bipolar, nonpermissive councils.

Figure 9–1 summarizes this discussion. The empirical classification is not a single scale on which councils are ordered on some single "most to least" dimension; rather it is a multidimensional classification. If the research can ferret out the several dimensions of a classification, its theoretical richness is correspondingly enhanced. Analysis will show that ordering the typology differently depending on the research question of interest is theoretically suggestive and empirically viable.

Complexity and Decisional Structures

The etiology of the decisional structure is as complex as the relations of councilmen, inside and outside the council, are complex. The anecdotal interview material revealed that a wide range of

---

[14] This information comes from research conducted by Peter A. Lupsha for the City Council Research Project. See Peter A. Lupsha, *Swingers, Isolates and Coalitions: Interpersonal Relations in Small Political Decision-Making Groups* (unpublished manuscript, 1970), p. 123, Table 6–16. In bipolar councils containing swingers, only 36% were accorded respect, while of the nonswingers—those who never crossed factional lines—54% were named as being respected.

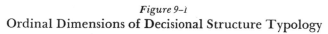

Figure 9–1
Ordinal Dimensions of Decisional Structure Typology

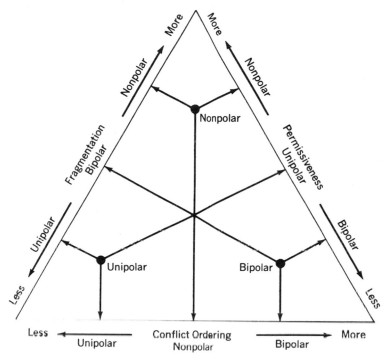

behaviors and social attitudes are implicated in the crystallization of particular voting structures. How the members of a group feel about one another, see one another, or conduct themselves toward one another is likely to be related to the total character of their environment—both the environment created by their own interactions and the larger environment in which they govern. Insofar as interpersonal relations of whatever kind are structured, therefore, one should expect that these structures are at least in part responses to the complexity of the total environment.

The decisional structures in their various dimensions are more or less systematically related to the complexities that stem from the council's own size and from the size of its city's population. It is difficult to formulate particular hypotheses about these rela-

Table 9–8
Relationships Among Decisional Structures,
Council Size, and City Size

Decisional structure	Large council N = 15	Large city small council N = 28	Small city small council N = 39
Unipolar	13%	36%	54%
Bipolar	27	18	28
Nonpolar	60	46	18
	100%	100%	100%
Gamma for fragmentation order = .49	Gamma for conflict order = .25		Gamma for permissiveness order = .37

tionships because each structure's several dimensions, though analytically distinct, are of course mutually entangled. Moreover, it is equally difficult to anticipate the extent to which internal or external complexity, or both jointly, contribute to the emergence of a particular decisional structure. It is best, therefore, to proceed heuristically and let the data guide the analysis.

Table 9–8 shows that internal and external complexity have a substantial impact on whether a council's decisional structure is

Table 9–9
Correlation Coefficients for Relationships
Between Decisional Structures and City and Council Size

Correlation of decisional structure and:	Fragmentation order	Conflict order	Permissiveness order
Council size (zero-order)	.57	.38	.30
Council size controlled by city size (large cities only)	.33	.38	.10
City and council size combined	.49	.25	.37
City size (zero-order)	.44	.20	.34
City size controlled by council size (small councils only)	.42	.12	.43

fragmented, and a moderate impact on whether it is permissive. In general, the more complex the total context, the more fragmented, permissive, and conflictual is the decisional structure, in that order. Nonpolar structures predominate among the large councils, mostly located in large cities, and characterize almost half the small councils in large cities, while the unipolar structure predominates among the small councils in small cities.

Of more theoretical interest are the contributions which internal and external complexity independently make to the decisional structure's three dimensions. In the first place, as Table 9–9 reports, the impact of council size on fragmentation of the decisional structure is reduced once city size is held constant (from a strong .57 to a moderate .33), while the independent effect of city size, once council size is controlled, remains substantial (.44 versus .42). Large city size, it seems, is especially conducive to shifting voting patterns, though large council size also contributes. The council in the more complex environment of the larger city, being subject to many more pressures from the outside than is the small-city council, responds flexibly to the multiplicity of demands made on it. Its own large size makes integration of the decisional structure all the more difficult. While the relationship between council size and the decisional structure in its permissiveness dimension is greatly reduced when controlled by city size (from .30 to .10), the correlation between city size and decisional structure is measurably improved (from .34 to .43) when city size is controlled by council size. Permissiveness in the more complex external environment is likely to be due to the fact that individual councilmen in the larger city, by being bound in their external relationships to particular and different clienteles, and coming from more diverse backgrounds with varied interests, accommodate one another by allowing each member a maximum of freedom in his other voting choices. This permissiveness reinforces the fragmentation of the decisional structure.

By way of contrast, and this is a most enlightening finding, it is council size rather than city size that seems to make for the possibility of conflict and the emergence of bipolar structures. As Table 9–9 shows, when council size is controlled by city size, the relationship remains undisturbed (.38). Indeed, large city size appears to ameliorate conflict to judge from the reduction of the coefficient to .25 once city size is introduced as a measure of complexity. Conflict on the council, it appears, is rooted in the problematics stemming from the multiplication of interpersonal relations in the larger group. The small group is more capable of establishing harmonious relations in the voting situation and of achieving the high degree of cohesive voting that characterizes the small unipolar council, while the large group provides more opportunity for conflict.

Insofar as the decisional structure is a response to complexity, then, it is variously influenced in its constituent dimensions. Both external and internal complexity are conducive to fragmentation; external complexity is especially conducive to permissiveness; and internal complexity is more conducive to conflict. The multidimensionality of the decisional structure is both a source of strength and a source of weakness in collective adaptation. We shall pursue this theme in the next chapter.

Chapter 10

Social Organization and Decision-Making

There is something definitive and final in the voting stage of the legislative process that sets it off from preceding stages. The voting stage is the point of no return, the point at which the legislature's collective choice emerges from the individual choices of its members. It is the point in the process of legislative decision-making when each individual participant commits himself and through his action commits the council. By participating in decision-making, each legislator defines his position vis-à-vis his colleagues. He lines up with some or all of his fellow legislators, or he opposes them.

The voting stage and the resultant decisional structure differ in another, indeed consequential, respect from previous stages and other structural features of the legislative process. In contrast to what goes on prior to voting, which is often known only to the participants themselves (although they may choose to reveal it to the press), voting is public. Public commitments are more difficult to reverse than the more tentative exploratory patterns of behavior that precede the vote. In combination, the near-finality of voting and having to take sides publicly lead to the institutionalization of the decisional structure. Once publicly committed and positioned, the individual legislator finds it difficult to escape from his commitments and positions. Over time, commitments and positions coalesce into the collective patterns of behavior that give the legislature its characteristic decisional structure which outlasts occasional deviations or temporary alignments.

189

Because of institutionalization, the decision-making structure can be treated, in the language of social research, as an independent, dependent, or contextual variable, depending on the assumptions that are made about institutionalization. If it is assumed that each new decision reinforces established legislative patterns and practices, the decisional structure is an independent variable. If it is assumed that decisional behavior making for reinforcement is the outcome of antecedent political arrangements and social circumstances, the decisional structure is a dependent variable. If it is assumed that the decisional structure provides the environment for interactions that are themselves interrelated in the process of decision-making, the decisional structure is a contextual variable.

However one proceeds, analysis is made difficult by the multidimensionality of the decisional structures. Nevertheless, because each type of structure is more characterized by one than another dimension, the types can be ordered so as to make theoretical sense. As was seen in the previous chapter, the orderings—along a fragmentation-integration dimension, a conflict-harmony dimension, and a permissiveness-constraint dimension—are implicated in various social relations within the council. The fact that theoretically meaningful ordering of the decisional structures is empirically possible suggests that they are not just artifacts of analytic construction.

While it is possible to order the decisional structures along each one of the three dimensions by rotating the three particular types from fragmented to integrated, conflictual to harmonious, and permissive to constrained, it may well be that one order has more power than the others over the distribution of other council properties or the shape of the interdependencies among these properties. This is an empirical question which cannot be prejudged. It is important to bear in mind, however, that each type of decisional structure contains within itself all three dimensions that give the typology its alternative orders. The following chart summarizes the mixes of each structure's implicit behavioral content. The bipolar structure is most characterized by conflictual behavior that fragments interactions along stable lines of cleavage and permits little freedom of conduct. In this structure the individual member

| Behavioral content | *Type of Decisional Structure* | | |
involved in structure	Bipolar	Nonpolar	Unipolar
Conflictual	High	Medium	Low
Fragmented	Medium	High	Low
Permissive	Low	High	Medium

is constrained to stick to his faction in the split that divides the council. The nonpolar structure is fragmented into shifting alliances among individuals or cliques that give each member much freedom of action and reduce the likelihood of severe conflict of a permanent kind. The unipolar structure has little conflictual behavior. But the harmony and integration of the unipolar structure constrain council members from doing as they please, though they have more leeway than councilmen in the conflictual bipolar setting. The mix of behavioral patterns will of course vary from council to council so that one should expect variations in the council's other organizational properties even within the same polar type. We turn first to the analysis of these variations, treating the decisional structure as an independent variable.

The Decisional Structure as Independent Variable

The variety of associations among the three types of decisional structure and a number of social relations, noted in the previous chapter, revealed the inherent multidimensionality of each decisional pattern. However, not each dimension carries the same weight in influencing the degree to which other social-structural, behavioral, or relational properties may be present in a council. The effects of the decisional structure on other properties will reflect the strength of one dimension over the others in each of the types. But the power of any one type of decisional structure to affect other council properties is predicated on the autonomy of the decisional structure as a component of the council's social organization.

This is a very demanding requirement because, as was shown in Table 9–8, the ordering of the decisional structures along the three dimensions is not independent of either the internal or external complexity. It follows that the power of a decisional structure will vary with the complexity of the council's social context.

If the relationships between decisional structures and the several kinds of social relations are observed by city size,[1] Table 10–1 shows that the original orderings of the decisional structure typology undergo some changes. Regardless of the original orderings, in five of the six associations between decisional structures and social relations—the exception being expertise—the effect of the conflict factor is reduced in the smaller and increased in the larger cities. While there are some other variations (for instance, respect declines in the large-city unipolar councils), it is the impact of the decisional structure's conflictual dimension that is most evident. As noted in Table 9–9, the decisional structure itself is least strongly associated with external complexity if ordered on the conflict dimension. Yet in the more complex context, as Table 10–1 shows, conflictual decision-making plays a more decisive role in shaping relevant dependent properties than do the fragmented and permissive aspect of the decisional structure.

Other evidence confirms the critical importance of the conflict dimension. Table 10–2 relates the decisional structures, ordered by the conflict dimension, to several of the council's properties examined in earlier chapters. In the overwhelming number of relationships these properties are ordered as dependent variables by the decisional structures along the conflict dimension. There are some disturbances in the pattern of the small cities (see boxes in Table 10–2), but only compromise is totally immune to the ordering power of the decisional structure's conflict dimension (as it is, we noted in Chapter 5, to environmental complexity).

Exceptions apart, conflict evidently plays a potent part in both shaping the council's decision structure (that is, giving it order) and engendering governing practices as well as social-psychological and interactional attributes. There is a good deal of consistency in the relationships between decisional structures and the depen-

---

[1] Ideally, one would want to observe these relationships also by council size and preferably by both joint council-city size. The small number of large councils ($N = 15$) and the miniscule number of large councils in small cities ($N = 2$) makes such analysis inadvisable and impossible.

Table 10-1
Relationships Between Decisional Structures
and Social Relations, by City Size

Original Order: Conflict

Percentage high on:	All cities			Large cities			Small cities		
	B N=20	N N=29	U N=33	B N=9	N N=20	U N=12	B N=11	N N=9	U N=21
Opposition potential	55	52	42	78	50	50	36	56	39
Friendship	60	55	38	78	55	25	45	56	38

Original Order: Fragmentation

	All cities			Large cities			Small cities		
	N N=29	B N=20	U N=33	N N=20	B N=9	U N=12	N N=9	B N=11	U N=21
Cosponsorship	59	50	33	60	56	33	56	45	33
Opinion leadership	59	55	33	55	78	17	67	36	43

Original Order: Permissiveness

	All cities			Large cities			Small cities		
	N N=29	U N=33	B N=20	N N=20	U N=12	B N=9	N N=9	U N=21	B N=11
Respect	62	52	35	60	33	56	67	62	18
Expertise	38	46	60	40	58	56	33	38	64

NOTE: Underlined percentages represent reversals of orderings from original order.

Table 10–2
Relationships Between Decisional Structures and Political Behavior Properties, by City Size

| | Decisional Structures: Conflict Order | | | | | | | | |
| | All cities | | | Large cities | | | Small cities | | |
Governing style	B N = 20	N N = 29	U N = 33	B N = 9	N N = 20	U N = 12	B N = 11	N N = 9	U N = 21
Political	50%	24%	6%	89%	30%	0%	18%	11%	10%
Pragmatic	0	17	30	0	20	17	0	11	38
Benevolent	50	59	64	11	50	83	82	78	52
	100%	100%	100%	100%	100%	100%	100%	100%	100%
Governing practices									
General exchange	20%	45%	67%	11%	35%	67%	27%	67%	67%
Limited exchange	65	31	6	89	35	17	45	22	0
Coalition formation	35	38	9	44	35	17	27	44	5
Ministration	15	35	61	0	40	58	27	22	62
Bargaining	50	35	12	78	35	8	27	33	14
Compromise	25	24	24	22	20	33	27	33	19

Table 10-2 (cont.)

Decisional Structures: Conflict Order

	All cities			Large cities			Small cities		
	B	N	U	B	N	U	B	N	U
	N = 20	N = 29	N = 33	N = 9	N = 20	N = 12	N = 11	N = 9	N = 21
Climate									
Collegial	25	41	70	11	35	58	36	56	76
Impersonal	10	34	24	11	40	33	9	22	19
Antagonistic	65	24	6	78	25	9	55	22	5
	100%	100%	100%	100%	100%	100%	100%	100%	100%
Interaction									
Political	50%	34%	50%	78%	40%	33%	27%	22%	29%
Public	35	45	13	22	45	34	46	44	9
Private	15	21	32	0	15	33	27	34	62
	100%	100%	100%	100%	100%	100%	100%	100%	100%

dent properties in both the more and less complex city settings.

Moreover, all the subtables in Table 10–2 show that despite the evident regularities in the relationships there are enough deviant cases suggesting the basically continuous character of the decisional structures; the unipolar structure is not compulsively harmonious, the nonpolar structure is not inflexibly permissive, and the bipolar structure is not obsessively conflictual. Each of the three types of decisional structure also produces responses that contravene the main patterns. For instance, just as there are bipolar structures with a collegial climate, there are unipolar structures with an antagonistic or impersonal climate. As responses to or effects of the decisional structure, therefore, these results are indicative of the continuity that underlies the discrete nominal decisional structure types as well as of the flexibility in any political group.

Finally, and again speaking generally, the problems created by whatever rigidities there may be in one or another decisional structure are emphasized in the more complex environment. From this perspective, the external environment makes for more politicized relationships in the larger cities. High politization in the more complex contexts and low politization in the simpler contexts create symbiotic relationships between the decisional structure and other council properties, even though, as in the bipolar situations, conflict is very pervasive in council organization and operation.

Stratification and role differentiation, as Table 10–3 shows, are differently affected by the decisional structure. Conflictual decision-making makes for high council stratification in large cities but not in small ones; stratification is unaffected by the other dimensions of the decisional structure. External complexity and internal conflict evidently accentuate interpersonal distinctions and, as a consequence, make for hierarchy. But if internal conflict is countervailed by environmental simplicity, stratification is low. In general, however, the council's status system is quite autonomous of its decision structure.

Role differentiation does not occur as a response to conflict but rather as a response to permissiveness and possibly fragmentation in the decisional structure, especially in large cities. Conflict in the

Table 10-3
Relationships Between Decisional Structures
and Stratification and Role Differentiation, by City Size

Decisional Structures: Conflict Order

	All cities			Large cities			Small cities		
Stratification	B N = 20	N N = 29	U N = 33	B N = 9	N N = 20	U N = 12	B N = 11	N N = 9	U N = 21
High	45%	52%	52%	78%	50%	50%	18%	56%	52%
Low	55	48	48	22	50	50	82	44	48
	100%	100%	100%	100%	100%	100%	100%	100%	100%
Role differentiation									
High	35%	72%	48%	56%	80%	42%	18%	56%	52%
Low	65	28	52	44	20	58	82	44	48
	100%	100%	100%	100%	100%	100%	100%	100%	100%

decisional structure also contributes to high role differentiation in the more complex environment. If the data reported in Table 10–3 are reordered along the permissiveness dimension, role differentiation is largely due to the lack of constraint and integration characteristic of the nonpolar structures. As the decisional structure gives councilmen few behavioral clues in the voting situation, the permissiveness so created would seem to stimulate a high level of role differentiation.

Conclusion

The decisional structure conceived as an independent variable has a pervasive and determinative effect on the council's properties immediately relevant to its decision-making tasks, notably its social relations, governing practices, social climate, and interactions. The social organization of the council is a response to the degree of conflict that characterizes one or another type of decisional structure and to the limitations on behavior created by the decisional structure. Role differentiation, also, is a response to these limitations, but in this regard it is the decisional structure's permissiveness rather than its conflict component that is the effective dimension. The decisional structure has no such effect on the council's status system, which appears to be relatively autonomous (though it is an important independent component of the council's social organization in other respects).

The Decisional Structure as Dependent Variable

The decisional structure's power to order the web of relationships among the components of council social organization suggests that these behavior patterns are not random and unpredictable, labyrinthine though they may be. Small legislative decision-making groups, like other formally organized collectivities, have an underlying and lawful social order. The treatment of linkages among the council's organizational components as interdependent variables can be helpful in explaining the decisional structures. The construction of models of council social organization, with the decisional structures as dependent variables, is the next step in the analysis.

Coping with the decisional structure as the dependent variable requires treating it in terms of its three behavioral dimensions, for the effect of any prior variable will be different, depending on whether the decisional structure is viewed in terms of conflict-harmony, fragmentation-integration, or permissiveness-constraint. Moreover, because the various components of the social organization are responses to social complexity, it is necessary to proceed in two ways: first, by holding social complexity constant so that the problem of adaptation can be divorced from the problem of organization; and second, by observing the social organization within the context of complexity so that it can be interpreted as a response to social complexity.

Because councils are small institutionalized groups in which social relations are relatively stable and permanent, the components that, along with the decisional structure, constitute the social organization are interdetermined rather than causally linked. This assumption facilitates treatment of the decisional structure as the genuinely dependent variable.

Figures 10–A and 10–B recapitulate the interdependencies of the five major organizational components by way of diagrams that depict the "tightness" of the organizational web. Figure 10–A eliminates the possibly disturbing influence of the decisional structure as an independent variable by holding it constant (i.e., it is based on the partials reported in Table 10–6 below). Figure 10–B controls the same relationship by city size. Both diagrams show the council's social organization as a net of rather loosely associated components. In both diagrams only one linkage—between stratification and governing style—is substantial. All the other relationships among the organization's components are only moderate or weak, and some are practically nonexistent. One is hard put to ascertain just which component property of the council's social organization has primacy over the others.

However, social organizations differ under varying conditions of environmental complexity, differences which indicate responses to the setting in which the council organizes itself for the task of governance. Figures 10–C and 10–D represent what occurs in

Figures 10-A to 10-D
Relationships Among Components of Council Social Organization

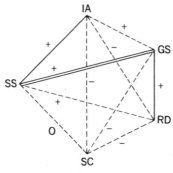

Figure 10-A
Components by Decisional Structure (Partials)

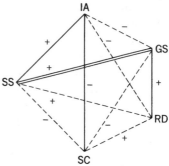

Figure 10-B
Components by City Size (Partials)

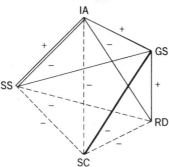

Figure 10-C
Components in Large Cities

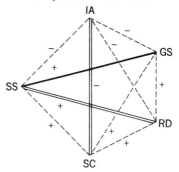

Figure 10-D
Components in Small Cities

Coda:
SS = Stratification
IA = Interaction
GS = Governing Style
SC = Social Climate
RD = Role Differentiation

-------- Weak (.00 − .24)
———— Moderate (.25 − .39)
======= Substantial (.40 − .54)
———— Strong (.55 − 1.00)

response to different degrees of environmental complexity. Figure 10–C shows that in the large cities the constraints of external complexity have a noticeable impact on the council's social organization. The net of relationships among the organizational components is more tightly knit than it is in the small cities. Not only are the interdependencies generally stronger in the more complex context, but the interdependencies of any significance vary from context to context. These relationships have been reviewed in detail, if seriatim, in earlier chapters. Overall, in the complex and heterogeneous environment, the council's organizational components are at least moderately interrelated. That strong environmental pressures are the source of more integrated structural arrangements is a "law of organization" widely demonstrated and accepted in social analysis. Clearly, even small governing groups such as city councils are not immune to this law.

Three Models

The three-dimensional character of the decisional structure requires three models, each geared to a different dominant dimension in the typology. For the nature and strength of the linkages between the council's organizational components and the decisional structure will vary depending on whether conflict, fragmentation, or permissiveness is stressed. The objective is to discover the relative impact of components of social organization on the decisional structure as well as to reveal pathways of causation that can be inferred as significant linkages. Figures 10–E, 10–H, and 10–K present the emergent models with city size held constant; Figures 10–F, 10–I, and 10–L locate the models in the complex context of the larger cities, and Figures 10–G, 10–J, and 10–M, in the simpler context of the smaller cities. The interdependencies among the organizational components have been omitted from these diagrams for the sake of graphic clarity. They can be easily inspected (and inserted) by reference to Appendix B10.1. We focus here on the direct linkages between the organizational components and the decisional structure.

The Conflict Model

When the linkages between organizational components and decisional structure are ordered on the conflict dimension and controlled by city size (Figure 10–E), three pathways, from governing style, interaction, and social climate, stand out as of at least moderate strength. Stratification and role differentiation, the latter at best only weakly linked to the other components (Figure 10–B), have no direct impact on the decisional structure in the conflict model. Most significant is the impact of social climate: the more antagonistic the climate, the more conflictual is decision-making. A political style and politicized interaction also contribute.

When external complexity is introduced, the greater cohesion in the larger cities is reflected in the greater impact each organizational component has on the decisional structure of the conflict model. Indeed, the differences from one setting to the other are rather spectacular, in regard both to the direction and the strength of the linkages. In the larger cities, stratification makes for bipolarity in the decisional structure, while in the small cities it makes for unipolarity. In the larger cities, a political governing style strongly makes for conflictual decision-making, while in the smaller cities it makes, moderately, for more harmonious decision-making. In the larger cities, political interaction has a substantial impact on the emergence of bipolar decisional structures, while in the smaller cities the impact is moderate. In the larger cities role differentiation has a substantial negative effect on the appearance of conflict in decision-making, while in the smaller cities it has a weak positive effect. Only social climate has a similar effect in both environments, and the effect is in both cases strong.

External complexity, it appears, makes for a social organization that facilitates the emergence of conflictual decision-making patterns. This is all the more noteworthy because, as was noted in Tables 9–8 and 9–9, environmental complexity is more conducive to the emergence of fragmented and permissive, rather than conflictual, decisional patterns. But the paradox is more apparent than real. For the data show that *if and when* external complexity and conflictual decision patterns converge, the latter are reinforced by organizational components which, we noted in earlier chapters,

Figures 10-E to 10-M

Social Organization and Decisional Structures

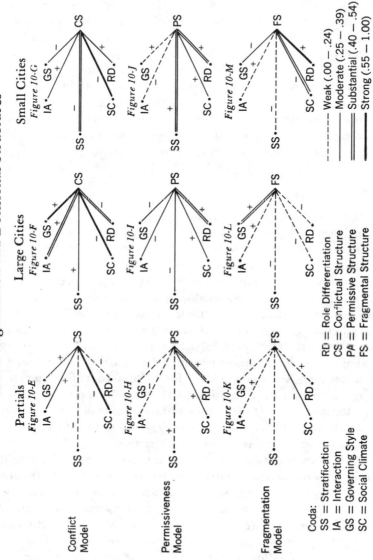

Coda:
SS = Stratification
IA = Interaction
GS = Governing Style
SC = Social Climate

RD = Role Differentiation
CS = Conflictual Structure
PA = Permissive Structure
FS = Fragmental Structure

---- Weak (.00 — .24)
—— Moderate (.25 — .39)
══ Substantial (.40 — .54)
▬▬ Strong (.55 — 1.00)

are themselves responses to external complexity. This is especially true of stratification (Tables 4–4 and 4–5), social climate (Tables 6–1 and 6–2), and interaction (Tables 7–1 and 7–2), but less true of governing style, which is more related to internal than to external complexity (Tables 5–7 and 5–8), though city size is also contributive. In general, then, conflictual decision-making is most likely if an externally complex environment produces a social organization which not only is relatively tightly knit but whose components are predominantly politicized. Given these circumstances, bipolarized decision-making structures are predictable consequences of politization in the social organization.

The Permissiveness Model

Different linkages characterize the effect of social-organizational components on the decisional structure when it is ordered on the permissiveness-constraint dimension. As Figure 10–H shows, when complexity is removed as a variable, the links between most of the organizational components and the decisional structure are not only weaker in three relationships but change direction in all relationships. Stratification continues to have practically no impact. Social climate, weakly related, is positively so: the more collegial the climate, the more permissive is decisional behavior. Only weak linkages exist between governing styles and interaction: neither a benevolent style nor private interaction contribute much to permissiveness in the decisional structure. But permissiveness in the decisional structure is a substantial outcome of role differentiation; the more the council is characterized by role differentiation, the more permissive is its decisional pattern.

Role differentiation remains an important factor affecting decisional permissiveness when external complexity is introduced. In both large and small cities, its impact is almost identical. Stratification now also has an impact, but it differs from one setting to the other. In the more complex setting, it is low stratification that makes for permissive decisional behavior, while in the small cities permissiveness follows upon high stratification. Governing style and interaction have a moderate effect in the larger contexts but almost none in the less complex contexts: in the more complex environment, it is a benevolent style and private interaction that are conducive to the emergence of a permissive decisional structure. Social climate has about the same moderate effect in both settings: a collegial climate favors permissiveness.

In general, the components of social organization have more impact on permissiveness in decision-making in the more complex context (where they are themselves more highly interrelated) than in the less complex environment. Only role differentiation has a substantial impact on the appearance of permissive decisional behavior in both contexts. Nonpolarity in the decisional structure results from internal and external complexity (Tables 9–8 and 9–9), but is also most likely if and when role differentiation is pronounced.

The Fragmentation Model

The impact of organizational components on the emergence of a decisional structure in its fragmentation-integration dimension is, in some respects, the most interesting because it reflects, more than the other two models, the adaptive quality of the council's social organization. When complexity is held constant, Figure 10–K shows, only social climate has at best a moderate effect on the decisional structure. However, when complexity is introduced as a variable, the direction of the linkages as well as their strength varies considerably.

As Figure 10–L indicates, only one linkage is at all significant in the more complex setting of the larger cities. A political governing style has a strong impact on fragmentation in the decisional structure. By way of contrast, as seen in Figure 10–M, three pathways lead to the decisional structure in the small cities. Stratification and interaction have little impact, though the latter has more than the former. Most significant in smaller cities is the influence of role differentiation; it has more of an impact on fragmentation than on the permissiveness or conflict dimensions. An antagonistic climate contributes to fragmentation, as does a nonpolitical governing style. Although fragmentation of the decisional structure is more common in the complex environment (Tables 9–8 and 9–9), the council's social organization is more conducive to fragmentation in the simpler context. Evidently, if the context is complex, the social organization's components have little elbow-room to contribute further to fragmentation.

Conclusion

If the council's decisional structure is treated as an outcome of social-organization patterns and processes that antecede its emergence, different components of the social organization have different but highly plausible consequences for the varying emphases in the decisional structure. These emphases depend on the degree of complexity in the council's external environment.

The effect of stratification is ambiguous. In the larger cities, high stratification makes for conflict and constraint in the decisional structure, while in the small cities it makes for harmony and permissiveness. Social climate has a more consistent effect. In both large and small cities, an antagonistic climate makes for conflict and fragmentation but favors constraint. The political governing style is conducive to fragmentation, conflict, and constraint in the large but not in the small cities. Politicized interaction makes for conflict and, to a lesser extent, constraint in the larger cities but for fragmentation and conflict in the smaller cities. Role differentiation favors harmony and permissiveness and, to a very limited extent, integration in the larger cities but makes for fragmentation, permissiveness, and conflict in the smaller cities.

As a dependent variable that is multidimensional, the decisional structure is evidently the outcome of a highly intricate configuration of external circumstances, internal organizational patterns, and, as we have yet to show in a later chapter, policy choices confronting the decision-makers.

The Decisional Structure as Contextual Variable

Contextual analysis does not ask about the power of one variable to determine another but about the relationship between two variables within the context provided by a third. The procedure is essentially heuristic; it provides insight in the literal sense of "in-sight."

As a preliminary, Table 10–4 presents the partial correlation coefficients obtained for the relationships among the council's social relations when the decisional structures are held constant. Two aspects of the matrix are noteworthy. First, it is symmetrical, with two exceptions. Second, the relationships are strongest among those properties previously identified as intrinsically political—opinion leadership, cosponsorship, opposition potential, and friendship. The symmetry of the matrix and the varying strengths of the associations among the six kinds of social relations suggest that even if removed from the contexts provided by the decisional structure, the council's social relations are not only interdependent but coexist in an orderly fashion.

The original symmetry of the partials matrix is differentially disturbed when the decisional structure is introduced as context. But each contextual matrix has its own characteristic and by no means arbitrary pattern. We shall emphasize, however, only those relationships that are substantial or strong (where gamma equals .40 or more), and we shall call attention to patterns or especially noteworthy relationships by cluster lines and by underlining the coefficients.

First of all, the politically most salient properties—opinion leadership, cosponsorship, opposition potential, and friendship—remain highly interrelated in each context (clusters A). There is one exception; in the fragmented and permissive context of the nonpolar structure, friendship is only weakly related to opinion leadership and opposition potential and is evidently not perceived as a political resource.

Second, within each of the political clusters the strongest relationships among the four properties vary from one context to the next. Each of these relationships provides insight into the particular decisional structures. The very strong relationship between opinion leadership and cosponsorship in the nonpolar context is consonant with fragmentation. As shown earlier (Tables 9–5, 9–6, and 10–1), both properties are independently ordered by the decisional structure's fragmentation-integration dimension. In the

Table 10-4

Correlation Coefficients for Relationships Among Council Social Relations, by Decisional Structures*

Partials	Cosponsorship	Opposition potential	Friendship	Expertise	Respect
Opinion leadership	.71 >	.64 >	.58 >	.48 >	.47
Cosponsorship	—	.65 >	.51 <	.54 >	.10
Opposition potential		—	.52 >	.41 <	.57
Friendship			—	.49 >	.23
Expertise				—	.39
Bipolar					
Opinion leadership	A .56	.88	.80	−.05	.81
Cosponsorship	—	.56	.40	.40	−.60
Opposition potential		—	.54	.17	.49
Friendship			—	.33	.36
Expertise				—	.50

Table 10–4 (cont.)

	Cosponsorship	Opposition potential	Friendship	Expertise	Respect
Nonpolar					
Opinion leadership	A .87	.57	.18	.88	.13
Cosponsorship	—	.48	.44	B .88	.13
Opposition potential		—	.20	.55	.68
Friendship			—	.54	.02
Expertise				—	.64
Unipolar					
Opinion leadership	A .61	.58	.77	.27	.59
Cosponsorship	—	.75	.61	.27	.35
Opposition potential		—	.75	.39	C .62
Friendship			—	.51	.35
Expertise				—	.52

* Bipolar = highly conflictual, medium fragmented, low permissive
Nonpolar = medium conflictual, highly fragmented, highly permissive
Unipolar = low conflictual, low fragmented, medium permissive

nonpolar structure the success of a proposal is best assured by searching for support among those whose voice counts—the opinion leaders.

In the conflictual bipolar context, two relationships—between opinion leadership and opposition potential and between opinion leadership and friendship—are especially noteworthy. Both opposition potential and friendship are independently ordered by the conflict dimension of the decisional structure (Tables 9–2, 9–3, and 10–1). In the bipolar setting opposition is a fact of political life and friendship is highly politicized as two factions, sensitive to each other's opposition, confront one another. In this context opinion leadership crystallizes lines of cleavage, and opinion leadership is located within factional bonds of friendship.

In the harmonious, integrated unipolar context, three relationships stand out—between opinion leadership and friendship, friendship and opposition potential, and opposition potential and cosponsorship. Friendship serves as a reference point for opinion leadership, but as the opposition of friends is a source of concern because it threatens the council's unity, it tends to be offset by a corresponding emphasis on cosponsorship to maintain the council's basic harmony through a kind of cooptational behavior.

In spite of variations, all three polar contexts are characterized by at least substantial linkages among the properties that constitute the political clusters of each contextual matrix. But there are also dramatic differences, especially between the unipolar and nonpolar councils with regard to the expertise and respect variables. In the nonpolar structure, expertise shows strong linkages to the political properties (cluster B). This is rather astounding because, as was noted earlier (Table 10–1), nonpolar councils are least characterized by a high level of expertise. Evidently, when expertise does reach a high level in the fragmented and permissive nonpolar context, it is precisely because explicit political (factional as well as consensual) cues are missing that those considered as most informed and knowledgeable are sought out as opinion leaders and cosponsors or identified, if to a lesser extent, as potential opponents or friends. By way of contrast, expertise is less politically linked in the bipolar and unipolar structures.

The place of respect in the three contexts is much more ambiguous. It is most in evidence as a correlate of the other properties in the unipolar settings—an indication of the mutual deference that accompanies social relations in the integrated and harmonious context (cluster C). In both the conflictual bipolar and the less conflictual nonpolar structures, respect for potential opponents makes for at least a substantial, if not strong, relationship between the two properties. It is at least substantially related to expertise in all three contexts, but especially in the nonpolar. Most interestingly, however, respect is given to opinion leaders in the conflictual bipolar structures (.81). As one must assume that opinion leaders are found on both sides of the division, the strong relationship between opinion leadership and respect in this setting perhaps attests to the integrative nature of conflict. Even though the council is divided, opinion leadership on either side is valued, thus reducing interpersonal conflict without, of course, affecting the basic division of the council.

Social Relations and Stratification

Contextual analysis can serve to give further meaning to the nature of the decisional structure if we observe the relationships between social relations and the system of stratification to which social relations give rise. As Table 10–5 shows, in the harmonious, integrated unipolar structure, cosponsorship and friendship are especially conducive to high stratification. The great bulk of these structures are in small councils and the majority of the small councils are located in small cities (Table 9–8). Both cosponsorship and friendship are substantially or strongly related to stratification in the less complex environments (see Table 4–6). Environmental simplicity and an integrated decisional structure provide a favorable context for cosponsorship and friendship—themselves basically harmonious kinds of social relations—to affect stratification.

Opposition potential and expertise contribute most to stratification in the nonpolar context. They do the same, we noted earlier (Table 4–6), in the more complex environments—precisely the environments in which most nonpolar councils are located (Table

Table 10–5
Correlation Coefficients for Relationships
Between Social Relations and Stratification, by Decisional Structures

Relationship between stratification and social relations in:	Co-sponsorship	Opposition potential	Friendship	Expertise	Opinion leadership	Respect
Unipolar structures	.77	.62	.77	.52	.35	.29
Nonpolar structures	.57	.75	.45	.61	.33	.20
Bipolar structures	.20	.02	.25	−.17	.41	.36
Zero-order	.54	.54	.50	.38	.33	.29

9–8). In the bipolar structures, largely unrelated to the external environment, only opinion leadership makes a substantial contribution to stratification, though respect makes a moderate contribution. Overall, the effects of particular kinds of social relations on stratification vary not only with internal and external complexity but also with the decisional context which is most closely related to complexity. In turn, each decisional context is saturated by relationships between various kinds of social relations and stratification that give it organizational relevance beyond the voting situation itself.

Social Organization in Context

The notion of context implies that the property involved is not so much parametric as perimetric. Context sets limits to the patterns, processes, or structures that constitute the council's social organization. Relationships among the components of the social organization are likely to be circumscribed by the boundaries set by the decisional structure as a contextual variable. But though

perimetric, context is also parametric in the sense that each decision structure's boundaries may be more or less closed or porous.
The different dimensions of the decisional structure reflect this
aspect of the context especially well. The nonpolar structure, internally fragmented and permissive, fails to contain or constrain
other relations so that behavioral patterns can be somewhat random and unpredictable. By way of contrast, the bipolar structure
is strictly bounded. Divided by conflict into two clearly identifiable factions, the boundaries of the conflict define the boundaries

Table 10–6

Correlation Coefficients for Relationships Among Stratification,
Governing Style, Interaction, Role Differentiation, and Social Climate,
by Decisional Structures

Partials	Governing style	Inter-action	Role differentiation	Social climate
Stratification	.45	.26	.18	—.00
Governing style	—	.08	.30	—.07
Interaction		—	—.06	—.24
Role differentiation			—	—.09
Bipolar				
Stratification	.81	.62	.36	—.50
Governing style	—	.50	.60	—.87
Interaction		—	.16	—.11
Role differentiation			—	—.26
Nonpolar				
Stratification	.00	.01	—.29	—.08
Governing style	—	.26	.19	—.54
Interaction		—	.00	.05
Role differentiation			—	—.43
Unipolar				
Stratification	.67	.32	.41	.29
Governing style	—	—.27	.27	1.00
Interaction		—	—.19	—.57
Role differentiation			—	.29

of the context. Under these conditions there is little freedom, and relationships are patterned and predictable. Relationships under conditions of unipolar decision-making fall in between. The unipolar structure is highly integrated, but precisely because it seeks to avoid conflict it is more permissive than the bipolar but less permissive than the nonpolar structure.

The relationships existing among the components of the council's social organization, reported in Table 10–6, confirm the differential contextual quality of the three decisional structures. In the nonpolar structures, only two relationships—between social climate and governing style and between climate and role differentiation—are at least substantial. The rest are only moderate, weak, or nonexistent. In the bipolar structures, on the other hand, seven of the ten relationships range from substantial to very strong. In the unipolar structures, the relationships of note vary from moderate to strong. The following chart summarizes the picture:

Strength of relationship between properties	Nonpolar	Unipolar	Bipolar
None (.00–.09)	5	0	0
Weak (.10–.24)	1	1	2
Moderate (.25–.39)	2	5	2
Substantial (.40–.54)	2	1	2
Strong (.55–.69)	0	2	2
Very strong (.70–1.00)	0	1	2
	10	10	10

Conclusion

Contextual analysis maximizes insight into the nature of the decisional structures as the most pervasive and institutionalized properties of the council. It shows that each type of decisional structure provides a special setting for the emergence of different associations among the council's relational, behavioral, and structural properties. Each type of polar structure facilitates or impedes certain associations among the properties that constitute a council's social organization. And each type accentuates or diminishes, in understandable ways, the strength of these associations (themselves of course found in all three settings). In general, bipolarization makes for stronger associations among other council properties than the existence of conflict would suggest, revealing the integrative character of conflict. Unipolarity is conducive to interdependencies among council properties, indicative of the basic integration of these structures but also revealing less rigidity than one might expect. Relatively weaker associations among council properties in the nonpolar structures are evidence of their great fragmentation and permissiveness, but, as was noted, strong association between political relations and expertise suggests why these structures do not succumb to the kind of diffuse conflict that, unlike factional cleavage, is difficult to resolve through strong majority rule.

Each structure contains within itself remedial processes that aid it in overcoming pathologies that might flow from undue emphasis on any one of the dimensions underlying each structure in varying mixes. The destructive potential of conflict is offset, in the bipolar structures, by integrative processes; the rigidity of unipolarity is offset by relaxation of constraints precisely because the underlying harmony of this context remains undisturbed. The fragmentation of the nonpolar structure is reduced by emphasis on instrumental bonds that keep it from flying apart. Each structure generates its own organizational arrangements that contribute to the council's collective adaptation.

Part III

Constitutive Processes as Linkages

INTRODUCTION

There is an unavoidable physical and social distance between the council as the tiny fraction which governs and the large body of citizens who are governed. This is a permanent condition of political life wherever the size of the community makes some form of representation mandatory. And because of this condition, the linkages established between governors and governed through institutional arrangements and political processes are critical components of governance. Because linkages vary in kind and extent, any government will be partly explained by investigating how the distance between governors and governed is bridged. The form and extent of the linkages will differ depending on the constitutional rules under which a polity is organized.

The linkages that appear in governments organized according to democratic assumptions and procedures are constrained by the value premises of the democratic tradition. This tradition stresses that the persons selected to make the day-by-day decisions concerning the collective life of the community should take into account the preferences of the citizenry. If "consent of the governed" is to be more than an empty slogan, it must be established as an operating principle of governance.

Making the principle of popular consent operable is not easy. Reliance on the goodwill of the governors—to suppose that they will inform themselves of the wishes of the people and act responsively—is not enough. Democracy does not trust its governors to seek and abide by the consent of the governed unchecked by any countervailing power. Constitutional democracy, from its beginnings in the eighteenth century, has involved a continuing search for ways to insure that men with great power will nevertheless be responsive to men with negligible power.

This search has made free elections the crucial instrument of leadership selection in democracies. By virtue of their centrality in leadership selection, elections constitute a major link between governors and governed. They are the tension point at which citizens exert leverage over political leaders. Large numbers of citizens play a role in government by choosing the men who actually manage the collective affairs of the community. By establishing a measure of popular control, elections are manifestly practical ways to bridge, in part at least, the distance between governors and governed, representatives and represented.

How elections introduce the principle of the consent of the governed into politics was well described in *The Federalist* when the author referred to the "elective mode of obtaining rulers" as an effective precaution for "keeping them virtuous whilst they continue to hold their public trust," and continued:

> Before the sentiments impressed on their minds by the mode of their elevation, can be effaced by the exercise of power, they will be compelled to anticipate the moment when their power is to cease, when their exercise of it is to be reviewed, and when they must descend to the level from which they were raised; there for ever to remain unless a faithful discharge of their trust shall have established their title to a renewal of it.[1]

This passage anticipates a line of reasoning about democracy that has been pursued to the present day. The "theory of democratic accountability" is a set of propositions attempting to show that citizens and leaders are linked together in the governing process by the institution of competitive elections. Men hold political office at the pleasure of the voters. Because governors wish to avoid electoral defeat at the hands of challengers, they select policies which they believe are in accordance with voter preferences. It is in the

---

[1] *The Federalist*, Number LVII, Max Beloff, ed. (New York: The Macmillan Company, 1948), pp. 292–294.

leaders' anticipation of voter response that a measure of popular control is introduced into the governing process. Governors and governed are thus linked through the institution of competitive elections.

This line of reasoning has been understandably popular in interpretations of democratic politics. The ancient task of preventing tyranny by the rulers is solved by the simple institutional device of elections. The quest for responsible and responsive government need not depend on Plato's hope that rulers can be taught not to take advantage of their powers. When government is organized under the rules of democracy, persons with great power will still consider the wishes of persons with negligible power. For at election time the power relationship is reversed; the electorate can punish the officials through eviction.

The conception of elections as central institutions linking governors and governed is important to our study in several respects. For one thing, it allows us to translate a major normative proposition in democratic theory into a set of research questions. We will analyze elections in the context of a tradition which takes "consent of the governed" as a core value. Whether elections do work to link governors and governed depends somewhat on whether the electorate is sufficiently alert and involved that it will evict from office those leaders who unfaithfully discharge their trust. And it is an empirical question whether electorates are involved in the process by which political leadership is selected and replaced. The degree of electoral involvement and the way in which involvement is expressed vary considerably from community to community.

There is a second, related reason for thinking of elections as linkage institutions. Elections are part of a more inclusive process through which certain men come to govern other men. The more inclusive process refers to such activities as political recruitment and political campaigning and can be summarized under the single label of leadership selection. Leadership selection includes a much more varied set of activities than just those normally associated with the election itself, though these activities will be affected by anticipation of the election. Because leadership selection is much more than just election, it provides several opportunities for linking the governed and their governors.

Nothing in political life is so closely considered by so many people as is the fate of powerful men. Citizens are fascinated by the movement of men into and out of high office, and certainly the high drama of politics is in those moments when men win or lose the powers of the throne or the chieftainship or the presidency or the party secretariat. In the United States, citizens huddle around television sets well into the night to hear election results; in the Soviet Union, citizens circulate rumors and seek out news when word comes that major shifts in the Politburo are in the offing; in Uganda, citizens flock to the streets for information and explanation when a coup occurs.

Political activists pay close attention to the making and unmaking of political careers. The removal of old leaders combined with the selection of new ones affects the policies and programs, the benefits of patronage, the privileges of access, the patterns of influence, and the career prospects of those who live for and off politics. Thus, information is continually circulated concerning who is maneuvering for position, whose strength is waxing and whose waning, whose career is being nursed and whose blocked by men in yet more powerful positions, and who scores high in popularity polls.

But interest in leadership changes is not restricted to the active stratum. Though not nearly so well informed about the preliminary maneuvering taking place in the corridors of power, the citizen at large sharply increases his political interest when public matters are dramatized as conflicts between personalities. The average citizen habitually defines public business in terms of individual men. Perhaps it is because citizens normally have only a distant and vague understanding of politics to begin with that the fate of persons rather than programs is given such attention. Perhaps it is because the earliest and strongest political attachments are formed in response to persons and the symbols of office rather than in response to ideologies, issues, or policies. But whatever the reason, elections, coups, political assassinations, the natural deaths of leaders, and even appointment to high office command, on the average, more attention among the citizenry than do court decisions, legislative enactments, administrative edicts, or even constitutional changes.

Because public matters are so often defined in terms of powerful men, the manner in which they come and go provides many opportunities for linking governors and governed. Of course, different modes of leadership selection differ in how effectively they establish linkages. Bureaucratic advancement according to merit examinations or seniority attracts little public attention. As a way in which to select leadership, bureaucratic advancement probably provides the fewest links between those who are elevated to positions of influence and those who are governed by them. Leadership change by violent methods presents a sharp contrast. Seldom in political life is public attention so fixed on political matters and seldom are the leaders so anxious about the public's response as when a coup is undertaken. Yet because coups or assassinations, as modes of removing and selecting leaders, are planned in secret and executed by only a few—besides being only sporadic events—they fail to establish regularized linkages.

As a means of building linkages between governors and governed, competitive elections have several advantages over alternative modes of leadership selection. Elections draw the attention of a citizenry which normally ignores political matters to what is happening at the centers of government; moreover, at election time, officeholders who normally remain distant from the daily lives of the citizenry grow sensitive to mass responses. Elections facilitate the participation of the public in the act of leadership selection on a regularized, predictable time schedule.

In some respects it is perhaps unfortunate that elections and related activities are so much at the center of political attention, for what happens to the careers of particular men is possibly less significant for the well-being of citizens than what happens in the legislatures, courts, or bureaucracies. But this does not alter one overriding fact. For the average citizen as well as for most political activists, it is elections and the general process of selecting leaders that attract attention in political life. The study of leadership selection is helpful in understanding what links those at the center of the political action to those at the periphery.

Because the task at hand is to explore the linkages established between council and community as collectivities rather than between individual councilmen and individual citizens, it is necessary to conceptualize elections and to handle the election data differently from common practice. A brief overview of how the election data were transformed to make them manageable as contextual properties of the council may be helpful even though a full description of the procedure must await presentation of the data themselves.

First, the election data are used in a way that emphasizes electorates rather than voters because the council as a unit is chosen by an electorate as a unit. Following Austin Ranney, it is necessary for analysis at the level of the council "to regard electorates not merely as arithmetic sums of individuals but rather as units playing special and significant roles in the political process and therefore worthy of analysis in their own right."[2] This is to think of electorates as action units; electorates can be described in terms of their attributes and in terms of their characteristic modes of action. They can be described as large or small, as homogeneous or heterogeneous, as acting in an assertive or passive manner, as being hostile or supportive, and so on. Once electorates have been classified as action units, it is possible to ask whether council structures, processes, and activities vary depending on the type of electorate in the community.

Second, the electorate is described in terms of its behavior over time. The operational procedure is to average the attributes and activities of city electorates for a period of five consecutive elections.[3] Averaging across several elections has the advantage of reducing the impact on fluctuations in the vote of situational factors like the weather, a controversial referendum at the time of a council election, or an occasional flamboyant candidate who attracts unusual public interest. More critical, however, is the need to treat the council data and the election data synchronically. Council properties are constructed largely from the behavior patterns reported by individual councilmen. In effect, then, these

---

[2] Austin Ranney, "The Utility and Limitations of Aggregate Data in the Study of Electoral Behavior," in Ranney, ed., *Essays on the Behavioral Study of Politics* (Urbana: University of Illinois Press, 1962), p. 99.

[3] Election statistics were collected for the decade preceding the time when councilmen were interviewed. In a few cases, where a city was incorporated recently, fewer than five elections had taken place.

properties are based on experiences and recollections that often span the careers of councilmen. For the most part, councilmen's relevant careers cover the decade prior to interviewing.[4] For this reason, the electorate is best described over the same span used to describe the council.

Finally, officeholders, as well as those who seek to displace them, probably have an image of the habitual behavior of the electorate. The most reliable index of habitual behavior comes from past election statistics. As a scholar who investigated campaign behavior has observed, politicians "find some analysis of the past election statistics in their districts a valuable means to determine roughly what will happen in the present election."[5] When a candidate estimates voter turnout, his calculation is bounded by the number of citizens who normally go to the polls. Because councils may vary in responding to the electorate's conduct, it is useful to have measures that approximate normal electoral patterns and indicate what councils most likely take into account when anticipating electoral behavior.[6]

The theoretical issues guiding the following chapters have to do with council constitutive processes, and especially elections, as linkages between the council and the citizenry. Two dimensions of the electorate's behavior—voter participation and electoral competition—and their interrelations in different urban and social environments are examined in Chapter 11. What emerges is the construct of an "electoral context" that is more fully developed and validated in Chapter 12. The electoral context is then used

---

[4] Most councilmen serve two terms, or eight years. A decade spans their incumbency plus a period immediately prior to their initial election or appointment to office. We assume that the electorate is salient to a person considering a council office and thus feel justified in creating electorate measures for a ten-year, rather than merely an eight-year, period.

[5] John W. Kingdon, *Candidates for Office: Beliefs and Strategies* (New York: Random House, 1966), p. 96.

[6] This procedure ignores trends in voter participation and electoral competition. Since many cities changed over the ten-year period in social composition and in other respects, secular trends in participation and competition rates probably also exist. We acknowledge the possibility of alternative ways of constructing electoral contexts that may be more fruitful; but our purpose is to neutralize secular trends precisely because we are more interested in reconstructing the politician's "psycho-political life space" than in describing "reality."

as the major analytic tool to investigate not only how elections directly affect the linkages between council and community but also, in Chapter 13, how it shapes recruitment practices and, in Chapter 14, political campaign activities. Throughout these chapters, the emphasis is on recruitment, campaigning, and elections as constitutive processes that, in principle, influence and determine the degree to which the "consent of the governed" is realized in the selection of the council as the community's governing body.

Chapter 11

Voter Participation and Electoral Competition

Councils are brought together in elections. Although some are occasionally activated by the appointment route, councils derive their legitimacy from having been elected. In this perspective, it does not matter whether many citizens or only a few turn out to vote; and it does not matter whether the vote outcome is close or not. It is the electoral process as such and acceptance of the electoral outcome that, in a democracy, legitimize governance.

Elections not only legitimize government, they also link government and citizenry. Because they permit citizens through their ballots to record approval or disapproval of past leadership and often to select new leaders, elections are linkage institutions between the council and the community. In this perspective, it makes an enormous difference whether many citizens turn out as voters or only a few and whether the election has been a close race or a landslide. For the fact that not all citizens bother to vote regularly, or the fact that those who vote may do so one-sidedly, affects the quality of the linkage between the governing few and the many who are governed that is made possible by the electoral process.

Voter Participation

Universal suffrage, everybody's right to vote, is one thing; universal voting, everybody's readiness to vote, another. After two

centuries of struggle to expand the electorate to include all members of the society without discrimination, many more citizens have
been enfranchised than take advantage of their right to vote. In
the United States, even presidential elections attract only about
three-fifths of those eligible to vote. Mid-term congressional contests on the average attract less than half the citizenry to the polls.
And local elections, especially when nonpartisan, draw even less
voter attention. The average turnout for the Bay Area city council elections is less than one-third (31 percent) when computed as
a proportion of the adult population and is still less than half (46
percent) when computed as a proportion of the registered voters.[1]
This situation conforms to what is known about local elections
elsewhere.[2]

There are many reasons why fewer citizens than are eligible trouble themselves to vote. Electoral turnout can be explained in
terms of the demographic and attitudinal attributes of individual
voters, in terms of situational factors, or in terms of legal and other
structural features of the polity. Investigating the causes or conditions of different rates of voter turnout is not our research concern.
Rather, in order to examine linkages between the council and the
community, the variation in voter turnout serves as an independent variable. Where the electorate is "small," relatively few citizens vote in council elections; where it is "large," a relatively
greater number participate. How are these electorates of different
size viewed by the council? What does the council see and experience as a governing group when it is located in a community with
a relatively small, as against a relatively large, electorate? If few
citizens vote in council elections, does this mean that there are
also fewer and possibly weaker links between the council and community than if many citizens participate? Does a small electorate

---

[1] This and the previous average are grand means, calculated on the basis of
average turnout for five elections.
[2] Since both region and form of election have been shown to influence voter
turnout in American city elections, it was expected that holding these factors
constant would reduce intercity variability. Although this is the case to some
extent, there is sufficient variability in the data to use turnout rate as a variable.
For a comparison of voter turnout in partisan and nonpartisan cities, and in
cities with different election forms, see Robert Alford and Eugene C. Lee,
"Voting Turnout in American Cities," *American Political Science Review* 57
(September 1968): 796–813.

imply that councils are less accountable to the populations they govern?

Questions like these suggest that there may be difficulties in interpreting differing levels of voter turnout. Relatively few voters in council elections might suggest that citizens are satisfied with how the community is being governed, that they do not bother to vote because their preferences are already reflected in council policies. Or it may be that citizens are indifferent to local governance. If you "can't fight city hall," why unduly trouble yourself on election day? Or low voter turnout may only reflect physical obstacles that citizens encounter in voting. Registration laws disenfranchise large numbers of citizens in communities with highly mobile populations.

Just as it is difficult to interpret low voter turnout, so it is equally difficult to give meaning to high turnout. A large electorate might suggest that citizens are disgruntled with community governance, and that they are voting in large numbers to bring about a change in policies. But the opposite interpretation is also plausible. Citizens turn out on election day because they are pleased with how things are going and because they wish to record their support. But neither of these interpretations may be adequate; perhaps the habit of voting is well established in the community and citizens participate in council elections simply to fulfill an important civic duty.

Theorizing about the meanings of different rates of voter turnout for the governance of cities is no substitute for empirical discovery. The number of citizens who go to the polls is an inadequate basis for inference about the viability of elections as linkage institutions. Because of this inadequacy the electoral context will be constructed along two dimensions—voter participation *and* electoral competition. It is to the form and extent of competition in council elections that we turn first.

Electoral Competition

It is the struggle among candidates for the control of political office that makes of elections not plebiscites but mechanisms for expressing voter choice. Competition for office is a minimum condition if elections are to establish consent of the governed. Unless men in office are challenged by others who want those offices, there is no way in which the electorate can threaten eviction. And if eviction is not a potential threat, the chain of events which allows the governed to control the governors lacks a vital link. Schumpeter's famous definition of democracy emphasizes this logic: "The democratic method is that institutional arrangement for arriving at political decisions in which individuals acquire the power to decide by means of a competitive struggle for the people's vote."[3] One cannot consider elections without also inquiring into the forms of political competition.

Competition for office has a direct bearing on whether elections link the governors and the governed. We can suggest this by several reasonable assumptions. A competitive struggle for office generates greater interest among citizens than the noncompetitive election.[4] The prospect of a change in personnel is sufficient in itself to attract the attention of the normally indifferent citizenry. And in close elections it is thought that one's own vote is more likely to make a difference. Moreover, the behavior of the leadership echelon is affected by the prospect of a close election.[5] Those in office busy themselves taking their case to the people. The challengers busy themselves by stirring up constituency support. The election campaign is a period of intense activity. All this makes for a greater variety and a larger number of links between the normally distant governors and the normally uninterested citizens.

---

[3] Joseph A. Schumpeter, *Capitalism, Socialism and Democracy* (New York: Harper & Row, Torchbook Edition, 1962), p. 269. First published in 1942.

[4] A study of voting behavior reports higher turnout among those who perceive the election to be close than among those who expect it to be one-sided, though this is mostly accounted for by those who have strong partisan preferences. See Angus Campbell, Philip E. Converse, Warren E. Miller, and Donald E. Stokes, *The American Voter* (New York: John Wiley and Sons, 1960), p. 99. Lewis A. Froman, Jr., reports consistently higher turnout in competitive, than in noncompetitive, congressional districts. See *Congressmen and Their Constituencies* (Chicago: Rand McNally, 1963), pp. 28–32, especially Table 2–8.

[5] John W. Kingdon notes that candidates present themselves differently depending on whether they seek office in marginal or safe districts in his *Candidates for Office: Beliefs and Strategies* (New York: Random House, 1966), pp. 128–129.

Three measures of electoral competition characterize city council elections, and with respect to each, cities vary in how competitive the elections are. One measure of competition is the number of candidates seeking council positions; the second is the closeness of the vote which separates the winners from the losers; the third is the frequency with which incumbents are evicted from office by an election defeat.

Office Contesting[6]

Competitive elections require at a minimum that there be more candidates for office than there are openings. Without at least two candidates for every opening, the electorate is unable to register its choice. Moreover, if the contestants are divided between incumbents and challengers, the electorate can do more than choose between alternative governors—it can use the ballot box to evict. Choice between the ins and the outs is provided when the incumbents want to remain and challengers aspire to replace them.

The situation most familiar from American national elections is when two candidates, each representing a major party, seek the same political office. Often one of the candidates will be the incumbent. Primary elections are a variant on this pattern, with two or more candidates seeking the designation of official party nominee.

Councilmanic elections follow neither of these patterns, the critical difference being that in any given election there will be two or more openings on the council. In five-member councils, for instance, elections will alternate in filling two or three openings. There will often be as many as ten or twelve candidates in the year when three seats are available. Multiple openings and mul-

---

[6] We speak of "contesting" with some risk of being misinterpreted. In normal electoral discourse, a "contested" election is one in which one or another candidate disputes or contests the election result, for whatever reason. This, clearly, is not the meaning we are giving to "office contesting." But as we are at a loss for another term—to set it off from competition or "closeness of vote"—we reluctantly retain the term "contesting" to refer to the number of candidates, both incumbents seeking reelection and their challengers.

Table 11–1
Distribution of Cities by Rate
of Office Contesting

Average number of candidates per council position, five elections	N = 81
1.00–1.50	7%
1.51–1.99	17
2.00–2.24	23
2.25–2.49	16
2.50–2.74	19
2.75–2.99	10
3.00–4.00	8
	100%

tiple candidacies present a picture of office contesting which differs in important respects from the familiar two-party race. Candidates in council elections do not run against a particular opponent for a particular opening, but rather compete against the entire field for one of two or more openings. Challengers can simultaneously compete against an incumbent standing for reelection and against other challengers where an incumbent has decided against another term.

The measure of office contesting used in the analysis computes the average number of candidates per council opening for each election and then computes the grand mean for the five-election period. Table 11–1 presents the distribution. The cities are clustered between the scores of 2.00 and 3.00, indicating that the electorate is presented with two or three candidates for each opening. However, there are cities at both extremes; in a few (7 percent), the average number of candidates is 1.50 or less, indicating that in some elections there is only one candidate for each opening. At the other extreme, 8 percent of the cities have on the average more than three candidates for each opening.

Closeness of the Vote

The second form which electoral competition takes has to do with the vote spread between winners and losers. It is a commonplace that the election is competitive when those who take office have but a few more votes than those rejected by the electorate. It is equally a commonplace that an election is noncompetitive when there are runaway winners. This usage of the terms probably derives from the language of athletic contests. A pennant race or track meet or boxing match is competitive when the performance of the winner is only slightly superior to the performance of the loser. The same is true of political contests, with performance being measured by the number of votes won.

The importance of the vote spread as a form of competition refers to the potential consequence for voter and candidate behavior. There will be a higher voter turnout among those citizens who perceive the election to be close than among those who expect it to be one-sided. Candidate behavior is also altered by these considerations, with candidates presenting themselves differently depending on whether they expect the vote to be close or not. The lore of campaigning has it that campaign contributors as well as campaign workers increase their investment and effort if the race is likely to be close.

However, assumptions about typical electoral competition should be applied to the city council situation with caution. The elections we study are formally nonpartisan, and candidates run at large and not from districts. Except in a few cases, plurality counting is used.[7] These electoral forms, when combined with multiple openings and multiple candidacies, make it difficult to apply a measure of closeness of the vote in the same manner as such measures are applied in two-candidate, single-opening political contests. Under these electoral conditions both voters and candidates will find it more difficult to estimate the likely vote spread in any one election than is the case in the more familiar races.

The measure to be used here compensates somewhat for these difficulties. As a sequence of five elections is being observed, if political participants were making a judgment about the closeness of the vote, it would not be about a single, forthcoming election

---

[7] Four cities have a primary, runoff system. Two of these cities (the two largest, Oakland and San Jose) plus two other cities also have a modified district election system. Candidates run in a particular district for an identified seat, but every voter in the city can cast a ballot in each district.

but about the habitual behavior of the electorate. The measure should capture, therefore, some sense on the part of voters and candidates that "elections are generally close in this city," or that "elections are seldom competitive here." To compute the measure, the average distance between each candidate's vote and the mean vote for all candidates was calculated.[8] A close election is one where all the candidates cluster around the mean: there is little dispersion. A noncompetitive election is one where candidates receive very unequal amounts of the total vote cast: there is significant dispersion.

Eviction from Office

The third measure of electoral competition is the frequency with which electorates remove their governors from office. This measure of competition is more important theoretically than the other two. Its importance derives from the probationary nature of political officeholding. The transitory aspect of political office is emphasized if electorates are able to control the actions taken by officeholders. To rephrase *The Federalist*, arbitrary exercise of power is prevented if the men in office are alert to the fact that their status is possible only at the pleasure of the voter.

Despite the centrality of this proposition in the theory of constitutional democracy, at all levels of officialdom men are in fact retaining elected office with great regularity. Eviction of incumbents is the exception more than the rule. Bay Area city councilmen, if they wish, are able to keep their positions. During the ten-year period, four of every five incumbents seeking reelection were returned.

However, as Table 11–2 shows, electoral eviction is not evenly distributed across all cities. In nearly a third of the cities fewer than one in ten incumbents seeking reelection suffered defeat. In contrast, 14 cities (17 percent) had electorates which evicted 40 percent or more of the incumbents attempting to be returned.

It is reasonable to infer, and subsequent analysis will bear out the inference, that electorates evicting incumbents are dissatisfied

---

[8] See Appendix B11.1.

Table 11–2
Distribution of Cities by Rate
of Incumbent Eviction

Incumbent eviction rate: proportion of incumbents seeking reelection who were defeated, five elections	N = 81
0–10%	30%
11–20%	20
21–30%	18
31–40%	15
41–50%	7
51–60%	5
61–100%	5
	100%

with the performance of their governors. More difficult are inferences about electorates that seldom evict incumbents. These electorates may be satisfied and supportive, but they may also be apathetic and ineffective. Possibly the challengers are viewed as no improvement over the incumbents, and electorates come to believe that it is a waste of effort to change the membership of the council. Or perhaps an electorate is rendered impotent because a politically organized minority consistently wins over a dispersed majority. This possibility is enhanced by plurality counting and multiple candidacies, for it takes only a small proportion of the total vote to return an incumbent.

The Politics of Electoral Competition

Each of the measures—office contesting, closeness of the vote, and incumbent eviction—refers to a different form of competition. The measures are not only operationally but also conceptually distinct. Thus each form of competition is likely to have different consequences for the emergence of linkages between councils and citizenry. However, their interrelatedness is an appropriate starting point for probing more fully into the nuances of electoral politics before examining their linkage potential.

There are various ways in which different forms of competition may be related to each other; it is difficult to predict just how they are related. For instance, a city may have numerous candidates (a high rate of office contesting) but still the electorate unfailingly returns the incumbents (a low rate of electoral eviction). Similarly, a city can have numerous candidates and yet the vote spread between winners and losers is so great that it would be inaccurate to refer to competitive elections. And the race for office can be closely contested but still result in victory for the incumbents.

As more challengers enter the electoral context, the likelihood of unseating incumbents should increase. Numerous challengers provide the electorate with a variety of choices, thereby increasing the probability that candidates more attractive than the incumbents would be among them. Moreover, a community with an electorate that habitually evicts incumbents should be expected to attract more challengers, for the politically ambitious have evidence that incumbents can be unseated.

The data do not support this reasoning. As Table 11–3 shows, the weakest relationship among the three forms of electoral competition is between office contesting and incumbent eviction (.14). Indeed, the relationship is weak enough for us to conclude that an electorate with many candidates to choose from evicts incumbents no more frequently than an electorate with more limited choices. A possible explanation for this result will be given in connection with Tables 11–4 to 11–8.

Table 11–3
Correlation Coefficients (r) for Relationships
Among Office Contesting, Closeness of Vote,
and Incumbent Eviction

	Office contesting	Incumbent eviction
Closeness of vote	.59	.32
Incumbent eviction	.14	

The moderate relationship between incumbent eviction and closeness of vote (.32) suggests that when incumbents are turned out of office, the vote strength of the several candidates tends to be more nearly equal. This is plausible. Unless defeated incumbents have completely lost the support of the constituency that initially elected them, a rare occurrence, the proportionate difference between their vote strength and that of the candidates replacing them should not be great.[9]

The strongest relationship in Table 11–3 is between office contesting and closeness of the vote (.59). As more candidates enter the race, the vote spread between winners and losers is reduced. Again there is a reasonable explanation. Many candidates each receiving some votes lessens the likelihood that a single candidate, or a pair of candidates, will overwhelmingly defeat all other candidates. Runaway winners occur less often when the total vote is divided among numerous candidates.

On the one hand, the three forms of competition covary. A community with many candidates seeking council positions also has more closely contested races and a slightly higher rate of evicting incumbents from office than does a community with fewer candidates. And where the vote spread is small between winners and losers, incumbents are somewhat more likely to lose their seats. On the other hand, the strength of the relationships hardly

---

[9] By this reasoning, the correlation should be even stronger than the .32 found. It is not stronger because the closeness of the vote is computed on the basis of the vote of all candidates, not just the vote of defeated incumbents and those who displace them. If it were, the correlation between eviction and closeness of the vote would undoubtedly be much greater. The measure, however, has sufficient slippage so that a city could have close contests between incumbents who lose and challengers who defeat them and yet be ranked low on the closeness of vote measure. This can easily be seen by the following hypothetical case. Imagine a five-man contest in which two of the five are incumbents standing for reelection. Assume a total vote of 2,000. One incumbent receives a thousand votes, a successful challenger receives 400, and a defeated incumbent receives 375. The remaining 225 votes are divided by the remaining two candidates. Moreover, assume that something similar to this pattern is repeated for each of five elections. Because half the incumbents standing for reelection are defeated, this city would rank high on the eviction measure. Yet the very unequal voting support for the candidates would rank it relatively low on the closeness of vote measure. This despite the obvious fact that the percentage difference between the defeated incumbent and his successor is slim, .0125 to be exact.

gives convincing support to the proposition that as one form of competition increases so do the others. There is sufficient slippage that a community can be very competitive in one regard but very noncompetitive in other regards. Contextual analysis will be helpful in further exploring patterns of electoral competition.

Electoral Competition and Community Wealth

There are theoretical reasons to suspect that political competition is not uninfluenced by a community's social structure or the complexity of its environment. If so, it may also be that the pattern of covariance among different forms of electoral competition will differ from one type of community to another.

Just as city size can be used as a surrogate variable of environmental complexity, so community wealth can be treated as a surrogate variable of social structure. It would be false to assume that a wealthy city has a comparatively homogeneous population and a poor city a comparatively heterogeneous population.[10] However, the dominance of one or another social class in wealthy or poor communities is probably less significant for electoral competition than is the relative social composition of the politically active stratum in wealthy and poor cities. This stratum in any community probably includes no more than from 5 to 10 percent of the total population.

Measured in terms of social origin and status-related experiences, the *politically active stratum* is more homogeneous in the wealthy city than in the poor city. The middle- and upper-middle-class citizens dominate the civic and political organizations of the community. Seldom will the uneducated citizen from a low-prestige occupation be found among the small group which takes

---

[10] Classifying cities as wealthy or poor is *not* the same as classifying them as homogeneous or heterogeneous. Rather, what distinguishes the cities is the proportion of the population which belongs to one or another social class. The city classified as wealthy has a high proportion of middle- and upper-middle-class citizens; the city classified as poor has a high proportion of working- and lower-class citizens. Nevertheless, the wealthy cities include some members of the working class and the poor cities have citizens who belong to the middle and upper-middle classes.

an active interest in local matters. In the wealthy community, the active stratum is likely to be overwhelmingly middle class both in composition and orientation. It is relatively homogeneous.

In the poorer community, where the ratio of middle- to non-middle-class citizens is skewed in favor of the latter, the politically active stratum has a more mixed membership. To be sure, the middle class retains its interest in local affairs and will be present in large numbers in the civic and political networks. But the greater number of working-class citizens permits the growth of civic organizations catering to their preferences, such as trade unions, ethnic associations, sports clubs, and so forth. The leaders of these organizations will be among the community leaders, contributing to a politically active stratum more varied in composition than is true of wealthier communities. Only in the wealthy community is political life so organized that lower-class citizens find it difficult to enter the active stratum. In the poorer community, the patterns of recruitment into the active stratum are such that members of the comparatively smaller middle class are represented just as are citizens from the working class.

With these considerations in mind it is possible to examine two hypotheses about the relationship between electoral competition and community wealth:

1. Wealthy communities are characterized by less electoral competition than poor communities.
2. However, when wealthy communities are characterized by relatively high levels of competition, its three forms—contesting, closeness of vote, and eviction—will be more closely related than they are in poor cities.

The first hypothesis refers to the *frequency* of competition as it varies with community wealth; the second hypothesis refers to the *pattern* of competition as it varies with wealth.

Table 11–4 confirms the first hypothesis. In regard to all three forms of electoral competition, high levels occur less frequently in wealthy than in poor communities. This does not mean that there is more political conflict in poor than in wealthy cities; but in the poorer community conflict is more likely to spill over into the electoral arena.

Table 11–4
Correlation Coefficients (r) for Relationships
Between City Wealth
and Forms of Electoral Competition

	City wealth*
Office contesting	—.35
Incumbent eviction	—.39
Closeness of vote	—.44

* Indexed by median market value of homes.

Both the results reported in Table 11–4 and their interpretation are plausible in terms of what has been said earlier about the social composition of the politically active stratum. In the wealthy city, the members of the active stratum are similar in social origins and social status; it is likely that they share a general view of community goals. Moreover, the organizational network which knits the active stratum together is composed of kindred civic-minded, middle-class clubs and associations. Political differences will not be sharp; the homogeneous active stratum can work out what political differences do occur within the network of similarly inclined civic organizations. Accordingly, there is less need to have electoral struggles over who will sit on the city council; rather, the recruitment process is the quiet search for talented members of the community who can be urged to perform their civic duty by serving a term or two on the council.

In the poorer community, with its more heterogeneous active stratum, political differences will be sharper. Moreover, the political struggle is likely to center on the control of the city council, leading to contested elections and greater electoral competition.

The second hypothesis stresses that *if* there is electoral competition in wealthy cities, the three forms will be more closely inter-related there than they are in poorer cities. Two considerations undergird this hypothesis. First, a homogeneous active stratum (as in the wealthier cities) which does have political splits is likely to be characterized by a more intense pattern of conflict than is the more loosely connected and heterogeneous stratum (as in the poorer cities).[11] Second, in the wealthy community, a comparatively large proportion of the total population has the socioeconomic resources normally associated with political involvement. Advanced education, prestigious occupation, and higher income covary positively with high levels of political information, efficacy, and awareness. If there is competition over who is to govern the wealthy community, a comparatively larger proportion of the population is available for political mobilization than is true of poorer communities. Candidates have the funds and the political resources to mobilize voter support, thus increasing the likelihood of closely fought elections. There are more persons in the wealthy than in the poorer community who consider themselves appropriate candidates for local office.

Table 11–5 supports the hypothesis that forms of competition cohere more in wealthy than in poor communities. The relative strength of the contingent coefficients in both types of city is the same as the original zero-order coefficients (Table 11–3). However, the relationships are consistently stronger in the wealthy than in the poor cities. Competition for political office occurs more fre-

Table 11–5
Correlation Coefficients (r) for Relationships
Among Three Forms of Electoral Competition
in Wealthy and Poor Cities

Relationship between:	Wealthy cities N = 41	Poor cities N = 40
Office contesting and closeness of vote	.63	.53
Closeness of vote and incumbent eviction	.37	.20
Incumbent eviction and office contesting	.23	.03

[11] The logic behind this assumption will be detailed more fully in connection with the analysis of the relationship between city size and competition, below.

quently in poor than in wealthy communities. But when competition does occur in wealthy communities, the three forms tend to coalesce, perhaps reflecting more intense conflict.

Electoral Competition and Urban Complexity

At least two politically relevant factors increase as urban complexity, measured by city size, increases: the complexity of the problems facing the council and the variety of different viewpoints in the community as to how such problems should be dealt with. Complex problems lead to mistakes and political failures, and these in turn lead to political opposition. A variety of political viewpoints and of social groupings in the community provides the organizational base necessary for many contestors for political office, as well as the mass electorates which can lead to electoral competition. Stated differently, the larger the population, the greater the critical mass that can be mobilized in support of political candidacies. The 500 blacks of a city of 5,000 probably do not provide the basis for a political organization, but the 5,000 blacks in a city of 50,000 do provide an adequate basis. It is not then the proportion of blacks but the absolute size of this group which is relevant for political organizational purposes, at least for those sorts of organizations likely to become involved in city elections.

Again two hypotheses—one concerning the *frequency* of competition and the other concerning the *pattern* of competition under varying conditions of urban complexity—will be examined:

1. Small cities are characterized by less electoral competition than large cities.
2. However, when small cities are characterized by relatively high levels of competition, its three forms—contesting, closeness of vote, and eviction—will be more closely related than they are in large cities.

The expectation that there is more electoral competition in large cities than in small cities is only partially confirmed, as Table 11–6 shows. It is moderately accurate with respect to vote

Table 11–6
Correlation Coefficients (r) for Relationships
Between City Size
and Forms of Electoral Competition

	City size
Office contesting	.38
Incumbent eviction	—.08
Closeness of vote	.25

spread and not at all with respect to eviction from office. But it is the relatively high level of office contesting in large cities *in combination with* the absence of any relationship between city size and incumbent eviction that has special import. The very fragmentation of political viewpoints that presumably produces many candidates in the large cities works to the advantage of incumbents.

The second hypothesis—that forms of competition are more interrelated in small than in large cities *if* there is a struggle for office in the former—derives from assumptions about the place of intimacy in more and less complex environments.

Small communities allow a more intimate, face-to-face type of politics than do large cities. If one assumes that one in 20 citizens belongs to the politically active stratum,[12] even a community of 10,000 would have as few as 500 citizens actively involved in local affairs. But a city of 100,000 would, under the same assumption, have close to 5,000 involved citizens. It is clear that 500 people engaged in the same set of activities and belonging to the organizational network will get to know one another fairly well over the years. The same can hardly be said of 5,000 people. Face-to-face politics, then, is possible and even likely in the smaller community; it is practically impossible in the larger community.[13]

---

[12]See Dwaine Marvick, "Political Recruitment and Careers," *International Encyclopedia of the Social Sciences,* Vol. 12 (New York: Macmillan and Free Press, 1968), p. 281.
[13] The connection between this observation and the hypothesis under discussion is suggested by the theories of political conflict developed by Simmel and Coser. We particularly take note of work by Gordon Black, who applies Simmel and Coser to the city council data.

The lack of diversity in smaller communities limits the frequency of political conflict; however, the relatively low association shows that some small cities will be characterized by political differences. When this happens, the political conflict will be more intense than it normally is in larger, more complex units. In the more intimate milieu of the small city, there is a greater tendency to personalize political differences. The absence of social distance among the political participants leads to a more intense form of political conflict. If these speculations are at all plausible, one should expect, as the hypothesis states, that when the small city (with its more intimate political life) has many candidates seeking council positions, there will also be more closely fought elections and more frequent displacement of incumbents through defeat at the polls.

Table 11–7 supports the hypothesis. The relationships between any two forms of electoral competition are consistently stronger in the small than in the large cities. Before drawing a final conclusion from the patterns, it would seem desirable to examine the joint effect that city wealth and city size as contextual properties might have on the politics of electoral competition.[14] Table 11–8 presents the data.

With one deviation, the overall configuration is highly consistent. Forms of electoral competition are more tightly interrelated in small, wealthy cities than in large, poor communities. Size, it appears, has more of an impact on the configuration than has wealth.[15] Just why closeness of vote and incumbent eviction are related in the large, poor cities but not at all in the small, poor cities or large, wealthy ones we cannot say.

Of particular interest remains the relationship between office contesting and incumbent eviction which, as a glance back to

---

[14] The correlation between city size and city wealth is −.11, indicating sufficient independence between the two variables that any pattern produced by controlling simultaneouly for size and wealth represents additive effects and not interaction between them.

[15] This can be seen by comparing the differences in the coefficients between different-size cities, controlling for wealth, with the differences in the coefficients between poor and rich cities, controlling for size. The differences between small and large cities are on the average twice as high as they are between wealthy and poor cities.

Table 11–7
Correlation Coefficients (r) for Relationships
Among Three Forms of Electoral Competition
in Small and Large Cities

Relationship between:	Small cities N = 40	Large cities N = 41
Office contesting and closeness of vote	.69	.39
Closeness of vote and incumbent eviction	.41	.22
Incumbent eviction and office contesting	.38	.05

Table 10–3 will show, had been found inexplicable. It had been thought that, of the various forms of competition, the number of candidates and the rate of eviction would show the highest correlation. An electorate presented with several choices should more easily find attractive candidates among the challengers than an electorate presented with fewer choices. Furthermore, a community in which incumbents are frequently defeated should attract

Table 11–8
Correlation Coefficients (r) for Relationships
Among Three Forms of Electoral Competition
in Four City Environments

Relationship between:	Small, wealthy cities N = 19	Small, poor cities N = 21	Large, wealthy cities N = 22	Large, poor cities N = 19
Office contesting and closeness of vote	.70	.67	.46	.25
Closeness of vote and incumbent eviction	.61	.09	.03	.32
Incumbent eviction and office contesting	.48	.24	.02	—.19

more candidates willing to invest in a council race than a community in which incumbents seldom suffer election defeat. This reasoning was not confirmed; the zero-order correlation between office contesting and eviction was low (.14).

It can now be seen that these two forms of competition are positively related in small, wealthy cities but that the relationship actually turns negative in large, poor cities (.48 and −.19, respectively). The negative relationship is of particular interest.

The electorate of the large and poor city, when faced with many contestors for office, is unlikely to turn incumbents out. This is an electorate which is comparatively short of such political resources as efficacy, information, and awareness. It is also an electorate of a community that is normally more fragmented in its politics than are smaller communities. Under these conditions too many candidates may well create such electoral confusion that the position of the incumbents is actually strengthened. Too many candidates would seem to prevent the electorate from examining the past performance of incumbents and perhaps evicting them.

By way of contrast, there is a substantial relationship (.48) between office contesting and eviction in the small and wealthy city. Here the social milieu is very different from the contrasting situation in large and poor cities. Political resources are more widely distributed throughout the population, as a larger proportion of the citizens belong to the educated middle class. Here, also, is generally less political fragmentation, and there are fewer single-issue groups. As more candidates enter the race for the council positions, the probability of incumbents being evicted increases. Challengers enter the race to displace the ins because there is some dissatisfaction with how the community is being governed. And there are segments of the population with enough political muscle to make some changes.

Contextual analysis of electoral competition in terms of city wealth and city size as surrogates for a host of theoretical variables thus serves to clarify the ambiguous pattern among forms of competition that earlier had been found puzzling. As Tables 11–4 to 11–8 have shown, electoral competition expresses itself and emerges as a pattern differently from one type of community to another. Both the frequency and the interdependence of forms of competition tend to vary as between large and small, poor and wealthy cities. Relevant assumptions about the social composition of the politically active stratum as well as about the intimacy and diversity of political life under different conditions of urban complexity explain this variability.

The data presented in this chapter are interesting in their own right because they provide a rich understanding of the nuances of electoral politics. This is important because electoral competition, combined with the role of citizen participation, provides an analytical tool to investigate just how the council's constitutive processes serve to bridge the social and political distance between the governing few and the many who are governed.

Chapter 12

The Electoral Context:
Explication and Typology

Councils as governing bodies should vary in what they do just as electorates vary in constituting the councils. Were this not the case, one would have to conclude that elections are defective as mechanisms that link governors and governed, and one would have to doubt the democratic character of the governing process. Democracy, perhaps needless to say, has a multitude of meanings; yet central to most meanings is the notion that those managing society will be sensitive to the moods and preferences of the citizenry. Because the moods and preferences of citizens are most regularly and forcefully expressed through elections, defects or weaknesses in electoral systems as linking mechanisms jeopardize the democratic process in which the electorate is presumed to be the basic political actor.

This is not to say that particular cities or states or the nation do in fact have governing processes in which the assumptions of democratic governance invariably or equally hold. Despite the wealth of accumulated knowledge about individual voters—their attributes, preferences, and behaviors—and about elections as aggregate processes, it remains difficult to say just how the electorate as a collective actor is linked to government and, through this linkage, how it affects the course of governance.

Needed for the purpose of examining elections as institutions that link governors and governed is an analytic tool that will meet two requirements. First, it should describe recurrent patterns in the behavior of electorates, on the assumption that it is the repetitive patterns in the electorate's behavior that are most salient to the council and most significant for the governing process. Second, the tool should describe the electorate's behavior in a manner congenial to analysis of the relationship between two units of action that are corporate entities—the council and the electorate.

The analytic tool meeting these conditions will be called "electoral context." Because the concept is novel, it requires some explication before it can be constructed. The notion of electoral context derives from the recognition that councils are collective actors and that much of what one wishes to understand about governance is best approached at the level of councils as decision-making groups rather than at the level of individual officeholders. This in turn directs attention to the contexts within which governance takes place. A context is established, for instance, by the demographic composition of the governed population, by the city's economic structure, or by other environmental factors impinging on governance. Insofar as they provide points of reference for the council, these contexts are council properties.

The regular behavior of the electorate over time constitutes the council's electoral context.[1] It differs from "nonhuman" contexts in that it arises from the behavior of a major actor in the political process—the electorate—which, according to democratic theory, should have considerable influence on how the community is governed.

It is the search for linkage between the few who govern the community and the large population remaining distant from the activities of the governing few that directs attention to the electoral context. It is exceedingly difficult for the council to learn much about the moods and preferences of the population at large;

[1] Most election studies investigate single elections or, in a few cases, types of elections. Some studies examine trends in elections and concern themselves with such important aspects as "critical elections" or with typologies such as deviating, maintaining, and realigning elections. However, even these studies take the single election and its various attributes as the phenomenon to be analyzed and interpreted. See V. O. Key, Jr., "A Theory of Critical Elections," *Journal of Politics* 17 (February 1955): 3–18, and "Secular Realignment and the Party System," *Journal of Politics* 21 (May 1959): 198–210; Angus Campbell, Philip E. Converse, Warren E. Miller, and Donald E. Stokes, *The American Voter* (New York: John Wiley and Sons, 1960), pp. 531–538, and *Elections and the Political Order* (New York: John Wiley and Sons, 1966), pp. 63–77.

and it is exceedingly difficult for a population to express its wishes or demands to the council. When the population is organized into an electorate, these communication difficulties are lessened. The electorate, as opposed to an amorphous population, is an actor in the political life of the community.

The Electoral Context: Two Terms of Reference

The electoral context will be constructed in terms of voter participation and competition for office. A measure of participation and a measure of competition are both needed. By itself, the level of voter turnout defies straightforward interpretation. A high turnout may mean voter dissatisfaction or its opposite, voter support. Low turnout may mean withdrawal and hostility on the part of citizens, or it may mean a political indifference born of satisfaction with how the community is governed. To explore what different levels of voter participation mean for the governing process, it is necessary to consider participation in conjunction with competition for office.

Competition for office is also difficult to interpret by itself, for it takes on very different meanings depending on the number of voters who participate in elections. There can be a struggle to control political office, but so few voters may go to the polls that the competition is just an intraelite contest. An intraelite battle has very different consequences for the governing process than does an elite competition for the favor of the voters. If in the struggle to control office the voters can be safely ignored, even very intense competition will not establish linkages between those in office and those indifferent to political affairs.

Participation and competition are thus interdependent instances of electoral behavior and constitute the electoral context. It remains to explicate the particular measures of voter participation and competition that will be used.

Voter Participation

Two measures of voter participation are available—the percentage of voters among the total adult population and the percentage of voters among the registered population. These two measures are correlated at .76, suggesting that choosing one over the other would not greatly affect the ranking of the cities.

However, because the electoral context will be constructed from dichotomized variables, it is desirable to determine just how many cities would change classification as between low and high voter turnout depending on the measure used. Nine cities, or 12 percent of the total number, do in fact change classification and would be assigned to a different electoral context, depending on how voter turnout is indexed. The number is high enough to require some justification of the choice to be made.

The voters of a city can be thought of in three different ways. The *eligible* electorate are those who meet whatever minimal restrictions are placed on suffrage; these are citizens above the minimum age who have lived in the city long enough to meet registration requirements, whose criminal status does not debar them from voting, and so forth. The *available* electorate are those who are registered to vote; these are the citizens who have completed the necessary preliminary steps and are able to vote, if they choose, on election day. The *actual* electorate are those who do vote in council elections.

The decision to be made is whether to compute the actual electorate as a proportion of the eligible citizens or as a proportion of the available citizens. Because the concept of electoral context should adumbrate those aspects of the electorate's behavior that are reasonably salient to the council, the proportion of voters among the registered citizens is the more useful index of voter participation. From the perspective of both incumbents and their challengers the actual electorate is most likely viewed as a subset of the available rather than of the eligible electorate. This is so because in council elections the number of registered voters is a given. Unlike presidential, statewide, and even congressional campaigns, no council campaign begins with a registration drive. The registration machinery is hardly visible during a council election, which is out of phase with partisan elections. Council candidates simply accept as given the proportion of citizens who are registered. Campaigns are directed at the registered voters. If turnout is to be increased, a higher proportion of registered voters must be attracted to a council election; if incumbents are to be defeated, allegiances among the registered voters must be shifted.

It is the available electorate, then, which is taken into account when estimates are made about the likely size and behavior of the actual electorate. Because the actual electorate is best thought of as a subset of registered voters, turnout will be computed as the proportion of voters among the registered citizens.

Competition for Office

Of the three measures of electoral competition that have been described, the rate of incumbent eviction rather than office contesting or closeness of vote is particularly germane to the construct of electoral context. The choice derives from its significance as an aspect of electoral competition in contemporary democratic theory.

Despite the rhetoric of democracy, skeptics such as Mosca or Michels argued, political rule has remained in the hands of the few.[2] Moreover, as long as social life was organized by principles necessary for coordinating complex, industrial societies, government would unavoidably remain in the hands of the few. The "iron law of oligarchy" was a severe challenge to democratic thought.

Responding to this challenge, liberal democratic theorists fashioned a set of propositions which, though admitting rule by the few as probably inevitable, stressed the competition among elites for the people's vote and control of political office. The emphasis on competition was an answer to those who saw in the organizational revolution a process which would retard the evolution of democratic forms of government. Competition among elites allows the society to resist tendencies toward self-perpetuating

---

[2] Gaetano Mosca, *The Ruling Class* (New York: McGraw-Hill, 1939), first published as *Elementi di Scienza politica*, 1896; Robert Michels, *Political Parties* (New York: Collier Books, 1962), with an introduction by S. M. Lipset. *Political Parties* was first published in German in 1911. A useful review of what the various elite theorists wrote in criticism of democratic pretensions can be found in James Burnham, *The Machiavellians* (Chicago: Henry Regnery Co., 1963), first published in 1943.

oligarchies; competition insures that leaders, who seek the favor and support of electorates, will not grow indifferent to citizen preferences. In such formulations, democratic politics are preserved despite the irrefutable fact that in all societies "two classes of people appear—a class that rules and a class that is ruled."[3]

This confidence in electoral competition rests on the assumption that the status of political officeholders is probationary. It is not competition as such but the transitory tenure of officeholding resulting from competition that protects a measure of democracy. *The Federalist* alludes to this in suggesting that men of power are "compelled to anticipate the moment when their power is to cease."[4] The modern formulation owes much to the writings of Joseph Schumpeter who argues "that the role of the people is to produce a government," and expands on this view as follows: "it should be observed that in making it the primary function of the electorate to produce a government (directly or through an intermediate body) I intended to include in this phrase also the function of evicting it. The one means simply the acceptance of a leader or group of leaders, and the other means simply the withdrawal of this acceptance."[5]

In this conception, then, the power of the electorate to evict its governors is more basic to the democratic process then simply a competition among elites. As Schumpeter observes, "electorates normally do not control their political leaders in any way except by refusing to reelect them or the parliamentary majorities that support them."[6] Lipset and his colleagues elaborate this point of view in noting that democratic government is practically synonymous with the permanent insecurity of the governors: "Thus every incumbent of a position of high status within a truly democratic system must of necessity anticipate the loss of his position by the operation of normal political processes."[7] Robert A. Dahl can be

---

[3] Mosca, *The Ruling Class*, p. 50.
[4] *The Federalist*, No. LVII, Max Beloff, ed. (New York: The Macmillan Company, 1948), p. 293.
[5] Joseph Schumpeter, *Capitalism, Socialism and Democracy* (New York: Harper & Row, Torchbook Edition, 1962), pp. 269 and 272.
[6] *Ibid.*, p. 272
[7] S. M. Lipset, Martin Trow, and James Coleman, *Union Democracy* (Garden City, N.Y.: Anchor Books, Doubleday & Company, 1962), p. 241.

read in this tradition as well, for he stresses that the influence of the electorate rests in its ability to remove leaders from office.[8] The "ambition theory of politics" recently suggested by Joseph Schlesinger provides yet another perspective; public officials are restrained in their choice of policies because of their desire for election and reelection.[9]

Incumbent eviction through electoral defeat is further related to a wide range of issues in democratic politics. It is through electoral eviction, for instance, that the difficult problem of leadership succession is handled in democracies. Authority to govern passes from one set of men to the next because those who displace previous leaders were chosen by an institutionalized and legitimated set of procedures. Electoral eviction also relates to the stress on political opposition. The significance of opposition in formulations of democracy has meaning only if the prior assumption is made that procedures exist which allow the opposition to agitate for the removal of incumbents in ways that stop short of violence. And electoral eviction undergirds the notion of a periodic review of public policy by the citizenry; this review is connected with the possibility of peacefully removing persons responsible for unsuccessful or disliked policies.

It might be thought that office contesting is a more accurate indicator of competition for the council than is eviction from office. This overlooks one consideration. The number of candidates seeking office mainly reflects events within the politically active stratum. A high rate of office contesting implies divisiveness and fragmentation within the active stratum, as when numerous candidates compete in a primary. A low rate of office contesting implies that the active stratum is cohesive and well organized politically, so that disputes do not erupt into the electoral arena. While office contesting may tell us a great deal about intraelite battles, it says little about the role of voters in these battles. The measure of electoral eviction, then, has an advantage over the

---

[8] Thus, for instance, Dahl writes that "elected leaders keep the real or imagined preferences of constituents constantly in mind in deciding what policies to adopt or reject." Robert A. Dahl, *Who Governs?* (New Haven: Yale University Press, 1961), p. 164.

[9] Joseph A. Schlesinger, *Ambition and Politics: Political Careers in the United States* (Chicago: Rand McNally, 1966).

measure of office contesting. Office contesting is a necessary but not sufficient condition for eviction. There can be no eviction of incumbents unless there are challengers, but having challengers does not in itself lead to eviction. It is the intervention of the electorate which converts intraelite battles into electoral competition.

Incumbent eviction is also more useful for constructing and ultimately understanding the electoral context than is the closeness of the vote. Incumbents presumably stand in fear of a close race only because it increases the chance of defeat. What ultimately counts is not the vote spread between winners and losers, but who the winners and losers are. The measure of incumbent eviction stresses the latter.

All this does not deny the importance of office contesting and closeness of vote as forms of electoral competition. Both will be retained as part of the analysis. The intent in stressing incumbent eviction is merely to show its particular theoretical relevance for constructing a measure of electoral context.

Constructing the Electoral Context

In order to construct the measure of electoral context, the proportion of registered voters who cast ballots in council elections was dichotomized to classify cities as having either low or high electoral participation; similarly, the frequency of incumbent eviction by election defeat was dichotomized to classify cities as either low or high.[10] Cross-tabulation of the dichotomized variables yields the typology of electoral contexts pictured in Figure 12–1.

---

[10] On both measures the median is used to dichotomize cities into a low and high category. Although the Pearson correlation for the continuous data is only .12, a gamma produced by dichotomizing the distributions is somewhat higher (.34). This relationship affects the number of cities which fall into each category, but does not affect how we use the classification. Figure 12–1 is used to generate a contextual variable of the council. In using this typology we do not ask how much variance in a dependent variable is due to turnout and how much to electoral eviction. Were we to do so, the intercorrelation would become relevant. We simply ask whether councils having different electoral contexts vary with respect to behaviors thought relevant to the electoral process.

In the *permissive* context comparatively few citizens bother to vote and the electorate seldom, if ever, evicts its governors. Officeholders can feel relatively safe in their positions because the small, placid electorate rarely turns them out of office. Officeholders have a great deal of discretion. The city with a permissive electoral context is perhaps similar to safe legislative districts also characterized by low voter turnout.

Figure 12–1
Classification of Electoral Contexts

| | Electoral Participation | |
Incumbent eviction	Relatively low	Relatively high
Relatively low	Permissive (N = 23)	Supportive (N = 17)
Relatively high	Discriminative (N = 16)	Volatile (N = 24)

The *supportive* electoral context is one in which relatively more citizens vote in council elections and yet the electorate seldom, if ever, evicts its governors. The electorate is supportive in approving of its officeholders and in recording this approval on election day. Officeholders, however, probably have less discretion than they do in a permissive context. It may be that electoral support is engendered by the council's close attention to citizen preferences. Certainly the larger electorate implies attentiveness by voters as to how they are being governed.

In the *discriminative* electoral context comparatively few citizens vote but regularly turn incumbents out of office. A small but judgmental electorate intrudes into the governing process. Officeholders face a relatively small electorate but one which asserts its prerogative to remove those incumbents it disapproves of.

The *volatile* electoral context consists of a large electorate that often evicts incumbents from office. Volatility suggests a rather unpredictable relationship between council and electorate. From the perspective of the officeholder, the electorate continually agitating for change is viewed as unstable in its preferences and difficult to manage. From the perspective of the citizen, the electorate frequently changing its leadership is perhaps viewed as composed of many political groupings each pursuing different goals. And if the active groups change with changing issues—not an unreasonable assumption to make about an electorate in non-partisan cities—there is further reason to view the electorate as transitory in its attachments, which again contributes to great volatility.

None of these labels is completely satisfactory. Any one of them emphasizes one aspect of the electoral context at the expense of other aspects. For instance, the permissive context might have been called "apathetic," the discriminative context, "dissenting," or the supportive context, "attentive." Indeed, the volatile context might have been called "democratic." We have avoided terms such as apathetic, dissenting, attentive, and democratic because they are already heavily loaded with normative and empirical meanings. Though labels are never completely neutral, those chosen here have the advantage of being novel and free of pre-existing meanings (with the possible exception of "supportive," but this is the least troublesome label in any case).

Validation of Typology

The typology's validity must prove itself across a broad range of research questions and cannot be prejudged until actually used in analysis. But its face validity can be assessed. It should be emphasized, in this connection, that the typology is constructed exclusively from aggregate election data and that no interview data were used. Interview data can therefore serve the purpose of validation. Two measures—a measure of "perceived voter interest in council elections"[11] and a measure of "council sense of control of the electoral situation"[12]—will be employed. The results obtained on each measure should be significantly related to one or another of the components that constitute the typology. Perception of voter interest should increase with voter turnout—that is, it

---

[11] The question was: "How about the voters here in (city)? Would you say there is much interest in council elections, some interest, little interest, or no interest at all?"

[12] For a description of the "sense of control" measure, see Appendix B12.1.

Table 12–1
Correlation Coefficients for Relationships
Between Four Types of Electoral Context and Measures
of Perceived Voter Interest and Council Sense of Control

	Electoral Context			
	Permissive	Supportive	Discriminative	Volatile
Council sense of control	.44	.11	−.28	.51
Perceived voter interest	−.57	.28	−.25	−.32

should be positively related to the supportive and volatile contexts but negatively to the permissive and discriminative contexts. Sense of control over the electoral situation should decrease with incumbent eviction—that is, it should be negatively related to the discriminative and volatile contexts but positively to the permissive and supportive contexts. Table 12–1 shows that these expectations are met.

For the purpose of clarification, Table 12–2 represents the data in a manner that emphasizes the typology's components in terms of the differences between low and high voter turnout and the differences between low and high incumbent eviction.

Councils in communities with high voter turnout report greater citizen interest in council elections than do councils in communities with low turnout. And councils governing where the electorate evicts incumbents report less of a sense of control over the electoral situation than do councils governing where the electorate seldom evicts incumbents. Moreover, turnout and eviction have a cumulative effect. The permissive electorate is seen as less interested than the discriminative electorate (though both are low turnout); the volatile electorate is seen as more interested than the supportive electorate (though both are high turnout). Furthermore, there is a higher sense of control in the permissive than in the supportive context (though both have low eviction rates), and there is a lower sense of control in the volatile than in the discriminative context (though both have high eviction rates). This is

Table 12–2
Correlation Coefficients for Relationships
Between Voter Turnout and Perceived Voter Interest
in Elections and Between Incumbent Eviction
and Council Sense of Control

Components	Context type	Citizen interest
High voter turnout Low eviction	Supportive	.28
High voter turnout High eviction	Volatile	.51
Low voter turnout Low eviction	Permissive	−.57
Low voter turnout High eviction	Discriminative	−.25
Components	Context type	Sense of control
High eviction Low voter turnout	Discriminative	−.28
High eviction High turnout	Volatile	−.32
Low eviction Low turnout	Permissive	.44
Low eviction High turnout	Supportive	.11

exactly what one should expect, for voter turnout can have an impact on sense of control over the electoral situation, and incumbent eviction can have an impact on the degree of citizen interest perceived by the council.

The validation of the typology with the interview data confirms that the electorate's behavior is salient to the council. It remains to be seen, of course, whether councils vary in their behavior from one electoral context to another. As used in the analysis, the typology has no intrinsic order. The very reason for constructing four different contexts is to emphasize that each will produce its own pattern of linkages between council and public.

The Electoral Context and Leadership Selection

There is more to the selection of leadership than just what happens on election day. At least two other sets of activities merit attention—those surrounding the recruitment of political office-holders and those surrounding the campaign for political office. Because recruitment and campaigning are significant aspects of the constitutive processes through which councils are installed, they both provide opportunities for linking council and community.

When governance is organized under the rules of democracy, the recruitment of officials and the campaign for office will have particular characteristics defined by the fact that elections finally decide who is to govern. Elections constrain the range of activities which might otherwise become part of the recruitment and campaigning processes. For instance, men recruited to candidacy are likely to have (or be thought to have) voter appeal, hardly a criterion of importance if recruitment is through cooptation by established leaders or through bureaucratic advancement. Because recruitment and campaigning cannot be considered separately from elections in democratic governments, variations in these aspects of leadership selection under varying conditions of the electoral context will be treated in the next two chapters.

Chapter 13

Elections and Political Recruitment

Not all citizens have a chance to govern, only a few do. The meaningful participation of the electorate in choosing the few who govern is a defining characteristic of democratic politics. The public and its officials are linked together because the public is also an electorate, and electorates choose governors. This was the logic of parliamentary government, the harbinger of the democratic transformation in Western societies and of the eventual accomplishment of near universal suffrage. Parliaments and elections were intended to produce a governing group generally representative of the interests in society. This was the promise which motivated revolution and reform alike. But over time practices have tarnished these early optimistic promises. Doubt has been cast on whether the simple advent of elected representatives has brought about a truly "democratic" mode of selecting leaders. These doubts have taken three forms.

Parliamentary government grew apace with the political eclipse of the aristocracy and the rise to prominence of the bourgeoisie. As it turned out, most parliaments, even when chosen under conditions of near universal suffrage, came to be dominated by men of middle-class origin and habits. As Mosca correctly recognized, the bourgeoisie supplied the recruits for political office and thus established itself as the ruling class. From time to time, spokesmen of particularly aggressive worker or peasant movements were coopted

261

into the ruling class, but this only strengthened the position of the already established rulers.[1]

To this day, elected legislatures, in the established democracies of the Western world as well as in the newer nations of Africa, Asia, and Latin America, are overwhelmingly chosen from the middle and upper-middle strata of society. This is the case whether the basic political organization of the society is along vertical or horizontal lines. If politics is vertically organized, as is true where ethnicity, religion, or geography is politically salient, political groups include members of the various social strata in the society, but tend nevertheless to be led by their middle- and upper-middle-class members. These leaders provide the pool from which most political officeholders are selected. If politics is horizontally organized, as is true where class is politically salient, the membership of political groups is more homogeneous and the leaders may be of the same social origin as the members. But even under these conditions, the bourgeoisie supplies the large majority of political leaders, for reasons made clear by Michels.[2]

Social background broadly conceived as including status at birth and educational or occupational achievement affects who gains control of government. The bias toward the middle and upper-middle classes in the selection of governors is apparent in the cities of this study. To record this fact, however, does not imply that the electorate has no influence on the selection of its governors. What is problematic is the interdependence of socioeconomic bias in leadership selection, on the one hand, and the electorate's participation in the process of choice, on the other.

Mosca is the source of a second set of doubts concerning the open access to political office in societies with elected legislatures. Contrary to the promises of democratic rhetoric, not all men— not even all men of a particular social class—have an equal chance of being selected for political office. Unless one has long since committed oneself to a politically active life, the chances of reaching elective office are slim indeed. What Mosca called the

---

[1] Gaetano Mosca, *The Ruling Class* (New York: McGraw-Hill, 1939), especially Chapter 10.

[2] Robert Michels, *Political Parties* (New York: Collier Books, 1962), especially Part IV.

second stratum of the ruling class, and what we today call the active stratum, provides the candidates for elected office.[3] The route to positions of authority is through this active stratum. And even if candidates for office are not chosen from within this stratum, it is probable that whoever holds office will have been ushered there by the politically active in society.

The decision as to who gains control of office is not the unfettered choice of an electorate. The small politically active stratum intervenes in the selection processes. The recruitment of governors, then, is constrained by the prior formation of the active stratum. The sentiments and experiences of this group will be reflected in the legislatures chosen by the intramural maneuverings among the activists.

Despite the fact that a small politically active stratum nominates candidates from among its own members, it does not follow that the electorate is without influence. Perhaps the behavior of the electorate alters the normally high correlation between membership in the legislature and prior involvement in the active stratum. It is this possibility which sets the research question: to what extent does the electorate's behavior affect the flow of persons from the active stratum to the elected councils?

The third doubt about leadership selection under the rules of democracy, and the most pessimistic account of selection processes, is found in the writings of Michels. The famous "iron law of oligarchy" holds that notwithstanding democratic elections a relatively small group of men controls any political organization, its resources and its membership. "It is organization which gives birth to the domination of the elected over the electors, of the mandataries over the mandators, of the delegates over the delegators. Who says organization says oligarchy."[4] The oligarchy made possible by the organization of political life has tendencies toward self-perpetuation. The advantages which accrue to those who control the organization are sufficient to allow them to choose their successors, thereby guaranteeing the survival of the policies as they have shaped them.

---

[3] Mosca, *The Ruling Class,* p. 404.
[4] Michels, *Political Parties,* p. 365.

Core propositions from Michels have been reworked and applied to American politics by C. Wright Mills. The men who command American society do so because they sit astride the great institutions which coordinate the complex activities of a modern, industrial state. As in Michels's argument, the thesis expands to include the proposition that men of power are able to transmit it to the next generation of power holders by selectively sponsoring careers and otherwise influencing who is to inherit the important command posts.[5]

In such formulations, elections are less acts of choice than acts of ratification. The fact of oligarchic self-perpetuation combines with the previously noted tendency for recruitment to occur within the active stratum to produce a selection process relatively immune to the influence of the electorate. However, one can ask whether, despite the tendency toward self-perpetuation, the electorate will by its behavior minimize the success of the governors in selecting their own successors.

Several decades of commentary on leadership selection under presumed rules of democratic election pinpoint the three issues just reviewed: socioeconomic bias in the selection of governors, the choice of governors from the active stratum of the dominant class, and the tendency among ruling groups toward self-perpetuation. Taken together, these three issues cast doubt on the meaningful participation of the electorate in selecting its governors; thus they cast doubt on the effectiveness of elections as linkage institutions bridging the distance between the public and its officials.

Elections and Status Bias in Leadership Selection

The great nineteenth-century debates about representative democracy often originated in conflict over the social composition of the legislatures. A parliament dominated by the privileged estates could not, the English reformers asserted, adequately represent

---

[5] C. Wright Mills, *The Power Elite* (New York: Oxford University Press, 1956), especially chapters 10 and 12.

the new social groupings and interests coming to the fore in the industrializing cities. In the United States, similar political debates preceded the expansion of suffrage, the direct election of senators, and, more recently, the "one man, one vote" rulings of the Supreme Court. Underlying each reform has been concern with the demographic composition of the legislatures.

The malrepresentation of different social groups in legislatures has concerned reformers on the assumption that it indicates greater representation of some social interests and the neglect of others. Not all men have an equal chance of reaching office, and thus not all interests have an equal chance of expression. Of course, this position presumes an isomorphism between the social origin of legislatures and their policy positions, an isomorphism which has never been demonstrated empirically. But leaving this aside, socio-economic bias in leadership selection is inconsistent with the promise of democracy that status criteria are irrelevant in choosing governors.

This inconsistency is as true in the cities of the San Francisco Bay region as it is of political communities elsewhere in the world. Councilmen are disproportionately chosen from the more prestigious occupations, the better-educated and otherwise privileged members of the community. If the population of a community is arranged along a social stratification scale, the council of that community is rarely selected from social groups below the point identified by the sixtieth percentile, which more often than not divides blue-collar from white-collar occupations. This pattern is displayed in Figure 13–1, a figure which summarizes modal tendencies across the sample of cities.[6]

Two important things are illustrated in Figure 13–1. The curve is not J-shaped. Thus, although councilmen come from the advantaged sectors of society, the *most* prestigious persons are not necessarily the holders of political office. If the curve were J-shaped,

---

[6] The procedures used in constructing Figure 13–1 are explained in Kenneth Prewitt, *The Recruitment of Political Leaders: A Study of Citizen-Politicians* (Indianapolis: The Bobbs-Merrill Company, 1970), Chapter 2; the figure itself does not appear here, but was first published in Prewitt, "From the Many Are Chosen the Few," *American Behavioral Scientist* 13 (November/December 1969): 177. The text interpreting the figure is drawn from this essay also.

Figure 13–1
Hypothetical Contribution of Socioeconomic Status Groups to Leadership Selection

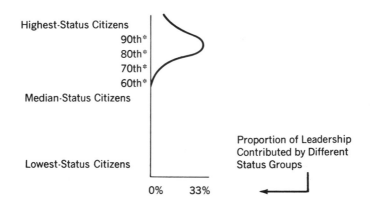

* Indicates percentile; that is, no citizens from below the 60th percentile of the population arrayed along status measures contribute to the leadership.

this would suggest that the higher one's social status, the greater the likelihood of being selected for political office. What is suggested by the shape of the curve is that in the competition for office, the most advantaged group is the one having 80 to 85 percent of the population below it on the status hierarchy but 5 to 10 percent above it.

Figure 13–1 implies another important point. The *absolute* value of the sixtieth percentile will shift from one community to another, or one state to another, or, of course, one nation to another. That is, the socioeconomic characteristics which put one in the upper two-fifths of the population differ from one setting to the next. In this study of city councils, for instance, the characteristics of the governing few shift according to the social composition of the community. In the working-class community, the lower limit of the socially eligible dips low enough to include union officials, public school teachers, craftsmen, and, from time to time, the skilled laborer. In the middle-class community, the lower limit is set a bit higher; the druggist, the successful car salesman, and the realtor fall within the upper two-fifths, but the union leader, school teacher, and so forth fall below the social threshold. And, of course, in the upper-class suburb, even the middle-class entrepreneur discovers his occupational status and bachelor's degree to be more liability than asset if he should seek office.

To show how the status of the council as a group varies with the socioeconomic setting of the city, councils were coded according to the occupation and education of their membership. The relatively high-status councils include a preponderance of members who have completed college and are either professionals and top managers or, in a few cases, large landowners. The relatively low-status councils are those in which most members have not completed college and are employed in less prestigious white-collar occupations.[7]

What we term low-status councils are not of low status in an absolute sense. The members of these councils are drawn from occupational groupings and an educational stratum well above the average and within the upper two-fifths range of a community's social structure. A council coded as low-status is so only in comparison with high-status councils.

As Table 13–1 shows, there is a strong and entirely consistent relationship between the socioeconomic type of community (measured by the median market value of homes) in which a council is located and the council's socioeconomic status. In the less wealthy cities, the status of the council is relatively low; in the more wealthy cities, the status of the council is relatively high. This pattern is *not* a statistical artifact. There are more than a sufficient number of high-status individuals in any community, even the lowest in socioeconomic character, so that a city council could include only the very wealthy, best-educated, and prestigious persons. Instead, as Table 13–1 shows, there is some regression

---

[7] Moreover, the polar classification disguises some of the internal ambiguities that stem from the difficulty of clearly assigning some councils to one or the other status category. See Appendix B13.1 for examples of four councils and how they were coded.

Table 13–1
Relationship Between Social Status of Council
and Socioeconomic Character of City

| | Socioeconomic Status of City* | | | |
Status of council	Low N = 22	Medium-low N = 18	Medium-high N = 22	High N = 20
Relatively low	82%	61%	41%	20%
Relatively high	18	39	59	80
	100%	100%	100%	100%

* Indexed by median market value of homes. Cities were divided into rough quartile ranges.

toward the modal socioeconomic characteristics of the city being governed. Although demographic malrepresentation is always present, the most prestigious in any population do not command all the leadership positions. Persons chosen to govern are above average in social status, but not so much above that they will be completely isolated from the sentiments and aspirations of the general citizenry.

It is an intriguing question, therefore, why the relationship between the community's socioeconomic character and the council's social status shifts as it does. The socioeconomic data by themselves are insufficient to answer it. The reasons must be found elsewhere.

Selection of councils takes place within the politically active stratum. This stratum is generally composed of citizens who tend to be the better educated and of middling or prestigious occupations. This politically active group includes a fair representation of the entire range of socioeconomic status groups found *above* the sixtieth percentile for the population as a whole. But while in all cities the council is recruited from the active stratum, recruitment need not be based on the candidates' absolute social status in this stratum.

On the one hand, therefore, the social composition of the governing group varies with the socioeconomic character of the entire community because the substantive meaning of the sixtieth

percentile point that defines the population pool out of which
the active stratum is selected also varies from city to city. On
the other hand, although these socioeconomic constraints are present, success *within* the active stratum is likely to be associated
with traits such as political ambition, political skill, appropriate
political contacts, suitable political beliefs, and so on. These political traits need not covary with the social status of those who are
politically active. Figure 13–2 illustrates this pattern.

There is a way, albeit indirect, to examine the assumptions implicit in Figure 13–2. As noted in connection with Table 13–1,

Figure 13–2

**Illustrative Graph Showing Hypothetical Relationship
Between Social Stratification System
and Processes of Leadership Selection**

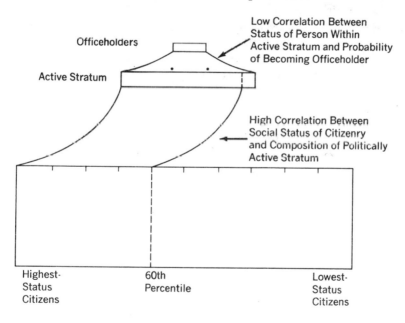

there is a fit between the council's and the population's socioeconomic character: relatively high-status councils govern in the
wealthier cities and relatively low-status councils govern in the

poorer cities. The relationship shows, however, that some council-city pairings are mismatched; there are high-status councils in poorer cities and low-status councils in wealthier cities. It is the presence of these "mismatches" which allows us to explore the notion that the relationship between the selection process and socioeconomic bias in selection will vary with differing electoral contexts.

Table 13–2 presents the relationship between the council's and the city's socioeconomic status (now dichotomized) for the different electoral contexts. A relatively high positive correlation would indicate that, within a particular context, the higher-status councils are more in wealthier cities and the lower-status councils are more in poorer cities; a zero correlation would indicate a random relationship between council status and the socioeconomic character of a city's population.

The results are striking and, in particular, reveal a suggestive difference between communities with high and low eviction rates. Selection patterns in contexts with supportive and, to a lesser extent, permissive electorates—both characterized by low eviction—suggest the possible relevance of socioeconomic congruence of social status between governors and governed. In contrast, the council's socioeconomic composition appears to be less germane where the electorate is volatile. In the discriminative context, finally, the relationship between the community's socioeconomic character and the council's social status is reversed but weak.

The theoretical implications to be drawn from these differences are best made by comparing cities with supportive electoral con-

Table 13–2

Relationship Between Status of Council
and Community Wealth Within Four Electoral Contexts

	Electoral Context and Community Wealth						
	Permissive		*Supportive*		*Discriminative*		*Volatile*
Council status	Poor	Rich	Poor	Rich	Poor	Rich	Poor Rich
Low	4	4	7	1	3	6	15	2
High	1	14	2	7	3	4	5	2
Gamma =	.87		.92		—.20		.50	

texts, a group which has only 18 percent mismatches, with cities in which the electoral context is discriminative, a group which has 56 percent mismatches. This comparison suggests that in the supportive context sharp political judgments are seldom made. As a result, considerations of status become more salient in leadership selection. It is sufficient, indeed, it may be politically important, that the city fathers be "representative" of the active stratum in occupational achievement, educational attainment, or personal wealth. The leaders will be modal, even though this modality is a statistical tendency in the upper two-fifths of a given city population. If the persons in that stratum typically are successful lawyers or business executives, the council will be composed of persons of similar status. If, however, the upper two-fifths is typically composed of small local businessmen or perhaps skilled craftsmen, the council will tend to be composed of persons of equivalent status.

The data cannot explain why this congruence emerges. It may be that voters, in the absence of political cues, elect to leadership persons higher in status than themselves, but not too much higher. If this tendency does occur, it is not surprising that it will be most evident in electoral contexts that are supportive or permissive, that is, in situations of low political content at election time. Neither partisan differences nor divisive issues give the electorate an opportunity to take sides across lines of socioeconomic cleavage. Under these conditions, in which the voter's political rationality is not tested, the activities and influence of the active stratum become decisive. As the electorate characteristic of supportive or permissive contexts does not intrude threateningly on leadership selection, the recruitment process is unhampered by possible electoral sanctions and leads to the nomination of candidates with "appropriate" (i.e., modal in terms of the particular active stratum) characteristics.

The nearly random relationship between the socioeconomic composition of the council and the community under conditions of a discriminating electorate, as well as the less pronounced relationship in the volatile electoral context, seem to follow from the greater emphasis on political involvement of the voters in such cities. Where the electorate frequently evicts, elections are likely to be more issue-oriented. Within both the general electorate and the active stratum there seems to be a greater stress on where a candidate stands on the issues of the day than on his social status. (Though, again, it should be emphasized that all candidates will be drawn from upper-status groups.) Within upper-status groups, the political ambitions, skills, and experiences of individuals are not likely to vary much with their relative status. Thus, where political rather than status traits of candidates are salient to the voter, as we expect is the case when electorates are discriminating or volatile, the relationship between council status and city wealth is less pronounced.

These, of course, are *post hoc* speculations about a pattern which emerges when the socioeconomic bias in leadership selection is examined under differing electoral conditions. There is no way we can test these explanations at present. But socioeconomic bias is a political variable too important to be ignored. The variance in the extent and the shape of the bias from one political setting to another is associated with the habitual behavior of the electorate.

Elections and Political Recruitment

City councils are selected and renewed from among the relatively small part of the population which is regularly active in political matters. Socioeconomic selectivity counts heavily in the formation of this active stratum (see Figure 13–2). Within this stratum the determination of who will govern is affected by the workings of the recruitment process. However, the significance of the active stratum as a source of leadership is not lessened just because offices are filled through elections. As Weber noted, the mass base of politics in parliamentary democracies must be organized. And the persons who assume responsibility for this organization, the political cadre, become the professionals who largely decide who will stand for office.[8] Yet the extent of reliance on the active stratum as a source of candidates might vary depending on the involvement

---

[8] Max Weber, "Politics as a Vocation," in H. H. Gerth and C. Wright Mills, *From Max Weber: Essays in Sociology* (New York: Oxford University Press, 1946), pp. 77–128.

of the electorate. Established recruitment channels will be more broadly construed and less firmly adhered to if the electorate is an active participant in the process of leadership selection.

The political stratum consists of those persons who take an active part in managing the affairs of the community; in numbers it will, of course, be considerably larger than the number of elective or appointive offices available and considerably smaller than the actual electorate, let alone all the adult citizens. Our estimate is that the active stratum, in both the public and private sectors, comprises about one in 20 adult citizens, with the better-educated and well-to-do segments of the population greatly overrepresented.

City councilmen in the San Francisco Bay region are typically recruited from two, often overlapping, sets of persons who constitute the community's active stratum. (1) There are persons who are part of what we term the "auxiliary government." These are persons who serve on public bodies, whether appointive or elective, such as the school board, the library board, the planning commission, and a variety of other local agencies. (2) There are persons who are part of what we call "civic leadership." They are the officers of the local chamber of commerce, service clubs, community chest, churches, and so on. In many cities these positions in the auxiliary government or civic leadership may be filled by the same people, making for much overlap, and individuals move from one position to the other as opportunity arises and civic duty calls. At one time they may play a civic leadership role, at another time they may serve in the auxiliary government, and at still other times they may serve on the city council. Men in these roles form the active stratum which manages the affairs of the community.

Yet, auxiliary government and civic leadership are quite distinct components of the active stratum. Auxiliary government agencies serve at the discretion of the city council, operating on budgets made available by the council, or they are, if separately elected commissions, in close touch with the city government. Civic leaders, in contrast, have budgets independent of what might be allocated from tax sources, and their incumbency in civic positions is not monitored by the electorate, directly or indirectly. Civic leadership is more autonomous of the city council than is the auxiliary government.

Councils are, of course, not exclusively recruited from the auxiliary government or the civic leadership. Some men enter political office without prior indication of interest or activity. The "lateral entrants" usually will have excelled in some occupational pursuit, gained renown for their achievements, and then transferred their prestige to politics. The five-star general, the astronaut, the athlete, or the movie star who has made a reputation and enters politics are examples of officeholders with lateral entry patterns. Similar transfers take place at the local level as well. Although relatively few individual councilmen—12 percent of the 435 who were interviewed—had careers which can be described as lateral entry, it is possible to classify the cities into those having a recruitment system which includes lateral entry (47 percent of all councils) and those without the practice (53 percent).[9]

To what extent, one may ask, does the active stratum vary as a supplier of governors from one electoral context to another? One would expect, in answer, that the larger electorate would decrease the number of officeholders recruited directly from the active stratum. A larger electorate tends to expand the talent pool from which the governing group can be renewed. The more active citizenry will be less content with the offerings provided by the relatively few people who already occupy the political and parapolitical leadership positions in the community.

The hypothesis can be explored in two ways. First, in Table 13–3, the contribution of the active stratum to the council is compared as between low- and high-turnout cities, controlling for electoral eviction. The hypothesis is moderately confirmed. In every instance a larger electorate is associated with less reliance on the active stratum as a council recruitment pool. Second, in Table 13–4, the extent to which lateral entry occurs in recruitment processes is shown for each electoral context. Again, in the high-voter turnout cities (supportive and volatile contexts) there are greater opportunities for persons outside the active stratum to reach office. In terms of the hypothesis, Table 13–4 shows that high turnout is associated with a somewhat more open and flexible

---

[9] A council was classified as facilitating lateral entry if at least one councilman reached office in this manner. See Appendix C, Questions 53 to 55.

Table 13–3

Percentage Differences in Recruitment
from Active Stratum in Low- and High-Turnout Cities,
Controlled by Incumbent Eviction

Low incumbent eviction	Difference between low- and high-turnout cities
Recruitment from auxil- iary government	10%
Recruitment from civic leadership	9%
High incumbent eviction	
Recruitment from auxil- iary government	19%
Recruitment from civic leadership	18%

NOTE: Figures indicate that x% fewer cities in high- than in low-turnout cities recruit in the manner described.

recruitment process. It is in the contexts established by a large electorate that political aspirants reach office without first serving an apprenticeship in the auxiliary government or civic leadership positions.

Taken together, the findings of Tables 13–3 and 13–4 suggest that renewal of the council more regularly emphasizes recruitment from the active stratum if the citizenry is comparatively withdrawn from electoral participation.

Table 13–4

Types of Electoral Context and Lateral Entry

Lateral entry	Type of Electoral Context			
	Permissive $N = 23$	Supportive $N = 17$	Discriminative $N = 16$	Volatile $N = 24$
Present	35%	65%	31%	58%
Absent	65	35	69	42
	100%	100%	100%	100%

Most writings about the composition of legislatures stress social origins. But a council, or any other governing group, can be described in terms of the recruitment origins of its members as well as in terms of its social origins. The value of such description lies in what it reveals about the prior experiences of those who govern. Stated more broadly, the study of political recruitment is the study of the formation of the governing group. Recruitment patterns do vary with the electorate's behavior, though in every respect the patterns only suggest tendencies.

As expected, councils are largely recruited from the active stratum. Only 12 percent of the total sample of individual councilmen report career lines that are not in one way or another movements through the established role network lying intermediate between the council and the public. The network has two major components—the auxiliary government and the civic leadership group. Though the tendency to recruit from these groups persists in all communities, reliance on these groups is somewhat lessened when there is greater electoral participation. A larger electorate is associated with less recruitment from the auxiliary government or the civic leadership and with a correspondingly greater tolerance for lateral entry patterns into the council.

Elections and Career Sponsorship

The eighteenth-century attack on aristocratic privilege and hereditary rule intended to open political office to any man of talent and ambition. Expansion of the suffrage was crucial to this goal. The public as a whole should sit in judgment of political worthiness, and its judgment would reward with office men of merit. Some observers believe that at least in industrial democracies movement into positions of social and political leadership is now largely a result of individual achievement and ambition. Modern societies have moved "beyond the ruling class" and thus have abolished the tendency for leadership groups to perpetuate themselves in power.[10]

---

[10] Suzanne Keller in her aptly titled *Beyond the Ruling Class* (New York: Random House, 1965) is a leading proponent of this argument.

Other observers are less sanguine about the historical trend. Max Weber called attention to the extent to which the organizational modes of an industrial society penetrated democratic processes and structure. Michels drew the conclusion that all organizations, even political parties with elected officeholders, tend to be managed according to the "iron law of oligarchy." Elections were no guarantee against self-perpetuation by the ruling group. Perhaps Mosca's pessimism is justified:

> When we say that the voters "choose" their representative, we are using a language that is very inexact. The truth is that the representative *has himself elected* by the voters, and, if that phrase should seem too inflexible and too harsh to fit some cases, we might qualify it by saying that *his friends have him selected*.[11]

This concern with oligarchic self-perpetuation is relevant in a study of leadership selection at the municipal level. It probably is a near universal tendency for governing groups to influence who their successors will be. A group of men who invest time, energy, and political capital in formulating public policies have reason to protect those policies. This is especially true if the policies work to their personal benefit, as is often the case when realtors on a council fashion land-use policy or businessmen on a council fashion taxation policy. But even setting aside the self-interest motive, it is reasonable that governors would prefer the public policies they have shaped to extend into the future and not to be radically changed just because a few of their members change. An important way in which to influence public policy even after leaving office is to have a hand in selecting like-minded successors. Concern over succession was expressed when councilmen had to consider whether they themselves would run again in the next election. "I can't afford not to run," a respondent stated, "because of some of the characters I've seen who want to run and might get elected." Or another respondent: "It depends on my potential successors; I want to see the balance on the council continue." And a third said that "if I can get someone that shares my viewpoint on policies and someone I can trust I'd be happy to step down and let him take over."

---

[11] Mosca, *The Ruling Class,* p. 154.

City councils thus attempt to renew themselves by affecting the next generation of officeholders. They do so primarily by sponsoring the careers of younger men in the active stratum. Key apprenticeship positions, especially appointment to the planning commission, are made available to some potential candidates but not to others. The civic leadership group is surveyed for possible recruits. The clearest examples of career sponsorship appear in councils where premature retirement from office by an incumbent is followed by appointment of a suitable successor. As reported in one council, "We are very careful about whom we appoint and we make sure that they want the community to develop in the same way the rest of us feel is best." From a different council comes a complete description of recruitment by appointment: "When you are not going to re-run you have to resign a few months before the election so that the present council can appoint some good man in order to get the same mood maintained in the council." Altogether, nearly a fourth (24 percent) of the councilmen first reached office by being appointed.

What does vary from community to community is the success with which the governing group influences the next generation of community leaders. Communities can be classified according to the extent of control over the recruitment process successfully exercised by those already in established positions. Councils vary in the extent to which membership consists of persons whose political careers were sponsored by their predecessors in office or by influentials closely associated with officeholders.[12] Where sponsor-

---

[12] The measure of sponsorship is particularly problematic in that we are summing not just individual experiences to get a group score but individual experiences which took place over a considerable span of time in some cases. It may be that the aggregation of individual career experiences into a council recruitment measure disguises more variance in the original data than the index should be burdened with. Councilmen enter the council at very different points in time, and recruitment as a system property may have undergone major changes since the entry experiences of the older members. For the present, however, we are trapped by our own data; when we began the study we were thinking of recruitment as an individual attribute and thus mainly collected data about individual careers. Despite the relatively weaker nature of our sponsorship measure, we are reluctant to give up our theoretical posture. A council was given a sponsorship measure by computing the mean of six alternative paths to office. The "sponsorship continuum" ranged from the case in

Table 13–5

Types of Electoral Context and Career Sponsorship

Career sponsorship	Type of Electoral Context			
	Permissive N = 23	Supportive N = 17	Discriminative N = 16	Volatile N = 24
High	65%	59%	50%	21%
Low	35	41	50	79
	100%	100%	100%	100%

ship is successfully practiced, the recruitment process is relatively closed and generally under the control of persons in office. Where sponsorship is less successfully practiced, the recruitment process is relatively open and free of control by persons in established positions.[13]

Table 13–5 shows the relationship between successful sponsorship and the four types of electoral context. Sponsorship varies with the joint effect of electoral participation and electoral eviction. Three times as many councils in permissive contexts than in volatile contexts have mostly sponsored members. The data in Table 13–5 are a remarkable confirmation of the proposition that differences in electorate behavior can affect the processes through which leaders are selected. To be sure, no community is completely

---

which an outside challenger initiated his own career and attained a council seat with minimum contact between himself and those already in established positions to the case in which a councilman was deliberately selected—either asked to run or appointed to the council—by those already in office. The means were then ranked and, for present purposes, dichotomized.

[13] A word of caution about the sponsorship measure is necessary. A city classified as having "relatively low sponsorship" may indeed have as much sponsorship taking place within the active stratum as a city classified "relatively high." There is no way of knowing how much actual sponsorship occurs since we must infer attributes of the recruitment process from evidence only about those who have won office. It is probably a natural tendency for a governing group to attempt to control its successors. The cities could be equal in the amount of sponsorship that takes place and differ only in the success of the council in selecting its own successors. When we classify cities as low or high in sponsorship, then, we are, more precisely, classifying them with respect to the *success* of persons in established positions in controlling the flow of newcomers to the council.

free of career sponsorship. But some communities are freer than others, and the variability is consistent with what one should expect to be the joint effect of electoral participation and eviction. The permissive electorate and to a lesser degree the supportive electorate evidently allow the council to run its own show, at least with respect to political recruitment. The volatile electorate especially, but also the discriminative electorate to a degree, imposes more constraints on the inclination of councils to sponsor succession.

Tables 13–3 through 13–5, which show how recruitment and sponsorship vary from one electoral context to another, can be summarized in terms of some general trends clearly showing that recruitment to office and the electorate's behavior are interdependent constitutive processes.

Recruitment in the *permissive* electoral context makes for a highly integrated structure. In this context, characterized by a small electorate and little eviction, the electorate does not intrude into the recruitment process. There probably are close bonds between the council, aware that it will not be displaced, and other local governmental and civic elites, aware that voter constituencies are not being mobilized against their programs. Both the auxiliary government and the civic leadership sectors provide personnel for elective office. Moreover, lateral entry is limited. This, coupled with the emphasis on career sponsorship, suggests that the permissive electoral context establishes conditions in which those in office can rather effectively control who their successors will be.

In the *supportive* context, where the electorate is large but seldom defeats incumbents, recruitment tends to stress both sponsorship and lateral entry rather than selection from distinct subgroups of the active stratum. It may be that the larger electorate active in the community explains the somewhat broadened recruitment net, but that the low rate of eviction allows for the comparatively greater emphasis on sponsorship. An electorate which turns out in good numbers but seldom evicts incumbents, we can assume, is an electorate not only satisfied with the leadership but also willing to endorse them. In this setting, the council is free to sponsor the careers of local notables, and, indeed, by searching for new recruits outside as well as inside the more visible active stratum, may add to its electoral strength.

In the *discriminative* electoral context a small and attentive electorate does not hesitate to evict incumbents from office when displeased with their performance. In this setting, a somewhat precarious one from the vantage point of the council, previously nonactive candidates appear reluctant to serve on the council. Lateral entry is limited. The most pronounced career line appears to be through the auxiliary government, suggesting that the discriminating electorate stresses greater governmental experience in its elected leaders.[14] Thus, despite personnel turnover, some continuity in the leadership is protected. And that sponsorship is practiced in at least half the cities would again indicate that continuity is not entirely absent, despite the relatively high rate of incumbent eviction.

The recruitment pattern in the *volatile* electoral context contrasts sharply with that of the permissive context. Where the electoral context is fluid, with a large electorate which frequently evicts incumbents, the recruitment system appears to be more open. Reliance on career sponsorship is significantly reduced and lateral entry more frequently practiced. Recruitment from the two groups of community apprentices—auxiliary government members and civic leaders—is less than under any other electoral conditions. If recruitment processes are integrated when the electorate is permissive, then they appear to be more fragmented when the electorate is volatile. A greater variety of political groupings are able to nominate candidates and, given the relatively high turnover in office, are likely to be successful in getting their candidates elected. The larger electorate probably makes for the expression of a greater variety of political viewpoints, and a certain political volatility in the community is the result.

Conclusion

Political leaders are not randomly selected from the population at large; they are recruited from definite citizen groupings. Both

---

[14] See Kenneth Prewitt and Heinz Eulau, "Social Bias in Leadership Selection, Political Recruitment, and Electoral Context," *Journal of Politics* 33 (May 1971): 312, Table 5.

socioeconomic traits and political characteristics define the pool of eligibles from which leadership is drawn. Evidence suggests the importance of considering how the electoral system and the leadership selection system interrelate. The pools from which leaders are selected and the nature of the selection process vary according to the size of the electorate and the tendency of the electorate to evict incumbents. The very fact of interrelatedness is of some importance. For though such relationships have long been assumed, there has been little empirical attention to whether—let alone how—the electoral context might constrain the type of leadership selection that occurs.

Two findings emerge. Although the men who govern the San Franscisco Bay Area cities are drawn from the middle and upper-middle strata of their communities, the extent to which they are representative of those strata varies from city to city. This in turn suggests that considerations other than those of social status affect movement from the active stratum into elected leadership. A recruitment process placing comparatively greater emphasis on political choices and judgments seems to be associated with an electorate that intrudes on the selection process. In contrast, recruitment practices evidently relying on the social background and accomplishment of candidates are associated with an electorate that is supportive or permissive.

Political as well as social-status characteristics help define the pool of citizens from which leaders are disproportionately drawn. Governors typically are chosen from among those citizens already actively involved in governmental and community affairs. But the relative emphasis on recruitment from the active stratum, as well as the incidence of career sponsorship and lateral entry, does vary from one electoral context to another.

Chapter 14

Leadership Selection and Political Campaigning

Rare are the occasions in the political life of the community when the governed and the governors are brought together to exchange viewpoints. Political campaigns are one of these occasions. During a political campaign, the men who hold office along with an additional few who challenge them present themselves and their ideas to the citizenry. Citizens are given an opportunity to review the policies of past leaders and to judge the promises of would-be leaders. It is in this regard that political campaigning is part of the linkage between council and community.

Campaigns do not work as some early proponents of universal suffrage had expected they would. The notion that citizens approach the political campaign with a view to informed evaluation of personalities and programs, and then vote the "best" man into office, is no longer viable, if it ever was. Campaigns may reinforce preexisting loyalties or perhaps activate a passive citizenry, but they seldom convert voters from one allegiance to another. Voters who are guided by long-standing partisan attachments remain poorly informed about the policy positions of the men for whom they vote. Research into voting behavior has led some observers to downgrade the significance of the political campaign in democratic politics, or, even more pessimistically, to bemoan its befuddling consequences.

If, however, attention shifts from voter choice to public involvement, the significance of campaigns for democratic politics

is seen in a different light. Campaigns can then be viewed as part
of a package of activities which selects governors and which provides opportunities to link governors with the electorate.

The political importance of campaigns derives from the fact
that they intervene between two other stages of leadership selection—recruitment and elections. To understand the campaign, it
is necessary to look backward in time to the recruitment of candidates and forward in time to the election of governors. The campaign grows out of the prior activities which select some men to
run for office and eliminate others. Because these recruitment
processes typically push forward more candidates for office than
there are vacancies to be filled, a campaign becomes necessary. But
whereas recruitment is comparatively private and attracts the attention only of the active stratum, campaigns are deliberately
public and invite the attention of a mass audience. In publicizing
that governors are to be chosen, campaigns take politics out of the
hands of the few and place it, however temporarily, in the hands of
the many.

Broadening the involvement of the public in political life is
abetted by the fact that campaigns look forward to election day.
In anticipating the election, campaigns announce in a loud and
oftentimes clamorous voice that the polling booths will be open
and citizens are invited to express their preferences. The importance of campaigns in this regard can be easily grasped by imagining elections without them. Whatever the consequences, or lack
of them, for rational voter choice, there is little doubt that campaigns do increase public involvement in activities which result
in a few men governing the rest. During the campaign the citizen-
at-large begins to play a role, usually that of merely interested spec-
tator but sometimes that of active participant, in choosing who the
governors will be, a role which reaches its maximum importance
on election day.

Campaigning: A State of Mind and Physical Effort

The more lively the campaign in a community, the greater the
scope and intensity of contacts between the public and the candi-

dates. A lively campaign involves the candidates in public explanations of past accomplishments and promised benefits. However
fanciful some of these explanations, the need to appear before the
electorate leads to an exchange of viewpoints between officeholder
and citizen. As expressed by one councilman, "When running for
election you make your views and attitudes well-known, you have
communicated."

It is worth underscoring that the candidates in city council
elections are not shielded from the electorate by a cadre of public
relations experts, media personalities, and professional staff. If
an active campaign is to be waged, it involves the candidate going
door-to-door and speaking to audiences in the community. Direct
contact is facilitated by the campaign characteristics of most city
elections.

The campaign can be thought of, then, as an attribute of the
general interaction patterns between council and public. This in
turn implies classifying communities according to their level of
campaign activity. Campaigning and electioneering are to be compared across the 82 communities rather than between candidates
seeking the same position, as is usually the case.[1]

Campaign activities were measured along four dimensions—the
campaign effort of councils, the enjoyment of campaigning expressed by councils, the extent to which councils use door-to-door
campaigning, and the extent to which they speak to large audiences as part of the campaign.

Councilmen were asked, "Would you say that you campaigned
fairly hard, some, not too much, or what?" as part of a general
series of questions on campaigning. Responses to this question, aggregated into a measure of campaign effort, reveal wide variability
across the communities and, incidentally, suggest why it is that
an active campaign effort presents opportunities for linkages. "I
went everywhere that I was invited, and talked before a lot of

---

[1] Students of political campaigning typically ask about the success of alternative
campaign strategies. A successful strategy is defined as one that enables a candidate who initially controls fewer resources than his opponent to nevertheless do
well in the contest for office. The research involves comparison between candidates seeking the same office, and the investigator collects data on how candidates and their supporters organize their efforts and marshal their resources.

groups," said one councilman. One of his colleagues reported that he "covered a lot of ground; we asked for opportunities to speak around and they gave them to us." Of course, in many cities there is not much effort put into campaigning. Sometimes this is attributed to lack of opposition: "No one ran against us, so there was no need to do much campaigning." A few councils even report that "it just wouldn't be appropriate to campaign hard here; we don't do things like that."

Councilmen were also asked what they liked and disliked about campaigning, and on the basis of these responses councils were classified into those where campaigning is enjoyed and those where it is not.[2] Again there is wide variability, and the responses suggest how a measure of campaign enjoyment can be considered in the context of linkage processes. Councils which enjoy campaigning are likely to be more involved with the public and to present themselves more eagerly through campaigning, whereas councils not liking to campaign will close off opportunities to exchange viewpoints with the public if possible. Thus one respondent who finds campaigning enjoyable says that "the electorate should be afforded a chance to see the men they are to choose from." Another who enjoys "contacts with people" notes that the campaign is "an opportunity to learn and get impressions of what voters have on their minds." A third respondent tells us that he likes campaigning because "it is interesting to wander around the city and get to know the various areas and the variety of persons in the community." But there are councilmen who actively dislike the pressures and nuisances of campaigning: "It gets awful tiresome talking to all those people. I dislike the time-consuming nature of it." Another who "doesn't like anything about campaigning" also doesn't "believe in coffee klatsches or ringing doorbells," thus breaking off the linkages which an active campaign might bring about.

Campaign techniques include door-to-door campaigning and speaking to large audiences.[3] Both involve person-to-person con-

---

[2] The question was: "Speaking of running for office, how do you feel about campaigning? Could you tell me a little bit about what you like or dislike about it?"

[3] See Appendix C, Item 5.

tact, but the former involves more intimacy than the latter. The councilman going door-to-door to introduce himself and to pass out campaign literature engages in informal chats with citizens from throughout the community (or at least those sections where he expects voter support). Perhaps nothing in political life so effectively, if only temporarily, bridges the distance between governors and governed. This campaign technique goes back to a day when the suffrage was sufficiently restricted that word-of-mouth and parlor caucuses carried the campaign to voters. Such intimate campaigning is no longer possible at the state or national levels, having been supplemented and even superseded by radio, television, and the press. But what is true of national and state-wide campaigning is less true of city elections, where size alone allows some retention of intimate campaign techniques.

Addressing large audiences is similar to the media campaigns of national figures in that sophisticated techniques of managing mass opinion can be employed. Slogans and symbols can be displayed more effectively when the trappings of large, public meetings provide the setting than when it is just the candidate and the voter in a door-to-door conversation. Still, directly addressing the voters— in contrast to media advertisements and television performances— can lead to relatively unfettered exchanges between candidate and citizen. This is likely when campaign meetings are organized by local civic groups, especially the League of Women Voters, in a manner designed to allow cross-examination and audience participation. Many meetings at the local level are of this type; specific community groups organize a candidate's night and this is what attracts the audience.

This analysis is less concerned with differences among the four indicators of campaign activity than with how the scope and intensity of campaigning vary with differences in political recruitment and the electorate's behavior. One should, however, at least consider the interrelationships among the four measures. Table 14–1 shows the strength of the associations.

As a state of mind, the enjoyment of campaigning is only weakly related to various forms of physical campaign activity. Evidently, some councils which do not enjoy campaigning nevertheless do so actively, while other councils which do enjoy it nevertheless

Table 14–1
Correlation Coefficients for Relationships
Among Four Indicators of Political Campaigning

	Campaign enjoyment	Door-to-door campaigning	Speaking to large audiences
Campaign effort	.24	.50	.73
Campaign enjoyment	—	.14	.21
Door-to-door campaigning	—	—	.33

minimize their activity. More will be said about this in connection with the political conditions that tend to increase or decrease campaign efforts.

Campaign effort, a general appraisal of their activity level by councils, is substantially related to door-to-door campaigning and very strongly to appearances before large audiences—as indeed it should be. A strenuous campaign effort necessarily implies the use of the two techniques; and, because of the relatively strong associations, it will be used as a shorthand measure to make subsequent table presentation and description less complex and cumbersome.

Political Recruitment and Political Campaigning

The election campaign grows out of a prior set of activities which recruits from within the active stratum a small number of persons who become candidates for council positions. Two subsets of the active stratum—the auxiliary government and the civic leadership—supply most council candidates, or at least supply most of those persons who eventually become councilmen.

It is relevant to note here that the role socialization of councils recruited from auxiliary governments differs in important respects from that of councils recruited from civic leadership circles. And these differences have particular relevance to campaign practices.

The role socialization of councils selected from auxiliary governments includes long-standing exposure to and involvement in campaigns, for two reasons. Auxiliary governments, it will be recalled, are composed of such persons as the city engineer, city attorney, and their staffs, as well as planning commission members and persons on the library board and similar committees. These positions in city government are filled by appointment, and such appointments often are rewards for service in the campaign of a friend or associate who gains a council position. As reported by one incumbent, "I had served on the planning commission, and prior to that I campaigned for councilmen and mayors." It is not unusual for the ambitious politician to route himself to office by first working in campaigns, then being appointed to a position in the auxiliary government, which in turn leads to candidacy for a council opening. This route to office implies sustained involvement in campaigning and electioneering, first for others and subsequently for oneself.

Even if membership in the auxiliary government is not a reward for prior campaign support, persons in the auxiliary government stand in a close and constant relationship to the life of the city council. And this implies proximity if not direct involvement in the biennial campaigns. Insofar as auxiliary government members do hold appointive positions, they hold them only so long as their friends and colleagues on the council continue the appointments. A sharp change in the composition of the council can lead to a turnover in the auxiliary government. For this reason alone members of the auxiliary government will take some active interest in campaigns and council elections.

By reason of prior experience in campaigning as well as close proximity to the council, the members of the auxiliary government will have been socialized into the habits of active campaigning. Therefore, councils recruited from the auxiliary government can be expected to campaign more actively than councils not recruited from the auxiliary government.

Civic leaders constitute the second important subset of the active stratum and the second significant source of recuits for the city council. Civic leaders include persons active in business-based groups, such as the Chamber of Commerce or a merchant association; persons active in service clubs, such as the Lions Club or the Rotary Club; persons active in homeowner associations and tax-payer groups; and persons active in such strictly civic organizations as the Little League, League of Women Voters, and so forth. Persons in civic leadership positions have undergone in-role socialization just as have persons in the auxiliary government. But their socialization is comparatively far removed from campaign and electioneering activities. Most civic groups are run with scarcely a thought being given to periodic elections or voter constituencies. To be sure, the internal politics of civic groups might from time to time involve the "election" of a new president or a chairman, but this kind of election does not have the trappings associated with formal governmental elections.

Councils recruited from the civic leadership are composed of persons whose prior experience involved little close association with political campaign activities. The socialization accompanying their journey from the active stratum to officeholding will not have habituated them to campaigning. They can therefore be expected to campaign less actively than councils not recruited from the civic leadership cadre.[4]

Table 14–2 presents the data pertinent to these hypotheses. Part A of the table shows a consistent tendency for councils more rather than less often recruited from the auxiliary government to campaign actively. Complementarily, Part B of the table shows a consistent tendency for councils less rather than more often recruited from the civic leadership to campaign actively. The reversals are demonstrably strong except for campaign enjoyment; in neither case is the council's state of mind regarding campaigning much affected by prevailing recruitment practices, suggesting that in-role socialization has more of an impact on campaign behavior than on predisposition toward campaigning.

The political campaign grows out of prior recruitment patterns, making for the relationship between type of recruitment and the

---

[4] The wording of this and the previous hypothesis is intended to indicate that recruitment from the civic leadership is not at the opposite end of a continuum which has recruitment from the auxiliary government as the other pole. Councils can stress both recruitment sources, or neither. The coding procedures simply identify how much recruitment from each source characterizes the community; in this sense they are independent measures.

Table 14–2

Relationships Between Patterns of Political Recruitment
and Extent of Campaign Activity

Part A	Councils Recruited from Auxiliary Government		
Proportion of councils high on:	Less often N = 40	More often N = 42	Index of difference
Campaign effort	40	59	+19
Campaign enjoyment	52	57	+ 5
Door-to-door campaigning	45	59	+14
Speaking to large audiences	47	71	+24
Part B	Councils Recruited from Civic Leadership		
Proportion of councils high on:	Less often N = 49	More often N = 33	Index of difference
Campaign effort	55	42	−13
Campaign enjoyment	57	51	− 6
Door-to-door campaigning	67	30	−37
Speaking to large audiences	67	48	−19

extent of campaigning noted in Table 14–2. But the campaign
also anticipates the election. A campaign thus simultaneously involves looking backward in time and forward in time; because of
this, the extent of campaigning should also reflect both what went
on before and what is likely to happen at the next stage of leadership selection.

This formulation can be put to the test by examining the interrelationships among political recruitment, political campaigning,
and electorate behavior. The electoral context typology, summarizing as it does the habitual behavior of the electorate, can be
taken as a guide to what the council considers as it looks toward
the next election. If the council has reason to expect strong activity on the electorate's part, campaigning is likely to increase; if the
council has reason to expect low involvement by the electorate,
comparatively little effort will be invested in campaigning. But
the hypothesis should be qualified by the previous finding that
recruitment patterns affect the extent of campaigning. Table 14–3
presents the three variables simultaneously.

Table 14–3
Proportion of Councils from Different Recruitment
Sources Reporting High Campaign Effort in Four Types
of Electoral Context

Part A

Electoral context in which councils are high in campaign effort	*Councils Recruited from Auxiliary Government*	
	Less often	More often
Permissive	10% (N = 10)*	85% (N = 13)
Supportive	22% (N = 9)	38% (N = 8)
Discriminative	33% (N = 6)	60% (N = 10)
Volatile	62% (N = 13)	64% (N = 11)

Part B

Electoral context in which councils are high in campaign effort	*Councils Recruited from Civic Leadership*	
	Less often	More often
Permissive	73% (N = 11)	33% (N = 12)
Supportive	20% (N = 10)	43% (N = 7)
Discriminative	67% (N = 9)	29% (N = 7)
Volatile	61% (N = 18)	67% (N = 6)

* Number in parenthesis indicates base on which percentage is calculated; for instance, of the ten councils located in a permissive context and less often recruited from the auxiliary government, only one reports high campaign effort.

Part A of Table 14–3 shows the proportion of councils in each electoral context reporting high campaign effort among those recruited and those not recruited from the auxiliary government. Part B of the table presents the data comparing councils more or less often recruited from the civic leadership corps. The electoral settings in which more than three-fifths of the councils report high campaign effort have been specially marked to facilitate inspection.[5]

Because Parts A and B of the table complement each other we shall interpret them jointly. In the volatile electoral context campaigning activity is sustained at a high rate irrespective of the recruitment patterns. The volatile electorate—large in numbers and given to evicting incumbents—evidently is sufficiently feared that candidates involve themselves in the campaign no matter what their prior socialization may have been. The political realities are pressing ones, and old habits must be cast off if office is to be gained and retained. Opposite conditions hold in the supportive electoral context. The recruitment source has some bearing on campaign habits, but councils tend toward comparatively little campaign effort where the electorate traditionally turns out on election day to express its support for the incumbents.[6] In the supportive context councils are perhaps sufficiently relaxed about reelection that the campaign habits acquired during the course of recruitment experience are no longer germane.

In the other two electoral contexts, permissive and discriminative, the relationship between recruitment sources and campaign effort is consistent with the hypotheses about in-role socialization. Councils more often recruited from the auxiliary government tend to be active campaigners, and councils largely recruited from civic leadership circles tend not to be active campaigners. Differences are particularly striking in the permissive context where, for instance, eight times as many councils chosen from the auxiliary government report high campaign effort as do councils not chosen

---

[5] To keep the amount of data presented manageable, we report only the measure of campaign effort; it is more central to our theoretical concerns than the measure of enjoyment and it relates strongly to the measures of campaign techniques.

[6] There is an anomaly in the data. In the supportive context, councils recruited from the civic leadership exert more campaign effort than councils not recruited from this source, reversing the pattern established by Table 14–2. A possible explanation, advanced in the spirit of *post hoc* reasoning, is that civic groups organize informational meetings in most communities and that councils selected from these groups and serving in a supportive context recognize attendance at such meetings to be part of their civic duty; effort, then, is not effort directed toward reelection but effort as part of a continuing series of civic responsibilities accepted by those who accept leadership in the supportive context.

from this source. It is not easy to account for this, for one might think that councils in communities where the electorate is small and not given to eviction of incumbents would scarcely worry about campaigning, irrespective of their recruitment experiences. We have no explanation for this, and simply note that the campaign habits rooted in recruitment experiences persist where the electorate is permissive or discriminative. However, these same habits are modified, in predictable manner, if the electorate is either supportive or volatile.[7]

As campaign effort and the electorate's behavior are related, the political characteristics of the public may tend to accelerate or depress the intensity and scope of campaigning. The campaign is more than just what the council wishes to make it; it also reflects the pressures, or lack of pressures, emanating from the public. For instance, as Table 14–4 shows, campaigning is intensified where the public, at least as perceived by the council, is actively interested in council elections.

Table 14–5 underscores the significance of this finding. When the electorate's actual behavior through electoral participation is taken into account, the scope and intensity of campaigning continue to be affected by perceived public interest despite differences

---

[7] Although our interest here is with the pattern of interrelationships among the three separate stages of leadership selection—recruitment, campaigning, and elections—the reader may wish to know the bivariate relationship between campaigning and the electoral context. We present the data here.

| | Electoral Context | | | |
	Permissive (23)	Supportive (17)	Discriminative (16)	Volatile (24)
High campaign effort	52%	29%	50%	62%
High campaign enjoyment	39%	29%	88%	62%
Much door-to-door campaigning	44%	51%	50%	71%
Speaking to large audiences	48%	53%	75%	71%

There is a consistent tendency for campaigning to be more frequent in the discriminative and volatile electoral contexts, with a corresponding tendency for campaigning to be less frequent in the permissive and supportive electoral contexts.

Table 14–4
Relationships Between Campaign Activities
and Perceived Interest of the Public
in Council Elections

| Proportion of councils high on: | Perceived Interest of Public | | |
	Low N = 42	High N = 40	Index of difference
Campaign effort	43	56	+13
Campaign enjoyment	50	60	+10
Door-to-door campaigning	40	65	+25
Speaking to large audiences	48	72	+24

Table 14–5
Relationships Between Campaign Activities
and Perceived Interest of the Public in Council Elections,
in Low- and High-Turnout Cities

| Proportion of councils high on: | Cities with Low Voter Turnout | | |
	Low interest N = 29	High interest N = 14	Index of difference
Campaign effort	48	64	+16
Campaign enjoyment	55	71	+16
Door-to-door campaigning	41	57	+16
Speaking to large audiences	52	64	+12

| Proportion of councils high on: | Cities with High Voter Turnout | | |
	Low interest N = 13	High interest N = 26	Index of difference
Campaign effort	31	54	+23
Campaign enjoyment	38	54	+16
Door-to-door campaigning	38	69	+31
Speaking to large audiences	38	77	+39

in the number of citizens actually voting in council elections. But campaigning intensifies when there is high actual turnout and high perceived public interest. The pattern is cumulative because a public can be interested in council elections and express that interest in ways other than by high voter turnout. The 13 electorates with high voter turnout yet "uninterested publics" are not necessarily inconsistent; nor are the 14 "interested publics" which vote at a comparatively low rate.

Two types of public behavior—interest in the election and voter turnout—affect the campaign activities of the council. The public influences campaigning in various ways independently of council attributes, such as its recruitment sources. Campaigning constitutes a part of the total pattern of interaction between council and community, and this interaction is shaped through the behavior of both those in office and those far removed from office.

Several specific findings in Table 14–5 give further insight into the nature of political campaigning. The smallest number of actively campaigning councils is in cities with high voter turnout reported to be relatively uninterested in council elections. What seems to be involved here is the conservation of resources. To reach a large electorate requires a heavy expenditure of time, energy, and money. To reach a large electorate that is comparatively uninterested and uninvolved in the campaign itself may require expenditures that are prohibitive. If the campaign is unlikely to reach many voters and yet there are very many of them, the campaign cost per voter is sufficiently high that the rational (that is, economic) strategy is not to bother.

A second suggestive finding is the relatively large percentage of councils (71 percent) that enjoy campaigning in cities having low voter turnout but highly interested electorates. This condition presents the least drain on campaign resources. The presence of relatively few voters, but many of whom take an interest in the election, reduces the frustrations typical of campaign situations. The target audience can be reached and is receptive, though not necessarily responsive, to the campaign message. By way of contrast, councils in cities with small though uninterested electorates express campaign enjoyment as frequently as do councils in cities with large and interested electorates, which suggests that the sheer size of the electorate puts a strain on limited campaign resources and thus reduces the enjoyment councils might otherwise feel in campaigning.

These observations are pertinent to an understanding of the campaign itself, but are less important than the general conclusion to be drawn about linkage processes. The campaign stands between the governed and the governors; it provides each of the main actors in the political drama an opportunity to make contact with the other. In this sense the campaign is part of the linkages which span the natural gulf separating the few who are selected from the many they represent. The significance of the campaign as linkage is affected by the interest which the public takes in the electioneering and by the number of votes cast on election day. At least with respect to campaigning, the public is a significant other whose expectations and activities help establish the extent of interaction between governors and governed.

Electoral Competition and Political Campaigning

An electoral campaign involves three major political actors— the public or electorate, the incumbent officeholders seeking re-election, and the challengers. Unfortunately, no interview data are available about challengers and unsuccessful candidates. Rather the council itself has been used as the source of information about all candidates—incumbents as well as challengers, the successful as well as the unsuccessful. This weakens the analysis,[8] but the defect can be partly remedied by introducing some of the measures of electoral competition developed in Chapter 11.

Electoral competition in the form of office contesting (the average number of candidates seeking a council position) and closeness

---

[8] It would be preferable to separate the part played by the council and the part played by the challengers in giving shape to the political campaign. The problem is even more complex than this paragraph indicates, though the complexity works to our advantage as well as to our disadvantage. When councilmen report on their campaign activities, they are reporting on campaigns associated with their first election, when they were challengers, as well as on campaigns associated with subsequent elections, when they are incumbents. It is for this reason that the campaign measures can be taken as summaries of general campaign activities and not just those of incumbents. This is one reason we have been content to use the campaign measures as attributes of the community as a whole.

Table 14–6
Relationships Between Political Campaigning and Political Competition

Proportion of councils high on:	Office Contesting		
	Low $N = 41$	High $N = 40$	Index of difference
Campaign effort	29	60	+31
Campaign enjoyment	49	60	+11
Door-to-door campaigning	51	55	+ 4
Speaking to large audiences	56	65	+ 9

Proportion of councils high on:	Closeness of Vote		
	Low $N = 38$	High $N = 38$	Index of difference
Campaign effort	42	58	+16
Campaign enjoyment	39	66	+27
Door-to-door campaigning	45	63	+18
Speaking to large audiences	55	66	+11

Table 14–7
Relationships Between Campaign Effort and Political Competition, Controlled by Recruitment from Auxiliary Government

	Recruitment from Auxiliary Government				
	Less often		More often		Index of cumulative difference*
Office contesting	Low $N = 23$	High $N = 16$	Low $N = 18$	High $N = 24$	
High campaign effort	35%	38%	56%	71%	+36%
Closeness of vote	Low $N = 20$	High $N = 18$	Low $N = 18$	High $N = 40$	
High campaign effort	25%	50%	67%	65%	+40%

* Index measures percentage difference between condition predicted to have lowest campaign effort and condition predicted to have highest campaign effort.

of vote (the average difference in the vote between successful and unsuccessful candidates) allows a partial discovery of how members of the active stratum, other than the council itself, affect campaigning. Because the political campaign is in some respects the behavioral manifestation of a competitive situation, high office contesting, for instance, implies a fragmented active stratum, composed of many political groupings promoting their own candidates. Similarly, a closely fought election implies that no single interest is able to dominate the community for long.

Given the nature of political competition, councils wishing to retain governing control will have to increase their campaign effort if they are challenged, and especially if there is a presumption that the contest will be close. Much less campaign effort is called for in the absence of challengers or if the council's electoral position is secure. The data presented in Table 14–6 generally confirm this hypothesis: all four measures of campaigning increase under conditions of high office contesting and closely fought elections. Not every measure is strongly related, but there are no reversals and the overall pattern is consistent.

It is tempting to infer from Table 14–6 that the characteristics of the active stratum, reflected in the competitive situation, have an effect on campaigning independent of the composition of the council or of the electorate. But it is also reasonable to assume that recruitment patterns or electoral context, already noted to be consequential for campaigning, might minimize the significance of competition in this respect. Tables 14–7 and 14–8 show the proportion of councils reporting high campaign effort by office contesting and closeness of vote, controlling respectively for recruitment from the auxiliary government and the civic leadership.

The effort put into campaigning increases with the number of candidates seeking a council opening and the closeness of the election irrespective of the source from which the councils are recruited. Although the pattern is not confirmed in every setting, the general tendency is sufficiently consistent to warrant the conclusion.[9] Tables 14–7 and 14–8 show as well that campaign effort is

---

[9] Thus, for example, if councils are not recruited from the auxiliary government, campaign effort remains uniformly low irrespective of how much office

Table 14–8
Relationships Between Campaign Effort and Political Competition, Controlled by Recruitment from Civic Leadership

	Recruitment from Civic Leadership*				
	More often		Less often		
					Index of
	Low	High	Low	High	cumulative
Office contesting	N = 19	N = 14	N = 22	N = 26	difference
High campaign effort	32%	57%	54%	58%	+26%
Closeness of vote	Low	High	Low	High	
	N = 16	N = 16	N = 22	N = 22	
High campaign effort	38%	50%	50%	64%	+26%

* Because high recruitment from the civic leadership is the complement of less recruitment from the auxiliary government, the order of the recruitment variable here is the reverse of that in Table 14–7, for convenience of interpretation.

influenced by recruitment patterns irrespective of the rate of office contesting and the closeness of the vote. Stated differently, the habits of campaigning which councils bring to the election by virtue of their recruitment experiences, and the competitive conditions, have a joint and cumulative effect on campaigns as links between council and public. The index of cumulative difference shows the increase in campaign effort between the conditions expected to produce the least campaign effort and the conditions expected to produce the most campaign effort. Recruitment patterns and the struggles within the active stratum each affect the level of campaigning.

Electoral Context and Political Campaigning

Because electoral context has had an impact on political campaigning, though varying with recruitment patterns (Table 14–3),

---

contesting there is; and if they are recruited from the auxiliary government, campaign effort remains uniformly high irrespective of the closeness of the vote.

it remains to determine whether conflict within the active stratum has an effect on campaigning irrespective of the electorate's behavior. Put differently, do the relationships between campaigning and political competition noted in Table 14–6 hold within each of the four electoral contexts? If so, it can be accepted that how councils are recruited, how strongly they are challenged, and how strongly the public is involved in leadership selection all have an impact on campaigning. If not, revisions in the assumptions guiding the inquiry are indicated.

Table 14–9 shows convincingly that in two electoral contexts—the permissive and the supportive—campaign effort is strongly associated with office contesting and closeness of the vote, the two indicators of conflict within the active stratum. These are the contexts, it should be recalled, which are both characterized by relatively little incumbent eviction but which differ in electoral participation.

It appears that a lively campaign ensues when there are many challengers or closely fought elections despite a low probability of evicting the incumbents. In this situation political differences and opposition are in themselves sufficient to generate active campaigning. Indeed, the very difficulty of displacing incumbents by election defeats calls forth increased campaign activity on the part of those who are dissatisfied with how the city is governed. What takes place is an intraelite conflict, with the electorate tending mostly to side with the "party" in office. The very low level of campaign effort in the permissive and, especially, the supportive contexts where there is relatively little conflict in the active stratum testifies to the political quiescence resulting from the absence of competitive elections. This quiescence is present even though large numbers of citizens may go to the polls, as is the case in the supportive context.

A very different pattern emerges in the discriminative and volatile electoral contexts. In cities with a discriminative electorate no differences in campaign effort are associated with increased challenges from within the active stratum. And in the volatile context the pattern is actually reversed. Much campaign effort occurs where there are comparatively few challengers and less closely fought elections. This reversal is especially significant for interpreting political competition and campaigning.

Table 14–9
Relationships Between Campaign Effort and Political Competition in Four Electoral Contexts

	Permissive			Supportive			Discriminative			Volatile		
	Low N=12	High N=11	ID*	Low N=8	High N=9	ID	Low N=10	High N=6	ID	Low N=11	High N=13	ID
Office contesting												
High campaign effort	33%	73%	+40%	12%	44%	+32%	50%	50%	0%	73%	54%	−19%
	Low N=12	High N=11	ID	Low N=8	High N=9	ID	Low N=10	High N=6	ID	Low N=11	High N=13	ID
Closeness of vote												
High campaign effort	33%	75%	+42%	20%	50%	+30%	50%	57%	+7%	88%	50%	−38%

* Index of difference: high minus low.

The volatile electoral context is characterized by relatively frequent electoral evictions and by high voter participation. The electorate intrudes forcefully into the leadership selection process. Such an electorate calls forth high levels of campaign effort, as one might expect. However, the campaign effort slackens off if there are numerous challengers and the probability of a close election. A reasonable though certainly *post hoc* explanation can be offered. Multiple candidacies per council opening, narrow margins of victory and defeat, high rates of eviction from office, and a large electorate combine in a manner producing great unpredictability. A council facing such conditions senses that a heavy investment of time and resources in campaigning will not, after all, make too much difference. There is an "iffy" quality about the electoral situation which contradicts the common sense assumption that well-conceived campaigns can spell the difference between victory and defeat.

Conclusion

The election campaign "stands between" the governors and the governed and thus helps in bridging the distance that characterizes the relationship. Although not empirically demonstrable, the notion of the campaign as a linkage mechanism led to consideration of how it fits into the sequence of activities to select councils that begins with recruitment and concludes with elections. As part and parcel of these constitutive processes, campaigns contribute to the linkages so necessary to democratic governance, for they deliberately involve the public in judging incumbent officeholders and evaluating prospective ones.

Two general findings are noteworthy. First, the effort that goes into campaigning is substantially affected by practices characteristic of other stages in the leadership selection process. For example, councils bring to their governing tasks habits acquired during earlier periods and resulting from previous experiences. These habits have a bearing on campaign activities: councils campaign differently depending on whether they are recruited from the auxiliary government or the civic leadership. Campaigning also differs depending on the competitive struggles going on within the active stratum. The campaign, in part, is the surface manifestation of differences of opinion and competing ambitions which regularly flow through the stratum supplying council personnel. The campaign is not an isolated political phenomenon.

The second general finding carries this conclusion a step further. An adequate explanation of campaigning as a linkage mechanism requires consideration of the electoral context as the indicator of the electorate's habitual behavior. The campaign is part of the ongoing interactions between the council and its publics. Prior political experiences and conflicts in the active stratum are related to campaigning differently, depending on how the citizenry constitutes itself as an electorate. The electoral context gives form and meaning to the linkages that connect the council and the community.

Part IV

Petitioning Processes as Linkages

INTRODUCTION

Democratic governance presumes that the affairs of the community are managed in accord with citizen preferences. Constitutive processes—political recruitment, campaigning, and elections—partly bridge the distance between governors and governed. But constitutive processes are not sufficient to reduce the distance that separates governors and governed.

While governors may be selected in ways that maximize public participation, even in a democracy they still stand apart once the selection has been made.[1] Though significant, the flurry of activity surrounding the election does not solve the long-range problem of linking choosers and chosen. When the excitement of election has dwindled, the governors once again retreat into the company of their peers and close advisors. A good deal of time elapses before either officeholders or members of the public again turn their attention to the question of who shall govern. Yet it is between elections that legislation is passed, statutes are written, taxes are raised, public monies are spent or misspent, commitments and

---

[1] See Heinz Eulau, "Changing Views of Representation," in Ithiel de Sola Pool, ed., *Contemporary Political Science: Toward Empirical Theory* (New York: McGraw-Hill, 1967), p. 80: ". . . I believe we must proceed from the behavioral assumption of a built-in difference between representative and represented—built-in in the sense that representation always involves a difference in status between representative and represented. And if this is so, a viable theory of democratic representation must be based on this assumption of an inevitable status difference rather than on the democratically pleasing, but false assumption of some basic similarity between representative and represented."

policies are made in the name of the community—in short, that governing occurs. The analyst of democratic governance is not content to know that the rules of democracy prevailed in the selection of governors; he wants to know whether the governed have access to their governors in the years intervening between elections.

Linkage can occur through the variety of activities usually summarized as petitioning or pressuring. The composition of the governing group may be settled for a time, but its decisions need not be taken for granted. Citizen-initiated activities making for petitioning—group lobbying and pressuring, letter writing, personal contacting between individuals, editorializing, demonstrating, attending meetings, and so forth—are opportunities for linking the council and its publics.

The interelection period also may be characterized by deliberate efforts on the governors' part to establish contact with the governed. Mass media and public meetings are available, though not always used, to explain programs and policies, usually with a view to attracting the support of the population. Councils, for example, often deplore the low level of political interest and information characteristic of their communities and devise various means to inform and involve the public. Each activity designed to mobilize public interest and attract support tends to link governors and governed.

Perhaps the most important factor in providing linkages between elections is the group life of the community. Certainly the group process has long been singled out for special attention. As aptly stated by Key, "In a regime characterized by official deference to public opinion and by adherence to the doctrine of freedom of association, private organizations may be regarded as links that connect the citizen and government."[2] Groups are said to aggregate diverse views and thus to strengthen the voice of any single citizen; they articulate to those in office the wants and wishes of those out of office. Officeholders, in turn, may use groups to mobilize public support. Moreover, groups are believed to shield citizens from the

---

[2] V. O. Key, *Public Opinion and American Democracy* (New York: Alfred A. Knopf, 1961), p. 500.

ever present threat of despotic, arbitrary rule and, at the same time, to protect governors from the pressures of diffuse mass sentiments.

Two distinct and familiar research traditions, each having to do with linkage processes, treat groups and political life. One tradition—primarily interested in pressure group activity and the role of groups within the established democratic ways of doing political business—stems from Bentley, Odegard, Herring, and others who seek to explain the relationship between group pressures and public policy. The other tradition—primarily interested in problems of state and society and in the part played by organizational life in facilitating and sustaining democratic rule—derives from theories of mass society and pluralism as expressed in the works of James Madison, de Tocqueville, Truman, and Kornhauser.[3] Though they are distinct theoretical traditions, much empirical research joins questions from each. For our purposes, both are relevant because they are concerned with how the group life of a community mediates between governors and governed.

The group approach to democratic politics emphasizes the double exchange occurring between the members of a group and its leaders, and between these group leaders and officeholders, especially legislators. Acting as lobbyists, group spokesmen transmit demands to officials and results back to citizens. The group approach takes as axiomatic that "group interests are the animating forces in the political process. The exercise of the power of governance consists in the promotion of group objectives regarded as legitimate, in the reconciliation and mediation of conflicting group ambitions, and in the restraint of group tendencies judged to be socially destructive."[4]

---

[3] For works in the pressure group tradition, see especially Arthur F. Bentley, *The Process of Government—A Study of Social Pressures* (Chicago: University of Chicago Press, 1908); Peter H. Odegard, *Pressure Politics: The Story of the Anti-Saloon League* (New York: Columbia University Press, 1928); and E. Pendleton Herring, *Group Representation Before Congress* (Baltimore: The Johns Hopkins Press, 1929). For works in the pluralism tradition, see especially James Madison, *The Federalist*, No. X; Alexis de Tocqueville, *Democracy in America* (New York: Alfred A. Knopf, 1945); David B. Truman, *The Governmental Process* (New York: Alfred A. Knopf, 1951); and William Kornhauser, *The Politics of Mass Society* (Glencoe, Ill.: The Free Press, 1959).

[4] V. O. Key, Jr., *Politics, Parties and Pressure Groups* (3rd ed.; New York: Thomas Y. Crowell Company, 1952), p. 23.

The organization of interests into more or less permanent political pressure groups has far-reaching implications for the linkage processes. As Key writes, "Pressure groups fill a gap in our formal political system by performing a function of representation beyond the capacities of representatives chosen by the voters in geographical districts." Because the elective principle does not adequately represent all special interests, organization is necessary so that citizens sharing a viewpoint will have spokesmen who "state their attitudes authoritatively before the government and the public."[5]

Key's formulation stresses that publics have two sets of representatives, those who are elected to office and those who represent special interests to the officeholders. The notion of a "dual representative system" is relevant to an understanding of linkages, especially those which relate to petitioning the governors rather than to selecting them.

The second research tradition emphasizes how an active group life can sustain a government democratic in form and benign in consequences. There are two components to this tradition. The first is specifically concerned with the role of groups in achieving accommodation of the different interests of the people. This perspective is well summarized by Salisbury: "The United States is a large and diverse nation with many different kinds of people holding many different values. The pursuit of these diverse values often occurs through the medium of interest groups which contend against one another for the influence and power to gain their values. The competition among so many groups moderates the claims and counterclaims by forcing compromise and bargaining. It disciplines the groups thereby, and they adjust and adapt to one another. If any sector of society is aggrieved, it may organize and seek redress through the bargaining among groups. Freedom for each group is thus maximized, goals are moderated, and social consensus is promoted."[6]

The other component emphasizes how associational activity in society mediates between the governed and the governors in a way that protects each from the excesses of the other. The excesses of the governors are found in aloofness, arbitrariness, and, finally,

---

[5] *Ibid.*, p. 152.
[6] Robert H. Salisbury, ed., *Interest Group Politics in America* (New York: Harper & Row, 1970), p. 2.

tyranny. The excesses of the governed are found in shifting mass moods, ill-informed and ill-formulated political viewpoints, unreasonable demands, sporadic spurts of activity, and, finally, social anomie. Tyranny on the one hand and anomie on the other are prevented only if the "space" between governed and governors is filled by an active group life. Groups monitor the behavior of governors and thus check their tendencies toward arbitrariness; groups also organize the political life of the governed and thus check their tendencies toward anomie.

The stress on groups as accommodating diverse interests, and the stress on organizations in political life as preventing mass society, share with the studies of pressure group activity a concern with linkage processes. Each research tradition recognizes the distance between governors and governed and each contains propositions about how this distance is bridged through group activities. Though our data do not allow investigating each of the many propositions contained in these traditions, the analysis does reflect relevant issues. From the pressure group literature, we derive hypotheses about the access of groups to the council and the conditions affecting differential access across the 82 communities. From the study of groups as accommodating diverse interests, we derive hypotheses about the diversity and intensity of group life. From mass society notions, we derive hypotheses about the role of groups in mediating the flow of demands from public to council and the role of groups in affecting how authority is exercised.

Group activities are not the only potential linkages in the interelection period. Citizens can contact councils in ways that are unrelated to elections or group-based activities. And councils have ways of approaching the public that do not involve recruitment, campaigning, or group mobilization. For instance, there is the role of spokesmen for particular sectors of the community, such as business interests, homeowners, minority groups, and so forth. By virtue of his effort to speak on behalf of such sectors, a spokesman is a liaison between the public and the council. An example is the lawyer who becomes a self-appointed watchdog for the interests of homeowners and who attends council meetings as well as sessions of the planning commission in order to speak on policies that affect homeowner interests. A spokesman might be a group leader, but this is not always the case; and his mode of operation is sufficiently different that he merits separate attention in considering the linkage processes.[7]

Spokesmen serve as more or less institutionalized links between the sector on whose behalf they speak and the council. In this context, "institutionalized" suggests that councils regularly turn to spokesmen for information about and interpretations of public sentiment, or at least the sentiment of particular sectors. However, this does not mean that spokesmen have direct influence over council policies. Furthermore, the sector in the community spoken for tends to rely on the spokesman for reports of council actions. The spokesman interprets council decisions and thus provides guidelines for seeing through to the implications of public policies.

This linkage role is theoretically suggestive in much the same way that the lobbying activity of groups is suggestive. Spokesmen are part of the dual representative system in that they represent the sentiments of selected citizen interests to officeholders. By thus increasing the way through which citizens contact councils and councils contact citizens, spokesmen help bridge the distance between governors and governed.

In addition to group activities and the role of spokesmen, there is the possibility of linkage through direct contact between council and public. Such direct contact, often of an informal sort, is particularly likely in the political units we are studying. Councilmen, unlike state and national legislators, live and work in the community they govern. Their children are in the same schools as are those of their constituents; their wives are in the same clubs as are those of their fellow citizens; and they themselves are involved in a network of nongovernmental activities, both of a social and a business sort, which involve citizens from throughout the com-

---

[7] Although we need not here be particularly interested in the motivation of spokesmen, we should note that they are often politically ambitious and use the spokesman role to create constituency support in anticipation of seeking elective office. And of course, some have pecuniary motives; being a spokesman for the business community creates contacts and publicizes one's own talents just as speaking on behalf of the homeowners makes known one's own skills and, especially important for the young lawyer, attracts clients. Some spokesmen simply appreciate the prestige which goes along with being "recognized" by both the council and interested members of the public.

munity. Direct contact between governors and governed is facilitated by the life-styles, business and professional associations, and
leisure-time activities of the councilmen. In this sense councils are
less set apart than are state and national legislatures.

Council meetings also provide opportunities for direct contact.
On the average, city councils meet biweekly; meetings are held in
public places and are well publicized, including prior announce-
ment of the agenda. Especially during times of community controversy, council meetings can attract as many as several hundred
citizens, some of whom participate by raising objections, hooting
or applauding decisions, and otherwise making their feelings
known.

The next four chapters continue the inquiry into linkage processes that result from the pressuring, petitioning, and contacting
activities of groups or individuals in the community as well as
from the informing and mobilizing activities of the council. Then,
in Chapter 19, linkages implicit in some of the council's and the
public's mutual perceptions and expectations will be treated from
the council's perspective.

Chapter 15

Governing and the Group Process

Publics behave politically in ways that make for a continuum. On one end of this continuum there are, in theory, no publics at all but only one public that is a single, undifferentiated whole acting as a collective political force. At the other end, the public is nothing more than discrete, individual citizens, each pursuing his interests independently of all other citizens. Neither "pure type" is likely to be found in the real world of contemporary democratic societies. Rather, it is more realistic to think of the community as being composed of many publics, more or less differentiated and organized and more or less inclined to formulate political goals and to act through political means.

Certainly the cities of the San Francisco Bay region have publics that are more or less organized and more or less politically active. They range from highly mobilized publics like those organized by merchant associations or neighborhood clubs to highly inert and fractionated publics like consumers or welfare recipients. The fact that publics are "more or less" organized or organizable, "more or less" politically efficacious or active, is critical to a range of factors that give city governance its distinctive characteristics.

City politics are influenced by the extent, variety, traits, and activity levels of organized political interests, and the variations in these characteristics give the politics of cities a distinct imprint. Although some publics and interests are effectively barred from participation in the political process, making the epigram "he who says politics, says groups"[1] somewhat dubious, the forms and consequences of a community's group life constitute an important social environment in which the city council orients itself to action and policy.

The Group Life of Cities

The number of groups active in city affairs is an important indicator of a community's group life. A very different governing process ensues when the city has numerous active organizations than when it has few. The difference can be sensed in the following quotations from interviews in two cities: "We have ninety-six service organizations, including the senior citizens. They not only ask for things, but volunteer services and money. Groups are a real prime part of the community. A portion of the budget for the Chamber of Commerce is underwritten by the council." "There are no groups active here, except maybe the Chamber of Commerce in a very, very minor way. There are no groups which appear before the council. If things go o.k. in a small town, no groups care. They just sit at home. We haven't had any organizations involved in our problems."

The sheer number of groups active in a city is likely to affect the governing process differently because it engenders a greater variety of *types* of active groups. Tautological though this may sound, it is possible to distinguish between the number and variety of groups. There can be many groups of the same type, as when a city has every known kind of service club but few other types of

---

[1] Arthur F. Bentley, in his classic *The Process of Government—A Study of Social Pressures* (Chicago: University of Chicago Press, 1908), p. 208, takes nearly this unqualified a position: "When the groups are adequately stated, everything is stated. When I say everything I mean everything. The complete description would mean the complete science in the study of social phenomena. . . ." Few students of the group process would today take such an extreme position. For a representative list of studies, see those noted in footnote 3 of the Introduction to Part IV. Recent and useful collections can be found in Betty H. Zisk, ed., *American Political Interest Groups: Readings in Theory and Research* (Belmont, Calif.: Wadsworth Publishing Company, 1969); and Robert H. Salisbury, ed., *Interest Group Politics in America* (New York: Harper & Row, 1970).

Table 15–1
Relationship Between Number and Variety
of Groups Active in City Affairs*

	Number of Active Groups	
Variety of groups*	Relatively few N = 42	Relatively many N = 40
One	43%	15%
Two	24	28
Three	24	22
Four or more	9	35
	100%	100%

* The types of groups into which those named were classed appear in Table 15–2. For the question on which the data are based, see Appendix C, Item E.

organization; or there can be only a few groups but each of distinct type. As Table 15–1 shows, the number and variety of groups reported by councils as active in their cities covary significantly.[2]

The covariation between the number and variety of politically active groups is significant because it affects the degree to which citizen preferences are articulated and brought to the council's attention. If, for instance, only the Downtown Merchants Association and the Chamber of Commerce are politically active, only a small segment of the citizenry has its viewpoint expressed through organizations. This segment, then, being restricted to the commercial class of white, middle- and upper-middle-class citizens, is more

---

[2] The two measures used in Table 15–1 come from wholly different questions in the interview. The measure of group activity comes from a count of groups which are reported to appear before the council and to take an active role in community affairs. See Appendix C, Question 45. The measure of variety of groups comes from a checklist item asking each councilman whether nine different types of groups (see Table 15–2 for a list) have active membership. This measure, then, does not inquire whether these groups appear before the council, or even whether the groups are involved in community affairs. It is a reasonable assumption, and one we make in the analysis, that if councils report particular types of groups to have active memberships, they are telling us something about whether these groups are active in local matters. See Appendix C, Item E.

effectively linked to the council than are other publics. If only trade unions are active, then the business and commercial interests lack an organizational channel. Only in the city with active civic groups, merchant associations, labor organizations, minority groups, and homeowners' groups is the full range of citizen wishes brought to bear on the city's decision-making process between elections. The number and variety of groups active in the community are indirect measures of the degree to which group spokesmen are available to represent different publics before the council.

There is another reason for attention to the covariation between the absolute number and the variety of types of groups. Three alternatives involving the activity level of groups are possible. First, the activity level of each type varies positively with the activity level of all or most other types of group. Organizational life begets organizational life. Second, the activity levels of different types of group are negatively related. Certain types of groups preempt the organizational space of the community. Depending on the pattern of negative association, this might mean that considerable activity by one group, such as a Chamber of Commerce, would render the activity of another, like a merchant association, superfluous; or it might mean that one type of group, like a civic association, would prevent another type, such as a reform club, from asserting itself in public life. And third, there is no relationship among the activity levels of different types of groups. This suggests that groups form and grow assertive, or fail to, for reasons altogether independent of what is happening elsewhere in the community's organizational environment. Table 15–2 presents the pertinent data.

It is the first alternative that prevails in Bay Area cities. Of 36 possible relationships among group-type activity levels, the coefficients for 33 are positive and range from at least moderate to very strong. Only three are weak or near-zero, and there is no negative correlation. Not only do the number and variety of groups covary, but both vary with the intensity of group life. For this reason, the *number* of active groups will be used in the following analysis as a stand-in indicator for the diversity and intensity of group life as well.

We expect group activity to vary significantly with the complex-

Table 15-2
Correlation Coefficients for Relationships Among Activity Levels of Nine Types of Groups

Type group	Civic	Chamber of Commerce	Reform/protest	Unions	Service clubs	Merchant associations	Political party	Garden clubs, library association
Homeowner groups and neighborhood associations	.36	.05	.32	.41	.01	.12	.52	.35
General civic affairs groups like League of Women Voters, Civic League		.44	.48	.62	.39	.47	.67	.69
Chamber of Commerce or Jaycees			.86	.74	.58	.72	.58	.27
Reform/protest groups				.87	.29	.55	.71	.38
Trade unions					.31	.58	.87	.53
Service clubs like Kiwanis or Rotary						.55	.41	.41
Merchant associations							.70	.40
Political party clubs or organizations								.69

ity and heterogeneity of the urban environment. A large city contains a more diverse universe of publics than a small city. But linkages between these publics and the council will be stronger and more effective if organized groups are more, rather than less, active. As Table 15–3 shows, the city's presumed social pluralism, measured by city size, is systematically related to and finds expression in the activity levels reported by councils for various types of groups.

These results can be variously interpreted. First, there is a statistical interpretation. The larger the population in absolute terms, the more numerous is the active stratum from which most organizations draw their membership. It is the critical mass of the large city that facilitates the formation of many diverse groups. The larger city's social pluralism—ethnic heterogeneity, religious diversity, occupational stratification, variety of interests, and so on—creates the conditions giving rise to extensive organizational activity.

Table 15–3
Relationships Between Group Activity Levels
and City Size

Councils reporting moderate to high activity for:	City Size			Total N = 82
	Large N = 17	Medium N = 33	Small N = 34	
Chamber of Commerce, Jaycees	94%	67%	41%	62%
Homeowner, neighborhood groups	76	50	41	51
Civic affairs groups	88	42	31	48
Merchant associations	65	54	31	48
Service clubs	41	45	41	43
Garden clubs, library association	35	33	28	32
Reform/protest groups	47	12	3	16
Political party clubs	18	15	6	12
Trade unions	23	12	3	11

Second, with an increase in population size come complex community problems that become politically relevant and call for governmental response. The greater number and variety of community problems in the larger city call forth a greater number and variety of organized interests. Social and economic growth accompanying urban development activates organizations intent on protecting vested interests, such as homeowner groups which seek to resist commercial and industrial expansion; or it mobilizes groups determined to shape city policies, such as civic clubs concerned that adequate services or amenities be provided for an expanding population.

The politization of the city's group life as it grows in population involves the articulation and aggregation of interests that, in the absence of organizations, would be too diffuse to have an impact on local governance. The large city makes it difficult for governors and governed to meet face-to-face. Organizations serve as channels of communication that link representatives and represented. A complex and extensive layer of organizations between the various publics and the governing body contributes to the ability of citizens to speak out and of councils to explain.

Whatever the merit of these interpretations, the relationship between city size and group activity is likely to have consequences for council conduct and public policy. The significance of sheer size is reinforced if, as in Table 15–4, the citizenry's wealth is taken into account as well. Wealth also has some influence on the activity level of the various types of groups, but not the same uniform impact. Some groups are more active in poorer communities, as are, for instance, the reform groups, service clubs, and trade unions. Other groups become more active in wealthier cities, as do homeowner associations and garden clubs. And there are group types which differ in their activity level depending on the wealth of the community when they are in small but not in large cities, as is illustrated by the civic groups.

Service clubs, on the one hand, and garden clubs and similar associations, on the other, are unaffected in their activity level by city size (see Table 15–3) but are clearly affected by community wealth. Service clubs are more active in the poorer cities, regardless of size. It may be that they play a role in the poorer communities

Table 15–4
Activity Levels of Different Types of Groups,
by City Size and Wealth

Proportion of councils reporting moderate to high activity of:	Small Cities		Large Cities	
	Poor N = 21	Wealthy N = 20	Poor N = 19	Wealthy N = 22
Chamber of Commerce	67%	30%	79%	73%
Homeowner, neighborhood groups	33	60	42	68
Civic affairs groups	10	50	68	64
Merchant associations	43	20	68	59
Service clubs	57	25	53	36
Garden clubs, library association	14	45	21	46
Reform/protest groups	5	0	42	18
Political party clubs	5	15	21	9
Trade unions	5	0	32	9
Summary index of general group activity*	14	35	68	64

* Additive index of groups listed in table. See Appendix B15.1.

that in wealthier cities is played by civic groups or homeowner associations. On the national scale, the membership of the Elks, Lions, or Rotary is middle class; in the poorer communities with a large working class, these clubs are likely to be composed of the local equivalent of the upper class. The relationship between city size and activity level is reversed in the case of garden clubs, library associations, and similar leisure-time groups. While city size is not related to their activity level, they are more likely to be active in wealthy than in poor cities. This type of organization tends to satisfy the needs and interests of housewives who are not occupationally employed, who have children of school age and a special stake in the community's cultural life.

The summary index of general group activity reported in Table 15–4 shows the importance of population size for level of group activity compared to wealth. Although the level is higher in the small, wealthy cities than in the small, poor ones, it is nearly twice as great in the large, poor cities than in the small, wealthy cities. Three conclusions can be drawn: first, the larger the city, the greater is its group activity level; second, wider distribution of wealth tends to increase group activity in the smaller, but not in the larger, city; and third, if an increase occurs as a result of a different distribution of social and economic resources among the citizens, different types of groups increase their activities.

More generally, governing in the large city is much more likely to be affected by an intermediate layer of organizational activity which links council and citizens than is governing in the small city. However, additional evidence is required to determine just how the availability of organizations as linkages between council and public does affect the governing process.

Organizational activity, Table 15–2 suggested, begets organizational activity. The consistency of the relationship between the activity level of one type of group and that of another suggests an expanding universe of group activities. There is not a limited amount of space for organized group activity to fill. Greater activity by one type of group does not reduce the activity levels of other types; on the contrary, different types of groups tend to increase their activity levels supplementarily. But the relationship might differ in small and large cities for the simple reason that in small cities the pool of persons who can be active is more limited than it is in large cities.

Table 15–5, comparing the activity levels of various pairs of group types in small and large cities, shows that in most instances the activity levels are more independent of each other in small cities and, in two cases, are negatively related.[3] No definitive interpretation is possible, but the hypothesis of the "limited pool" is intuitively persuasive. The organizational types presented in Table 15–5 tend to draw their members from the same sectors of the

[3] Pairs appearing in Table 15–5 are those for which the difference in gamma is .40 or greater between small and large cities.

Table 15–5

Correlation Coefficients for Relationships
Between Various Active Group Types
in Small and Large Cities

Relationship of activity levels between:	Small cities N = 41	Large cities N = 41
Civic affairs and homeowner groups	.13	.55
Chamber of Commerce and homeowner groups	—.22	.43
Merchant associations and homeowner groups	—.38	.20
Political clubs and home- owner groups	.28	.81
Civic affairs groups and Chamber of Commerce	.15	.68
Reform and civic affairs groups	.10	.49
Service clubs and civic affairs groups	.28	.61
Chamber of Commerce and merchant associations	.85	.18
Reform groups and merchant associations	.65	—.01

population: the middle- and upper-middle-classes supply the members and officers for civic groups, neighborhood associations, political clubs, the Chamber of Commerce, and so on. High levels of activity by each one of these types of group are difficult to sustain if the pool of potential members is relatively small. Moreover, in the smaller and less differentiated city it may be easier for one type of group, say a civic league, to represent the range of interests that in a larger city would produce a more differentiated group life.

As Table 15–5 also shows, activity levels for two pairs of group types are more strongly associated in small cities than in large cities. One of the pairs is the combination of reform groups and merchant associations—both of which types are highly active in large cities. But while these types are independent in level of activity in the large cities, in small cities the possibility of conflict between them may make for a relationship. For instance, an active merchant association, especially if it is aggressively promoting downtown business interests, can become the occasion for citizen protest groups to form and assert themselves around the issue of protecting the community from further commercial development.[4]

The two reversals notwithstanding, the strongest pattern is for the activity levels of various types of groups to be much less inter-dependent in the simple small-town environment than in the more complex big-city environment. If organized political action begets organized political action, this is more likely to be the case where the population base for membership recruitment is larger and where urban complexity makes for group activation.

The Council Views Its Publics

Linking governors and governed through interest groups and their spokesman is not possible on a one-way street. The community's group life may be rich in diverse and active organizations that seek to influence the course of public affairs; but unless the council is receptive to the articulation of group interests by group spokesmen and willing to utilize groups in the governing process, neither the incidence nor activity of groups will have much of an impact on council conduct and policy.[5]

---

[4] The other pair which reverses the general pattern shown in Table 15-5 is the Chamber of Commerce and merchant association coefficient, showing a gamma of .85 in the small community and .18 in the larger community. There is no ready explanation for this and we report it for whatever it may be worth.
[5] The literature on interest groups has paid little attention to the views that persons holding elected office take toward the group process. But see John C. Wahlke, Heinz Eulau, William Buchanan, and Leroy C. Ferguson, *The Legislative System* (New York: John Wiley and Sons, 1962), Chapter 14; Harmon Zeigler and Michael Baer, *Lobbying: Interaction and Influence in American State Legislatures* (Belmont, Calif.: Wadsworth Publishing Company, 1969); and Roger H. Davidson, *The Role of the Congressman* (New York: Pegasus, 1969), Chapter 5.

Councils differ markedly in how they evaluate the activity of groups in the community's political life. Some see group expression as an important and appropriate part of public life. "It is the only way a democracy can work," testified one. Groups "give the council a better understanding of what people want. People have spokesmen in these groups, they are a go-between." Some councils "wish there were more organized representation going on" and complain about how difficult it is "to know what the people want." Councils often provide very specific reasons for their favorable view of groups: "We appreciate any help we can get. The groups have a lot of facts and are interested in what the council is doing or can do for them." Group spokesmen help councils anticipate likely public response: "We like to know about any disagreements that may be coming up ahead of time."

But not all councils speak so favorably. At times they distinguish "pressure" from "information" groups and welcome the latter but reject the former. Moreover, groups can be divisive: "They should not attempt to divide the council and express opinions independently." They also "distort, and place a burden on the functioning of the council." Some councils actively dissuade groups from coming before them, though such a position is usually couched in cautious language which reaffirms the right of all citizens to be heard. Nevertheless, since "groups are too often emotional, not factual," it is important that they not be allowed to change public policies. The most frequent complaint has to do with the parochialism of groups, their "limited viewpoint" and indifference to the public welfare. The difficulty with paying too much attention to groups is "that there are other sides which aren't heard. We have to be concerned about the non-represented." Of course, among those councils which take a dim view of the group process are some which distinguish between cooperative and obstructive groups. "Do you mean the good or bad groups? The psychotic groups we are not interested in. They create turmoil just for their own glory."

These comments illustrate some of the wide differences in council attitudes toward the group process as a political phenomenon. For the purpose of analysis, councils are separated into those more favorable and those less favorable toward the efforts of groups to participate in the governing of cities.[6] Although the focus is primarily on the evaluative stance of the council as an independent variable, some of the features of the city's group life may predispose the council to look with more or less favor on groups voicing political views or seeking to influence public policy. The amount of group activity alone may affect the council's judgment of the group process as harmful or beneficent.

Table 15–6 presents the relationships between the council's general orientation toward groups and two measures of group activity. The first, called "group petitioning," is constructed from a count of the number of groups reported to be active in public affairs and to appear before the council to express their views. It is a direct measure of whether many or few groups present claims on community resources and petition the council for specific programs. The second measure, termed "general associational activity," was introduced in connection with Table 15–2 and is computed from the activity level of the nine types of group listed there. This measure indicates the extent to which the city is characterized by a rich and varied group life; it does not specifically reveal whether groups contact or otherwise petition the council.[7]

There is a weak tendency for councils to be more favorably disposed toward groups where there is greater petitioning activity, but the extent of general associational activity is not related to council judgment of the group process. But these relationships may be spurious because the nature of the urban environment, already noted as relevant, is ignored. They are controlled, therefore, in Parts B and C of Table 15–6, by city size. The relationship between group petitioning and council attitude is nearly identical in small and large cities. The weak though positive relationship results from the tendency of councils to be in contact with more groups when they are favorably inclined toward them. The nature of the urban environment does not alter the pattern.

---

[6] For the question on which the measure is based, see Appendix C, Question 46.2.

[7] See note 2. Of course the two measures are related; the gamma is .49, since petitioning activity cannot take place in the absence of at least some active groups in the community. Nevertheless, there is a distinction to be made, and the somewhat less than strong association confirms this.

Table 15–6
Relationships Among Council Attitudes Toward Groups,
Group Petitioning, and General Associational Activity,
Uncontrolled and Controlled by City Size

Part A	Group Petitioning		Associational Activity	
Council attitude toward group activity	Low N = 42	High N = 40	Low N = 45	High N = 37
Unfavorable	57%	48%	53%	51%
Favorable	43	52	47	49
	100%	100%	100%	100%
Gamma =	.19		.04	

Part B				
Group Petitioning	Small Cities		Large Cities	
Council attitude toward group activity	Low N = 26	High N = 15	Low N = 11	High N = 25
Unfavorable	58%	47%	56%	48%
Favorable	42	53	44	52
	100%	100%	100%	100%
Gamma =	.22		.16	

Part C				
Associational Activity	Small Cities		Large Cities	
Council attitude toward group activity	Low N = 31	High N = 10	Low N = 14	High N = 27
Unfavorable	48%	70%	64%	44%
Favorable	52	30	36	56
	100%	100%	100%	100%
Gamma =	−.43		.38	

By way of contrast, the random zero-order relationship between
favorability to groups and general associational group activity is
clearly spurious. When it is controlled by city size, it is evident
that too much activity leads to disapproval of the group process

by councils in the smaller cities, whereas too little activity leads to disapproval of the group process by the councils governing in the larger cities. In the latter, the higher the level of general associational activity, the more favorably inclined are councils toward groups.

The contrary relationships between general associational activity and council attitude toward groups tend to confirm some themes that can be culled from the pluralist interpretation of American politics. This interpretation stresses the existence and consequences of an intermediate organizational layer between individual citizens and their leaders. A strong, varied pluralism of groups and associations protects the community from the specter of "mass society" in which "elites and non-elites are directly accessible to one another by virtue of the weakness of groups capable of mediating between them."[8] Social pluralism is prevalent in the more, rather than the less, complex urban environment. No wonder, then, from the pluralist perspective, that in the larger cities councils look favorably on the greater activity and wider variety of groups. Councils in the larger cities will feel cushioned from the diffuse individual demands and complaints if a strong and active interest-group system intervenes between the council and its publics. In the small cities, however, councils are less favorable if group activity becomes too intense and varied, perhaps because there is less need for groups to link the governors and the governed. Councils in the smaller cities may take a dim view of the political agitation that a rich and varied life can bring about. The stable presence of a Chamber of Commerce or of service clubs whose behavior is predictable does not cause concern; but the more general activity of homeowner groups, reform organizations, civic improvement associations, and so on means that interests of a wider range seek access to the council. They are felt to be a nuisance. What is experienced and interpreted as desirable and beneficial in the more complex context of the large city is viewed as harassing in the simpler context of the small city.

In general, then, how group activity is evaluated is differentially affected by its extent and intensity in small and large cities. Hy-

---

[8] William Kornhauser, *The Politics of Mass Society* (Glencoe, Ill.: The Free Press, 1959), p. 228.

potheses concerning the politics of mass society are relevant in the more complex urban setting, as they should be; they are less germane in the simpler environment of the small city.

However, the actual amount of group activity does not exhaust what is worth knowing about the conditions leading councils either to favor or to disapprove of the active presence of interest groups in the governing process. The quest to account for differences in evaluation is continued in the next chapter; and we then ask how council evaluations affect the linkage process established by group life.

Chapter 16

Group Influence
and Council Response

If, as Lasswell put it, "the study of politics is the study of influence and the influential,"[1] inquiry turns to the relationship between group influence and council response as the politically most salient question that one can ask in this connection.

Council Attitudes and Group Influence

After reporting on the groups perceived as active and influential in city affairs, councils were asked: "What are the main reasons for their influence?"[2] Three reasons were given. First, there are the resources and strengths of the group. A civic improvement association in one community is seen as influential "because of their numbers, this makes them an effective pressure group."[3] In another city, Rotary has influence because "they give money at

---

[1] Harold D. Lasswell, *Politics: Who Gets What, When, How* (1936), in *The Political Writings of Harold D. Lasswell* (Glencoe, Ill.: The Free Press, 1951), p. 295.

[2] For the question, see Appendix C, Question 45.B.

[3] Although we occasionally speak of "influence," what is being reported is, of course, "perceived influence." Convenience of expression makes us occasionally drop the qualification. We are equally aware of the fact that asking people about influence does not yield a measure of "real influence"—if real influence is measurable at all. If people see groups as influential, and if there is reasonable consensus to this effect, influence may be a consequence of the perception.

election time to their friends who are running." Organizations which can produce voting blocs are often cited as influential. So also are those groups to which councilmen belong. Thus voting strength, cohesion, financial support, overlapping membership with the council, and ability to involve their members in community action are viewed as resources making for group influence.

A second explanation is related to the stake in the community of different groups. This reason was most frequently given in connection with the Chamber of Commerce and merchant associations. A property owners' association is seen as influential because "they represent a very heavy investment here," or the Chamber is deferred to because "it represents the merchants in town with whom we're in close partnership." In another community it is again the Chamber which is singled out for special attention, though the rationale is voiced somewhat differently. "The Chamber is the most important. Their membership is representative of most of the voters—they represent a geographic and socioeconomic cross-section." And in yet another city the Chamber "is a broad cross-section of the community" and hence is listened to. The last two quotations are suggestive of a mobilization of bias; to the extent that councils consider such a specialized group as the Chamber of Commerce as "broadly representative," it is plausible why certain sectors of the community may find it difficult to gain an audience.

The third explanation has broadly to do with respect for the group as a reason for its influence. Groups which have active memberships, which know the facts about community issues, which have excellent leadership, which work for the good of the community, and so forth are cited as being influential. One council defers to the local improvement association because "it is made up of the senior citizens and the active citizens within the city. The city actually originated from the association—so we listen very carefully when they promote something. Generally it is them helping us—they seldom ask for anything." This sentiment is voiced often when respect for the group is cited as justifying its influence; such groups collaborate with the council rather than act as adversaries. The Lion's Club is influential in the governing process because "of their accomplishments toward community betterments —tree planting, beaches, etc. If they did not do it, it would cost the city money." Here is a private organization actually taking over something the council might do, gaining respect for its actions, and, understandably, being cited as influential in the community.

Part A of Table 16–1 shows that the city in which groups are seen as influential because of their objective resources is as likely as not to have a council which is favorably disposed toward the group process. But if groups are seen as influential because they have a stake in the community or are generally respected, councils respond favorably to their participation in the governing process.

The relationship between group influence and council response is likely to be affected by the prevailing level of general group activity. Both the amount of group activity and group characteristics can alter the council's evaluation of the group process. Part B of Table 16–1 shows that this is the case. If only a few groups are active, their strength is evidently a cause for council discomfort. A few groups with political resources make the council look with less favor on group involvement in local governance. Where many different types of groups are active, however, the same resource base leads to a more positive evaluation of the group process. In this situation, it is not implausible to assume, groups balance other groups—in the classic veto group politics described by Riesman, Galbraith, and others.[4] But in the former case, it is more likely that a few groups with considerable political resources may effectively oppose council policies. Instead of being able to use groups and their resources in the governing process, councils will have to be cautious that they do not offend the one or two dominant organizations in the community.

This interpretation is supported by the changes in the relationship between favorable attitudes and respect felt for influential groups. A low level of organizational activity greatly accelerates the positive association between looking with favor on the group process and seeing influential groups as meriting respect. Groups influential because they are respected, it will be recalled, are those cooperating with the council in community projects. Such groups

---

[4] See David Riesman, *The Lonely Crowd* (New Haven: Yale University Press, 1950), Chapter XI; and John Kenneth Galbraith, *American Capitalism: The Concept of Countervailing Power* (Boston: Houghton Mifflin, 1952).

Table 16–1
Relationships Between Council Attitude Toward Groups
and the Perceived Bases of Their Influence
in the Governing Process, Uncontrolled and Controlled
by Associational Activity

	Reasons for Influence					
Part A Council attitude toward group activity	Objective resources		Stake in community		General respect	
	No N = 46	Yes N = 36	No N = 41	Yes N = 41	No N = 42	Yes N = 40
Unfavorable	52%	53%	61%	44%	62%	42%
Favorable	48	47	39	56	38	58
	100%	100%	100%	100%	100%	100%
Gamma =	.01		.33		.37	

	General Associational Activity			
Part B	Low		High	
Objective resources Council attitude	No N = 29	Yes N = 16	No N = 17	Yes N = 20
Unfavorable	48%	62%	59%	45%
Favorable	52	38	41	55
	100%	100%	100%	100%
Gamma =	−.28		.27	
Stake in community Council attitude	No N = 22	Yes N = 23	No N = 19	Yes N = 18
Unfavorable	59%	48%	63%	39%
Favorable	41	52	37	61
	100%	100%	100%	100%
Gamma =	.22		.46	
General respect Council attitude	No N = 25	Yes N = 20	No N = 17	Yes N = 20
Unfavorable	68%	35%	53%	50%
Favorable	32	65	47	50
	100%	100%	100%	100%
Gamma =	.60		.06	

can serve as an auxiliary arm of the government, as in cases where the council subsidizes programs of the Chamber of Commerce. If organizational activity is carried out by very few groups, and these groups tend to be cooperative, councils favor the group process. This condition reverses the case where there are just a few groups active; but those which are influential are so because they have political muscle. The former condition should lead to a collaborative arrangement; the latter, to an adversary one.

Both the amount of group activity and the nature of that activity affect the council's disposition toward group politics in the legislative process. Observers of legislative behavior, particularly exponents of the group process approach, point out that groups are important to legislatures because group spokesmen and lobbyists provide much-needed information and advice. Council comments cited earlier lend anecdotal support to this assertion. If correct, then legislatures which do view groups as usual sources of information and advice will look with favor upon their political activities. Table 16–2 confirms this to be the case for the city councils.

Again, the complexity of the urban environment is likely to affect council dispositions toward the group process. In small cities, Part B of Table 16–2 shows, the results are rather inconclusive. However, in the large cities the relationships between whether groups are seen as useful informants or advisors and council attitude toward them is strong. The relationships are interdependent. Useful groups probably benefit from favorable council attitudes; and councils finding groups useful are favorable. Councils unfavorably disposed toward the group process are those governing a large population without benefit of reliable information and advice from group spokesmen. They may feel that an important, even desirable, partner in governance has let them down. Governing the large city is difficult under the best of circumstances; it is a task made only the more difficult if community groups, by failing to give information and advice, also fail to provide much-needed links between governors and governed.[5]

---

[5] When group petitioning and general associational activity are introduced as controls, the zero-order correlation between usefulness and favorability remains unchanged. This further confirms that the sheer difficulty of managing the affairs of the larger community is what contributes to the pattern in Table 16–2.

Table 16–2

Relationships Between Council Attitude Toward Groups
and the Perception of Groups as Sources
of Information or Advice, with and without City Size as Control

	Groups Are Important as			
Part A	Information source		Source of advice	
Council attitude toward group activity	No N = 39	Yes N = 43	No N = 32	Yes N = 50
Unfavorable	64%	42%	59%	48%
Favorable	36	58	41	52
	100%	100%	100%	100%
Gamma =		.42		.22

Part B	Small Cities				Large Cities			
Council attitude toward group activity	Information		Advice		Information		Advice	
	No N = 21	Yes N = 20	No N = 16	Yes N = 25	No N = 18	Yes N = 23	No N = 16	Yes N = 25
Unfavorable	57%	50%	44%	60%	72%	35%	75%	36%
Favorable	43	50	56	40	28	65	25	64
	100%	100%	100%	100%	100%	100%	100%	100%
Gamma =	.14		−.32		.66		.68	

Three generalizations are now possible. First, there is a correspondence between the number, the variety, and the types of organizations active in community affairs and the size of the city. Although hardly unexpected, this finding is not without importance in understanding variations in how governors relate to, and represent, the governed. The links connecting citizens and officials are more likely to be formal organizations as the ratio of citizens to officials increases. What difference this makes to the general governing process will be explored later.

Second, city size and the extent of group activity are related in a manner that affects the probability of councils being favorably disposed toward the group process. The council tends to be less favorable in the small city if there is too much organizational activity and less favorable in the large city if there is too little.

Finally, in addition to city size and extent of organizational activity, the characteristics of groups affect whether councils view the group process favorably or not. The reasons why groups are seen as influential and the usefulness of the information and advice provided by groups can affect whether councils welcome the involvement of groups in the governing process.

These generalizations provide the necessary background for examining the critical problem of group access. Under what conditions will legislatures facilitate the access of groups? Under what conditions will they deliberately mobilize group support for legislative programs?

Facilitating the Group Process

Group access varies with group characteristics—their numerical strength, their economic resources, the effectiveness of their leaders, the persuasive skill of their spokesmen, and so on.[6] By comparing different groups in these terms, it is possible to explain their success or failure in securing access and affecting legislation. In turn, legislatures will differ in the degree to which they facilitate access to interest groups and their spokesmen.

Many councils follow an open door policy and welcome expressions of political interest and policy preference from the various groups in the community. A typical response to the question of whether councils should make it easy for groups to contact them is as follows:[7] "If a citizen or groups want to contact, they should have easy access either in or out of council meetings." For some, it is a matter of principle to be available: "I am their representative. It is why I am elected to office." Others are available because there are political benefits to be gained: "It keeps interest in groups up by listening to them. It helps us get information, too.

---

[6] See especially David B. Truman, *The Governmental Process* (New York: Alfred A. Knopf, 1951).

[7] For the question, see Appendix C, Question 46.3.

It helps keep up the contact of the city with the council." For still others, it is a calculation of the political costs to be paid if groups are not given access: "Being a politician you run into problems if you avoid influential groups."

Not all councils are so accessible, however. Some only reluctantly make themselves available, as, for instance, the council which "doesn't advertise that we want to hear from them," or the councils which are available if there "really is a problem" but which in general do not favor making group access too easy. Of course, there are also councils which actively avoid groups, either because they feel the expression of group opinion to be unnecessary or because they have learned to distrust the advice and information provided by group spokesmen. As one outspoken critic of the group process put it, "First thing you know they'd have you twenty-four hours a day listening to a lot of nonsense"; he goes on to ask, "If you cannot make decisions on your own, why are you there?"

Councils favorably disposed toward groups should facilitate their access. Part A of Table 16–3 shows this to be the case, and the relationship is strong. Moreover, as Part B shows, it remains basically the same in small and large cities, though it is stronger in the latter than in the former; it is the same whether a few groups or many are actively petitioning the council; and it is the same whether general organizational activity is limited or extensive. How councils, and presumably legislatures generally, evaluate the group process affects their accessibility independently of the number of groups seeking access and the intensity of their activity.

There remains the possibility that a group's characteristics affect its access independently of council attitudes toward the group process. Part C of Table 16–3 is, therefore, an indirect test of the hypothesis that group attributes rather than council attitudes determine the degree of access granted groups.[8] However, the table

---

[8] The test is indirect because specific groups are not being compared; we compare cities where influential groups are characterized as having resources, a stake in the community, or respect. The relationship between evaluation and access was also controlled by the perceived usefulness of groups—that is, whether they provide information and advice to the council. Again the zero-order pattern remained stable even though we varied how useful groups are to the council (data not presented).

Table 16–3
Correlation Coefficients for Relationships
Between Attitude Toward Groups and Council Access Facilitation,
Controlled by City Size, Group Petitioning,
General Associational Activity, and Reasons for Group Influence

Part A	Attitude Toward Group Process	
Council facilitates group access	Unfavorable N = 43	Favorable N = 39
Less	58%	28%
More	42	72
Gamma = .56	100%	100%

Part B

Relationship between council attitude and access facilitation in:	Gamma
Small cities (N = 41)	.44
Large cities (N = 41)	.66
Cities with little group petitioning (N = 42)	.54
Cities with much group petitioning (N = 40)	.56
Cities with low associational activity (N = 45)	.56
Cities with high associational activity (N = 37)	.56

Part C

Relationship between council attitude and access facilitation according to reasons for influence in:	
Cities where objective resources not stressed (N = 46)	.63
Cities where objective resources are stressed (N = 36)	.46
Cities where community stakes not stressed (N = 41)	.47
Cities where community stakes are stressed (N = 41)	.71
Cities where general respect not stressed (N = 42)	.56
Cities where general respect is stressed (N = 40)	.52

shows that controlling for group characteristics does not alter the direction or the general strength of the association between councils' evaluations of the group process and their readiness to facilitate group access. Influential groups in the city may be viewed as having political muscle or not, as having a stake in local issues or not, as meriting respect or not. But variations in these conditions do not affect the access of groups nearly as much as the disposition of the council toward them.[9]

The stability of the basic association between the disposition of councils toward the group process and the degree to which they facilitate group access is remarkable. This confirms the importance of the legislature's evaluation in any attempt to explore group politics. It is insufficient to measure only group attributes—their numbers, organizational unity, leadership skills, and so on—if the research task is to describe the conditions which make for accessibility. The significance of Table 16–3 is underscored if another dimension of the group process is considered—whether councils deliberately foster the active involvement of groups in the governing process.

Group Activation for Governance

One of the biases in democratic theorizing is a preoccupation with the conditions under which citizen control of or access to political leadership are established and a corresponding disinterest in the processes by which the leadership mobilizes and involves the public. Thus the assumption is normally made that groups become politically active if and when *they* perceive that there are clear benefits to be gained and when *they* feel it is necessary to establish linkages with the governors. But this is a misleading assumption, or at least it disguises an important aspect of group politics. Groups do not always become active on their own initiative; they may be drawn into the political process by the legislature itself.

This is the case with Bay Area city councils. One council, which lists nearly a dozen influential groups in the community, reports that "We call on all these groups when we have a selling job to do in the city and we want to promote something." This, then, is

---

[9] This is consistent with findings reported in a study which interviewed lobbyists as well as legislators: "Legislators are more likely to accept interaction with lobbyists toward whom they have a more favorable attitude." Harmon Zeigler and Michael Baer, *Lobbying: Interaction and Influence in American State Legislatures* (Belmont, Calif: Wadsworth Publishing Company, 1969), p. 82.

not a case of groups petitioning and pressuring their elected representatives. Rather, groups are being used by these representatives to exert pressure on their fellow members and to argue in the political arena at large. As put in another council, "Cities cannot stir up active support themselves on some of these issues, you need a group." The point made here is important. There is not necessarily spontaneous support for council programs; such support will come only if there is an organized effort to create it. And it takes formal groups to invest this effort. At least some of the councils recognize that the task of promoting programs is as urgent as the task of representing. The relationship between council and organizations here is one where the council "tries to sell them on a project" so they will "get out and talk it up with other citizens." An activated group process is due at least in part to the deliberate mobilization by councils rather than to lobbying.

Group activation can be useful for putting pressure on persons other than citizens or group members. Councils or council factions do not hesitate to enter into a coalition with groups in order to force a particular council action. As put bluntly by a respondent, "I phone key leaders and ask them to put the heat on other councilmen, whatever is necessary." A mayor who must manage an unwieldy council of nine members reports that "If I don't have five votes, I contact groups and have them call the councilman whom I feel is ready to cave in. And I pick the group which best fits the problem and the councilman to be called." This type of group activation, however, is reported less frequently than is the type which has as its goal the building of community support.

Councils are, of course, likely to vary in their willingness to actively engage interest groups in the governing process. As with access facilitation, those holding a favorable view of the community's group life should be expected to mobilize groups more frequently than those having an unfavorable view. As Part A of Table 16–4 shows, there is only a moderate relationship between attitude vis-à-vis groups and group activation. Why is the relationship not stronger?

The complexity of the urban setting and the level of group activity may be factors influencing the relationship. As Part B of Table 16–4 indicates, if the city is small, if there is little petitioning, and if general associational activity is limited, there is practically no relationship between the attitude of the council and the likelihood that it will actively involve groups in the governing process. However, under other conditions, the evaluation of the group process by the council becomes critical in whether it deliberately fosters group activation. Where the urban setting is complex, where many groups are active in local affairs, or where organized activity is extensive, councils looking with favor on the group process are much more likely than those which do not to draw groups into the governing process. In large cities or where group activity is extensive, councils can ill afford not to muster support by activating groups. But if councils do not look with favor on the group process, they will not lend their own prestige to group efforts.

Table 16–4
Relationships Between Council Attitude
Toward the Group Process and Group Activation,
Controlled by City Size, Group Petitioning,
and General Associational Activity

Part A	Attitude Toward Group Process	
Group activation by council	Unfavorable N = 43	Favorable N = 39
Does not take place	56%	41%
Takes place	44	59
Gamma = .29	100%	100%

Part B

Relationship between council attitude and group activation in:	Gamma
Small cities (N = 41)	—.07
Large cities (N = 41)	.60
Cities with little group petitioning (N = 42)	—.03
Cities with much group petitioning (N = 40)	.55
Cities with low associational activity (N = 45)	—.05
Cities with high associational activity (N = 37)	.63

Table 16–5

Relationships Between Council Attitude
Toward Groups and Group Activation Under Varying Conditions
of Group Influence

	Objective Resources			
	No		Yes	
Group activation	Unfavorable N = 24	Favorable N = 22	Unfavorable N = 19	Favorable N = 17
Takes place	38%	50%	53%	71%
Does not take place	62	50	47	29
	100%	100%	100%	100%
Gamma =	.25		.37	

	Community Stake			
	No		Yes	
Group activation	Unfavorable N = 25	Favorable N = 16	Unfavorable N = 18	Favorable N = 23
Takes place	60%	56%	22%	61%
Does not take place	40	44	78	39
	100%	100%	100%	100%
Gamma =	−.08		.69	

	General Respect			
	No		Yes	
Group activation	Unfavorable N = 26	Favorable N = 16	Unfavorable N = 17	Favorable N = 23
Takes place	38%	69%	53%	52%
Does not take place	62	31	47	48
	100%	100%	100%	100%
Gamma =	.56		−.02	

The relationship between council attitude and council activation of groups also varies with the reasons given for group influence in the community. Table 16–5 presents the pertinent data.
Two patterns are of particular interest. Groups influential because
of objective resources are more likely to be mobilized than are

groups lacking such traits, regardless of whether councils favor the group process or not. But councils favoring group politics will mobilize such influential organizations more readily. Organizations presumably having political muscle cannot be easily ignored, no matter what the council's attitude toward the group process.

A different pattern emerges when the relationship is examined in terms of group stakes in the community. In general, where group stakes are seen to be low, council attitude makes no difference. But if groups have a stake in the community, they will not be deliberately activated unless councils entertain a generally favorable view of the group process. Respected groups are likely to be activated regardless of the council's stance toward the group process. But in the absence of respected groups, councils mobilize groups only if they generally recognize the group process as a vital feature of democratic governance.

Public-Private Partnership

A layer of voluntary associations and formal organizations mediates between the public and its officials. It offers citizens a means of aggregating their voices and thus increasing their influence in governing councils; it gives leaders regularized contact with citizens and a method of involving them in the governing process; it facilitates the flow of information between those inside and outside formal governmental institutions; it protects against social anomie and its consequences of diffused mass agitation; and it provides leaders some maneuvering room in their dealings with an often ill-informed and impatient public.

Two qualifications are in order. While groups do present political demands to the councils and, incidentally, councils at times deliberately foster group involvement in governance, the amount of group activity varies considerably from one city to the next. As the amount varies, so do other important features of the group process. Under certain conditions, governance occurs with only minimal reliance on groups seeking out the council and petitioning or on group-organized political activity. This is particularly true in smaller communities where environmental challenges are less demanding. In larger political units, the intermediate layer of group activity will probably always be present, but in smaller units, it is not a given that governing involves adaptation to the group process.

Since the extent, the variety, and the intensity of group politics will vary across political communities, it is possible to locate cases where such group activity is at a minimum. This in turn permits comparative investigation of the conditions which alter the amount of group activity, as well as comparative investigation of the correlates and consequences of lesser and greater involvement by groups. What we find is that the conditions of their presence or absence have a great deal to do with how the governing process works itself out, a finding which suggests a second qualification.

Whether groups have ready access to the governing circles depends not only on their own resources but also on the evaluation placed on group activity by governors. Although there is a certain circularity, for groups can act in ways that improve their image, there is a council viewpoint on the group process independent of specific group behavior. Councils may take such a dim view of the group process that they deny the very access necessary for group leaders to prove their worth as purveyors of information and sources of advice. Antagonism of elected leaders toward groups, then, can substantially affect the type of role groups play in the governing process.

With these qualifications in mind, it is possible to distinguish between cities where groups play a minimal role in linking council and public and cities where there exists an intermediate layer of groups. In the latter set of cities it is possible to distinguish between those with a more collaborative and those with a more adversary group process. Table 16-6 shows the resultant tripartite classification, including—because of its importance—a breakdown by city size. This analysis summarizes the major findings of the previous two chapters.

Groups play a less significant role in connecting council and public in smaller cities than they do in large cities, as is to be expected on the basis of previous analysis. Where councils and publics are linked by the intermediate layer of organizational activity, the quality of relationship which is established between

Table 16–6
Classification of the Group Process, by City Size

Classification of group process	City Size			
	Small N = 32	Medium N = 33	Large N = 17	Total N = 82
Groups play minimal role in linking council and public	47%	33%	12%	34%
Groups play more extensive role in linking, and relationship between council and public is collaborative	19	30	64	33
Groups play more extensive role in linking, and relationship between council and public is adversary	34	36	24	33
	100%	99%	100%	100%

governors and group spokesmen also differs by city size. This was not expected. But the pattern of the relationship is suggestive. *If* there is an active group life in the smaller political unit, it more often produces an adversary relationship than a collaborative, cooperative one. In sharp contrast, councils in large cities are much more likely to form a collaborative than an adversary relationship with groups.

Table 16–6 confirms several findings already reported in this and previous chapters. More often than the large city, the small community is politically quiescent. But when it is not quiescent, its politics will be conflictual. This finding was initially presented in connection with electoral behavior; it is now repeated in the arena of public life having to do with the processing of group demands. Indeed, it may be the very act of shattering the political quiescence in small communities which leads governors to view the group process with hostility. This sets in motion a cycle in which group leaders attempt to unseat the governors, thereby only increasing the antagonism felt by the governors toward the group process.

Officials faced with the difficulties of governing large cities take a very different stance toward the political activities of groups. Whether they fully appreciate groups or not, they recognize the important role that groups play. Councils in larger cities, therefore, foster a more collaborative relationship. They rely on groups for advice and information and they encourage groups to mobilize community support behind city programs.

Chapter 17

Group Activity
and Recruitment

"If a pressure group wishes to shape policy to its interests," Bone has noted, "it can hardly ignore the necessity for electing persons sympathetic to its views."[1] But, as Key has pointed out, the maxim that "private groups, displeased with the performance of legislators and other officials, would respond by punishing their enemies and rewarding their friends at the polls" is unduly simplistic.[2] Fortunately, the argument is not immune to empirical resolution. To resolve it empirically, it is best to assume that politics cannot be neatly separated into what happens in elections and what happens in the legislative chambers during the interelection period. The activities through which governing bodies are selected and the activities through which they are petitioned may be, but need not be, connected.

The separate treatment of constitutive processes and group processes is largely a matter of convenience—one cannot deal with everything at once. Both processes, however, are components of the total set of linkages between representatives and represented. Because the question over their interrelations is open, it behooves us to be modest in approach and cautious in interpretation, espe-

---

[1] Hugh A. Bone, "Political Parties and Pressure Group Politics," *Annals of the American Academy of Political and Social Science* 319 (1958), reprinted in Betty H. Zisk, ed., *American Political Interest Groups* (Belmont, Calif.: Wadsworth Publishing Company, 1969), p. 170.
[2] V. O. Key, Jr., *Public Opinion and American Democracy* (New York: Alfred A. Knopf, 1961), pp. 518–519.

cially as we are dealing with a very specific political arena at the local (and predominantly nonpartisan) level of government. Nevertheless, the search is guided by the assumption that the recruitment of governors and the group life of the community are not altogether independent of each other.[3]

Political Campaigning and the Group Process

In the folklore of American politics, interest groups are active participants in the campaigning that precedes election day. Indeed, groups do not seem reticent about endorsing candidates known to be, or expected to be, favorable to group interests.[4] And campaign efforts by organizations frequently extend beyond endorsement as they provide money, precinct workers, contacts, mailings, and audiences as well as moral support.

Group support can be thought of as a trade-off of benefits between the candidate and the group. The organization works

---

[3] It should be recorded that some political scientists hold that such independence is the actual political condition. In his *Party Government*, Schattschneider describes a pressure group as "an association that tries to bring about the adoption and execution of certain public policies without nominating candidates for the great offices, without fighting election campaigns, and without attempting to get complete control of government." It sounds here as if Schattschneider believes the compartmentalization of recruitment activities and group petitioning to be sound. He later writes that pressure activities and winning elections are lodged in different spheres of the political order, the one belonging to groups and the other belonging to parties. Perhaps, however, Schattschneider's empirical claims are too much colored by his hopes that effective party government will, in his words, "shut out the pressure groups." The weight of most informed opinion is that groups are as involved in nominations, campaigning, and electioneering as they are in lobbying and petitioning. Still, Schattschneider's observations bid us treat this as a proposition to be confirmed (or rejected) by empirical analysis rather than as an assumption which can be passed over and simply incorporated into our political models. See E. E. Schattschneider, *Party Government* (New York: Farrar and Rinehart, 1942), pp. 187–192.

[4] Systematic studies of the campaign process and the role of groups in it are in short supply. But see M. Kent Jennings and Harmon Zeigler, eds., *The Electoral Process* (Englewood Cliffs, N.J.: Prentice-Hall, 1966); John W. Kingdon, *Candidates for Office: Beliefs and Strategies* (New York: Random House, 1966); and V. O. Key, Jr., *Public Opinion and American Democracy*, especially Chapter 20.

toward the nomination and election of candidates who can be counted on to promote their interests, or at least to be neutral. And the candidate deliberately seeks out group support at campaign time to build as broad a constituency as possible. The mutual benefits to be gained would go far toward explaining the relationship between campaign activities and group processes.

Group presence in nominating, campaigning, and electioneering is probably more critical in local, nonpartisan elections than it is in state and national elections. The absence, at least formally, of political parties leaves a political vacuum into which flow the energies and efforts of interest groups. In nonpartisan elections, writes one student of group politics, "the support of interest groups is often of paramount importance and eagerly sought. Because a nonpartisan nominee lacks the organizational and financial backing of a political party, interest groups have an excellent chance to influence the outcome of these elections and may aid candidates without being charged as being pro-Republican or pro-Democratic." Citizens groups frequently rate the candidates for local offices; and these "recommendations are eagerly sought by candidates for nonpartisan offices." The recommendations play a significant role in voter choices because "in the absence of a party label, a number of voters are guided by the endorsements—or lack of them—given by a municipal league to candidates for nonpartisan office."[5]

Reasonable as these speculations are, they have yet to be tested empirically. In the San Francisco Bay region, Table 17–1 shows, campaign effort on the part of councils varies with the level of active group life in the community. The measure of group life refers to group involvement in the local legislative process, not to group activity in election campaigns. Yet the substantial relationship indicated in Table 17–1 suggests the possible interdependence of the politics of the election period and the politics of the inter-election period.

Insofar as there is such a relationship, it has implications for linkage processes. The campaign has a higher probability of linking representatives and represented where there is extensive

---

[5] Hugh A. Bone, "Political Parties and Pressure Group Politics," p. 171.

Table 17–1
Relationship Between General Group Activity
and Council Campaign Effort

	General Group Activity	
	Low	High
Campaign effort	N = 28	N = 54
Relatively little	64%	43%
Relatively much	36	57
Gamma = .42	100%	100%

campaign effort by candidates; the group process has a higher probability of linking governors and governed where there is an extensive group life in the community. Table 17–1 indicates that linkages operating at one point in the political process may reinforce linkages operating at a second point. That group activities and campaign activities are mutually reinforcing is indirectly confirmed by two additional findings. Cities in which there is active campaign effort also have councils which mobilize and involve organized interests in the legislative process (gamma = .46); and they have councils which show a willingness to facilitate access to group leaders and their requests (gamma = .20).

Of course, these findings cannot sort out cause and effect in the interdependence between the general activity of groups in the legislative process and the level of council effort in campaigning during the electioneering phase. Campaigning itself may serve to activate latent groups and to lead to their involvement in the governance of the community. An effective campaign can rally taxpayers and homeowners around a common issue, and in this sense the campaign is the catalyst for the emergence of new community organizations. The ambitious but little-known candidate can thus create a group for election purposes and perhaps become its leading community spokesman. But even in the absence of such deliberate efforts, the campaign publicity given to an issue or cause can transform a latent interest into an organization. This happens particularly during recall elections, usually a time of heated community feelings. The possibility that campaign efforts can initiate group formation underscores the possible interconnections between what might initially appear to be separate components of the linkage process.

The more likely interpretation of Table 17–1 and the supportive evidence is simply that the greater the number of groups in the community, the more campaign activity is generated. Groups do seek out particular candidates and do lend them campaign support. Councilmen were asked the direct question: "In your last campaign for the Council, were there any community groups or organizations which supported you?" Some quotations from the interview protocols are helpful to interpretation: "There was an organization generated for the reelection of O'Connor, Althoff, and Meynaud. They got posters out, had matchbooks out, cards, and went door-to-door." In another city, a local betterment league "organized several meetings so that candidates could appear before goodly numbers of people. They helped distribute literature."

Table 17–2 shows a strong relationship between the extent of active group intervention in the campaign and the council's own campaign effort. The proportion of councils reporting relatively much campaign effort is twice as great where groups play an active role in the campaign as where they play a lesser role.

Organized interests, the evidence suggests, attempt to influence the choice of governors. This, however, says little about the more interesting, if difficult, question of whether groups are successful in these attempts. As Key wrote some time ago, "the actual influence exerted by pressure groups in nominations and elections is a matter about which there is little precise knowledge."[6] And despite journalistic accounts of the alleged influence of groups in the election process, there is little specific information on this question one way or another.

In addition to being asked about the activity of groups in the campaign, councils were also queried as to whether there was "any group active during the last campaign that you particularly disliked." In many cities, councils had no difficulty identifying disliked groups: "The John Birch Society was irresponsible in their attacks on some of the candidates and used the election as a

---

[6] V. O. Key, Jr., *Politics, Parties, and Pressure Groups* (3rd ed.; New York: Thomas Y. Crowell Company, 1956), p. 163.

Table 17-2
Relationship Between Group Campaign Activity
and Council Campaign Effort

| Campaign effort | Level of Campaign Activity by Groups | |
	Low N = 37	High N = 45
Relatively little	68%	36%
Relatively much	32	64
Gamma = .58	100%	100%

forum for criticism of the city council and staff." In another community it was the "socialists, Commies, and left-wing radicals" who used unfair campaign tactics: "They are newcomers and are trying to corrupt the city, drag it down." Sometimes it was the discarded leaders, "the old power clique," as one respondent put it, who organized the opposition to the current incumbents.

One might expect that the presence of disliked groups in the campaign would accelerate the council's own campaign effort. And if this should be so, it is indirect evidence that councils view groups as potentially influential in election outcomes. Heightened campaign effort is a defensive posture taken in the face of opposition from certain organized interests in the community. The underlying assumption here is, of course, that groups are disliked because they oppose certain candidates. This, as the interview protocols reveal, is the reasonable assumption. The Little League was resented in one city because it "attempted to coerce all candidates into election eve promises by threatening opposition." In another community, "The editor of the paper and the Chamber of Commerce came out against us, and they didn't have the facts."

Table 17-3 shows a strong relationship between the presence of disliked groups and council campaign effort. Whether groups actually do influence election outcomes cannot be ascertained from the table, but that councils fear that they might is at least suggested by the association.

A more direct indication of group influence on electoral outcomes is provided by calibrating the reasons councils give for group influence into the analysis. Councils report groups to be

Table 17–3

Relationship Between Presence of Disliked Groups
in Campaign and Council Campaign Effort

	Disliked Groups in Campaign	
	Absent	Present
Campaign effort	N = 48	N = 34
Relatively little	67%	26%
Relatively much	33	74
Gamma = .67	100%	100%

influential if they command respect, have a stake in the community, or control political resources, including, it should be recalled,
voting strength. Insofar as councils believe that groups can affect
electoral outcomes, therefore, one should expect that council campaign effort will be accelerated if groups have political muscle,
but not if one of the other factors accounts for their influence.
Again, an increase in campaign effort on the council's part can be
interpreted as a defensive posture in the face of opposition, but
it is necessary only if the groups involved in the campaign have
sufficient *political* resources to affect election results.

Table 17–4 shows that campaign effort is increased where influential groups have political resources, is unaffected where groups
are influential because of their stake in the community, and actually decreases slightly if groups are influential only because they are
respected. Influence through respect, it should be recalled, occurs
when groups are largely cooperative with the council in promoting
commonly shared community goals. Councils have no reason to
fear the electoral opposition of such groups; less campaign effort is
needed where the community's organized interests are seen as
influential because they are respected.

Tables 17–3 and 17–4 provide only indirect evidence, but together they give some ground for inferring that councils at least
consider it prudent to increase their campaign efforts under certain
conditions of the group process. This does not prove that groups
are influential, that they can elect friends and defeat enemies. But
it indicates that their active presence in the selection process is
not without impact on how vigorously councils take their record

Table 17–4
Relationships Between Three Conditions
of Group Influence and Council Campaign Effort

	Reasons for Group Influence	
	Political Resources	
	Low	High
Campaign effort	N = 46	N = 36
Relatively little	59%	39%
Relatively much	41	61
Gamma = .38	100%	100%

	Stake in Community	
	Low	High
Campaign effort	N = 41	N = 41
Relatively little	51%	51%
Relatively much	49	49
Gamma = .00	100%	100%

	General Respect	
	Low	High
Campaign effort	N = 42	N = 40
Relatively little	45%	55%
Relatively much	55	45
Gamma = −.19	100%	100%

to the public through campaign efforts. Additional perspectives on
the interdependence between the group process and leadership
selection is provided by shifting attention from the campaign to the
prior activities through which candidates are recruited.

Career Sponsorship and the Group Process

Groups may not only support their political friends and oppose
their political enemies during an electoral campaign but may also
seek to have a say in who will run for office in the first place. The
activity of groups in promoting council candidacies should reveal

itself in two respects. First, a higher level of general group activity should generate more candidacies for office and lead to a more closely contested election. Second, and related to this proposition, a higher level of group activity should reduce the council's success in selecting its own successors. To this second proposition we turn first.

Many councils attempt to control who their successors will be; or, if control be too harsh a word, councils look with favor on certain potential successors and perhaps provide those who are favored with help by way of desired appointments, contacts with key people in the inner circles, beneficial public exposure, and advice regarding campaign strategies. But if many councils attempt in some degree to sponsor careers as a means of perpetuating their policies, some councils are more successful than others. There is a limit to how effectively any council can influence the flow of new recruits through manipulating the apprenticeship system, having a say during the screening and nomination of candidates, or swaying the opinions of voters. As shown in Chapter 13, the electoral context sets limits to the practice of career sponsorship. An active group life also imposes limits.

The hypothesis implicit in this argument contradicts a common notion about the role of interest groups in the selection of political candidates. It proposes that an active group life opens up the recruitment process by taking it out of the hands of an inner circle or power structure. Conventional wisdom has it that undue group influence in nominating and electioneering spells the end of an open recruitment process. Powerful group leaders, meeting in secret and possibly promising extravagant campaign funds, circumvent the democratic process of candidate selection. But the discrepancy between the position put forward and the conventional position is more circumstantial than real.

The dim view of group influence over the selection of candidates is focused on partisan politics. The political party is seen as the proper locus of candidate selection. Being heterogeneous in membership and diverse in viewpoint, the party is more representative of the public interest than is the homogeneous, sectarian special interest group. The selection of candidates rightly belongs to the parties and beyond them to the people, and this right is infringed if group leaders pick and choose who is to run for office. Whatever the empirical merits of this belief, it is plausible that the veto power exerted by influential groups over state and national candidates does narrow the definition of candidate acceptability and in this regard imposes constraints on the recruitment process.

Very different circumstances hold in the local, nonpartisan setting. These different circumstances suggest that active group politics may open up the recruitment process. In the local, nonpartisan setting there are relatively few major political actors, though one of them is the council itself along with its circle of friends and advisors. The council often attempts to establish the routes to office and to influence who shall move along these routes. In the absence of any major competitor in the recruitment process, the council is likely to be relatively successful in choosing its successors. But if organized groups become active in recruitment, they also are political actors in the community. And if they promote their own candidates, their activity should have the effect of reducing effective career sponsorship by the council. Only the absence of an active group life would sustain a more quiescent politics which would give the council an opportunity to have sole say in the recruitment of new members.

Table 17–5 shows a moderate tendency for successful career sponsorship to vary inversely with an active group life. Moreover, this is entirely a small-city occurrence. In the small city alone

Table 17–5

Relationship Between Career Sponsorship
and Group Activity in All, Small, and Large Cities

	Group Activity					
	All Cities		Small Cities		Large Cities	
	Low	High	Low	High	Low	High
Sponsorship	N = 28	N = 54	N = 19	N = 22	N = 9	N = 32
Little	43%	57%	37%	59%	56%	56%
Much	57	43	63	41	44	44
	100%	100%	100%	100%	100%	100%
Gamma =	−.29		−.42		.00	

is there a comparatively substantial tendency for career sponsorship to be curtailed when groups play an active role in local politics. There is no such relationship in the large cities. How can this result, which gives the hypothesis some reprieve, be explained?

The number of politically active citizens in a community tends to vary with the size of the population. Approximately one in 20 adult citizens becomes actively involved in political matters. This estimate of 5 percent will not hold in the smallest cities, where a somewhat higher proportion might be politically active, or in the largest cities, where a somewhat lower proportion might be politically active, but it is a serviceable estimate and can be used to advantage in accounting for Table 17–5. In the small cities, the active stratum, combined with the inner governing circles, numbers relatively few people, perhaps as few as two or three hundred even in a city approaching 10,000. The small number of people makes career sponsorship relatively easy *unless* an active electorate or organized interests intrude into the leadership selection processes. This intrusion broadens the constituencies represented in the politically active stratum and serves to loosen up the cohesiveness of the governing circles. This in turn places constraints on the self-perpetuating tendencies of the governing group. Councils of the small cities which do succeed in sponsoring their successors might resent any moves toward greater group involvement in the governing process. Such councils very clearly refrain from deliberately mobilizing groups, and they even tend somewhat to make access difficult.[7] The opposite practice is true in the larger cities.

In the large city, then, group activity and career sponsorship are independent political phenomena. It may be, however, that in attempting to perpetuate its own kind the council of the larger city casts its net more widely, if for no other reason than that there is a more sizable pool of potential recruits than there is in the small city. Councils practicing career sponsorship in the large city may take a more relaxed attitude toward groups and collaborate with them in determining the succession. Indeed, councils practicing sponsorship in the large city do tend even more than nonsponsor-

---

[7] In the small cities the gamma measure of association between the practice of career sponsorship and group mobilization is −.42; between sponsorship and facilitating group access it is −.15.

ing councils to facilitate group access and to mobilize groups into the governing process.[8] It is as if councils were dependent on groups rather than, as in the small cities, trying to avoid them. Nevertheless, the lack of relationship between group life and career sponsorship in the large cities partially negates the hypothesis that group activity opens up the recruitment process.

Political Competition and the Group Process

The activity of groups in promoting candidacies as well as in campaigning for or against candidates should be reflected in the number of candidates competing in the council race and in the closeness of the competition. An active group life should engender a greater number of competitors for council openings and more closely fought elections.

A rich group life reflects and partially creates divisions both within the active stratum and within the general electorate. Organizations provide a collective means of expressing citizen sentiments and a platform for the politically ambitious who would represent those sentiments in the legislative chamber. As shown earlier, the sheer number of groups does indicate a greater variety of interests finding organized outlets not only because organization begets organization, but also because a rich organizational life opens up group outlets for even the most specific of interests.

Where a wide variety of specific interests have an organized voice in the community, the active stratum, composed as it is largely of group leaders, will have a correspondingly greater number of factions and internal divisions. And because this stratum is the locus of recruitment processes and the source of most council candidates, the greater the number of separate interests represented, the greater will be the number of candidates likely to seek council positions. Morover, the electorate will also be divided into more voter groupings if political organizations are many and

---

[8] In the large cities the gamma measure of association between the practice of career sponsorship and group mobilization is .29; between sponsorship and facilitating group access it is .37, in each case reversing the pattern of the small city.

varied in the community. In the absence of party labels it is likely that endorsements by group leaders have some effect on voter choice. And if the candidate himself is the president of the civic club or an officer in the Rotarians or a leading figure in the Chamber, it is all the more likely that members of the respective organizations will vote in accordance with group loyalties. Thus a large number of politically active groups fragments the vote and tends to create close vote divisions between the winners and the losers.

Confirmation of these hypotheses would be further evidence that groups are involved in the nomination of candidates as well as in the election; and it would be another indication of the interdependence of the city's constitutive and petitioning processes. As Table 17–6 shows, both office contesting and the closeness of the electoral contest are associated with an active group life in the community.

Unlike the case of career sponsorship, the patterns are stable regardless of city size (data not shown). Table 17–6 supports the notion that an active group life can open up channels of recruitment, at least in the sense of providing a greater number of avenues to the council and a more varied choice for the electorate. But this does not mean that group endorsement is tantamount to election. Only most generally does an active group life determine who will

Table 17–6
Relationships Between General Group Activity
and Office Contesting and Closeness of Vote

	General Group Activity	
	Low	High
Office contesting	N = 27	N = 54
Low	63%	44%
High	37	56
Gamma = .35	100%	100%
	Low	High
Closeness of vote	N = 25	N = 52
Not close	68%	40%
Close	32	60
Gamma = .52	100%	100%

occupy the seats of government. To isolate a political condition—that is, an active group life—that contributes to more competition and, at least in small cities, to less sponsorship is certainly to say something about the composition of the council. The interdependence of the group process and constitutive processes indicates that councils will be chosen from a wider pool of recruits in communities with an active group life than in communities lacking this political condition. But the data do not indicate that specific groups have this or that consequence for the success or failure of specific candidates.

Why councils respond to organized interests differently in more or less complex urban settings can be clarified by looking at the relationship between office contesting and closeness of the vote, on the one hand, and the inclination of councils to mobilize groups in the governing process, on the other. If pressed by challengers, the small-city council is unwilling to activate groups and legitimate their involvement in the legislative process.[9] There is much reluctance to generate more political activity than is necessary. By refusing to mobilize interest groups, the council seeks to curtail the effectiveness of groups. But the opposite occurs in the large cities. If challenged in the election, the big-city council goes out of its way to involve groups in the governance of the community.[10] Although the challengers will be recruited from the ranks of these groups, the large-city council under electoral pressure makes allies where it can. Organized interest groups are sufficiently entrenched in large cities that councils there have fewer options in controlling the political process than they do in small cities.

Incumbent Eviction and the Group Process

The strength of pressure groups "is often supposed to rest ultimately on the probable actions of their members at the polls."[11]

---

[9] The gamma measure of association between office contesting and mobilizing groups in the small city is $-.28$; between closeness of the vote and mobilizing groups it is $-.31$.

[10] The gamma measure of association between office contesting and mobilizing groups in the large city is $.37$; between closeness of the vote and mobilizing groups it is $.40$.

[11] V. O. Key, *Politics, Parties, and Pressure Groups,* p. 127.

In these words, V. O. Key sums up the common notion that group leaders threaten unfriendly legislators with retaliation at the polls as well as promise their friends unwavering electoral support. As the authors of one of the most systematic investigations of group politics note, "the electoral threat is the only type of fear-arousing communication that legislators and lobbyists perceive as available to the lobbyists."[12]

This belief that groups can influence electoral outcomes would seem to indicate that higher group activity leads to higher rates of incumbent eviction. The hypothesis must be treated with caution because it does not take into account that the electoral effectiveness of groups must be measured in terms of keeping friends in the council as well as in terms of removing enemies. If groups are successful in influencing the electoral outcome, it will be reflected in the rate at which certain incumbents retain office despite the presence of challengers, as well as in the rate at which incumbents whose policies are viewed as detrimental to group interests are defeated. Still, if the time period is long enough, eviction itself can be taken as some indication of the ability or inability of groups to influence the outcome.

Table 17–7 indicates only a moderate relationship between group activity and incumbent eviction, with a higher rate of eviction tending to be associated with a more active group life. Groups may influence the electoral outcome as well as be consequential in the earlier stages of candidate selection and electoral campaigning, but the relationship here is not sufficiently strong to be accepted at face value. However, it is evidently not an artifact of urban complexity. When controlled by city size, the relationship between group activity and incumbent eviction is nearly identical in both small and large cities (.27 in the former and .30 in the latter). A higher level of group activity in local, nonpartisan governance is systematically, if only moderately, associated with a higher rate of leadership turnover.

Although incumbent eviction varies with the degree of group activity prevalent in the community, the relationship may in turn

---

[12] Harmon Zeigler and Michael Baer, *Lobbying: Interaction and Influence in American State Legislatures* (Belmont, Calif.: Wadsworth Publishing Company, 1969), p. 120.

Table 17–7
Relationship Between General Group Activity
and Incumbent Eviction

| | General Group Activity | |
| | Low | High |
Incumbent eviction	N = 27	N = 53
Low	59%	44%
High	41	56
Gamma = .26	100%	100%

vary with the level of voter turnout. An activated electorate and a high level of group activity may cumulate in accelerating the tendency to evict incumbents. Table 17–8 presents the data and reveals two matters of interest. First, the association between eviction and an active group life persists in both low and high turnout cities, though the association is nearly twice as strong if more voters go to the polls than if fewer do. Groups evidently find it easier to remove incumbents when large numbers of voters can be mobilized. Second, group activity and electoral participation do have a cumulative effect on the rate of eviction. Where there is an active group life and a large electorate, almost two-thirds of the councils suffer high rates of incumbent defeat. By way of contrast, approximately a third of the councils are similarly affected where groups are absent and the electorate is comparatively apathetic.

Table 17–8
Relationship Between General Group Activity
and Incumbent Eviction, Controlled by Voter Turnout

| | Low Voter Turnout | | High Voter Turnout | |
| Group activity | Low | High | Low | High |
Incumbent eviction	N = 14	N = 25	N = 13	N = 28
Low	64%	56%	54%	36%
High	36	44	46	64
	100%	100%	100%	100%
Gamma =	.18		.35	

Incumbent eviction, one should suppose, will be higher in cities where critical groups are present than where they are absent; and, indeed, there is a moderate association (gamma = .25) between these variables. But unlike voter turnout, as Table 17–9 shows, the presence or absence of critical groups, though having a cumulative effect on incumbent eviction along with the level of general group activity, also has a depressing effect on the direct relationship between the latter and the former.

The highest rate of incumbent eviction occurs in cities with a great deal of general group activity, much of it evidently fostered by groups critical of what the council is doing. Organized opposition faced by incumbents from time to time most likely comes from groups that have been critical during the prior legislative period. Criticism of policies is translated into electoral opposition. In conjunction with the prior evidence, Table 17–9 gives support, indirect though it may be, to the notion that groups are not entirely without influence on electoral outcomes.

Groups do more than generate candidacies, campaign actively, and tighten the election contest. They may also meet with success in actually evicting incumbents from office. Though this is a reasonable inference to be drawn from the evidence, it should be stressed that every test has been indirect. We have explored the relationship between two systemic variables, the level of group activity and the rate of incumbent eviction, and not the fortunes

Table 17–9
Relationship Between General Group Activity
and Incumbent Eviction, Controlled by Presence
and Absence of Critical Groups

Group activity Incumbent eviction	Critical Groups Absent		Critical Groups Present	
	Low N = 19	High N = 28	Low N = 9	High N = 28
Low	63%	54%	44%	36%
High	37	46	56	64
	100%	100%	100%	100%
Gamma =	.19		.18	

of a specific candidate either blessed with group support or hounded by group opposition.

Conclusion

The group life of the community is not without consequences for recruitment practices in the selection of the few who govern the many. Although general group activity, as measured here, refers to petitioning and pressuring in the legislative context rather than in other stages of the political process, it is related in predictable ways to the recruitment of candidates, electoral campaigning, and even the probability of defeating incumbents.

Groups do not limit their political activities only to the legislative process but expand their efforts into the electoral arena as well. The goal is to influence the selection of candidates and the election of persons sympathetic to group interests. This is accomplished by penetrating the recruitment process, by working in campaigns, and by seeking to defeat or otherwise undermine the position of legislators deemed unfriendly to the group. It is not easy to gauge the success of such efforts, especially with measures that describe systemic attributes of group politics and constitutive processes. But success must be frequent enough, the evidence suggests, that the appetite to influence the "who" of governance remains whetted. Groups define their political role more broadly than simply lobbying and informing their members about legislation. And the governors themselves help in defining a broader role for groups. They rely on groups not only for aid in governance, as noted in the previous chapter, but for assistance in their quest for office.

At the more abstract level of linkages, the evidence is relevant to a core notion in democratic thought—that citizens should have access to their governors by participating in the choice of these governors. Like many other propositions of democratic theory, the access axiom is silent on the actual mechanics by which the linkage can come about. The data show that if citizens are organized into politically effective groups, they have a dual leverage on their leaders. Leverage is exerted through the activities associated with

recruitment and election; and leverage is also exerted through pressuring and petitioning the council. Two seemingly distinct political processes are thus joined through effective organization, and
both processes are conducive to linking the governors and the
governed. Linkages, the evidence suggests, are mutually reinforcing
across different sets of group activity, at least across such important
sets as are involved in selecting and making claims on the
governors.

Chapter 18

Channels
of Communication

The petitioning and contacting activities which link governors and governed also occur through channels other than those provided by organized groups. Two such channels were identified: first, the activities of spokesmen who represent particular sectors of the community; and second, the direct and largely informal contacts which result from the daily activities of the councilmen in the community. Spokesmen and direct contacts supplement and in some respects extend the channels established through group-based activities.

Figure 18–1 pictures the three channels of contact between the council and the public. Spokesmen along with organized groups serve as intermediaries between council and public, whereas direct contacts bypass the role of the intermediary. A distinction between mediated and unmediated contact is important to the notion of a "dual system of representation."

A public has two sets of representatives—legislators elected to public office and intermediaries who represent the public to the elected officials.[1] The notion of intermediaries stresses their role in bridging the distance between governors and governed, while the

---

[1] Easton refers to intermediaries as "gatekeepers" and describes them as occupants of structural points in the political system who convert wants into political demands. Our usage is somewhat different from Easton's, for our concern is with linkages rather than with the flow of demands. Hence we use the term "intermediary" to stress how the distance between governors and governed is bridged. See David Easton, *A Systems Analysis of Political Life* (New York: John Wiley and Sons, 1965), pp. 86–88.

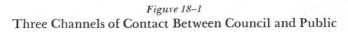

Figure 18–1
Three Channels of Contact Between Council and Public

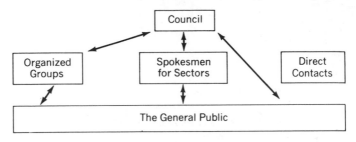

term "represent" is appropriately used for two reasons. First, the intermediary claims to speak on behalf of (to represent) a particular constituency, as when a group leader presses for legislation in the name of group members. Second, the intermediary may be seen by the legislature as a typical (representative) member of a community sector, as when a council listens to a businessman in the belief that it is hearing a viewpoint shared by all businessmen. The intermediary is expected to summarize the wishes of the people on whose behalf he speaks. In this role he claims the status of spokesman.

Direct contacts between council and public circumvent the dual representative system, at least occasionally and for particular purposes. Direct contacts can be initiated by the council as well as by citizens. There will be occasions when the council prefers to get information and advice directly from its publics by bypassing the occupants of intermediary positions like group leaders or formal spokesmen.[2]

Spokesmen for Public Sectors

When a council reports that a local businessman "comes before the council in support of things the merchant community would

---

[2] Easton discusses the circumstances under which gatekeepers might be bypassed and speaks of the direct and unmediated conversion of demands. His usage is suggestive, for it points out that members of the public can in principle address themselves directly to their governors. Our usage of "direct contacts" is an extension of Easton's usage. See Easton, *A Systems Analysis of Political Life,* pp. 88–90.

like to have" and then describes this person "as sort of a liaison man," it is clearly identifying a spokesman for a sector of the community.[3] Liaison activities connect an interest sector with the council, and in this sense we see spokesmen as part of the linkage processes of local government.

Spokesmen, as here defined, are not occasional or casual contact men between council and some sector of the public but persons who regularly appear at council meetings or otherwise regularly present claims on behalf of an interest cluster. So defined, eight different types of spokesman or, more accurately, eight different sectors of the public with specifically named spokesmen were identified. Most sectors were infrequently cited by any one council, six of them appearing in less than one-fifth of the communities. The remaining two were mentioned by a sizable number of the councils. Forty-two percent of the councils identified a spokesman for what might be called "Main Street business interests," a category including the downtown merchants and the local realtors primarily. Thirty-eight percent of the councils identified a spokesman for what might be called the "quasi-governmental sector," a category including local commissions and boards. The remaining spokesmen served one of the following: a public-interest conservation sector; large landowners and related "upper-class" economic elites; industrial and manufacturing interests; taxpayer and homeowner groups; and a recreation and education sector.

Not all councils could name particular spokesmen. Some (17 percent) actually denied that any sector was regularly represented

---

[3] The questions on the basis of which spokesmen were identified inquired about "influential" persons in the community. However, we are not interested in whether these persons are influential in the sense of affecting council policy; we are intersted only in the likelihood that they serve as go-betweens. We coded as spokesmen those persons who frequently appeared before the council or otherwise communicated the viewpoint of a sector of the community. For a spokesman to be coded as such, he (she) had to be cited by two members of a five-member council or by at least three of a larger council. The questions eliciting the necessary data were: "Now I would like to ask you about some of the individuals outside the Council who are actively involved in what the Council does here in (city). Are there any persons who are particularly influential here—I mean people whose voices are really important in Council decisions affecting the city? Who are they? On what kinds of things are they influential? Lets take Mr. ———, in what matters is he influential? And what makes for his influence? What does he actually do to affect decisions made by the Council?"

before the council. About a third (35 percent) reported only one spokesman for a particular sector. Slightly more than half the councils, then, do not rely on intermediaries or, if they do, the intermediaries represent only one interest. The remaining councils (48 percent) reported contacts with from two to four spokesmen. In these councils the linkage process is indeed strengthened by inter-mediaries between the council and its several publics.

Direct Contacts

In addition, direct exchanges of viewpoint between council and public also play a part in linkage processes. These direct and largely informal contacts occur by virtue of the social life and work patterns of local councilmen. Councils differ in this respect a great deal from the houses of Congress or state legislatures, which, by virtue of their political situation, are more dependent on formal agents as intermediaries. The national and state legislatures are nearly always at some geographic distance from their con-stituencies. The populations they represent are comparatively large—a circumstance that makes intermediaries who aggregate and articulate claims and requests all the more important. More-over, the national and state legislatures are organized by political parties, which serve to bridge the distance between them and their various publics.

In contrast, councilmen reside in the communities they govern. They are part of the daily life of the community and thus have opportunities to establish direct contacts. And in most though not all cases the populations are smaller than is true of con-gressional and even state districts. Besides, each city has five or more councilmen while a legislative district often has only one representative. The nonpartisan councils cannot rely on a regu-larized political party network to keep them informed of commu-nity happenings, and thus will build their own networks.

Contrasts between city councils and other elected legislatures are, however, differences in degree and not in kind. Especially in larger cities, councils cannot hope to be acquainted with the politi-cal interests of citizens from every sector of the community. In their social and work lives, councilmen move in narrow circles, usually composed of persons of similar social standing. They will find at least some intermediaries indispensable if they are to maintain contact with all sectors of the community.

Responses to two sets of questions provide the data for analysis of direct contacts. Each respondent was asked to evaluate the importance of eight sources of advice about issues before the council, and each was asked to evaluate the importance of five sources of information about controversial matters in the community. Because the distinction between sources of advice and information is not particularly germane in this connection, the two sets of data are combined to present a general picture of the council's direct and informal contacts with the public.[4]

Analysis revealed that certain sources are nearly always ranked as important, and these sources tend to be, first, city staff or colleagues on the council and, second, newspapers or organizational leaders. Councils rely more on their immediate associates and, to a somewhat lesser degree, on established intermediaries than they do on informal and direct contacts. Yet there is a good deal of variability from council to council, with such sources of information as friends, people in the neighborhood, work associates, and so forth receiving higher rankings in some cities than in others.

Figure 18–2 presents the data classified by city size. Direct contacts, if relevant at all, will be most pronounced in smaller communities. The figure should be interpreted as follows: above the center line is listed each information source according to the size of the city in which it is ranked as most important; below the line is listed each source according to the size of the city in which it is ranked as least important. Newspapers, for instance, are comparatively more important in large cities and less important in small cities; friends, by way of contrast, are comparatively more important in small cities and less important in large cities.[5]

---

[4] For the questions on which the direct contact measure is built, see Appendix C, Items F and G; for construction of the measure, see Appendix B18.1.

[5] It should be stressed that this does *not* mean that friends are *absolutely* more important than newspapers in the smaller city. Indeed, the mean ranks (in parentheses in Figure 18–1) show that the ordering of the various items remains roughly constant across the classification by city size. It means that newspapers receive a higher ranking in large cities than they do in either medium-size or smaller cities and that friends as sources of information receive a lower ranking in large cities than in either medium-size or small cities.

Figure 18–2
Comparative Importance of Sources of Information and Advice
in Different-Size Cities

	Large cities	Medium cities	Small cities
Relatively more important	Newspapers (2.4) Organizational leaders (3.3)	City staff (1.9) People in the neighborhood (4.7)	Colleagues on council (2.6) Friends and acquaintances (3.0) People in general (3.5) Influentials (3.9) Work associates (4.2) People at council meetings (4.4)
Relatively less important	Colleagues on council (3.1) Friends (3.8) Work associates (4.1) People in general (4.4) People at council meetings (4.8) People in the neighborhood (5.0)	Influentials (4.1)	City staff (2.5) Organizational leaders (3.6) Newspapers (3.9)

Note: Figures in parentheses are the mean scores computed for each item. The lower the score, the greater the importance assigned to the source by the council.

The pattern is striking and consistent. Of the information sources which suggest direct contact between council and public, including friends, acquaintances, people in general, work associates, and people who come to council meetings, nearly all receive high rankings in the smaller cities and lower rankings in the larger cities. The only exception is people in the neighborhood receiving the highest ranking in the medium-size cities. The pattern is reversed with respect to newspapers and organization leaders, the clearest example of intermediaries.[6] As sources of information and advice, they receive relatively high rankings in the large cities and relatively low rankings in the small cities.

To the extent that councils rely on informal, direct contacts, this is most likely to happen in small cities. There is an individualized network which supplements the more institutionalized channels in the small city. Councils in large cities are not totally indifferent to direct contacts, but certainly place comparatively less stress on them.[7] The picture in medium-size cities is mixed. Councils in such cities tend not to devalue any source of information or advice, at least in comparison to large-city and small-city councils. Thus six of the ten items receive their lowest ranking in the large cities, and three of the ten items receive their lowest ranking in the small cities; yet only one item is ranked lowest in the medium-size cities. Councils governing middling-size cities pursue a mixed strategy in regard to contacts with the public, relying on both direct and indirect channels of communication.

Figure 18–2 confirms the self-evident. The governing process in large political units proceeds as formal agencies articulate and aggregate demands from the population. The public is too vast and diffuse for elected leaders to do anything but use group leaders,

---

[6] Unfortunately, "influentials in the city" was an item poorly worded in that it does not distinguish between what we have called spokesmen and what may only be friends of the city councilmen who also happen to be viewed as influtials in the city. It is unclear whether to call this item part of the direct, informal channels of communication or part of the intermediaries.

[7] This can be seen by considering the mean rank of each item. If the mean rank is 5.0, this would indicate that every council in one of the three size categories ranked that item low. This happens only once; "people in the neighborhood" are never seen as important by councils in large cities, and "people who come to meetings" are nearly as unimportant to councils in large cities. Other items tend to get at least some higher rankings from councils.

spokesmen, newspapers, and similar sources for information. The same is true of smaller political units, but evidently to a lesser degree. Governing in the small community can include at least some direct contacts for learning what the public wishes.

Though self-evident, these results are not without significance for linkage processes and, eventually, for political representation. The possible importance of direct contact between public and council can be assessed by constructing a summary measure based on the items in Figure 18–2. Councils are scored as placing comparatively greater stress on informal, direct contacts, such as friends, neighbors, people in general, and so forth; or as placing comparatively little stress on such sources of information and advice.

Council reliance on direct contacts should be inversely related to reliance on spokesmen for broad sectors of the public. Table 18–1 shows this to be the case, though the association is at best moderate. A council benefiting from spokesmen who serve as liaison with the public can more readily dispose of the information and advice which might come through the informal and direct network of friends and associates. Lacking such spokesmen, however, a council will more readily turn to direct contacts and informal channels. This pattern persists in large and small cities (gamma $= -.29$ and $-.33$, respectively).

Linkage Interrelationships

Group activity, representation through spokesmen, and direct contacts are all major means of linkage between governors and governed in the interelection period. Sector representation and direct contact, it was seen in Table 18–1, are inversely related. Table 18–2 examines the effect of group activity on whether spokesmen play a role in local governance.

Spokesmen are less frequent in cities with more limited group activity generally. They are evidently not a substitute for group-based linkages—a conclusion one would draw if the relationship were negative. Rather, linkages established through general group activity and through the exchange between council and spokesmen

Table 18–1
Relationship Between Presence of Spokesmen
and Council Reliance on Direct Contacts

	Number of Spokesmen		
Direct contacts	None N = 14	One N = 29	Two or more N = 39
Relatively less	36%	45%	60%
Relatively more	64	55	40
Gamma = −.32	100%	100%	100%

are complementary. Indeed, organized interests probably provide in part the constituencies serviced by spokesmen who act as intermediaries between the council and its various publics. Moreover, the pattern persists in small as well as in large communities, though in the latter, councils very infrequently report spokesmen in the absence of organized interests. The population of the large city is too diffuse for the role of spokesman to gain much prominence without being organized by groups. In the small city, a spokesman can have some success collecting a constituency even if the public is not already organized.

We also expect reliance on direct contacts to be stressed in the absence of an active group life and depreciated if groups do play important intermediate roles. This, as Table 18–3 shows, is the case. The relative stress on direct contacts is inversely related

Table 18–2
Relationship Between Presence of Spokesmen
and General Group Activity, in All, Small, and Large Cities

	General Group Activity					
	All Cities		Small Cities		Large Cities	
Number of spokesmen	Low N = 28	High N = 54	Low N = 19	High N = 22	Low N = 9	High N = 32
None or one	64%	46%	58%	45%	78%	47%
Two or more	36	54	42	55	22	53
	100%	100%	100%	100%	100%	100%
Gamma =	.35		.25		.60	

Table 18–3
Relationship Between General Group Activity
and Direct Council Contacts, in All, Small, and Large Cities

	General Group Activity					
	All Cities		Small Cities		Large Cities	
	Low	High	Low	High	Low	High
Direct contacts	N = 28	N = 54	N = 19	N = 22	N = 19	N = 32
Relatively less	46%	59%	37%	59%	67%	59%
Relatively more	54	41	63	41	33	41
	100%	100%	100%	100%	100%	100%
Gamma =	−.25		−.42		.16	

to the level of group activity. However, stress on direct contacts in
the absence of groups changes depending on the size of the population with which the council must deal. Where group activity is
low, the council of the small city will seek out friends and associates
to provide it with necessary information and advice. Even if groups
are present but the relationship is an adversary one, councils in
small cities nevertheless place comparatively greater stress on
direct, unmediated contacts with the public.[8] In other words, the
dual representative system is replaced by direct contacts under
either of two conditions: there are no groups available to link the
public and the council, or the groups which are available are
looked upon with disfavor by the governors.

Leadership Selection and Linkages

Just as groups may play an active role in the recruitment and
election of councils, so may the presence of spokesmen and direct
contacts be related in patterned ways to recruitment practices.

---

[8] The notion of an adversary relationship with groups was briefly introduced at
the end of Chapter 15. There are nine small cities in which the relationship of
councils to groups is an adversary one; of these, 78% place relatively greater
stress on direct contacts. This compares to only 33% of the councils of large
cities having adversary relationships with groups (N = 18).

From what has been discovered, it is possible to suggest a very general working hypothesis.

As a mode of linking citizens and council, direct contacting is more compatible with a politics that allows councils to control the succession through sponsoring the careers of new members; that stimulates relatively few candidacies for open council seats; that does not lead to closely competitive elections; and that has a comparatively tempered campaign. In other words, if recruitment practices and selection processes are quiescent and closed, the council is more likely to seek out direct, informal ways of dealing with the public. It simply limits its effective clientele to friends, neighbors, or work associates and goes about the business of governance without much attention to organized groups or unorganized interests.

Contrariwise, spokesmen will play a greater role as linkage agents where the route to office is more open and career sponsorship is limited; where there are numerous candidates and closely fought election contests; and where the council actively campaigns for reelection. In other words, more lively and open selection processes will bring spokesmen of various publics into the governing process. The council in this politically more active environment will seek links to the various interest sectors of the community; and the public, more highly involved in leadership selection, will try to maintain the linkage by having spokesmen before the council in the interelection period.

Table 18–4 is an economic summary of the data, comparing the relative strength of the two linkages—spokesmen and direct contacts—under differing conditions of leadership selection.[9] In every case, direct contacts are stressed more frequently than are spokesmen under the conditions taken as indicative of a comparatively quiescent recruitment process: high sponsorship, low campaign

---

[9] Table 18–4 should be read as follows: the direction of the arrow indicates the relative stress on spokesmen or direct contacts. The percentages of course do not total 100%, for the table reports on two separate measures. A council can both identify spokesmen and stress direct contacts, or do neither, though, as Table 18–1 shows, these measures are negatively associated. A measure of career sponsorship places "high" at the top of the table and "low" below it, which is consistent with how the measure is conceptualized in terms of the present hypothesis.

Table 18–4

Relative Emphasis on Spokesmen and Direct Contacts
Under Different Conditions of Leadership Selection

| Conditions of leadership selection | | *Type of Communication* | | |
		Two or more spokesmen		Relatively more direct contacts
Career	High (N = 39)	42%	<	56%
sponsorship	Low (N = 43)	54%	>	44%
Campaign	Low (N = 41)	36%	<	68%
effort	High (N = 41)	59%	>	32%
Office	Low (N = 41)	49%	<	54%
contesting	High (N = 40)	47%	>	45%
Closeness	Low (N = 38)	34%	<	55%
of vote	High (N = 38)	60%	>	48%

NOTE: The table shows the proportion of councils which identify two or more spokesmen where there is high sponsorship. This is a separate measure from that of stress on direct contact, and the two measures will not add up to 100%. If they total less than 100%, this indicates that some councils are high on neither of these measures; if they total more than 100%, this indicates that some councils are high on both of the measures.

effort, low office contesting, and low electoral competition. And in every case, spokesmen are stressed more frequently than direct contacts under the conditions indicating a comparatively more open and lively recruitment process: low career sponsorship, high campaign effort, numerous contesters, and closely fought elections. Though the contrasts which appear under differing conditions of office contesting are negligible, they do not disconfirm the hypothesis. Of the eight separate opportunities to show the hypothesis as unsound, in not one instance does this occur, though the differences are usually moderate.[10]

---

[10] As a check, Table 18–4 was recomputed for small and large cities. No arrows changed direction in the small cities; and most of the differences were accelerated. Two arrows did change direction in the large cities; spokesmen were given more emphasis than were direct contacts despite few contesters and despite high sponsorship. On balance, however, the hypothesis resists falsification irrespective of the size of the city.

The patterns reflected in Table 18–4 add weight to a conclusion drawn in the previous chapter. Although political activities for choosing governors can be distinguished from political activities involving various forms of petitioning them, the two types of activity are interrelated in the governing process. Consent of the governed is not only institutionalized, if it is, through public participation in selecting leaders and through public participation in petitioning them, but it is institutionalized in the interdependence of the two forms of political activity. It may be that the recruitment process leads to particular forms of public petitioning and pressuring. Or it may be that the manner in which the public is organized to pursue its political goals spills over into the ways by which legislatures are constituted at election time. The probability is that this interdependence reaches back into the history of the political community, and it becomes impossible to call one process cause and the other effect. Selecting leaders and petitioning them merge into one general set of processes which more or less effectively links the governors with the governed.

Electoral Context and Linkages

It is through its behavior on election day that the public most clearly expresses its level of involvement in community governance. The electoral context should be sufficiently critical for the shape and substance of local politics that it affects the type of communication channels used by council and public. One may ask whether the comparative stress on spokesmen over direct contacts or on direct contacts over spokesmen shifts from one electoral context to another. It is expected that spokesmen play a more prominent role in community politics if the electorate is actively involved, and that informal and direct contacts are cultivated if the electorate is comparatively uninvolved.

In the large cities, Table 18–5 shows, the hypothesis does not hold. But the role of spokesmen and the importance of direct contacts vary sharply as between cities where the electorate does not evict incumbents and cities where it does. Direct and informal contacts supplant the more formalized linkage through spokesmen only if the electorate signals its comparative satisfaction or lack of interest in matters of governance. The pressure is off those councils where the electorate is permissive or supportive. If the city is also small, the council turns to a network of friends and associates to collect what information and advice is needed. What is politically significant, however, is that the comparative stress on informal contact does not just vary with city size; for when the electorate is volatile or, especially, discriminative (both cases where incumbents are frequently evicted), the emphasis on direct contacts drops off and the stress on intermediaries increases.

The political conditions established by the permissive and supportive electorates in the small community allow the comfortable governing style of simply checking things out with a broadened

Table 18–5

Relative Emphasis on Spokesmen and Direct Contacts
in Four Electoral Contexts, in Small and Large Cities

Mode of linkage	Electoral Context: Small Cities			
	Permissive $N = 6$	Supportive $N = 15$	Discriminative $N = 6$	Volatile $N = 12$
Two or more spokesmen	33%	33%	83%	59%
Relatively more direct contacts	∧ 83%	∧ 80%	∨ 67%	∨ 25%

Mode of linkage	Electoral Context: Large Cities			
	Permissive $N = 17$	Supportive $N = 2$	Discriminative $N = 11$	Volatile $N = 12$
Two or more spokesmen	36%	—	50%	50%
Relatively more direct contacts	36%	—	50%	42%

circle of friends and neighbors. Politics is face-to-face rather than dependent on intermediaries who facilitate the flow of information and demands between council and public. It is likely, of course, that the proportion of the public involved in this intimate politics of friends and acquaintances is comparatively small, especially in the permissive context, where few bother even to vote.

A discriminative or volatile electorate establishes very different governing conditions. And some of the consequences are evident in the type of contacts which predominate in the small cities. Both spokesmen and direct contacts receive considerable emphasis where the electorate is discriminative. Councils faced with a small electorate but a high eviction rate tend to establish channels of communication wherever they can. A small city with a discriminative electorate means few voters, in the absolute as well as the relative sense. If these voters are highly judgmental, and the high rate of eviction suggests that this is so, a council will continually try to mend its fences. These councils, by the way, show a very high rate of group mobilization (83 percent) and nearly as high a rate of group access facilitation (67 percent).[11] The discriminative electorate of the small city has the greatest success in establishing multiple linkages with its council.

---

[11] These proportions are higher than for councils of any other electoral context in either small or large cities, except that 67% of the councils in large cities with a volatile electorate also facilitate group access.

Chapter 19

Images
of the Public

Many citizens do not express themselves politically,
at least not in ways which can be easily seen by officeholders.
They do not participate in selecting the governors or in petitioning them. Only about a third of the eligible voters in the 82 Bay
Area cities cast ballots in council elections; undoubtedly many less
than a third are active in campaigns. Perhaps half the population
belongs to organizations,[1] but since many of these organizations
play a negligible role in local affairs, the proportion of citizens in
contact with the council through membership in organized groups
is substantially less. It is only a part of the public and not *the* public that is linked to the council in one way or another.

These rather simple facts create some of the knottiest problems
of democracy and complicate understanding the workings of democracy. Persons democratically chosen to manage the collective
affairs of the community are supposed to attend to the well-being
of the entire population—the nonvoters as well as the voters, the
unorganized as well as the organized. Politicians do not speak of

---

[1] In the absence of data about actual group memberships in Bay Area cities, this
estimate can only be a guess. It is based on the assumption that the proportion
of citizens belonging to voluntary associations in the Bay Area is unlikely to
deviate markedly from what has been recorded by national surveys. The proportion is likely to be slightly more than half in the wealthier cities and
slightly less than half in the poorer cities. See, for instance, V. O. Key, Jr.,
Public Opinion and American Democracy (New York: Alfred A. Knopf, 1961),
pp. 501–508; and Gabriel A. Almond and Sidney Verba, *The Civic Culture*
(Princeton University Press, 1963), pp. 301–306.

serving the electorate or organized interests; rather, they claim to be "serving the public"—a phrase that symbolizes the sentiment presumably animating the workings of representative democracy. Sentiment aside, it is exceedingly difficult for officeholders to respond to something as elusive as the public weal even under the best of conditions; and under the conditions normally prevailing it is perhaps impossible.

Many questions are set by the fact that only some citizens express themselves politically in democracies. Some of these questions are germane to the problems of representation that will be treated in Part V; some of them still refer to linkages more directly. So far, linkages have been described in terms of specific activities which connect council and public, such as recruiting, campaigning, electing, organizing, contacting, and informing—in short, activities through which citizens participate in selecting and petitioning councils. But there are also other factors which, though associated with these activities, are sufficiently distinct to call for a different perspective on linkage processes. They derive from the expectations or perceptions that officeholders and citizens have of each other.

The public has a view of its governors, and the officeholders have a view of those they govern. The interplay of these views helps establish the norms that hold governors and governed together in the same political system. The reciprocal relationship involved has largely eluded systematic analysis.[2] On the one hand, population surveys have reported how citizen attitudes toward political leaders reflect the public's moods and behaviors. On the other hand, much less is known about how governors see the public, and even less about how such views affect the type of relationship that is formed between governors and public.

---

[2] One of the few such studies is Carl D. McMurray and Malcolm B. Parsons, "Public Attitudes Toward the Representational Roles of Legislators and Judges," *Midwest Journal of Political Science* 9 (May 1965): 167–185. Related also is the analysis in Warren E. Miller and Donald E. Stokes, "Constituency Influence in Congress," *American Political Science Review* 57 (March 1963): 45–56, though this study reports on differing issue positions more than on mutual images and expectations. The Miller and Stokes article also includes evidence on the paucity of information which elected leaders have regarding constituents.

A legislative body is likely to have a generalized view of the public—as more or less attentive to political matters, as more or less patient with officialdom, as more or less satisfied with policies, as more or less manageable in its political behavior, as more or less supportive of the government, and so on. Traits of the public as a whole such as attentiveness, patience, satisfaction, manageability, or supportiveness—and their opposites, of course—are dimensions along which governors view the public and, as a result, see themselves in one or another type of relationship with the governed.

The public's views of the leadership, the leadership's views of the public, the behavior of the public, and the behavior of leaders are all interdependent. Although the analysis to follow can consider only a part of this interdependent package of perceptions and behavior, the degree of interdependence is crucial for governance. Moreover, when a governing group like a city council looks beyond its chamber and envisages the public, it is undoubtedly many publics that are seen rather than a single public. Yet, it is plausible to assume that the views of various publics cumulate into a more generalized picture of the public as a whole. An attentive public, for instance, is one so seen in the shared image of five or so councilmen. This is not to ignore the great variability in any population of some size, but personalization and even reification of large aggregates is a psychological shorthand that few in public life do without. Populations, however much internally differentiated in an objective sense, take on composite characteristics in the perceptions of those who regularly assess and deal with them.

Three Perceptions of the Public

Council perceptions of the public include three aspects of interest: first, the attentiveness or alertness of the public regarding council actions and community affairs; second, the agreement or shared assumptions of council and public regarding the duties of the council and the tasks of governing; and third, the manageability of political relations, or the council's sense of control in its dealings with the public.

Perceptions of these matters constitute a psychological context that is part of the political culture in which governing takes place. The degree to which the public is seen as attentive, as agreed with the council on its roles or tasks, and as manageable or controllable establishes conditions allowing certain kinds of governing behavior and precluding others.

A council governing where the public is attentive might initiate community projects which depend on widespread community cooperation and participation, whereas a council governing where the public shows little interest in local matters might initiate only such projects as can be financed from public sources and brought to fruition without wide community involvement. A council sensing a lack of agreement between its self-expectations and what the public expects will, other things being equal, turn increasingly to the staff for allies and support, whereas a council feeling itself to be in agreement with the public is more likely to involve citizens in the governing process. The degree to which councils feel a sense of control in their relations with the public affects whether they take a defensive or confident stand on community issues or whether they placate immediate pressures or formulate long-range plans.

The psychological context implicit in the council's perceptions of its relations with the public gives insight into the governing process in two ways. First, some of the problems stemming from attentiveness, agreement, and manageability in the relationship between council and public are pertinent to problems of representation. More immediately, however, these problems affect the linkages between council and public. One may ask, therefore, to what extent the council perceives the public independently of its electoral and petitioning behavior. The dilemma for democratic government is that, on the one hand, citizens express themselves as voters and, especially through organizational memberships, as petitioners; but that, on the other hand, not all citizens vote or belong to organizations. This being the case, the electorate and organizations may so dominate political life that councils will be unable to define their relations with the public except in the context of electoral and interest-group politics.

Attentiveness

Many councils govern in communities with an inattentive public, or at least one so perceived.[3] In such communities, citizens only express interest in public affairs "when they have an axe to grind" or "when it directly concerns them." For the most part they remain indifferent: "Most citizens live their own cloistered lives. They go to work and back and spend weekends at the lakes. Unless it involves them in their own home or work, they have no vital interest in local government."

Of course, such inattentiveness is not characteristic of the public in all cities. Councils sometimes report high levels of consistent political attention by citizens, as in the following case: "Participation goes back into our history. Local politics have always been of interest to the public. There have always been two sides, two factions, and therefore the people have an opportunity to choose."

Councils vary not only in how much attentiveness they ascribe to the public but also in the valuation they place on attentiveness. Illustrative of one viewpoint is the council which places high value on citizen attentiveness because "then the council is more reflective of city majority wishes," a sentiment echoed in another city where attentiveness is seen as facilitating "a type of government which follows the wishes of the people more closely."

Other councils are less sanguine or more frank about the implications of high citizen interest in local matters. In one community it is reported that lack of attentiveness actually "helps in that we are not distracted by lots of people giving their opinions which are usually based on incomplete facts. We have to base our decisions on the good of the whole." A variation on this theme stresses that citizen interest can hamper efficient operations. A councilman comments on a neighboring community's difficulties: "They are having a hell of a time with all that interest over there. They cannot operate as efficiently in some cases with that high an interest." The pressures of public scrutiny are felt in yet other ways, as reflected in the fear that "the more people watch us, the more self-conscious we get and the less able to reinforce each other's thoughts

---

[3] See Appendix C, Question 20.

Table 19–1
Correlation Coefficients for Relationships
Between Attentiveness of Public
and Four Types of Electoral Context

Type of electoral context	Attentiveness of public
Permissive	—.02
Supportive	—.04
Discriminative	.03
Volatile	.04

and come out with the best answer. If people are all watching and listening, it requires going up more blind alleys and appearing uninformed."

Differences in the extent of civic attentiveness and in the valuation placed on attentiveness suggest the importance of asking whether attentiveness is reflected only by the electoral and petitioning activities of citizens or whether it might, instead, be part of a relationship that connects council and public independently of electoral and petitioning activities. There is good reason for expecting the perception of the public's attentiveness to vary from one electoral context to another. For the activities of the electorate are visible and regular expressions of citizen involvement in and concern for community affairs. Publics constituting large electorates might be viewed as more attentive than publics constituting smaller electorates; and publics often evicting incumbents might be seen as more alert and concerned than publics less inclined to evict incumbents. Table 19 1 altogether falsifies these expectations.[4]

A council judges the attentiveness of the public quite independently of how that public acts as an electorate. This is all the more striking if one recalls that council estimates of public interest *in elections* are consistently related to the electorate's actual behavior (see Table 12–1). This is clearly not the case when it comes to

[4] To compute the coefficients, each city was classified as having or not having each context. Thus 23 cities are classified as having a permissive context and the remaining cities as not having one, etc. This procedure is also followed in Tables 19–3 and 19–5.

a more general perception of public attentiveness to local affairs. Table 19–1 suggests that councils are evidently sensitive to the variety of ways in which citizens might express themselves regarding local matters and that they are careful not to confuse a segment of the public—the electorate—with the public as a whole.

But what of the public's petitioning activities? Are they also unrelated to the council's evaluation of public attentiveness? The notion of the dual system of representation is useful in exploring this question. As noted earlier, publics at times rely on intermediaries to petition and otherwise contact their councils. If many groups are active in community affairs, if spokesmen play an important role in providing access for sectors of the community, and if direct, informal contacts are deemphasized, then organizations act as intermediaries between council and public. Few politically active groups, an insignificant role for spokesmen, and a stress on direct, informal contacts indicate the comparative unimportance of an intermediary system with its emphasis on organizations.

Table 19–2 shows that councils are more likely to view publics as attentive and alert when the dual system of representation is operable. A public gains the reputation of being politically attentive if it is represented in the legislative chamber not only by elected officials but also by spokesmen and group leaders. Communities in which political life is characterized by dual representation benefit doubly. The small governing circle in which decisions are made includes two different sets of persons claiming to act on

Table 19–2
Correlation Coefficients for Relationships
Between Attentiveness of Public and Extent
of Organizational Activity

Extent of organizational activity	Attentiveness of public
Many groups active	.67
Spokesmen are important	.41
Low emphasis on direct contacts	.14

behalf of the public. While these two sets of representatives can be in collusion to the detriment of the public, the data in Table 19–2 indicate that this is not a pervasive pattern. The presence of a second set of "representatives" leads the council to perceive the public as attentive and alert to what is going on in the community. This probably heightens their feeling of being watched, which, in turn, is conducive to effective representative government.

Councils are evidently able to, and in fact do, distinguish between what happens on election day and what happens in the course of the more continuous petitioning activities, at least as reflected in their judgment of the public's attentiveness. Insofar as public attentiveness has implications for the responsiveness of governing groups like councils, it is interest-group organizations or spokesmen for certain sectors of the public that facilitate relevant relationships. This inference must be treated with caution. No evidence has been presented as to whether the public that is perceived includes persons who are not organized or represented by spokesmen. Additional data are needed to determine whether the unorganized are within the purview of the council when it forms its picture of the public as a whole.

Agreement

Even under optimal political conditions, a public and its office-holders will have some differences of view about how the affairs of the community should be managed. Perhaps it is the distance separating the general public from the few who govern which makes it inevitable that some disagreements will characterize the relationship. The men who actually govern will see the constraints on the governing process in ways that escape the notice of the citizenry at large. Legal, bureaucratic, and financial constraints have as much bearing on their decisions as do calculations of public preferences; yet the public is likely to give little thought to the many ways in which choices are hampered and options foreclosed by precedents, regulations, and resources.

When councilmen were asked, "Are there important differences between what you think the job of councilman involves and the way the voters see it?" the question produced a shopping list of problems in the relationship between public and leadership. Thus, in one council, it is reported that "Most citizens do not see the council as performing a public function. They have no idea of public policy and that the council is where this is hammered out." Here then is a basic misunderstanding on the part of the public regarding the role of the council in community affairs; there is no shared understanding as to what public policy is and how it is formulated. This council is not an isolated case; from another comes the complaint that citizens "just often don't know enough about the process of government; they fail to distinguish between the council as a policymaking body and the staff that implements the policy."

Reflected in these comments are more than just differences of opinion about specific policies. They reflect differences about the very tasks of the council and the management of the community's affairs. The degree of agreement or disagreement ferreted out by the question refers to the expected role of the council, not to the content of particular decisions or policies. Certain disagreements are perhaps inevitable, but they are very much a matter of degree.

Although councils report neither complete agreement nor complete disagreement as regards their own view and the public's view of the governing task, councils differ across cities regarding how much agreement characterizes their relationships with the public. Some indicate a bleak condition, but others report a happier state of affairs, as illustrated in the following comment: "This is an enlightened community. The citizens have some grasp of what the duties of councilmen are."

Councils differ in their perceptions as to the amount of agreement with the public concerning the governing task, but they are nearly unanimous in commenting on how difficult it is to know what the public thinks. The interview question frequently was countered by: "But how can you know whether they differ with you or not?" And though respondents would sometimes offer educated guesses, they generally lamented their lack of information about this vital aspect of their relationship with the public.

This lament raises the question of whether the behavior of the electorate holds clues concerning the proper role of the council. The interview protocols suggest an affirmative answer. Typical of many comments was the observation that "every two years some councilmen get elected and then for four years they serve in office. You can tell by the vote how people respond to their council." This is an understandable retort to the question about agreement, but as Table 19–3 indicates, there are complications. In two electoral contexts, there is no relationship between electorate behavior and council judgments about agreement. In the remaining two contexts, electorate behavior has considerable bearing on whether the public is perceived as being in agreement with how the council is conducting itself.

A supportive electorate understandably leads to a sense that community and council have come to some sort of agreement concerning the role of officeholders. An electorate large in size but seldom inclined to evict its governors seems to be the optimum condition for communications between council and public to be built on mutual trust. The significance of this is reinforced by the absence of any relationship in the permissive electoral context. The permissive electorate is no more likely than the supportive electorate to evict its governors, but it is apathetic. Under these conditions, the council must make a judgment about the extent of agreement independently of voter behavior. Despite regularly returning incumbents, the electorate which involves comparatively few voters does not communicate a sense of agreement with how the council is carrying out its tasks. For agreement to be communicated, it takes active support and not the indifference suggested by

Table 19–3

Correlation Coefficients for Relationships
Between Perceived Agreement Regarding
Council Tasks and Four Types
of Electoral Context

Type of electoral context	Council-public agreement*
Permissive	.00
Supportive	.59
Discriminative	—.71
Volatile	.00

* A positive coefficient means high agreement for that electoral context as against all other contexts; a negative coefficient means low agreement.

permissive electoral behavior. The council in the permissive electoral context remains unclear as to how much agreement characterizes its relations with the public. On the one hand, it is not
voted out of office; yet on the other, not many citizens bother to
cast ballots. A comparison of the permissive and supportive contexts shows that under favorable conditions a large number of
voters does communicate agreement in a way that few voters do
not.

This inference is jeopardized, however, in the other two contexts. The discriminating electorate leaves little doubt in the
council's view that its relationships with the community are problematic, for the council with a discriminating electorate reports
very little agreement between itself and the public as regards its
general role in the community. The volatile electorate, in contrast,
appears to present no regular clues; the public is as likely to be
viewed as being in agreement as in disagreement.

There is, then, one reasonably firm conclusion and one puzzle.
Just as a supportive electorate generates a sense of council-public
agreement, so a discriminative context generates a sense of disagreement. In both cases, the electorate has a plausible impact on
how the public is perceived. This is the firm conclusion. The
puzzle has to do with the effect of the electorate's size on the
council's interpretation of the public mood. A large electorate
rarely evicting incumbents, as in the supportive context, facilitates
perception; but it does not when, as in the volatile context, it often
evicts the incumbents.

The relationship between a community's organizational life and
perceived agreement between council and public is less problematic. A dual system of representation emerges, one can assume, if
the linkages between governors and governed are strained. In this
situation the latter will seek alternative means for bringing their
voices to bear on public issues. If the elected representatives do
not meet or satisfy public expectations, then, in a manner of
speaking, a second set of representatives is sent to the seats of
government. The message is not likely to be lost on the officeholders. One would expect, therefore, that in communities where
many groups are active, where spokesmen play an active role, and
where direct contacts are limited, councils will be especially sensitive to disagreements between their own conception of council

Table 19–4

Correlation Coefficients for Relationships
Between Perceived Agreement Regarding Council Tasks
and Extent of Organizational Activity

Extent of organizational activity	Council-public agreement
Many groups active	—.46
Spokesmen are important	—.52
Low emphasis on direct contacts	—.50

tasks and the conceptions held by the public. Table 19–4 shows this to be the case.

An alternative explanation may be noted, though Table 19–6 will lead us to reject it. Lack of agreement between council and public, one might suppose, would lead the council to deny an important role to group leaders or to spokesmen and would lead it to turn instead to informal, direct contacts as a way of going outside the dual representative system. However, as we shall see, when relations with the public are most problematic, councils appear to welcome whatever means are available for establishing contact with the public.

The pattern in Table 19–4 adds support to the observation made in connection with Table 19–2: it is difficult for the council to have a viewpoint regarding its relations with the public that is not refracted through the prism of community organizations. The absence of a dual system of representation conveys to the council that the public is comparatively inattentive to local issues and generally in agreement with how business is being conducted. The presence of a dual system of representation conveys the opposite message: the public is alert to what is happening and is not in full accord with what it witnesses.[5]

---

[5] Although we are not interested in the interrelationship between attentiveness and agreement, it should be noted that there is practically no association; the gamma is .05. We mention this because readers might think that the two sentences concluding this paragraph actually report only one finding on the mistaken assumption that high attentiveness and low agreement go together. That this is not the case only makes the findings of Tables 19–2 and 19–4 all the more important.

Manageability

Governing groups differ with respect to whether they feel themselves in control of the political situation.[6] For instance, does the council report that things are going along smoothly? Does it act as if it has been empowered by the community to make decisions? Does it indicate some sense that there is room to maneuver in selecting from alternative policies? In short, is there slack in its relations with the public?

Conversely, does the council report many difficulties and complications in its relations with the public? Does it act hesitantly, and with the sense that what it does is always looked upon with suspicion? Does it feel that mistakes, however small, will arouse the wrath of citizens? In short, is there a taut quality about its relations with the public?

The interview protocols usually made it very clear whether the council thought the political situation was manageable or whether, instead, it felt anxious about how things were going and how the public was responding to its leadership. Compare, for example, the council where "the people passed direct legislation in the form of a referendum to protest and overthrow the council actions" with the council reporting that the people "are not much interested because things are running smoothly and problems are handled well." Indeed, despite the difficulties of providing a precise definition of sense of control or manageability, councils clearly fall into two categories—those with a relatively low, and those with a relatively high, sense of control. A low sense is illustrated by these comments:

> The interest of pressure groups is increasing; there are some councilmen who are inclined to act from fear or panic, or whoever spoke to them last.

> Our meetings are just like a football game—a whole flock of Monday-morning quarterbacks sitting out there second-guessing you. Ninety-eight percent of the people do not understand. Someone can rouse them and say, "Did you hear what's going on in the council?" and they run down here and jump up and speak out without knowing any of the facts.

---

[6] See Appendix B12.1.

By way of contrast, the following two comments illustrate council feeling that relationships with the public are under control or well managed:

> We are a peaceful, quiet community. We don't have all those problems. It is all kind of stabilized.

> The people in town approve of what we are doing; their letters indicate that the people really respect what is going on in the community.

To use the language introduced earlier, there is considerable slack in the relationships between public and council in the last two examples and considerable tautness in the relationships in the first two.

A council's sense of control is likely to vary with electoral conditions that may generally set the tone for council-public relationships. Table 19–5 presents the data. As one would expect from what is known about the character of each type of context, the council's position as a governing unit is seen as being least secure in the discriminative and volatile situations with their assertive and judgmental electorates.

The opposite occurs when the electorate is permissive; then the council tends to take a more relaxed view. Quiescence in the electorate allows the luxury of feeling that matters are under control, and indeed they probably are. As noted earlier, councils do at times describe their communities as politically "quiet, peaceful, and stabilized"; such a description is perhaps most apt when few citizens vote, and those who do simply register their assent to the

Table 19–5
Correlation Coefficients for Relationships
Between Sense of Control in Council Relations
with the Public and Four Types
of Electoral Context

Type of electoral context	High sense of control
Permissive	.44
Supportive	.11
Discriminative	—.28
Volatile	—.32

current order of things. But if a permissive electorate gives the council a feeling of security, the supportive electorate does so less despite also being an electorate which seldom evicts. The low, though positive, association indicates that councils with supportive electorates must perhaps work to maintain that condition. The relationship is much less taken for granted than it is in the permissive context, probably because the electorate is large.

The effect of a community's organizational life on the council's control is difficult to anticipate. On the one hand, an active organizational life should reduce a council's sense of control in that the council will be under pressure from many clienteles. On the other hand, a network of groups and spokesmen which mediate between council and public can make for effective, regularized government, as we had occasion to observe in Chapter 15. In contributing to a smoother, if more complicated, politics, the dual system of representation may reduce certain anxieties inherent in governing a distant and so easily misunderstood public. Table 19–6 leaves this theoretical issue unresolved. On the one hand, as the negative signs show, the data tend to support the first hypothesis: a more active organizational life consistently tends to reduce the council's feeling that it is managing the community without facing much public recalcitrance. On the other hand, the coefficients of association are less strong than those found in Table 19–2 (regarding attentiveness) and Table 19–4 (regarding perceived agreement). The comparatively weaker associations may mean that in some cities a good deal of organizational activity actually strengthens the council's sense of control.

Table 19–6
Correlation Coefficients for Relationships
Between Sense of Control in Council Relations
with the Public and Extent of Organizational Activity

Extent of organizational activity	High sense of control
Many groups active	−.30
Spokesmen are important	−.41
Low emphasis on direct contacts	−.15

Conclusion

In descending order of generality, the analysis can be sum-marized in terms of three findings. First, the relationship which councils say they have with the public is significantly affected by how the public expresses itself as an electorate and by how thoroughly organized the public is. Although some qualification will follow, the general pattern is unmistakable. It suggests one of two things. Either the council actually forms a relationship with only that part of the public which is the electorate and which is organized; or the council attempts to form a relationship with the entire public, nonvoters as well as voters and the unorganized as well as the organized, but has its perceptions and evaluations substantially shaped by the behavior of a small part of the public. Either alternative excludes the possibility that the council-public relationship is independent of electorate behavior and organizational life.

Second, the extent of organizational life, or what has been called the dual system of representation, has a more consistent association with how the public is perceived than does electorate behavior. Despite the great emphasis put on elections in democratic theory, from the perspective of officeholders electorates come and go. Although elections take place every two years, they actually affect the career of any given councilman only once in every four years, this being the usual term of office. The organizational life of the community stands in marked contrast to elections. If groups and spokesmen are active, they are likely to be continually active, not only in the election period but also in the interelection period. Whether the dual system of representation is firmly established in a community is perhaps a more pervasive and significant aspect of its political life than how the electorate behaves. However, this generalization goes well beyond the data presented in this chapter, which simply indicate that, on balance, organizational life has a more decisive bearing on council-public relationships than does electorate behavior.

Third, the association of electorate behavior with the council-public relationship is highly variable, showing no pattern with respect to judgments about attentiveness, a mixed pattern with respect to judgments about agreement, and a consistent pattern only with respect to judgments about manageability. The more elusive and evaluative the phenomenon to be judged, the more the council turns to electorate behavior for clues as to the public's character. Attentiveness is easily described, and councils indicate little difficulty in estimating the extent to which citizens are attentive and alert to local affairs. Agreement is more difficult to estimate as far as the councils are concerned; to a greater extent than in regard to attentiveness, councils are being asked to evaluate their relationship with the public and not just to describe an attribute of the public. The distinction between description and evaluation is even clearer in the case of a judgment about manageability or being "in control" of the general political situation. Here the electorate provides important feedback. Furthermore, how the electorate behaves is an important component in the creation of the conditions which can be seen as manageable or not. A quiet electorate not only indicates that council-public relations are under control; it brings about that condition. The volatile electorate not only indicates that relations with the public may be problematic; it creates that condition.

Part V

Representation
as Political Activity

INTRODUCTION

Representation, wrote James A. Mill, is "the grand discovery of modern times."[1] His sentiment is shared by most modern democrats. Representation is central to democracy because it permits its adaptation to the conditions associated with urbanization, industrialization, nationalism, and mass participation in governance. These conditions, in turn, facilitate the growth of political equality and self-government. Above all, the concentration of citizens in urban centers and the spread of political boundaries to include ever greater numbers of people in one jurisdiction make some form of representation indispensable. Representative institutions facilitate indirect citizen participation in governance when direct participation is impractical. *The Federalist* No. 52 described a representative scheme "as a substitute for a meeting of the citizens in person."[2]

If self-government is to grow and survive under modern conditions, political representation is imperative for another reason. Democratic governance has been profoundly affected by the growth of bureaucracy, the specialization of labor, and the increased role of government in organizing collective effort and allocating collective goods. Commentators like Weber and Michels and, to a lesser extent, Mosca recognized that democratic forms are

---

[1] Quoted without citation in Carl J. Friedrich, *Man and His Government* (New York: McGraw-Hill, 1963), p. 301.
[2] *The Federalist*, No. LII, Max Beloff, ed. (New York: The Macmillan Company, 1948), p. 270.

398

not immune to the modes of organizing and exercising authority associated with the industrialized, rationalized society. These modes penetrated political life as quickly and effectively as they penetrated economic life. The rhetoric of democratic reform and the institutionalization of democratic practices notwithstanding, political rule seemed concentrated in the hands of the few. Michels's "iron law of oligarchy," Weber's "politics as a profession," or Mosca's "ruling class" are variants on a common theme: political power will not be equally dispersed in society but will tend always to be controlled by those who are delegated, or usurp, leadership in managing collective affairs.

Although there will always be rulers or governors distinct from the ruled or governed, this need not mean a relationship of absolute domination and submission. In the context of counterpressures toward democratization, there is a continuing search, in both theory and practice, for ways of organizing politics so that the governors will be responsible and responsive to the governed. If rule is inevitably in the hands of a tiny fraction of the population, arrangements are needed to insure that these few will represent the interests and welfare of the many.

Theorizing about political representation has proven difficult largely because the concept "political representation" is so elusive. As Hanna Pitkin observes, "Learning what 'representation' means and learning how to represent are intimately connected."[3] Because it is difficult to state what representation is, it is difficult to specify the conditions, institutional or otherwise, which establish it. Inquiry into the conditions making for representation is not separable from attention to the meaning of representation.

There are a variety of approaches for inquiring into the meaning of representation. One can consider alternative arguments for what the representative should do, an approach illustrated by Burke's well-known speech to the Electors of Bristol. One can investigate how the term is used, an approach suggested by ordinary language analysis and admirably illustrated in Pitkin's work on representation. Or one can turn immediately to the various institutional

---

[3] Hanna Pitkin, *The Concept of Representation* (Berkeley: University of California Press, 1967), p. 1.

arrangements thought to produce representative government, an approach found whenever constitution making is the order of the day, as, for instance, in *The Federalist.* Each of these approaches finds its way into the following chapters, but none exclusively.

The scientific problem stems from the anomalous situation that though representative institutions or institutions so described are abundant, there is no theory about how representation works. In the United States alone there are nearly 90,000 different governing units in which certain citizens are selected to represent other citizens. There are school boards, special district commissions, township and city councils, county boards, state and national legislatures, and many other types of committees, all of which share the designation "representative." The same phenomenon—governance by a few in the name of the many—pervades the nongovernmental sectors of society; every organization from neighborhood clubs to giant corporations, from the local P.T.A. to million-member labor unions, is governed by a small number of members designated to represent the interests of the collectivity. Because of flourishing activity of representation and the enormous diffusion of representative institutions, sustained effort is required to explain how the representational process works.

Such effort has been partially retarded by the obsolete conceptions of representation which continue to guide empirical investigation. Though most empirical work on representation has been cast in the vocabulary of Burke, this vocabulary is inappropriate for thinking about representative government two centuries later. But more is necessary than breaking the spell of Burke. Various ways of looking at representation which have long dominated theoretical work need to be modified and possibly discarded.

The way in which we have organized analysis holds the clue to at least one major modification considered necessary. Two linkage processes between the council and the public have been examined at length—those through which the council is constituted and those through which it is petitioned. Either might have been taken as synonymous with political representation, and have been by some theorists. We distinguish between these two major forms of linkage, on the one hand, and representation, on the other. For viewing representation in terms of selection or petitioning leads to an insufficiently behavioral theory of representation. In reviewing briefly why this is so we make clear that our conceptualization emphasizes what councils *do* in carrying out their representational tasks.

The Selection and Composition of Legislatures

A dominant theme in representational theory turns on the term "representative*ness*"; it is a term which stresses the characteristics of the membership of governing groups. A legislature is said to be more or less representative depending on how it is selected and on how accurately it mirrors the population with respect to its members' social origins or political viewpoints. Debates about proportional representation reflect a concern for the appropriate process of selecting legislators and for the numeric reflection in the legislature of the distribution of population characteristics. An assembly is representative when it mirrors the population it "stands for." Friedrich, for instance, comments on proportional representation as the attempt to "secure a representative assembly reflecting with more or less mathematical exactness the various divisions in the electorate."[4]

The familiar criticism of proportional representation is based on difficulties of governance. When the selection of legislators is such as to reflect in the assembly every shade of political opinion, instability at best and paralysis at worst is the likely outcome. The early debates over proportional representation did not give much attention to the meaning of representation implied by the concern with the selection and composition of legislatures.

More recent criticism has noted that a preoccupation with the representative*ness* of legislatures fails to uncover the conditions under which legislatures can be said to be actually *representing*. Attention turns from the characteristics of legislators to the activities of legislatures. Pitkin, for instance, includes a review of proportional representation in a much broader discussion of "de-

---

[4] Carl J. Friedrich, *Constitutional Government and Democracy* (rev. ed.; Boston: Ginn and Company, 1950), p. 286.

scriptive representation," a term she borrows from Griffiths, who writes that "if our concern is that a country's assembly should be the forum for every given opinion that the country contains, it is natural and reasonable to suggest that the assembly should be composed of descriptive representatives drawn from every opinion-holding group."[5] Pitkin concludes that this view of representation "has no room for any kind of representing as acting for, or on behalf of, others; which means that in the political realm it has no room for the creative activities of a representative legislature, the forging of consensus, the formulation of policy, the activity we roughly designate by 'governing.' "[6]

This critique of proportional representation or, more broadly, descriptive representation guides us in distinguishing an analysis of the selection of councils from an analysis of their representational behavior. We thereby avoid several difficulties. First, we avoid confusing an empirical and a definitional issue. Who the legislator is and what he does may well be empirically related, but to define representation as in some manner synonymous with the characteristics of legislators, their typicalness, is to mistake a formalistic for a behavioral theory of representation.

Second, viewing representation in terms of the selection and composition of legislatures is to force on analysis an unnecessary complexity. What is behind such viewpoints is nearly always a concern with what legislatures are doing, along with the implicit hypothesis that what they do must relate to who they are. When the trade union movement asserts that Parliament would be more representative if only it included more working-class members, there is the presumption that social origin is highly correlated with, first, political viewpoint and, second, ability to represent the interests of the workers. Even the proportionalists, Pitkin comments, "are interested in what the legislature does; they care about its composition precisely because they expect the composition to determine the activities."[7]

---

[5] Quoted in Pitkin, *The Concept of Representation,* p. 83. The article cited is A. Phillips Griffiths and Richard Wollheim, "How Can One Person Represent Another?" *Aristotelian Society Supplement* 34 (1960): 187–224.
[6] Pitkin, *The Concept of Representation,* p. 90.
[7] *Ibid.,* p. 63.

If the concern is with what legislatures do, then it is preferable to make that the central analytic task rather than to approach it through the indirect and cumbersome path of presuming a correlation between composition and activity. Two purposes then are served by distinguishing the selection of leaders and the composition of legislatures, on the one hand, from representation, on the other. It allows viewing representation in terms of what leaders do rather than who they are (or how they are selected), and it permits treating the relationship between these as a matter for empirical inquiry.

Petitioning the Legislature

Congress, declares the First Amendment to the United States Constitution, shall make no law "abridging the freedom of speech, or of the press; or the right of the people peaceably to assemble, and to petition the Government for a redress of grievances." The right to petition political leadership is a cardinal tenet of democracy; so also is the need of the leadership to be informed of the viewpoints and preferences of the public, though the latter is not formalized in constitutions.

Writings on parliamentary democracies contain the thread of an argument, stretching back to thirteenth-century England, to the effect that the petitioning process itself is a form of representation. In this argument, or at least in its contemporary formulation, governments are said to be representative when citizens (or estates) have opportunities effectively to voice their preferences on public issues. We find this formulation of representation deficient. The reasons for distinguishing the activity of representation from the extent and form of petitioning relate in large part to the legal status of city councils, a status which is best reviewed in the context of two different roles that elected assemblies have played throughout the history of parliamentary government.

When the monarchs of feudal England brought together the Lords Spiritual and Temporal, as well as delegates from the counties and boroughs, they were not of course convening a legislature in the current sense of that term. The Parliament was not a law-making body so much as an instrument of rule, a means of tightening the centrally directed administrative apparatus through which the royal treasury was replenished. But these forerunners of modern-day legislative assemblies also communicated the viewpoints of the various estates to the monarch. And this role of parliamentary bodies has its twentieth-century equivalent.

This is especially so in the parliamentary system where the legislature forms and then supports the government, as well as houses the loyal opposition. Parliament is to keep itself and the administrative branch informed of the currents of opinion abroad in the society. All legislatures play this role to some extent, but in some cases this role is so dominant that perhaps it is inappropriate to use the term "legislature" to describe them. In certain new nations, for instance, where government is patterned on the Westminster model but where the executive and the civil service are far stronger than the parliament or the party, the legislature has not much of a role other than to reflect the diversity of viewpoints in the society and to act as a channel of communication between the public and the effective governors.

When the primary task of the parliament is to serve as a sounding board for the sentiments of different groups in the society, a case can be made for viewing representation in terms of the petitioning process. Because the elected assembly does not govern, it makes no sense to equate representation with the responsiveness of the assembly to the expressed preferences of the public, a conception of representation shortly to be advanced. But because the assembly does tell the executive agency what is wanted and not wanted by the constituencies, it makes some sense to view representation as closely related to the accessibility of the assembly, to the openness of the communication channels, in short, to the effectiveness of the linkage processes between representatives and represented.

City councils fall well outside a parliamentary tradition stressing the communication role of the representatives. The councils *are* the governments in their communities. They are not even limited by the separation of powers found at the state and national level. The councils legislate and control the administration of their own enactments, at least in a *de jure* sense. In studying councils, one can rightly claim to be studying governance, and not simply petitioning or even legislating.

When the prime task of the elected assembly is governance, it would be misleading to define representation in terms of the petitioning process. Such a definition focuses on the expression of preferences by the public and neglects whether these preferences are translated into policy by the council. A public can express itself vigorously and through many channels; yet the council may fail to enact policies responsive to these preferences. Or a public can express itself weakly and infrequently; yet the council may still select policies thought to be in accord with public preferences.

Insofar as the assembly governs, in the quest to understand whether it also represents we must ask not what it hears but how it responds. The availability of channels for the expression of citizen viewpoints may well be empirically related to how representative the government is, but the linkage process should not itself be taken as representation. Distinguishing the petitioning of councils from their representational activities serves a purpose similar to that served by distinguishing between the selection of councils and representation. It allows us to examine empirically the relationship between petitioning and representation, and it frees us to search for a substantive and behavioral conception of representation.

At one point in her study of the concept of representation Pitkin comments that representation "is a certain characteristic activity, defined by certain behavioral norms or certain things a representative is expected to do. The greater part of the literature on political representation takes such an assumption for granted. . . . But to understand that literature and master its controversies, we need to be clear about what is entailed in viewing representation as activity, and how such a view differs from what has gone before."[8]

That representation involves activity has too long been ignored. By taking it for granted, theory cannot possibly come to grips with the reality of representing institutions. The behavioral study of politics provides a corrective to the definitional formalism in theorizing about representation. It leads to inquiry about the

---

[8] *Ibid.*, p. 112.

activities of those citizens who are chosen to represent their fellow citizens and to a search for criteria to decide when representation is taking place and when it is not.

In working toward a theory of representation, much underbrush needs clearing away. Chapter 20, taking off from Burke's concern with the proper relationship between representative and represented, the mandate-independence formulation, examines some representational activities associated with political trusteeship. The analysis leads us to discard trusteeship as well as the mandate-independence formulation as useful approaches to understanding representation. This leads, in Chapter 21, to a search for an empirically viable alternative conception of representation, a task guided by Pitkin's work that makes "responsiveness" the core term in assessing representational activity. Finally, in Chapter 22, analysis turns to one of the central problems of democracy—the conditions which facilitate or impede representation now defined in terms of the responsiveness of the governors to the governed. In groping for a "theory of electoral accountability," the assumption shared by many theorists of democracy is that it is when the public can hold the representatives accountable for what they are *doing* that a responsive relationship between governors and governed is most likely to occur.

The theoretical interest in accountability provides the clearest and most significant reason for holding to the distinction between constituting and petitioning the council, on the one hand, and representation as responsiveness, on the other. If representation is taken to mean the numeric reflection of population characteristics in the legislature, then it is not possible to connect accountability and representation, for voters do not hold the legislator to account for who he is but for what he does. Similarly, if representation is taken to mean the openness and effectiveness of petitioning, then it is not possible to connect accountability and representation, for voters do not hold the legislator to account for what he hears but for how he responds to what he hears. To introduce accountability into a theory of representation, which we believe necessary, representation must be conceived as activity, as something which the legislature *does* and for which it can be held to account.

Chapter 20

Representation as Trusteeship

For the overwhelming majority of San Francisco Bay region city councilmen the classic question about political representation—whether a representative should do what his constituents want and be bound by instructions from them, or whether he should be free to act as seems best to him in the pursuit of their welfare—poses few difficulties. Of the 435 individual councilmen interviewed, 60 percent opted for the role of "trustee," 18 percent for the role of "delegate," and only 22 percent either could not choose between one role or the other or claimed to follow one strategy of representation in some circumstances and the other strategy in other circumstances.[1]

It would seem, therefore, that the theoretical tension between the two classical interpretations of representation, between mandate and independence, is in practice not very salient to the practitioners. This may be so because both trustees and delegates agree that it is their job to promote the welfare of the community and disagree only on the style of behavior involved in performing this task. While the delegate believes that the welfare is best served by a close translation into legislation of expressed constituency wishes, the trustee believes that the public interest is best served by resisting immediate constituency wishes through the exercise of

---

[1] For an analysis of the individual-level data on representation, see the companion volume by our collaborator Katherine Hinckley, *The Fabric of Urban Representation* (Indianapolis: The Bobbs-Merrill Company, forthcoming).

independent judgment. Either position is meritorious, depending on some initial assumptions, and for this reason, perhaps, a reconciliation of the conflicting imperatives has eluded theoretical solution. Indeed, as with most dualisms in human as in scientific affairs, it may be that the manner in which the issue is posed makes for a false question. As Pitkin has observed, "what is most striking about the mandate-independence controversy is how long it has continued without coming any nearer to a solution, despite the participation of many astute thinkers."[2]

Empirical research is not likely to solve a normative problem, even though it may take off from it. However, there are theoretical considerations that are, at least in principle, if not in practice, soluble. This is so because theoretical considerations can be placed in an empirical context that serves to circumscribe what is demonstrable. A case in point is the city setting in which councilmen approach the representational task. It is a setting which, we noted in Chapter 5, is especially congenial to what was called a benevolent governing style—a kind of paternalism, or "father knows best" attitude, more characteristic, probably, of amateur than of professional politics. And city councilmen are amateurs par excellence. The claim that one's own judgment should prevail over instructions from one's constituents is part and parcel of the amateur's paternalism. Little attention has been given in political theorizing about the representative's would-be independence to this component of his role.

Yet it is a component that deserves some attention because it points up an ironical paradox in Edmund Burke's defense of the independence theory of representation. If the role of trustee incorporates the role of father, it is evident that the representative's "independence" contains its own brand of parochialism—that is, it evinces a tendency toward exactly that representational style which independent judgment is presumably intended to avoid. Fathers, there is reason to suspect, are prone to take a narrow view of their families' interests. If this is so, Burke's defense of independence as the proper style of representation is more parochial and limited than meets the eye.

---

[2] Hanna Pitkin, *The Concept of Representation* (Berkeley: University of California Press, 1967), p. 148.

Whatever Burke seemed to tell the voters of Bristol in his famous election speech of 1774, it contained more than an exegesis of contrary theories of representation. This is not to deny its seminal importance for the theory of representation. But it was presented in a historical context, and knowledge of that context is necessary for understanding Burke's meaning. As pointed out elsewhere, Burke was above all a party man, and his party was the aristocratic Whig faction in Parliament which, by virtue of its members' status, considered itself the true custodian of England's interests as a nation.[3] When Burke argued that "parliament is a *deliberative* assembly of *one* interest, that of the whole,"[4] he in fact questioned the representational role and celebrated the deliberative role of the legislature. While he seemed to oppose the parochial interests of the constituencies as harmful to the welfare of the community, he in fact substituted for local interests the interests of the parliamentary faction he served—interests no less parochial than those of the good merchants of Bristol with whom he found himself at loggerheads and whose disagreement with his policy positions finally forced him to decline reelection in 1780.

Although Burke himself was what one would call today a professional politician, the noblemen he served were not. Politics was for them a matter of *noblesse oblige*, so at least they claimed, or a pleasant pastime; but in their hearts they were aristocratic amateurs who knew best what England's interests were and who had no difficulty in making their own interests the nation's interests. In articulating and defending the conception of the representative's role as an independent trustee, Burke promoted the interests of the class which had coopted him. Modern city councilmen are not aristocrats but, as was noted in Chapter 13, of the middle class. But, like Burke's parliamentarians, they are amateurs, and their interest in politics is largely restricted to the confines of the city they serve.[5]

[3] See Heinz Eulau, "Changing Views of Representation," in Ithiel de Sola Pool, ed., *Contemporary Political Science: Toward Empirical Theory* (New York: McGraw-Hill, 1967), pp. 69–76.
[4] Edmund Burke, "Speech to the Electors of Bristol" (1774), *Works*, Vol. II, p. 12.
[5] Less than a third (29%) of the councilmen expressed some wish for higher office. Of these 127 with higher ambitions, almost half (48%) did not aspire higher than to another local office or to the position of county supervisor; 18% of the 127 aspirants looked forward to state legislative service and 11% to the

Just as in the case of Burke's Parliament, there is a strong current of paternalism underlying most city councils' conceptions of trusteeship. Parliament (read city council) is a small group of especially talented men who "care for" the welfare of those who are either not willing or not able to look after their own interests. If the voters are wise, they will elect representatives who embody the best of the community; these will be men of judgment, discernment, and competence. By means of deliberation, Parliament (read city council) can advance the welfare of the whole community if only its members remain committed to the values of trusteeship and are not swayed by selfish interests and narrow prejudices. These sentiments are unmistakably voiced in the city councils: "The council has to lead and exercise political courage. A city will stagnate if we follow the lead of the people. Progress and new programs come with the council leading and the community following in behind after a while." Councils frequently claimed "the benefit of more knowledge of the problems" and thus justified their paternalistic governing style: "The general public does not necessarily know what the issues are and what is even best for them, thus we use our own best judgment."

Although councilmen may see themselves as having been elected by a particular group, or even by voters from one area of the city, they are, with a few exceptions, elected at large. The logic of this electoral system runs counter to the representation of a geographic unit within the city, and there is a strong presumption that the council as a whole represents the entire population as a whole. In this context the role of representative becomes identified with the role of city father as readily as the role of Burke's representative was identifiable with that of the English nobleman.

As a result, moreover, the *focus* of representation is not likely to be especially salient to councilmen.[6] Though possibly differing in

Congress. The remainder had an eye on a judicial post or were not clear as to what they might prefer. See Kenneth Prewitt, *The Recruitment of Political Leaders: A Study of Citizen-Politicians* (Indianapolis: The Bobbs-Merrill Company, 1970), pp. 183–185.
[6] Councilmen clearly differ in this respect from state legislators elected from geographic constituencies. See John C. Wahlke, Heinz Eulau, William Buchanan, and Leroy C. Ferguson, *The Legislative System: Explorations in Legislative Behavior* (New York: John Wiley and Sons, 1962), pp. 287–310: "The Legislator and His District: Areal Roles."

style of representation, city councils see the city as a whole as their proper focus of attention.

Because of the strong concentration of trustee orientations at the individual level and the skewed distribution of the three orientations across the 82 councils, it was advisable to classify the councils in terms of the relative strength of the trustee orientation in each. While ideally one would want to compare predominantly trustee councils with delegate councils and with councils of highly mixed composition, there were too few councils in the latter two categories to serve the purpose of analysis. Councils were classified, therefore, as being either trustee or nontrustee councils, with the latter being residual as they include, in varying combinations, a variety of orientations possible at the individual level of analysis.[7]

Two consequences should follow from trusteeship. First, the council strongly pervaded by the values of trusteeship should be willing to stand up against and defy the expressed wishes of the majority—not necessarily always but often enough to show that the willingness is there. For it is not the immediate wishes of even a majority but the long-term welfare of the entire community that is the criterion against which the soundness of policy is to be judged. Second, the council highly committed to trusteeship should be able and willing to resist the claims of specific interest groups in the community. For independent judgment of an issue's merits is no less threatened by particularistic, and presumably selfish, demands than it is by majority wishes. If majority wishes are viewed as possibly in conflict with the general welfare, it is even more likely that the claims of a particular interest will be deficient when measured against the welfare of all.

Defying the Majority Will

In the course of the interview, councils were asked: "Do you ever have to take a stand that the majority of the voters seem to disagree with?" Although this proved to be a difficult question for many respondents, they indicated the general direction in which they leaned. Thus in one council where "it is hard to know what

---

[7] For the question on which the measure is based, see Appendix C, Question 38.

the voters want," there nevertheless is the attempt "to ascertain what most of them want for the city and then vote for that." In another council which seldom takes stands counter to majority preferences, it is reasoned that "it is their city, they are paying for it."

Not all councils are willing to defer to expressions of majority preferences. Among those which do stand against the majority it was frequently commented that the public is too ill informed to decide on intricate matters before the council, a common argument against plebiscitary democracy. It is thus the responsibility of the council to consider those issues which the public has failed to take into account. "Many times the public does not have the basic facts before them. Given all the facts, the time, and the same degree of interest, the public would vote as we do." Here is the distinction between "wish" and "welfare" so prominent in discussions of representation. What the public wishes is all too often based on insufficient evidence and an inadequate review of the matter at hand; their wishes therefore run counter to the public interest. The importance of the deliberative assembly is that it can protect the welfare of the public even against its own at times misguided wishes.

Other councils defying the majority may do so out of simple opposition to what is wished. A clear case of this appears in a city with a large and vocal black population where formal government remains under the control of downtown business interests. According to a member of this council, taking stands against the majority "happens now more than ever because of the conditions we face. There is great social unrest. People want a Police Review Board because of police brutality charges, but that is not going to solve things. The policeman has to be the law in my opinion."

It is evident why a trustee council might frequently find itself in opposition to the majority. If the majority has poor information on which to make judgments; or, even worse, if it makes "wrong" judgments such as showing insufficient respect for the legal foundations of the community, then the trustee council will use its discretion to protect the majority from itself. Although inadequate information, poor judgment, narrow interests, desire for short-term gratifications, and a host of ills are attributed to the political majority by the council, there is no reason to expect that these traits cluster more in high- than in low-trusteeship cities.[8] However, there is good reason to expect that high-trustee councils will take note of such traits and will employ them in explaining, to themselves and to others, why it is often necessary to contravene the majority. If correct that there is more than a trace of paternalism in trusteeship, then the trustee council will be hypersensitive to the inadequacies of the majoritarian position on issues of governance. Paternalism implies a certain caution toward the opinions of those one is obligated to care for. Moreover, in trusteeship the council has readily available a justification for preferring independent judgment over majority expressions.

Table 20–1 shows that councils relatively high on trusteeship do take stands counter to the majority on a more regular basis than do low-trustee councils. The logic is well stated in one council: "Responsibility is not always what the majority want you to do, but what is best for the entire city."

However one evaluates the appropriateness of trusteeship in representative democracies, the argument of the trustee that responsibility may imply ignoring majority preferences must be taken seriously. It is possible that on a particular issue at a certain time a small group of men presumably chosen for their competence and judgment will indeed "know better" than even the majority of citizens what is best for the community. Perhaps no more persuasive evidence is available than the part played by the law courts (small groups of specially selected men) in protecting civil liberties and minority rights against the contrary wishes of even sizable majorities. The fact that the majority has been wrong in the past

---

[8] It might be thought that councils would adopt the trustee role in response to a public which was poorly equipped to guard its own welfare. There is a logic to this expectation, but it is here rejected on two grounds. First, trusteeship, or lack of it, appears to be more a part of an officeholder's individual political philosophy than an orientation growing out of his interactions with the public. Second, the data available indicate no relationship between trusteeship and perceived traits of the public, though the particular measures constitute only a partial test of the notion that trusteeship is not adopted in response to public traits. Using the measures introduced in Chapter 18, we find that the association between trusteeship and perceived attentiveness by the public is .00; between trusteeship and perceived agreement regarding community management .05; and between trusteeship and sense of control in relations with the public .08.

Table 20–1

Relationship Between Trusteeship and Whether
Council Frequently Takes Stands Counter
to Majority Preferences

Take stands counter to majority	Trusteeship		
	Low N = 34	Medium N = 24	High N = 24
Seldom	62%	46%	29%
Often	38	54	61
	100%	100%	100%
Gamma = .43			

and the possibility that it might be wrong in the future sustains the
tradition of trusteeship in democratic politics, despite the paternalistic and even elitist tendencies involved. That majorities may
sometimes have to be opposed is recognized in the establishment
of representative government rather than plebiscitary democracy
and in the laws which exclude certain principles from the agenda
of political debate.

Our immediate interest is not with the complicated issue of
majoritarian power versus minority rights; it is with trusteeship
and what it implies. Table 20–1 shows that councils widely adopting trusteeship as the basis of a relationship with the citizenry
more often and more willingly oppose the expressed preferences
of the majority than do councils less comfortable with the norms of
trusteeship. When and where it is felt necessary, the high-trustee-
ship councils will allow independent judgment to prevail.

Serving a Special Clientele

Legislatures, whether actually petitioned or not, often pay attention to the preferences of particular clienteles. This can happen
in several ways. Sometimes, as in Congress, one or another legislator is supported by and becomes known as the spokesman for
an identifiable organized interest, say, the oil industry or certain
labor unions. Sometimes one or more legislators take on the cause

of a broad interest, say, public education, or even an unorganized interest like consumers. Sometimes an entire legislative committee may form an alliance with a specific client, as that between the House Agriculture Committee and the farm interests. However it comes about, regular attention to the latent or manifest preferences of a clientele is an important aspect of the legislative process in state and national politics.

Similar phenomena occur in local politics. In some 50 cities, councils reported being regularly attentive to the preferences or well-being of a clientele group when considering policies.[9] In such instances the council would enact policy in conformity with the declared or undeclared interests of a group, or it would at least avoid policy alternatives opposed by that group. More than a dozen councils, for example, stressed the importance of protecting downtown merchants and other local business interests. This might involve city-supported parking facilities, zoning areas for commercial development, resisting pressures for a sales tax, or generally promoting business-related community services.

That the business sector is a client of the council does not mean that business interests control the council. It only means that the council recognizes the importance of enacting policies which protect this client's interest, that it is willing to defer to business groups on matters considered their legitimate concern, and that it protects in a general way the cluster of values relevant to a "healthy business atmosphere."

This council-client relationship can work itself out in several ways. In some instances the council for all intents and purposes

---

[9] Two things about the conceptualization and coding of clienteles merit note. The procedures used did not allow for the possibility that an entire community could be considered a clientele; it is always an identifiable group *within* the community, usually a relatively cohesive group the members of which share economic interests. What brings a clientele to attention is that it has some specialized interests which it promotes to the exclusion of other interests. Second, the coding procedures identify a clientele only if its preferences are regularly attended to by the council. Simply pressing claims was not enough, or else a clientele would not differ from the groups and spokesmen we have already discussed in connection with linkage processes. A clientele, then, has two characteristics: it is a part of and never the entire community; and it is attended to, even serviced, by the council. For a description of the measure, see Appendix B20.1.

merely ratifies legislation fashioned outside the council by the clientele group. In other instances the council so completely shares the values of the clientele group that there is no question but that in matters affecting it the "appropriate" decisions will be made. For example, councils intent on conserving the residential nature of the community have an interest identical with that of certain homeowner groups. The developers, realtors, and other expansionists are in this case resisted as a matter of course.

As a clientele is a part of and never coincident with the entire community, as well as favored by the council, one should expect that trustee councils would show little regard for clientele groups. To be attentive to a clientele would mean relinquishing independent judgment, at least in those matters in which the clientele had an interest. And giving continuous preferential treatment to a clientele would make it difficult to guard the interests of the entire community, for there are undoubtedly occasions when the clientele's interests conflict with those of the community.

Resisting clientele groups as an aspect of trusteeship is what Burke had in mind when he proposed independence as the appropriate norm for organizing representative legislative bodies. In the absence of trusteeship, the preferences of a single client might dominate legislation; this would happen if a single sector of the community were able to control the recruitment processes. In that case, legislators, in line with the mandate principle, would be beholden to the client who promoted their candidacies and possibly elected them to office. But the mandate theory violates the democratic principle that the welfare of the whole, or even the wishes of the majority, should be reflected in legislative deliberations. Trusteeship is a form of prudent social insurance because it allows the legislature, as Burke put it, to be a body "where, not local purposes, not local prejudices ought to guide but the general good, resulting from the general reason of the whole."[10]

Table 20–2 presents the relationship between trusteeship and clientele servicing. Neither Burke's reasoning nor the hypothesis derived from his reasoning are supported. In fact the relationship, though weak, is the opposite of what was expected; trustee councils

---

[10] Burke, "Speech to the Electors of Bristol," p. 12.

Table 20–2
Relationship Between Trusteeship
and Whether Council Services a Clientele

	Trusteeship		
Whether a clientele is serviced	Low N = 34	Medium N = 24	High N = 24
No	47%	37%	33%
Yes	53	63	67
	100%	100%	100%
Gamma = .20			

are actually *more* likely to service a clientele regularly than are nontrustee councils. This is a surprising pattern, for it is difficult to understand how a trustee council can be attentive to a clientele and yet insist that it relies on independent judgment, the hallmark of the trustee orientation. Either our reasoning about trusteeship is in error, or there are trustee councils behaving counter to the imperatives of their professed representational values.

This finding presents a perplexing problem which can be formulated most clearly, and a tentative explanation offered, by presenting the evidence in the two previous tables jointly; this is done in Table 20–3. It would seem that the high-trustee councils trade off majoritarian preferences for the preferences of a clientele. More than twice as many high-trustee councils are attentive to a clientele as are attentive to the majority. The councils in which trusteeship is least present are relatively attentive to both the majority and a clientele. These are the councils which come closest to a mandate position and thus should be sensitive to instructions coming from various sources.

If, as in Table 20–3, the relative emphasis given to one source of cues over the other is compared, a tendency in trusteeship little noticed by either its critics or defenders is evident. Critics despair that trusteeship is not true representativeness because it implies distance and aloofness from majority preferences. Apologists defend trusteeship for exactly those reasons, stressing that the representative needs discretion if he is to bring to bear his own judgment on matters of state. But the distance which the trustee

Table 20–3
Relationship Between Trusteeship
and the Relative Emphasis Given
to Majority Preferences and Clienteles

	Trusteeship		
Council is attentive to:	Low N = 34	Medium N = 24	High N = 24
Majority (seldom defies it)	62%	46%	29%
Clientele (regularly services it)	53%	63%	67%
Index of relative emphasis*	+9%	−17%	−38%

* Percentage difference as measure of relative emphasis
given to one source of cues over the others.

maintains between himself and the majority opens up an entirely
new possibility in political representation, a possibility which
serves neither the goal of the mandate position nor the goal of the
independence position.

The trustee council, in turning a deaf ear to the majority's voice,
allows for the possibility that the voice of a clientele group will
be heard all the louder. This is most likely if the clientele group
claims that its specialized interests are in harmony with the general
welfare. It is the paternalistic element in trusteeship which allows
a council to rationalize a harmony of interests between what is
judged to be the general welfare and what is preferred by a clientele. The council exercises its judgment when majority wishes are
thought to be in conflict with the public welfare, but defers in that
judgment when a clientele's wishes can be seen as consonant with
the public welfare.

Facilitating Conditions

To consider this interpretation more than plausible, it is desirable to identify the conditions which facilitate or impede the

likelihood that trustee councils will attend to or service a clientele. One such condition is given by the differing relationships between the council and the public in general; another is given by the different types of electoral context. The general hypothesis holds that the tendency of trustee councils to service a clientele will be facilitated if the council's relations with the public are not problematic, but that it will be impeded if these relations are disturbed. Where community politics are relatively free of tensions and difficulties in the relationship between governors and governed, a council inclined to act as trustee can harmonize a clientele's wishes with its own judgment of the public interest.

Table 20–4 partly confirms the hypothesis. A positive coefficient means that councils placing high value on trusteeship are more sensitive and helpful to a clientele than are councils placing low value on trusteeship; they behave counter to expectations. A negative coefficient indicates that trustee councils are less amenable to clientele interests than are nontrustee councils.[11] Although the public's attentiveness, as perceived by the council, has no effect on the relationship between trusteeship and a clientele orientation, both council-public agreement and the council's sense that the public is manageable have a striking effect. The contradictory implications of trusteeship and commitment to a clientele are adjusted more easily if the public is agreeable and viewed as being manageable.

Very much the same results are obtained under the different conditions provided by the four types of electoral context. As Table 20–5 shows, under the less problematic and more congenial conditions provided by supportive and, to a lesser extent, permissive electorates, the trustee council is more likely than the low-trustee council to defer to the preferences of a clientele group. In the supportive and permissive electoral contexts the trustee council can more readily insist on exerting its own independent judgment

---

[11] In Table 20–4 and the remaining tables of this chapter the measure of trusteeship is a dichotomous one, collapsing for purposes of computing a gamma the categories of moderate and high as used in earlier tables. The gamma association between trusteeship and a client orientation for the uncontrolled 2 × 2 table is .24; for Table 20–2, where trusteeship is a trichotomous measure, it is .20.

Table 20–4
Correlation Coefficients for Relationship
Between Trusteeship and Clientele Orientation
Under Different Conditions of Council-Public Relations

Public is viewed as:	Relationship between trusteeship and clientele orientation
Relatively less attentive (N = 41)	.26
Relatively more attentive (N = 41)	.24
Relatively little agreed (N = 49)	−.24
Relatively more agreed (N = 32)	.76
Relatively unmanageable (N = 43)	−.14
Relatively manageable (N = 39)	.58

in matters of public concern and yet incorporate the viewpoints
of a clientele. This tendency is not likely when the electorate
intrudes into the governing process as in the discriminative and
volatile electoral situations.[12]

Table 20–5
Correlation Coefficients for Relationship
Between Trusteeship and Clientele Orientation
in Four Types of Electoral Context

Type of electoral context	Relationship between trusteeship and clientele orientation
Permissive (N= 23)	.27
Supportive (N = 17)	.77
Discriminative (N = 16)	−.03
Volatile (N = 24)	−.28

---

[12] It should be stressed that this analysis makes no assumptions about the frequency of trustee councils in different electoral contexts. Indeed, we have no
reason to expect that the trustee style is more congenial with one type of electorate than another. And, with the exception of a slight increase in the volatile context, the proportion of trustee councils is practically random across the
four categories: Permissive = 56%; Supportive = 53%; Discriminative = 56%;
and Volatile = 67%.

The more harmony prevails between council and community, the more will trustee councils view the general welfare from the perspective of a *part* of the community. By identifying with a clientele, the council projects special interests into the public arena and rationalizes them in terms of the public interest.[13]

High- and low-trustee councils may also differ in commitment to clientele interests depending on the community's group life. One should expect that a looser and less institutionalized set of linkages between the council and interest groups would be associated with a greater tendency of trustee councils to accommodate a clientele. Tenuous linkages make for the kind of discretion that permits a council to claim free agency and yet to satisfy a favored clientele. But if the space between council and public is filled by an intervening layer of politically active groups and their spokesmen, then the council insisting on independent judgment as its prerogative will find it more difficult to behave inconsistently with its representational stance.

The more established the dual system of representation, then, the less likely it is that a trustee council will differ significantly from a low-trustee council in its clientele orientation. Table 20–6 shows this to be the case. In the absence of much group activity and many spokesmen, the trustee council tends to accommodate a clientele. But where the dual system of representation is well established, there is almost no relationship between trusteeship and clientele orientation.

Only under certain circumstances does trusteeship mean what it is presumed to mean—the independent judgment of the legislature applied to the welfare of the community as a whole. Some trustee councils sympathize with and accommodate the special interests of some clientele. These councils deviate from their declared representational style not under pressure from the majority but in response to the preferences, declared or undeclared, of a

---

[13] This group-level formulation will undoubtedly remind the reader of Harold D. Lasswell's famous formula for the developmental history of the political man as one who displaces private motives on to public objects and rationalizes them in terms of the public interest. See Harold D. Lasswell, *Psychopathology and Politics* (1930), in *The Political Writings of Harold D. Lasswell* (Glencoe, Ill.: The Free Press, 1951), pp. 261–262.

Table 20–6
Correlation Coefficients for Relationship
Between Trusteeship and Clientele Orientation
Under Varying Conditions of Organizational Activity

Conditions of organizational activity	Relationship between trusteeship and clientele orientation
Few groups active (N = 28)	.52
Many groups active (N = 54)	—.06
Minor role for spokesmen (N = 43)	.52
Major role for spokesmen (N = 39)	.09
Emphasis on informal contacts (N = 41)	.43
Little emphasis on contacts (N = 41)	—.21

single interest. Deviant trustee councils appear most consistently where neither their relations with the public and the electorate nor the linkage processes connecting them with different publics make close public monitoring of council actions possible.

Conclusion

Trusteeship appears to contain an element of residual elitism, in two respects. In one respect, it refers to the actions of a competent and intelligent group of men who in relying on their own judgment work to protect the welfare of all, even if, from time to time, this requires resisting the wishes of the majority. There are elements of paternalism and moralism, but also of realism, in this aspect of trusteeship. The trustee council is being realistic in admitting the mandate uncertainty which characterizes representational situations. The aspect of trusteeship which stresses the independent judgment of the elected assembly has long been accepted as a defensible position within the principles of democratic governance. In pointing out the dangers of mandatory democracy or decision-making by plebiscite, the advocate of trusteeship does not see himself as an antidemocrat. Indeed, trusteeship is viewed as necessary if minority rights and the general good are to be protected.

In a second respect, however, the elitism implicit in trusteeship has its dark side. In this perspective, majority wishes are ignored but clientele preferences are favored. This distortion of the majority will is made possible by the trustee council's tendency to substitute, willy-nilly, the needs of a special clientele for the welfare of the whole. This predilection is facilitated by the council's paternalistic bias. But it is predicated, in turn, on a relatively placid political relationship between council and public.

If trusteeship is little more than an excuse to defy the majority so that a clientele can be better served, then the values which trusteeship is designed to further are aborted. The independence which Burke so resolutely defended undergirds an elitist type of representation.

In the scientific perspective, the various modes of behavior possible under the norms of trusteeship cast doubt on its utility as a conceptual tool. A concept which points toward very different types of representational conduct depending on prevailing political conditions may be useful to the political practitioner, but it is of little use to the empirical scientist. For it tells us nothing that cannot be better learned by examining the political conditions which do hold. For this reason, the concept of trusteeship will not be employed in the next two chapters, which continue the inquiry into political representation.

Chapter 21

Representation as Responsiveness

Theories of representation are eminently concerned with the relationship between the representative and the represented. This was especially true of Burke's formulation. As one abandons the notion of trusteeship, therefore, and with it the mandate versus independence controversy over the role of the representative, it is all the more necessary to find a conception of representation that does not suffer from the empirical disabilities of the classical theory and yet retains the *relationship between* governors and governed as the core problem to be explored. A new formulation should meet at least three criteria. First, it should illuminate the relationship between representatives and represented. Second, it should focus on the behavioral rather than the formal-normative aspects of this relationship. And third, it should direct attention to representation as a property of the collectivity rather than as an attribute of individual persons. All three criteria are met in Pitkin's definition which, with modifications, we adopt and apply: "representing here means acting in the interest of the represented, in a manner responsive to them."[1]

Representation conceived of as responsiveness is rooted in the relationship between officeholders and citizens without making assumptions about mandate or independence. The free agent, at least normatively speaking, acts as much in the interests of the represented as does the instructed agent, for both are presumably

---

[1] Hanna Pitkin, *The Concept of Representation* (Berkeley: University of California Press, 1967), p. 209.

responsive. Of course, responsiveness is a broad and vague term, but it has empirical grounding. Governments place priorities on societal challenges (guns versus butter, commerce versus conservation); they decide what resources will be mobilized to pursue collective goals (taxes, manpower, or land); they determine the instrumentation of resource collection (military conscription versus a volunteer army, income versus property taxes); and they shape the patterns of distribution of the benefits provided through collective action (laissez-faire, welfare policies, nepotism, and so on). A government represents when it defines priorities, collects and distributes resources, and otherwise manages the affairs of the community in a manner responsive to the interests of its citizens.

The formulation of representation as responsiveness is also substantive or behavioral rather than formalistic. Representation is not a matter of essence in the definitional ways of Aristotle. Rather, representation is implied in the behavior toward each other and the interactions of two sets of persons—the elected assembly and the electorate which chooses the assembly. Representation as responsiveness can therefore not be taken for granted, but it may emerge in the course of interaction between governors and governed. This formulation is congenial to empirical analysis because it leads to questions about the conditions under which responsiveness may or may not occur.

Finally, the formulation of representation as responsiveness makes it a matter of intergroup rather than of interindividual relationships. In stipulating that governments are representative when they act in a manner responsive to the public, Pitkin suggests that political representation is best viewed as a relationship between two collectivities—governors and citizens. Representation, she writes, is "primarily a public, institutional arrangement involving many people and groups, and operating in the complex ways of large-scale social arrangements. What makes it representation is not any single action by any one participant, but the overall structure and functioning of the system, the patterns emerging from the multiple activities of many people."[2]

---

[2] *Ibid.*, pp. 221–222.

Representativeness, then, characterizes the relationship between council and community when the former governs in a manner responsive to the expressed interests of the latter. This definition begs two important questions. First, and this appears to be Pitkin's view, representation emerges when the legislature stands ready to be responsive and when the public has an interest to declare. It might be said, then, that a particular legislature is responsive even in the absence of specific instances of response. Although there is merit in Pitkin's view that a potential for responsiveness is as important as acts of responsiveness, it is difficult to work empirically with a concept that stresses the possibility of behavior rather than the behavior itself. For this reason our analysis stresses the occurrence of rather than the potential for responsiveness.

Second, responsiveness involves reaction to expressed interests and not simply to "the interest of the represented." This formulation turns on the act of governing rather than on the consequences of governing. This, again, is a matter of empirical necessity. While we can determine whether policies are enacted in response to the public, we cannot determine whether they are in the interest of the public. To say that a council is representing when it governs in response to publicly expressed preferences does not preclude that the policies of a nonresponsive council may be in accord with the interests of its public. But we have no way of ascertaining this.

Although our formulation deviates from Pitkin's perspicacious analysis of representation, it is more viable in empirical research with the data at hand. Hopefully, it illuminates the relationship between governors and governed that is involved in representation; it is certainly behavioral rather than formalistic; and it refers to the behavior of collectivities rather than to the behavior of individuals.

Slightly less than half (44 percent) of the city councils could be classified as nonresponsive.[3] These councils appear to be altogether immune to pressures emanating from the public; no identifiable public voices, whether sporadically or permanently organized, intrude into their deliberations. These councils may or may not be acting in the interests of the represented, but they are clearly

---

[3] For a description of the classification, see Appendix B21.1.

not acting in response to the represented. They entertain self-defined images of community needs and preferences. And it is in terms of these images that the nonresponsive councils tackle the problems which come to their attention.

The remaining councils, all of which are classified as responsive, fall into two categories. There are councils which consider the views and expressed preferences of attentive publics, that is, of identifiable and permanent interest clusters in the community. These attentive publics may have differing community goals, in which case the responsive council will adjust and compromise. Or the attentive publics may share common goals, in which case the responsive council need only determine these goals and act upon them. A particularly apt description of responsiveness to attentive publics is provided by one council: "Most of the time we bow to the wishes of the people, not necessarily the majority of all the citizens, but the majority of the people who are interested." Approximately a quarter (24 percent) of the councils are responsive to attentive publics.

The second type of responsive council concerns itself with transitory issue-groups. Neighbors, for instance, may organize on a temporary basis in order to demand a neighborhood service. A council responsive to such demands is classified as responsive to *ad hoc* issue-groups. This response style is illustrated in the following comment from an interview: "There are no pressure groups in the city. There are factions that apply pressure on individual issues and then dissolve when that issue is over." To be responsive under such conditions is perhaps even to placate these action groups, or even individual citizens. About a third of the councils (32 percent) are classified as responsive to *ad hoc* issue-groups.

The most important distinction of course is between responsive and nonresponsive councils, for it is this distinction which permits analysis of the conditions under which representation emerges. In the next chapter the dichotomous classification will be sufficient for theoretical purposes. But the distinction between responsiveness to attentive publics and responsiveness to issue-groups is useful, especially in the present chapter where we shall explicate and elaborate the notion of representation as responsiveness.

Responsiveness: Associated Views of the Public

Because responsiveness refers to how a council works out its relations with the public, it will be associated with how the council views the public. This is so because representation emerges, if it does, from the multiple patterns of behavior and perceptions which characterize the relationship between governors and governed.

This analysis involves descriptive elaboration rather than hypothesis testing because the same data were used in constructing the responsiveness classification and the measures of the council's views of the public. And although the same data were coded on wholly different dimensions, it is yet possible that the variables are not truly independent of each other.[4] Moreover, there is no way of determining the causal order of the association between responsiveness and council views of the public.[5] Because of these logical and empirical difficulties, the analysis is at best heuristic in that it can enrich understanding of responsiveness by relating it to council views of the public. Table 21–1 presents the relevant data.

Most immediately apparent are the insignificant differences between the two types of responsive councils. With a minor exception in the relationship between sense of control and responsiveness, council perceptions of the public differ hardly at all as between those councils responsive to permanent interest clusters and those responsive to more transitory issue-groups. The differ-

---

[4] The classification of responsiveness was coded from a variety of questions, including those which generated the measures of the public's attentiveness, agreement, and manageability. And while very different dimensions were being coded —that is, responsiveness in no way is thought of as a view of the public, nor are council views of the public thought of as necessary parts of any particular response style—it is possible that a coder judgment about one dimension affected judgment about the other.

[5] Thus it might be argued that the way in which a council perceives the public it governs necessarily affects how the council responds or fails to respond to that public, and the argument would have merit. It can also be argued that the response style adopted by the council affects the behavior of the public and, eventually, how the council sees the public, and this argument would again have merit.

Table 21-1

Relationships Between Responsiveness and Council Perceptions
of the Public

Council views of the public		Nonresponsive councils N = 36	Responsive to issue-groups N = 26	Responsive to attentive publics N = 20
Attentiveness of public to local affairs	Low	59%	42%	45%
	High	41	58	55
		100%	100%	100%
Agreement between council and public on council tasks	Low	40%	77%	75%
	High	60	23	25
		100%	100%	100%
Sense that council-public relations are under control	Low	31%	65%	75%
	High	69	35	25
		100%	100%	100%

erences of interest are clearly between the nonresponsive and responsive councils.

Responsiveness is consistently associated with a view of the public that underscores the problematic nature of council-public relations. There is, first, a tendency for responsiveness to be associated with a view that the public is indeed aware of and interested in community affairs. There is a much sharper difference in regard to whether agreement is perceived between council and public and whether relations with the public are thought to be under control by the council, with approximately twice as many of the responsive councils indicating disagreements and difficulties as do the nonresponsive councils. Stated differently, the inattentive public which is thought to be in agreement with how the council is handling its duties and which is viewed as presenting few difficulties of governance is the public governed by a nonresponsive council.

Two comments about Table 21-1 are in order, one specific and the other much more general. The specific patterns in the data indicate a consistency between the views held and the relationship formed. Indeed, given the traits of the publics they govern, perhaps the responsive councils have little choice but to respond. These publics are active and even difficult partners in the governing process. Responsiveness grows out of the interactions between public and council because the public is attentive and, even more, because the public takes little for granted. There are comparatively few shared assumptions; it is as if the council must constantly prove itself. And governance is not always the smooth, managerial process so often wished for by the architects of nonpartisan "businesslike" city councils; politics surfaces in the public, as well as in the private, arenas of governance.

The specific patterns in the data also enhance understanding of the councils which are comparatively immune to external pressures, the nonresponsive councils. These councils are concentrated in communities where the public is comparatively uninterested in local matters, is viewed as sharing norms with the council regarding the tasks of governing, and is seen as presenting no great problems of governance. Nonresponsiveness is congenial to the political conditions established by a reticent and agreeable, perhaps compliant, public—or at least one so perceived.

Different interpretations are possible. There may be a measure of virtual representation: the council embodies the values of the public to such an extent that neither attentive publics nor issue-groups form and press claims. Although possible, this is hardly likely to explain all instances of nonresponsiveness. For there surely will be some issues, even of such an insignificant nature as a neighborhood club's wish for a street light at a school crossing, that cannot be anticipated by the council. This would lead to an articulated preference by members of the public, but it appears as if councils, under certain conditions, will turn a deaf ear. An alternative interpretation is that the public presses claims but is not troublesome when the council fails to acknowledge or respond to these claims. What accounts for quiescent publics is not our concern here, but that they exist can hardly be denied. A council governing where the public is politically quiescent may simply decide to entertain only its own views of what the community needs, and thus resist publicly expressed preferences in the security that the public will, in the end, not press its claims vigorously or make trouble when confronted with nonresponsiveness.

There are more general conclusions to be drawn from Table 21-1 as well. Responsiveness, and thereby nonresponsiveness, are facets of the representational process embedded in a coherent set of notions about the public and its characteristics. Responsiveness is council behavior certainly, but it is behavior that cannot be isolated from the existential context established by what the public is and is seen to be. This is so because responsiveness emerges from a multitude of council-public interactions; from, to again cite Pitkin, "not any single action by any one participant, but the overall structure and functioning of the system, the pattern emerging from the multiple activities of many people."[6]

Responsiveness is not an orientation which an individual council decides to adopt or reject, as might be said about trusteeship. Indeed, it is instructive to consider the lack of association between trusteeship and council views of the public in light of the associations indicated in Table 21-1. The contrast between responsiveness as something which emerges out of relationships with the pub-

---

[6] Pitkin, *The Concept of Representation*, pp. 221–222.

Table 21–2

Comparison of Correlation Coefficients for Relationships
Between Council Perceptions of the Public
and Responsiveness and Trusteeship

	Public is viewed as attentive	Public is viewed as in agreement	Public is viewed as under control
Trusteeship	.00	.05	.08
Responsiveness*	.29	—.65	—.64

* For the purpose of computing the gamma measure, councils are divided into responsive and nonresponsive.

lic and trusteeship as a style which councils adopt irrespective of the public is evident in Table 21–2. The table demonstrates that responsiveness cannot be considered, as might trusteeship, as something immune to the network of perceptual and behavioral relationships linking a council and its public.[7]

Responsiveness: Associated Behavior

Responsiveness is the behavior emerging out of the patterns of many activities in which the council and public are engaged. Councils are representing when these patterns indicate that the elected representatives are responsive to their publics. It should therefore be possible to identify specific behavior patterns that are associated, first, with whether councils are responsive or not and, second, with the kind of responsiveness—to issue-groups or attentive publics—that occurs.

---

[7] Having reintroduced trusteeship, we might note that it and responsiveness are nearly independent measures. The gamma association is a negligible .11. An independent study, using 88 school boards selected from throughout the United States, employed a measure of responsiveness and of trusteeship nearly identical to ours. The authors find very little relationship ($r = .15$) and conclude, as do we, that "the classic roles appear to tell us very little about these particular behavioral manifestations of representation." See M. Kent Jennings and Harmon Zeigler, "Response Style and Politics: The Case of School Boards," *Midwest Journal of Political Science* 15 (May 1971): 297.

The analysis continues to be elaborative or configurative rather than causal. We do not ask whether behavior patterns cause different response styles or whether different response styles cause certain behavior patterns. The task is only to show that specific types of behavior are associated with the more general behavior that is captured by the measure of responsiveness. Two of the behavioral variables have been introduced previously—the council's tendency to stand up against majority wishes and its servicing a clientele; running errands for constituents is a third indicator of its representational behavior that can be used to advantage in clarifying the meaning of different response styles.

Taking a Stand With or Against the Majority

As Table 21–3 shows, council responsiveness is strongly related to whether councils do or do not take a stand against the majority. The great majority of nonresponsive councils claim that their actions seldom contravene majority preferences. These are not councils claiming to respond to the majority as a matter of course, but councils which see a correspondence between their decisions and the presumed wishes of the majority. There are, therefore, several and generally compatible reasons for finding this form of behavior to be associated with nonresponsiveness. Councils resisting specific demands from attentive publics or issue-groups undoubtedly need a rationale for their nonresponsiveness. This rationale is provided in the claim that they resist specific pressures in order better to serve the wishes of the (silent) majority. Furthermore, as noted,

Table 21–3

Relationship Between Responsiveness
and Taking a Stand Counter to Majority Preferences

Take a stand against majority	Non-responsive N = 36	Responsive to issue-groups N = 26	Responsive to attentive publics N = 20
Seldom	72%	38%	15%
Often	27	62	85
Gamma = .70	100%	100%	100%

communities with nonresponsive councils also have more quiescent publics; it may be that the reduced volume of messages flowing into the council allows it to believe that it is governing in accordance with majority wishes, even if it is not responsive to the preferences which do get expressed. Finally, it is possible that virtual representation does characterize at least a few of the communities in which the publics are nondemonstrative and the councils nonresponsive. Councils here would embody majority preferences, and their conception of the general welfare would correspond to the conception held by the majority.

In sharp contrast, the responsive councils are more likely than not to behave in ways they consider counter to majority preferences. It could hardly be otherwise, for these are councils which do respond to the "intense minorities" in their communities. It is the people who speak out who are listened to. A council which responds to issue-groups or attentive publics cannot also act in accordance with perceived majority preferences, at least not in those cases where the vocal minority pushes for actions contrary to what the majority might prefer. When councils continually take account of and respond to the preferences of articulate groups, they recognize that legislation will not always conform to (usually unexpressed) majority wishes.

Table 21–3 also shows an interesting difference between the two styles of responsiveness. Responding to *ad hoc* issue-groups involves somewhat fewer stands against the majority than does responding to attentive publics. Thus, while nearly two-fifths (38 percent) of the one category of responsive councils seldom go against the majority, only 15 percent of the second type of responsive councils are able to make this claim. Councils which are responsive to the highly specific demands of transitory issue-groups are able to alternate this response style with policies thought to reflect majority wishes. The requests of issue-groups run to such matters as a stoplight, a dog leash regulation, a more efficient librarian, a new parking lot downtown, and similar relatively isolated appeals. These requests can be satisfied without, except marginally, affecting the interests of the majority one way or the other. Councils which are responsive to the regular, persistent presence of attentive publics make the adjustment much less easily. What characterizes attentive publics is their involvement across a wide range of community issues. An attentive public, for instance, might be pro-development, in which case it would take a position on everything from street lights to tax legislation. At some point and perhaps at many points, its demands may be contrary to majority preferences. It is correspondingly more difficult for the responsive council to bow to the wishes of an attentive public or an intense minority and yet claim to govern consistently with the wishes of the majority.

Servicing a Clientele

Councils vary in clientele orientation, though, as reported in the previous chapter, as many as three-fifths very regularly accommodate the preferences of a clientele. Table 21–4 shows that this kind of representational behavior is especially characteristic of councils that are responsive to attentive publics, in a ratio of four to one. The councils in the other two response style categories are about as likely to take clientele interests into account as not.

The difference between councils responsive to attentive publics and those responsive to issue-groups shows the former's representational stance as part and parcel of a syndrome of behavior patterns emerging from the activities of the public as well as from those of the council. Where clientele groups are to be accommodated, a response style stressing responsiveness to broad clusters of attentive publics is appropriate. The form of responsiveness is embedded in the conditions established by the alternative ways in which the public expresses itself. But, as Table 21–4 also shows, servicing a clientele is so pervasive that it appears in over half the nonre-

Table 21–4

Relationship Between Responsiveness
and Servicing a Clientele

Council services a clientele	Non-responsive N = 36	Responsive to issue-groups N = 26	Responsive to attentive publics N = 20
No	47%	46%	20%
Yes	53	54	80
Gamma = .32	100%	100%	100%

sponsive councils as well as in over half those responsive to *ad hoc* issue-groups. Behavior involved in accommodating clientele groups cannot therefore add much to an understanding of response style.

Running Errands for Constituents

In the course of the interview, respondents were asked: "In your work as a Councilman, do you spend a lot of time doing services for people—giving information, helping them with requests, and so on? Or some time, or not much time?" The answers to this question were usually explicit and incidentally provide a lengthy list of the types of requests which citizens take to their local representatives. One councilman reported that he had responded to citizen requests about "grease on their sidewalks, dogs in their backyard, untrimmed hedges, and parking strips." Another was expected to do something about "barking dogs, noisy children, and streets needing repair." A third councilman spoke of assisting citizens on everything from "sick kids to sick street lights." In some councils it is taken for granted that errands are part of the job, though not always the most agreeable part. "It is the job I asked for, although it doesn't mean I like it. It's frustrating but interesting," commented one respondent.

Not all councilmen are so open to citizen requests for such services. Active resistance is possible, if somewhat disguised. As a councilman admitted, "I do nothing for individual whims. If small problems come up, I direct them to the proper people, but I seldom do much of the errands." And another reported, "People don't bother me with details. If so, I refer them to the City Manager. I'm busy." For these councilmen, the job does not include doing services for individual citizens.

Councils were classified into those spending a great deal of time running errands for citizens or otherwise aiding them individually and those spending less time in this manner. Table 21–5 crosstabulates council response styles and the relative amount of time councils spend in running errands for citizens.

Responsive councils spend more time running errands than do nonresponsive councils, indicating once more the way in which responsiveness is part of a network of activities. Although responsiveness as a general behavioral style is not the same thing as an-

Table 21–5
Relationship Between Responsiveness
and Running Errands for Citizens

Time spent by councils running errands	Non-responsive N = 36	Responsive to issue-groups N = 26	Responsive to attentive publics N = 20
Relatively little	72%	35%	60%
Relatively much	28	65	40
Gamma = .42	100%	100%	100%

swering dozens of specific requests by individual citizens, it is likely that at least one of the ways responsiveness can emerge in council-public relations is through just such behavior. A council which invests itself heavily in performing services for citizens will over time establish conditions amounting to responsiveness.

This can be seen more clearly in the difference between the two forms of responsiveness. A greater amount of time and more effort running errands is expended by councils responsive to *ad hoc* groups than by councils responsive to attentive publics, though the latter still spend more time on such citizen services than do the nonresponsive councils. Attentive publics can so preoccupy council attention that the council intent on responding to them may notice little else, and especially not the isolated individual wanting a street light repaired or a barking dog quieted. Responsiveness to *ad hoc* groups is more compatible with errand running. For one thing, this form of responsiveness has in it an element of placating irate citizens, a form of representational behavior that would certainly extend to running errands for them. For another thing, the line separating responsiveness to *ad hoc* groups from running errands for citizens is not easily drawn; the same behavior may be interpreted under both rubrics. The neighborhood group pressing for a dog leash law and the citizen angry because a dog has torn up his shrubs can be simultaneously satisfied by the council responsive to issue-groups or the council willing to run errands for individual citizens.

Not all legislatures are responsive to the electors who have selected them, and this simple fact presents a fascinating (and consequential) problem for representative democracy. The problem of course refers to the political conditions under which responsiveness does emerge as an important element in the relation between governors and governed. Responsiveness appears to be part of a set of behavioral and perceptual patterns which generally characterizes the relationship between council and public. The evidence amply validates the conception that responsiveness refers to the multiple activities of many political actors in the community.

Linkages and Responsiveness

The feasibility of defining representation in terms of the selection and composition of the governing group was previously considered and rejected. Also considered and rejected was the feasibility of defining representation in terms of the public's petitioning activities. Instead, constitutive and petitioning processes were thought of as providing linkages between the governors and the governed. The reason for this approach should now be clear. The core issue in representation is not how leaders are chosen or petitioned, but whether they are responsive. It is entirely possible that governors are selected by the most democratic of procedures and yet are nonresponsive; and it is entirely possible that they are regularly petitioned and yet are nonresponsive. The crucial question in a theory of representation as responsiveness is, therefore, how governors behave *after* they have been chosen and *after* they have been exposed to the preferences of the public.

Nevertheless, linkages through constitutive or petitioning processes and representation should not be thought of as altogether independent phenomena, even logically. If responsiveness is to be a measure of representation, it is important to remember that it involves not just the isolated act of a single individual, or the interaction of a pair of individuals. It involves not even the actions of one group alone, like the council, considered as something apart from a larger context. Responsiveness emerges from the multiple activities of many groups and people as they are variously involved in the political life of the community.

The ways in which governors are chosen and petitioned may well also be parts of the manifold of activities through which responsiveness emerges. Although it is not theoretically useful to define representation in terms of leadership selection or petitioning, it would also not be useful from the theoretical perspective to divorce these processes from a general account of political representation. All of these processes constitute what can be called, at least loosely, the system of representation. It remains to be shown, then, that the activities connected with selecting and petitioning representative bodies are associated with the emergence or nonemergence of responsiveness.

Table 21–6 presents evidence relevant to two leadership selection variables—the extent to which councils are recruited through processes of sponsorship, and the amount of campaign effort invested in seeking council office. Both measures are chosen for obvious reasons. Both indicate something about the extent of public involvement in choosing the councils. When sponsorship is low, recruitment processes are more open and public. When campaign effort is high, there is sustained interaction between council and public during the election period. Insofar as responsiveness emerges as part of the activities which select leaders, it should be more pronounced in those communities where these activities involve the public to a greater degree.

As Table 21–6 shows, responsiveness and the activities surrounding the recruitment of representatives are interconnected, and the associations are from moderate to strong. There is greater responsiveness in those communities where sponsorship is less the practice and where more effort goes into campaigning. Put differently, where councils are composed of men who owe their offices to predecessors who coopted them and where councils are composed of men who reach office without extensive campaigning, the council-public relationship tends to be characterized by nonresponsiveness.

A similar set of interconnections should be true of petitioning activities, the other major linkage process between governors and governed. When governors are accessible to the public because channels for exchanging viewpoints are well established, the conditions for responsiveness should also be present. Although petitioning and accessibility do not in themselves constitute representation, they are likely to be part of the net of activities from which council responsiveness to public preferences emerges. When groups and spokesmen are active in the community and correspondingly

Table 21–6
Relationship Between Responsiveness
and Constitutive Processes

	Career Sponsorship	
	Relatively little	Relatively much
Council responsiveness	N = 43	N = 39
To *ad hoc* issue-groups and attentive publics	65%	46%
Nonresponsive	35	54
Gamma = .37	100%	100%

	Campaign Effort	
	Relatively high	Relatively low
	N = 41	N = 41
Responsive	71%	42%
Nonresponsive	29	58
Gamma = .55	100%	100%

less emphasis is placed on informal contacts, responsiveness is facilitated. In the absence of such institutionalized linkages through groups and spokesmen, and with a greater emphasis on informal, direct exchanges, the pattern of political activities provides less support for responsiveness to emerge.

Table 21–7 indicates this to be the case. Responsiveness is more likely to emerge where groups are active in promoting constituency viewpoints, where spokesmen serve as effective bridges between council and public, and where informal contacts are not given too much emphasis. Responsiveness is not simply due to the predispositions of the elected leaders. It is anchored in the patterns of activities established by citizens and by community leaders as well as by the council. It takes the articulation of citizen preferences to provide something for councils to respond to, and this articulation is facilitated in the dual system of representation.

Tables 21–6 and 21–7 suggest that linkages increase the probability that responsiveness will emerge. But, one may ask, are these linkage processes necessary conditions, sufficient conditions, or both necessary and sufficient conditions? The data in Tables 21–6 and 21–7 will be presented in a format that gives a partial answer, though strictly speaking necessary and sufficient conditions can only be identified if the contingency table contains empty cells.[8]

To answer the question about necessary and sufficient conditions, we can ask whether the ratio of responsive to nonresponsive councils is greater when the linkage conditions are comparatively present or absent. In other words, for each of the five separate variables in the two tables one compares the rows rather than the columns. For instance, Table 21–8 shows how many nonresponsive and responsive councils there are when campaign effort is relatively high—the favorable condition—and when it is relatively low. There are 2.73 times as many responsive as nonresponsive councils when campaign effort is high (29 and 12, respectively), but only 1.41 times as many nonresponsive as responsive councils when campaign effort is low (24 and 17, respectively). Table 21–8 presents the full array of ratios. In all but one instance (group activity) the ratio of responsive to nonresponsive councils where linkage conditions facilitate contact is considerably higher than the

---

[8] The logic of specifying necessary and sufficient conditions for 2×2 tables is relatively straightforward. The following table indicates that the cause is both necessary and sufficient for the effect to occur:

		Cause	
		−	+
Effect	−	100%	0%
	+	0	100

If the left-hand column indicated a random relationship, 50% in each cell, but the right-hand column remained as we have it, this would indicate that the cause is sufficient but not necessary for the effect to occur. If the right-hand column indicated a random relationship, 50% in each cell, but the left-hand column remained as we have it, this would indicate that the cause is necessary but not sufficient for the effect to occur. These patterns are illustrated in the following tables:

Cause is sufficient condition		
−	+	
50%	0%	
50	100	

Cause is necessary condition		
−	+	
100%	50%	
0	50	

Table 21–7
Relationship Between Responsiveness
and Petitioning Processes

Council responsiveness	Number of Active Groups	
	Many N = 54	Few N = 28
To *ad hoc* issue-groups and attentive publics	68%	32%
Nonresponsive	32	68
Gamma = .64	100%	100%

	Importance of Spokesmen	
	High N = 39	Low N = 43
Responsive	67%	47%
Nonresponsive	33	53
Gamma = .39	100%	100%

	Emphasis on Informal Contacts	
	Little N = 41	Much N = 41
Responsive	63%	49%
Nonresponsive	37	51
Gamma = .29	100%	100%

Table 21–8
Ratios Between Responsive and Nonresponsive Councils
Under Relative Presence and Absence of Linkage Conditions*

Type of linkage condition	Ratio of responsive to nonresponsive councils when condition is present	Ratio of nonresponsive to responsive councils when condition is absent
Career sponsorship	1.87	1.17
Campaign effort	2.73	1.41
Group activity	2.18	2.11
Spokesmen important	2.00	1.15
Informal contacts	1.73	1.05
Mean difference	2.10	1.38

* Computed from differences in cell frequencies of Tables 21–6 and 21–7.

opposite set of ratios (that of nonresponsive to responsive councils when the linkage conditions are comparatively absent). On the average, there are slightly more than twice as many responsive as nonresponsive councils if linkage conditions are present. There are only 1.38 times as many nonresponsive as responsive councils when these conditions are absent.

Linkages, whether stemming from constitutive or petitioning processes, are sufficient conditions for the emergence of responsiveness, but not necessary conditions. This is shown by the fact that responsiveness is about as likely as nonresponsiveness when the linkage activities are absent, but that responsiveness is much more likely than nonresponsiveness when these activities are present.

This finding provides additional support for the approach which treats representation as analytically distinct from how a governing group is constituted and how it is petitioned. For it is now evident that responsiveness can emerge even if the processes which select governors do not much involve the public, and even if the activities for petitioning governors are not such as to build many bridges between them and the public. Responsiveness is present in the myriad activities, behaviors, and perceptions which link the governors and the governed, and not just in those more specialized activities which have to do with selection and petitioning. Still, we are yet lacking what might be called a "theory of representation" which would provide a firmer sense of what political conditions actually bring about responsiveness.

Chapter 22

Responsiveness and Accountability

Even under the most favorable conditions provided by the social environment and the immediate political context, governors will be responsive to community wishes or needs if, and perhaps only if, they are held accountable for their actions and decisions. Linkages between the council and the community stemming from constitutive and petitioning processes, the previous chapter concluded, are sufficient but not necessary conditions for the emergence of responsiveness. Something else is needed to guarantee the kind of responsiveness which in a democracy is the defining property of representation. That guarantee is the possibility of holding governors accountable.

Accountability means that there are standards against which the performance of officeholders can be measured. If these standards are not met or are violated, officeholders will be removed from office. In a democracy, these standards are not just legal and formal requirements for appropriate conduct, but the wishes and welfare of the citizenry the governors are chosen to represent. Governors failing to meet these exacting standards are held accountable, and it is for this reason that there is a strong presumption that they will strive to be responsive to the citizenry.

The Search for Accountability

In the American political tradition, accountability has been sought in a variety of ways. One of these ways is through constitutional restraints. An elaborate constitutional system of checks and balances, the framers of the American Constitution thought, would allow the different branches of government as well as different levels of officialdom to check tendencies toward the abuse of power by another branch or level. Moreover, the separation of powers, both between the executive and the legislature and between the two houses of the bicameral legislature, would make for the representation of different classes of constituency. Accountability would be assured as one subset of governors could countervail and check another subset.

Accountability through a system of checks and balances is an important facet of constitutional democracy, but it is doubtful that it serves the needs of representative democracy. It is by no means clear that different branches of government, or even different levels, do serve different constituencies, at least not in the sense intended by the framers of the Constitution. Moreover, so many formal agencies and informal arrangements cut across the different branches and levels of government today that it is unlikely that one branch or level will check another in any significant sense relevant to accountability.

Another way of guaranteeing accountability is through internalization. Governors in a democracy are accountable, it is believed, because as a result of their training and practice in democratic rule they have been socialized into and have internalized the norms of accountability. Appropriate standards of democratic behavior, including responsiveness, are part of the elite's political culture, and members of the elite are held accountable by each other as well as by their own consciences if they fail to meet these standards. Dahl, for instance, suggests that the members of the active political stratum understand and agree on the norms of the democratic creed and support these norms. And within this stratum, "the professionals tend to agree even more on what the norms should be, what they are, and the desirability of maintaining them substantially as they are."[1] Indeed, endorsement of existing norms is a criterion for political recruitment and advancement: "complex processes of

---

[1] Robert A. Dahl, *Who Governs?* (New Haven: Yale University Press, 1961), p. 320.

political selection and rejection tend to exclude the deviant who challenges the prevailing norms of the existing political system. Most of the professionals might properly be called democratic 'legitimists.' "[2]

Although the stress on democratic norms as a source of accountability should not be minimized, as a guarantee of accountability such a source is flawed in an important respect. It involves the proposition that the criteria by which governors are to be evaluated and are in fact evaluated are set by the governors themselves, or at least by their predecessors. Governors, then, are "accountable" to standards largely shaped and given operational meaning by the actions and viewpoints of those in a position to determine the political norms of society. V. O. Key has made much of the fact that the distribution of opinions and values in society is often a consequence of the positions taken by the leadership.[3] One is left in doubt, however, whether there are criteria independent of those established by the leadership or active stratum. Such independent standards are desirable if a citizenry is to judge whether governors conform to the democratic rules.

Finally, there is a way of assuring accountability through the people's vote. Electoral sanctions, in the judgment of many theorists of democracy, effectively join the issues of responsiveness and accountability. The men who rule are responsive to the preferences of the ruled because the rulers, as elected officials, can be and are held accountable through the simple mechanism of eviction from office. In the words of Dahl, political elites operate within limits "set by their expectations as to the reactions of the group of politically active citizens who go to the polls,"[4] a proposition that is generally confirmed in his empirical study: "elected leaders keep the real or imagined preferences of constituents constantly in mind in deciding what policies to adopt or reject."[5]

---

[2] *Ibid.*

[3] See V. O. Key, Jr., *Public Opinion and American Democracy* (New York: Alfred A. Knopf, 1961). As Key writes in his concluding chapter, p. 343, "it has been repeatedly noted that the political activists may shape the opinions of the rest of the people."

[4] Robert A. Dahl, *Preface to Democratic Theory* (Chicago: University of Chicago Press, 1956), p. 72.

[5] Dahl, *Who Governs?* p. 164.

The burden of the argument, then, is that elections in establishing accountability also establish the conditions for responsiveness on the part of the governors toward the governed. However, proof of this proposition is difficult because the term "accountability" is not entirely unambiguous. In at least one of its usages it directs attention away from rather than toward political responsiveness. As Pitkin points out, the conception of the representative as "someone who is to be held to account, who will have to answer to another for what he does," is devoid of substantive meaning.[6] For this conception says nothing "about what goes on *during* representation, how a representative ought to act or what he is expected to do, how to tell whether he has represented well or badly."[7] Formal accountability allows for the possibility of completely irresponsible actions which can only be remedied when the officeholder is removed at the end of his term.

Electoral accountability, as the term is used here, does not suffer from the formalism that is Pitkin's concern. Representation is not defined as accountability; rather, the conditions of accountability are said to *increase the likelihood* that governors will be responsive and, in this sense, represent. Pitkin recognizes this conception in observing that the accountability view can be restated as an empirical hypothesis: "Accountability theorists mean to say that a man who will be held to account for what he does, and knows that he will, is most likely to act responsibly and respond to the desires of those to whom he must account."[8]

Representation, then, is not identical with selecting and removing governors. Rather, governors *are more likely* to be responsive

---

[6] Hanna Pitkin, *The Concept of Representation* (Berkeley: University of California Press, 1957), p. 56.

[7] *Ibid.*, p. 58.

[8] *Ibid.* In the final chapter of her work, Pitkin comes very close to accepting the central terms of the theory of electoral accountability. In her search for the conditions which establish "regular, systematic responsiveness," she comments that "We require functioning institutions that are designed to, and really do, secure a government responsive to public interest and opinion." The institutions most noteworthy in this regard are elections and some sort of collegiate representative body. About the former it is noted that "Our concern with elections and electoral machinery, and particularly with whether elections are free and genuine, results from our conviction that such machinery is necessary to ensure systematic responsiveness."

because they were selected by and can be removed by the governed. Accountability connects the machinery of elections, on the one hand, with a responsive relationship between governors and governed, on the other. Electoral accountability actually implies two major propositions or, stated more accurately, involves two major sets of conditions likely to bring about responsiveness. It is useful to distinguish carefully between them.

Institutional Conditions

Schumpeter defines the democratic method as "that institutional arrangement for arriving at political decisions in which individuals acquire the power to decide by means of a competitive struggle for the people's vote."[9] He is echoed by Lipset, who writes about a "social mechanism which permits the largest possible part of the population to influence major decisions by choosing among contenders for political office."[10] Dahl comments that organized opposition to the government in power may be regarded "as very nearly the most distinctive characteristic of democracy itself."[11] Pitkin concludes that "representative government is not defined by particular actions at a particular moment, but by long-term systematic arrangements—by institutions and the way in which they function."[12]

All these and many other theorists of democracy share the assumption that certain institutional conditions are necessary to the working of political representation. The core terms of these institutional arrangements are inevitably free and regular elections, competitive political parties or other organized groups, the peaceful transfer of power from the defeated to the victorious, and the continuing right to form opposition groups. It is through the workings of elections and related institutions that officeholders

---

[9] Joseph Schumpeter, *Capitalism, Socialism and Democracy* (New York: Harper & Row, Torchbook Edition, 1962), p. 269.
[10] S. M. Lipset, *Political Man* (Garden City, N.Y.: Doubleday & Company, 1960, Anchor Books, 1963), p. 27.
[11] Robert A. Dahl, ed., *Political Oppositions in Western Democracies* (New Haven: Yale University Press, 1966), p. xvi.
[12] Pitkin, *The Concept of Representation*, p. 234.

are held to account and therefore are likely to be responsive to the electors.[13]

However persuasive this reasoning about the institutional conditions of accountability, institutions are for nought unless coupled with a second set of conditions. For in the final analysis it is not institutions but groups of men who either are or are not responsive. Theorizing about accountability must connect institutional arrangements with behavioral tendencies.

Psychological Conditions

As used here, the term "psychological conditions" refers to the predispositions or habits of mind of the officeholder. Friedrich's "rule of anticipated reactions,"[14] for instance, captures the notion that officials are responsive to electors because they are anticipating, and trying to avoid, the sanctions available to the voters. This also seems to be what Dahl has in mind when he comments that elites are limited in the choices they make because of their expectations as to the reactions of voters.[15] A psychological condition of accountability is, then, an awareness on the officeholder's part that electoral sanctions may be effectively forthcoming if he is not responsive to voter preferences, at least over the long haul.

Schlesinger's ambition theory of politics takes an additional step. The reason that officeholders do anticipate voter reactions and thus govern in accordance with voter preferences is that the officeholder has made an effort to reach office and wishes to retain it. He is politically ambitious. For Schlesinger, representative government depends on a supply of men driven to gain and then to hold political office: "the desire for election and, more important, for reelection becomes the electorate's restraint upon its public officials."[16] Political ambition stands behind the willingness, even

---

[13] See especially Anthony Downs, *An Economic Theory of Democracy* (New York: Harper & Row, 1957).

[14] Carl J. Friedrich, *Constitutional Government and Democracy* (Boston: Ginn and Company, 1946), pp. 589–591.

[15] Dahl, *Preface to Democratic Theory*, p. 72.

[16] Joseph A. Schlesinger, *Ambition and Politics: Political Careers in the United States* (Chicago: Rand McNally, 1966), p. 2.

eagerness, of the officeholders to anticipate voter wishes and to govern in a manner responsive to those wishes.

Friedrich's rule of anticipated reactions and Schlesinger's ambition theory of politics supply the necessary link between elections and group competition, on the one hand, and responsiveness by governors, on the other. This link is well illustrated by the quotations from councils which indicate that if the psychological conditions are absent, the institutional conditions are unlikely to establish responsiveness. In response to the question as to whether it is easy or difficult to go against majority preferences, one councilman remarked, "It is easy, I am an independent type of individual. I don't feel the weight of voter responsibility. I am not all fired up for a political career"; and another commented, "I am free to do as I feel. In general it is easy to vote against the majority because I don't have any political ambitions."

The importance of distinguishing between the institutional and the psychological conditions of accountability is now apparent. It is insufficient to apply the term "representative" to a political system just because there are elections. Men can be elected to office, and face removal through electoral eviction, and yet not be responsive. It is an empirical question whether elections and responsiveness are associated. Moreover, there are reasons to expect that elections will have little effect on responsiveness unless additional conditions are met, most notably, unless officeholders think in terms of electoral sanctions.

Toward a Model of Electoral Accountability and Responsiveness

These notions can be empirically tested by separately measuring the institutional and the psychological conditions of accountability and then determining how both sets of conditions relate to political responsiveness. Three measures of the institutional conditions which establish electoral accountability will be used.

Office Contesting

The availability of more candidates than political openings is a necessary, though not sufficient, condition for electoral accountability. Only one candidate for each political office deprives the electorate of choice, and elections become ceremonies which ratify rather than institutions through which choices are made. Often electoral accountability is promoted by the presence of a competitive party system. While nonpartisan elections lack competitive parties, they do involve forms of political opposition in which challengers seek to defeat other challengers and work to unseat incumbents. The measure of office contesting—the average number of candidates who seek council openings—will be used as a surrogate of the competitive party system.

Incumbent Eviction

In stressing that responsiveness occurs because officeholders are held accountable through competitive elections, the critical dimension of competitiveness is the possibility of evicting incumbents. However many candidates there are and however closely fought an election, the conditions of accountability are not met unless there is some probability that officeholders can be punished through election defeat. Electoral eviction is a second institutional condition of electoral accountability.

Voter Turnout

Voter turnout as an institutional condition of accountability is more problematic. What is the expected form of the relationship between responsiveness and different levels of voter turnout? It may be that there is a linear relationship; the larger the electorate, the more do the conditions of accountability hold and the more likely is responsiveness to emerge. Or a threshold effect might be operable; beyond a certain minimum, the number of voters going to the polls has no independent bearing on whether officeholders are responsive or not. The emphasis on electoral sanctions implies the latter. An electoral defeat by a few voters is no less a sanction than a defeat by many voters. Voter turnout will be included, but whether it influences responsiveness independently of office contesting and electoral eviction is an open question.

Two measures of the psychological or predispositional conditions which establish electoral accountability will be used, one suggested by Friedrich's rule of anticipated reactions and the other by Schlesinger's ambition theory of politics.

Perceived Electoral Sanctions

The rule of anticipated reactions cannot operate unless councils are aware that citizens have available the sanction of electoral defeat. Of course, all councils are aware of this in the sense that they know there is universal suffrage, periodic elections, limited tenure of office, and so forth. But councils vary in the extent to which this awareness penetrates their daily operations. Some councils give very little thought to the fact that voters can react to policies and programs by defeating incumbents; other councils seem to give it much more attention. In other words, though electoral sanctions are a constant, the concern of the councils with this constant is variable.

Political Ambitions

Councils have been classified according to the effort expended in gaining office and the pervasiveness of aspirations for higher office. This measure is an approximation of the concept of political ambition implied by Schlesinger's theory. The conditions of electoral accountability hold when councils are composed of men who were eager to reach office and who desire higher office; they do not hold when councils are composed of men more indifferent to office-holding. As Schlesinger notes, "No more irresponsible government is imaginable than one of high-minded men unconcerned for their political futures."[17]

A parsimonious technique for investigating the pattern of relationships between the institutional and psychological conditions of accountability, on the one hand, and the responsiveness of councils, on the other, is provided by causal modeling. Figure 22–1 summarizes a theory of electoral accountability in terms of

---

[17] *Ibid.* For a description of the measure of "political ambition," see Appendix B22.1. Appendix B12.1 describes the measure of "perceived electoral sanctions."

the variables we have introduced and diagrams the relationships hypothesized to hold among them. The diagram indicates that both the institutional and psychological conditions should have a direct effect on responsiveness. However, part of the effect of voter turnout, office contesting, and electoral eviction will flow through the intermediate psychological conditions. That is, councils which are sensitive to electoral sanctions and intent on holding office will be more responsive if the electorate is large, challengers are many, and defeat a distinct possibility.

Figure 22–1
A Model of Electoral Accountability
and Political Responsiveness:
Hypothesized Relationships

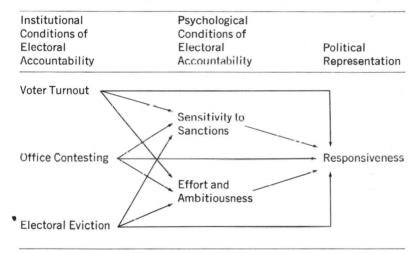

Some caution is called for in interpreting the causal model. Though the arrows would seem to indicate a fixed ordering of the variables, no independent test is available to determine whether the correct order is being suggested. Moreover, there is no way of determining if the relationships might not be reciprocal. For instance, lack of responsiveness could give rise to incumbent eviction; or lack of sensitivity to electoral sanction could be the occasion for a high degree of office contesting.[18] Finally, the attempt to fit the data into a causal model does not deny logically alternative models. Rather, the intent simply is to evaluate the relative importance of different connections in the formal model.[19] Modeling the two distinct themes about electoral accountability is heuristically valuable.

Figure 22–2 presents the model. In a very general sense the effect of electoral accountability appears to be confirmed. The combined impact of the five independent variables explains 22 percent of the variance in responsiveness. The findings revealed in the patterns internal to the model suggest four points.

First, and most striking, voter turnout is neither directly nor indirectly connected with responsiveness. Although it takes some minimum number of voters to have an election, differences in the number of voters beyond this minimum level do not appear to influence the probability that a council will be responsive to the preferences expressed by the public. Even a council's awareness of voter sanctions is no greater where the electorate is large than where it is small. Not voters as such, but voters in combination with candidate competition lead to greater responsiveness on the part of elected officials.

Second, the two aspects of electoral competitiveness, office contesting and incumbent eviction, do have a direct impact on responsiveness. The connections are not strong, but they are noticeable.

---

[18] At least partially in favor of the causal model is the fact that the institutional conditions of accountability derive from election returns over a ten-year period, whereas the remaining measures derive from interview data collected at the end of this period. This, however, is at best a partial justification for the ordering of the variables. Councilmen responded to our questions and probes in terms of a history of experiences in local government. Certainly our coding procedures weighed reports of past events and perceptions as heavily as reports of present perspectives.

[19] For this purpose path coefficients are computed and interpreted in much the way that partial correlations would be. The three measures based on election statistics are entered into the equation at one step, followed by the measure of sensitivity to electoral sanctions, the measure of effort/ambitiousness, and then the dependent variable, political responsiveness. Thus, for instance, the path coefficient between effort/ambitiousness and responsiveness is similar to a partial correlation with all previous variables being held constant. The direct path between any one of the three measures of institutional conditions and responsiveness indicates the correlation when the other two measures are held constant.

Figure 22–2
Path Coefficients Between Conditions
of Electoral Accountability and Responsiveness*

Institutional Conditions of Electoral Accountability	Psychological Conditions of Electoral Accountability	Political Representation

High Voter Turnout

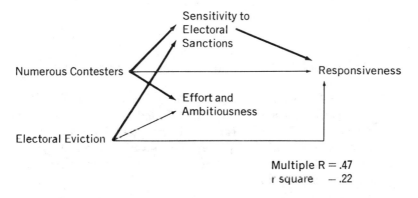

Multiple R = .47
r square — .22

---

* See Appendix B22.2, Table A, for path coefficients. No arrow indicates that path coefficients are less than .11. Light arrow indicates that path coefficients are from .12 to .24. Heavy arrow indicates that path coefficients are .25 or higher.

Councils, irrespective of how sensitive they are to electoral sanctions and irrespective of how strongly they feel about holding office, appear to respond directly to expressions of electorate discontent.

Third, part of the impact of office contesting and incumbent eviction on responsiveness is indirect, being mediated by the extent to which the council thinks in terms of electoral sanctions. The rule of anticipated reactions receives partial confirmation. Councils are more likely to be aware of electoral sanctions where objective conditions suggest that they would be, that is, where challengers are relatively common and where eviction is relatively frequent. And councils are more likely to be responsive where they are sensitive to the sanctions available to the electorate.

Finally, although the effort expended in seeking a council position and the aspiration for higher office are related to contesting and eviction, political ambition does not in turn affect the emergence of responsiveness in council-public relations. The ambition hypothesis of politics is not supported, at least not when the other factors establishing accountability are taken into account. Moreover, even the uncontrolled relationship between responsiveness and ambition, though positive, is weak (.24). Despite the fact that both indicators of electoral competition relate to ambition, as part of a more general model of electoral accountability political ambition appears not to affect responsiveness.

Accountability, Responsiveness, and Urban Complexity

The relationships between conditions of electoral accountability and political responsiveness may be affected, at least in part, by the complexity of the urban context. The model might work differently, therefore, in different-size cities for several reasons. Political intimacy and frequent face-to-face exchanges in the smaller community can make electoral discontent more visible to the council. The more institutionalized layer of organizations and spokesmen in the larger city will reduce the consequences of electoral behavior for responsiveness. Moreover, because the larger city often presents the council with a more complex set of social problems and a wider variety of groups pressing specific claims than does the smaller city, the manner in which electoral conditions impinge on the councils might differ.

Figures 22–3 and 22–4 show the model as it unfolds empirically in small and large cities. Responsiveness is more strongly affected by the conditions of electoral accountability in the small communities than in the large communities. Whereas in small cities, the five measures account for 35 percent of the variance in the responsiveness of councils, in large cities they account for only 23 percent of the variance. One possible reason for this has already been suggested. The behaviors and perspectives associated with the emergence of responsiveness, especially a dual system of representation and open constitutive processes, are more characteristic of

Figure 22–3
Conditions of Electoral Accountability
and Political Responsiveness in Small Cities*

Institutional Conditions of Electoral Accountability	Psychological Conditions of Electoral Accountability	Political Representation

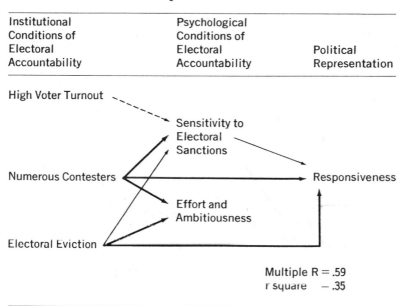

Multiple R = .59
r square   — .35

* See Appendix B22.2, Table B, for path coefficients. No arrow indicates that path coefficients are less than .11. Light arrow indicates that path coefficients are from .12 to .24. Heavy arrow indicates that path coefficients are .25 or higher. Broken arrow indicates negative coefficient.

the larger cities. The council of the large city evolves a relationship with the public stressing responsiveness for a variety of reasons and not just because the conditions of electoral accountability are present. In the small city, where the patterns of activity associated with the emergence of responsiveness are less pervasive, the conditions of electoral accountability bring about a sharper increase in the extent of responsiveness.

Perhaps most interesting in Figures 22–3 and 22–4, however, are the internal workings of the model. What is strikingly apparent is that office contesting for council positions and incumbent eviction, the two most important institutional conditions of accountability, have a direct effect on responsiveness in the small cities and no

Figure 22–4
Conditions of Electoral Accountability
and Political Responsiveness in Large Cities*

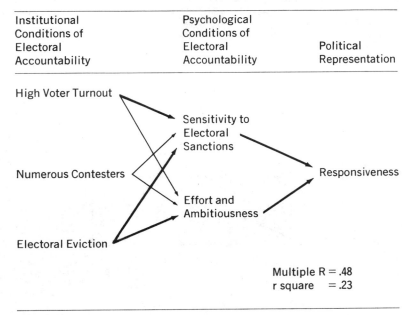

Institutional Conditions of Electoral Accountability	Psychological Conditions of Electoral Accountability	Political Representation

High Voter Turnout

Numerous Contesters

Electoral Eviction

Sensitivity to Electoral Sanctions

Effort and Ambitiousness

Responsiveness

Multiple R = .48
r square   = .23

* See Appendix B22.2, Table C, for path coefficients. No arrow indicates that path coefficients are less than .11. Light arrow indicates that path coefficients are from .12 to .24. Heavy arrow indicates that path coefficients are .25 or higher.

direct effect on responsiveness in the large cities. Furthermore, the psychological conditions of accountability have comparatively little effect in the small cities and a much more persistent effect in the large cities. These patterns merit more detailed attention.

Electoral Accountability in Small Cities

Even a city of 17,000 persons, the largest of the cities here classified as small, has very few citizens actively involved in council elections and community affairs. As few as a thousand voters can send a man to office and keep him there. And most of the small cities of course have many fewer citizens than 17,000; the politically active stratum often numbers only in the hundreds. The council in small communities will often know directly or indirectly most of the active and concerned citizens. If there is widespread discontent among the citizenry, this will be obvious to councilmen as well as to those with whom they have frequent political, social, and business contacts.

Bearing these observations in mind, the data presented in Figure 22–3 gain significance. Councils are responsive when there are challengers and when there is a tradition of eviction *even if* the councils are not ambitious to hold office. Furthermore, the awareness of electoral sanctions has only a weak bearing on responsiveness. To be sure, there are councils in small cities which do manifest a strong interest in holding office and which do show awareness of electoral sanction. And these perceptions and aspirations are related to the number of contestants and the rate of eviction, though not to the size of the electorate.

What is the significance of the direct associations between the institutional conditions of accountability and responsiveness and the weak or nonexistent associations between the psychological conditions of responsiveness? Councilmen live and work and raise their families in the communities they govern. The smaller the community, the larger will be the proportion of the population that the council is involved with in a network of social relationships. Councils will be sensitive to discontent and to implied criticism, and no stronger manifestation is likely than the appearance of challengers and the experience of electoral defeat. This sensitivity will not depend on their own ambitions or concern about the termination of their political careers. Rather it will depend on patterns of social relationships and involvements, often of a face-to-face nature.

The point can best be made by distinguishing between a "career in politics" and a "career in the community." A career in politics refers to the sequence of political offices held and to the length of time one remains in office. A career in the community refers to the less precise but no less significant sense of being respected, well liked, and accepted by one's neighbors and associates. It may

also refer to such tangibles as whether one's professional skills—
legal or medical, for instance—are in demand or whether one's
merchandise is purchased.

No matter what their political aspirations, or lack of them, councilmen cannot easily be indifferent to their career in the community, to how they are being judged by their fellow citizens. These
political and social judgments are bound to be more significant in
the smaller city. For it is in the nature of political life in small
cities that these judgments are being made by business associates
and customers, by professional clients, by parents of one's children's playmates, by people who attend one's church and who
belong to the same social and civic organizations, and even by
persons known more or less directly by the councils. They are not
being made by some unknown, impersonal mass electorate.

Electoral Accountability in Large Cities

A very different pattern of relationships holds in the large city.
First, all three of the institutional conditions of accountability are
connected with the psychological conditions, but none of the three
is directly associated with responsiveness. Second, both awareness
of electoral sanctions and ambitiousness directly affect responsiveness. In short, the electorate has an impact on responsiveness only
if councils tend to worry about electoral sanctions and have political aspirations. When political careers are of concern, then a mass
electorate which chooses among many challengers and frequently
evicts incumbents increases the likelihood of responsiveness.

The large city is the setting for impersonal politics. Social roles
are likely to be more segmented than they are in the small community. The persons with whom councilmen deal politically are
not necessarily the same persons with whom they socialize or with
whom they are engaged in business associations. To have a career
in the community need not involve concern with a large proportion of the citizenry. It means concern with one's particular niche
in the community, with one's neighbors, friends, fellow church
members, business and professional associates, and social circles.
The larger the city, the smaller will be the proportion of the total
population having anything to do with the "community" in

which officeholders live, raise their children, and view their future. To be held in social disrespect by salient circles is as serious as it is in the small city, but it is much less likely that widespread electoral discontent in the large city indicates disrespect by the people "who count."

Of course Figure 22–4 does not indicate a lack of relationship between the conditions of electoral accountability and responsiveness. It only indicates that electoral discontent or pressures do not bring about an increase in responsiveness *unless* political careers are important. The electorate cannot bring about responsive behavior on the part of the council unless the intermediate conditions, such as the rule of anticipated reactions and the ambition hypothesis of politics, hold.

Conclusion

Whether government is representative of the citizens whose lives it regulates, whose taxes it collects, whose well-being it affects, and whose support it requests surely ranks as one of the central issues of democracy. The issue of political representation is particularly critical because, in the nature of things, it is always the few who govern the many, even in a democracy; yet, that the many can control the few is equally critical in assessing a political regime as more or less democratic. Hence the central question: do governors represent the governed?

In the absence of certain institutional and psychological conditions—a mass electorate, political opposition, incumbent eviction, perceived voter sanctions, and career ambitions—the council is free to be unresponsive. Where these institutional and psychological conditions are present, making accountability a reality, a council cannot as easily behave unresponsively.

In general, council responsiveness is more likely if electoral conditions maximize the probability that officeholders can be held to account for their actions. However, the way in which this comes about differs with the complexity of the urban environment. Social pressures explain responsiveness under conditions of electoral accountability in the smaller cities, while career ambitions explain responsiveness in the larger cities. A career in the community is the mechanism which connects electoral discontent with council responsiveness when the setting of political life involves smaller numbers of people and more face-to-face exchanges. The more familiar career in politics is the mechanism which connects electoral discontent with council responsiveness when the political setting is more depersonalized and when there is more distance between the council and the electorate.[20]

---

[20] It should be emphasized that the analysis has not considered marginal distributions of the measures of electoral accountability. That is, to discover that the theory of electoral accountability does help explain responsiveness should not be confused with any statement about how frequently these conditions are met. Indeed, many of the cities have election systems and council perspectives which systematically undermine the potential of elections to hold officeholders to account for their actions. See Kenneth Prewitt, "Political Ambitions, Volunteerism, and Electoral Accountability, *American Political Science Review* 64 (March 1970): 5–17.

Part VI

Public Policy and Collective Adaptation

INTRODUCTION

Cities are places where people work, sleep, and play. For some people the city is primarily a place to make a living; for others it is primarily a place to relax; and for still other people it is both. How well the city satisfies these needs, singly or in combination, depends not only on social choices and economic decisions, or nondecisions, in the private sector, but also on governmental decisions. The quality of urban life is in part the product of governance.

What city government can or cannot do is severely circumscribed by the territorial scope of its jurisdiction and by statutory limitations. It is also restricted because agencies at other levels of government—federal, state, regional, county, or district—have a hand in urban governance, often the upper hand. Yet city dwellers expect their councils to govern in ways that are conducive to the attainment of collective goals, and they seek to influence city governance in ways which translate private preferences into public policies. Regardless, therefore, of what city government can or cannot do, people turn to it to listen to their desires, solve their problems, redress their grievances, or adjust their conflicts. And among the agencies of city government whose actions affect the public good, the city council is central. By virtue of their formal authority, councils shape the city's public life-style through initiating, nurturing, or blocking appropriate policies.

Public policy, it is sometimes argued, is the *raison d'être* of politics. There is merit in the argument, for government is justified by the policies that accrue to the public good. But policies are not and cannot be ends in themselves. Undue emphasis on policy as the end-all of governance neglects the means by which policy comes about. If policy as the end of politics becomes too precious, the use of any means is not only acceptable but justifiable, even if the means are repugnant. There is no inherent virtue in an emphasis on the content of public policy, just as there is no inherent virtue in an emphasis on the process by which policy comes about. Indeed, it is the relationship between the what for and the how of politics, between the product and the process of governance, that sets the major normative questions of political science.

The chapters that follow explore the interdependence of certain policies and certain aspects of policy-making under different conditions of urbanization. Neither all policies of importance to city life nor all aspects of the policy process are treated. On the contrary, the exploration is highly stylized in approach and limited in objective.

Policy is a strictly theoretical construct inferred from the patterns of relevant choice behavior by political actors and from the consequences of choice behavior. Policy is distinguished from policy goals, policy intentions, and policy choices. Policy is defined as a "standing decision" characterized by behavioral consistency and repetitiveness on the part of both those who make it and those who abide by it. Because it stems from uniformities and regularities in political behavior, policy is treated as an emergent property of the polity, a response to environmental challenges and pressures. The response involves adaptation to as well as control of the environment. But though policy is caused by environmental forcings, it is also directed toward a goal and, therefore, purposive. The problematics of policy arise out of this polar, but by no means dualistic, quality of the policy process.

Because policies cumulate over time, they establish an environment within which new policy-making takes place and new policies evolve. The policy environment is as restrictive in this respect as the physical or social environment. It is a product of governance and also a frame of reference for governance. Indeed, of all the environments within which governance takes place, the policy environment is probably the most salient. It reduces policy options and makes for what has been called "bounded rationality." Because it pervades any polity, the policy environment is more productive in comparative policy research than are itemized policies. This rather abstract conception of policy will be more fully explicated in Chapter 23.

The policy environment, as an emergent, is the outcome of developmental sequences in the decisions of councils as revealed by their budget allocations over a period of eight years. City expenditures for planning and amenities serve as indicators of policy behavior. Planning serves to control the urban environment, and amenities are adaptations to the urban environment. Both represent policy areas in which the council has a maximum of discretion, with the result that cities differ more significantly in these respects than in policies involving traditional city services or the administration of justice.

Because the policy environment emerges from the confluence of particular policies through time, at any one point in time it represents a stage or phase of policy development. By using the annual variations in city expenditures for planning and amenities as indicators of policy behavior, Chapter 24 identifies three stages—retarded, transitional, and advanced—and two phases—emergent and maturing—of policy development. At the terminal (and admittedly arbitrary) point of the time sequence under observation, each city can be located in the stage or phase of development that constitutes its current policy environment. Although the word development has an evolutionary ring, development may be progressive or regressive. Chapter 24 includes a validity test of the empirical operations performed in constructing the developmental typology that supports the notion of policy environment as a variable in its own right.

Governments face difficulties in mobilizing natural, material, and human resources for the goals of collective action because such resources are scarce or are resistant to political manipulation. But the legacy of ongoing policies as they have developed through time also weighs heavily on what is or is not done by government as well as on what is likely to be done. Perhaps no condition is more constraining than is the legacy of established public policies. For this reason policies themselves constitute an environment within which governors approach their decision-making and other tasks. Just like any other environment, the policy environment cannot easily be changed at will, much as governors and governed alike may wish to change policies. Policies are not simply instruments of collective adaptation and control; they intrude on and constrain governance.

Nevertheless, the policy environment is also relatively malleable because policies are partly purposive responses to the challenges of the physical and social environments. The very factors that challenge the ingenuity of policy-makers also provide them with opportunities. Thus a large population gainfully employed in commerce and industry creates problems for government, but is also a resource potential to cope with these problems.

We have referred to two very different types of environment: one given by the physical and social conditions of the community, the other resulting from the cumulation of specific policies over time. The relationship between these different environments constitutes the vital context of governance. It is a highly interactive or collinear relationship and, as a result, constitutes a single "eco-policy system." This concept describes the patterned relationship between public policy, on the one hand, and the physical and social conditions of the community, on the other.

Although the eco-policy system is in reality a perhaps irreducible, if multidimensional, whole, it must be artificially constructed. It can, therefore, also be analytically decomposed. Chapter 25 examines the ecological, demographic, and institutional correlates of policy development that show, despite some irregularities in patterns, a high degree of interdependence between the physical-social and policy environments. The symmetry of this interdependence makes it difficult to estimate the true path of causation. If policies are responses to the challenges of the urban environment, they also create and shape the urban environment. But the degree of equilibrium between policy and challenges varies among cities, and when, as shown in Chapter 29, policy development is out of step with the challenges of the natural environment, policy analysis encounters its most puzzling task.

Policy development depends not only on resources that provide capabilities for policy change, but also on institutional arrangements that either impede or facilitate appropriate policy-making. Policy-making is never automatic. Resource potential does not guarantee that governors will respond to environmental pressures and steer their city appropriately. Neither does the immediate availability of needed resources always delay efforts to deal with challenges. The introduction of institutional arrangements, such as a change in property assessment procedures or the permissible tax limit, can mobilize resources that are not presently available. This interpretation assumes, of course, that policy-makers, be they citizens in elections or councilmen in office, recognize and are willing to respond to environmental challenges—a condition as necessary for policy development as the challenges themselves. Policy-makers respond to environmental pressures less in terms of the resources available than in terms of their willingness to generate and mobilize them. For this reason, inquiry into councilmen's perceptions of city problems, their policy positions, and policy images is an important and necessary part of policy analysis.

Chapter 26 introduces the novel notion of the policy map as an instrument of analysis. The construct of policy map assumes that councils do, in reality, project in their cognitions the "territory" within which they are called upon to make decisions and shape policies. As they orient themselves to action, they take cognizance of the problems that confront them; they formulate goals or images of the future; and they take positions on issues. Although these components refer to past, present, and future, they are in fact synchronous and, as a result, constitute a policy map. Unlike the decision-making process that necessarily follows a real time sequence, from initiation through a series of intermediate steps to termination, the policy process is not time-bound in the same way. The perception of environmental challenges as problems, the formulation of attainable goals, and the elaboration of policy stands go hand in hand. How a council perceives, formulates, and elaborates is of interest because it may reveal continuities and discontinuities in the policy process.

Because the requirements of data analysis are such that the substantive content of the policy map must be treated in a rather stylized manner, particular problems or positions are dimensions of each component that deserve measurement. Similarly, the degree of agreement on problems, images, and positions obtained in each council cannot be ignored. Chapters 26 and 27 undertake this analysis.

Problem perceptions are classified into two broad areas—those relating to urban growth and those relating to city services; images refer to constructs of the future that either envisage a residential city or a balanced city where residential and commercial and/or industrial land uses coexist in varying mixes; and positions refer to stands taken in favor of further land use development or in favor of providing for life's amenities. The degree to which these dimensions in each map component are interrelated reveals continuities and discontinuities in the policy map as a whole. Moreover, as shown in Chapter 28, the continuity or discontinuity among map components varies with urban complexity; policy map-making is in fact differentially responsive to the challenges of the ecological environment.

But map-making is also constrained or facilitated by the policy environment. And if, as was suggested, policy environment and ecological environment are interactive, the effect of their interaction on policy mapping is a question for analysis. Chapter 28 explores a causal model of the policy process that derives from the propositions developed in the previous chapters. The model is rather simple, as it employs only five variables. In constructing it we were mindful of Stouffer's injunction that "exploratory research is of necessity fumbling, but . . . the waste motion can be reduced by the self-denying ordinance of deliberately limiting ourselves to a few variables at a time."[1]

However, one can entertain serious doubts about the viability of causal modeling the policy process. Given the purposive aspect of policy-making, the attempt to explain public policy by way of causal models may be something of an anomaly. At issue, clearly, is the question whether the research design in causal modeling of public policy is sufficiently homomorphic with policy-making as a behavioral process in the real world to warrant confidence in the inferences that are made about the emergence of policy. Thought-

---

[1] Samuel A. Stouffer, *Social Research to Test Ideas* (New York: The Free Press, 1962), p. 297.

lessly imposing a causal model on the policy process will not yield
valid knowledge. Therefore, Chapter 29 presents a *post facto,*
quasi-longitudinal design of the policy process that uses basically
synchronous data in a rather unorthodox manner but that is inspired by another comment of Stouffer that we need "many more
descriptive studies involving random ratlike movements on the
part of the researcher before we can even begin to state our problems so that they are in decent shape for fitting into an ideal
design."[2]

The design presented in Chapter 29 is based on the notion of
the eco-policy system as an interactive configuration of the ecological and the policy environments. This system is in equilibrium
if the policy environment and the ecological environment are in
commensurate states. Concretely, a less developed policy environment is commensurate with a less complex urban environment,
and a more developed policy environment is commensurate with
a more complex urban environment. If the policy environment is
more developed than the urban environment demands, the eco-
policy system is not problematic; but if the policy environment is
less developed than a more complex urban environment calls for,
the city may be in trouble. The question to be asked, therefore, is
why relevant policies, in the present case measured by expenditures for planning and amenities, have not kept up with or responded to the challenges of the urban environment. Chapter 29
explores the hypothesis that the eco-policy system, now treated as
the dependent variable, is in disequilibrium if there are serious
incongruities in the policy maps of the councils in those cities that,
though relatively strongly urbanized, have a policy environment
that is out of step with the level of urbanization.

By treating the eco-policy system as a dependent variable, we
restore government and the processes of governance to their right-
ful place at the apex of the political order. Analysis that uses environmental variables—be they indicators of the physical, social,
or, as in this study, policy environments—only as causal factors
tends to be unduly deterministic and to underrate the voluntaristic
nature of politics. While it would be naive to assume that a com-

---

[2] *Ibid.*

munity can achieve all it wants to achieve just by wishing for it and resorting to collective action, it would be sheer fatalism to assume that environmental constraints alone determine what is achieved. The multiple environments in which governmental processes take place are themselves both pliable and adaptable, and in coping with these environments government and politics are active agents of transformation in the polity's multiple environments. In this perspective, then, policies are both outcomes of governmental processes and instrumentalities of political action. To treat them only as outcomes or as instruments is to ignore the complexity of politics.

Chapter 23

Policy Perspective and Policy Environment

Policy is a governing body's "standing decisions" by which it regulates, controls, promotes, services, and otherwise influences the community's collective life. The governing body may be the whole citizenry whose choices in elections or referenda cumulate into policy over time, or it may be a small elected group, like a city council, which acts or fails to act in behalf of the people.

This initial and brief definition of policy is sufficiently different from the few other definitions one finds in the scientific literature to warrant explication. Although policy is a common sense term of ordinary discourse that seems easy to use, it is in fact extraordinarily abstract. Paradoxically, both its common sense usage and its abstract nature make possible reasonably unambiguous communication among policy-maker, policy consumer, and political scientist. But this ease of communication may be deceptive.

A definition of policy cannot be the same definition as may be given to composite terms with which the word policy is often associated. Policy must clearly refer to something other than what policy-making, policy process, policy output, policy evaluation, or similar composite terms refer to. Moreover, because the term policy is not separable from its content, it is almost invariably used in connections that become the term's defining and, as a result, limiting characteristics, as when we speak of "urban policy" or "agricultural policy" or "foreign policy," and so on. For, when so used, definition and explication are more likely to refer to the object of policy than to policy as a subject term. Yet, the meaning of policy in these connections cannot be taken for granted, nor can it be derived from them. Therefore, no matter how simple the usage of policy-related terms may be in ordinary discourse, their use in scientific work requires prior clarification of "policy."

What Policy Is Not

The term "policy" is sometimes used as a synonym for goal, objective, purpose, or end-in-view: "It is the council's policy to make our city a better place to live in," or "it is the council's policy to achieve racial integration in housing." Making the city a better place to live in or eliminating racial segregation are goals of governmental action that imply problems to be solved and values to be realized. They are not policies. For if no distinction is made between policy and the goals of policy, it is impossible to say whether a given policy achieves its stated goals or purposes. Without a distinction one cannot evaluate the policy that is being pursued, regardless of whether the goals are implicit in the policy or explicit and regardless of whether they are deliberate or unanticipated consequences of policies.[1] Indeed, if the consequences of policy are in conflict with preferred goals, the occasion is given for changes in policy. The very dynamics of the policy process require a clear-cut distinction between "policy" and "policy goal" as analytical terms.

Equally incorrect is the use of the term policy in referring to a declaration of intent to do something. This is the usage implied in a phrase like "in order to attract business, it is the council's policy to keep taxes down." Here the term refers to the position or program that is contemplated, the step or series of steps that might be taken to achieve a goal. The assumption is that there is

---

[1] Compare our naturalistic exposition with the normative formulation by Carl J. Friedrich, *Man and His Government* (New York: McGraw-Hill, 1963), p. 79: ". . . a proposed course of action of a person, group or government within a given environment providing obstacles and opportunities which the policy was proposed to utilize and overcome in an effort to reach a goal or realize an objective or a purpose. . . . It is essential for the policy concept that there be a goal, objective or purpose."

a goal and that it is the intent to achieve it through relevant programs. There is a demand that something be done, a statement of willingness to do it, and possibly an expectation that it will be done.

But such declarations of intent are not policies. They are at best guidelines for action, specifying what things should be done or how they are to be done. These statements are really in the nature of exhortations—"let us keep the taxes down." They may orient the policy-maker's behavior; they do not necessarily describe the behavior of those who are directed to do something or of those whom the appeal is designed to influence. Programs are not policies.

Finally, policy is not a synonym for particular events in the policy process, such as decisions or actions of the governing body. Decisions or actions may occur in the pursuit of programs or goals, but they are not themselves policies, even though they may be authoritative or sanctioned.[2] Decisions—whether designed to regulate the conduct of governors and governed, or involving the allocation of resources, or distributing and redistributing governmental costs and benefits—become policies only under certain conditions. The discrete events that constitute part of the policy process are not themselves policies.

The distinction between policy and decisions or actions "making for" policies is necessary because policies result not only from events but also from nonevents. While things that do not occur, or

---

[2] For this formulation we are indebted to Robert H. Salisbury, "The Analysis of Public Policy: A Search for Theories and Roles," in Austin Ranney, ed., *Political Science and Public Policy* (Chicago: Markham, 1968), p. 152. This definition derives, of course, from David Easton's formula of the object of political analysis: "the authoritative allocation of values for a whole society." Salisbury notes: "It [policy] refers to the 'substance' of what government does and is to be distinguished from the processes by which decisions are made. Policy here means the outcomes or outputs of governmental processes." While Salisbury's statement is useful in distinguishing between the "substance" of what government does and decision processes, not all that government "does" is policy. Government may have programs that do not become policy, and even enactments may not become policy if they do not guide conduct because they are not accepted. Finally, Salisbury confuses the terminology by defining policy as "outcomes or outputs." As we argue in the text, policies are invariably outcomes of governmental action or inaction, but outputs do not constitute policy.

nondecisions, are necessarily hypothetical constructs which cannot themselves be directly observed, their results may be only too obvious. In other words, policy may be the outcome of a failure to make decisions or to allocate values. Such failure may be intentional and, if verbalized, constitute a program; or it may be inadvertent, due simply to the policy-makers' inactivity. The consequences are the same. For instance, a city council's failure to cope with racial discrimination results in policy as much as an authoritative effort to remedy the situation. Discrimination is the effective policy, though it may be counter to a stated program or goal. Problems of governance often arise when manifest statements of policy, either programmatic or purposive, are in conflict with practices due to a failure to make decisions. Such failure nonetheless has as a consequence the emergence of a policy.

Two Properties of Policy:
Consistency and Regularity

Policy, then, is a term which should not be equated or confused with "political goal," "program," "decision," or "action."[3] It might appear, therefore, that the term does not have an empirical referent, that it cannot be used without a designative adjective or noun, as when we speak of "city policy," "foreign policy," "policy development," or "policy-making." It has been said, for instance, that "policy is necessarily an abstraction, therefore, to be approached through aggregative or summarizing analytic procedures."[4] But to say this is to make at most an operational suggestion that leaves the theoretical problem of definition unsolved. For policies are phenomena, not epiphenomena.

To define the term policy, one must deal with those properties of the phenomenon to which the term presumably refers and

---

[3] See, for instance, one of the few formal definitions in the literature by Harold D. Lasswell and Abraham Kaplan, *Power and Society* (New Haven: Yale University Press, 1950), p. 71: "Policy is a projected program of goal values and practices." This composite definition is operationally useless and theoretically confounding. If it is decomposed, it leads to noncommensurate empirical referents.

[4] Salisbury, "The Analysis of Public Policy," p. 153.

which characterize the phenomenon independently of other designative characteristics. To speak of "urban renewal policy," for instance, is to specify the scope and domain of a given policy. Policy content is a generic property of policy, but it is not sufficient to define the phenomenon itself. We shall suggest two additional properties.

In the first place, policy refers to consistency in behavior with respect to *what* is being done or *how* it is done in a given domain of public activity. Consistency in behavior may be observed either among those who participate in governmental action or among those who are affected by it. This is possible because people customarily conduct themselves in given ways, or because their behavior is highly sanctioned, or because they voluntarily abide by prescriptions. There is, then, a strongly normal as well as normative component in conduct, and insofar as practices relevant to the scope and domain of governmental activity exhibit normalities, policy may be said to be operative. For instance, if the city council follows identical or near-identical behavior patterns in granting variances to all petitioners, then this is the policy with respect to variances.

But consistency is only one component of policy. The behavior is also characterized by repetition. That is, it occurs not just at one point in time but through time. This refers to the behavior of both governors and governed. For instance, the council's policy in granting variances involves not only consistent behavior but also behavior that is of some duration. The council's variance policy is said to be well established if, more often than not, its decisions through time are permissive rather than restrictive. As a result of such repetition, citizens can entertain reasonably stable expectations with regard to what the council will do in particular situations.

Consistency and repetitiveness in behavior, then, indicate whether a policy is operative. For conceptual purposes we can ignore how much consistency and repetition is required to infer policy from a pattern of conduct. This is a matter of empirical determination. Of course, the more consistent and repetitive a pattern of conduct, the more established is the policy.

Permissive and restrictive decisions may alternate in repetitive fashion, making for a policy cycle. For instance, just as the Federal Reserve Board may increase or lower the interest rate, so may a city council periodically increase or decrease expenditures for a particular budget item. Such cyclical behavior is both consistent and repetitive, although it makes it more difficult to infer the operation of a policy. In short, cyclical behavior is not random behavior. Whether a policy is operative is probably best ascertained by comparison between different policy arenas.

It is the actual norm of conduct in a specific substantive area of governmental action, then, that constitutes policy. Observation of consistent and repetitive behavior patterns in the governmental decision-makers' conduct allows us to define policy as "standing decision."[5] If a policy is operative, it is *as if only one decision* had been made all along and had been effective in guiding governmental conduct. To go back to our example of a permissive variance policy, it is as if the council had said only once, "from here on any petitioner can expect us to grant his application for variance." In fact, of course, no such single decision was made, but rather a great many actions were taken, and these actions were consistent through time. Pending disturbances in the behavioral patterns involved—either because of changes in the behavior of the governors or of the governed—policy is a standing decision precisely because it engenders consistent and repetitive conforming behavior.

As a governing body's standing decision, policy is truly an emergent phenomenon that is more than the sum of its parts. In other words, policy is not simply the adding together of discrete decisions or actions; rather, it reveals itself in behavioral uniformities and regularities that are built in to what governors and governed do

---

[5] We are using the notion of "standing decision" as the long-term, cumulative set of previous decisions in the same way in which Key and Munger used it in referring to the relatively stable balance of electoral voting attachments over time. See V. O. Key, Jr., and Frank Munger, "Social Determinism and Electoral Decision," in Eugene Burdick and Arthur J. Brodbeck, eds., *American Voting Behavior* (Glencoe, Ill.: The Free Press, 1959), p. 286: "In fact, there tends to be a standing decision by the community, although as a descriptive term 'decision' has connotations of deliberate choice that are apt to be misleading. The 'decision' may simply represent the balance between two opposing party groups each with striking powers of self-perpetuation."

and how they do it. Another example—one that stems from our research—may be helpful. The council, over a period of years, annually allocates a certain proportion of the total city budget to libraries, museums, playgrounds, swimming pools, and other things called amenities. Its particular actions do not constitute its amenities policy, but the fact that it does so year in and year out suggests that a policy to provide for amenities is operative. On close inspection, we may also note certain patterns in the council's behavior that are indicative of its options. It can keep the proportion of the budget allocated to amenities constant from year to year, it can incrementally increase the proportion, or it can alternately increase or decrease the proportion. Whatever the pattern, it is the council's budget behavior as observed in dollar allocations from which the council's amenities policy is inferred.

Policy as Emergent

The conception of policy as standing decision calls attention to the time perspective, for something that "stands" does so through time. Some policies may require a relatively long time span to be identified, while others may require relatively little time. In any case, one cannot think of policy as being unaffected by time or by what happens through time. In this perspective, then, policy is not only sanctioned behavior—whether formally through authoritative decisions and actions or informally through expectations and acceptance, regardless of whether specific decisions have been made; it is truly "sanctified" by time.

It may appear that the notion of policy as standing decision implies the absence of change. This is not the case. Because a policy is ongoing, it does not follow that it is not also changing. That statics is only a special case of dynamics is now generally recognized in ontology. Especially in human affairs, the perception of permanence is more illusion than reality. It is only the weakness of our observational tools that makes us think that something is rather than becomes, though it may be convenient to *assume* that a behavioral pattern is in a static state. If, therefore, we define policy as a standing decision, we are not suggesting that there is no process of change. Policy emerges from consistent and repetitive behavioral patterns that are in fact changing through time; they appear to be stable only because behavioral changes themselves are probably more or less regular and subject to laws of change.

The usage of standing decision as the defining characterization of policy does not preclude our pinpointing the emergent quality of policy. Policy is "made," but it is made in special ways. It emerges from the chain of actions and interactions of those involved in the process of governance, be they governors or governed. It is partly made through decisions, though any one decision does not constitute a policy. It is partly made through compliant behavior, regardless of whether compliance is enforced or voluntary. Even if the behavioral patterns appear to be vacillating, at times following one line of action and at another time a different line, policy emerges. Of course, if the behavior involved is altogether random, what emerges is not policy but chaos. But the extreme case does not preclude the notion of policy as changing, nor does the specification of policy as changing deny its characterization as a standing decision. That policies undergo cyclical movements is well known. In this case, the cycle is itself a property of the policy.

Although the conception of policy as an emergent strongly implies that policy evolves by accretion due to new action, taken deliberately or not, or to nonaction, this does not mean that the changes involved are necessarily or only incremental.[6] Policy as an emergent may be affected by highly visible, spectacular events that bring about sudden behavioral change, such as a constitutional decision of the Supreme Court or the adoption of a radically new legislative program.[7] But what ensuing policy "really is" cannot be simply inferred from court decisions or legislative enact-

---

[6] "Incrementalism" is a policy that is usually observed in budget behavior where indeed, as research shows, figures tend to increase slowly over time, especially if the time series observed is a long one. But change may also be due to inaction or reversal of behavior; that is, policy may be decremental.

[7] Most "policy research" deals with such spectacular events. But few studies trace out the consequences of such events and subsequent policy as an emergent. Most definitions of policy are therefore tailored to fit these spectacular events and, as such, are deficient for the observation of policy as an emergent property of governance.

ments. Even spectacular events must be implemented, accepted, and absorbed to become policies as standing decisions of the community.

Whether the outcome of slow accretions, of spectacular actions, or of governmental inaction, it seems clear that policy not simply is but becomes, that specification of the nature of policy at any point in time is necessarily partial and time-bound, for one does not in that case really know whether it is a standing decision.[8] In reality, policy emerges through time, and it can for this reason only be observed through observing the behavior of governors and governed in time. What the observer sees when he identifies policy at any one point in time is at most a stage or phase in a sequence of events that constitute policy development.

Policy, in short, is nothing less than governance in the pursuit of collective adaptation and control. For this reason, policy is always a property of the collectivity—be it a nation-state, a province, a city, a tribe, a party, or a faction—and never a property of individuals. Policy may affect individuals alike or differentially, it may benefit some and harm others, it may be approved by some and disapproved by others, but it is a collective response to the problems of collective life.

Policy as Response

Policy has been defined as standing decision, but it remains to suggest "what policy does" in the process of governance. For this purpose, we shall think of policy instrumentally, as something created by stating goals, deciding issues, and implementing programs, and as something that becomes institutionalized by compliant behavior. We ask, therefore, about the conditions which bring the governing process into motion. There is reason to be-

---

[8] Prohibition "policy" in the twenties is a classical example of such uncertainty. Both enforcement of prohibition legislation by the governors and compliance by the governed varied almost incessantly. It was probably more a program than a policy, for it was devoid of uniform or regular conduct among governors and governed alike.

lieve that, in this respect, policy does not differ from other aspects of human behavior, and that, therefore, the propositions of behavioral psychology are relevant.

In behavioral psychology, action is a response to stimuli in the organism's environment; appropriate conduct is learned because certain responses are rewarded. If no reward is forthcoming, the response is unsuccessful and ceases. If, on the other hand, the action is rewarded, the response will be reinforced so that when similar conditions recur as stimuli, similar responses are likely to occur as well. As a result of the sequence of these behavioral events, human behavior becomes predictable.

Policy is the community's learned and reinforced response to conditions of the physical and social environment. Generally, a policy is operative so long as it is successful, that is, so long as the response it represents proves rewarding. In fact, it is "success" that makes policy what it is—a set of consistent and repetitive behavioral patterns through which governing units cope with environmental conditions. Changes in policy presumably occur when there are changes in the environmental conditions. If there is no response to changed circumstances, if no new policy emerges, the old response pattern or policy is obsolete and may become harmful if insisted on.

As a response to environmental conditions, policy is either an adaptation to environmental changes or it controls further changes in the environment. Whether the policy involves adaptation or control depends on many factors—some of which are characteristics of the environment, and some characteristics of the governing unit. In general, it is probably safe to say that the more surmountable environmental conditions appear to be, the more will governors make decisions and undertake actions that promise to control the environment; and the more overwhelming environmental obstacles appear to be, the more will they pursue policies that are adaptive and adjustive. But the characteristics of the governing unit are also relevant—its political structure, its human and physical resources, the degree of citizen involvement in governance, the vitality of interests making public demands, and, of course, the perceptions, preferences, and orientations of the governors.

The problematics of policy arise out of the relationship among environmental changes that call for response, the ways in which these changes are experienced as issues requiring solutions, and the goals pursued in responding to changes. Policy, then, is a means of responding to environmental conditions, both physical and social, that involves anticipating a future state of affairs. If so, a change in policy is both causal and purposive: it is caused by environmental stimuli, but it is also directed toward a goal and shaped by a purpose. The tension arising out of the simultaneous impact of causal and purposive "forcings" is a basic issue in the scientific study of governance.

The Policy Environment

Policies in all domains of social activity cumulate over time and constitute a policy environment which, like other environments, shapes and is shaped by political processes. The policy environment in which governors and governed are mutually implicated is intuitively nothing less than the set of policies that has evolved through time and culminated, at any given moment, in a stage or phase in the development of policy. Policies, whether major or minor innovations and whether departures from or confirmations of earlier policies, constitute a policy environment very much the way a formal constitution, its amendments, court interpretations and practices make for a constitutional environment. The policy environment is a historically evolving context in which governors and governed respond to the problems of collective adaptation and control and to the task of attaining collective goals.

We are at this point in a curiously paradoxical scientific position. On the one hand, we are using the notion of policy environment in a loosely intuitive way that seems to make sense. On the other hand, we have not given it precise operational meaning. What is clearly lacking is a theoretical explication that, especially because the conception of policy environment is novel to political science, is necessary if we are to use the term in analysis.

Policies are a governing unit's standing decisions or standing responses to challenges from the physical and social environment.

They develop through time and envelop diverse and distinct areas of governmental activity. Policies, in cumulating over time and by area, constitute a *space-time manifold* that we term policy environment. The policy environment is a contextual property of cities and thus of the council and of the public affected by council decisions.

Of the multiple environments in which governors and governed are enmeshed, the policy environment represents a special type of constraint on the processes and outcomes of governance. This is so because the policy environment is a threshold for further policy development. Those involved in the governmental process—whether the city council, the city bureaucracy, special clienteles, or the general public—are participants in the policy environment; it orients their interactions and relationships. The policy environment is perhaps the most salient of all the environments in which governance takes place, and it is perhaps the most pervasive because, as a partly normative component in the total configuration of environmental structures and events, it has implications for the direction and purpose of governance.

The policy environment, though apparently stable at any one point in time, is in fact an emergent phenomenon that constantly changes as old policies are modified or reversed, new policy decisions are made, allocations reflecting policies are increased or decreased, and so on. As an emergent phenomenon, the policy environment is developmental, without a clear beginning that can be unambiguously dated and without a sharply identifiable future. What we observe is invariably a cross section in time which may give the impression of stability but which in fact is a stage or phase in the developmental process as new policies are adopted, old policies neglected, continued, or revised, or as policies just "happen" without decisions in fact having been made. As an emergent, the policy environment has characteristics that are novel and not simply characteristics of its component policies. For instance, the policy environment may be homogeneous as individual policies are ideologically similar, or it may be heterogeneous as some policies move in one direction and other policies in the opposite direction. The policy environment may be activist, as it emerges from actively and deliberately pursued policies, or it may be inert, as little emphasis is placed on conscious or purposive policy-making.

The policy environment influences what new policies are acceptable or tolerable. New policies or substantive changes in old policies cannot easily be made without reference to it. Paradox-ically, the policy environment not only constrains but also liberates governance. Because it reduces the options open in policy-making, it frees governing units from having to consider all rationally possible alternatives. It makes for what Simon called "bounded rationality." It defines for governors and governed alike what is practical or feasible in the making of policies. Because policies are established ways of doing things—standing decisions—the policy environment makes for its own continuance. Once a city has taken on providing a certain level of fire or police protection, once it has begun planning its land use and zoning, once it has embarked on promoting and developing its recreational facilities or economic resources, governmental action will only rarely reverse or undo these policies, although reversal is always possible.

We can also think of the policy environment as intervening between policy-making units and the challenges and pressures from the physical or social environments. For how the physical and social environments are perceived and responded to may depend on the state of the policy environment. Under some conditions, changes in the physical or social environments may be seen as "problems," while under other conditions they may not. For instance, the availability of financial resources may be a severe problem in a city which stresses increases in services, but less of a problem where there is satisfaction with a relatively low level of such services or where they are already adequately provided. Where services are not highly valued, though there is in fact a need for them, the unavailability of resources may be treated as a nuisance rather than as a problem.

There are two reasons for using the policy environment rather than individual policies or types of policy as a variable in the analysis of governance. In the first place, it is a composite phenomenon and is thus more pervasive in the actions of governing units than discrete policies are. It is particularly suitable in an analysis of macro-units such as cities because as an outcome of the governmental process it is a more characteristic property of the collectivity than discrete policies can ever be. For this reason it is probably a more powerful independent variable, that is, it likely explains more of the variance in governance than can discrete policies.

Second, if used as a dependent variable, the policy environment is probably easier to explain than are discrete policies or types of policy. Attempts made in recent years to explain policy outputs in terms of governmental variables such as party competition, interest-group demand patterns, or formal institutional characteristics have not been successful—"a devastating set of findings," as Robert H. Salisbury has noted.[9] Instead, the findings have been that physical resources and demographic factors explain both governmental processes and policy outputs. Paradoxically, although the investigators working in this genre of policy research seem to accept Easton's notion that outputs are the ultimate dependent variable to be accounted for,[10] they do not heed Easton's caveat: "My approach to the analysis of political systems will not help us to understand why any specific policies are adopted by the politically relevant members in a system."[11] We have reason to believe that the policy environment, as a composite variable that is holistic rather than itemistic, is a theoretically more rewarding variable than are discrete policies or policy outputs.

Focus on Planning and Amenities

Charting the policy environment of a modern community in all its possible dimensions is probably not feasible; but it is also not necessary because not all policies are of equal theoretical relevance or operational utility. Which policies are of interest depends on the focus of research attention and the research problem. As a result, the policy environment that may be constructed empirically

---

[9] Salisbury, "The Analysis of Public Policy," p. 164.
[10] See, for instance, Thomas R. Dye, *Politics, Economics, and the Public* (Chicago: Rand McNally, 1966), pp. 3–4.
[11] David Easton, *A Systems Analysis of Political Life* (New York: John Wiley and Sons, 1965), p. 89.

is necessarily a partial and selective aspect of the cluster of available policies.

Of the policies that seem especially germane to urban governance, four substantive types stand out: policies that provide for the traditional services, such as fire and police protection, maintenance of streets and utilities, and so on; policies that manage conflicts between more or less diverse interests if and when they occur; policies that enrich the quality of urban life by providing for such amenities as parks, libraries, museums, and similar facilities; and policies that protect the city's character, whatever it may be—residential, commercial and industrial, or balanced.[12]

These types of policy differ in an important respect. The first two—providing services and managing conflicts—are almost defining properties of urban governance. In other words, a city is, by definition, a collectivity that sees to it that the immediate needs of its inhabitants are satisfied. It is difficult to conceive of a city, as we know it, that would not provide its citizens with fire and police protection, street repair, housing ordinances, waste disposal, minimal justice, and so on. Although it may provide these services directly or indirectly and with varying levels of performance, no city has an option but to pursue relevant policies. On the other hand, a city has considerably more discretion as to whether it wishes to provide for life's amenities through public action and as to whether it wants to protect the use of land through planning and zoning. A city, depending on the preferences of its citizens or governors, may decide not to invest in amenities, leaving this activity to the private sector, and it may control public and private land haphazardly or not at all.

Because cities have more leeway with respect to amenities and planning than they do with respect to the more traditional policies, the former are both more interesting from a policy perspective and more useful in identifying and distinguishing various kinds of policy environment. Put differently, the strong voluntaristic

---

[12] Although our classification of policies deviates in several respects from the "role of government" classification advanced by Oliver P. Williams and Charles R. Adrian in *Four Cities: A Study of Comparative Policy Making* (Philadelphia: University of Pennsylvania Press, 1963), we greatly benefited from it and we wish to acknowledge our indebtedness to the authors.

component inherent in amenities and planning policies is helpful in determining the extent to which policies are governmental responses to conditions in the physical and social environment. Moreover, the nature of the response appears to be more clear-cut than in the case of policies involving conventional city services or conflict management. Amenities policies can be unambiguously thought of as adaptive responses to environmental conditions, while planning and zoning policies can be readily considered as control responses.

Chapter 24

Policy Development: Stages and Phases

The policy environment is a stage or phase in the development of policy. The concept of development, particularly when specified as "political development," is bothersome. The task here cannot be to evaluate such uses as have been made, although we shall occasionally refer to them in order to clarify our own usage. This is all the more necessary because we shall try to adhere to a strictly analytic interpretation of the term.

What do we mean if we say that we are using "development" in a strictly analytic sense? In the first place, development takes place quite independently of the criteria that may be used to make inferences about the direction of the developmental process. In other words, development is not to be confused with growth or expansion. The growth of administrative services, or of budget allocations for planning, or of the influence of interest groups, is not so much development as the result or consequence of development. If administrative services are reduced, budgets cut, or interest group influence declines, there is also development, although the process of development is in the opposite direction. Both growth and decay are consequences of development.[1] This conception of development is analytically neutral in that it is not by itself predictive of a future state of affairs.

---

[1] The notion that development may involve decay as well as growth was brought to scholarly attention by Samuel P. Huntington, "Political Development and Political Decay," *World Politics* 17 (April 1965): 386–430.

Second, our conception of development is also normatively neutral; it avoids built-in substantive criteria that involve judgments about the outcome of development. In part, the difficulties surrounding the notion of political development have been due to confusing the properties of governance, such as differentiation, legitimacy, stability, or integration, with development. Indicators of such phenomena are constructed in systemic rather than in developmental terms,[2] and a judgment is made—sometimes implicitly—that the presence of the property in question represents development. If the property is absent, the system is characterized as undeveloped or underdeveloped. Involved in this usage of development is an a priori judgement, usually a progressive bias. But it could just as well be argued, for instance, that simplicity rather than complexity is the more developed form of a system. A simple administrative structure may be more efficient than a complex one, or bloc allocations in budgets may be more conducive to discretion than item allocations. Changes in system properties may be laden with value preferences, but they are to be treated as neutral from a strictly developmental perspective.

This is not to say that the measurement of development does not involve valuation. Any kind of measurement involves points on a scale that assume values—such as the values of a thermometer or a yardstick. In measuring policy outputs, for instance, our measurement points will be the proportions of dollar values of total expenditures. We measure increases or decreases in policy outputs by observing the dollar proportions that are allocated to various governmental activities. But whether an increase or a decrease is "good" is another matter. What is approved by one observer may be disapproved by another. Yet both can agree that something has changed and both can agree on the validity of the measurement.

Development is more than change through time in the thing being measured. While the discovery that something has changed

---

[2] As Fred W. Riggs has pointed out, "Neither Lasswell nor Almond place their functional categories [of decision-making] in a developmental framework. . . . Both assume that these categories are universal functions in any political system." See Fred W. Riggs, "Administrative Development: An Elusive Concept," in John D. Montgomery and William J. Siffin, eds., *Approaches to Development: Politics, Administration and Change* (New York: McGraw-Hill, 1966), p. 234.

requires measurement at two points in time, so that one can say whether the thing measured has increased or decreased, the change may be random. Development, therefore, is a useful conception only if it can be shown that the changes observed through measurement are not random but follow an orderly process through time. If the process of change through time is orderly, the phenomenon observed and measured has also been *transformed*. In other words, as the term transformation suggests, the thing observed has changed in quality, in the sense that *something new has emerged* that was not present when the first measurement was made. Development, then, means that the unit has moved from one state of affairs to another and that it has been transformed in the course of such movement. Put differently, development means that there are identifiable "states of affairs" at different points in time, and that the thing observed has moved or will move from one state (or stage or phase) into another in an orderly manner. The identification of such states of affairs in the real world is a matter of empirical determination.

States of affairs or stages of development, then, are themselves the outcomes of orderly processes of change through time. The transformation of the unit whose behavior is observed or its movement from one stage of development into another is of course never "seen" but inferred from the measurements that are conducted at different points in time. The movement may be forward or backward, depending on the measurements conducted at time 0 as against time 0 + 1. The direction of movement is not immanent in development, but depends on the *conditions* affecting development. Under one set of conditions there may be progress, under another set, regress. Scientific interest is in the conditions that move a unit from one state of affairs into another, whatever the direction, or with the conditions that make for the absence of development.

Because development involves transformation, it is impossible to think of development without time-bounded stages or phases as characteristic components in the sequence of events from which development is inferred. Developmental analysis must make, therefore, two simplifying assumptions. First, the assumption that a unit "is" in a given stage or phase of development is a simplification. The simplifying assumption is made that a unit located in a stage of development is undergoing only slow, minor, or occasional changes that are quantitatively and qualitatively insignificant. In fact it is the crudity of the measuring device—usually a nominal or weak ordinal scale—that conceals whatever changes may be taking place.

Second, developmental analysis assumes that a sequence of events has a beginning state and an end state and that these can be identified. In reality, of course, terminal states are not easy to specify. Moreover, implicit in thinking about termini of development is the further assumption that these terminal stages are stable states, at least as long as the conditions making for stability are present. Both assumptions—that there are identifiable terminal stages and that these stages are stable—are simplifying but useful, for they provide threshold criteria for measurement. Without them, there would be no lower or upper limits on the measurement scale, and we could not think in theoretically fruitful ways about the dynamics of development.

Policy Development: A Typology

Policy development will be measured in terms of policy outputs that follow each other sequentially through time. If the annual outputs are similar, we refer to the sequence as a *stage* of policy development. We locate cities in three developmental stages which we call *retarded, transitional,* and *advanced.* These terms are analogous in some respects to terms like traditional, transitional, and modern used in writings on the politics of new nations.[3]

Two points need to be made about the analogy to national development and our nomenclature. As to the nomenclature, it would seem to suggest a bias toward the progressive hypothesis—that development invariably implies change from a less to a more developed state of affairs. No such implication is intended by the nomenclature itself. The word is not the thing. As we shall point

---

[3] See, for instance, David E. Apter, *The Politics of Modernization* (Chicago: University of Chicago Press, 1965); or Lucian W. Pye, *Aspects of Political Development* (Boston: Little, Brown, 1966). Also Robert A. Packenham, "Approaches to the Study of Political Development," *World Politics* 17 (October 1964): 108–120.

out later on, development may be reversed, that is, a unit may move from a more developed to a less developed state of affairs. The direction of the movement is a matter of empirical determination, and the explanation of the direction is a matter of theoretical stipulation. The nomenclature here is not intended to prejudge what is yet to be discovered.

Second, it is important to keep in mind that our observations cover only a moment of the historical developmental process, a very small segment that is essentially "modern." We can illustrate this in Figure 24–1:

Figure 24–1
Three Historical Stages of Development

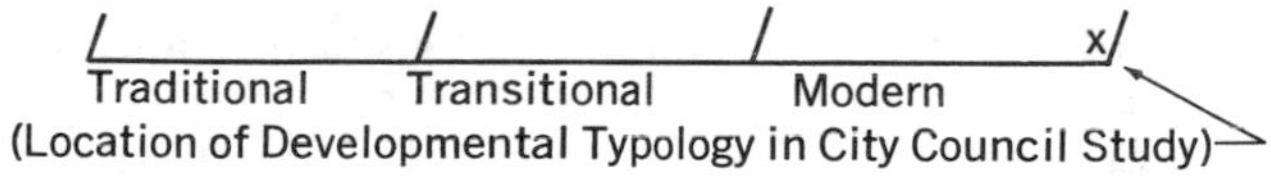

Traditional   Transitional   Modern
(Location of Developmental Typology in City Council Study)

It is therefore all the more significant that, even within this miniscule segment of history, we can locate cities in clearly different stages of policy development. This suggests that a concept like modern disguises a great deal of variation that detailed analysis can reveal. The point to be made is that our stages correspond only analogically to similarly named stages used in the long-term analysis of social development.

The conception of a set of sequential outputs as constituting a stage implies continuity and stability. But the notion of development means that one stage, sooner or later, will yield to another. Yet it is unlikely that a given stage will suddenly be replaced by another. Unfortunately, some of the writings on development that use the concept of stage as an analytical tool give just this impression. It stands to reason, however, that the developmental process does not neatly subdivide into only clear-cut stages. The transformation from one stage to another likely involves a simultaneous movement forward and backward, some actions appropriate to Stage A and some to Stage B. In this case development appears uncertain. Or, put differently, this case gives rise to a situation from which we cannot easily extrapolate whether a city will remain where it started or whether it will be transformed.

For instance, to take an extreme example, let us assume that we are observing eight policy outputs that follow each other in an annual sequence. Outputs$_{1,2}$ can be assigned to Stage A; outputs$_{3,4,5,6}$ will fit Stage B; but they are followed by outputs$_{7,8}$, which are characteristic of Stage A again. In other words, in the period of observation the outcomes are sufficiently dissimilar so that the sequence as a whole cannot be simply assigned to a single stage of development.

To cope with this possibility, we define a set of sequential but dissimilar policy outputs as a *phase* of development. The notion of phase suggests that the sequence is less clearly bounded and, perhaps, of shorter duration than a stage. As we are constructing three stages of development, we must provide for two phases—an *emergent* phase, located between the retarded and the transitional stages, and a *maturing* phase, located between the transitional and advanced stages.

A word is in order on "reversed" development. While stages of development (as constructed by the historian dealing in epochs) are inevitably consecutive and irreversible, as when we say that the Middle Ages followed Antiquity, for analytical purposes development is in fact reversible. In other words, even though we assume that stages and phases follow one another in temporal order, no assumptions need be made concerning the direction of change. Reversal is always a possibility.

Before describing how we actually constructed our typology of policy development and assigned cities, Figure 24–2 diagrams the developmental sequence. In the three stages—retarded, transitional, and advanced—development is relatively stable, while in

Figure 24–2
The Developmental Process

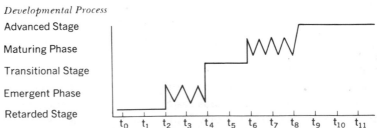

Developmental Process

Advanced Stage

Maturing Phase

Transitional Stage

Emergent Phase

Retarded Stage

t_0 t_1 t_2 t_3 t_4 t_5 t_6 t_7 t_8 t_9 t_{10} t_{11}

the two phases—emergent and maturing—development is unstable, as symbolized by the zigzag lines. The purpose of the typology is to locate each city's sequence of policy outputs during the
period of observation in the particular stage or phase of development that constitutes its current policy environment.

Construction of Development Typology

To measure each city's policy environment, we have constructed
an eight-year policy profile that permits us to assign a city to a
stage or phase of development. It will be recalled that, for theoretical reasons, we focus on amenities and planning policies as the
components of the policy environment. The indicator of amenities
policy is the percentage of *total* government expense spent for
health, libraries, parks, museums, recreation, and so on.[4] The
major accounting categories used to report expenditures presumably include the more important amenities offered by cities. A
city with a high expenditure level for amenities differs from a city
with a more traditional service orientation in that it spends pro-
portionately less of the city's income for fire and police services,
public works, and so on.

The measure we shall use to indicate a city's land-control policy
is the percentage of all general government expenses spent by the
planning commission. General government expenses include
essentially all administrative expenses and salaries *not* included
under fire, police, amenities, or other categories.[5]

Figure 24–3 illustrates how annual policy outputs are assigned

---

[4] Since education and public welfare policies are not made at the city level in
California, we cannot use expenditures in these areas as measures.

[5] Expenses by the planning commission include both operating expenses and
outlays, therefore encompassing the range of items from paper supplies to salaries of full-time city planners to special outside studies commissioned by the city
planning commission. California state law requires every city to have a planning
commission, but this body may be, and frequently is, a standing committee of
citizens appointed by the city council which incurs no expenses charged against
the city. Therefore, the actual dollar amount spent by the planning commission
would seem to be a good indicator of the extent of a city's commitment to the
idea of planning as a way of controlling the environment. General government
expenses are used as the percentage base rather than total government expenses
in order to make planning definitionally independent of amenity expenditures.

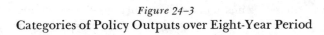

Figure 24–3

Categories of Policy Outputs over Eight-Year Period

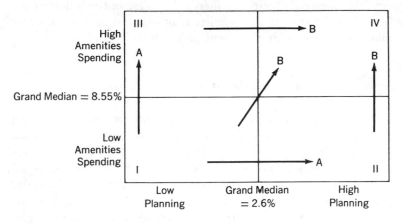

to a stage or phase of policy development. If planning and amenities expenditures both fall below the grand medians of expenditures in every year of the eight-year sequence, the policy profile is
classified as retarded (cell I); if one type of expenditure falls above
and the other below the grand medians, the profile is designated
as transitional (cells II and III); and if both planning and amenities expenditures are above the medians in all eight years, the
profile is assigned to the advanced stage of development (cell IV).
If, during the eight-year sequence, expenditures cross the median
lines, the profiles represent phases of development: outputs moving from cell I to cells II and III (arrows A) are classified as constituting the emergent phase; those moving from cells II or III
(and, occasionally, cell I) into cell IV (arrows B) are assigned to
the maturing phase. To illustrate further, Figures 24–4 to 24–11
show typical policy profiles for the eight fiscal years, 1958 to 1965,
used in the analysis.

   In the assignment we had to make decisions about deviant cases.
As Table 24–1 shows, for the 82 cities over a period of eight fiscal
years there were 536 opportunities for a change in outputs.[6] Of

----

[6] This calculation was made as follows: if all 82 cities had been in existence over
the whole eight-year period of measurement, there would have been a total of
82 × 7, or 574, opportunities for reversal. However, eight of the cities incorporated after 1958 reduced the actual opportunities to 536.

Table 24–1
Developmental Typology of City Policy Profiles
with Opportunities for Change and Reversals

Development type	Cities N =	Oppor- tunities N =	Number of Reversals				Total Reversals	
			One	Two	Three	Four	N =	% =
Retarded	10	58	5	1			7	12
Emergent	15	92	3	5	1	1	20	22
Transitional	27	176	9	6			21	12
Maturing	15	105	6	4	1		17	16
Advanced	15	105	4	1			6	6
	82	536	27	34	6	4	71	13

these opportunities, 13 percent represented reversals from one year to the next. In the other 87 percent of opportunities, there either was no change—that is, all outputs remained in the same stage over all eight years—or change occurred in an incremental direction making for a phase of development. Reversals in profiles assigned to stages of development are due, of course, to the assignment of some deviant cases where an annual reversal in the magnitude of output seems to be only a temporary deviation from the regular pattern.[7]

A Validity Test

To test the validity of the typological constructs, we assume that policy development in fact proceeds in the direction of growth rather than of decline, in other words, that in the normal course of things a city will move from the retarded through the emergent,

---

[7] To reduce arbitrary assignment as much as possible, the technique used was similar to unidimensional scaling. We gave each city a score for each policy output—1 if the output located the city in cell I; 2 for cell II and III outputs; and 3 for being in cell IV. The individual scores were then totaled and assignments made. For instance, a city that in all eight years had policy outputs in cell I would have a score of 8; cell II and III would total 16; and cell IV outputs, 24. Cities with total scores lying between the limits imposed by each "ideal" cell score were assigned to stages or phases in such a way that "reversal errors" would be minimized.

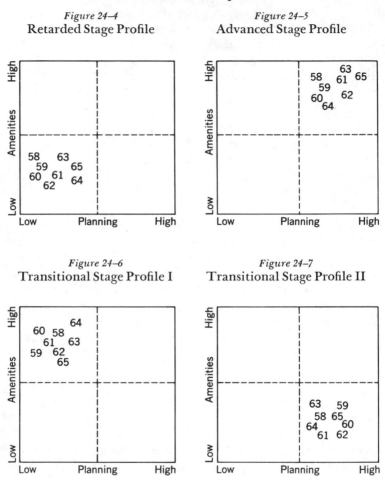

Figures 24–4 to 24–11
Assignment of Cities to Stages
and Phases of Development

Figure 24–4
Retarded Stage Profile

Figure 24–5
Advanced Stage Profile

Figure 24–6
Transitional Stage Profile I

Figure 24–7
Transitional Stage Profile II

Note: Numbers in cell refer to fiscal years 1958 to 1965. In Figure 24–4, for instance, the city was low in spending for amenities and planning in all eight years and was therefore assigned to the retarded stage. For assignment of cities to stages or phases of development, see text.

Figure 24–8
Emergent Phase Profile I

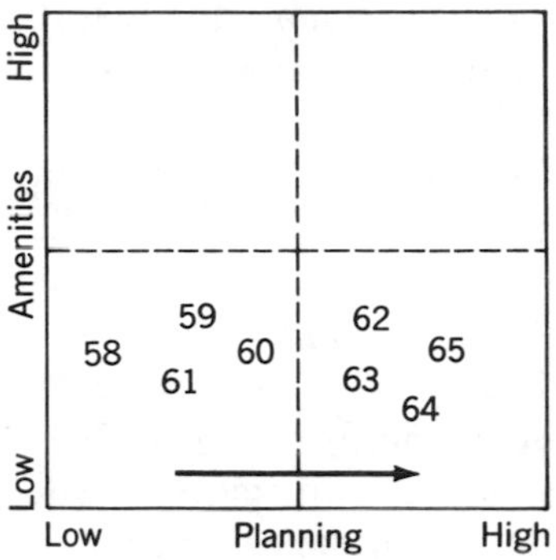

Figure 24–9
Emergent Phase Profile II

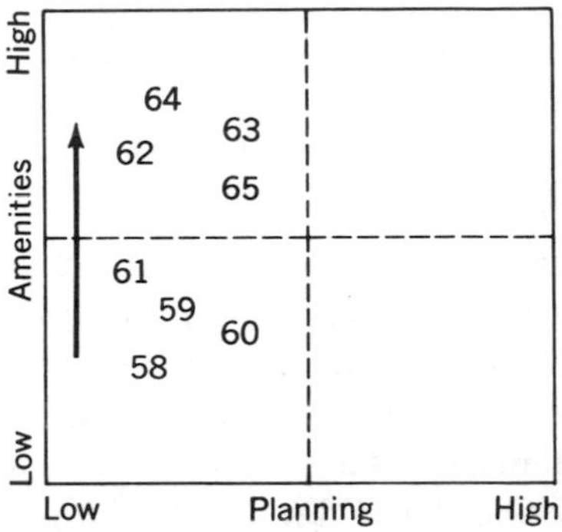

Figure 24–10
Maturing Phase Profile I

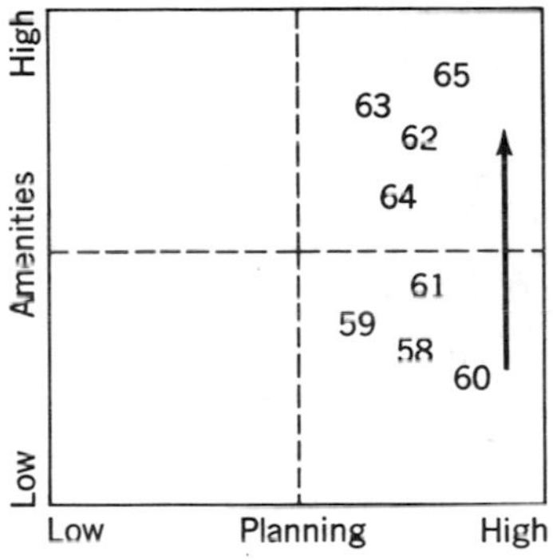

Figure 24–11
Maturing Phase Profile II

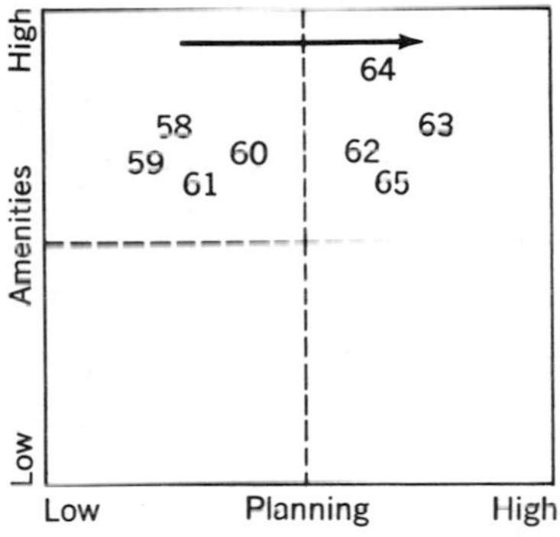

transitional, and maturing to an advanced state of affairs. We test this assumption, and with it the validity of the developmental typology, by dividing the eight-year period into two four-year periods and assigning each city to either a stage or phase of policy development for both periods. Cross-tabulation reveals the internal movement from one period to the next. If our assumption and assignments are reasonably valid, we should be able to predict, from knowledge of a city's location on the development scale in

the first four-year period, where it will be located in the second
four-year period. We predict that cities in a stage of development
are less likely to move than cities in a phase of development. We
also predict that when there is movement, it is more likely to be
in the hypothesized growth direction than in a reversed direction. Table 24–2 presents the results.

It is readily evident that both predictions are generally supported by the data. Of the 47 cities in stages of development during the 1958–1961 period, 62 percent remained in the same stage
during the following period; but of the 29 cities in a phase of development during the earlier period, only 28 percent remained
there in the later period. If we consider the direction of movements, it appears that of the 18 cities in stages during the earlier
period that did move, 14 (78 percent) moved in the expected direction. But this result of course is largely due to the boundaries set
by the typology: retarded cities can only move forward and advanced cities can only move backward. More significant, therefore,
is the fact that none of the advanced cities reverted, suggesting that
once this plateau is reached, institutionalization of policies makes

Table 24–2
Policy Development of Cities in Developmental Sequence
from 1958–1961 to 1962–1965

State of development, 1958–1961	State of Development, 1962–1965				
	Retarded (N = 11)	Emergent (N = 13)	Transitional (N = 28)	Maturing (N = 14)	Advanced (N = 16)
Retarded (N = 14)	6	7			1
Emergent (N = 13)	2	1	8	2	
Transitional (N = 23)	1	3	13	5	1
Maturing (N = 16)			5	7	4
Advanced (N = 10)					10
No data*	2	2	2		

*City not incorporated 1958–1961.

reversal unlikely; and the further fact that of the ten transitional cities that did move, six moved forward and four backward. Similarly, of the 12 emergent cities that moved, ten (83 percent) moved forward as expected and only two returned to the retarded stage in the later period; but of the nine moving maturing cities, only slightly more than half (55 percent) reverted to the transitional stage. Of course, these results may be influenced by the original data. Some policy outputs as measured are in some cases very close to the cutting point that serves as the criterion for assignment, so that we may be dealing here with errors that are due to the crudity of our measuring instrument. Nevertheless, we believe that the weight of the evidence is sufficient to warrant our interpretation of Table 24–2. It is also noteworthy that few of the movements, either forward or backward, exceed one step at a time. Of the 24 cities moving forward and having an opportunity to do so by more than one step (that is, those retarded, emergent, and transitional in the first period), 20, or 83 percent, moved one step only; and of the nine cities moving backward and having an opportunity for more moves (that is, those transitional and maturing in the first period), all but one reverted only one step.

Reversed development is a fact of social life. While stages of development as conceived by historians are inevitably consecutive and irreversible, policy development is in fact reversible. Altogether, 11 out of 76 cities did revert in the second period to an earlier stage or phase. Although we assumed, for the purpose of the validity test, that stages and phases in general follow each other in an orderly process from less to more of the outputs, an assumption that Table 24–2 certainly does not falsify, no rigid assumptions need or should be made about the direction of change. Policy is the creation of men and can be changed by men, within certain constraints imposed by environmental conditions, in whatever direction they prefer. Otherwise the concept of policy would make little sense.

Policy Development and Policy Environment

It is important to recognize that the development typology is not a simple continuum. While the five types constitute a weak ordinal ranking on a scale from less to more developed, they also represent qualitative differences associated with different levels of development. In other words, a city's movement from one stage into another may be due to structural changes in causal factors rather than to simple gradual increases. This means that variables related to city policy development may well exhibit sharp changes at certain points in the developmental sequence rather than incremental changes from one stage to another. For instance, a council's orientation to action may change radically after it has left the retarded stage and entered the emergent phase and then not change at all. Also, variables need not change monotonically across the five developmental types. For instance, development may be related to city growth in the early stages or phases but not in subsequent ones. Or cities at the three intermediate levels of policy development may show characteristics not shared by the least and most developed cities. Or cities in the two phases of development may be more similar to each other than to cities in the immediate neighboring stages.

As policies emerge and cumulate over time they come to constitute a policy environment that is not something static and invariable but a stage or phase in a sequence of development through time. In other words, what may be experienced by the political actor as his policy environment and, perhaps, as something that is fairly stable is in fact only a segment in the sequence of policy events that connects past and future. The human perspective, and especially the political perspective, is generally short-range. Only a few participants in the political arena are sensitive to the past, and only a few envisage the future. Most political actors limit their focus of attention to the present and, if thinking developmentally at all, assume that present trends will continue indefinitely into the future. In fact, we conclude, the policy environment is only a stage or phase in the development of policies. Nevertheless, the policy environment is significant, like other environments, in defining the situation in which the processes of governance and the behavior of governors and governed unfold.

Chapter 25

Policy Context: Challenges and Opportunities

That policies are purposive responses to challenges from the physical and social environment rather than conditioned reflexes is not a trivial notion, for the conception of policy as purposive implies the intervention of human actors in the sequence of events that links the natural-social with an appropriate policy environment. The policy environment is not simply an automatic or spontaneous effect of external causes.

Policy research cast in a conventional stimulus-response design is unlikely to be theoretically interesting. It can generate a multitude of correlation coefficients between itemistic indicators of policy and environmental variables, but it is not at all clear just what has been demonstrated if and when a relationship is found to exist.[1] A strong relationship does not *ipso facto* mean that policy has been explained; or the absence of a relationship does not mean that policy is unaffected by environmental conditions. Whatever the strength and direction of the relationship, therefore, the policy-*making* process and the conduct of political actors in that process cannot be ignored.

---

[1] Richard I. Hofferbert, in "Ecological Development and Policy Change in the American States," *Midwest Journal of Political Science* 10 (November 1966): 480, has rightly observed that "such correlations provide a starting point for analysis rather than a logical culmination of inquiry. . . . They do not specify the links between ecology and policy, i.e., the behaviors of the human actors who must ultimately make the policy decisions."

The reason for caution in making inferences from direct relationships between environmental conditions and policy is obvious. Policy is not simply caused by environmental pressures but, in turn, has an effect on the environment. This is so because policy is partly purposive. One of its purposes often is to bring about changes in the physical and social environment. Indeed, the environment is never the same once policy-makers have injected themselves. This means that the relationship between environment and policy cannot possibly be asymmetrical. In a technological society the relationship is more likely to be reciprocal, if not asymmetrical in the opposite direction. Human intervention, whether deliberate or not, is as likely to shape the physical and social environment as the latter is likely to affect human governance. If not reciprocal, therefore, it may well be that environmental pressures and governing responses cancel each other, with the result that the direction of the relationship between environment and policy may be even more complex than is normally suspected. In the language of statistics, the relationship may be strongly interactive and collinear.

The Urban Challenge

A broad conception of urbanism, as proposed in Chapter 3, and of policies as themselves constituting an environment is probably more conducive to theorizing about city governance than correlating specific policy outputs with specific economic, ecological, or demographic variables. Although one must, of necessity, use particular indicators of urbanization, such as population size, density, growth rate, or employment data, these itemistic variables are of interest only insofar as they broadly express the urban challenge as a complex social, psychological, and physical phenomenon. It is the city as a whole that constitutes the policy-relevant environment. Population size, for instance, is relevant not because it engenders particular problems—say, housing—but because it is a surrogate for a whole range of environmental conditions connected with urbanism. If one says "size," therefore, one says complexity, diversity, congestion, large-scale organization, specialization, areal stratification, and other corollaries of urbanism.

The conception of the policy environment is equally broad-gauged. The policy development typology introduced in Chapter 24 harnesses what Easton has spoken of as an "aggregate of outputs over an interval of time."[2] Although the indicators used—amenities and planning expenditures over a period of eight years—are partial, each stage or phase of development in these policy outputs can be more broadly conceived as constituting the city's policy environment. As a consequence, policy environment should not be thought of as simply being a dependent variable in the conventional sense. Rather, it is to be conceived as a contextual variable which, along with the urban environment, orients governmental action. And it is not merely a feedback stimulus. It is a pervasive property of the total environment in which governance is carried on.

It is within the policy environment, especially as it is related to the urban environment, that the council governs the city. Particular policies are not simply direct responses to challenges stemming from the urban environment; nor are they merely expressions of the ongoing policy environment. Rather, the context of policy-making consists of the *relationship* between the urban context and the policy context. This relationship makes for a configuration of environmental properties that gives governance its peculiar form from one locale to another. The relationship is of a theoretical interest, therefore, not because the urban environment somehow "explains" the policy environment, but because it represents the total context of governance.

The policy environment is intermediate between changes in the urban environment, including social demands generated by that environment, on the one hand, and the willingness and capacity of governing bodies to cope with the challenges of urbanism, on the other. While the relationship between the urban and the policy environments is not sufficient to set governance in motion, it is a necessary condition. If there were no relationship between the urban and policy environments, if there were no identifiable configuration, governance would be largely whimsical, subject to the temporary moods of policy-makers or to the arbitrary decisions of

---

[2] David Easton, *A Systems Analysis of Political Life* (New York: John Wiley and Sons, 1965), p. 400.

power holders. Yet this is not the case, not even in political systems in which arbitrariness is sanctified as a form of government. It is not the case because the policy environment, as a purposive response to challenges from the physical and social environments, serves as a constraint on policy-making. Much of what policymakers do they do because the relationship between policy environment and ecological environment, as it emerges through time, orients their conduct and action. The degree of freedom available in governance is invariably limited by this relationship.

This theoretical reasoning, rather than a search for causal linkages, leads to Table 25–1. There we present some selected ecological and demographic characteristics of the 82 Bay Area cities in relationship to the five stages and phases of policy development that constitute, at the terminus of the period, the ongoing policy environment. Although there are a few disturbances in particular relationships, the overall pattern is highly linear. In general, the more developed the policy environment, the greater is the proportion of cities having a large population, high density, growing density, high growth rate and increasing growth rate, more change in land area, more land in commercial or industrial use, an industrial character, a high ratio of employment in manufacturing, high ethnic diversity, and greater proximity to a major city. In the less developed policy environments these relationships are reversed.[3]

In spite of some irregularities, the overall pattern of relationships presented in Table 25–1 suggests that cities evolve policy environments that are congruous with changes in and challenges

---

[3] Most of the serious deviations from the main pattern occur in the environments that represent the two terminal stages of policy development—the retarded and the advanced. This is probably due to the artificial boundaries that had to be set to the typology. Had the data from which the typology is constructed covered a longer time series than the years 1958 to 1965, the disturbances might not have occurred (though, perhaps, others might have appeared). But the deviations from the linear pattern also represent real phenomena. While the retarded cities have many "rural" characteristics like small population, low density, small growth rate, and so on, some of them are in fact industrial working-class cities with a relatively high ethnic diversity. At the other end of the development continuum there is, as one might expect, a leveling-off of the growth rate and density. Evidently, once policy development has reached the advanced stage, further changes in the physical environment have less of an impact on policy development because relevant policies are in fact operative.

from the urban environment. The more urbanized the physical and social environment, the more likely it is that a city has evolved a more developed policy environment. Conversely, policies giving rise to a given policy environment tend to shape the city's physical and social environment. Whatever the declared policy objectives of urban governors, they seem to pursue policies that either adapt the city to the urban environment or serve to control that environment and all that urbanization implies.

Urban Opportunities

The policy development typology, it will be recalled, includes two variables—expenditures for planning and zoning, and expenditures for amenities. The former may be thought of as indicators of the city's regulative capability, while the latter may be thought of as at least partial indicators of its distributive capability. Regulation and distribution are significant components of a governing unit's total capability. Levels of expenditure in the case of both planning and amenities depend on physical and economic resources as well as on the willingness to mobilize these resources. For it is most unlikely that lacking resources or a willingness to use them, a city will respond to pressures in terms that are relevant to policy development. Entertaining an extreme view, one might suspect that policy development is wholly dependent on wealth and willingness to spend for the purposes of governance. This, however, is not the case, as will soon become clear. Nor is the mobilization of resources itself a simple response to environmental pressures.

Paradoxically, what in some respects appear to be deprivations from the policy perspective are, in other respects, opportunities. Increasing population size and density or a high degree of industrialization and employment in manufacturing, for example, cannot be treated as if they were burdensome factors in a city's environment. They create problems for governance, but they also contribute resources. A growing population that is gainfully employed, buys land, builds homes, and spends income probably makes a net contribution to the city's arsenal of resources. The growth of

Table 25–1
Urbanization and Policy Development in 82 San Francisco Bay Region Cities

Urban environment	Proportion of Cities in Stages and Phases of Development				
	Retarded (N = 10)	Emergent (N = 15)	Transitional (N = 27)	Maturing (N = 15)	Advanced (N = 15)
1965 Population size > 50,000	0	0	11	40	53
< 10,000	90	80	37	7	0
1965 Population density > 4,000	0	13	33	33	53
< 2,000	70	60	26	33	0
1960–1965 Increase in density	38	54	63	67	53
Decrease in density	24	31	33	33	47
1960–1965 Population growth > 25%	20	27	41	67	40
= 0%	50	33	7	0	0
1960–1965 Growth > 1950–1960 growth	10	13	22	47	47
1960–1965 Growth < 1950–1960 growth	60	53	44	33	53
1960–1965 Land area change > 4%	20	53	52	60	73

Table 25-1 (cont.)

Urban environment	Proportion of Cities in Stages and Phases of Development				
	Retarded (N=10)	Emergent (N=15)	Transitional (N=27)	Maturing (N=15)	Advanced (N=15)
1965 10% Land area in commercial or industrial use	30	13	33	73	67
1965 10% Employed in manufacture	0	7	22	27	33
2% or less employed in manufacture	80	60	59	33	13
Chiefly residential	40	60	59	40	7
Chiefly agricultural	30	27	15	13	20
Chiefly industrial	30	13	26	47	73
High in ethnic diversity	40	13	22	40	47
Low in ethnic diversity	0	47	33	27	27
Located within 10 miles of major city	30	33	44	60	53

commerce and industry broadens the tax base and creates new resource bases.

Institutions and Policy

The impact of formal institutional arrangements on governance, and especially on substantive policy formation, is ambiguous. At the level of the American states, the bulk of the evidence, though not uncontradicted, seems to show that formal structural variables have relatively little effect on policy outputs once physical and economic variables are controlled.

But what can be learned about political structure and policy formation depends on how the problems of governance are conceptualized, approached methodologically, and translated into reasonable propositions. First, institutional variables are simply too gross to account for highly particularized data, and thus policy analysis cannot achieve meaningful theoretical closure if it is restricted to an itemistic approach. These data are more likely to be historically determined—that is, they are unique events subject to temporary variations.[4] Policy analysis seeking to include institutional factors as possible explanations is therefore better served by treating policy as a "manifold of events."[5] The notion of the policy environment as a stage or phase in long-term development represents such a manifold of events. As such, it is both more inclusive and stable through time than are itemistic outputs of policy, and it is more likely to be meaningfully related to systemic phenomena like institutions.

Second, too strict an adherence to causal modeling of the policy process may account for the failure of an itemistic procedure to discover significant relationships between policy outputs and institutional variables. Institutions—by definition, patterns of behavior

---

[4] Hence Sharkansky's incrementalist approach is more powerful in explaining variations in policy outputs than is correlational analysis at one point in time. See Ira Sharkansky, *The Politics of Taxing and Spending* (Indianapolis: The Bobbs-Merrill Company, 1969).

[5] This expression is, of course, classically Lasswellian. See Heinz Eulau, "The Maddening Methods of Harold D. Lasswell: Some Philosophical Underpinnings," *Journal of Politics* 30 (February 1968): 3–24.

occurring over a long period of time and giving rise to formalized structures of behavior—cannot readily be incorporated into causal models of the policy process. For a causal model not only makes assumptions about the primacy of one variable as against another, but the asymmetry of the model also presupposes an ordering of the variables along a time dimension. But institutions do not "precede" or "follow" policies. They constitute a context within which decisions are made, outputs are enacted, and policies emerge. They are powerful constraints on the policy process, but they are constraints that are synchronic with the policy process and not its antecedents.

Finally, institutions, especially those formalized in constitutions and statutes, are instrumentalities of governance that can be manipulated. This is an important consideration if one wishes to understand the process by which policies develop and through which a policy environment emerges. The choice involved in adopting one or another institutional arrangement is likely to take account of the advantages and disadvantages that may ensue. For instance, councils intent on promoting commerce and industry in their cities are likely to opt, if they can, for institutional arrangements that will facilitate rather than impede this goal.

Among the institutional arrangements relevant to the governance of California cities, the city's legal status, its form of government, its statutory tax limitations, and its tax assessment procedures are especially germane to the policy process.

Legal Status of Cities

An intricate history of institutional development following the adoption of the California State Constitution of 1879 culminated in two major forms of legal status for cities—general law and local charter status. Charter cities have greater flexibility in their own governance, such as determining the size of the council and municipal structures and activities, because they do not have to seek state legislative authorization before setting up additional departments and services. In fact, the state legislature has come to grant such broad authority to general law cities as well that in recent years most cities eligible for charter status (those with a population of over 3,500) have not made use of the opportunity.[6] As a result, the main differences between these two types of legal order seem to be: (1) charter cities have the authority to levy all kinds of taxes not prohibited by the state or federal constitutions or by the charter itself; and (2) charter cities have more leeway to alter the forms of local government.

Form of Government

Both charter and general law cities can adopt either the council-manager form of government and its variation, the council-administrator form, or the council-weak mayor form. Only the council-strong mayor and commission forms are denied to general law cities, but in fact these two forms are rarely used even in charter cities. General law cities have been able to elect the mayor independently since 1959, but this does not give him additional authority, and only a few California general law cities elect their mayors. The chief difference between the council-mayor and council-manager forms is the greater professionalization of city government and the greater integration of city activities under the council-manager form. There are other differences, but they need not be spelled out here. Although the council-administrator form does not give the administrator formal authority over other city personnel and subjects him to more council control than the manager, in actual practice city managers and many city administrators follow identical routines.[7]

Tax Assessment Procedures

Assessment of property value is, in the great bulk of California cities, in the hands of the county tax assessors, who perform this

---

[6] See Winston W. Crouch, Dean E. McHenry, John C. Bollens, and Stanley Scott, *California Government and Politics* (Englewood Cliffs, N.J.: Prentice-Hall, 1964), p. 245: "Although the power to write and adopt a home rule charter has been widely acclaimed as an important victory for a large number of cities in California, it has not been extensively used in recent decades. . . . Thus, most cities that are eligible to have charters have not made use of the opportunity."

[7] See *ibid.*, p. 249: "In actual practice, however, city managers and many city administrators function identically. Councils do not make a meaningful distinction between the two positions, and appointed general executives who have operated in both forms say that they perform the same way in one as in the other."

work for most cities under contract. However, a number of cities, for various reasons, prefer to assess property locally with their own staffs.[8]

Statutory Tax Limitation

The property tax remains the most important source of municipal revenue. However, although the value of taxable property has been rising, the use of the property tax has in effect been declining because the tax rate is generally fixed at $1 per $100 of the assessed valuation of property. Some special property taxes for particular purposes such as financing employee retirement plans or maintaining some amenities are permitted to exceed the $1 limit, but the overall property tax rate is limited.[9]

Cities will choose institutions as instruments of governance depending on their policy stance—whether they wish to slow down or speed up policy development. Because development toward the more advanced stage is likely to be facilitated by a maximum of freedom of action on the part of policy-makers, we expect that the more developed the city, the more likely it is that it has a charter, the council-manager form, a relatively open property tax limit, and self-assessment of property. As the adoption of these institutional arrangements is also a matter of city size, controlling the relationship between institutional arrangements and policy development is essential. Table 25–2 presents the data, both uncontrolled and controlled by city size.

Whether a city has a charter is largely a matter of city size, but it is also a matter of policy development, especially in the larger cities. Similarly, the council-manager (including the council-administrator) form of government predominates in all the larger cities regardless of policy development, but in the smaller cities the city's stage of development clearly makes a difference in whether it has the more professionalized form of administration. Both large and small cities rely heavily on county assessment of their property taxes, but there is a tendency in both for city assessment to vary with policy development, especially in the maturing

---

[8] *Ibid.*, p. 199.
[9] *Ibid.*, p. 201.

Table 25–2

Relationships Between City Institutional Arrangements
and Policy Development

Institutional arrangements	Re-tarded (N = 10)	Emer-gent (N = 15)	Transi-tional (N = 27)	Matur-ing (N = 15)	Ad-vanced (N = 15)
Charter city	0%	0%	11%	47%	73%
General law city	100	100	89	53	27
Council-manager	20%	27%	67%	80%	93%
Council-administrator	20	27	22	20	7
Council-mayor	60	46	11	0	0
County assessment	100%	93%	93%	87%	67%
City assessment	0	7	7	13	33
$1 Property tax limit	90%	87%	70%	33%	20%
Large cities	(N = 0)	(N = 2)	(N = 15)	(N = 10)	(N = 14)
Charter city	—	0%	13%	50%	79%
General law city	—	100	87	50	21
Council-manager (incl. admin.)	—	100%	87%	90%	93%
Council-mayor		0	13	10	7
Council assessment	—	100%	100%	90%	64%
City assessment	—	0	0	10	36
$1 Property tax limit	—	100%	67%	30%	21%
Small cities	(N = 10)	(N = 13)	(N = 12)	(N = 5)	(N = 1)
Charter city	0%	0%	8%	40%	—
General law city	100	100	92	60	—
Council-manager (incl. admin.)	40%	36%	75%	100%	—
Council-mayor	60	64	25	0	—
Council assessment	100%	92%	83%	80%	—
City assessment	0	8	17	20	—
$1 Property tax limit	90%	85%	75%	40%	—

and advanced cities. Most striking, however, is the possible effect of the city's option to stay within or exceed the $1 property tax limitation. Regardless of city size, cities opting against the limit are more likely to be in the more developed phases or stages of policy formation, and the relationship is highly linear in both large and small cities. More than the other institutional arrangements, the greater flexibility permitted by the property tax limit option is clearly reflected in its connection with policy development. As cities move toward the more advanced stage of policy development, the more will they manipulate the property tax limitation as a tool of governance that is conducive to policy development. In general, then, the data presented in Table 25–2 support the contention that freedom in the manipulation of institutions is related to policy once appropriate indicators of policy are harnessed in molar measures which, like the types of policy development, permit commensurate treatment of institutions and policy.

Resource Capability

Resources, whether human, economic, or environmental, must not be confused with resource capability. Resource capability is in part objectively determined by the level of actual wealth in the city, tax rebates from county and state governments, federal or state grants, and so on. But it also depends on the tax rate citizens are willing to tolerate and on whether city councils seek rebates or grants. High resource capability is necessary for policy development, but it is not sufficient.

Ideally, resource capability should refer to the maximum amount of income a city can expect annually when serious efforts are made to tap all possible income sources, including current revenues from taxes, borrowed funds, grants-in-aid, or income from utilities, and so on. To collect such data was beyond the scope of our research. Nor can one use a measure equivalent to per capita gross national product, as in the comparative study of nations, for a high proportion of the production of any city crosses city boundaries and is not available to support local government expenses. What is needed is a measure of resource capability that is based on the wealth remaining wholly within city limits and available to local taxation or to such state taxation as is refundable to the city.

The impossibility of forming any absolute measure of potentially available resources leads to the use of the most readily accessible indicator of relative resource capability. The measure is the total assessed valuation per capita subject to local taxation for fiscal 1965–66, as determined by the California State Board of Equalization. Assessed valuation includes private houses and property, commercial property, and industrial property. From private property a city government will receive personal property tax revenues and a portion of state income tax revenues; from commercial property it will derive property tax revenues and sales tax revenues; and from industrial property it will get property tax revenues. In using per capita assessed valuation, the assumption is made that wealth in any of these three forms is a potential source of income and that total valuation per capita is thus a rough indicator of a city's resource capability. A city will hesitate to institute new programs or expand old ones if it has a low level of assessed valuation per capita, but may be more inclined to do so if it has a high level.

Initially, the critical problem is to determine whether and to what extent resource capability accounts for the variance in policy development. If, as in the state studies of policy outputs, we were to find that economic resources alone accounted for policy development, much of our argument about policy development as a purposive response to environmental challenges would be jeopardized. However, policy development is dependent on policymakers' willingness to mobilize resources, and their willingness to do so depends on the intensity of the pressures from the urban environment *regardless* of available resources.

From this theoretical perspective, the results reported in Table 25–3 are reassuring. There does not appear to be a direct relationship between policy development and resource capability as measured by per capita assessed valuation. Although there is a slight tendency for the maturing and advanced cities to have relatively

Table 25-3
Relationship Between Resource Capability
and Policy Development

Assessed valuation per capita	Re- tarded (N = 10)	Emer- gent (N = 15)	Transi- tional (N = 27)	Matur- ing (N = 15)	Ad- vanced (N = 15)
$2,600 or more	50%	36%	26%	40%	46%
$1,700–$2,599	20	36	22	47	27
Less than $1,700	30	28	52	13	27
	100%	100%	100%	100%	100%

high per capita valuation, as many as five of the ten retarded cities show the same level. The overall distribution of the cities in the different valuation categories tends to be random.

To investigate the hypothesis that policy development takes place in response to urban environmental challenges regardless of resource capability, it is necessary to control the relationship between policy development and the indicators of urbanism by per capita valuation. To protect cell entries from being overly small in the multivariate tables, the data are dichotomized. Table 25–4 presents the results.

The findings are unequivocal. Although there are some irregularities in the patterns of the low capability cities in connection with density and growth rate, even here the general pattern is sustained. The pattern is highly regular in the low capability cities with respect to the influence of city size and in the high capability cities with respect to all three indicators of urban environmental pressures. Regardless of whether they have high or low assessed valuation per capita (resource capability), the less developed cities are relatively small, thinly populated, and slow-growing, while the more developed cities are relatively large, thickly populated, and fast-growing. Policy development appears to be a response to challenges from the urban environment, and the greater the challenge, the more developed is the policy environment. Resource capability, at least as measured by per capita assessed valuation, contributes relatively little to the variance in policy development.

City trait	Retarded (N = 3)	Emergent (N = 4)	Transitional (N = 14)	Maturing (N = 2)	Advanced (N = 4)
	Per Capita Assessed Valuation				
	<$1,700				
Size					
<25,000	100%	100%	57%	50%	25%
>25,000	0	0	43	50	75
	100%	100%	100%	100%	100%
Density					
<2,000	33%	50%	14%	0%	0%
>2,000	67	50	86	100	100
	100%	100%	100%	100%	100%
Growth rate					
<10%	67%	0%	36%	0%	25%
>10%	33	100	64	100	75
	100%	100%	100%	100%	100%
	>$1,700				
	(N = 7)	(N = 11)	(N = 13)	(N = 13)	(N = 11)
Size					
<25,000	100%	100%	69%	54%	9%
>25,000	0	0	31	46	91
	100%	100%	100%	100%	100%
Density					
<2,000	86%	64%	38%	38%	0%
>2,000	14	36	62	62	100
	100%	100%	100%	100%	100%
Growth rate					
<10%	71%	50%	31%	23%	18%
>10%	29	50	69	77	82
	100%	100%	100%	100%	100%

Conclusion

Public policies, such as those relating to planning and amenities, are in various stages or phases of development, with each stage or phase constituting a temporary policy environment. This policy environment is, more or less, a response to the challenges of the city's physical and social environment. In general, the more complex, diverse, or specialized the physical and social environment, the more developed is the policy environment.

However, the physical and social environment not only presents challenges but also provides opportunities. The same factors that create problems for the city, such as a large and dense population, commerce and industry, and so on, also provide opportunities for policy development. Growth in population and in commerce and industry strengthens the city's resources to cope with the social and physical environment. And there are other opportunities as well. Relevant institutional arrangements facilitate policy development. However, resource capability is not sufficient to set a city on a course of policy development. For resource capability to have an effect on policy development, policy-makers must be willing to tap the resources available to them. Whether they will do so or not depends on the severity of the environmental challenges and on their policy orientations—the problems they recognize, the future they envisage, and the policy stands they take.

Chapter 26

Policy Maps:
I. Perspective
and Problems

The map is not the territory. But without maps, there is only *terra incognita*. In orienting themselves to action, city councils draw mental maps that aid them in meeting the challenges and seizing the opportunities provided by the physical and social environment. Policy map-making need not be a conscious intellectual process; and, for this reason, the analogy between the policy-maker's mental mapping of the environment and the geographer's mapping of the territory should not be pushed too far. However, the analogy is suggestive: even if policy-mapping is not a conscious process, it is not altogether arbitrary and random. The bits and pieces of information that come to the policy-maker's attention, the demands that are made on him or that he makes on himself, and the expectations that he entertains about the future provide a more or less accurate guide to what is possible or desirable in the making of public policy.

Mapping of the policy terrain may be more or less tutored by a council's sense of reality—of what it knows, sees, and hears about the physical and social environment within which it governs. Part of this total environment is, of course, also the policy environment. Policy maps are likely to differ, therefore, depending on the character of the urban setting and the prevailing policy climate. Both contexts set constraints on the policy-maker's orientation to action.

Policy, however, is not simply a reaction to environmental challenges and opportunities. Being purposive, it is also an effort to mold the future. Although most policy-making is incremental, some concern with the long-term future is felt by even the most pragmatic policy-makers. But the future is uncertain and unknown. Its exploration is enlightened by a knowledge of past and present, but it also calls for imagination concerning the shape of things to come.

Space is easier to explore than time. The past is forever elusive, not just because new facts are added to knowledge as a result of discovery, but because old facts acquire new meanings with the changing perspective made possible by discovery. The future is even more elusive—for nothing is certain about it, and the imagination needed to fathom it is not a matter of anticipatory cognition alone. If the discovery of the past is often accompanied by affect, the anticipation of the future is even more so. If men like to see in past and present what they wish to see, their conceptions of the future are even more likely to be molded by their preferences.

The notion of a policy map involves a search for the links in policy-makers' orientations toward past, present, and future. How do they perceive the environment and what do they perceive? What expectations or preferences do they hold concerning the more immediate and more distant future? Are these expectations or preferences rooted in accurate perceptions of current realities, or are they purely the products of imagination? How do policy-makers propose to move from present to future? Do their policy maps, like the geographer's map of the territory, provide the landmarks and directions that make travel possible? Or are they drawn on the assumption that whatever the destination, any road will get there? Put more formally, how structured is the policy-maker's mapping of the policy terrain? What landmarks stand out? How much direction does it give? How much agreement is there among policy-makers on the map's components—the problems that come to attention, the issue positions that can be taken, or the images that are held of the future?

Not all of these questions can be answered here. Policy maps are partial representations at best. Moreover, we review only those aspects of policy that lie exclusively within the jurisdictional boundaries of the city. This limitation naturally introduces much artificiality into map construction, for no city in a metropolitan region is an island unto itself. The recognition that the city's problems are, to a large extent, the region's problems has been the source of innumerable observations, lamentations, and recommendations for change. However, as the primary task is to explain the policy environment as defined, and as it was defined in terms of policy outputs exclusively within the jurisdiction of cities, omitting the map's metropolitan component is a self-imposed denial that is mandatory if the analysis is to remain within its initial premises.[1]

Components

Policy is set in motion by challenges from the physical and social environment. But not all environmental challenges are recorded on the policy map. Challenges first have to be perceived as *problems*. Unless situations or events in the environment are seen as problems, no responses can be expected to occur (although a "nonresponse" may also be a response with consequences of its own). No matter how real an environmental challenge is in an objective sense, only if it is perceived and experienced as a problem will it be entered on the policy map. Without being mapped as problems, environmental challenges as such are unlikely to lead to the making of policy decisions.

But how is it that some challenges are seen as problems and others are not? Or, put differently, how is it that some men see something as a problem while other men do not see it? It is insufficient to say that some men are "blind" to challenges while others are not. For if they are blind, their blindness requires explanation.

Facts, even if fully agreed on, rarely speak for themselves. Rather, environmental challenges are perceived as problems if the facts involved are differently judged and evaluated. Of course,

---

[1] The data collected by the City Council Research Project on councilmen's perceptions of and attitudes toward metropolitan problems are being analyzed by Dr. Thomas E. Cronin of the Brookings Institution in a monograph entitled *The Metropolitan Crucible: Intergovernmental Relations* (Indianapolis: The Bobbs-Merrill Company, in preparation).

values and goals may change in the face of facts that are incontrovertible and, in turn, influence the perception of environmental challenges as problems. But more often than not situations or events in the environment, challenging though they may be objectively, become problems only if they are seen as threatening what is cherished and valued. If the environment is seen as endangering what is valued, the objective condition becomes a subjective problem.

Values and goals, therefore, like problem perceptions, are important components of the policy map. They are important precisely because the perception of challenges as problems may be shaped by them. In exploring the environment and mapping the policy terrain, policy-makers are perhaps initially more aware of the destination they wish to reach then of their point of departure or of the road that will get them where they want to go. But goals or images of the future also set limits to policy issues and aid in crystallizing the policy positions that are taken to solve problems and to achieve preferred objectives.

Policy positions, as components of the policy map, refer to means rather than to ends, to the recommendations for action needed to solve problems and attain policy goals. Policy positions are the options or alternatives open to policy-makers that are either brought into the decisional situation by individual participants or that evolve in the course of collective choice-making. The ways in which policy positions are related to the perception of problems, on the one hand, and to goal images, on the other, are crucial in the shaping of policy. They are its most immediate determinants.

Dimensions

The components of the policy map—problems, images, and positions—are related to one another on a number of dimensions that give the map its contours.

In the first place, policy maps differ in the content of things they highlight for the user, very much the way a land-use map outlines the areas devoted to industry, commerce, residence, and recreation.

The components of the policy map may refer the user to the particular content of problems, images, and positions. Differences in content will affect the structure of the policy map as a whole. To anticipate, the problems perceived by councils are predominantly matters of urban growth or traditional city services; policy positions stress commercial/industrial development or the amenities of life; and policy images either envisage a residential future or some balance between residential and commercial/industrial land use.

Second, the policy map may be more or less diverse. One policy map may be glutted with the details of a multitude of problems, images, and positions that make the map both diffuse and confusing. Another map may show only the broad outlines of its contents; the map is simple and easy to read. The map's degree of diversity greatly affects its potential use. A map that is too detailed and highly diverse in what it shows can prevent important decisions from being made; a map that is too simple and unspecific can lead to inappropriate action.

Finally, maps differ in the degree of agreement reached among policy-makers. Just as geographers can disagree on mapping, so policy-makers can disagree on the content of the policy map. The degree of agreement they reach in perceiving problems, specifying images, or formulating positions affects not only the structure of the policy map as a whole but also the policies that emerge from their actions or nonactions.

Whether the components of the policy map and their analytic dimensions constitute a single, unified "perspective," as Harold Lasswell might say, is a matter of empirical determination. It is more than likely that the map is differently structured under different conditions of the urban and policy environments. The fit between policy map and environment cannot be prejudged.

Problems: Triggers of Policy

Environmental challenges are not inevitably self-evident. Only if they are perceived as problems do they serve as triggers of policy. To recognize a problem means to realize that conventional ways of doing things are inadequate or, at least, that their adequacy is in question. It is through the perception of problems, then, that policy is set in motion.

In collegial bodies a problem is a problem if enough members are aware of it. The number of members who "must" see a problem for it to be a group problem is quite arbitrary. Although the councils range from five to nine members, a problem was assumed to be at the focus of the council's attention if it was so recognized by at least three members, regardless of council size. This is a rather relaxed criterion, but it is probably sufficient to get a problem on the council agenda, even in the larger councils. In order to identify the policy problems perceived by the councils, the following question was asked:

> Mr. Councilman, before talking about your work as a councilman and the work of the council itself, we would like to ask you about some of the problems facing this community. In your opinion, what are the two most pressing problems here in (city)?

Table 26–1 presents the particular local problems that seem most pressing to the councils in the San Francisco Bay region. Two aspects of Table 26–1 are noteworthy. First, although the criterion for problem articulation was hardly demanding, not more than 13 percent of the councils consider any *one* problem as most pressing. Indeed, there is a wide spread in the particular kinds of problems pinpointed, and many of them are perceived by only one or two councils. Moreover, in a fifth of all councils no single problem is recognized at all by at least three members. In regard to particular problems, then, intercity differences are greater than one might expect, given the fact that all the cities are located in the same region.

Second, not a single council perceived problems related to what are sometimes called the amenities of life, such as parks, playgrounds, museums, libraries, and so on. Amenities are either thought of as luxuries to be given high priority only after more pressing problems have been solved, or their provision is not problematic because it is already handled satisfactorily. As will be seen, the former is more likely than the latter. Though not perceived as problems, amenities do in fact rank high as council policy positions.

Although problems are highly diverse, they fall into broad area categories such as urban growth problems (transportation and traffic, zoning and planning, renewal, business expansion, etc.); traditional city services (financing, sewerage and drainage, water sources, etc.); social or remedial matters (pollution, housing, education, racial tensions, etc.); and governmental affairs (personnel, annexation, participation, etc.). Table 26–2 presents the distribution of councils in these broad problem areas.[2]

Table 26–1
Policy Problems Perceived as "Most Pressing"
by San Francisco Bay Region Councils

Problem	N	Percentage
Financing services	11	13
Transportation and traffic	11	13
Sewerage and drainage	9	11
Zoning and maintenance	8	10
Planning	5	6
Urban renewal and development	4	5
Water sources and service	3	4
Attract business and industry	3	4
Assessment and taxes	2	2
Annexation	2	2
Sanitation and disposal	1	1
Water pollution	1	1
Race and ethnic tensions	1	1
Educational matters	1	1
Housing	1	1
Local government personnel	1	1
Citizen participation	1	1
Not classifiable by criterion	17	21
Total	82	98

NOTE: A council was classified in one of the "single problem" categories if at least three members perceived the same specific problem (regardless of council size). Percentage does not total 100% due to rounding.

---

[2] In assigning the councils to a problem area category, the category receiving "most mentions" among all mentions was recorded, regardless of council size

Table 26–2
Areas of Policy Problems Perceived as "Most Pressing"
by San Francisco Bay Region Councils

Problem area	City Size			
	<10,000 (N = 32)	10–50,000 (N = 33)	>50,000 (N = 17)	Total (N = 82)
Growth (N = 54)	44%	82%	76%	66%
Services (N = 25)	50	18	18	31
Social-remedial (N = 2)	3	0	6	2
Government (N = 1)	3	0	0	1
	100%	100%	100%	100%

NOTE: A council was classified in a problem area category provided the category included 30 percent or more of all responses (regardless or council size).

A number of observations are in order. Growth and service problems are preponderant and significantly related to city size. Problems of growth are perceived as most pressing in cities where the population exceeds 10,000 and where greater urbanization challenges policy-making, while service problems predominate in the smallest cities, where the challenge of urbanization is less severely felt. Problems related to social, remedial, or governmental matters are clearly of secondary importance. Because these two areas are minimally salient in only three councils, these councils will be omitted in some subsequent analyses. Finally, even if only broad areas are treated, and individual items are aggregated at the council level, the provision of amenities does not emerge as a problem.

While what is perceived as a problem depends on the intensity of the environmental challenge, it may be that the city's resource capability to meet challenges rather than the challenges themselves makes for this result. If so, one should expect that in larger cities the perception of growth problems would be especially related to low capability, while in smaller cities the perception of service

but provided it included at least 30 percent of all responses made by individual councilmen. The criterion, then, is even more relaxed than the criterion used in classifying particular problems, which required that at least three members mention the same problem.

Table 26–3
Relationship Between City Size and Problem Area Perceptions,
Controlled by Resource Capability

	Resource Capability			
	High		Low	
City Size	Small	Large	Small	Large
Problem area	(N = 25)	(N = 26)	(N = 13)	(N = 14)
Services	52%	15%	38%	21%
Growth	48	85	62	79
	100%	100%	100%	100%
Partial = .65				

problems would be related to low capability. But, as Table 26–3
shows, this is not the case. In the large, low-capability cities
problems of growth do stand out (79 percent), but they stand out
even slightly more in the large, high-capability cities (85 percent).
And service problems are more salient in the small, high-capability cities than in the small, low-capability cities. The urban
challenge as such rather than the city's ability to cope with it determines just what kinds of problems are recognized as pressing.

Problem Diversity

Although the great variety of problems can be subsumed under
broad categories, this does not mean that council policy maps are
easy to read. The map's categoric content constitutes only one
dimension of the problem component. Also relevant is that the
council's policy map, like that of any collegial decision-making
body, can be more or less diverse. Categoric treatment of content
disguises within-council variances in problem perceptions.

To measure the degree to which the members of a council *among
themselves* perceive particular problems, account is taken of both
diversity and council size.[3] For councils in which many diverse

---

[3] For discussion and construction of the measure of problem diversity, see Appendix B26.1.

Table 26–4
Relationship Between Problem Diversity
and City Size

Problem diversity	City Size		
	<10,000 (N = 32)	10–50,000 (N = 33)	>50,000 (N = 17)
Relatively low	41%	58%	59%
Relatively high	59	42	41
	100%	100%	100%
Gamma = −.26			

problems are perceived the policy map is highly detailed. Presumably, the council with such a map will have more difficulty in orienting itself to action than the council with a map that highlights relatively few particular problems. The degree of diversity in problem perceptions, then, has important consequences for the council's action potential.

As Table 26–4 shows, diversity in problem perceptions is relatively high in the smallest cities and relatively low in the larger cities. Where environmental challenges are urgent, fewer and perhaps more significant problems come to the attention of councils than in situations where environmental pressures are of less urgency.

Problem Agreement

For a problem to be tackled rather than merely put on the agenda, at least a majority of the council must agree that an issue or issue area should call forth a response. Two measures of agreement assess the consensual potential of councils: a measure of interpersonal agreement on the single most frequently mentioned problem and a measure of agreement on the most frequently named problem area. The two measures, as Table 26–5 shows, are related, but not as strongly as one might suppose. As the marginals show, relatively high agreement on a single problem seems easier to come by (40 percent) than is high agreement on a problem area (27 percent). And while only 27 percent of the councils do not reach agreement on a single problem, more than half (56 percent) are not agreed on a broad problem area.

Where environmental challenges are strong, as in the larger cities, there will also be more pressure for agreement on particular problems or problem areas, while this is less the case in the smaller cities, where environmental challenges impinge less on the policy process. The hypothesis is supported by the data for problem area agreement but not for particular problems. City size has no effect on whether a high level of agreement is reached with regard to a particular problem (−.08, table not shown); it has some effect, as Table 26–6 indicates, on problem area agreement. In the cities under 10,000 population, three-fourths of the councils lack minimal majority agreement on what broad issue area is problematic, whereas in the cities over 10,000 about three-fifths of the councils have at least majority agreement.

A council's ability to reach agreement at least on a problem area should be greater if its policy map is of low diversity. If a given problem area is forcefully at the council's focus of attention, fewer alternative problem formulations will be forthcoming and the potential for consensus will be maximized. But as Table 26–7 shows, this is not the case. Rather, it is the nature of the urban

Table 26–5
Relationship Between Agreement
on a Single Problem and a Problem Area

Problem area agreement	Single Problem Agreement			Total
	67–100% (N = 33)	51–66% (N = 27)	<50% (N = 22)	(N = 82)
67–100%	39%	22%	14%	27%
51–66%	19	11	23	17
<50%	42	67	63	56
Gamma = .32	100%	100%	100%	100%
Partial* = .34	40%	33%	27%	

* Controlled for city size.

Table 26–6
Relationship Between Problem Area Agreement
and City Size

	City Size		
Problem area agreement	<10,000 (N = 32)	10–50,000 (N = 33)	>50,000 (N = 17)
67–100%	16%	40%	24%
51–66%	9	15	35
<50%	75	45	41
Gamma = −.34	100%	100%	100%

environment that makes for differences in the level of problem area agreement. Regardless of problem diversity, more councils in the larger than in the smaller cities are at least minimally agreed on one or another problem area. Indeed, it is where diversity in problem perceptions is high that city size has more of an impact on whether agreement is reached. As high diversity is more characteristic of the smaller cities (Table 26–4), the most plausible explanation for the results in Table 26–7 is that it is precisely when many diverse problems are at the big-city council's focus of attention that the challenge of the urban environment forces the council to

Table 26–7
Relationship Between Problem Agreement*
and Diversity, by City Size

	Small Cities		Large Cities	
	Diversity			
	Low	High	Low	High
Problem agreement	(N = 17)	(N = 24)	(N = 25)	(N = 16)
>50%	35%	17%	60%	69%
<50%	65	83	40	31
	100%	100%	100%	100%
Partial = .12	Gamma = .46		Gamma = −.19	

* Problem agreement, size by diversity = .66 (partial); problem agreement, size in low-diversity cities = .47; problem agreement, size in high-diversity cities = .83.

concentrate on one problem area. It is the paradoxical mix of great diversity, on the one hand, with urban complexity and heterogeneity, on the other, that maximizes the council's potential for consensus.

Problem agreement should also be meaningfully related to problem content. Reaching agreement is more urgent in situations where the city is beset by problems of growth than where it is beset by problems involving traditional services. But as both dimensions are related to city size (Table 26–2 and 26–6), any direct relationship may be spurious. While, as Table 26–8 shows, the partial rela-

Table 26–8
Relationship Between Problem Area Content
and Agreement, by City Size

Problem area agreement	Small Cities		Large Cities		All Cities	
	Growth (N = 21)	Service (N = 18)	Growth (N = 33)	Service (N = 7)	Growth (N = 54)	Service (N = 25)
51–100%	29%	22%	70%	43%	54%	28%
0–50%	71	78	30	57	46	72
	100%	100%	100%	100%	100%	100%
Partial = .32	Gamma = .17		Gamma = .51		Gamma = .50	

tionship between problem area content and agreement, with city size controlled, is moderate, it is substantial in the larger cities. In these cities the presence of growth problems further increases the pressure for agreement already noted. That the perception of problems created by urban growth has an effect on the potential for agreement may be accepted as evidence of the continuing capacity of cities to cope with the urban environment.

Chapter 27

Policy Maps: II. Images and Positions

Values are ends-in-view which, like dreams, may never be realized; or they may be goals that are attainable. Goals are at least plausible projections of ongoing policies. Of course, the more distant the future, the more are goals likely to be discontinuous with current policies. But this need not prevent their being guides in the present. Because policy is in part purposive, the policy map necessarily includes a futuristic component.

Cognitive considerations make it preferable to speak of the policy map's images rather than of values or goals. Ends-in-view may be normative, in the sense that expectations of the future are demands which, if realized, turn out to be self-fulfilling prophesies; or they may be factual expectations in the sense of being genuine predictions of the shape of things to come. Although the distinction between a preferred and a predicted future is clear enough analytically, in cognitive reality it rarely is. Political practitioners, pragmatists though they are, do not carefully distinguish between what will be and what ought to be. Their expectations of the future are both valuational, or judgmental, and factual, or predictive. It is difficult to say, therefore, whether questioning councilmen concerning the city's future evokes a normative response as to what they prefer or a predictive response as to what they expect to happen. To tap the futuristic or image component of the policy map, councilmen were asked the following question:

Now, taking the broadest view possible, how do you see (city) in the future? I mean, what kind of a city would you personally like (city) to be in the next twenty-five years or so?

Images: Guides to the Future

The question was sufficiently open to permit a great variety of responses. Moreover, councilmen sometimes answered it in predictive, and sometimes in preferential, language; and some, as the following response shows, included both predictive and normative considerations: "I see it as a commercial area with continuous growth problems—a large growth area with inadequate financing for twenty years ahead. I would like to see it as a balanced commercial and industrial city with adequate housing to support a labor force for this growth. I would like more cluster type housing which provides for more open spaces and a park-like atmosphere."

Individual responses could be aggregated at the council level into two major classes: councils with a residential image and those with a balanced (residential-industrial/commercial) image. In only seven of the 82 councils was it impossible to detect a broad common theme because the councilmen were disagreed, and in three other councils insufficient data made it impossible to construct an image. Of the 72 councils in which at least a majority of the members were agreed as to what the city's future would or should look like, 33 held a residential, and 39 a balanced, image of the future. As Table 27–1 shows, images are significantly related to

Table 27–1
Policy Images of San Francisco Bay Area Councils,
by City Size

	City Size		
Policy image	<10,000 (N = 27)	10–50,000 (N = 29)	>50,000 (N = 16)
Residential (N = 33)	63%	45%	19%
Balanced (N = 39)	37	55	81
Gamma = .52	100%	100%	100%

city size.[1] Whether preferential or predictive, council images of the future appear to be tied to current realities. As smaller cities are actually more residential and larger cities more balanced, the relationship between image and level of urbanization suggests that pragmatic politicians do not stray far from the present when envisaging the future.

Image Specificity

Images articulated by individual councilmen could be quite specific, giving a very detailed picture of what the city's future would or should be, as already illustrated; or they could be vague, limited to expressions such as "Same as it is now in character but possibly expanded in size; I like it this way, that's why I moved here"; or, "I would like to see a model city so that people would be proud to live here. We need more beautification; we got to do something so they'll come here." Individual responses were rated on a five-point scale from low to high specificity and averaged for the council as a whole.

Table 27–2 presents image specificity by city size. The relationship is curvilinear. In both the smallest and largest cities, the majority of councils hold very specific images; in the medium-size cities, they do not. The latter are in a state of transition from low to high urbanization. In these cities also, a glance back to Table

Table 27–2
Relationship Between Image Specificity
and City Size

	City Size		
	<10,000	10–50,000	>50,000
Image specificity	(N = 32)	(N = 33)	(N = 17)
High	56%	39%	53%
Low	44	61	47
Gamma = .11	100%	100%	100%

[1] However, images are not significantly related to resource capability (gamma = −.14). When city size is controlled by resource capability, the relationship between city size and image content remains undisturbed (partial = .62).

27–1 shows, councils are almost evenly divided between those holding a residential and those holding a balanced image.[2]

Image Agreement

In 72 councils, it was noted earlier, at least a majority of the
members agreed on the policy image of their city's future. The
degree of agreement, however, varied a good deal. As the totals
in Table 27–3 show, two-thirds of the councils were unanimous,
and this great amount of unanimity is unrelated to the content of
the image or, for that matter, to image specificity (table not shown).
However, as Table 27–4 indicates, unanimity seems to stem from
the particular mix of image and environmental conditions. Where
image and environment are congruent, as in the smaller cities with
a residential image and the larger cities with a balanced image,
unanimity is more readily forthcoming than in situations where
the image is less adapted to environmental circumstances. The
results obtained in Table 27–4 confirm what has been hinted at
earlier—that council images of the future tend to be rooted in
reality rather than in imagination. But if the relationship between
city size and level of agreement is controlled by image, it is strong

Table 27–3
Relationship Between Image Content
and Level of Agreement

	Policy Image		
Level of agreement	Residential (N = 33)	Balanced (N = 39)	Total (N = 72)
Unanimity	70%	67%	68%
Majority	30	33	32
Gamma = .07	100%	100%	100%

---

[2] There is no indication that the content of policy images is related to the degree
of specificity that characterizes them. Councils with a residential image are just
as likely to have a specific or a general map as are councils with a balanced
image; and this absence of a relationship is not affected by city size (table not
shown).

Table 27–4
Relationship Between Image Content
and Image Agreement,* by City Size

Level of agreement	Small Cities		Large Cities	
	Residential (N = 22)	Balanced (N = 13)	Residential (N = 11)	Balanced (N = 26)
Unanimity	82%	69%	45%	65%
Majority	18	31	55	35
	100%	100%	100%	100%
Partial = .07	Gamma = .33		Gamma = −.39	

*Image agreement, size by image = .36 (partial); image agreement, size in residential-image cities = .69; image agreement, size in balanced-image cities = .09.

in cities with a residential image (.69), but almost nonexistent in cities with a balanced image (.09). It is councils in the larger cities clinging to a residential image that find it difficult to be wholly agreed on what the future will or should look like.

Attitudes Toward Change

Policy images necessarily contain a valuational aspect regarding the prospects of change. In some councils, the image is favorable to social, economic, and governmental change, while in others the dominant orientation to the future is conservative and opposed to change. Still other councils are ambivalent.

Councilmen with images favorable to retaining the city's residential character are likely to be inherently conservative and opposed to change: "Pretty much the way it is—upper middle class residential. . . . Hopefully it will be a bedroom community with no industry. . . . A relaxing, livable, enjoyable, beautiful area. . . . The way it was 15 years ago, being one of the most desirable communities to live in. . . . Exactly as it is, a bedroom community of low density that we have at the present time, although we do need to reduce the minimum-sized lots to below an acre."

Those with an image of the future envisaging growth in commerce and industry are likely to seek improvement of the urban condition and to be favorable to change: "Industrial growth is coming. We should develop a good industrial park that is productive and efficient. We also want to balance industry with a residential bedroom community. . . . The population will triple. This will change the entire nature of the city. New people and new ideas will come in. . . . We could put in restaurants—people could come in boats and have fish dinners and visit the antique shops."

Finally, there is the ambivalent orientation with regard to change: "Our objectives—we have the only wooded area in a town in our county. Park-like, with trails, country homes. We incorporated to keep that atmosphere. That is the ambition of the citizens here. We now have urban development crushing us from all sides. It is my opinion that we should study carefully the needs of the San Francisco water supply to the north, the development of Redwood City to the east and Stanford's changing property development. It's a problem because of their changing economic needs and scientific development. The Federal Government is putting a 6-lane highway through. We should study all these things and see how much we can keep, how much will be left."

To measure the attitudinal dimension of the policy map's image, individual responses were scored on a six-point scale from those favoring basic changes in the nature of the city to those preferring no change at all. The responses were averaged for each council and the councils were rank-ordered. As one might expect, and as

Table 27–5
Relationship Between Image Content
and Attitude Toward Change, by City Size

Attitude toward change	Small Cities		Large Cities		All Cities	
	Resid. (N = 22)	Bal. (N = 13)	Resid. (N = 11)	Bal. (N = 26)	Resid. (N = 33)	Bal. (N = 39)
Chiefly anti	86%	23%	73%	27%	82%	26%
Chiefly pro	14	77	27	73	18	74
	100%	100%	100%	100%	100%	100%
Partial = .88	Gamma = .91		Gamma = .76		Gamma = .86	

Table 27–5 shows, the relationship between the content of policy images and the accompanying attitudes toward change is very strong. Councils with a residential image tend to oppose change, while councils with a balanced image tend to favor it. Because attitudes toward change are also related, if only moderately, to city size (gamma = .27, table not shown), Table 27–5 controls the relationship between image content and attitudes by city size. The relationship is especially strong in the smaller cities where a residential image prevails, but is also strong in larger cities. Whatever the cognitive quality of the policy image—whether it is normatively or factually futuristic—it is not independent of the council's more general orientation toward social, economic, and governmental change.

On the other hand, image specificity and attitude toward change are only weakly related. Councils with highly specific images tend to be somewhat more favorable to change than those whose images are more general. Evidently, opponents of change more readily express themselves in generalities, while advocates of change will be more specific. But, as Table 27–6 shows, these tendencies are especially pronounced only in the smaller cities. In the larger cities, the majority of councils favor change regardless of the degree of specificity in the image component of their policy maps. Pressure for change in the more complex environment of the

Table 27–6
Relationship Between Image Specificity
and Attitude Toward Change, by City Size

Attitude toward change	Small Cities		Large Cities		All Cities	
	Specificity					
	Low (N = 20)	High (N = 21)	Low (N = 22)	High (N = 19)	Low (N = 42)	High (N = 40)
Chiefly anti	75%	48%	36%	42%	55%	45%
Chiefly pro	25	52	64	58	45	55
	100%	100%	100%	100%	100%	100%
Partial = .22	Gamma = .53		Gamma = −.12		Gamma = .19	

larger cities makes for reduction of dissonance with respect to change even in councils whose images are poorly articulated.

By way of summary, then, councils entertain broadly defined images of their city's future, and these images are rooted in current environmental realities. In the smaller cities which are in fact more residential, councils tend to see a residential future; in the largest cities, councils tend to envisage a balanced future. Cities that are medium-sized are more closely divided on their images (Table 27–1). If image and environmental conditions are congruent, as in smaller cities holding a residential image and larger cities holding a balanced image, agreement is likely to be highly consensual (Table 27–4). Councils with residential images are more likely to be opposed to social change, while councils with a balanced image tend to be more favorable (Table 27–5).

Positions: Steps to Action

Images are inscribed on decision-makers' policy maps, and their dimensions—content and agreement—orient the policy process. Within this orientational context, the policy-making group, be it a large legislature or a small city council, evolves policy positions— the steps that lead to action. Policy positions are the stands taken by governing groups as they approach the task of decision- making.

A policy position of the council, whether agreed to by all members or only a majority, emerges out of its interactions, delib- erations, and negotiations, and it is not simply the summation of individual members' policy preferences. What is constructed, then, when individual responses concerning policy positions are aggre- gated, is not the council's stand as it appears in the voting situa- tion, but rather the council's preference orderings before the legis- lative process has had a full opportunity to affect the decisional outcome. Nevertheless, one can also assume that these responses are not just indicative of private preferences. Because councilmen are members of a continuously interacting group, their individual policy positions are likely to be influenced by the common membership.[3] In order to tap the position component of the policy map, data from the following interview question were used:

> Now, looking toward the future, what one community-wide improvement, in your opinion, does this city "need most" to be attractive to its citizens?

From the metaphorical perspective that guides our construction of the policy map, policy positions can be thought of as the "signs" or "pointers" that give direction to the policy-making process. This is not to say that the process is a one-way street—that policy-makers first identify problems, then stipulate goals, and then take positions, or that they first define goals, then discover problems, and finally take positions. On the contrary, the *intellectual* process involved in policy-making probably does not follow the *decisional* process.[4] It is only convenient to conceive of policy positions initially as the product of convergent problem perceptions and image formulations and as immediately prior to a policy decision.

Position Content

Perhaps the first and most intriguing aspect of the policy map's position component is its heterogeneity, if specific suggestions for improvements serve as indicators. Although the procedure for aggregation required that only three members of the council, regardless of its size, would have to advocate the same specific im-

---

[3] One could argue the case more liberally on statistical grounds and possibly test it if there were more diverse legislative bodies available for analysis: the larger a legislative body, the more likely it is that averaged individual preferences will approximate, if not correspond to, the preferences of the collectivity.
[4] Although we are committing this comment to a footnote, we would like to call attention to the distinction we are making between the policy-making process and the decision-making process. Conceptions of the latter are predicated on a sequential process through time, as, for instance, in Harold D. Lasswell's seven-category functional model—Intelligence, Recommendation, Prescription, Invocation, Application, Appraisal, and Termination. See Harold D. Lasswell, *The Decision Process: Seven Categories of Functional Analysis* (College Park, Md.: Bureau of Governmental Research, University of Maryland, 1956). By way of contrast, our model of the policy map is configurative and makes no a priori assumptions about the time order of map components and their dimensions.

provement in order for it to be considered as indicative of the council's position, Table 27–7 shows that only 28 out of the 82 councils, or about a third, could be classified as having a policy position by this very relaxed criterion. In 54 councils no three members mentioned exactly the same improvement.

This lack of agreement seems to suggest that councils are composed of highly idiosyncratic individualists. This, however, is very implausible. Perhaps it is the lack of political structuring in nonpartisan settings that makes for the heterogeneity of individual preferences. This is more plausible but also unlikely. Most plausible is the explanation that the coding categories used in Table 27–7 are too itemistic—that it is too much to expect that individual councilmen will articulate their preferences in similar ways. If this is so, then it is more appropriate to subsume the particular responses under broader categories before aggregating them at the group level of analysis.

Table 27–7
Policy Positions on "Most Needed" Improvement
by San Francisco Bay Region Councils

Improvement needed	N	Percentage
Parks or recreation areas	9	11
Urban renewal or downtown development	7	9
New civic center or facilities	7	9
Open space and conservation	1	1
Waterfront or bay development	1	1
Beautification, undergrounding, sidewalks, etc.	1	1
Street repair, new streets, or transit system	1	1
Better street lighting	1	1
No one item mentioned by at least three members	54	66
Total	82	100

Councils were therefore classified in terms of a number of broad categories into which the discrete positional responses could be placed, such as services, amenities, development, social or remedial matters, and governmental affairs. This procedure made for successful and, in an important respect, revealing results. In the first place, as the totals in Table 27–8 show, for slightly more than half the councils, action in the area of amenities is their most salient policy position, followed by about a third of the councils stressing further city development as desirable. Second, and this is especially noteworthy, amenities are widely favored, but services practically not at all. This suggests that the problem and position components of the policy map are clearly distinguished. For, it was noted in Chapter 26, the provision of amenities is not perceived as a problem at all, while the provision of services is seen as a prominent problem. A plausible hypothesis for this difference in problem perceptions and policy positions has been suggested already. Although the provision of amenities is a desired good, its absence is not necessarily experienced as a deprivation. Amenities, it can now be

Table 27–8

Policy Position Areas Most Salient
in San Francisco Bay Region City Councils, by City Size

	City Size			
Position area	<10,000 (N = 32)	10–50,000 (N = 33)	>50,000 (N = 17)	Total (N = 82)
Amenities (library, civic center, recreation, etc.)	53%	57%	41%	52%
Development (planning, zoning, urban renewal, attract business, etc.)	37	33	41	37
Services (finance, police, fire, disposal, street lights, water, etc.)	0	3	0	1
Other or ties	10	7	18	10
	100%	100%	100%	100%

seen, are something the city may want or need, but they are luxuries that are given low priority on the agenda of *problems* facing
the council. On the other hand, even though services rather than
amenities are considered problems, councils recognize the value
of amenities and would presumably provide for them once services are adequate. Dealing with problems of service is something
councils must do, whether they want to or not. Hence services do
not appear as positions on the policy map. But providing for
amenities is something that councils clearly consider desirable.

Finally, Table 27–8 shows that the provision of amenities is
preferred by more councils in the smaller cities, while development is preferred by slightly more in the largest cities. But the relationship between city size and policy position is weak. It may be,
however, that what councils consider preferable is circumscribed
by their sense of what is feasible, and what is feasible is a matter
of resource capability. If, as in Table 27–9, both city size and resource capability are related to council policy positions, there is,
indeed, a stronger relationship between policy position and resource capability (partial = .41) than between policy position and
city size (partial = .16). Especially in the smaller cities does resource capability make a significant difference in what policy
position councils include in their policy map: where capability
is high, three-fourths of the councils favor amenities; where it is

Table 27–9

Relationships Among City Size,
Resource Capability, and Position Content*

	Small Cities		Large Cities	
	Resource Capability			
Position content	High (N = 24)	Low (N = 12)	High (N = 23)	Low (N = 13)
Amenities	75%	33%	57%	54%
Development	25	67	43	46
	100%	100%	100%	100%
Partial = .41	Gamma = .71		Gamma = .05	

* Position content, size by capability = .16 (partial); position content, size in
high-capacity cities = .40; position content, size in low-capacity cities = −.40.

low, two-thirds favor development. But in the larger cities capability has. no such effect: in both high- and low-capability cities, slightly more than half the councils favor amenities. Size, in turn, has opposite effects in high- and low-capability cities: where capability is high, more of the small-city councils advocate amenities (.40); where capability is low, more of the large-city councils stress amenities (−.40). Development is probably seen as most desirable by the small-city, low-capability councils precisely because it is considered conducive to strengthening the city's resource base.

Position Diversity

The construct of position content is a highly abstract feature of the policy map, a product of analytic simplification and only a very approximate reproduction of reality. Yet one must remain cognizant of the great variation that the construct disguises. As with problem perceptions, therefore, it is desirable to introduce a measure of diversity, that is, a measure of the degree to which council members articulate few or many special positions.

The measure of position diversity, like the index of problem diversity, takes account of both the number of particular improvements articulated by individual councilmen and council size. Councils in which many different improvements are recommended have high position diversity, while councils in which few different improvements are suggested have low diversity on the map's position component. Again, as in connection with problems, position diversity presumably has an effect on the council's action potential.

As Table 27–10 shows, councils in the larger cities are more likely to have policy maps with low position diversity than are councils in the small cities. The pattern is nearly the same as that found in connection with problem diversity (Table 26–4). In the larger cities the range of options for policy change open to councils appears to be more limited than it is in the smaller cities. More of the councils with an amenities preference than of those with a development preference reveal low diversity on the position component of their policy maps (Table 27–11). The data, however, are perplexing, for an amenities position is more characteristic of

Table 27–10
Relationship Between Position Diversity
and City Size

	City Size		
Position diversity	<10,000 (N = 32)	10–50,000 (N = 33)	>50,000 (N = 17)
Low	37%	52%	59%
High	63	48	41
	100%	100%	100%

Gamma = −.28

councils in the smaller cities (Table 27–8), and position diversity is relatively high in the smallest cities (Table 27–10). There is the possibility, then, that the relationship between position content and diversity is spurious. But, as Table 27–11 shows, it is not. Regardless of city size, more councils taking an amenities position are characterized by low position diversity than are councils taking the development position. But city size does make a difference. In the larger cities, councils favoring amenities are evidently under very strong constraints to limit the alternatives that they consider. On the other hand, in the smaller cities, both councils favoring amenities and councils favoring development seem to have more leeway in specifying alternative proposals. The constraints imposed by the more complex and heterogeneous environment of the larger cities

Table 27–11
Relationship Between Position Content
and Diversity, by City Size

	Small Cities		Large Cities		All Cities	
Position diversity	Amenit. (N = 23)	Devel. (N = 14)	Amenit. (N = 20)	Devel. (N = 16)	Amenit. (N = 43)	Devel. (N = 30)
Low	39%	29%	75%	44%	56%	36%
High	61	71	25	56	44	64
	100%	100%	100%	100%	100%	100%
Partial = .25	Gamma = .25		Gamma = .59		Gamma = .37	

have the effect of pinpointing more sharply the alternatives open to councils in planning for amenities.

Position Agreement

The council's action potential is, in part, circumscribed by the level of agreement it can reach on policy positions. Agreement on broad position areas, like amenities or development, is easier to obtain than agreement on specific measures. As the marginal distributions in Table 27–12 show, of the 82 councils, 59, or 72 percent, did not reach simple majority agreement on single positions; but only 18, or 21 percent, were not agreed on a position area. Yet, of the 59 councils incapable of generating simple majorities on a single proposal, 39 percent were agreed by simple majority on a broad position area and another 31 percent by a two-thirds majority or better. Agreement on a broad position area is probably more conducive to maximizing action over the long haul than is agreement on specific positions, which is much more difficult to come by.

This is reflected in the relationship between position area agreement and position diversity. As the distributions in Table 27–13 show, low position diversity facilitates high position agreement in broad areas of policy. And this is more so in the larger cities than in the smaller cities. But as Table 27–13 also shows, high diver-

Table 27–12
Relationship Between Single Position Agreement
and Position Area Agreement

Position area agreement	*Single Position Agreement*			
	67–100% (N = 6)	51–66% (N = 17)	<50% (N = 59)	Total (N = 82)
67–100% (N = 34)	100%	59%	31%	42%
51–66% (N = 30)	0	41	39	37
<50% (N = 18)	0	0	30	21
Gamma = .73	100%	100%	100%	100%
	7%	21%	72%	100%

Table 27–13
Relationship Between Position Area Agreement
and Position Diversity, by City Size

	Small Cities		Large Cities		All Cities	
	Position Diversity					
Position area agreement	Low (N = 15)	High (N = 26)	Low (N = 24)	High (N = 17)	Low (N = 39)	High (N = 43)
67–100%	53%	27%	67%	18%	62%	23%
51–66%	40	35	29	47	33	40
<50%	7	38	4	35	5	37
	100%	100%	100%	100%	100%	100%
Partial = .68	Gamma = .57		Gamma = .79		Gamma = .68	

sity—the stipulation of many options—is not a complete obstacle to reaching agreement on at least a broad position area. The council's ability to muster such agreement on at least broad position areas in spite of great diversity within has implications for its decision-making structure and policy process.

One must ask whether it is easier to reach agreement on one rather than another broad policy position. As the totals in Table 27–14 indicate, the differences in agreement between amenities and development are minimal, slightly favoring the former. However, if city size is accounted for, agreement is more readily reached on

Table 27–14
Relationship Between Position Content
and Agreement, by City Size

	Small Cities		Large Cities		All Cities	
Position area agreement	Amenit. (N = 23)	Devel. (N = 14)	Amenit. (N = 20)	Devel. (N = 16)	Amenit. (N = 43)	Devel. (N = 30)
67–100%	30%	50%	70%	31%	49%	40%
51–66%	43	29	20	50	33	40
<50%	27	21	10	19	18	20
	100%	100%	100%	100%	100%	100%
Partial = .13	Gamma = −.27		Gamma = .53		Gamma = .12	

amenities in the larger cities and on development in the smaller cities. The choice of policy positions is not independent of the nature of the environmental challenges facing the council, a question which will be explored more fully in Chapter 28. In general, the council's potential for action is greater if it concentrates on a few issue areas and does not spread itself too thin.

Conclusion

Great diversity in council positions on the city's "most needed improvement" characterizes San Francisco Bay Area councils if particular single preferences are considered (Table 27–7). However, if these single positions are clustered into broad position areas, a majority of the councils favor amenities and somewhat more than a third prefer development, with an ever so slight tendency for the former to be more salient in the larger cities and the latter in the smaller cities (Table 27–8). However, it is resource capability more than city size that enters the calculation of whether amenities or development will be considered preferable, with amenities being preferred in the high-capability cities and development in the low-capability cities (Table 27–9). There is less position diversity in the larger cities (Table 27–10), and in the larger cities councils favoring amenities are less likely to formulate a great variety of specific proposals (Table 27–11). In general, agreement is more easily reached on broad policy positions than on particular positions, but even councils little agreed on particular positions can be agreed on broad position areas (Table 27–12). Position specificity facilitates position agreement on broad areas of policy, especially in the larger, but also in the smaller, cities (Table 27–13). But whether agreement is reached on amenities or development varies with city size and does not seem to be inherent in a given position area: it is easier to reach agreement on development in the smaller cities and on amenities in the larger cities (Table 27–14). One should not conclude, however, that the choice of position through agreement is simply due to the nature of the environmental challenge. It is likely to depend on the whole structure of policy map components.

Chapter 28

Policy as Process:
Continuities
and Discontinuities

The policy map, like the geographer's map, is a reductive and thematic tool of orientation; it treats only special classes of data and ignores others. Although the policy map as a set of components is, therefore, only a "partial whole," the parts are related to each other in ways that constitute the map's structure. Moreover, the components are related to each other not only structurally but also, by virtue of their nature, sequentially. The time perspective involved in the map's configuration of components is, therefore, a critical aspect of orientation to action. For it is precisely because its components have sequential referents that the policy map is a guide in policy choice. At issue is the order of sequence among the components.

In the perspective of time, the perception of problems refers to past events, the taking of policy positions to present events, and the formulation of policy images to future events. Although the cognitions of map components are contemporaneous, their reference points are past, present, and future. Insofar as map components are associated, therefore, the policy map as a structure of orientations is a more or less accurate replica of the policy-making process (though not, as pointed out earlier, of the decisional process). But cognitions of past, present, and future are not necessarily sequential. The future may be dimly seen before the past is rediscovered or the present unfolds.

The conception of process employed here does not deviate from its conventional usage in political science. "In the other social sciences," stated a report of some years ago, "the concept of process refers to change over time or the activities within a structure, but political scientists normally use the concept to identify every kind of activity, structured or otherwise, that plays a part in shaping public policy. Political process is equivalent to the idea of interaction of all political variables viewed as a complex totality."[1] This conception, then, assumes both continuities and discontinuities in the structure of the policy map. Continuities and discontinuities are important because they serve to explain the relationships between environmental challenges and policy response. For this reason, description of the relationships among the policy map's components will have to precede analysis of the possible linkages among policy map, policy challenges, and policy response.

Ideally, one would want to describe simultaneously the whole configuration of relationships among the policy map's components and their dimensions. One would want to know, for instance, how a council with a specific and conservative image of the city as a residential community perceives the problems it must deal with, how much diversity in problems it recognizes and how much it is agreed on the existence of problems, as well as what position it takes on policy issues, its degree of consensus in this respect, and the options it sees for action. Given the limited number of cases, a complex multivariate analysis of this kind is not feasible. Therefore, the description will be largely bivariate, though an attempt will be made, in the latter part of this chapter, to specify at least some of the major patterns in the policy map as a whole.

Content Linkages

Because map components are being treated as obverse types, the meaning of the directional signs in the correlations must be clearly understood. The following chart presents these meanings.

---

[1] Social Science Research Council, Committee on Historiography, *The Social Sciences in Historical Study* (New York: Social Science Research Council, Bulletin 64, 1954), p. 71.

Chart 28–1
Meanings of Directional Signs
in Correlations Among Policy Map Components

If correlation is between:	and sign is:	then meaning of sign is that:
Image and problem	+	Balance image is related to growth problems, *and*
		Residence image is related to service problems
	—	Balance image is related to service problems, *and*
		Residence image is related to growth problems
Image and position	+	Balance image is related to development position, *and*
		Residence image is related to amenities position
	—	Balance image is related to amenities position, *and*
		Residence image is related to development position
Problem and position	+	Growth problem is related to development position, *and*
		Service problem is related to amenities position
	—	Growth problem is related to amenities position, *and*
		Service problem is related to development position

Because the policy map may assume different contours under different conditions of environmental challenge, the analysis will treat the data as conditional correlations by city size and as partial correlations with city size held constant.

Figures 28–1 and 28–2 show that the policy map's content components are more highly integrated in the larger cities than in the smaller cities. Moreover, while in both large and small cities the direction of the association between images and positions, on the one hand, and problems and positions, on the other, is the same, the association between images and problem perceptions varies in direction with city size. In the larger cities, councils with a residential image perceive growth as a problem and those with a bal-

Figures 28–1 to 28–3
Linkages Among Policy Map Components

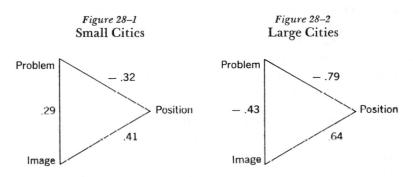

Figure 28–1
Small Cities

Figure 28–2
Large Cities

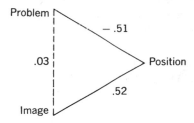

Figure 28–3
All Cities (Partials)

anced image see services as problems; in the smaller cities this is reversed—those with a residential image perceive service problems and those with a balanced image see growth problems.

This result is evidently due to different orientations to urban growth under different environmental conditions. In the more complex and challenging environment of the larger city, a council with a residential image is likely to take a dim view of urban growth because growth threatens the community's continued future as a residential city. In contrast, in the simpler and more manageable environment of the smaller city, in which the council with a residential image need not fear urban growth as much, it will see services as problems because unsatisfactory services make the city less attractive as a residential community. And councils with a balanced image in the smaller cities are less afraid of growth, though it creates problems, precisely because these problems can be remedied by amenities policies designed to cope with urban growth.

These different orientations to growth as a problem, then, seem to be interdependent with the viability of the images of the future held under different environmental conditions. Images are viable if they lead to policy positions that are conducive to the solution of the city's problems. In both large and small cities, Figures 28–1 and 28–2 show, councils with a residential image prefer amenities to development policies, and councils with a balanced image prefer development to amenities policies. Given the meanings of the images, these appear to be appropriate policy positions. A residential city is, by definition, a city that seeks to provide its citizens with a pleasant environment relatively free of urban discomforts. Maximizing life's amenities thus serves to make the city more attractive. In contrast, in a balanced city, further development improves the city's urban potential. Not that development is totally rejected in residential cities or that amenities are totally disdained in balanced cities. But it is more than likely that the councils with a residential image will prefer amenities to development policies, and that councils with a balanced image will prefer development to amenities policies. City size itself strengthens these proclivities more in the larger than in the smaller cities. In both cases, however, there is a great consistency between policy images and positions that indicates genuine continuities in the policy process.

Moreover, policy positions are appropriate responses to problem perceptions in both large and small cities, though the tendency is again stronger in the larger than in the smaller cities. Where municipal services are problems, this is likely to be due to limited resources. Improving services means generating new resources, and new resources can best be mobilized through new development projects. Similarly, councils perceiving growth problems favor amenities policies because they will alleviate, at least in some respects, the troubles associated with urban growth. As the city's population increases, it is in continuous need of new facilities for recreation and leisure. Again, this does not mean that all councils stressing growth as a problem disavow development, or that all councils perceiving service problems underrate amenities. It only means that different emphases are placed on one or another mix of policy positions. Again, the relationship between problem perceptions and policy positions suggests considerable continuity in the policy process.

The continuities between policy problems and positions, on the one hand, and policy images and positions, on the other, suggest that the policy process as reflected in council policy maps is rational. The discontinuity between policy images and problem perceptions is evidently an artifact of different interpretations of what growth means in large and small cities. If city size is controlled, as the partial correlation in Figure 28–3 shows, the discontinuity is complete. There is no relationship between policy images and problem perceptions. This means, clearly, that the perception of problems is direct—a significant consequence of environmental circumstances rather than of the long-term ends-in-view or goals that councils may entertain. There is, then, a good deal of reality-testing going on, and it is the city environment rather than the image concerning the future that defines what the council perceives as a problem. But the image, along with problem perceptions, orients the council's policy position, and policy positions are meaningful responses to both the definition of the problematic situation and the definition of the future included in the policy image.

Alternative Designs for Policy Research

Research on public policy is severely hampered by obstacles to genuine experimentation that inhere in real-world conditions. If public policy is a political unit's response to challenges from the environment, and if it is to be proved that policy is due to the intervention of policy-makers, research in terms of the classical design would have to deal with at least two political units whose behavior is to be compared—an experimental unit in which policy-makers intervene in very much the way an experimental stimulus is introduced into the laboratory experiment, and a control unit in which the stimulus is absent. Pictorially, the design would look like Figure 28–4. If, on measurement, $A_{0+1} - A_0$ is significantly differ-

Figure 28–4
The Classical Experimental Design

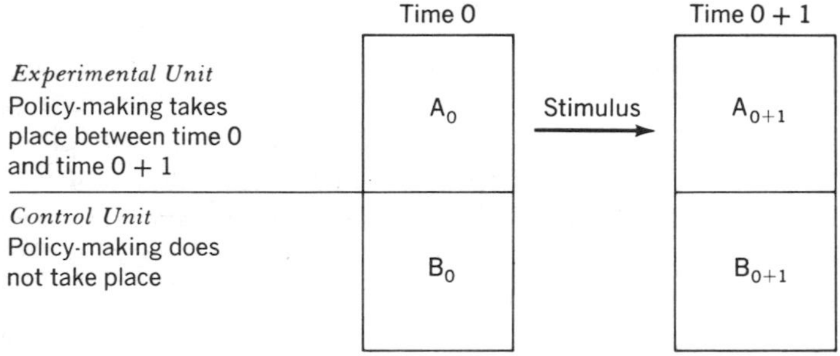

	Time 0		Time 0 + 1
Experimental Unit Policy-making takes place between time 0 and time 0 + 1	A_0	Stimulus $\longrightarrow$	A_{0+1}
Control Unit Policy-making does not take place	B_0		B_{0+1}

ent from $B_{0+1} - B_0$, the result may be taken as proof that the difference in outcomes is due to the intervention of policy-makers.

An experimental design of this kind is extraordinarily difficult to execute in the real world of politics. There is no need to dwell at length on the many obstacles involved in meeting the requirements of this design, such as the random assignment of the experimental stimulus so that any change in the experimental unit's conditions at time 0 + 1 can be attributed with confidence to the

intervention of policy-makers,[2] or the problem of obtaining a sufficient number of units through time so that the intervention of
policy-makers in the experimental units can be observed and
measured.

The purpose of reviewing the classical experimental design is
not to set up an unduly perfectionist criterion of proof. Rather, it
is to show that *any* research design, no matter how simple, is a
derivative of the classical design. This is true even of the design
which, in practice, is no design at all and which has only minimal
truth value. For instance, the proposition is advanced that there is
today a generation gap that is greater than it was yesterday, and an
attempt is made to explain the gap in terms of some cause. The
design implicit in this proposition is represented by Figure 28–5.
In stating the proposition, the observer fills in the "before situation" with imagined data (represented by the cell with the broken
lines). The design is highly truncated, for there is no control group

Figure 28–5
Case Study Design

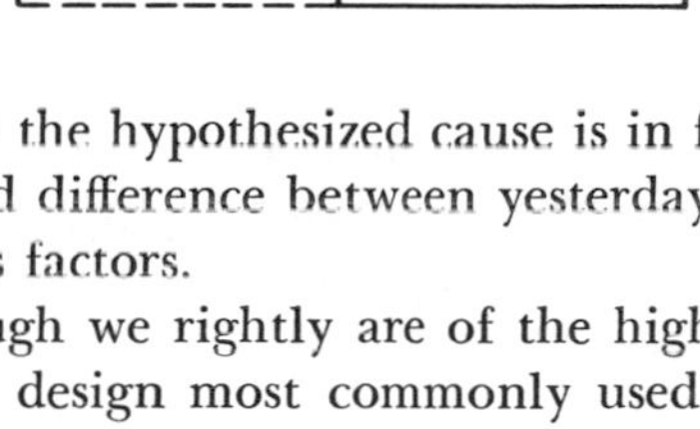

Time 0	Time 0 + 1
A_0	A_{0+1}

to make sure that the hypothesized cause is in fact operative and
that the presumed difference between yesterday and today is not
due to extraneous factors.

Suspicious though we rightly are of the highly truncated case
study design, the design most commonly used in contemporary
policy research, although considerably more sophisticated and

---

[2] See Ronald A. Fisher, *The Design of Experiments* (Edinburgh: Oliver and
Boyd, 1937), pp. 20–24.

creditable, is also truncated in that it lacks a "before situation." In this design—let us call it the after-correlational design—two units or sets are compared by way of cross-tabulation or correlation, and statistical controls are used in order to hold any number of variables constant so that the effect of a test variable can be identified and measured. As Figure 28–6 shows, the two units are compared in terms of a test variable at time $0 + 1$, but nothing is known about the state of the units at time 0. Causal modeling is only a special case of the after-correlational design.

Figure 28–6
After-Correlational Design

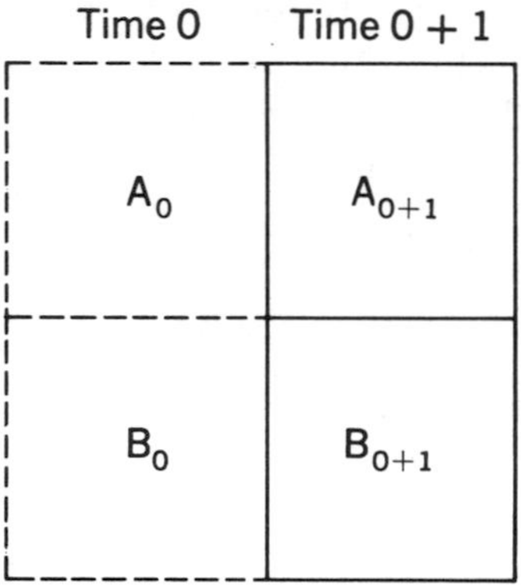

There are several other truncated designs, but only one other will be reviewed here because it is relevant to the design to be employed in the next chapter. In this design—let us call it the random-panel design (as distinct from the longitudinal-panel design in which the same unit is observed at two points in time)—two *different* units or sets of units are compared at different times. As shown in Figure 28–7, the assumption is made that if the unit observed at time 0 had also been observed at time $0 + 1$, it would have the characteristics of the second unit actually observed at that time. Vice versa, the assumption is made, of course, that if the unit actually observed at time $0 + 1$ had been observed "before" at time 0, it would have been identical in properties with the unit actually observed at that time.

Figure 28–7
Random-Panel Design

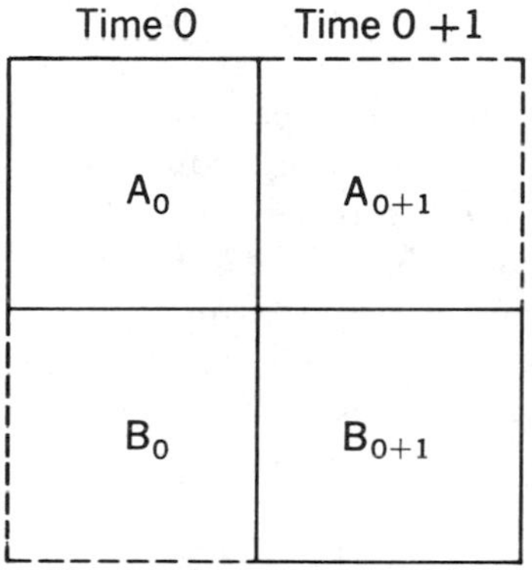

Time 0	Time 0 +1
A_0	A_{0+1}
B_0	B_{0+1}

The juxtaposition of a number of truncated or quasi-experimental designs and the classical experimental design serves to sensitize the analyst to the truth value of his inferences. None of the quasi-experimental designs satisfies the theoretical assumptions and technical requirements of the classical design. However, because they are not satisfactory from the perfectionist perspective, it does not follow that they are not creditable; it only follows that the proof of any hypothesis tested by the design is at best partial.

The validity of the propositions to be advanced can therefore not be proved in any strict sense. The best proof derives from subjecting the propositions to alternative designs in order to determine whether they predict observations. There are two designs possible with the kind of data we have. We shall present one in this chapter and another in the next.

A Causal Model

The consistencies and continuities evidently characteristic of policy mapping recommend more systematic treatment. This involves some kind of modeling of the policy process consonant with the conceptualization of policy presented in Chapter 23. The model of the policy process that emerges from this conceptualization consists of three major variables—the physical-social environment, the policy environment (that is, the configuration of relevant policies that evolves through time), and what has been called the policy map. The policy map, explicated in Chapters 26 and 27, consists of three components: perceptions of the environmental challenges or problems on which councils are called to act; the goals or images of the future they have in mind as they respond or fail to respond to the environment; and the positions they take in regard to the problems confronting them. The model we test is predicated on the initial empirical observation of a close and strong relationship between urbanization as the environmental challenge and policy environment as the response. Table 28–1 presents the data.

In exploring the relationship between policy environment and policy map it is important to keep in mind that the data used to measure level of urbanization and degree of policy development refer to a time period clearly prior to the time period in which the data for the policy map components were collected. In other words, the possibility that any one of the policy components has an antecedent effect on either urbanization or policy development, or both, can be ruled out, and the relationship between urbanization and policy development need not be subjected to "control" in order to determine whether it is spurious. Both variables are exogenous to

Table 28–1
Policy Development and Urbanization

City size	Re-tarded (N = 10)	Emer-gent (N = 15)	Transi-tional (N = 27)	Mature (N = 15)	Ad-vanced (N = 15)
<10,000	90%	80%	37%	7%	0%
10–50,000	10	20	52	53	47
>50,000	0	0	11	40	53
	100%	100%	100%	100%	100%
Gamma = .82					

the model. Moreover, the strength of the relationship suggests that there may be a strong interaction effect on observed relationships as between each of the two variables and the components of the policy map and among the latter themselves.

The physical-social environment and the policy environment are interdetermined. For instance, there is a reciprocal relationship between urbanization as an environmental stimulus and policy as a response. But policy can also influence the course of urbanization, as when land is set aside for industrial or commercial growth, or taxing policies favor urbanization. As an interdeterminate relationship, it is subject to the conditions of a moving equilibrium. A change in environmental stimuli engenders a change in policy, and a change in policy alters the environment.

The propositions that constitute a theoretical model of the policy process can be derived as follows:

1. An environmental challenge calling for a policy response has the expected effect only if it is perceived by policy-makers as constituting a problematic situation. Unless environmental challenges are experienced as problems, policy responses are not likely to be forthcoming.

2. Environmental challenges may be, but need not be, directly related to policy-makers' images of the future. They need not be related because goals or images refer to the future and can be independent of past or present conditions. But images may be related indirectly to environmental conditions if the latter are perceived as problems and suggest a reformulation of images.

3. Environmental challenges are not directly related to policy positions, for positions need only be taken if the challenges are seen as problems and become issues to be settled.

4. The policy environment, that is, the set of ongoing policies that has emerged through time, may be, but need not be, related to the perception of challenges from the environment. It will not be related to problem perceptions if the relationship between policy environment and the environmental challenge is in equilibrium; it will be related if the latter relationship is disturbed. Put differently, if ongoing policies successfully cope with environmental challenges, the latter are unlikely to be perceived as problems.

5. The policy environment is related to policy-makers' images of or goals for the future. The policy environment is, by assumption, rewarding. And if the policy environment is rewarding, images and goals are not likely to deviate widely from the images or goals that are implicit in ongoing policies; in fact, they are likely to be congruent with them.

6. The policy environment is not directly related to policy positions. For positions are at best intentions that may or may not be consonant with ongoing policies.

7. The relationship between the perception of problems and policy images is ambiguous. On the one hand, one can assume that images as views of the future are totally independent of perceptions of current problems. On the other hand, one can assume that the perception of strong challenges from the environment leads to a reformulation of images, or one can assume that the perception of problems, even if rooted in the reality of environmental challenges, is colored by the preferences or expectations inherent in images. Put differently, what policy-makers perceive as problems and what they envisage for the future may be at loggerheads; but perceptions of problems may reshape images, or images may shape the perception of problems. As a result, the relationship between problem perceptions and policy images as such is indeterminate and depends largely on antecedent conditions.

8. Policy images are directly related to policy positions. Because positions are policy-makers' declarations of how they intend to cope with environmental challenges, they are likely to be tutored by their images or ends-in-view.

9. Perceptions of problems, stimulated by environmental challenges, are directly related to policy positions. For if environmental conditions do not give rise to problems, then policy positions are not dependent on problem perceptions.

For the purpose of modeling the relationships among the variables of the theoretical model, level of urbanization and state of policy environment will be treated as independent (exogenous) variables, problem perceptions and policy images as intervening variables, and policy positions as the dependent variables.

The first task is to determine the independence of the relationships between the two exogenous variables and the dependent variable (Propositions 3 and 6), for only if these relationships are zero, as hypothesized, can it be assumed that problem perceptions and policy images are truly intervening variables. To test the null hypothesis, we control the relationships by both problem perceptions and policy images. The resulting second-order partial correlation coefficients are .07 for the urbanization-position relationship, and −.03 for the policy environment-position relationship. Clearly, we can discard the possibility of a direct relationship between the two independent variables and the dependent variable. Problem perceptions and policy images can be treated as intervening variables.

We shall deal next with the bothersome question of the relationship between the two intervening variables (Proposition 7). The relationship was characterized as indeterminate. Because this relationship has important implications for all the model's linkages, we shall present it as a zero-order relationship, and as a partial relationship, controlling successively for the other three variables individually and jointly.

It appears, from Table 28–2 A, that if uncontrolled, the relationship between problem perception and policy image is weak (.24). In other words, there is only a slight tendency for policy makers with a balanced (rather than a residential) image to perceive growth problems (rather than service-related matters). When the possible reactive effect of policy position on the relationship is partialed out, the relationship becomes substantial (.50). However, it declines when controlled for the possible effect of policy environment (.32), and it altogether vanishes when controlled for level of urbanization (.04). To explore the relationship further, we controlled for the possible simultaneous effect of urbanization and policy environment. The result, as Table 28–2 A shows, is highly instructive. The relationship changes significantly in direction. It now appears that it is policy-makers with a residential (rather than a balanced) image who perceive problems of growth confronting them, while those with a balanced image now perceive service-connected matters as problems. However, the relative weakness of the relationship confirms our initial proposition that the direction of the relationship is indeterminate.

The implications of this indeterminacy require elaboration. One

Table 28–2
Zero-Order and Partial Correlations
Among Components of Policy Map

(A) $g_{PI,PP} = .24$

$g_{PI,PP/PoP} = .50$

$g_{PI,PP/PoEn} = .32$

$g_{PI,PP/Urb} = .04$

$g_{PI,PP/PoEn,Urb} = -.32$

$g_{PI,PP/PoP,PoEn,Urb} = -.26$

(B) $g_{PP,PoP} = -.42$

$g_{PP,PoP/PI} = .-.61$

$g_{PP,PoP/PoEn} = -.35$

$g_{PP,PoP/Urb} = -.51$

$g_{PP,PoP/PoEn,Urb} = -.62$

$g_{PP,PoP/PI,PoEn,Urb} = -.90$

(C) $g_{PI,PoP} = .54$

$g_{PI,PoP/PP} = .54$

$g_{PI,PoP/PoEn} = .54$

$g_{PI,PoP/Urb} = .52$

$g_{PI,PoP/PoEn,Urb} = .57$

$g_{PI,PoP/PP,PoEn,Urb} = .66$

Code:

PI = Policy image
PP = Problem perception
PoP = Policy position
PoEn = Policy environment
Urb = Urbanization

way of doing this is by examination of the relationship between problem perception and policy position (Table 28–2 B). If this relationship is controlled for the possible effect of policy image, it is strong ($-.61$), as expected (Proposition 9). Its direction has already been discussed. One might have expected that policy-makers perceiving growth problems would advocate further development. This is clearly not the case. Instead, those perceiving growth as a problem take an amenities position, and those perceiving service problems favor further development (hence the negative sign of the coefficient).

We can also shed at least some light on the indeterminate relationship between problem perception and policy image by examining the relationship between policy image and policy position

(Table 28–2 C). The relationship is substantial (.54) and reveals that those with a residential image favor amenities in taking a position, while those with a balanced image favor further development.

If we juxtapose the findings concerning the relationship between problem perception and policy position, on the one hand, and between policy image and policy position, on the other, the indeterminacy of the problem perception-image relationship becomes explicable. It appears that policy-makers with a residential image perceive problems of growth because these problems probably jeopardize the residential future that they prefer. They therefore take an amenities position that is congenial to their image of the future. Vice versa, those seeing or preferring a balanced city do not perceive problems of growth as threatening and, seeing service problems instead, favor further development, presumably because further development will maximize the city's resources needed for the effective provision of services. It would seem, therefore, that policy positions are "double-caused" by problem perceptions and policy images. This seems to be a true double-causation relationship and explains, therefore, the weak relationship between problem perceptions and policy images.

However, it would be unduly hasty to accept this interpretation. As both policy images and problem perceptions were assumed to be related to policy environment (Propositions 4 and 5), a third-order partial test controlling for policy environment, level of urbanization, and successively for each component of the policy map seemed indicated. Table 28–2 shows the outcome. Not only is the relationship between policy image and problem perceptions further weakened (−.26), but the relationships among the policy map's other components are strengthened (−.90 and .66, respectively). We infer that the major pathway of environmental conditions and ongoing policies moves, in fact, through the cognitive screen of problem perceptions, although the effect of policy images on policy positions is also strong. The relationship between policy image and problem perceptions is not a crucial link in the chain of causation.

We shall turn now to the independent variables of the model. We have noted already that level of urbanization and policy environment are not directly related to policy positions. However, both independent variables, being highly related to each other and interdeterminate, are likely to be stimuli for problem perceptions (Propositions 2 and 5). The question of causal ordering is hardly at issue because the time order of the variables is clear— the independent variables preceding the intervening ones.

Of interest, therefore, is which of the two independent variables contributes more to the variance in problem perceptions and policy images. Table 28–3 presents the zero-order correlation coefficients and the first-order partials (controlling for one of the independent and one of the intervening variables). Some of the consequences of the sequentially introduced controls are noteworthy. In the first place (Table 28–3 A), a fairly strong positive relationship links level of urbanization and problem perceptions and withstands all controls (in support of Proposition 1). The more urbanized the environment, that is, the more intense environmental challenges are, the more likely it is that policy-makers will perceive problems connected with growth. Second (Table 28–3 B), the relationship between urbanization and policy image almost vanishes when it is controlled (in support of Proposition 2). Third (Table 28–3 D), the state of the policy environment has a strong

Table 28–3
Zero-Order and Partial Correlations
Among Urbanization, Policy Environment,
and Components of Policy Map

(A) $g_{Urb,PP} = .57$ (C) $g_{PoEn,PP} = .08$

     $g_{Urb,PP/PoEn} = .73$ $g_{PoEn,PP/Urb} = -.32$

     $g_{Urb,PP/PoEn,PI} = .64$ $g_{PoEn,PP/Urb,PI} = -.53$

(B) $g_{Urb,PI} = .58$ (D) $g_{PoEn,PI} = .81$

     $g_{Urb,PI/PoEn} = .30$ $g_{PoEn,PI/Urb} = .75$

     $g_{Urb,PI/PoEn,PP} = .10$ $g_{PoEn,PI/Urb,PP} = .80$

effect on the formulation of policy images and withstands successive controls (in support of Proposition 5). In other words, the more mature or advanced the policy environment, the more do policy-makers hold a balanced image of the city's future. In entertaining policy goals, it seems, policy-makers do not entertain "far-out" views. Finally (Table 28–3 C), and this is perhaps the most interesting finding, the relationship between policy environment and problem perceptions, evidently nonexistent when uncontrolled, grows increasingly stronger as it is controlled by urbanization and policy image. As suggested in Proposition 6, this relationship is likely to vary with the degree of equilibrium in the relationship between environmental challenges and policy environment. The negative coefficients show that the *less* developed the policy environment, the *more* are policy-makers likely to perceive problems related to growth.

This result, however, pinpoints a problem that the causal model cannot successfully tackle. We can best state the problem in the form of a syllogism that reflects the data, as follows:

> The more urbanized the environment, the more developed is the policy environment (.80).
>
> The more urbanized the environment, the more are problems related to growth perceived (.64).
>
> ---
>
> The more developed the policy environment, the more are problems related to growth perceived.

The data, however, show that the logical conclusion derived from the premises is not empirically viable. In fact, the opposite is true: the less developed the policy environment, the more are problems of growth at the policy-makers' focus of attention. It would seem, therefore, that there is a condition present in the relationship between urbanization and policy environment that eludes the causal model. This condition may be the degree of equilibrium in the relationship between the urban and policy environments. The equilibrium condition is concealed in the causal model and can only be ascertained by a design that manipulates the data in a different way. As we shall see in the next chapter, there are a number of cities which are, in fact, in disequilibrium—those that are highly urbanized but whose policy environments are less developed than one should expect from an equilibrium point of view.

Figure 28–8 summarizes all the relationships obtained by partial correlation analysis. It is of the utmost importance to emphasize the tentative nature of the results, because "all other things" are probably not "equal," and relevant error terms are probably not uncorrelated. Determining causal directions under these conditions is difficult. While in the present model there is no doubt as to the true independence and priority of the urbanization and policy environment variables, and while direct relationships between them and the dependent variable—policy position—probably would not exist even if additional variables were introduced, the flow of causation through the two intervening variables is not self-evident. For instance, are the effects of urbanization or policy environment on the taking of policy positions mediated more through policy images or through problem perceptions? To answer this question, we can compare the predictions that are possible with the actual results that were obtained for the intermediate links of the causal sequence.

If problem perceptions or policy images are truly intervening between the independent and the dependent variables, we should predict that the relationship between the independent variable (x) and the dependent variable (y) equals the product of the correlations between each and the intervening variable (z). In other words, we predict that $r_{xy} = (r_{xz}) \cdot (r_{zy})$. Table 28–4 presents the calculations.

Comparison of the predicted and actual outcomes shows that, while far from perfect, the fit is excellent for the chain in which urbanization and policy positions are linked by problem perceptions, and good for the chain that runs through policy images. The fit is fair for the chain that links policy environment to policy positions through policy images, so that we need not reject it. But it is poor for the chain from policy environment to policy positions through problem perceptions. We conclude, therefore, that policy positions are primarily taken in response to the perceptions of problems that stem from environmental challenges (Path 1–4–5),

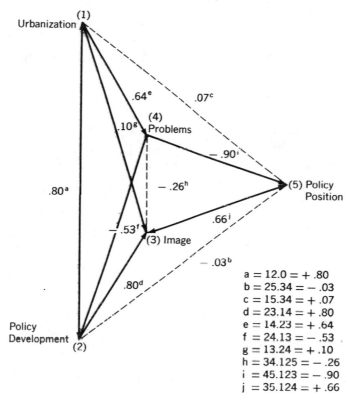

Figure 28–8
Causal Model of Policy Process

$$a = 12.0 = + .80$$
$$b = 25.34 = - .03$$
$$c = 15.34 = + .07$$
$$d = 23.14 = + .80$$
$$e = 14.23 = + .64$$
$$f = 24.13 = - .53$$
$$g = 13.24 = + .10$$
$$h = 34.125 = - .26$$
$$i = 45.123 = - .90$$
$$j = 35.124 = + .66$$

CODE FOR INTERPRETING DIRECTION OF COEFFICIENTS

Image—Problem Perception:
(+) = Balance-Growth or Residential-Service
(−) = Balance-Service or Residential-Growth

Image—Policy Position:
(+) = Balance-Development or Residential-Amenities
(−) = Balance-Amenities or Residential-Development

Problem Perception—Policy Position:
(+) = Growth-Development or Service-Amenities
(−) = Growth-Amenities or Service-Development

Table 28–4
Test of Models of Policy Process

	Predicted	Actual	Fit
1. Urbanization (x)	*Predicted*	*Actual*	*Fit*
↓ .57			
Problem perception (z)	$r_{xy} = .24$	$= .25$	Excellent
↓ .42			
Policy position (y)			
2. Urbanization (x)	*Predicted*	*Actual*	*Fit*
↓ .58			
Policy image (z)	$r_{xy} = .31$	$= .25$	Good
↓ .54			
Policy position (y)			
3. Policy environment (x)	*Predicted*	*Actual*	*Fit*
↓ .08			
Problem perception (z)	$r_{xy} = .03$	$= .29$	Poor
↓ .42			
Policy position (y)			
4. Policy environment (x)	*Predicted*	*Actual*	*Fit*
↓ .81			
Policy image (z)	$r_{xy} = .44$	$= .29$	Fair
↓ .54			
Policy position (y)			

NOTE: Predictions are based on uncontrolled correlations between variables.

and in response to the policy images strongly dependent on the environment of ongoing policies (Path 2–3–5). Although the relationship between level of urbanization and policy image is weak, it has also some effect on what policy positions are taken (Path 1–3–5). We can reject the assumption that ongoing policies have an effect on policy positions through the intervention of problem perceptions (Path 2–4–5).

Conclusion

A partial model of the policy process linking environmental challenges (urbanization), policy environment (state of development in the ongoing policies concerning planning and amenities), and the three components of the policy map (problem perceptions, images of the future, and policy positions) shows both continuities and discontinuities in the policy process. Neither level of urbanization nor level of policy development has an independent effect on policy position, the map's component most proximate to the decisional situation. Rather, policy positions are responses to both types of environment variously mediated through problem perceptions and images of the future. While level of urbanization affects policy positions through the intervention of both problem perceptions and images, the policy environment has an effect only through the intervention of images. Although problem perception is not unrelated to the policy environment, and though the latter is related to the formation of images, the discontinuity between images and problem perceptions nullifies the influence of ongoing policies on policy positions through the mediation of problem perceptions. But as policy images do mediate between policy environment and policy positions, discontinuities may actually make for just that minimal amount of discretion that is at the core of policy-making. Otherwise the making of policy would be unduly deterministic. As they are called on to take policy positions prior to actual decision-making, policy-makers balance what the problematic situation calls for against what their images of the future suggest as desirable. In doing so, the data suggest, they do not let their sense of reality, reflected in problem perceptions related to environmental challenges, be distorted either by ongoing policies or images of the future. And as the latter are not independent of the policy environment and in fact mediate between it and policy positions, images themselves are not devoid of reality. Policy positions, it appears, are realistic contemporary adaptations to multiple environments in spite of the fact that their influence is screened by perceptions of past problems and images of the future. This is so because neither problem perceptions nor future images are lacking in a sense of reality.

Chapter 29

The Eco-Policy System: A Reconstruction

If the policy process seems to evince a good deal of rationality, this does not mean that policy-making is rational in the procedural sense. Councils do not simply perceive a problem, specify the goal to be achieved, and then choose the policy position that would solve the problem and achieve the goal. Rational behavior of this sort could occur only if councils had full control over all aspects of the policy process. In fact, they have only limited control.

The council has control, within limits set by the imagination, over its goals. But it has no such control over the problems with which it may have to deal. Problems are pressed on it by environmental challenges. Although challenges become problems that call for solution only if they are seen as in conflict with valued goals, they do not go away just because they may not be perceived. Moreover, environmental challenges, if perceived as problems, may be so strong as to force the policy-making group to reassess and possibly change its goals. Goals are variable, although perhaps less so than the positions taken to attain them, and goals may change as new values are stimulated in the course of responding to environmental challenges and taking appropriate policy positions. Finally, as challenges from the environment present themselves, whether experienced as problems or not, policy positions can be taken such that they do not guarantee solutions that would satisfy preconceived goals.

All this is particularly likely to be the case in legislative policy-making groups. Unlike a shoe factory whose goal is to manufacture shoes, the council's goals are not necessarily given but rather evolve in the process of policy-making. Changes in style and fashion may bring about changes in the shoe factory's production; they do not alter its primary goal of producing shoes. But changes in demands and values, as well as changes in the physical and social environment, bring about changes in the goals of public policy. Indeed, it is the peculiar attribute of legislative policy-making that the chain of means and ends is not unidirectional, so that the familiar model of procedural rationality so congenial in the study and practice of administration (whether actually true or not) is not necessarily appropriate and in fact is only rarely so. For the goals of public policy are seldom clear (as they are in the case of the shoe factory). Because positions must often be taken in the absence of clear and unambiguous goals, the latter do not easily provide guidelines for action and are often the unanticipated consequences of policy problems or policy positions.

These considerations raise the question as to whether the causal model of the policy process explored in Chapter 28 sufficiently resembles policy-making in the real world to be given face-value credence, for the model is clearly built on the assumptions of procedural rationality. It assumes that environmental challenges precede policy mapping, that goals or images of the city's future, as they were called, are given, that challenges are in fact perceived as problems and that policy positions emerge rationally from the confluence of antecedent conditions. Yet there is reason to doubt that the legislative process follows this sequence, not only because of theoretical considerations but also because of empirical discrepancies between the condition of the physical and social environment and the policy environment as a response to these conditions. As was noted in the previous chapter, contrary to expectations, councils in less developed policy environments are more likely to perceive problems of growth than are councils in the more developed policy environments. The fit of the predicted relationships between policy environment, problem perception, and policy position, on the one hand, and the observed relationships, on the other, is poor (Path 2–4–5 in Figure 28-8). The disturbance in the real-world situation is due perhaps to a condition of disequilibrium in the relationship between urbanization as the environmental challenge and policy environment as the response that antecedes policy-mapping. As the causal model assumes equilibrium, its absence is also likely to disturb its built-in assumption of procedural rationality. An alternative design, providing for the possibility of disequilibrium, is therefore in order.

A Hypothetico-Longitudinal Design

The critical weakness of the causal model in policy research is that it lacks longitudinal depth. Assumptions were made about the time ordering of the relationships between each of the two independent variables and the two intervening variables, but not about any time ordering between the two independent variables themselves. They were treated as synchronic, although it was suggested that the reciprocal relationship between them could alternately be one of equilibrium and disequilibrium. But if this assumption is made, it follows that the relationship at any one point in time is only a special case of alternating asymmetries at different points in time.[1] There is an observed relationship between the independent variables that is synchronic, and hypothetical relationships that are diachronic. What is required is a design that would allow inferences from the observed to the hypothesized relationships.

One of the drawbacks of the causal model cast in the after-correlational design is that it disguises original relationships in the data among the variables of the model. For instance, as shown in Table 28-1, the relationship between level of urbanization (measured by city size) and the state of the policy environment is so strong from the correlational perspective that we are prone to ignore deviant cases. In order to pinpoint these deviant cases more sharply, Table 29-1 presents the data in bivariate and dichotomized form. It shows that we are dealing with two kinds of deviant situations. First, in cell "c" we note six cases of cities which are

---

[1] See Morris Rosenberg, *The Logic of Survey Research* (New York: Basic Books, 1968), pp. 8–9.

Table 29–1

Policy Environment and Urbanization (Size)
Variables Dichotomized

Development dichotomized		Size Dichotomized	
		Small (Less urban) N = 41	Large (More urban) N = 41
(Retarded, emergent, transitional)	Less (N = 52)	a) 35	b) 17
(Mature, advanced)	More (N = 30)	c) 6	d) 24

more developed in spite of limited environmental challenges. These cases are "truly" deviant. They cannot be accounted for by the contingent relationship between urbanization and policy environment. In other words, the observed outcome can be attributed simply to policy-makers' purposes, preferences, and efforts.[2]

But this is not possible with the 17 cases in cell "b." Although they are statistically deviant, they could be considered truly deviant only if one were to assume that the relationship between urbanization and policy environment is invariably in equilibrium. But this is unrealistic. If we conceive of a reciprocal relationship as a succession of alternating asymmetries, it is more realistic to assume a lag between stimulus and response—in other words, that as urbanization proceeds and challenges the policy-maker, an appropriate response is not immediately forthcoming. This reasonable assumption allows us to construct a dynamic model of the policy process: (1) As long as environmental challenges are weak (the city is small, less urbanized), the policy environment is less de-

---

[2] We drop these six cases from further analysis for two reasons: first, they are theoretically uninteresting from the perspective pursued here; and second, the small number involved makes further quantitative breakdowns not viable. It would, of course, be interesting to find out why the policy-makers in these six cities behave as they do, but this would take us too far afield.

veloped—challenge and response are, indeed, in equilibrium; (2) as the city grows and environmental challenges become urgent (the city is now large, more urbanized), there is an initial lag in policy response—the policy environment remains less developed so that challenge and response are in disequilibrium; (3) as the challenges from the environment are not likely to abate, and as ongoing policies are not appropriate, policy-makers as purposive actors will, sooner or later, adopt positions that reestablish the equilibrium between urbanization and policy environment.

This transformation of the static into a dynamic model of the relationship between environmental conditions and the policy environment suggests that the 17 cases in cell "b" are not truly deviant. They represent situations that can be expected to occur normally in the sequence of events linking past and future. In searching for a design appropriate to the analysis of data that are synchronic but which, nonetheless, should be interpreted diachronically, it is useful to combine familiar assumptions made for the after-correlational design with assumptions made for the random-panel design, as follows:

1. As in the panel design, the less urbanized, less developed cities are assumed to be control groups. Not having been exposed to the stimulus of urbanization, they have had no opportunity to respond. The two sets of cities that are more urbanized (whether less or more developed) are assumed to be experimental groups. Both have been exposed to the stimulus of urbanization.

2. As in the panel design, it is assumed that if both experimental group cities had been observed at an earlier time, they would have looked like the control group cities; or that the second experimental group of cities (more urbanized, more developed) would have looked like the first experimental group (more urbanized, less developed) at an earlier time. A corollary assumption is that if it were possible to observe the control group cities at a later time, after more urbanization had taken place, they would in sequence look like the two experimental group cities.

3. As in the after-correlational design, it is assumed that the two experimental group cities are similar in all respects except for the differences in policy environment; and the control group and the first experimental group cities are assumed to be similar

in all respects except for the difference in level of urbanization.

4. As in the after-correlational design, the difference in policy environment between the two experimental group cities is assumed to be due to a third factor (or several other factors) that is the test variable—in our case, the policy map.

Although the set of assumptions made in constructing the design is complex, it merely combines a number of assumptions now routinely made in quasi-experimental designs for the analysis of real-world data. What the design shows is that once-latent assumptions are made explicit; comparison of evidently static situations can be used to test hypotheses about change in the real world for which direct data are not available. Although the three sets of cities being compared are actually observed at the same point in historical time, longitudinal assumptions derived from adaptations of the classical experimental design serve to infuse an element of dynamic interpretation into comparative analysis—a recognition of the fact that comparative statics is, indeed, a special case of dynamics.

As Figure 29–1 shows, the design permits three kinds of comparison by way of test variables: (1) comparison of A_0 and B_{0+1}; (2) comparison of A_0 and C_{0+2}; and (3) comparison of B_{0+1} and

Figure 29–1
Quasi-Longitudinal Design of Policy Process

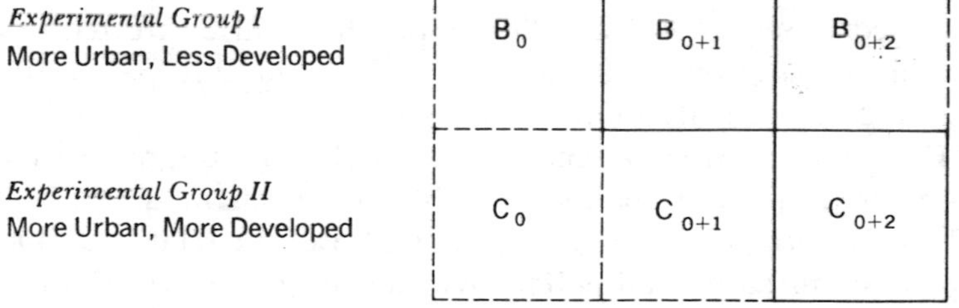

	Time 0	Time 0 + 1	Time 0 + 2
Control Group Less Urban, Less Developed	A_0	A_{0+1}	A_{0+2}
Experimental Group I More Urban, Less Developed	B_0	B_{0+1}	B_{0+2}
Experimental Group II More Urban, More Developed	C_0	C_{0+1}	C_{0+2}

C_{0+2}. As we postulate that urbanization is a necessary but not sufficient condition for policy change, the comparison between A_0 and C_{0+2} is not enlightening, for while the two situations can be expected to differ significantly on test variables, we cannot say whether the difference in the policy environment is due to the test factors or to change in urbanization. Moreover, both situations are in equilibrium. Of the other two comparisons possible, that between A_0 and B_{0+1} serves as a control test. As no change in policy environment is observed, yet there is a change in urbanization, it follows that increased urbanization is not sufficient to bring about a change in policies. The comparison between B_{0+1} and C_{0+2} is the most relevant because it is the appropriate test for rejecting the null hypothesis that a change in the policy environment is not due to purposive action.

The research question asked is why is it that in situation B_{0+1} the policy environment has not developed in spite of a change in the necessary condition for such change, that is, increased urbanization. Our hypothesis is, of course, that policy change has not taken place because of policy positions taken by policy-makers that impede it.

Quasi-Longitudinal Analysis

The data will be analyzed within the constraints of the quasi-longitudinal design in three ways: first, as marginal distributions; second, as conjunctive patterns; and third, as correlations.

Marginal Analysis

Table 29–2 shows the marginal distributions of councils on the three components of the policy map. They will be treated *as if* the data were genuinely longitudinal. From this perspective, Table 29–2 is highly informative.

First, growth is experienced as a problem by the majority of councils in all three periods, but it is most felt in time $0+1$ when the "eco-policy system" (as we shall call the relationship between urbanization and policy environment) is in disequilibrium.

Table 29–2
Distribution of Councils on Policy Map Components
by States of the Eco-Policy System

Components of policy map	*Time 0* Less urban, less devel. (N = 27)	*Time 0 + 1* More urban, less devel. (N = 14)	*Time 0 + 2* More urban, more devel. (N = 18)
Growth is problem	56%	93%	78%
Development is position	37%	36%	56%
Balance is image	33%	50%	89%
Problem-position differential	19%	57%	22%

NOTE: Table includes only those councils which could be classified on all three components of policy map.

In the third period, when there has been an appropriate policy response to restore the equilibrium, the urgency of problems connected with growth is somewhat reduced, but these problems continue to concern policy-makers.

Second, in view of the prominence of growth problems at time $0 + 1$, it is revealing that so few councils (36 percent) at that time take policy positions in favor of development. In fact, they do not differ at all from time 0. Only in the third period, when the eco-policy system is again in equilibrium, do a majority of councils take positions that are presumably capable of coping with the problems of growth. It may be noted that a discrepancy between perceiving growth as a problem and taking pro-development positions also occurs in the equilibrium situations at time 0 and time $0 + 2$, but it is considerably less than in the disequilibrium state at time $0 + 1$ (19 percent and 22 percent, respectively, versus 57 percent). The need for services and not growth-related problems, the earlier causal analysis has shown, makes for policy positions favoring development. But as service problems are not seen as critical at time $0 + 1$, it becomes understandable why positions preferring amenities are more widely held in this period by comparison with the third period.

Third, as Table 29–2 shows, policy images change dramatically and systematically through time. While at time 0 only 33 percent of the councils envisage a balanced future for their cities, 89 percent do so at time 0 + 2. Of particular interest, however, is the fact that at time 0 + 1, when the eco-policy system is in disequilibrium, the councils are exactly split, with half holding an image of a balanced future and another half holding an image of a residential future. In the disequilibrium situation, in spite of the fact that councils are keenly aware of problems connected with growth, they do not uniformly adopt policy positions in favor of development. These problems, it would seem, are looked upon as nuisances that can be wished away by pursuing amenities policies; and if problems connected with service are not perceived, further development is an option that does not enter the policy map.

Although we cannot prove, with the data at hand, that the policy environment as a response to the challenge of urbanization is facilitated or impeded by the policy map, we inspect the data *as if* they could be used as tests, provided we read them cautiously. In treating the same data in this hypothetical manner (as if the policy map components were the independent variables and the eco-policy system the dependent variable), we should read Table 29–3 as follows: while of the councils with a residential image, 67 percent are "found" at time 0 (in the less urbanized, less developed

Table 29–3

Distribution of Councils on States
of the Eco-Policy System by Policy Map Components

Eco-policy system	Policy Map Components					
	Image		Problem		Position	
	Bal. (N = 32)	Resid. (N = 27)	Growth (N = 42)	Serv. (N = 17)	Devel. (N = 25)	Amenit. (N = 34)
Time 0	28%	67%	36%	71%	40%	50%
Time 0 + 1	22	26	31	5	20	26
Time 0 + 2	50	7	33	24	40	24
	100%	100%	100%	100%	100%	100%
Gamma =		−.69		−.45		−.24

state of the eco-policy system), of those holding a balanced image, 50 percent are "found" at time $0 + 2$ (when the system is more urban, more developed); and so on. If we read the data in this way, it is evident that the image component of the policy map discriminates most strongly among the three states of the eco-policy system ($g = -.69$); that problem perceptions discriminate moderately ($g = -.45$); and that policy positions discriminate very little ($g = -.24$). This is not surprising; as we noted in the causal model (Figure 28–8), neither urbanization nor policy environment as separate variables have a direct effect on policy positions. As the causal model demonstrated, the perception of problems and policy images are critical intervening variables that link reality to policy positions. But the marginal distributions also suggest that the topography of the policy map differs at different periods or in different states of the eco-policy system. We shall pursue this theme further by looking next at the conjunctive patterns in the policy map that can be observed in different states of the eco-policy system.

Conjunctive Patterns

The data can be looked at in terms of the particular combinations formed by the components of the policy map. These conjunctive patterns probably constitute the most realistic representations of the policy maps as wholes. Eight such patterns are possible, and our interest is in the frequency of particular patterns at different points in time or in different states of the eco-policy system. Table 29–4 presents the data.

It appears from Table 29–4 that some conjunctive patterns occur only at time 0, that some occur mainly at time 0 and time $0 + 1$, and that some occur in all three periods, although dominantly at time $0 + 2$. (One pattern, B–S–A, does not occur at all.) Councils with a residential image perceiving service problems are found exclusively at time 0, regardless of their positions on policy. However, when councils with a residential image experience growth problems, they are not only found at time 0 but also at time $0 + 1$ when the eco-policy system is in disequilibrium. As a balanced image is adopted but problems of growth continue to be

Table 29–4

Distribution of Councils by Conjunctive Patterns
of Policy Map Components in Three States
of the Eco-Policy System

Conjunctive patterns	*Time 0* Less urban, less devel.	*Time 0 + 1* More urban, less devel.	*Time 0 + 2* More urban, more devel.	Total
R–S–D (N = 3)	100%	0	0	100%
R–S–A (N = 7)	100%	0	0	100%
R–G–D (N = 4)	50%	25	25	100%
R–G–A (N = 13)	46%	46	8	100%
B–G–D (N = 11)	27%	27	46	100%
B–G–A (N = 14)	29%	21	50	100%
B–S–D (N = 7)	14%	29	57	100%
B–S–A (N = 0)	—	—	—	—

Code: R = Residential image   B = Balanced image
　　　 S = Service problems   G = Growth problems
　　　 A = Amenities position   D = Development position

experienced, councils are now more often found at time 0 + 1 and time 0 + 2, but especially in the latter period. When a balanced image is combined with recognition of service as a problem and a pro-development position is taken, most councils have reached the state of the eco-policy system that is characteristic of the last time period, although some remain in the earlier states as well. This arrangement of the data gives more detailed insight than do the marginal distributions into why it is that some councils experience disequilibrium in their eco-policy systems. These are evidently councils in which, because residential images prevail, growth is experienced not as a problem to be handled by appropriate policies but as a problem that is unwelcome. However, when a balanced image comes to be accepted, policies to cope with growth problems are adopted and, in due time, the eco-policy system regains equilibrium.

Correlation Analysis

It remains to look at the transformation through time of the relationships among the components of the policy map. It is likely

that at different times one or another component is more relevant
to the adoption of a particular policy position. Moreover, as the
relationships among policy map components are more or less
interdependent, it is desirable to observe the flow of the effects of
one component on the other. Figure 29–2 presents the models using
the phi coefficient.[3]

The relationships among map components not only take on
different values in different states of the eco-policy system, but the
map seems to undergo structural change. At time 0, when the chal-

Figure 29–2
Structure of Policy Map in Three States
of the Eco-Policy System (Phi)

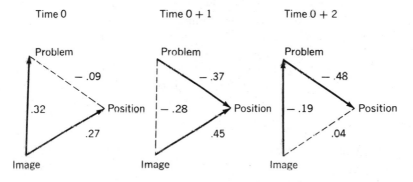

lenges of urbanization are weak and the policy environment is
relatively little developed, councils with a balanced image perceive
growth problems and those with a residential image perceive
service problems (.32). In turn, councils with a balanced image
prefer further development, and those with a residential image
favor amenities (.27). But the perception of problems is practically
unrelated to policy positions (−.09). In fact, of course, we know

[3] We opt here for the phi measure because it is not subject to a difficulty arising in gamma for 2 × 2 tables, also known as Yule's Q. For in the case of the
latter, if one of the cells vanishes, the measure appears as unity (+1 or −1) in
spite of an imperfect relationship between the variables. Phi, like Q, is a
symmetric measure and may be interpreted as the Pearson r. Its values are likely
to be less than those of Q. Hence the phi and gamma values are not directly
comparable.

that in this state the policy environment is little developed, that is, as compared with later states. Ongoing policies do not particularly stress either development or amenities. Available resources are invested in meeting the minimal service needs of these communities. The policy environment is static and in equilibrium with the urban condition.

At time 0 + 1, as the challenges of urbanization come to be felt, the structure of the map changes sharply. Councils with a balanced image now perceive service problems and those with a residential image see growth problems (−.28). Both the perception of growth as a problem and a residential image engender a policy position that favors amenities. This is rather anomalous mapping, but it is the R–G–A pattern observed in Table 29–4 that seems to be characteristic of this state of the eco-policy system. The anomaly may be due to the effect that policy images have. Although problems are seen realistically, policy images have a fairly substantial effect on policy positions (.45). But, more significantly, there is now a linkage between problem perceptions and policy positions. Councils seeing growth problems favor amenities, while those perceiving service problems advocate further development (−.37).

An anomalous situation is unlikely to persist. Sooner or later the policy map will be restructured to fit the exigencies of urbanization. The quasi-longitudinal design permits observation of how the policy map is restructured. Most notable at time 0 + 2 is the fact that the relationship between policy images and policy positions vanishes (.04), while the relationship between problem perceptions and policy positions becomes stronger (−.48). Moreover, the relationship between problem perceptions and images is reduced and becomes weak (−.19). As we saw in Table 29–2, 16 of the 18 councils (89 percent) entertain an image of balance at time 0 + 2. As a result, there is little room for images to discriminate among policy positions or problem perceptions. And, as a further result, it is the perception of problems that now almost alone influences the policy positions that are taken. Councils seeing service-connected problems favor development policies, presumably to mobilize the resources needed to pay for swelling demands for such services in the wake of increased urbanization; while councils experiencing the pangs of growth tend to favor amenities, presumably to offset the unpleasantness of urbanization. The policy map at this time is, not unexpectedly, in congruence with the policy environment. By operational definition, it is an environment in which ongoing policies are geared to both development and amenities policies. In any case, the policy map no longer blocks, as it did at time $0 + 1$, the taking of positions congenial in a policy environment that is in equilibrium with the challenges stemming from heightened urbanization.

If we say that not only the values in the relationships among policy map components change but that the structure of the map itself changes, we mean, of course, that different models define the linkages between the map's points. To determine the adequacy of alternative models, Table 29–5 presents the predicted and actual results for the following three models of three-variable relationships:

Dual effect model	$x \overset{z}{\underset{y}{\diagdown}}$	$r_{yz} = (r_{xy}) \cdot (r_{xz})$
Dual cause model	$\overset{x}{\underset{z}{\searrow}} y$	$r_{xz} = 0$
Intervention model	$x \rightarrow z \rightarrow y$	$r_{xy} = (r_{xz}) \cdot (r_{zy})$

Note: x = images; y = positions; z = problems.

Table 29–5 shows that the Dual Effect Model best characterizes the policy map structure at time 0. Policy images, it seems, have a pervasive effect on the structure of the map, influencing both the perception of problems and the positions that are taken. The fit of prediction and result is only fair, but it is adequate enough to retain the model. At time $0 + 1$, the effect of the policy image on policy positions is complemented by a relatively independent effect of problem perceptions, as predicted in the Dual Cause Model. In the last period, insofar as policy images are still relevant, their effect tends to be mediated through the intervention of problem perceptions. They have no independent effect on policy positions,

Table 29-5

Predicted and Actual Relationships
Among Policy Map Components in Alternative Models
During Three States of the Eco-Policy System

	Predicted	Actual	Fit
Dual effect model at time			
0	.08	−.09	Fair
0 + 1	−.13	−.37	Poor
0 + 2	−.00	−.48	Poor
Dual cause model at time			
0	−.02	.32	Poor
0 + 1	−.17	−.28	Good
0 + 2	−.02	−.19	Fair
Intervention model at time			
0	−.03	.27	Poor
0 + 1	−.10	.45	Poor
0 + 2	.09	.04	Very good

which are strongly determined by problem perceptions. The fit of the Intervention Model at time 0 + 2 is very good.

Although the data cannot be used to test the validity of the inferences made about the course of policy through historical time, it appears that comparative cross-sectional data can be analyzed by way of a *post facto,* quasi-longitudinal design, and that this analysis yields models of policy that not only are plausible but that would in principle be testable in a genuine natural-state experiment if appropriate data were collected at the proper time.

Predicting the Eco-Policy System

If policy is both determined and purposive, policy mapping should prove useful in predicting the future state of the eco-policy system. If one knew a council's policy map and nothing were known about the city's physical and policy environments, one should be able to predict, from knowledge of the map, the current state of the eco-policy system and, by simulating changes in the map, the future state of the system. For instance, if one knew that the policy map consisted of a residential image, a perception of services as problems, and an amenities position, one should predict the eco-policy system to be less urbanized and less developed.

This turning around of the original causal model does violence to the data, but it is a worthwhile intellectual exercise because it unmasks some hidden assumptions that are made in policy analysis. Figure 29–3 simulates possible compositions of the policy map and the expected states of the eco-policy system. It is, in fact, a rough approximation of the conjunctive patterns found in em-

Figure 29–3
Predictive Model of the Eco-Policy System

	Observations on Policy Map at		
	Time 0	Time 0 + 1	Time 0 + 2
Policy image	Residential	Equivocal	Balanced
Problem perception	Services	Growth	Services and growth
Problem position	Amenities	Amenities	Development and amenities
Predicted eco-policy state	Less urban, less devel.	More urban, less devel.	More urban, more devel.

pirical reality as reported in Table 29–4. If it were possible to collect data on policy maps prior to conducting observations on the state of the eco-policy system, the outcome should be as predicted in Figure 29–3.

The hypothetical predictions in Figure 29–3 make explicit the assumption of the causal model that there is a time differential between the policy mapping and the crystallization of a particular eco-policy state. While in fact the eco-policy system is measured as the outcome of increasing urbanization and policy development over time, the policy map is graphed at one point in time at the very end of the developmental process. Yet the eco-policy system can also be treated as the cumulative outcome of urban growth and policy development, in which case it is no more than contemporaneous with policy mapping. But policy mapping would precede the eco-policy developmental process if the policy map were to be considered, as in Figure 29–3, a truly determinative factor in its emergence. The quasi-longitudinal design can only be interpreted as being of heuristic value.

Conclusion

Policy as a response to challenges from the physical and social environment is an emergent property of politics contingent on purposive political behavior. But it is also related to changing environmental conditions. Because political behavior is imbued with purposes that are its goals or ends-in-view, policy inferred from behavioral patterns may, at times, be at odds with environmental requirements. The resultant disequilibrium in the relationship between environment and policy is resolved as the configuration of relevant orientations—what we have termed the policy map—undergoes structural change. This change, it appears, is largely due to cognitive adjustments to environmental pressures. It serves to ease the inconsistencies between policy and environment so that a satisfactory equilibrium can be reestablished. Put differently, what is and what ought to be are dimensions of political behavior which constitute an interlocking series of events through time. In this moving manifold of events, policy emerges as a resultant of causal and purposive forcings which are themselves interrelated in ways that seem commensurate with ongoing policies—what has been termed the policy environment.

Chapter 30

Governing Structures and Policy Outcomes

Policy serves to solve public problems but often creates fresh ones in the process of governance. Bringing new industry and people into the city will strengthen its resource base and its ability to provide needed services; but there may be unintended and undesired side effects such as insufficient housing or crowded transportation. New problems, then, come to disturb the balance between the challenges posed by the urban environment and policy as a response. Cities vary in how successfully they achieve a desirable balance. In some cities public policy is out of phase with the urban challenge. These are large cities which still have policies appropriate to the conditions of the less complex environment of smaller communities. The 17 cities in which policy and challenges are in disequilibrium, the previous chapter has shown, are governed by councils with inconsistent policy maps. It is evidently difficult for the council to evolve a uniform and appropriate response to the stresses and strains of urbanization.

The inadequacy of their policy response to urban growth has not gone unnoticed by councils themselves, as can be seen in Table 30–1. It is in cities at time $0 + 1$, those which have yet to bring policy into line with urbanization, that councils rate the performance of their own or previous councils as unsuccessful. Nearly 2.5 times as many of these councils admit failure as claim success.[1]

---

[1] The question eliciting the relevant responses was: "As far as you can remember, at the time of your last campaign, did you consider the *previous* council as having been a pretty successful council, or not successful?" It is evident that

Table 30–1
Relationship Between Success
of Council and States of the Eco-Policy System

	Time 0	Time 0 + 1	Time 0 + 2
Council was judged to be successful	Less urban, less devel. (N = 35)	More urban, less devel. (N = 17)	More urban, more devel. (N = 24)
No	37%	71%	46%
Yes	63	29	54
	100%	100%	100%

They recognize that all is not well, that the council is (or has been) inadequate in adjusting public policy to the demands of prevailing conditions. One council reports itself very unsuccessful because it failed "to take stands on issues and allowed too much spot planning." Difficulties are traced to an incumbent "who forever blocked measures." In another unsuccessful council, the members are reputed to " lack political conviction, they were unable to stand up to the private demands made against them." In this city, it appears, parochial pressures prevented the council from starting the communitywide programs which might have brought policy to the point where it could effectively cope with the probems of urban growth. The inadequacy of councils (and their policy maps) can also be caused by selfish interests on the council: "Councilmen have been working for personal gain and not for the good of the community. There was a recall election and resignations from office before the council was able to get moving again."

A very different chord is struck by councils at time 0; they evaluate their performance in generally successful terms: "The men on the council have had long terms of service; they have much experience and they handle things in a fairly effective and quiet way."

---

the initial purpose of the question was to explore the reasons persons have for seeking a council seat and perhaps to ascertain the type of campaign waged. We did not then think that we would be interested in the type of analysis attempted in this chapter. Thus the question is not ideal for our immediate purposes, but it does serve to illustrate that very different self-evaluations are made in the different eco-policy states.

Another council reports that "we accomplished a lot and were able to pretty well keep the city the way we want it." Councils at time $0 + 2$ also express satisfaction with their programs and progress, but their answers reveal more sensitivity to the need for planning and responsiveness to changing conditions: "We had a good session and started to get many programs into action—like redevelopment and rehabilitation of neighborhoods that were run down." The importance of the makeup of the council to its success is stressed in the following remark: "We were very successful, we did things. We got several good new men on the council. We got redevelopment and the stadium moving. I think we have made a good start, and have made the council more respectable." Frequently councils at time $0 + 2$ attribute their success to planning for the future: "We laid the groundwork for the future by making important policy decisions affecting the city."

These self-judgments not only indicate that councils can admit failures as well as claim accomplishments; they also point to some of the political conditions which make policy either relevant or irrelevant to the challenges of the urban environment. Locating these political conditions in a more precise and systematic manner is the task of this chapter. It is a task which leads us to ask whether the politics of the council and the community are related in any meaningful way to the state of the eco-policy system.

The nature of this relationship, however, is complex. Because policy, as we interpret it, is a cumulative phenomenon through time that constitutes an environment of its own, it has a reciprocal impact on the structures and processes through which issues are formulated and decisions made. We stress the interdetermination of politics and policy because policy is not simply made and processed through political structures as antecedent conditions; political structures and processes are themselves the consequence of policy in different states of the eco-policy system. Political structures and processes, then, both influence and are influenced by the eco-policy system. Cause and effect are interdetermined: politics is as much a response to policy as policy is a response to political conditions.

The typical investigation of the relationship between politics and policy has not been altogether satisfactory. Specific decisions—

to escalate a war, to integrate public facilities, to undertake tax reform, and so forth—are traced to the preferences and activities, or nonactivities, of governing groups or citizens, especially as the latter become collective political actors in and through electoral and petitioning processes. The linkages between governors and governed are assumed to be interrelated with the substance of public policy. But the tracing of policy back to the policy intentions of governors and the preferences of citizens as expressed in voting choices or interest group demands, and especially the linkages between them, has proven enormously difficult. Several decades of refined and often sophisticated analysis have left unclear the basic issue: to what extent and under what conditions is public policy a reflection of political structures and processes, and to what extent and under what conditions are political structures and processes themselves consequences of cumulative and incremental policies?

We do not claim that we can answer these questions satisfactorily. But we propose to inquire into the relationship between politics and policy, as typically formulated, from a fresh perspective. If policy and the political activities of the council and/or community are separate and independent, this will be revealed by the lack of systematic relationship between the eco-policy system, on the one hand, and political activities as well as linkage processes, on the other hand. Conversely, if what is going on in the politics of the council and the community and what is going on in the policy sphere are mutually affecting each other, then the political process in councils, their selection and being petitioned as well as their representational behavior, should vary depending on the state of the eco-policy system.

This is not a test, then, of whether specific political structures or processes bring about particular public programs or of whether particular states of the eco-policy system have an impact on political structures and processes; but the analysis has a theoretical affinity with these questions. If politics and policy are unrelated using aggregated unit measures, there is reason to doubt whether the cumulation of specific policy-relevant activities on the part of governors and governed alike results in a policy environment reflective of the former's policy intentions or the latter's policy preferences—just as there is reason to doubt that the policy environment in turn has an impact on political structures and processes. If, however, there are interrelationships of a meaningful sort, there is reason to conclude that the council and/or the public do affect the standing decisions of the community, and that these standing decisions make for political structures, processes, and linkages that are themselves adaptations to the state of the eco-policy system. Although the test is indirect, it is relevant to a persistent question of democratic theory: do the political activities of the public and its elected representatives give shape and substance to policy, and is policy in turn conducive to the maintenance and strengthening of democratic processes?

The specific hypothesis is straightforward. The state of the eco-policy system of a city is more likely to be in disequilibrium if the structure of the council itself and the linkages between the council and its constituencies are impaired or ineffectual. That is, cities at time 0 + 1 will have more irregular or less effective structures and linkages than cities at either time 0 or time 0 + 2.

No illusions need be harbored about the inferential leaps involved in this hypothesis, but theorizing is not served by backing away from the hardest questions confronting the student of democratic politics. And though caution is called for, apologies are not. What we can do is to make clear some hidden assumptions. We assume that it is in the interest of the council and of citizens for policy and environmental challenges to be in balance. They are not in accord at time 0 + 1. If cities are in the disequilibrium state, then, councils and citizens are assumed either to have failed in recognizing their interests or to be unable to translate their preferences into a public policy conducive to coping with the environment. Either of these conditions can result from insufficient structural adaptation or faulty linkages, and their policy consequences can in turn aggravate antecedent structures and processes.

Criteria for Testing the Hypothesis

The logic of the hypothesis can be made more explicit by stating in advance the data patterns which would reject or confirm it.

Figure 30–1 shows two data patterns which indicate a lack of meaningful relationship between politics and policy. The X axis represents the three states of the eco-policy system, with the middle state, time $0 + 1$, being the disequilibrium state. The Y axis represents a given political condition. In Part A of the figure, each of the three eco-policy states is similarly characterized by the political condition. In fact, the political condition is not only independent of policy development but also of the urban environment. In Part B, the political condition in small cities is unlike that in large cities—that is, it may well be a response to level of urbanization; but policy development in the large cities has no relationship to the political condition—that is, policy as such has no reciprocal impact on the political response to urbanization. If either of these data patterns occurs in the analysis, we conclude that policy and politics are independent phenomena.

Figure 30–2 presents data patterns which confirm the hypothesis that political conditions in cities at time $0 + 1$ are affecting and being affected by a lack of equilibrium between policy development and urban environment. This is revealed in one of three ways. First, as shown in Part A, political conditions at time 0 and time $0 + 1$ are similar, despite the fact that the latter is located in large cities and the former in small cities. There is evidently an obstruction in the politics at time $0 + 1$ that prevents the emergence of a policy appropriate to the level of urbanization reached in that state of the eco-policy system; or, vice versa, failure of policy development may reinforce the political condition. Second, and a variation of this pattern, there can be a linear relationship between political condition and the three states of the eco-policy system, as shown in Part B of Figure 30–2. However, the political condition at time $0 + 1$ is lagging behind that found at time $0 + 2$. This lag pattern also confirms the hypothesis; though the political condition at time $0 + 1$ differs from that characteristic of time 0, whatever is going on in the politics at time $0 + 1$ has failed to bring policy in line with the requirements of the urban challenge as evidenced at time $0 + 2$. A final pattern is shown in Part C; this deviant pattern indicates serious disturbances in the political condition at time $0 + 1$. There is either an excess or absence of some political condition. A clear example of this was the data pattern

Figure 30–1

Hypothetical Data Patterns Showing
No Meaningful Relationship
Between Political Conditions and State
of Eco-Policy System

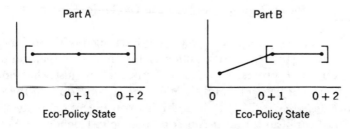

Part A Part B

Eco-Policy State Eco-Policy State

Figure 30–2
Hypothetical Data Patterns Showing
Political Conditions as Differing
in Meaningful Ways When Eco-Policy System
Is in Disequilibrium

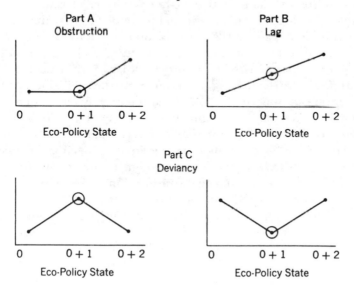

Part A
Obstruction

Part B
Lag

Eco-Policy State Eco-Policy State

Part C
Deviancy

Eco-Policy State Eco-Policy State

shown in Table 30–1; councils at time 0 + 1 deviated sharply from councils at time 0 and time 0 + 2 in reporting in undue proportions that they had not been successful as governing bodies.

Social Organization and the Eco-Policy System

It is through and by way of a governing body's social and political organization that policy is formulated. Organizational structures and processes of course cannot tell us just what policy decisions will be made, and the effect of organization on the substance of policy is likely to be so highly contingent on many other political conditions that it is best to assume independence. Yet, as noted in Part II, the council's internal structures and processes are adaptations to the exigencies of the external physical and social environment, and some are also especially conducive to internal adjustments. It is not unreasonable to assume, therefore, that even if no causal inferences in one or another direction can be made, the disequilibrated state of the eco-policy system at time 0 + 1 is interdependent with difficulties in the council's social and political organization. Table 30–2 tends to confirm the hypothesis that at least some of the council's internal structures and processes at time 0 + 1 are characterized by obstruction, lag, or deviancy.

Indeed, obstruction, lag, or deviancy are the rule rather than the exception at time 0 + 1 of the eco-policy system. Councils at time 0 + 1 and 0 + 2 are similar only in the proportions with the same governing style, nonpolarity in decisional structure, and collegial social climate. Policy-making in the direction one would expect in response to the urban challenge is evidently obstructed at time 0 + 1 by low internal stratification and low role differentiation; insofar as policy development, as at time 0 + 2, is a correlate of high stratification and role differentiation, an undue proportion of time 0 + 1 councils are deficient in these respects. Lag combined with deviancy in time 0 + 1 councils is especially marked in regard to decisional and interaction patterns. And just as a disproportionate number of time 0 + 1 councils are characterized by public interaction, so are a disproportionate number characterized by an impersonal social climate. Both types of political condition are symptomatic of tensions internal to the council that may well be consonant with the unresolved state of the eco-policy system at time $0 + 1$. The uncertain state of policy development at time $0 + 1$ may, in turn, feed back on the kind of political immobilism that is facilitated by a lack of privacy in interaction or an impersonal climate.

The configuration of distributions as a whole in Table 30–2 presents a structural profile that is only contingent and tendentious, but it is symptomatic of an unsettled state of affairs in the council's internal social and political organization if and when the policy context is in disequilibrium. The obstructions, lags, and deviancies in council social and political conditions at time $0 + 1$ suggest that the disequilibrated policy situation may be implicated in the structural profile that emerges. In turn, councils with these deficiencies in social and political organization can hardly be expected to be forceful and consistent policy-making bodies.

Constitutive Processes and the Eco-Policy System

The electorate's intervention in the policy process is infrequent and mostly cursory. Yet by electing their governors the voters have the opportunity to influence the direction of policy. Both in the act of voting and in the campaigning activities which elections call forth the citizen can establish links with the council. If electoral politics and policy are meaningfully interrelated, we should find that cities at time $0 + 1$ differ from those at time $0 + 2$. Parts A and B of Table 30–3 soundly reject this hypothesis. Neither in voter turnout nor in incumbent eviction, the two dimensions of the electoral context, are there noticeable differences. A similar lack of relationship characterizes campaign activities; irrespective of policy development, large-city councils look alike as regards campaign efforts, whether they enjoy campaigning or whether there are disliked groups active in the campaign. It appears that if there are disruptions in the linkage processes especially prominent at time $0 + 1$, these are not to be found in electoral activities.

Leadership selection, however, involves more than campaigns and elections. It begins at the point when candidates are being re-

Table 30–2
Relationships Between Indicators
of Council Social Organization and Three States
of the Eco-Policy System

	Time 0 Less urban, less devel. (N = 35)	*Time 0 + 1* More urban, less devel. (N = 17)	*Time 0 + 2* More urban, more devel. (N = 24)
A. *Governing Style*			
Benevolent	66%	53%	50%
Political/pragmatic	34	47	50
	100%	100%	100%
B. *Stratification*			
High	43%	41%	67%
Low	57	59	33
	100%	100%	100%
C. *Role Differentiation*			
High	43%	47%	75%
Low	57	53	25
	100%	100%	100%
D. *Decisional Structure*			
Unipolar	57%	35%	25%
Bipolar	29	18	25
Nonpolar	14	47	50
	100%	100%	100%
E. *Interaction*			
Political	26%	35%	54%
Public	31	41	33
Private	43	24	13
	100%	100%	100%

Table 30–2 (cont.)

	Time 0 Less urban, less devel. (N = 35)	Time 0 + 1 More urban, less devel. (N = 17)	Time 0 + 2 More urban, more devel. (N = 24)
F. Social Climate			
Collegial	60%	35%	38%
Impersonal	20	41	25
Antagonistic	20	24	37
	100%	100%	100%

NOTE: Broken line boxes enclosing times 0 + 1 and 0 + 2 show political condition at time 0 + 1 to be similar to political condition at time 0 + 2; broken line boxes enclosing times 0 and 0 + 1 show obstruction in political condition at time 0 + 1; broken line arrows show lag pattern for political condition at time 0 + 1; and solid line boxes show deviancy in political condition at time 0 + 1.

cruited and even prior to this when political careers are being differentially affected within the active stratum. Perhaps it is in these earlier recruitment stages that councils face differing political conditions depending on the eco-policy state. Parts C and D of Table 30–3 lend support to this supposition. There is, first, less career sponsorship at time 0 + 1 than at either of the other two eco-policy states. It should be recalled that career sponsorship is a way of insuring policy continuity despite leadership turnover. Though individual councilmen come and go, policies set in motion by their decisions and programs persist if their successors are generally committed to maintaining what has been started. It is, then, suggestive that half or more of the councils at both stable eco-policy states practice successful sponsorship whereas only about a third of the councils at time 0 + 1 are effective in perpetuating policy by the expedient of sponsoring careers.

Recruitment processes exhibit deviant patterns at time 0 + 1 in a second way. Two talent pools provide most of the new recruits for the councils: the auxiliary government and the civic leadership. A balanced recruitment process would select from both sources. This occurs more in cities with equilibrated eco-policy systems, whether the less developed policy states of the small cities or the more devel-

599

Table 30–3
Relationships Between Indicators
of Council Constitutive Processes
and Three States of the Eco-Policy System

	Time 0	*Time 0 + 1*	*Time 0 + 2*
	Less urban, less devel. (N = 35)	More urban, less devel. (N = 17)	More urban, more devel. (N = 24)
A. Electorate Behavior			
High voter turnout	67%	35%	33%
High incumbent eviction	42%	53%	54%
B. Campaign Activities			
High campaign effort	29%	71%	67%
High campaign enjoyment	43%	65%	50%
Disliked campaign groups	31%	53%	50%
C. Career Sponsorship			
Successfully practiced	54%	35%	50%
D. Recruitment Source			
More auxiliary government	40%	71%	50%
More civic leadership	43%	34%	46%
IMBALANCE INDEX*	−3%	37%	4%
E. Active Stratum Behavior			
High contesting	32%	82%	50%
Close races	42%	63%	46%

* Measures excess of one recruitment source over another.

oped policy states of the larger cities. But political imbalance prevails in cities where policy and environment are not in accord. And the direction of the imbalance is suggestive. Councils at time 0 + 1 are much more likely to be renewed from the auxiliary government than from the civic leadership. Thus, at the same time, they rely on persons already involved with ongoing public policies and they are shut off from sources of new ideas. The recruitment pattern is imbalanced and also encapsulated—the latter in the sense that there is a breakage in the relationship between council and immediate associates, on the one hand, and the active stratum, or some parts of it, on the other.

The data in Parts C and D of Table 30–3 are an important corrective to hasty conclusions drawn on the basis of the electoral and campaign data. Though no patterns emerge when we consider electoral and campaign activities, this evidently does not mean that leadership selection processes are unrelated to eco-policy development. Election data which inform us about the active stratum rather than the general electorate may be relevant.

Indeed, as Part E of Table 30–3 shows, the electoral situation at time 0 + 1 is more deviant than seemed to be the case on inspecting Parts A and B. The deviancy emerges in measures which reveal the activities of the active stratum rather than those of the general electorate. There are more contesters and more closely fought races under conditions of policy disequilibrium (time 0 + 1) than there are under either of the equilibrium conditions. Despite this, the eviction rate is not noticeably higher for cities at time 0 + 1 than for those at time 0 + 2. Something is evidently awry within the active stratum, or between it and the council. The politically competitive situation at election time is unable to increase the pace at which incumbents are removed. But before speculating about the meaning of this for the politics of cities at time 0 + 1, it is necessary to shift our attention from constitutive to petitioning processes.

Petitioning Processes and the Eco-Policy System

As the active stratum seems less integrated into constitutive processes where policy development is out of phase with environmental challenges, it is reasonable to conjecture that groups and organizations as instruments of the active stratum play different roles in the politics of cities at time $0 + 1$ and time $0 + 2$. Pertinent data are presented in Table 30–4.

Part A of the table shows that if group politics differ depending on the kind of balance in the eco-policy system, it is not because there is an impoverished group life or an excess of critical groups at time $0 + 1$. Nearly identical proportions of councils report an active group life and the presence of groups critical of the council and its policies in both stages of the eco-policy process. However, as Part B of Table 30–4 indicates, council behavior and attitudes toward the group process differ significantly at times $0 + 1$ and $0 + 2$. As pointed out in Chapter 16, council stands in this respect affect the type of partnership that emerges between governors and organizations. One should expect, therefore, that group politics would disturb the policy process in the disequilibrium state of the eco-policy system. But the data disconfirm this hypothesis. Although councils at time $0 + 1$ differ from councils at time $0 + 2$, they do so in exactly the opposite direction from what one might expect. Not only are more time $0 + 1$ councils favorably disposed toward the group process, but they seek to facilitate group access and actively mobilize groups in the governing process.

The data present a puzzle. Constitutive processes at time $0 + 1$ reveal weakened links between the active stratum and the councils which have yet to bring policy into line with the challenges of urbanization. But there do not seem to exist serious difficulties in the relationships between councils and interest groups at time $0 + 1$. If anything, councils in the disequilibrium situation seem to go out of their way to insure compatible working relationships with organizations. We can only speculate why this is so. The community's associational life may be dominated by older, more conservative persons, and these group leaders may cooperate with the council in keeping planning and amenities expenditures relatively low, so that the city remains less developed. There is no direct evidence on the conservatism or progressivism of groups, but the speculation makes sense when it is recalled that high office contesting and close races at time $0 + 1$ do not result in unusual voter participation or especially high rates of incumbent eviction. A few

Table 30–4
Relationships Between Indicators
of Council Petitioning Processes
and Three States of the Eco-Policy System

	Time 0	Time 0 + 1	Time 0 + 2
	Less urban, less devel. (N = 35)	More urban, less devel. (N = 17)	More urban, more devel. (N = 24)
A. Group Process			
Active group life	34%	59%	62%
Many critical groups	34%	53%	50%
B. Council Behavior Toward Groups			
Favorable to group process	49%	65%	42%
Facilitates group access	51%	71%	46%
Mobilizes groups	37%	65%	54%
C. Contact Patterns			
Reliance on informal contacts	66%	47%	33%
Spokesmen as linkages	43%	12%	71%

dominant organizations may team up with the council in order to maintain traditional ways of doing things despite urban growth. And the large, unorganized mass of citizens has not yet been activated. Thus the *political* pressure for change lags behind the *social and environmental* pressures for change.

If this inference is sound, it should be confirmed by the types of contact that councils have with their publics. Part C of Table 30–4 is suggestive. The data represent the lag pattern, more councils at time 0 + 1 than at time 0 + 2 rely on informal contacts with immediate associates and friends for information and advice. To practice a friends-and-neighbors brand of politics in the large city is to invite only limited contacts with the broader public.

Perhaps it is also to give favored access to groups reluctant to see many changes taking place.

The data on the role of spokesmen in the relationship between council and interest sectors in the community are even more revealing. Only two out of the 17 councils at time $0 + 1$ have the regularized institutional links to various sectors provided by spokesmen. This is astounding because the association of group activity and spokesmanship is generally substantial.[2] It is not easy, then, for councils simultaneously to report high group activity *and* few spokesmen. But this is exactly what occurs in cities at time $0 + 1$. Though there are no fewer groups here than in other large cities (Part A of Table 30–4), nearly seven times as many councils at time $0 + 2$ as at time $0 + 1$ have spokesmen linking them with broad segments of the public. Indeed, despite collaborative relationships with groups, councils at time $0 + 1$ have even fewer spokesmen than do councils in the small cities where less emphasis is placed on intermediaries who link council and public.

There is clearly something deficient in the linkage processes of those large cities whose councils cling to policies appropriate to the pre-growth years. Linkages are not disrupted across the full range of activities that connect governors and governed; most notably, no serious disturbances are evident in the specifically electoral behavior or group life of the community. But the linkages that are deviant form a consistent pattern, having primarily to do with the relationships a council might have with the active stratum and certain significant sectors in the community. Although the general electoral situation exhibits nothing unusual, there are numerous contesters attempting to gain council positions. And though there are many close races, incumbent eviction is not especially high. Furthermore, associational life appears to be well established and generally cooperative. Yet the pattern of contacts between council and public includes unusual reliance on informal contacts for large-city councils. And there is nearly a total absence of spokesmen who might link entire sectors of the public with the policy-making process.

---

[2] Of councils which report no spokesman, 29% say groups are active. For those which report one spokesman, 41% say groups are active; for those which report two spokesmen, 56% say groups are active; and for those which report three or more spokesmen, 75% say groups are active. The gamma is .43.

Representational Processes and the Eco-Policy System

Ruptured linkages with at least some components of the active stratum and the predominance of a politically apathetic electorate at time 0 + 1 should be reflected in the council's representational behavior. For instance, time 0 + 1 councils should differ in their images of the public from councils in either of the two other eco-policy states. As Part A of Table 30–5 shows, the distributions of councils support the hypothesis.

Fewer time 0 + 1 than time 0 + 2 councils, and only slightly more than time 0 councils, view the public as being interested in city affairs; but more time 0 + 1 than time 0 + 2 councils, though slightly fewer than time 0 councils, feel that their relations with the public are well under control. If, in these respects, time 0 + 1 councils more resemble time 0 councils than time 0 + 2 councils, they resemble the latter more in that relatively few (29 percent and 21 percent, respectively) see agreement between their own conception of how to manage city affairs and how the public views these matters. In this respect, then, time 0 + 1 councils resemble other large-city councils which face a multitude of conflicting demands and challenges. And insofar as time 0 + 1 councils differ from time 0 councils, one should not expect agreement between the council and the public, given the laggard response to environmental challenges fashioned in time 0 + 1 councils; but despite the fact that few sense agreement, the public is evidently not enough interested or agitated to do anything about it.

How the council perceives its relations with the public is an important aspect of its representational stance, yet it is difficult to explain how such perceptions come about, especially in the disequilibrium situation of the eco-policy process. Part B of Table 30–5 provides an indirect clue. The public is not very issue-oriented in what it expects from the representative body. An excessive proportion of the time 0 + 1 councils (65 percent) report that the public prefers the council to spend its time running errands. This corroborates the image of the public as relatively uninterested in city affairs and as easily managed. Pressures from the public are experienced as requests for personal services or particular errands rather than as organized demands for solving policy issues. If this is

Table 30–5

Relationships Between Indicators
of Council Representational Processes
and Three States of the Eco-Policy System

	Time 0	*Time 0 + 1*	*Time 0 + 2*
	Less urban, less devel. (N = 35)	More urban, less devel. (N = 17)	More urban, more devel. (N = 24)
A. *Images of Public*			
Interested in city affairs	40%	47%	67%
Relations with public seen as under control	63%	53%	29%
Public seen as in agreement	56%	29%	21%
B. *Perceived Public Preferences*			
Council to run errands	49%	65%	50%
Council to deal in issues	51%	35%	50%
	100%	100%	100%
C. *Representational Style*			
High trustee orientation	49%	77%	62%
Low trustee orientation	51	23	38
	100%	100%	100%
D. *Response Style*			
Nonresponsive	52%	41%	37%
Responsive to *ad hoc* groups	31	47	21
Responsive to attentive publics	17	12	42
	100%	100%	100%

so, then it is not surprising (as Part C of Table 30–5 shows) that an unusually large proportion of time $0 + 1$ councils, confronting these conditions, adhere to the trustee orientation in their representational style. The paternalism inherent in this orientation is conducive to slowing the rate of policy response to urbanization.

It remains only to discover whether different representational responses evolve in the varying states of the eco-policy process. It will be recalled that a responsive relationship between council and public may or may not emerge as a systemic phenomenon; if it does emerge, councils may be either sensitive to transitory and specialized pressures from *ad hoc* groups or to the more permanent interest clusters of the attentive public. Part D of Table 30–5 presents the data.

While large-city councils are more likely to be responsive than small-city councils, comparison of time $0 + 1$ and time $0 + 2$ councils indicates that the state of policy development influences the nature of responsiveness under conditions of environmental complexity. Councils at time $0 + 1$ are especially responsive to *ad hoc* pressure groups and correspondingly less responsive to stable, attentive publics. Where policy is in accord with environmental challenges, as at time $0 + 2$, twice as many councils are responsive to attentive publics as to *ad hoc* groups. Where policy does not meet urban challenges, as at time $0 + 1$, four times as many councils are responsive to *ad hoc* pressures as to attentive publics.

Their representational response style at time $0 + 1$ is consonant with the other characteristics of councils in the disequilibrium state of the eco-policy system. Councils' internal social and political organization is deficient. Their recruitment base is narrow and restricted, and their sources of information and advice about community needs are limited and parochial. Broad interest clusters are not visible in the politics at time $0 + 1$; they neither assert themselves through constitutive processes nor form links with the council through intermediary petitioning processes. Insofar as the general public makes demands on the council, they are for particularized services. What is missing at time $0 + 1$, but appears to be generally present at time $0 + 2$, is a broadly based and articulate political force which calls for both adaptation to and control of the environmental conditions created by increasing urbanization. If an attentive public does not intervene in the policy-making process by making relevant claims, the council finds itself in the position of having to placate a variety of specialized and temporary pressures. The response style is not conducive to forceful and effective policy-making in terms of the city's needs.

This conclusion is supported by the data presented in Table 30–6. The table shows the correlation coefficients for the relationships between response style and task-role orientation in each of the three states of the eco-policy system. A negative association means that the more responsive the council, the less likely is it to have a pro-development policy position and a task orientation that stresses the need for change.

Responsiveness at time $0 + 1$, in contrast to the two equilibrium states of the eco-policy system, implies a rejection of development-oriented policies. This result conforms with the previous speculation that councils at time $0 + 1$ may be collaborating with conservative interests in the community. Insofar as they are responsive at all to attentive publics, they are not likely to stress development as a policy. Moreover, as the second set of coefficients shows, respon-

Table 30–6
Correlation Coefficients for Relationships
Between Response Style, Policy Position,
and Task-Role Orientation in Three States
of the Eco-Policy System

Relationship between:	Time 0 Less urban, less devel.	Time 0 + 1 More urban, less devel.	Time 0 + 2 More urban, more devel.
Response style[1] and policy position[2]	.34	−.41	.45
Response style and task orientation[3]	−.08	−.33	.22

[1] Scale order: responsive to attentive publics > responsive to *ad hoc* pressures > nonresponsive.
[2] Scale order: development (+), amenities (−).
[3] Scale order: program > adapt > maintain (from most to least change-oriented).

sive councils at time 0 + 1 avoid a programmatic orientation and lean toward the maintaining role. But where policy has been adjusted to the increased urban challenge, as at time 0 + 2, it is the responsive councils which tend to choose development rather than amenities as their policy position and which define their task as planning for the city future. These findings give added significance to the earlier interpretation that inconsistent internal organization and lack of broadly based, organized pressures might account for the laggard policy development in some of the large cities.

Conclusion

Policy as a response to environmental challenges varies with the social and physical complexity of the environment. Policies stem from official programs and political decisions, or nondecisions, setting in motion behavioral regularities among both governors and governed which cumulate over time into the community's standing decisions which in turn constitute its policy environment. By identifying some cities in which policy is out of step with environmental challenges, it was possible to explore some political structures and processes—but only some—which affect policy-making and its outcomes. One set of factors is internal to the governing group, including its policy map and organizational adaptation. A second set of factors is external and refers to the various linkages, social and symbolic, which connect governors and governed.

In some respects, the policy environments of cities in which policy development has not been brought into line with the challenges of urbanization may be classical examples of decisional failure by governors and governed alike. Evidently, in the absence of political pressures for change, councils are either unwilling or unable to reorient old programs and to invest in new ones. Policy remains essentially what it was when the city was small and environmental challenges less urgent. Political as well as environmental pressures seem necessary to bring about substantial changes in public policy. Even challenges by counterelites may be insuf-

ficient and make little difference. Not until broader segments of
the public are mobilized, through elections or group petitioning
activities, do the governors redirect the policies of the community.
Organizationally adaptive, constitutive, petitioning, and representational processes are clearly germane to the formulation of
public policy. Policy emerges from the interactions between governors and governed just as it emerges from the governing group's
policy maps and internal organizational relationships. In turn,
existing political structures and processes may be reinforced by
the inertia prevailing in the eco-policy system. The flow of cause
and effect in the interchanges between politics and policy is interdeterminate and labyrinthine.

Epilogue:
The Labyrinth
of Governance

The most one can hope for on completing a piece of research is that ignorance has thereby been reduced and knowledge advanced. Whatever, the task of research remains unfinished. This has been a study of democratic governance in a particular place at a particular time. Even if it were possible to identify all the relevant variables, and even if our tools of inquiry were perfect, democratic governance would prove elusive as a topic of investigation. The more we know and the more reliably we know it, the more complex will democratic governance appear to be. For one thing, there is continuous change in the assumptions, ways, and goals of democratic governance; but there is no adequate theory of political change, and the empirical study of change remains primitive.

For another, the ways of democratic governance are labyrinthine. We use the metaphor of the labyrinth self-consciously. Metaphors have disadvantages and advantages when used in theories about human relations. They are disadvantageous because, as the history of social and political thought has amply shown, they can be misleading. But metaphors can also be useful because they may point toward a new reality, before only dimly seen.

We find the metaphor of governance as a labyrinth preferable to other metaphors used in politics. A labyrinth is an enclosure with many entrances and exits. Its layout consists of a maze of pathways, but the pathways can be marked by signs that help one to avoid false moves and lead the seeker where he wants to go. If the paths are not marked, trial and error may yet lead to discovery and the long way back. Democratic governance resembles the labyrinth. The labyrinth has walls that serve as boundaries but are more or less porous; it has major arteries and places of assembly but also byways, detours, nooks, and crannies. Passing through the labyrinth may take more or less time, depending on the continuities and discontinuities in the journey occasioned by what is known or unknown about the terrain.

There are a great number of variations in the behavior of governors and governed as they seek to adapt themselves in and to the maze of governance, as they seek to establish linkages, and as they seek to organize and regulate collective existence through policies that make the community livable. It is not helpful to reduce the maze of democratic governance to a simple formula. There are no simplistic solutions to the problems arising out of the need for adapting to or controlling the internal and external environments; for establishing linkages between those who inhabit the governmental labyrinth regularly (the active stratum and the governors) and those who visit only occasionally (the electorate) or not at all; or for settling differences, disagreements, and conflicts through responsive behavior on the part of the governors and supportive behavior on the part of the governed.

Our analysis has been alternatively marginal, correlational, multivariate, causal, contextual, or configurative, depending on what the data seemed to permit and what our theoretical notions called for. We behaved as analysts very much like citizens trying to find their way through the labyrinth. "Muddling through" may not be the best or most rational way of governing, but it seems to be the way in which democratic governance solves its problems; the metaphor or model of the labyrinth appears to be the most appropriate way to describe what happens in democracies.

We conclude this epilogue with three observations in the nature of a prologue. First, although Western thought and experience rightly celebrate the individual as the paragon of human accomplishment, it has in fact been the group, which, from the Greeks on down, has been the effective agent of political destinies. Despite the emphasis on the hero in history as the mover and shaker, there is reason to believe that the group as an instrumentality of governance is superior to the individual, especially in democracies, where, by definition, the "consent of the governed" is the ultimate criterion of legitimacy. The discovery of the group as something worthy of inquiry in its own right, apart from the individuals who compose it, has been one of the most significant contributions that modern social science has made to the understanding of human affairs.

Second, the history of mankind can be written as the history of its struggle with the environment, both the man-made and the natural environments. In this struggle the institutions of governance play a significant role. However one evaluates that role, and in today's world the evaluation is more likely to be negative than positive, there is no other way to mediate the struggle except through governance. It is more than likely that in the future, under the conditions of the postindustrial or technetronic era, governance will play an even greater role in the solution of man-milieu relationships. The control of the technological wonders or horrors in store for us is likely to remain in the hands of the governing few.

Finally, therefore, as long as the few govern the many, the problem of the distance between governors and governed will continue to be high on the agenda of theorizing about democracy. But theoretical defense of democracy is not enough. What is needed, and what we hope to contribute to in this work, is empirical inquiry into how the institutions of representative democracy work, and especially inquiry into the conditions under which the governors and governed are linked so that political responsiveness and responsibility are obtained. We take it for granted that the institutions of representative democracy in the United States will withstand the challenges of the new technological age, adapt to them, and control them. We do not take it for granted that these institutions always work in the ways set forth by democratic theory. But we believe that the problems of democratic governance cannot be wished away by slogans of popular sovereignty or participatory democracy. If muddle through we must, at least be it enlightened by theory tested in the crucible of empirical research.

Appendixes

Appendix A

The Research Project and the Data

This Appendix provides a brief *description* of the *context* for the analyses and interpretations reported in this and the other monographs of *The Urban Governors* series. These analyses and interpretations are grounded in or inspired by data collected at a specific "point" in time—actually over a period of some eighteen months, from January 1966 to June 1967—in a particular region of the United States. The data are "representative," therefore, in only a very limited sense. Although none of the writers of each monograph would claim greater universality for his interpretations than the data warrant, the temptation on a reader's part to forget or ignore the limitations of a clearly bounded space-time manifold is always present. The reader is entitled, therefore, to information about the setting of each study, if only for comparison with settings which are more familiar to him and which serve as his own frames of reference.

Needless to say, we cannot describe here the San Francisco Bay metropolitan region, its cities, or its people in their full richness and diversity. Clearly, only certain aspects of the environment are relevant, and this relevance must be determined by the objectives of the particular research project in which we were engaged. Before presenting the relevant context, therefore, the research project itself will be described in brief outline.

The City Council Research Project

As mentioned already in the Preface, the Project was a research and training program with as many as twelve participants working together at one time. Because the Project was intended, from the beginning, to maximize the independent research creativity of each participant, the research design had to be sufficiently flexible to permit the collection of data which would satisfy each Project member's research concerns. The monographs in this series reflect the heterogeneity of the research interests which found their way into the Project. At the same time, each researcher was necessarily limited by the Project's overall objective, which was, throughout, to gather data which would shed light on the city council as a small political decision-making group.

Our interest in the city council as a decision-making group stemmed from prior research on governance through democratic legislative processes. Political scientists have been traditionally concerned with the variety of "influences," external to the legislative body as well as internal, that shape both the legislative process and the legislative product. It was an assumption of the research that these influences could be studied more intensively in the case of small bodies than in the case of larger ones, like state legislatures or Congress, that already have been widely investigated. In particular, it was assumed that a decision-making body is both the sum of its parts and greater than the sum of its parts. Therefore, both the council as a collective unit and the councilman as an individual unit could be selected for the purpose of analysis. In the present book the council as such serves as the unit of analysis. In the accompanying monographs, individual councilmen primarily serve as the units.

Convenience apart, the choice of the universe to be studied was dictated by the research objective. On the one hand, we needed a sufficiently large number of decision-making groups to permit systematic, quantitative, and genuinely comparative analyses at the group level. On the other hand, we needed a universe in which "influences" on the individual decision-maker and the decision-making group could be studied in a relatively uniform context.

In particular, we sought a universe which provided a basic environmental, political, and legal uniformity against which city-by-city differences could be appraised. We therefore decided on a single metropolitan region in a single state in which we could assume certain constants to be present—such as *relative* economic growth, similar institutional arrangements and political patterns, identical state statutory requirements, and so on.

The price paid for this research design should be obvious. The San Francisco Bay metropolitan region is quite unlike any other metropolitan region, including even the Los Angeles metropolitan area, and it differs significantly from the Chicago, Boston, or New York metropolitan complexes. Undoubtedly, metropolitan regions, despite internal differences, can be compared as ecological units in their own right. But as our units of analysis are individual or collective decision-makers in the cities of a particular, and in many respects internally unique, region, the parameters imposed on our data by the choice of the San Francisco Bay metropolitan area recommend the greatest caution in extending, whether by analogy or inference, our findings to councils or councilmen in other metropolitan regions of other states.

All of this is not to say that particular analyses enlightened by theoretical concerns of a general nature cannot be absorbed into the growing body of political science knowledge. The City Council Research Project consciously built on previous research in other settings, seeking to identify and measure influences that have an impact on legislative processes and legislative products. The effect of the role orientations of councilmen with regard to their constituents, interest groups, or administrative officials may be compared with the effect of parallel orientations in larger legislative bodies. Their socialization and recruitment experiences, their differing styles of representational behavior, or their political strategies are probably influences not unlike those found elsewhere. Similarly, the relationships among individuals in a small group and the norms guiding their conduct may be compared with equivalent patterns in larger legislative bodies. Perceptions of the wider metropolitan environment and its problems, on the one hand, and of the city environment and its problems, on the other hand, and how these perceptions affect council behavior and outputs are of general theoretical interest. In terms of the developing theory of legislative behavior and process, therefore, the data collected by the Project and utilized in the monographs of this series have an import that transcends the boundaries of the particular metropolitan region in which they were collected.

The Research Context

San Francisco and its neighboring eight counties have experienced an extraordinary population growth rate since the end of World War II. Many of the wartime production workers and military personnel who traveled to or through this region decided to settle here permanently in the postwar years; they and thousands of others were attracted by the moderate year-round climate, several outstanding universities, closeness to the Pacific Ocean and its related harbors, headquarters for hundreds of West Coast branches of national firms, and, of course, the delightful charm of San Francisco itself. Other resources and assets exist in abundance: inviting ski resorts and redwood parks are within short driving distance; hundreds of miles of ocean lie to the immediate west; mile after mile of grape vineyards landscape the nearby Livermore and Napa valleys. All of these, linked by the vast San Francisco Bay and its famous bridges, make this one of the nation's most distinctive and popular metropolitan regions.

Larger than the state of Connecticut and almost as large as New Jersey and Massachusetts combined, this nine-county region now houses four million people. At the time of the study, ninety cities and at least five hundred special districts served its residents.

As has been pointed out already, no claim can be made that the San Francisco Bay region is typical of other metropolitan areas; indeed, it differs considerably on a number of indicators. Unlike most of the other sizable metropolitan regions, the Bay region has experienced its major sustained population boom in the 1950s and 1960s. This metropolitan area is also atypical in that it has not one major central city but three—namely, San Francisco, Oakland, and San Jose. And while San Francisco continues to be the "hub" and the region's dominant city, Oakland and San Jose are rival economic and civic centers. San Jose, moreover, anticipates that its population will triple to nearly a million people in the next twenty years. Of additional interest is the fact that this region has pioneered in the creation of one of the nation's prototypes of federated urban governmental structures. Its Association of Bay Area Governments, organized in 1961, has won national attention as one of the first metropolitan councils of local governments.

Although in many respects unlike other metropolitan regions, the San Francisco Bay region resembles some in the great diversity among its cities. Omitting San Francisco proper, 1965 city populations ranged from 310 to 385,700. Population densities in 1965 ranged from 71 to 12,262 persons per square mile. The rate of population growth between 1960 and 1965 ranged from zero to 204 percent. Median family incomes ranged from $3,582 to $23,300, and percentage nonwhite from 0.1 to 26.4.

Institutionally, the governments of the cities in the San Francisco Bay region are predominantly of the council-manager or council-administrator form, although some of the very small cities may rely on the chief engineer rather than on a manager or administrator. Cities may be either of the "charter" or "general law" type. Charter cities differ from general law cities in having greater control over election laws, the size of their councils, the pay of municipal officers, and tax rate limitations. General law cities have five councilmen, while charter cities may have more than this number. Among the cities included in the research, the number of councilmen per city ranged from five to thirteen.

All local officials in California, including, of course, those interviewed in the City Council Research Project, are elected under a nonpartisan system. With a few exceptions, councilmen run at large and against the entire field of candidates. In five cities there is a modified district election plan in which candidates stand in a particular district but all voters cast ballots for any candidate. Ten cities elect the mayor separately; in the remaining cities the mayor is either the candidate receiving the highest number of votes or is selected by vote of the council.

Council candidates must have been residents of the community

Map A–1
Bay Area Place Names

N

Cloverdale

Gualala R.

Russian R.

SONOMA

Healdsburg

Fort Ross

Guerneville

Calistoga

Lake Berryessa

St. Helena

NAPA

Sebastopol

Santa Rosa

Bodega Bay

Glen Ellen

Napa R.

Dixon

Vacaville

SOLANO

Petaluma

Tomales Bay

Sonoma

Napa

Fairfield

Drakes Bay

MARIN

San Rafael

San Pablo Bay

Vallejo

Benicia

Sulsun Bay

Rio Vista

Bolinas

MT. TAMALPAIS

Port Costa

Richmond

Martinez

Pittsburg

Antioch

Sausalito

Berkeley

Concord

Orinda

CONTRA

Lafayette

Walnut Creek

Brentwood

San Francisco

S.F.

Oakland

Alameda

Moraga

Alamo

Danville

MT. DIABLO

COSTA

Byron

Daly City

S. San Francisco

San Leandro

Hayward

Pacifica

San Mateo

Union City

Livermore

Pleasanton

Half Moon Bay

SAN

Redwood City

Fremont

ALAMEDA

MATEO

Palo Alto

Pescadero

Santa Clara

San Jose

SANTA

Big Basin

San Lorenzo R.

Saratoga

Los Gatos

Guadalupe R.

MT. HAMILTON

CLARA

SANTA

Morgan Hill

Santa Cruz

CRUZ

Gilroy

Monterey Bay

Watsonville

0   5   10   20   30
Miles

622

for at least one year prior to their election. For the most part they are elected to serve four-year terms, though charter cities may vary this. Only three cities have tenure limitations. The great majority of councilmen receive no compensation for their services or, if any, only a token compensation to cover expenses. For most, the council is a part-time activity.

The powers of the city councilmen may be exercised only as a group; that is, individual councilmen have no power to act alone. The council may meet only at duly convened public meetings and at a place designated by ordinance. Council meetings must be regularly scheduled and held no less than once a month, but when council action is required between regularly scheduled meetings, the statutes allow procedures for calling special meetings. The "Brown Act," passed in 1953 and in effect during the time our interviewing took place, requires all council meetings to be public and publicized, except for executive sessions on personnel matters.

The Data Bases

Five sets of data were generated or systematized by the Project. First, data from the U.S. Census of Population for 1960 and estimates for 1965 served a variety of analytical purposes. Because the data included in the census and its categories are well known, we need not say more about this data set. Specific uses made of census data and the rationale for such uses are explained in each monograph wherever appropriate. All members of the research team were involved in readying the census data for analysis.

Second, data concerning city income, resources, and expenditures were available in the State Controller's *Annual Report of Financial Transactions Concerning Cities of California*. These reports include breakdowns which are suitable for comparative analysis of Bay region cities for the years 1958–1959 through 1965–1966. How the measures derived from this data set were handled is described in appropriate places of the monograph series where the data are used. Robert Eyestone was largely responsible for preparing this data set.

Third, local election data over a ten-year period, 1956 through 1966, were collected by Gordon Black, with the collaboration of

Willis D. Hawley of the Institute of Governmental Studies, University of California, Berkeley. These data were obtained directly from the various cities, and they include the voting returns for each of five elections in each city, the registration figures for the city at each election period, and a variety of facts about individual candidates. These facts include incumbency, partisan affiliation, length of time in office, and the manner in which the incumbents gained office, whether by appointment or by election. A number of measures were constructed from these data, including measures of competition, partisan composition, voluntary retirement, forced turnover, and so forth. Descriptions of these measures can be found in the monographs which employ them.

Fourth and fifth, the core of the data on which the analyses are based came from interviews with city councilmen or from self-administered questionnaires filled out by councilmen. These two data sets need more detailed exposition.

1. Interview Data

With the exception of a city incorporated while the field work was under way (Yountville) and the city of San Francisco itself, interviews were sought with 488 city councilmen holding office in all the other eighty-nine cities of the San Francisco Bay Area. Although interviews were held with some members of the board of supervisors of the city-county of San Francisco, these interviews are not used in this and the other monographs owing to the city's unique governmental structure and the highly professionalized nature of its legislative body.

In two of the eighty-nine cities (Millbrae and Emeryville), all councilmen refused to be interviewed. In the remaining eighty-seven cities, 435 incumbent councilmen were interviewed. This constitutes 89 percent of the target population or 91 percent of the 478 councilmen from the eighty-seven cities which cooperated in the study. The interviews were conducted by members of the research team or by professional interviewers. Most of the respondents were interviewed in their homes, places of business, or city hall offices. All of them had been invited to visit the Stanford campus, and a small number accepted the invitation and were interviewed there.

Although the bulk of the interviewing was done between January and April 1966, some councilmen were interviewed as late as June 1967. The interview schedule was an extensive one. It included some 165 major open-end questions and additional probes ranging over a wide variety of topics. Every effort was made to record verbatim the comments which most councilmen supplied in abundance. The interviews lasted from two to five hours or longer and averaged about three hours. Parts of the interview schedule were pretested as early as 1962 and as late as 1965, with councilmen in the metropolitan region itself and with councilmen in a neighboring county.

The interview data were coded by members of the research team responsible for particular analyses. The coded data were recorded on seventeen machine-readable storage cards. They will be made available for secondary analysis on tape in due time, upon completion of all studies in *The Urban Governors* series.

2. Questionnaire

In addition to the interview, each respondent was asked to fill out a questionnaire made up of closed questions. These included a set of thirty-five checklist items, two pages of biographical items, and a set of fifty-eight agree-disagree attitude items. The strategy of self-administered questionnaires was dictated by the length of the interview, for, in spite of its length, the data needs of the team members could not be satisfied by the interview instrument alone.

Table A–1
Interview Success and Failure

	Number of councils	Number of councilmen
Interview targets	89	488
Access refused by entire council	—2	—10
Councils in which only three or fewer members were interviewed	—5	—13
Other interview failure	—	—30
Available for analysis	82	435
Percentage of success	92%	89%

The questionnaires were left with each respondent by the interviewer. If at all possible, interviewers were instructed to have the questionnaires filled out by the respondent immediately upon completion of the interview, but the length of the interview often did not permit this, and respondents were then asked to return the questionnaires by mail. As a result, there was some loss of potential data because councilmen neglected to return the completed forms. Nevertheless, of the 435 councilmen who were interviewed, 365, or 84 percent, completed the questionnaires. Perhaps the greatest strategic mistake in this procedure was our failure to administer the biographical and demographic background items as part of the interview.

The Sample: A Brief Profile

Although individual demographic data for all 435 councilmen who were interviewed are not available, our sample of 365 for which the data are at hand is probably representative. We shall present, therefore, a brief profile of these respondents.

On the average, San Francisco Bay region councilmen are well educated and have comfortable incomes (see Figure A–1). They are engaged in either business or professional activities. Table A–2 shows the principal lines of work of those council members who are not retired or housewives.

Table A–2
Principal Employment of City Councilmen
(Of Employed Councilmen) (N = 351)

Manufacturing, utilities	22%
Banking, insurance, accountancy	21
Business, commerce, real estate	13
Law	10
Construction, trucking	16
Civil service, public administration	14
Agriculture	4
	100%

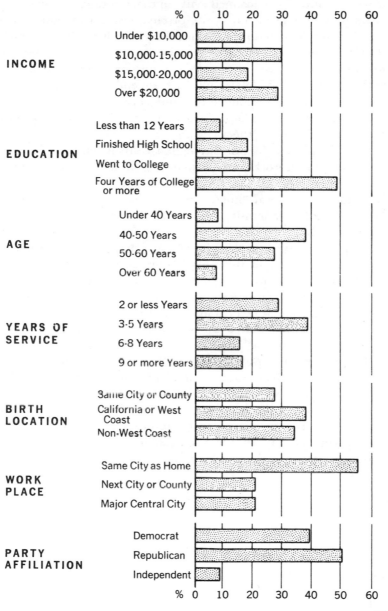

Figure A–1
Background Profile of San Francisco Bay Region
City Councilmen

Councilmen in the Bay region are predominantly middle-aged, usually coming to the council while in their forties or around fifty years of age. The turnover rate of city councilman positions is relatively high, with only a few members staying in office for more than three or four terms. The data in Figure A–1 show that close to 70 percent of the councilmen came into office for the first time within the previous five years. In open-end conversations with councilmen, many responded that they looked upon the job as a community service, as something that should be rotated among the local activists like themselves.

Fifty-six percent of the Bay region councilmen who are currently employed work in their home community, the community on whose city council they serve. This is not too surprising, for it is customary for local "home town" businessmen and lawyers to be involved in community service and civic undertakings, which often constitute the chief recruitment vehicle for the identification of city political leadership. While a majority of the councilmen are employed in their local communities, it is instructive to note that most of the councilmen are not natives of their present city or county. Most, however, are California or West Coast natives. Approximately a third moved to the Bay region from other parts of the United States, with about a dozen having been born in some other country.

The background profile data also indicate that Republicans outnumber the Democrats by an 11 percent margin in the Bay region's nonpartisan city council posts, although during recent years the party registration rates for the general electorate have favored the Democratic party in approximately a three-to-two ratio. Nine percent of the councilmen identify themselves as Independents.

Appendix B

Indices and Measures

B2.1 *The Gamma Statistic*

Social scientists are disagreed on the kind of statistics most appropriate to the analysis of their data. Some hold that the "poorer" and "softer" the data base, the more will highly sophisticated statistical analysis yield satisfying results—satisfying, presumably, in terms of some hypothesis being tested. We do not accept this view. It seems to us that the choice of a statistical measure should be determined by the nature of the data at hand and the task of measurement to be performed. Similarly, the evaluation of the statistical result cannot be absolute by comparison with other statistical measures. In the case of a correlation coefficient, for instance, the relative strength of a relationship should be assessed in terms of the upper and lower limits of the coefficient's values as they emerge in the total set of data or perhaps in a given subset of data. This is all the more important if, as in this research, the nature and quality of the data are very diverse, ranging from exceptionally "soft" to very "hard" variables.

Apart from inspection of percentage distributions, the measure of association most frequently used will be Goodman and Kruskal's *gamma*. This measure recommends itself for a number of reasons. First, as an elaboration of Yule's Q statistic for 2×2 tables, it is a symmetric measure that is responsive to one-way association; it varies between -1 and $+1$; and it has clear conceptual meaning: the proportion of positive pairs in the cross-tabulation less the proportion of negative pairs.[1] As such, gamma is a descriptive measure of association that only summarizes the data and adds little to the substantive interpretation of the findings—that is, it says nothing that cannot be seen through direct inspection of the data. It is a kind of average of a number of percentage differences in a multivariate table. But, in contrast to inspection of percentage differences, it makes possible *comparative* rankings of the degrees to which different combinations of variables are related. It is, therefore, a statistical tool well suited to comparative analysis.

Second, although gamma assumes ordinality, it is applicable to weakly ordered measures as well. This is so because no corrections need be made for ties as these are practically "invisible" when the association deals only with the presence or absence of a property in the cross-tabulation. Being flexible, gamma indicates both positive and negative associations between variables and can be directly interpreted. Moreover, in tables larger than 2×2, small cell frequencies are no obstacle to its computation.[2]

Third, gamma can be used to test a hypothesis because it assumes that in a bivariate relationship one value or "force" pulls the association in the direction of the hypothesis, while the second pulls it in the opposite direction. The cross-product of these pulls is, then, the measure of association. If the two forces are equal, there is no relationship. This is most evident in 2×2 tables, but, as Galtung points out, the logic of the 2×2 table can be generalized to more complex tables because it is always the same: "this measure of correlation is what we get when we *add* the conditions that an hypothesis of a relation between two ordinal variables shall hold in a set of four-fold tables that can be formed from the original table. . . ."[3]

The major weakness of gamma is that it can be $+1$ or -1 even if there is not maximum predictability, that is, if one variable takes only one value and the other variable takes two or more values. In that case, the cell frequency on one value for one vari-

[1] See Robert S. Weiss, *Statistics in Social Research* (New York: John Wiley and Sons, 1968), pp. 198–201.
[2] See Dean J. Champion, *Basic Statistics for Social Research* (Scranton, Pa.: Chandler Publishing Company, 1970), p. 223.
[3] Johan Galtung, *Theory and Methods of Social Research* (New York: Columbia University Press, 1969), pp. 195–196.

able is zero. This, however, is empirically more likely to occur in 2 × 2 tables than in tables of higher dimension. In a few instances where it occurred and where a coefficient of plus or minus one would have been misleading, we used the *phi* coefficient, which is not subject to this weakness. Of course, as the values of phi are generally lower than those obtained for gamma, the two measures are not directly comparable though the *order* of their magnitudes is the same.

In interpreting gamma, we generally accepted the following criteria:

If gamma is:	*Interpretation is:*
.00 — .09	Zero or near-zero
.10 — .24	Weak
.25 — .39	Moderate
.40 — .54	Substantial
.55 — .69	Strong
.70 — .99	Very strong

To test for spuriousness or, as in Chapter 28, to build a causal model, the relationships among variables were subjected to a "partial gamma" technique by controlling for the effect of prior variables in the chain. Davis has defined the partial gamma coefficient as "how much more probable it is to get like than unlike orders in measures A and B, when pairs of individuals [or other units being measured, H.E. & K.P.] differing on A and on B and tied on C but unselected on any other measure [are] chosen at random from the population."[4]

We have not subjected the data to significance tests because we are dealing with a near-universe of the cases as defined by the research locale.

B4.1 *Sociometric Index of Expansiveness*

This index measures the pervasiveness or incidence of a social-relational property in the group as a whole; it does not identify

---

[4] See James A. Davis, "A Partial Coefficient for Goodman and Kruskal's Gamma," *Journal of the American Statistical Association* 62 (March 1967): 189–193, at 190.

or measure the structure of social relations. Its virtue is that it permits group members to nominate as many other persons as they wish. The measure is labeled "expansiveness" by Charles H. Proctor and Charles P. Loomis, "Analysis of Sociometric Data," in Marie Jahoda, Morton Deutsch, and Stuart W. Cook, *Research Methods in Social Relations* (New York: Dryden, 1951), Vol. II, p. 572. The formula:

$$E = \frac{N}{M}, \text{ where}$$

E = expansiveness,

N = the number of all nominations made in the group, and

M = the number of all members (size of group).

Although the index appears to be very simple, it actually hides other properties. It takes account of the number of individuals named, regardless of the number of individual choices they received, and the average choices made in the group:

$$\frac{N}{M} = \frac{P}{M} \times \frac{N}{P}, \text{ where}$$

P = the number of individual persons named.

B4.2 *Stratification Index*

The stratification index measures the sum of the "distances" that separate one group member from the next in terms of the total nominations each received on the six measures of cosponsorship, oppositional potential, opinion leadership, expertise, respect, and friendship. If an individual's "star status" is determined by the number of nominations he received on the six measures compared with the number of nominations he might have received if all other group members had chosen him, the formula is:

$$S_i = \frac{C}{6(R - 1)}, \text{ where}$$

S_i = an individual member's star status,

C = the number of choices received by an individual, and

R = the number of respondents.

After each member's star status has been determined, the group index of stratification can be constructed. The formula:

$S = S_a - S_n$, where

$S =$ stratification,

$S_a =$ star status of most-chosen group member, and

$S_n =$ star status of least-chosen individual.

The difference $S_a - S_n$ is equal to the sum of the differences between each member's star status, as follows:

$$S_a - S_n = (S_a - S_b) + (S_b - S_c) + \ldots.$$

It follows that the greater the difference between the highest and lowest score, the steeper is the council's stratification or status order. Councils were rank-ordered from lowest to highest difference and divided into high and low stratified categories.

B5.1 *Measure of Governing Style*

Councils were classed into one of the three coding categories by imputation from a variety of questions. The following sample responses are drawn from the following question in the interview schedule: "Overall, just what makes the Council tick? I mean, *besides* the manager, the staff, or charter prescriptions, who decides what the Council should do, and how does it work?" It is interesting to note that the responses elicited by this question were not what it was designed to elicit. That it yielded the responses it did emphasizes the pervasiveness of "benevolence" as a governing style. Because of the element of subjectivity involved in coding the three governing styles, a systematic effort was made to err on the conservative side—on the a priori assumption that, given the tradition of manager government and nonpartisanship, the political style would be least likely to occur, the pragmatic style somewhat more frequently, and the benevolent style most often. In other words, a council was coded as having a political or a pragmatic style only if the evidence was strong and cumulative. While, as Table 5–1 shows, 48 of the 82 councils seemed to be primarily characterized by the benevolent style, the political style was slightly more prevalent (in 19 councils) than the pragmatic style (in 15 councils).

BENEVOLENT STYLE:

General willingness to work for the good of the city. There is no undue pressure. They must all feel like I do—a sense of satisfaction in performing an underpaid job.

The council is objective and all five councilmen are independent in thinking with the best interests of the city at stake. Their decisions are based on this.

PRAGMATIC STYLE:

In the normal course of events, we have a planning consultant, the city administrator, and the planning commission. These three are the ones who recognize conditions that are supposed to keep us attuned to the trends and the times and working with the Chamber of Commerce. We know they need parking, and they know we know they need it—we work together. This comes to us. We just have to be alert to things that will make this a better place to live.

It all comes about from just daily things that occur—as a problem arises, the Council meets it. I would like to see more planning for the future like Rapid Transit, parking, expectations of the Public Works Dept., etc. There is a need for more advance planning—there is some thinking on this but we need an administrative man to handle these future problems so we can work things out before they get to the point where they are very difficult to handle.

POLITICAL STYLE:

My views are closely aligned with those of two members. I am more aggressive, I will fight for principles. The old boy [mayor] is too slow, doesn't understand, I have a majority, and so I don't feel a need for compromise. There are variations and degrees—Jones will only vote with me four times in a row and that is the end.

Oh boy, there are lots of influencing factors—special interest groups; we have on the Council representatives from different social and economic backgrounds which do represent the views of most groups.

B5.2 *Measures of Governing Practices*

Governing practices were coded for each council from responses to a variety of questions concerned with the council's internal operations, but especially from these two: (1) "We just spoke about *what* you should do as a councilman. Now I would like to ask you whether there are particular strategies that you employ to accomplish what you want to do as a councilman? Just what's the best way of doing what you want to do?" (2) "City councilmen sometimes talk about decisions in terms of bargaining—do you think this goes on in your council?" If yes: "Could you explain a bit what this bargaining implies? Just what does one do in bargaining?" If no: "If there is no bargaining, what other ways are there to make decisions?" The following quotations from interview protocols illustrate the various governing practices.

EXCHANGE:

> I like to discuss a problem beforehand if possible, and it's hard to discuss it freely in a meeting. I like to talk about it with individuals and the councilmen beforehand so we can look into doubtful areas before the meeting.
>
> On some problems you cannot state your position publicly. You can go to individual councilmen—one at a time. You can get their opinions and their line of thought, so when it comes before the council as a whole, you can see whether it will survive.
>
> I don't wait for our council meeting. I talk with the mayor on the train, or have lunch with him or other councilmen in S.F. We get a feel of the views, so when you meet you know how they feel about various matters that are coming.

BARGAINING:

> There might be a little bit. Not as a result of one going to the other, but a couple of councilmen are getting sophisticated, and I think there is a little reciprocation. I don't see anything too wrong with it. Traditionally from what I've heard and read, this is what makes the wheels go round. At first blush, it may seem wrong, but I think it is a necessary part of the mechanics.

There can be implicit agreements, I guess. You're prone to support someone who supported your measure. You can't bargain effectively in public; therefore, little goes on since there's little informal contact. But you remember someone deferring to you.

You know what's coming up from the agenda. You talk to people, get phone calls, you try to compromise—you scratch my back, I scratch yours. I tell them [council] the little guy pays the bill. The Arts Council, the Symphony, always get donations from the city because they have the backing. The other night, the Filipinos came up and wanted a $200 donation for their festival which they have held for two years without asking for any help. The council was against it; they said let them wait till budget time. So I put my light on at the right time—the little Filipino was practically in tears—and I said "the Filipino people are the least trouble of anybody, they are good citizens and they deserve this donation."

COMPROMISING:

Occasionally, but not to a large extent. I have had one or two on the council ask me to trade votes. I have not agreed. I don't like vote trading. Compromise should be done by looking at one issue at a time. Give in on a point on one issue. I've considered doing it myself on a couple I wanted *very* strongly, but you don't actually know if they really would vote your way. What if you voted the way they wanted, what's to guarantee that they will vote your way? Are they going to give you a slip of paper saying so?

You supposedly have five intelligent people and you think something should be accomplished. If you can't get the whole cake, you take what you can get. Same in Congress and State Assembly. I personally would like a golf course, and I personally feel we should plan and zone the surrounding areas to avoid a hodgepodge. There is a lot of opposition to that so I settle for just a golf course. I aim at a high plateau, but have to settle for something less because otherwise I can't get it through.

To a limited extent it probably does. On some issues, somebody will say—I'll go for this but not for that; it has the effect of setting up ranges, limits of action. This can be done for harmony . . . or for power reasons, I suppose. Take the Bridgeway widening [2 in favor, 2 against]. Irish was in the middle. A compromise was proposed which he voted for [one lane in the middle of the street for emergency vehicles only]. Sometimes your vote is contrary to your intention. We recently considered the bond issue for parks [which would provide the city with $11,000]. The Recreation and Planning Commission hadn't taken a stand—I wanted them to consider it and take a stand before we voted [on endorsing the bond issue]. Two city councilmen called for a vote, so rather than vote no, against parks, I voted yes.

COALITION FORMATION:

I plant seeds all the time. If I trust people, I give them the word to get it accomplished. I get someone else to get a job started, to present an idea. I get someone else to pick up the ball. If I got their vote, I got two votes. If I do it myself, I only have one vote. I talk to people in business, industry, etc., to spread word of necessary projects. I feel the pulse of the community at large, and the members of the community.

Keep the majority of the councilmen with you. Take care of their needs and make them feel important. Appoint their favorite people to positions as long as they aren't complete jackasses. Keeping the four councilmen with me, we four compromise among ourselves.

We have a five-man board, we need three votes. You have to convince your colleagues it's a good idea. For example, we wanted to build a new city hall. As Mayor, I formed a citizen's committee to go around and feel the public pulse. Have a group with you, not against you, that's the way to get things done.

If you want to be effective you have to have support. At least two other guys on that council, or things die aborning. A great deal of time is spent trying to convince others. I try to see if I can get support. If I think it is worthwhile and will enjoy the support of the people I try to take it to the council chamber where there will be newspapers, so if it is defeated—somebody has to pay. I try not to embarrass my colleagues.

MINISTRATION:

It's simply that we discuss the problem as a group, as a board of directors, and arrive at a decision of the majority. We don't hold an axe over somebody's head and say, "if you don't vote for this we don't vote for that." That's what you mean. We try to operate as a business board of directors. We hire a city manager to run things. If he doesn't, we get someone who does. We make the policy, he takes care of the administering. There is no bargaining, no petty politics.

You notify the councilmen by letter what a problem is and the facts concerning it, with a very logical conclusion, and try to get a determination of the way they think it should go. If not my way, why? If they don't go along, I take it before the council at a meeting to the people there, if there are enough people there to approve or disapprove. If enough people are told what the problem is and the solution, there should be enough support.

B6.1 *Measure of Social Climate*

For a council to be coded as "collegial" or "antagonistic" there had to be pervasive evidence that the property in question was actually present. For instance, if all or most respondents referred to one another by first names and if there was other evidence of mutual deference, the council was coded as collegial. If there was pervasive evidence of an internal power struggle, competition for status, and frequent negative references to other members, the council was coded as tense. Collegiality and tension are emergent properties that cannot be either computed from individual data or imputed from direct information by one or a few individual respondents. What we are coding is a configuration of many aspects of legislative behavior that seems to characterize the group as a whole. Councils not codable as collegial or antagonistic were categorized as "impersonal."

B7.1 *Index of Interaction*

Question 16.5 (Appendix C) sought to elicit information about the frequency and intensity of interaction. It was assumed that intensity is related to frequency. Persons who often see each other have intensive contacts; persons who occasionally see each other have less intensive relationships, though they are more intensive than the relationships of persons who see each other only formally.

The question asked respondents how well they know each other, and in order to give them a cue as to what "knowing well" might mean, the frequency aspect of the interaction was given a contextual definition. While on the frequency dimension the three alternatives are unambiguous, the contextual specification yielded an unexpected finding. It turned out that the middle category—"we drop into each other's office occasionally or have lunch together"—is the most salient from the perspective of political communication, while the third category—frequent visiting in the home—is the least salient from this perspective.

Interaction was measured by a simple additive index which averaged individual scores for each council as a whole. If a member was given a formal contact choice, the score was 1; if he was identified as being occasionally and informally in contact with the respondent, the score was 2; and if intimate contact was reported, the score was 3.

The formula, then, is:

$$I = \frac{W_1 + W_2 + \ldots W_n}{M}, \text{ where}$$

I = the Interaction Index,

W = the sum of weighted choices received by each member, and

M = the number of all members in the council.

Alternative measures, such as mutual pairing, did not significantly alter the ordering of the councils on the simple I measure. For instance, cross-tabulation of the Interaction Index with a Cohesion Index based on the same data yielded these results: Gamma = .96; Chi square = 163.062; d.f. = 9; p = .00.

The mean score for all 82 councils was 1.64, the low score 0.90, and the high score 2.60. In other words, the total distribution of scores is somewhat skewed toward the more intimate end of the interaction continuum. (However, the mean of 1.64 is very close to the median of 1.60.)

Preliminary analysis of cross-tabulations of the interaction measure, using rough tercile ranges, with other council properties indicated curvilinear relationships: the middle (casual interaction) tercile was especially strongly related to other properties that had a political content. This finding confirmed our suspicion that it was indeed the occasional and informal kind of interaction which is politically most significant, followed by interaction in public and, in turn, by interaction of a private kind. The interaction tercile ranges were therefore conceptualized in terms of their potential for political communication. In other words, the middle range was treated as being politically most salient and intensive, while the high range, involving private interaction, was treated as being politically least relevant.

B8.1 *Role Orientation Classification*

For the purpose of classifying councils in terms of a *leading* role orientation, individual primary orientations were counted for each council, and a council was identified as having a *maintaining*, *adapting*, or *programming* orientation if at least two members subscribed to one of the three primary orientations. In other words, if at the individual level a primary orientation was articulated by only one person, the datum was sacrificed in this connection lest aggregation at the group level be too complicated. Of course, the information was not sacrificed in the construction of the role *differentiation* measure. *Leading* role orientation is, then, a council property and must not be confused with *primary* orientation at the individual level of analysis. The content of the three role orientations is described in the text.

B8.2 *Measure of Role Differentiation*

Councils were divided into "high" and "low" in terms of the distribution of primary role orientations among their members. When all three primary orientations were taken, the council was classified as high in differentiation; if only one or two orientations were present, the council was classified as low in differentiation. The following table presents and exhausts all the allocative patterns that occurred in the councils and the number of small or large councils with each pattern.

There are two difficulties with the classification. First, response failure (in the 2–2 or 3–3 pattern, for instance) may make for overrepresentation of the low-differentiated structure. This difficulty

Patterns of Differentiation
in Purposive Role Structure

High Differentiation			*Low Differentiation*		
Pattern	Council size	N	Pattern	Council size	N
6–3–3	Large	1	2–2	Small	5
5–1–1	Large	1	3–3	Large	1
3–1–1	Small	13	4–3	Large	2
4–2–1	Large	1	3–2	Small	10
3–2–1	Large	2	3–1	Small	4
3–2–2	Large	3	4–1	Small	10
4–4–1	Large	1	5–2	Large	1
3–3–1	Large	1	4–0	Small	1
2–2–1	Small	12	5–0	Small	4
2–2–1	Small	9			
		44			38

is unavoidable. Second, differentiation has more opportunity to occur in the larger councils. However, as the table shows, the high- and low-differentiation patterns appear to be quite randomly distributed between large and small councils.

B9.1 Classification of Decisional Structures

In 69 of the 82 councils, coding councils as unipolar, bipolar, or nonpolar structures created no difficulties. In 13 cases the data were ambiguous. The following decisions were made in classifying the councils:

Unipolar. A council was classified as unipolar when:

1. the question concerning vote lineups (see Appendix C—Q34) either did not elicit any response or called out such response as "this never happens here"; and when, in response to lineup questions on "problems" (see Appendix C—Q2, Q3), no conflict was indicated; and when, in response to a question concerning "swing-voting" (see Appendix C—Q34.5), there was no response (N = 28);

2. a cohesive group of four members, for instance, confronted a single deviant; although this structure might be considered bipolar, evidence from the other questions indicated that the one deviant did not affect the basic pattern of no conflict or no vote shifting (N = 2);

3. members, though not giving names, asserted that "it shifts"; but evidence from other questions suggested that this does not in fact occur (there are no conflicts on problems or swing-voting, for instance); although this response pattern might justify classifying the council as nonpolar, it seemed more appropriate to class it as unipolar (N = 3).

Bipolar. A council was classified as bipolar when:

1. there was high consistency in the identification of factions and swing-voters, and when in addition the same factions appeared in response to the "problem" questions (N = 17);

2. when a council with a nonaligned swing-voter seemed basically bipolarized and conflictual; in other words, though a 2:2:1 pattern might be considered nonpolar, other evidence pointed to a highly conflictual situation (N = 3).

Nonpolar. A council was classified as nonpolar when:

1. either members gave varying and inconsistent lineups or asserted that the lineups shifted, and when there was supporting evidence of flexibility from the other questions (N = 24);

2. the response pattern seemed to suggest a unipolar structure, but responses to the problem and swing-vote questions indicated that denial of split voting or shifting should be doubted (N = 4);

3. a bipolar lineup was given, but the evidence was confused because so many swing-voters were named that a permanent bipolar situation seemed very doubtful (N = 1).

B10.1 *Correlation Coefficients*
for Figures 10–A to 10–M

| A. | Partials | | | | | B. | Partials | | | | |
| | by Decision Structure | | | | | | by City Size | | | | |
	SS	IA	GS	SC	RD		SS	IA	GS	SC	RD
SS	—	.26	.45	.00	.18		—	.18	.43	−.02	.15
IA		—	.08	−.24	−.06			—	−.10	−.31	−.15
GS			—	−.07	.30				—	−.21	.19
SC				—	−.09					—	.03

| C. | Conditionals | | | | | D. | Conditionals | | | | |
| | (Large Cities) | | | | | | (Small Cities) | | | | |
	SS	IA	GS	SC	RD		SS	IA	GS	SC	RD
SS	—	.52	−.33	−.20	−.13		—	−.17	.62	.21	.40
IA		—	.27	−.23	−.29			—	−.12	−.40	−.03
GS			—	−.69	.25				—	.23	.13
SC				—	−.13					—	.21

| E–M. | Partials | | | Large Cities | | | Small Cities | | |
	CS	PS	FS	CS	PS	FS	CS	PS	FS
SS	−.06	.08	−.11	.30	−.30	−.08	−.41	.46	−.14
IA	.39	−.17	.15	.50	−.27	.07	.27	−.08	.23
GS	.31	−.15	−.01	.82	−.30	.55	−.36	.05	−.35
SC	−.62	.29	−.26	−.64	.28	−.14	−.59	.31	−.41
RD	−.09	.45	.21	−.41	.46	−.14	.23	.45	.58

Code:

SS = Stratification	RD = Role differentiation
IA = Interaction	CS = Conflictual structure
GS = Governing style	PS = Permissive structure
SC = Social climate	FS = Fragmented structure

B11.1 *Measure of Closeness of Vote*

The measure of "closeness of the vote" is the absolute mean deviation of the vote, a measure similar to the standard deviation ex-

cept that extreme scores are not weighted more heavily than close scores in computing the mean deviation. It is computed in the following manner: the mean number of votes per candidate is determined; then the deviation of each candidate's vote from the mean is calculated; these deviations are summed and divided by the number of candidates. This measure was constructed by Gordon Black, and the data prepared by him. The formula for the mean deviation is:

$$\frac{\sum(x_i - X)}{n}$$

B12.1   *Measure of Sense of Control*

This measure derived from a judgment made after reading through the protocols for the entire council. Councils were classified according to a three-category scheme:

1. Councils in which few or no remarks were made about elections or the power of the ballot box to sanction. These councils, in response to a wide variety of questions in which they discussed council affairs and their relations with the public, failed to make passing references to elections or to describe the public as an electorate. Forty-five councils (55 percent) were coded into this category.

2. Councils in which references were made to elections and to voters. These councils indicated awareness that the public could exercise some control over public policy by its use of the ballot box, but the councils did not seem to concern themselves with how the electorate might vote. Twenty-four councils (29 percent) were coded into this category.

3. Councils which indicated awareness of elections and electorates and which indicated some concern about how the voters might respond to initiatives, or lack thereof, by the council. The 13 councils (16 percent) in this category might be said to conform to Robert A. Dahl's theoretical proposition that effective political elites operate within limits "set by their expectations as to the

reactions of the group of politically active citizens who go to the polls." *A Preface to Democratic Theory* (Chicago: University of Chicago Press, 1956), p. 72. Indeed, this measure was suggested by Dahl's observation, and we were somewhat surprised to discover that fewer than half the councils made any mention of elections and in only 13 could it be said that council decisions might be made in anticipation of voter response. Reasons for this "discovery" are reviewed in Kenneth Prewitt, "Political Ambitions, Volunteerism, and Electoral Accountability," *American Political Science Review* 64 (March 1970): 5–17. There we report that "volunteeristic" councils indicate much less concern about elections than do nonvolunteeristic councils (29 percent and 60 percent, respectively).

In addition, and again on the basis of judgmental coding, councils were coded as indicating a sense of security in their general relationships with the public. This code refers to more than just the electoral situation, for it refers to the many dealings which councils have with publics. Councils were coded as expressing or not expressing this sense of security on the basis of data deriving from the entire interview. In this case the residual code is expressing sense of security. That is, we accepted as direct evidence the testimony of two or more councilmen, if not contradicted by other reports, that relations with the public were problematic. (For illustrative quotations, see Chapter 19.) If such materials were not forthcoming, the council was automatically coded into the "sense of security" category.

The measure used in Table 12–1 combines the two codes just described. A council coded "1" in the first measure and coded "sense of security" in the second measure is a "high-control council." A council coded "lack of sense of security" but not sensitive to electoral sanctions is a "moderate-control council." And a council which is both concerned about electoral sanctions and indicates a low sense of security in its dealings with the public is a "low-control council." There are 39 councils in the high category, 30 in the moderate category, and 13 in the low category. In cross-tabulation analysis, the moderate and low categories are usually combined.

B13.1 *Council Status Classification*

The assignment of councils into "relatively lower" or "relatively higher" status was accomplished in the following manner:

We first looked at the formal education of each councilman; if fewer than half the councilmen have completed college, the council is coded into the lower category, *unless* there are noncollege-educated councilmen who hold high-status occupations. For instance, the college dropout who has nevertheless moved into a top management position or the high school graduate who is a large landowner receives a "high status" and contributes to a summary score in that direction.

When more than half the councilmen have completed college, the council is coded into the higher category, unless among those who have college educations are some who hold lower-status occupations. A college graduate who is a barber receives a "low status" code and thus contributes to a summary score in that direction.

The overall council score is based on the modal status of individual councilmen. If three, four, or five councilmen are "high status," the council is assigned to the relatively higher category.

In a few cases where there were only four respondents, two of each status code, we allowed the extreme individual scores to pull the council either up or down. If the high-status councilmen were much higher than the low-status councilmen were low, the council would be assigned to the higher category. Two attorneys and two college-incomplete businessmen would be a high council; two college-complete businessmen and two high school-educated blue-collar workers would be a low council.

The authors coded the councils independently and then adjusted differences. Five cases (6 percent) had to be adjusted.

The following provides four illustrative cases, two councils coded into the "relatively high," and two coded into the "relatively low," status categories. We have provided examples of clear coding decisions as well as examples of more ambiguous coding decisions so that the reader will see how we treated borderline cases:

Social Status of Council

Higher	Lower
Council A (Clear)	*Council B (Clear)*
Electrical engineer, college complete	Business manager of valve shop, high school incomplete
National sales manager, college complete	Foreman, education not recorded
Surgeon, advanced degree	Assistant to Superintendent of Schools, graduate degree
President of company, college complete	Owner of small business, high school incomplete
Attorney, advanced degree	Bail bond insurance agent, high school complete
Council C (Ambiguous)	*Council D (Ambiguous)*
District manager of gas company, college incomplete	Newspaperman, education not recorded
Painting contractor, some graduate work	School Superintendent, advanced degree
Lobbyist for N.E.A., advanced degree	Steel fabrication contractor, high school complete
Advertising executive, high school incomplete	Dentist, advanced degree
	Sign painter and manufacturer, high school complete

B15.1 *Additive Index of General Associational Activity*

The activity level of each of nine different types of groups was computed for each city. See Appendix C, Item E, for a list of the groups and the question. A city was then scored as high or low for each group depending on whether it was above or below the median for all 82 cities. The additive index sums, for each council, the number of group types which are high on activity. Councils above the median on this additive index are said to have high general associational activity and those below the median are said to have low associational activity.

B18.1 *Measure of Communication Channels*

Each councilman was given two checklists. One checklist instructed him to rank the following in terms of the best advice he gets about issues before the council: city manager or other city officials, other councilmen, newspapers, organizational leaders in the community, influential individuals in the city, people in the city generally, people in the neighborhood, people who come to council meetings. The second checklist instructed him to rank the following in terms of the most important source of information about controversial matters in the community: appearance of individuals or representatives from organizations at council meetings, running into friends or acquaintances in the city, newspapers, business or work associates, contacts with organizational leaders.

Aggregate scores for councils were computed by multiplying the number of councilmen giving a particular rank, adding these figures, and then dividing by the total number of respondents. This provided a mean score of the importance of each item on the checklists.

An additional measure, used in Figure 18–2, was then computed. Councils were classified according to city size into three groups. A mean score of importance for each individual item was computed for all large cities, medium cities, and small cities. Thus, for instance, the importance assigned to "business or work associates" was separately computed for all councils in large cities, in medium cities, and in small cities. Figure 18–2 places a particular source of advice or information according to where it receives the highest ranking and where it receives the lowest ranking. For instance, newspapers receive the highest ranking in large cities and that is where newspapers appear above the dotted line in Figure 18–2; and newspapers receive the lowest ranking in small cities and that is where newspapers appear below the dotted line.

B20.1 *Measure of Clientele Identification*

Specific client groups were coded on the basis of a judgment after reading through the entire set of interviews for each council. The testimony of at least two councilmen, corroborated by supportive evidence, was necessary before a clientele was coded. Specific client groups included business/merchant interests, public interest groups, developers/realtors, conservation/homeowners, ethnics, and blacks. Some councils (24) reported more than one clientele group. But for purposes of the present analysis no distinction is made between single-clientele and multiple-clientele situations. Councils are simply classified into those which report no clientele and those which do.

B21.1 *Measure of Responsiveness*

The three-part classification of responsiveness was based on a judgment code after reading through the entire set of interviews for each council. The classification was as follows:

a. *Nonresponsive,* or responsive only to self-defined images of community needs. The interview protocols produced no evidence of attentiveness to publicly expressed demands or wishes (44 percent of the councils).

b. *Responsive to* ad hoc *issue groups,* usually sporadically organized in order to press a particular claim. The interview protocols generated significant numbers of illustrative accounts of how the council attended to *ad hoc* groups. To be coded into this category it was not sufficient for the council simply to identify such groups; it was necessary that there be evidence from a majority of councilmen that there were acts of responsiveness to the groups (32 percent of the councils).

c. *Responsive to attentive publics.* As with the previous code, it was not sufficient for councils to identify attentive publics; it was necessary that there be evidence of responsiveness to them. Attentive publics are generally permanent clusters which have an identifiable viewpoint on local matters and which make that viewpoint known to the council. There can of course be differences of opinion within the attentive public, which is to say that there can be attentive publics. But the coding procedures did not consider the degree of differentiation, only the extent to which councils were responsive to the expression of demands and interests emanating from attentive publics (24 percent of the councils).

B22.1 *Measure of Effort/Ambitiousness*

The measure of effort/ambitiousness is an approximation of the interest shown by councilmen in staying on the council. The simple measure of whether councils intended to stand for reelection is not satisfactory for the present analysis. Councils can be interested in reelection and yet serve where incumbents are automatically returned (in 20 cities no incumbent standing for reelection failed to be returned; see Table 11–2). Thus to learn that a council intends to stand for reelection provides little clue as to ambitiousness of the type identified in Schlesinger's theory. Our substitute measure is a combination of campaign effort (see Chapter 14) and desire to reach higher office. On both items a mean score for the council as a whole was computed and the range of means was collapsed into quartiles. The two quartiles were used to form an additive index that is used in the present analysis.

B22.2 *Path Coefficients for Figures 22–2, 22–3, and 22–4*

| | Figure | | |
| | A | B | C |
	22–2	22–3	22–4
Voter turnout and electoral sanctions	−.04	−.25	.26
Voter turnout and effort/ambitiousness	−.07	.11	.15
Voter turnout and responsiveness	.11	.02	.09
Contesters and electoral sanctions	.25	.41	.12
Contesters and effort/ambitiousness	.43	.29	.22
Contesters and responsiveness	.12	.35	−.06

| | Figure | | |
	A 22–2	B 22–3	C 22–4
Eviction and electoral sanctions	.26	.12	.26
Eviction and effort/ambitiousness	.21	.26	.27
Eviction and responsiveness	.15	.30	−.11
Electoral sanctions and effort/ambitiousness	−.07	−.10	−.01
Electoral sanctions and responsiveness	.29	.16	.39
Effort/ambitiousness and responsiveness	.08	−.08	.24

The zero-order correlation coefficients for the variables in the model are as follows, with the first coefficient being for a sample of 80 cities, the second coefficient being for the 39 small cities, and the third coefficient being for the 41 large cities:

	Con- testers	Eviction	Sanctions	Effort	Respon- siveness
Turnout	.07 .48 .01	.12 .01 .34	.01 −.06 .35	−.01 .26 .24	.14 .16 .24
Contesters		.12 .33 −.05	.28 .33 .11	.47 .40 .20	.27 .48 .04
Eviction			.29 .25 .35	.26 .33 .31	.29 .44 .13
Sanctions				.22 .05 .16	.39 .34 .41
Effort					.24 .17 .27

B26.1   *Measure of Problem Diversity*

The measure of diversity, to be viable, had to take account of the number of diverse problems perceived and the number of respondents in a council. For instance, if of ten problem mentions in a five-member council all of the responses referred to ten different problems, problem diversity would be maximal ($10/10 = 1.00$). If only two different problems appear in ten responses, diversity would be quite low ($2/10 = .20$). Diversity, however, must be weighted by an articulation score because in a council larger than five more particular problems had a chance to be mentioned. Therefore, diversity scores were adjusted for articulation by multiplying each score by an articulation ratio—the number of respondents over all responses. The formula, then, is:

$$\text{Diversity} = \frac{\text{N problems} \times \text{N respondents}}{\text{N mentions}^2}$$

Appendix C

Interview Schedule
and Questionnaire

Council Interview Schedule

Mr. Councilman:

Before we get started, I want you to feel assured that anything you tell me will be treated in strictest confidence. The information and opinions you give me will be coded and processed along with material from all other councilmen, here in (CITY) and in the other cities of the area. No names will be used, and what you tell me will be off the record.

We want to do a thorough job of this, and because this is a pretty thorough interview, I just want to outline to you what we shall try to cover.

We will begin with some questions about the problems facing your city and the Bay Area in general. Then we want to explore your job as a councilman, the work of the council as a whole, and all that is involved. We will then ask you some questions about the people in your city, both individuals and organizations. Toward the end of the interview we will have some questions about how you became a councilman and about city elections.

We will also have a questionnaire for you to fill out at the end of the interview, which you may prefer to complete at your leisure and send back to us through the mail.

1. Mr. Councilman, before talking about your work as a councilman and the work of the council itself, we would like to ask you about some of the problems facing this community.

In your opinion, what are the two most pressing problems here in (CITY)?

1.1   Why is (FIRST PROBLEM) a problem here in (CITY)?

1.2   And what about the other problem? Why is (SECOND PROBLEM) a problem?

2.   On the first problem (NAME FIRST PROBLEM) we just talked about, would you say that the council members are mostly in agreement on how to handle it, or do their views conflict?

Agree ( )   Conflict ( )   DK ( )   NA ( )

IF DISAGREE: In general, what is the lineup in the council on this? Who usually sides with you?

3.   And now on the second problem (REPEAT SECOND PROBLEM), would you say that the council members are mostly in agreement on how to handle it, or are they disagreed?

Agree ( )   Conflict ( )   DK ( )   NA ( )

IF DISAGREE: Could you tell me who among your colleagues usually sides with you on this problem?

4.   On a key problem such as we just talked about, is there any council member you would especially like to have join you as cosponsor of a proposal you might have?

INTERVIEWER: IN FIVE-MEMBER COUNCIL DO *NOT* PRESS FOR MORE THAN *TWO*. IF ANSWER IS "ALL," TRY TO GET ONE OR TWO NAMES.

4.1   Why would you like to have these members join you?

4.2   If there is disagreement in the council in regard to some key problem, which member's opposition would you be most concerned about?

PROBE: Just why would his opposition be of concern to you?

5.   In the past year, a number of cities have been troubled by

problems relating to the Negro. Are there such problems here?

Yes ( )　　No ( )　　DK ( )　　NA ( )

IF YES: What are these problems?

IF NO: SKIP TO Q. 5.2

5.1 Is the city attempting to do anything about this?

Yes ( )　　No ( )　　DK ( )　　NA ( )

IF YES: Just what is the city trying to do?

5.2 Regardless of what the city is doing, what do you personally think should be done about such problems?

6. Now, looking toward the future, what *one* communitywide improvement, in your opinion, does this city "need most" to be attractive to its citizens?

DK ( )　　NA ( )　　IF DK OR NA, SKIP TO Q. 7.

6.1 What community groups can be expected to support this improvement?

PROBE: What makes you think that these groups will give their support?

6.2 And what groups in the community are most likely to oppose this improvement?

PROBE: Why do you think that these groups will be in opposition?

6.3 What would you say are the main difficulties in getting this improvement?

DK ( )　　NA ( )

6.4 Now, taking the broadest view possible, how do you see (CITY) in the future? I mean, what kind of a city would you personally like (CITY) to be in the next twenty-five years or so?

7. Now, I have a few questions about some matters that concern all cities. Some people feel that every city has problems which it cannot solve by itself, but which require some kind of areawide solution. What three problems in the Bay Area are you most concerned about?

7.1 Just why are you concerned about these problems? Let's take

the first (second, third) problem you mentioned.
INTERVIEWER: RESTATE PROBLEM *AS MEN-
TIONED BY R.*

8.   It has been suggested that the Association of Bay Area Gov-
       ernments or other Bay Area agencies should play a greater
       role in the solution of metropolitan problems. How do you
       feel about this?

8.1   Speaking of the ABAG, do you feel that it is very useful, use-
       ful, not so useful, or not useful at all?
       Very useful ( )   Useful ( )   Not so useful ( )
       Not useful at all ( )   DK ( )   NA ( )

8.2   Would you be in favor of combining a few of the single-
       purpose special districts in the Bay Area with ABAG, thus
       giving ABAG increased responsibilities, or would you be
       opposed?
       In favor ( )   Opposed ( )   DK ( )   NA ( )
       COMMENTS:

8.3   Does your city belong to ABAG?
       Yes ( )   No ( )   DK ( )   NA ( )

8.31   IF YES: How long has it belonged?
       IF NO: Skip to Q. 9

8.4   Have you served as a delegate from your city or as an ob-
       server at ABAG meetings?
       Yes ( )   No ( )   NA ( )

8.5   How did it come about that you were selected to be a dele-
       gate or observer at these meetings?

8.6   Are there conditions or circumstances under which you
       would want your city to withdraw from ABAG?
       Yes ( )   No ( )   DK ( )   NA ( )
       IF YES: What are these?

9.   How, in your opinion, should the federal government take
       part in solving municipal or metropolitan problems?

9.1   How do you feel about federal aid for urban renewal? Would
       you say you approve of it, or disapprove?
       Approve ( )   Disapprove ( )   DK ( )   NA ( )
       PROBE: How's that?

9.2 Do you think that the federal government should undertake a full-scale program of mass transportation in metropolitan areas?
Yes ( )   No ( )   DK ( )   NA ( )
PROBE: How's that?

9.3 And how, in your opinion, should the state government participate in solving municipal or metropolitan problems?

9.4 What about the citizens here in (CITY)? What three problems of an areawide scope do you feel *they* are most concerned about?
INTERVIEWER: RECORD ALL COMMENTS.

10. Now I would like to ask you some questions about the job of city councilman. First of all, how would you describe the job of being a councilman—*what* are the most important things you *should* do as a councilman?
INTERVIEWER: PROBE THOROUGHLY: Anything else? Etc.

11. We just spoke about *what* you should do as a councilman. Now I would like to ask you whether there are particular strategies that you employ to accomplish what you want to do as a councilman?
PROBE THOROUGHLY: Just what's the best way of doing what you want to do?

12. Are there any important differences between what *you* think the job of councilman involves and the way the voters see it?
Yes ( )   No ( )   DK ( )   NA ( )
IF YES: Just what are these differences?
IF NO: How do you account for this lack of differences?
PROBE THOROUGHLY!

13. Would you say that being a councilman has helped you or hindered you in your private occupation? Or doesn't it make a difference?
Helped ( )   Hindered ( )   No Difference ( )
NA ( )
PROBE: How's that?

14.   Do you feel that city councilmen here in (CITY) receive the kind of respect from the community they deserve?
Yes ( )   No ( )   DK ( )   NA ( )
PROBE: How's that?

15.1* Now some questions about the council and how it works. City councilmen sometimes talk about decisions in terms of bargaining—do you think this goes on in your council?
Yes ( )   No ( )   DK ( )   NA ( )
IF YES: Could you explain a bit what this bargaining implies? Just what does one do in bargaining?
IF NO: If there is no bargaining, what other ways are there to make decisions?
INTERVIEWER: If NO TO Q. 15.1, SKIP TO Q. 15.4.

15.2   IF YES TO 15.1: When in decision-making would you say that bargaining usually occurs? Informally before meetings? At committee meetings? At council sessions themselves? After meetings when you sit and talk?

15.3   IF YES TO 15.1: In general, do you think there is too much bargaining going on, too little, or is it just right?
PROBE: Why is that?

15.4   If a group of your neighbors came to you with a proposal that you thought was worthy, although it was costly, how would you go about getting this passed?

16.   Does the council here (CITY) use a committee system?
Yes ( )   No ( )   DK ( )   NA ( )
IF YES: Which committees do you serve on?
INTERVIEWER: IF NO COMMITTEES, SKIP TO QUESTION 17.

16.1   How are committee assignments made?

16.2   Of all the council committees, which one would you personally like most to serve on?
PROBE: Why is that?

16.3   Quite regardless of your own preferences, which committee do you consider the most important?
PROBE: Why is it the most important?

---

* No question 15.

16.4   Speaking of this most important committee, whom do you consider its most influential member?

16.5   Here is a list of your fellow council members. We would like to know just how well you know each one. Would you please check the appropriate box?

    a.   I see him only at council sessions or in connection with council work.

    b.   We drop into each other's office occasionally or have lunch.

    c.   We visit each other quite often as guests in each other's home.

    INTERVIEWER: YOU MUST BE SURE, BEFORE INTERVIEW, THAT NAMES OF ALL COUNCIL MEMBERS EXCEPT RESPONDENT'S ARE INSERTED.

17.   I would next like to ask you some questions about the job of the mayor and the city manager (OR OTHER TOP ADMINISTRATOR). Let's take the mayor first: what should the mayor do to be most effective in his *relations with the other city councilmen?*

17.1   And what about his relations with the citizens? What should he do to be most effective?

18.   Now, what about the city manager (OR OTHER TOP ADMINISTRATIVE OFFICIAL)? What should he do, or not do, to be most effective in his relations with the council? PROBE: How about in policy matters?

18.1   One of the continuing controversies in city government concerns the city manager. Some people think the city manager has too much say in city policies; others think he doesn't have enough. How does this look to you here in (CITY)?

18.2   Just one more question about city personnel. Could you tell me something about the city attorney? What should he do or not do to be most effective *in his relations with the council?*

18.3   How would you rank in importance the influence of the mayor, the manager, and the city attorney on the decisions of the council?

(1) Who of the three would you   *Rank*
    say is the most important?   _____ Mayor
    PROBE: What makes you say so?   _____ Manager
(2) And who is the least important?   _____ City Attorney
    PROBE: What makes you say so?

19. Now I'd like to talk with you a little about your relations
    with the voters. Do you ever have to take a stand that the
    majority of voters seem to disagree with? Would you say
    this happens often, sometimes, rarely, or never?
    Often ( )   Sometimes ( )   Rarely ( )   Never ( )
    DK ( )   NA ( )
    COMMENT:

20. In general, how would you rate citizen interest in what the
    council is doing here in (CITY)? Would you say it is high,
    moderate, low, or nonexistent?
    High ( )   Moderate ( )   Low ( )
    Nonexistent ( )   Depends ( )   DK ( )   NA ( )
    PROBE: How do you account for this interest (lack of
        interest)?

21. In what kinds of local problems do people seem to be most
    interested?
    PROBE: Why is that?

22. How do you think this interest (lack of interest) affects the
    functioning of the council?

23. A few questions now about the budget. When the council is
    planning the upcoming budget, what major considerations
    affect your thinking about new programs and increases?
    IF NO MENTION IS MADE OF PROPERTY TAX: Does
        the property tax play a part in your thinking on these
        matters?
    Yes ( )   No ( )   DK ( )   NA ( )
    PROBE: How's that?

24. Let's suppose that the people in this city were all agreed

that the city budget and local taxes *both* had to be reduced. Would you have any preferences as to what services should be cut as a consequence and what ones should not be cut?

25. If federal money is available for locally administered programs—like rebuilding of secondary roads or the acquisition of additional "open spaces"—do you favor having the city staff make application for these federal grants-in-aid?
Yes ( )   No ( )   Perhaps ( )   DK ( )
NA ( )
PROBE: How's that?

26. *In comparison* with your fellow councilmen, are you *usually* in favor of "holding the line" on the budget, or do you "go along" with new requests?
Hold line ( )   Go along ( )   Depends on request ( )
DK ( )   NA ( )
PROBE: What makes you say so?

27. Let me go on to something else. Is there any aspect of council work on which you consider yourself particularly expert? I mean, when it comes to fire or police protection, ordinances, or other matters?
Yes ( )   No ( )   DK ( )   NA ( )
IF NO, SKIP TO Q. 28.
27.1 IF YES: In just what area do you consider yourself especially expert?
27.2 How did you come to be an expert in this?
27.3 Do you feel that the other councilmen accept and follow your suggestions in this matter (THESE MATTERS) always, usually, only occasionally, or what?
Always ( )   Usually ( )   Occasionally ( )
DK ( )   NA ( )   Other (SPECIFY):

28. I would like to ask you about other councilmen in this connection. Is there another councilman, or several, who is especially expert on some aspects of council work?

29. In most city councils there is usually one member who gives

the whole council "leadership and direction." From your experience here in (CITY), who would you say fills that role on
your council?

There is no one leader (   )

IF THERE IS *NO ONE* LEADER, SKIP TO Q. 29.3.

29.1 Just what is it, in your opinion, that makes Mr. _____
a leader?

29.2 Do you feel that Mr. _____'s leadership makes a
difference in how the council works?
PROBE: Just how's that?

29.3 Overall, just what makes the council tick? I mean, *besides*
the manager, the staff, or charter prescriptions, who decides
what the council should do, and how does it work?

30. In your opinion, what explains why one council member
may be listened to by his fellow council members, while
another may get hardly any attention from the others?

31. Who among the present council members would you say are
the most likely to have their opinions accepted by other
council members?
PROBE: Why is that?

32. Who, among the present councilmen, would you say is the
most respected? I mean, the kind of man a new member
would look up to when he's just learning about the council
and how it works?
INTERVIEWER: ONE NAME SUFFICES, DO NOT
        PRESS: IF MORE ARE MENTIONED, RECORD
        ONLY FIRST THREE.

32.1 What makes for his being so respected?

33. We've been told that every city council has its *unofficial*
rules—its rules of the game—certain things members must
do and certain things they must not do if they want the
cooperation of their fellow members.

33.1 What are some of these things—these "rules of the game"—
that a member must observe to get the cooperation of his
fellow members?

33.2 And what are some of the things that may cause a member to lose the cooperation of his fellow members?
IF NA TO Q. 33.1 AND 33.2, SKIP TO Q. 34.

33.3 How do the other members make things difficult for a councilman when he doesn't follow the rules of the game?

33.4 How about a new councilman? Is it difficult for him to discover and learn about these rules?
PROBE: Why is it difficult (or easy)?

34. When the council is in disagreement on an issue, would you say that there is more or less the same lineup of votes here in (CITY)? I mean, do some members seem to vote together on controversial issues?
Yes ( )   No ( )   DK ( )   NA ( )
IF NO: SKIP TO Q. 35.
IF YES:

34.1 With whom do *you* usually vote on controversial matters?

34.2 Why is it that you like to vote with these men?

34.3 Now, what about the others? Are they united or split?
United ( )   Split ( )   DK ( )   NA ( )
IF SPLIT: Who would you say votes most often together when the others are split?
RECORD ALL COMMENTS:

34.4 How do you account for the fact that the council divides as it does?

34.5 When the council is split over an issue, are there one or two members who sometimes vote with one side, sometimes with the other? Who are they?
Yes ( )   No ( )   DK ( )   NA ( )

34.6 Why do you think they behave that way?

34.7 If the council splits on an issue, is it ever along political party lines? I mean, do members of the same party vote together?
Yes ( )   No ( )   DK ( )   NA ( )
IF YES: Would you say this happens often, occasionally, rarely, or what?
Often ( )   Occasionally ( )   Rarely ( )
DK ( )   NA ( )   Other (SPECIFY):

34.8   IF YES TO 34.7: On what kinds of issues is the council
       likely to split along partisan lines?

35.   It is a general impression that most city councils vote unani-
       mously on many things. Could you give me an idea why you
       think this happens?

35.1   But what about important policy issues? On such issues,
       would you say that here in (CITY) unanimity occurs very
       often, often, only sometimes, or rarely?
       Very often ( )   Often ( )   Sometimes ( )
       Rarely ( )   DK ( )   NA ( )

36.   From your experience, would you say that personal friend-
       ships among the councilmen play an important part in the
       way they vote, some part, or no part at all?
       Important part ( )   Some part ( )   No part ( )
       DK ( )   NA ( )
       PROBE: How's that?

36.1   Whom among all the councilmen do you personally like
       best?
       RECORD ANY COMMENT:

37.   Now I would like to ask you about some of the individuals
       outside the council who are actively involved in what the
       council does here in (CITY).

37.1   Are there any persons who are particularly influential here
       —I mean people whose voices are really important in coun-
       cil decisions affecting the city? *Who are they?* (GET NAMES
       AND IDENTIFICATION)

37.2   On *what kinds of things* are they influential? Let's take
       Mr. _____. In what matters is he influential?

37.3   And what makes for his influence? *What does he actually do*
       to affect decisions made by the council?
       INTERVIEWER: RECORD ANY *GENERAL* COM-
       MENTS MADE ON INFLUENCE.

37.4   Would you say that the people you named as influential
       here in (CITY) are pretty much agreed on what kind of a
       community this *should* be, or disagreed?
       Agreed ( )   Disagreed ( )   DK ( )   NA ( )
       PROBE: How's that?

37.5 Generally speaking, would you say that these people contact you on issues before the council regularly, occasionally, not very often, seldom, or what?

Regularly ( )   Occasionally ( )   Not often ( )
Seldom ( )   DK ( )   NA ( )

37.6 Of the important people you mentioned, are there any whose judgment you particularly trust and whose advice you might generally want to seek? Who are they?

Yes ( )   No ( )   NA ( )

37.7 Are there important people in the community who *might have* influence on council decisions but who don't use their influence?

Yes ( )   No ( )   DK ( )   NA ( )
PROBE THOROUGHLY: How's that? IF YES: Why do they *not* use their influence?

37.8 Are there people who, as far as you can see, exercise political influence in (CITY), but who for some reason don't work through the council?

Yes ( )   No ( )   DK ( )   NA ( )
IF YES: How do they exercise their influence?

38. Now I would like to ask you some questions about your relations with the people here in (CITY). There are two main points of view concerning how a representative *should* act when he has to make up his mind.

(1) One is that, having been elected, he should do what the voters want him to do, even if it isn't his own personal preference.

(2) The second is that he should use his own judgment, regardless of what others want him to do.

Which of these views comes closest to your own view?

View 1 ( )   View 2 ( )   Can't say ( )   NA ( )
PROBE INTENSIVELY FOR R's REASONS: Why do you hold this view? Any other reason? Etc.

38.1 Do you find it difficult or easy to act in the way you just described?

Difficult ( )   Easy ( )   DK ( )   NA ( )
PROBE: Why is it difficult (easy) to act that way?

38.2 How do you think the voters feel about the two points of view? Do you think they want you to use your own judgment or to follow *their* wishes even if you disagree with them?
Use own judgment ( )   Follow voter wishes ( )
DK ( )   NA ( )
PROBE: What makes you think so?

39.   In your work as a councilman, do you spend a lot of time doing services for people—giving information, helping them with requests, and so on? Or some time, or not much time?
Lot of time ( )   Some time ( )   Not much time ( )
DK ( )   NA ( )

39.1 Just what sorts of things are you called on to do?

39.2 Do you feel that this is a burden on you in your work as a councilman?
Yes ( )   No ( )   DK ( )   NA ( )
PROBE: How's that?

40.   Would you say that people are more interested in your taking care of these personal things for them or in your stands on issues before the council?
Personal things ( )   Stands on issues ( )
DK ( )   NA ( )
PROBE: How's that?

41.   If you disagree with people on an issue that is before the council, do you ever try to swing them over to your point of view?
Yes ( )   No ( )   DK ( )   NA ( )
IF YES: Just what do you do to swing them over?
IF NO: Just why are you not trying to persuade them to your point of view?

42.   There is always much talk about a councilman's "responsi-bilities." Could you tell me just what "responsibility" means to you?

42.1 Just whom do you really feel responsible to?

42.2 Do you ever feel any conflict between your responsibility to

the people who voted for you and your responsibility to the
city as a whole?
Yes ( )   No ( )   DK ( )   NA ( )
PROBE: How's that?

43. How do you let people know how you stand on an issue that
is before the council?

44. Of course, cities differ a great deal in terms of their eco-
nomic, racial, occupational, and residential characteristics.
From this point of view, how would you describe your city?
What are its most important characteristics?
PROBE: Anything else?

45. Now, let us talk a bit about the groups and organizations
here in (CITY) which are active in community affairs and
sometimes appear before the council.

45.1 Which of these groups or organizations would you say are
the most influential when it comes to council decisions?
INTERVIEWER: GET NAMES FIRST, THEN ASK
     RESPONDENT FOR EACH.

45.2 Now, what would you say makes these groups so influential
—what are the main reasons for their influence?
REASONS FOR INFLUENCE:
INTERVIEWER: RECORD HERE ALL *GENERAL*
     COMMENTS MADE ON GROUPS AND GROUP
     INFLUENCE.

46. Do any community groups or organizations ever contact you
personally to seek your support?
Yes ( )   No ( )   DK ( )   NA ( )
PROBE: How's that?

46.1 When these groups contact you, how do they go about doing
it?

46.2 How do you feel about the efforts of groups to make their
views known to you and to win your support?

46.3 Do you feel that, in general, you should make it easy for

them to contact you, or should you try to avoid them?
Make it easy ( )   Avoid ( )
Pro/con, depends ( )   DK ( )   NA ( )
PROBE: Could you say a little more about this?

46.4   Before a council decision is made, do you ever actively seek support from any of the groups you have mentioned?
Yes ( )   No ( )   NA ( )
IF YES: What kind of support do you seek?

46.41 ONLY IF YES TO 46.4: May I ask from which groups you have sought support?

46.5   In your opinion, what kind of activity weakens a group's ability to influence the city council?

46.6   Are there any groups here in (CITY) which are consistently critical of what the council is doing?
Yes ( )   No ( )   DK ( )   NA ( )
IF YES: Which groups seem to be critical?
INTERVIEWER: LIST NAMES, THEN FOLLOW WITH 46.61.

46.61 What, in your opinion, makes them so critical?

50.*   I would like to shift our talk a bit and ask you a few questions about your background. We would like to find out how people first become generally aware of and interested in government and public affairs. Now, if you think back as far as you can, how did you first become aware of public matters? For instance, what is your very first recollection of being interested?
IF NOT CLEAR JUST WHEN FIRST INTERESTED, ASK: In just what period of your life would you locate this earliest interest?
Childhood or grammar school period? ( )
High school period? ( )
After high school or in college? ( )
After college? ( )
At time of making up mind to join council? ( )

51.   As far as you can recall, was there any particular situation that stimulated your earliest interest in government?

---

* No questions 47–49.

52. Do you remember, when you were growing up, whether your father thought of himself mostly as a Democrat or as a Republican, or did he shift around?
Democrat ( )   Republican ( )   Shifted ( )
DK ( )   NA ( )   Other (SPECIFY):

53. Now, thinking back over your own career in public life, can you recall when you first considered being actively involved in public matters?

54.1* As far as you can recall, was there any particular situation that stimulated your earliest activity?
54.2 Were there any particular persons instrumental in getting you active?
PROBE: Who were they? (INTERVIEWER: DO NOT SEEK NAMES OF PERSONS BUT RATHER THEIR ROLES—AS NEIGHBORS, FRIENDS, WORK COLLEAGUES, ETC.)

55. Now, just to make sure we won't miss anything, can you spell out for us the steps between your earliest activity in public affairs and your initial candidacy for the city council?
INTERVIEWER: ASK ONLY IF PREVIOUS ACCOUNT IS NOT CLEAR.
PROBE, IF NEEDED: Before coming on the council, had you held any other local government position, such as on the school board?
Yes ( )   No ( )   DK ( )   NA ( )
IF YES TO PROBE: What were these positions?

56. Before running for the council, did you know any of the incumbent councilmen pretty well?
Yes ( )   No ( )   NA ( )
PROBE: Who were they?

57. Now, when you first came on the council, were you elected or appointed?
Elected ( )   Appointed ( )   NA ( )

---

* No question 54.

57.1   IF APPOINTED: Had you expressed an interest in being
        appointed to any members of the council or their
        friends?
        Yes ( )   No ( )   NA ( )
57.2   IF APPOINTED: If you had *not* been appointed, do you
        think you would have run for the council sooner or
        later anyway?
        Yes ( )   No ( )   DK ( )   NA ( )
        PROBE: How's that?
57.3   IF ELECTED: What sort of things did you stress in your
        first campaign for office? For instance, did you stress
        any personal traits or any campaign themes, things
        that could be called platform planks?
        PROBE: Just what did you stress?
57.4   WHETHER APPOINTED OR ELECTED: When you
        first came on the council, were there any particular
        organizations or groups in the community which gave
        you encouragement or support?
        Yes ( )   No ( )   DK ( )   NA ( )
        PROBE: Who were they?

58.   We are wondering what in your previous experience, before
        you became a councilman, has been of most help to you in
        your work on the council?
        IF RESPONSE IS "NOTHING," ASK: Why is that?

59.   When you first came on the council, was there anything in
        particular you hoped to accomplish as a councilman?
        Yes ( )   No ( )   DK ( )   NA ( )
        IF YES: Just what did you hope to accomplish?
        IF NO: Why is that?
59.1   As a result of your service, have you changed your opinions
        about any important aspects of the work of the council?
        Yes ( )   No ( )   DK ( )   NA ( )
        PROBE: How's that?
59.11 Do you now have any different ideas about what can be ac-
        complished in city government from those you had before
        first joining the council?

Yes ( )   No ( )   DK ( )   NA ( )
WHETHER "YES" OR "NO": Why is that?

59.2 When you first became a councilman, do you remember how you learned about the job? I mean, how did you learn the routines of being a councilman?

59.3 Now, in addition to learning the routines, were there any informal things that one had to learn in order to get things accomplished?
Yes ( )   No ( )   DK ( )   NA ( )
PROBE: What sort of things?

59.4 IF YES TO 59.3: How would you say you learned about these sorts of things?

59.5 Did you attend the League of California Cities Institute for new councilmen?
Yes ( )   No ( )   DK ( )   NA ( )

60. In general, what do you think makes a person want to become a councilman?

60.1 In your work as a councilman, do you feel that, at times, undue demands are made on you from outside the council?
Yes ( )   No ( )   DK ( )   NA ( )
IF YES: Who makes these demands? How are they made?

61. Do you expect to continue to run for the city council?
Yes ( )   Perhaps ( )   No ( )   DK ( )
NA ( )
PROBE: Why is that? What are your reasons?

62. Are there any other political or governmental positions—local, state, or federal—which you would like to seek?
Yes ( )   Perhaps ( )   No ( )   DK ( )   NA ( )
IF YES OR PERHAPS: What are they?
PROBE: Why do you wish to seek these positions?
INTERVIEWER: PROBE THOROUGHLY AND RE-CORD ALL COMMENTS.

63. We are almost finished, but I would like to ask you a few

questions about elections here in (CITY). When was the *last* time you ran for election? _____

                                          Year

63.1   Were you opposed by other candidates in that election?
       Yes ( )   No ( )   DK ( )   NA ( )
       INTERVIEWER: IF RESPONDENT *NEVER RAN*
           FOR OFFICE, RECORD HERE ( ) AND SKIP
           TO Q. 64.
           IF RESPONDENT WAS UNOPPOSED, DO ASK
           ALL QUESTIONS.

63.2   Would you say that you campaigned fairly hard, some, not
       too much, or what?
       Fairly hard ( )   Some ( )   Not too much ( )
       DK ( )   NA ( )

63.3   In general, about how much campaigning is there in city
       elections here in (CITY)? Would you say it is considerable,
       moderate, or not too much?
       Considerable ( )   Moderate ( )   Not much ( )
       DK ( )   NA ( )

63.4   In your last election, what aspects of your campaign do you
       think contributed most to your success?
       PROBE: Could you tell me why?

64.   How about the voters here in (CITY)? Would you say there
       is much interest in council elections, some interest, little
       interest, or no interest at all?
       Much ( )   Some ( )   Little ( )   None ( )
       DK ( )   NA ( )
       PROBE: Could you tell my why this is so?

65.   Speaking of running for office, how do you feel about cam-
       paigning? Could you tell me a little bit about what you
       like or dislike about it?

65.1   In general, what is your impression about a councilman's
       chances for reelection here in (CITY)? I mean, how often
       do councilmen get defeated for reelection? Would you say it
       happens often, occasionally, rarely, or what?

Often ( )   Occasionally ( )   Rarely ( )
DK ( )   NA ( )
PROBE: How do you account for this?

66. In general, about how much would you say a campaign for the city council costs here in (CITY)?
$_____ DK ( )   NA ( )

66.1 In your *last* campaign, could you estimate approximately how much you spent yourself and how much was spent on your behalf by others?
$_____ by self $_____ by others
DK for self ( )   DK for others ( )
PROBES *RE* 66.1: Can you be more specific?

67. In your last campaign for the council, were there any community groups or organizations which supported you? What kinds of things did they do?
Yes ( )   No ( )   DK ( )   NA ( )
IF YES: PROBE FOR NAMES OF GROUPS FIRST, THEN FOR THEIR ACTIVITIES.
ONLY IF YES TO Q. 67:

67.1 As far as you know, did any of these groups or others remain active in city politics *after* the election?
Yes ( )   No ( )   DK ( )   NA ( )
PROBE: Which groups, and what are they doing now?

67.2 Was there any group active during the last campaign that you particularly disliked?
Yes ( )   No ( )   DK ( )   NA ( )
PROBE: Which group? Why did you dislike it?

68. As far as you can remember, at the time of your last campaign, did you consider the *previous* council as having been a pretty successful council, or not successful?
Successful ( )   Not successful ( )   DK ( )   NA ( )
IF YES: In what ways was it successful?
IF NO: Why did you think it was not successful?

69. Looking back to your last campaign, would you say that it

required more effort on your part than you expected before the election, or less effort?

More ( )   Less ( )   Neither more nor less ( )

DK ( )   NA ( )

PROBE: How's that?

70. In the last campaign, did you run with some others on a slate? Who were they?

Yes ( )   No ( )   DK ( )   NA ( )

71. If, in the next election, there were to be a slate of incumbents, seeking another term, with whom of your colleagues on the present council would you most like to run?

All of them ( )   None of them ( )   DK ( )

NA ( )

RECORD ANY COMMENT:

72. We know that elections to the city council are nonpartisan, but are the political parties at all active in council elections here in (CITY)?

Yes, active ( )   No, not active ( )

Sometimes active ( )   DK ( )   NA ( )

PROBE: How's that?

72.1 IF ACTIVE OR SOMETIMES ACTIVE: Would you say that this party activity in local elections is pretty open or disguised?

Open ( )   Disguised ( )   DK ( )   NA ( )

PROBE: Could you say a little more about this?

73. Do you think local government would be better off, or worse off, if councilmen were elected on a party ticket, or would it make no difference?

Better off ( )   Worse off ( )   No difference ( )

DK ( )   NA ( )

PROBE: What makes you say so?

74. It has been said that the parties are interested in councilmen because they can recruit among them for partisan office

on other levels of government. Do you feel this is the case, or not?

Yes ( )   No ( )   DK ( )   NA ( )

RECORD ANY COMMENT:

75. Do you feel that better people run and get on the city council in nonpartisan elections?

Yes ( )   No ( )   DK ( )   NA ( )

PROBE: What makes you think so?

76. Do people from either party organizations or party groups ever contact you on issues before the council?

Yes ( )   No ( )   DK ( )   NA ( )

IF YES: Who are they? How do they go about it? What do they want?

77. Is there anybody in either of the two major parties with whom you find it sometimes useful to consult?

Yes ( )   No ( )   DK ( )   NA ( )

IF YES: Just what kinds of things do you find it useful to consult about?

END OF INTERVIEW: Thank you very much. Now, I have a list of things I would like you to fill out and then we are finished.

Council Questionnaire

Dear Mr. Councilman:

We very much appreciate your permitting us to talk with you. We hope you enjoyed the interview, and we are looking forward to sending you the results of our survey with over 400 city councilmen in the Bay Area region.

Because of the length of the interview, we couldn't ask you about many other things that are of interest. We therefore would be very grateful if you could take another half hour and fill out the attached questionnaire. We feel that the questions are self-explanatory, and we think that you will have no trouble in answering them.

For your convenience, we have attached a self-addressed en-
velope. All you need do is to seal it and put it in the mail.

A. Here is a list of some Bay Area problems (water pollution, air
    pollution, rapid transit, traffic and highways, Bay fill, recre-
    ational developments, preserving open spaces, crime and juve-
    nile delinquency, job and housing discrimination). Would
    you please indicate which level of government you feel should
    take the principal responsibility for handling and solving
    these problems. CHECK ONE.
    1. City
    2. Special District
    3. County
    4. ABAG
    5. Other Bay Agency
    6. State
    7. Federal Government
B. Here are some additional statements that pertain to the job
    of city councilman. Which of these statements seems to fit
    best your own conception of the job? PLEASE READ AND
    CHECK *ONE*.
    1. The councilman should primarily consider proposals and
       requests by the city staff or other specialists, and then ac-
       cept, reject, or amend these proposals or requests.
    2. The councilman should concern himself primarily with
       advocating new programs or revising existing policies, and
       try to "sell" his ideas to his fellow councilmen.
    3. The councilman should seek out the viewpoints of others—
       colleagues, city staff, community groups, or private indi-
       viduals—debate and discuss the issues involved, and nego-
       tiate some agreement.
C. Here are some statements which reflect different viewpoints
    about the job of city manager or top administrator. We would
    like to know how you feel about these viewpoints. Would you
    please read each one and then check how much you generally
    agree or disagree with it.
    The city manager or other top administrator should:

1. maintain a neutral stand on any issues which may divide the community.
2. consult with the council before drafting his own budget proposal.
3. assume leadership in shaping municipal policies.
4. act as an administrator and leave policy matters to the council.
5. advocate policies even if important parts of the community seem hostile to them.
6. give a helping hand to good councilmen who are coming up for reelection.
7. advocate major changes in city policies if necessary.
8. encourage people whom he respects to run for the council.
9. work through the most powerful members of the community to achieve his policy goals.
10. work informally with councilmen to prepare important policy proposals.

D. We would like to know how some things are actually done in your city. Would you please check the answer which most closely describes municipal operations there?

1. *Hiring of department head:* a. council chooses; b. council joins with manager or administrator in choice; c. manager seeks council approval of his choice; d. manager chooses, but informs council before acting so that he can reconsider in case of strong objections; e. manager appoints and then informs council; f. other (PLEASE SPECIFY).

2. *Preparing the budget:* a. council draws up the budget with or without assistance of manager or administrator; b. council instructs manager regarding the main aspects of each departmental budget before he prepares budget; c. manager gets general indication of whether the council favors an "economy" or "expanded services" budget before he draws up the budget; d. manager prepares both an "economy" and "expanded services" budget for the council's choice; e. manager prepares budget without prior council consultation; f. other (PLEASE SPECIFY).

3. *Requests for new or expanded services:* a. manager takes

no part in initiating or commenting on proposals for new or expanded services; b. council proposes and gets manager's opinion; c. manager asks council whether it would consider expansion of services only in informal ways; d. manager does not hesitate to propose expanded services which he feels are advisable; e. other (PLEASE SPECIFY).

4. *Initiation of policy matters*: a. council initiates all policy matters; b. council initiates most policy matters; c. manager initiates most policy matters; d. manager initiates all policy matters; e. manager and council equally initiate policy matters; f. other (PLEASE SPECIFY).

E. We would appreciate your helping us rate the *participation of the membership* in the activities of some organizations in your city.

Please check the appropriate box (high, moderate, low, not applicable). If no such organization exists in your city, check "not applicable." If you don't know, leave blank.

1. Homeowner groups and neighborhood associations
2. General civic affairs groups like the League of Women Voters, civic league
3. Chamber of Commerce or Jaycees
4. Reform or protest groups
5. Trade unions
6. Service clubs like Kiwanis or Rotary
7. Merchant associations
8. Political party clubs or organizations
9. Garden clubs, trail clubs, library association

F. Please tell us how *controversial matters* in your community come to your notice. For this purpose, we would like you to consider the following items in terms of their importance to you.

PLEASE RANK THE FOLLOWING IN ORDER OF THEIR IMPORTANCE:

1. Appearance of individuals or representatives from organizations at council meetings
2. Running into friends or acquaintances in the city
3. Newspaper(s)

    4. Business or work associates

    5. Contacts with organizational leaders

    IF YOU HAVE OTHER IMPORTANT SOURCES OF INFORMATION ON *CONTROVERSIAL* MATTERS IN THE COMMUNITY, PLEASE LIST THEM BELOW.

G. We just asked you about sources of information. Now we would like you to tell us from whom you think you can get the *best advice* about issues before the council.

    PLEASE RANK THE FOLLOWING IN TERMS OF THE BEST ADVICE YOU CAN GET:

    1. City manager or other city officials

    2. Other councilmen

    3. Newspaper(s)

    4. Organizational leaders in city

    5. Influential individuals in city

    6. People in the city generally

    7. People in the neighborhood

    8. People who come to council meetings

H. We would like to know something about your interest in local affairs as compared with national affairs.

    1. Which of the following statements comes closest to how you feel about this? PLEASE CHECK ONLY ONE:

        a. I am *much more* interested in local than in national affairs.

        b. I am *a little more* interested in local than in national affairs.

        c. My interest in local and national affairs is about the same.

        d. I am *a little less* interested in local than in national affairs.

        e. I am *much less* interested in local than in national affairs.

    2. What newspapers do you read regularly? PLEASE LIST.

    3. What magazines do you read regularly? PLEASE LIST.

    4. Are there any columnists or news commentators whom you follow regularly through the newspapers, radio, or TV? Who are they? PLEASE LIST.

I.   The following statements are concerned with *elections* to the city council. Please consider each set from the point of view of which statement comes closest to your own experience. PLEASE READ *EACH SET* AND CHECK *ONE* STATEMENT ONLY:

1. Council candidates are occasionally treated rather rudely in the course of an election campaign. Which of the following statements best reflects your own experience during your *last* campaign?

    a. I encountered *no* rudeness at all from the supporters of other candidates.

    b. Only occasionally did I encounter any rudeness and hostility from the supporters of other candidates.

    c. I generally ran into several people at meetings who went out of their way to make things difficult for me.

    d. Things really got very unpleasant at times, so much so that I wondered if running for a council seat was worth the effort.

    e. Not applicable (there was no campaign; I was appointed, etc.).

2. Which of the following statements do you think best characterizes the relationships among the candidates during your *last* election campaign?

    a. Things were by and large pretty cordial. If there existed any animosity between anyone, I wasn't aware of it.

    b. There was some friction present, but one expects that in an election.

    c. In the midst of the campaign, people got fairly heated up and one could detect hostility between some of the candidates.

    d. There was considerable hostility among candidates and their supporters over some of the issues.

    e. Not applicable (there was no campaign; I was appointed, etc.).

3. Which one of these statements most accurately reflects your confidence, or lack of confidence, in winning at the time of your *last* campaign?

a. I felt fairly certain of winning.
b. I thought I would win, but I felt the election would be close.
c. I thought the election could go either way.
d. I expected to lose, but I thought if I worked, I could make it a close race.
e. I was fairly certain that I wouldn't be elected.
f. Not applicable (there was no campaign; I was appointed, etc.).

4. Which of the following statements most closely approximates your desire and efforts to be elected to the council during your *last* campaign?
   a. I really didn't work too hard at being elected.
   b. I wanted the office, but, for the most part, I limited my efforts to what I and a few friends could do by ourselves.
   c. I wasn't able to do as much as I might have liked, but during the later stages of the campaign I and my supporters worked quite intensively.
   d. I devoted a great deal of time and effort to the campaign.
   e. Not applicable (there was no campaign; I was appointed, etc.).

J. We would like you to tell us just what you envisage the role of city government to be in the future of your city. Would you please read all of the following statements and check the one that comes closest to your opinion.
PLEASE CHECK *ONE*.

1. I would like to see the city paying off most of its debts while maintaining its present level of services to citizens.
2. I would like to see the city providing more services to its citizens than it does now.
3. I would like to see the city maintaining its present level of activities.
4. I would like the city to cut back on many of its more expensive programs.
5. I would like to see the city taking an active part in promoting city growth.

K. Just to make sure that we have not misunderstood your feelings about being a city councilman in the course of the interview, would you please check *one* possible response in the following three sets of statements.

PLEASE CHECK *ONE* IN EACH SET.

1. Which of the following would you say comes closest to your conception of the requirements for the job of city councilman?

   a. Being a councilman is a tough political job—it requires that you be a real politician.

   b. Being a city councilman requires some political skills, but it is not really a political job.

   c. Being a city councilman requires the ability to get along with people, but I wouldn't say it's political.

   d. Being a city councilman is a matter of public service but in no way a matter of politics.

2. Which of the following statements would you say best *summarizes* your feelings about being a city councilman?

   a. It's a job for a hard-nosed political type.

   b. It's a lot of hard work with little pleasure.

   c. It's hard work, but there are satisfactions and rewards.

   d. It's a service to the community and I feel good about it.

   e. It's like a game, it's real fun.

3. In your opinion which of the following best describes the way the people in your community view the job of being a city councilman?

   a. They see the councilman as a real politician.

   b. They see the councilman as a public servant with little political involvement.

   c. They see the councilman as just another citizen and by no means a politician.

   d. Other (IF SOME OTHER VIEW, PLEASE WRITE YOUR COMMENTS IN THE SPACE PROVIDED BELOW.)

L. Here are four statements sometimes made in texts on local government. They are not mutually exclusive, but we would like you to rank them in the order which fits most closely your own conception of the job of a councilman.

PLEASE READ AND *RANK* THESE ITEMS IN ORDER OF IMPORTANCE.

1. It's the job of the councilman to be acquainted with the business before the council, attend all council sessions regularly, do the chores of the job, and vote on the issues before the council.
2. The councilman should try to get an overall picture of all the problems that exist in the community, be fair to all sides, and try to balance and harmonize conflicting demands that are made on the council.
3. The councilman should know or try to find out what the people in the community want, express their needs and wants at the council table, and protect the interests of the people in the community.
4. The councilman should propose programs which advance the city as a good place to live in, work for better local government, and try to solve the city's problems even before they arise.

M. There are always some conflicts in a community. Here is a list of possible lineups that occasionally occur. How would you rank these particular lineups according to their relative importance in your city?

PLEASE RANK THE FOLLOWING CONFLICTS IN ORDER OF THEIR IMPORTANCE IN YOUR CITY.

1. Business vs. labor
2. Republicans vs. Democrats
3. Old residents vs. new residents
4. White people vs. minorities
5. Supporters of new taxes vs. opponents
6. New subdivisions vs. old part of city
7. Liberals vs. Conservatives
8. Supporters of city planning vs. opponents
9. Others (PLEASE INDICATE)

N. Here is a list of things which, some say, city councils must do. We would like you to rank these four items in the order of their importance in your city.

PLEASE RANK THE FOLLOWING ACCORDING TO THEIR IMPORTANCE.

1. The council should find imaginative solutions for the city's many problems.
2. The council needs to do only what is required by charter or statute.
3. The council should adjust the conflicts of different interests.
4. The council should do what the people want it to do.

O. When the council is divided and tempers seem to fly high, which of the following do you try to do? PLEASE CHECK ONLY *ONE*.
1. I try to calm the others down by a light remark or a joke.
2. I remind the others that the council has a job to do.
3. I try to form a working majority for my point of view.
4. I usually sit back and wait until things calm down.

P. Here is a list of statements concerning why unanimity occurs in legislative bodies. Would you please indicate how relevant, in your opinion, these reasons are in your city? Are they often relevant, sometimes relevant, never relevant? PLEASE CHECK FOR EACH ITEM AS YOU SEE FIT.
1. There simply is no disagreement on many issues.
2. We usually talk an issue over and try to reach agreement.
3. We just don't like to disagree whenever possible.
4. We go along with the others to get support for our own proposals.
5. You go along with the others even if you disagree a bit because it is uncomfortable to be in the minority.
6. We try to iron differences out in private before the issue comes up in open session.
7. There is an unwritten rule that it is better to agree than to disagree.

Q. We are wondering from whom you think you get the *best* information about city affairs. Could you rank the following as to their importance? Are they very important, important, not very important, not at all important? PLEASE RANK FOR EACH AS YOU SEE FIT.
Information from:
1. City manager or other city officials
2. Other councilmen
3. People at council meetings

4. Organizational leaders in the community
5. People in the city generally
6. Newspaper(s)
7. People in the neighborhood
8. Influential individuals

R. In seeking advice or information in general, could you rank the following in terms of their *usefulness* to you in your work as a councilman?
PLEASE RANK THE FOLLOWING IN ORDER OF THEIR IMPORTANCE.
1. Business leaders
2. Ministers
3. Leaders of racial groups
4. Union leaders
5. City officials
6. Personal friends
7. City planners
8. Neighbors

S. Here is a list of the kinds of things campaigning may involve. Would you please check off the things you are likely to do in a campaign here?
PLEASE CHECK ALL RELEVANT ITEMS.
1. Run advertisement in newspaper
2. Speak to large audiences
3. Print cards or posters
4. Do door-to-door campaigning
5. Speak to small, informal groups
6. Ask others to campaign for me

T. Here is a list of different qualities which it has been said a city councilman might find useful. Which ones would you say are absolutely essential, which ones fairly essential, not very essential, or not essential at all?
PLEASE CHECK *EACH* AS YOU SEE FIT.
1. Ability to judge people
2. Knowledge of politics
3. Acquaintance with business leaders in community
4. General education
5. Long residence in city
6. Technical training in city government

    7. Acquaintance with political leaders
    8. Business ability
    9. Ability to deal with public
  10. Capacity to make friends
  11. Acquaintanceship with labor union leaders
  12. Knowledge of city

U. PLEASE READ THE FOLLOWING AND CIRCLE THE ANSWER THAT YOU THINK FITS BEST.

  1. How often do you read the local paper to see how council affairs are reported? Regularly? Occasionally? Rarely? Never?

  2. Do you feel that the paper's reporting of council affairs is: Always accurate? Mostly accurate? Mostly inaccurate? Always inaccurate?

  3. Would you say that the amount of coverage the paper gives to council affairs is: About right? Too much? Too little?

  4. How about editorials on city matters? Would you say they are: Always fair? Mostly fair? Mostly biased? Always biased?

  5. How useful are the editorials to you? Are they: Very useful? Of some use? Not very useful? Not useful at all?

  6. Do you pay much attention to the letters to the editor on city matters? Do you do so: Regularly? Occasionally? Rarely? Never?

  7. How do you feel about these letters? Do you find them: Very useful? Of some use? Not very useful? Not useful at all?

  8. How much influence would you say the paper has on how this city is run? Has it: Much influence? Some influence? Little influence? No influence?

V. Would you please check the item on this list which comes closest to describing your family's involvement in public affairs when you were growing up?
PLEASE CHECK ONLY *ONE* ITEM ON THIS LIST.

  1. They were very active in public affairs; family member(s) held public office.

  2. They were quite active, but no one ever held office.

3. They were somewhat active and discussed public matters a lot.
4. They were never actually active in public affairs, but they did discuss such matters a lot.
5. Public affairs were only infrequently discussed, just around presidential elections and times like that.
6. Family members were not at all interested in public affairs when I was growing up.

W. If the pressures of your occupation interfered with your work on the council, which of the following would you most likely do?
1. Give up the council job to meet my other obligations.
2. Complete my present term, but not run again.
3. Continue on the council and try to lighten my job load.
4. Put in extra time to be able to serve on the council.
5. Can't say what I would do.

X. TO COMPLETE OUR SURVEY, WE WOULD APPRECIATE YOUR ANSWERING THE FOLLOWING QUESTIONS AS FULLY AS POSSIBLE.
1. Where were you born? _____
                    (city)   (county)   (state)
2. In what year? _____
          (year)
3. Where were you brought up—when you went to grammar or high school? ___ _____
                    (city)   (county)   (state)
4. Your father's birthplace? _____ (country)
Mother's birthplace? _____ (country)
5. How would you describe the place where you grew up? Was it a city ( ), a small town ( ), or a farm ( )?
6. How many years have you lived here in (council city)? _____ (years)
7. What is your principal occupation—what do you actually do in your work? _____
          (description of actual work)
IF RETIRED, PLEASE INDICATE WHAT YOU DID BEFORE RETIREMENT AND CHECK HERE ( ).
8. Who is your employer? _____
         (name of firm and type of enterprise)

9. Are you self-employed ( )? In a partnership ( )?
10. Has this been your main occupation all your working
    life?
    Yes ( )   No( )   IF NOT, what other occupation
                              have you had?
    Other job:_____Years (from-to)_____
11. Where is your place of work?
    Here in city ( )? In neighbor city ( )?

    _____

                    (name of neighbor city)
12. What is your marital status?
    Married ( ) Single ( ) Divorced ( ) Widowed ( )
13. Do you have children? How old are they?

    _____

14. What was your father's principal occupation?

    _____

                      (father's occupation)
15. What was the *last* grade of school you completed?
    CHECK ONE.
    a. Less than high school   ( )
    b. High school (graduate)   ( )
    c. College incomplete   ( )
    d. College completed   ( )
    e. College (graduate work) ( )
    f. Trade school   ( )
16. Which of these rough income categories do you belong to?
    a. Less than $5,000 ( )   d. $10,000–14,999   ( )
    b. $ 5,000– 7,499   ( )   e. $15,000–19,999   ( )
    c. $ 7,500– 9,999   ( )   f. $20,000 and over ( )
17. What church do you belong to? (PLEASE NAME
    CHURCH, NOT JUST DENOMINATION)

    _____

                       (name of church)

18. What local clubs or organizations—professional, fraternal, or service—do you belong to? Are you an officer now, active or inactive?
19. Do you usually think of yourself as a Republican ( ), Democrat ( ), Independent ( ), or other (SPECIFY)?
20. And how do you register in state or federal elections? As: Republican ( ), Democrat ( ), or Independent ( )?

Y. How many years, including the present one, have you served on the council?

PLEASE CIRCLE NUMBER OF YEARS.

1   2   3   4   5   6   7   8   8+

Z. Have your terms on the council been continuous or interrupted?

Continuous ( )   Interrupted ( )

IF INTERRUPTED: Could you just indicate in a few words how this happened?

Index of Authors

Subject Index